THE HISTORY OF CIVILIZATION

THE FEUDAL MONARCHY IN
FRANCE AND ENGLAND

THE HISTORY OF CIVILIZATION

General Editor C. K. Ogden

The *History of Civilization* is a landmark in early twentieth Century publishing. The aim of the general editor, C. K. Ogden, was to "summarise in one comprehensive synthesis the most recent findings and theories of historians, anthropologists, archaeologists, sociologists and all conscientious students of civilization." The *History*, which includes titles in the French series *L'Evolution de l'Humanité*, was published at a formative time in the development of the social sciences, and during a period of significant historical discoveries.

A list of the titles in the series can be found at the end of this book.

THE FEUDAL MONARCHY IN FRANCE AND ENGLAND

From the Xth to the XIIIth Century

C. Petit-Dutaillis

Translated by
E. D. Hunt

Routledge
Taylor & Francis Group
LONDON AND NEW YORK

First published in 1936 by Routledge, Trench, Trubner
Reprinted by Routledge
in 1996, 1999

2 Park Square, Milton Park,
Abingdon, Oxon, OX14 4RN
Simultaneously published in the USA and Canada by Routledge
711 Third Avenue, New York, NY 10017

Routledge is an imprint of the Taylor & Francis Group, an informa business

Transferred to Digital Printing 2008

First issued in paperback 2013

© 1996 Routledge

All rights reserved. No part of this book may be reprinted or utilized in any form or by any means electronic, mechanical, or other means, now known or hereafter invented, including photocopying and recording, in any information storage or retrieval system, without permission in writing from the publishers.

British Cataloguing in Publication Data

ISBN 978-0-415-15604-2 (hbk)
ISBN 978-0-415-86811-2 (pbk)

Publisher's Note
The publisher has gone to great lengths to ensure the quality of this reprint but points out that some imperfections in the original may be apparent

CONTENTS

	PAGE
LIST OF MAPS AND GENEALOGICAL TABLES	ix
PREFACE	xi
INTRODUCTION	1

BOOK ONE

THE MONARCHY IN FRANCE AND ENGLAND FROM THE END OF THE TENTH CENTURY TO THE CREATION OF THE ANGEVIN EMPIRE

CHAPTER
  I. CHARACTERISTICS OF THE PRIMITIVE CAPETIAN MONARCHY 7
    I. The Events of 987, 7.—II. The Kingdom of France, 8.—III. The Diversity of France in the Eleventh Century—the Great Lordships, 13.—IV. The Royal Demesne, 17.—V. The Early Capetians and the Church, 19.—VI. The Sacred Character of the Monarchy and its Popular Backing, 23.—VII. Elective Monarchy. Association in the Throne, 27.—VIII. The Court, 30.

  II. THE ANGLO-SAXON MONARCHY. THE DUCHY OF NORMANDY 36
    I. The Primitive Social Elements of England, 36.—II. The Anglo-Saxon Monarchy, 42.—III. Anglo-Saxon Society at the Period of the Norman Conquest, 48.—IV. The Duchy of Normandy, c. 1066, 51.

  III. FOUNDATION OF THE ANGLO-NORMAN MONARCHY 56
    I. The Conquest, 56.—II. The Early Anglo-Norman Kings and Anglo-Norman Institutions (1066-1135), 60.

  IV. THE CAPETIAN MONARCHY AND ITS DOMAINAL POLICY (1060-1152) 76
    I. The Kings of France and their advisers, 76.—II. Political constriction. The liberation of the Demesne, 81.—III. Gregorian Reform. The Popes in France, 85.

BOOK TWO

THE ANGEVIN EMPIRE AND THE CAPETIAN MONARCHY

I. FORMATION OF THE ANGEVIN EMPIRE. THE NEW MONARCHY. THE MEN AND THEIR IDEAS . 99

    I. The House of Anjou. The Marriages of the Plantegenets. The Reign of Stephen and the Anarchy in England, 99.—II. Henry II and Richard Cœur de Lion, 107.—III. The Ministers, 111.—IV. Different Conceptions of the Monarchy. The Ideas of Lawyers, Church, and Nobility, 113.

II. ADMINISTRATION AND LEGISLATION IN ENGLAND (1154–1204) 125

    I. Pacification of the Kingdom, 125.—II. Local and Central Administration, 126.—III. Legislation. The Assizes. The Jury, 137.—IV. The Revenues of the Monarchy, 140.—V. Army and Navy, 144.—VI. The King and his English Subjects, The Conflicts, 145.

III. THE PLANTEGENET'S POLICY OF OVERLORDSHIP. THE CONTINENTAL POSSESSIONS . . 155

    I. Ireland, Scotland, Wales, 155.—II. The Continental Possessions, 157.—III. Normandy, 159.—IV. Anjou, Touraine, and Maine, 167.—V. Aquitaine, 169.—VI. Relations of the Plantegenets with Nobility, Clergy, and Towns of the Continental Possessions, 172.—VII. Ambitions in the Mediterranean, 177.

IV. RESISTANCE OF THE CAPETIANS TO THE ENGLISH HEGEMONY. PROGRESS OF THE FRENCH MONARCHY (1152–1201) 179

    I. The Resources of the Monarchy, 179.—II. Allies and Opponents, 193.—III. Attitude of the Emperors and Popes, 206.—IV. Conflicts with Henry II and Richard Cœur de Lion, 210.

V. THE VICTORY OF THE CAPETIANS . . . 214

    I. Philip Augustus and John Lackland, 214.—II. The Disinheritance of John Lackland, 216.—III. Anglo-German Coalition. Bouvines, 222.—IV. Last Conflicts. Treaty of Paris, 226.

CONTENTS

BOOK THREE

THE APOGEE OF THE FEUDAL MONARCHY IN FRANCE AND THE ARISTOCRATIC REACTION IN ENGLAND

I. THE INSTITUTIONS OF THE CAPETIAN MONARCHY FROM THE CONQUEST OF NORMANDY TO THE DEATH OF SAINT LOUIS . . . 233

    I. Residences and Homes of the Kings. The Household, 233.—II. The Court, 235.—III. Masters and Councillors, 242.—IV. The Demesne and the Local Administration, 245.—V. The King's Revenues, 248.—VI. Expenditure. Financial Balance of the Period, 254.

II. RELATIONS OF THE FRENCH KINGS WITH THE CHURCH AND THE HOLY SEE 1202–1270. THE CRUSADES AGAINST THE ALBIGENSIANS AND IN THE EAST 259

    I. Principles of the royal policy, 259.—II. Services rendered by the Church. Royal favours to the Church, 262.—III. The Liberties of the Church and the Supremacy of the Crown, 263.—IV. Relations with the Holy See, 268.—V. The Crusade against the Albigensians. The Inquisition, 275.—VI. Saint Louis' Crusades against the Moslems, 284.

III. HEGEMONY OF THE CAPETIAN MONARCHY IN FRANCE. PRESTIGE IN THE WEST, 1202–1270 288

    I. The Anarchy, 288.—II. Military Repression, 291.—III. Administrative Action. Bailiffs and Seneschals, 294.—IV. Inquests and Ordinances, 298.—V. The King Overlord, 301.—VI. The King above Feudalism, 310.—VII. The Attempt to subject the Towns, 314.—VIII. Assimilation of the Annexed Territories, 319.—IX. Prestige of the Capetian Monarchy about 1270. Peace and Arbitration, 322.

IV. THE ARISTOCRAT REACTION IN ENGLAND. THE GREAT CHARTER AND THE BARONS WAR . 327

    I. The Church and Barons against John Lackland, 327.—II. The Great Charter, 333.—III. Progress of the Opposition under Henry III, 339.—IV. The Revolution. Government by Council. Provisions of Oxford and Westminster, 342.—V. The Barons War and the Protectorate of Simon de Montfort, 347.—VI. Character and Results of these Crises, 350.

CONCLUSION 372
LIST OF REFERENCES 381
INDEX 411

LIST OF MAPS AND GENEALOGICAL TABLES

	PAGE
Map of the Kingdom of France in 987	9
Map of the Overseas Possessions of the Angevin Empire	160
I. Descent of William the Conqueror	102
II. Descent of Henry Plantegenet	103
III. Descent of John Lackland	103
IV. Descent of Louis VI and Louis VII	228
V. Descent of Philip Augustus, Louis VIII, and Saint Louis	229

PREFACE

INSTITUTIONS AND INDIVIDUALS

HERE is a book which, among other merits, has that of showing quite clearly how the work of scholarship can finally lead to a good historical synthesis and even to a truly scientific synthesis.

Charles Petit-Dutaillis has collected here the results of scholastic work on the period from the tenth to the thirteenth centuries, a work to which he has himself made important contributions,[1] to which, on certain points, he makes contributions even here.[2] He does not attempt to hide the gaps in our knowledge of facts and he points out those which are particularly serious and urgently need to be made good.[3] Already, however, sufficient has been prepared and it is sufficiently familiar to him for its presentation in a synthesis which is new.

It appears to him that France and England, during the period he has been studying, were in such close communication through the coming and going not only of individuals but of certain elements in the population that the language, in some measure, that the bond of vassalage, the unfixed character of territorial boundaries at a time when the idea of State and national frontiers was just developing (p. 12), that the mutual borrowings, the repercussions of all sorts, and even the conflicts, bound their history so closely together that we are justified or rather forced to attempt a new historical construction and to arrive at a combined history of England and France.[4] He traces the life of two countries which, at this period, lived in such close association, according to a cleverly articulated plan, which while consistently

---

[1] *Étude sur la vie et le règne de Louis VIII ; La Deshéritement de Jean sans Terre ; Querimoniae Normannorum ; Studies and Notes supplementary to Stubbs' "Constitutional History"*, 3 vols.

[2] For example: On the frontiers of the kingdom of France, the preparation of the Norman Conquest, on the origin of the institution of the bailiffs, on the peers of France in the thirteenth century ; on the process which ended, in France, in the royal ordinance applicable to the whole kingdom.

[3] On the gaps in scholarship see, for instance, pp. 157, 368 ; on the task of scholarship, pp. 241, 242.

[4] pp. 154 (The history of England at this period should not be separated by scholars from the history of the Angevin Empire), 372.

bringing them into relationship gives every opportunity to appreciate the differences in their evolution.

There can be no question of summarizing here a volume which the author himself has condensed to the essential minimum in the pages of sober clarity which form his conclusion; a volume full of knowledge in which, however, from beginning to end, the presentation of facts, particulars and hypotheses has been reduced to the minimum essential to appreciating the development of the institutions. We can undoubtedly see here a France and an England built up; we take part in the difficult advance of French unity beginning from the tiny geographical region, France (p. 10), in the formation of an English nation which survived the collapse of the cosmopolitan Anglo-French empire (pp. 108, 112, 178); we realize the full importance of the date 27th July, 1214, Bouvines. But Ch. Petit-Dutaillis is here less anxious to recount than to explain. If "history is more complex and contains more things than it is possible for one historian to know and tell" (p. 85) it is fortunately not necessary for the historian to know everything or, still less, to tell everything in order to produce some valuable generalizations. If we were seeking to astonish our collaborator himself, we would say that he had conceived and produced a volume of sociology—not, of course, a theoretical and abstract but a historical sociology. For what it is, this book falls excellently into its place. Our tasks here, therefore, will be to mark its precise place in the Evolution of Humanity *and to show how it conforms to the main purpose of the latter—which is its explanation.*

From the beginnings of humanity we have seen a tendency towards unification demonstrated in social forms and political organizations. The most striking examples of this have been the Empires. In the course of centuries we have met the Empires of the East, the Macedonian Empire, and the Roman. The idea and form of Empire was not destroyed in the eclipse of the power of Rome. It continued to appeal to some minds, particularly the minds of the ambitious.[1] *For we have similarly seen how the ambitions of individuals fitted in—in a more or less self-centred, more or less noble fashion*[2]—*with this tendency towards unity which the human masses have displayed, a*

---

[1] See vols. xxxii, xxxiii, xxxvii, xxxix.
[2] See, for example, p. 207.

PREFACE

tendency which is itself in part a social instinct, in part due to the need to " live and grow " [1] *which frequently reflects both.*

When an Empire falls into disintegration—whatever the cause—when the State is losing its authority in general, when, over large areas, anarchy is supreme, a social arrangement tends to establish itself on the basis of the need for protection, " recommendation "; it is the feudal system, the vassal's devotion, the suzerain's patronage—which is sporadic order, a tempered anarchy. Elsewhere, we have studied this regime of order in disorder [2]; here, we are concerned with the origins of the order which was imposed on disorder; we have to follow the progress of a unifying authority. It is a curious picture provided by this monarchy which established itself actually within feudalism which, moreover, remained essentially feudal—as Ch. Petit-Dutaillis has clearly shown—and which in the natural process of developing its principles went to the extent of reviving or rediscovering the idea of Empire. Henry II has been accused of aspiring to universal dominion. This old dream of the Romans appealed to many men of the Middle Ages. " The positive and practical spirit of Philip Augustus was not immune to chimerical dreams of universal empire." A contemporary says of him that he thought " that one man was sufficient to govern the world ".[3] More interesting, however, than the excesses of these avowed pretensions was the gradual consolidation of monarchical institutions and the development of its organs. Our collaborator has made a penetrating study of the renaissance of the State which succeeds in revealing its causes in all their complexity. While he weaves the institutional into the texture of events—and even all the better because of this method—he allows the reader to understand *the evolution;* that, as we have already said, is his merit and his art.

We know that the grouping of men into societies involves certain essential institutions; and that, in some measure, institutions are regulated by the structure of those societies, i.e. by their volume and density. From this, results social laws or what are, in effect at least, social laws.

---

[1] See p. 179.
[2] Vol. xxxiv. On the anarchistic violence of that period, see pp. 221, 288, 373; on the swarms of adventurers and brigands, pp. 58, 83, 169, 173, 376.
[3] Cf. pp. 108, 109, 157, 270.

These essentials are, themselves, born of a fundamental need, of an internal logic which operates amid many contingencies—some favourable, others the contrary—but which also translates and realizes itself in clear ideas.[1] In the process which is to end in the organization of the State, Ch. Petit-Dutaillis distinguishes what he calls " reasons of fact " and the " reasons of a spiritual character "—in other words the material contingencies and the reflected logic.[2]

The role of contingency—which, from its character, is necessarily ambiguous—appears here to be very considerable. There is the admission of collective groups—with their ethnic character [3] : that of individuals—with their abilities or defects, their apathy or their ambition—from which, in such impulsive periods, arises intrigues, manœuvres, traffickings, corruption, treasons, and recantations.[4] There is the game of marriages and divorces, of accession to the throne by association or heredity.[5] There are the general circumstances of politics and religion, the atmosphere common to France and England: Feudalism, Church, and Papacy: circumstances peculiar to France: greater importance of the towns and the bourgeoisie.[6] There are events which had very distant repercussions; the revolution of 1066, one of the most fundamental changes that has ever transformed a country (p. 374) and, after the conquest of England and the outburst of imperialist megalomania, the defeat of Bouvines.

At the beginning of the period which this book covers we find lordships but no State. The idea of the subject was lost (pp. 12, 302, 310). The king was nothing but a " higher suzerain " at the peak of the " feudal pyramid " (p. 2). Kingship represented a title rather than a power. It did not imply a kingdom ; the

[1] See our Synthesis of History ; the General Introduction to the *Evolution of Humanity*, preface to vol. vi.

[2] p. 64. Opposition of the " needs " and " tendencies " which lead society to " theoretical views " ; pp. 368-9. A profound movement which led to the English revolution.

[3] See, in particular, pp. 53-5, 374 (Normans), 348, 376 (English).

[4] See pp. 22, 34, 96, 214 (Philip Augustus' neurasthenia), 215-16 (cyclothymia of John Lackland), 375 (the misfortune of incompetent and disreputable kings) ; p. 377 (the luck of having good kings for almost a century) ; pp. 108, 208, 214, 227, 327 (ambition).

[5] See pp. 100, 305 (the chance of profitable marriages, profitable unions), 210 (the " Roman events " which interfered in the policy) ; 375 (the chance of the queen's fertility ; the uncertain expedient of association in the throne).

[6] By a few sober but full pages on Paris, Ch. Petit-Dutaillis makes its history from the twelfth century part of the general history. See pp. 197 ff., 234.

PREFACE

king's personal demesne, in the beginning was " broken up and scattered." The kingdom and the unity of France were built up once more only gradually, particularly by the victories over the English and the Albigensians. The degree of " Civilization ", therefore, had no relation to the progress of the monarchy which, for a long time, played no part of moral or intellectual importance (pp. 96, 376).

It remains, however, a fundamental truth that the attributes of this higher suzerain became more and more clearly defined and applied (p. 200) at the same time as the sacred character of the monarchy grew stronger. On the whole, in spite of conflicts, Feudalism and the Church served the cause of the king.

This is particularly true of the Church and in various ways. It was the natural enemy of war, brigandage, and unbridled passions. By tradition and interests, it upheld the authority on which its own position was based.[1] " It believed in the king's mission and propaganded on its behalf." (pp. 3, 19). In this way the King of France found a peculiar growth of his prestige which distinguished him " from other mortals ", even from the barons themselves.[2] This " mystery of royalty " linked up with the Carolingian legend and the remembrance of unity in the minds of people and poets.[3] In England the Church played the part of a supporter less consistently for " it occasionally figured among the opposition " (p. 72).

But it was not only through an " alliance [4] " either continuous or intermittent that the Church served the State ; it was also, in France and England alike, by the example and influence of its own organization. " It was within the Church that political understanding and the spirit of juridical and administrative organization grew up." " It had everything which the world of laymen lacked as the basis for a political society ; . . . it had established methods for the election of delegates, for the conduct of meetings, for preserving written records of the discussion, for the formulation of decisions." It was the " tutor " (pp. 72, 113).

More and more ideas interfere to reinforce circumstances to establish, in its feudal setting, this medieval monarchy with all the essential characteristics which distinguish it from the monarchy of to-day (p. 234). In addition the Normans had

[1] See pp. 23, 120 ff.
[2] pp. 22, 23, 34, 125.
[3] pp. 10, 25, 84.
[4] See pp. 195, 258. Even in France it had suffered setbacks. pp. 86, 89.

contributed "*a certain sense of government*"; *they had a* "*legal outlook*" (p. 55). *The logic* (p. 2) *which demanded that the feudal pyramid should culminate in* "*the sovereign*" *and that anarchy should be remedied by his power finished by becoming conscious in a growing number of brains.* " *The Capetians of the eleventh and twelfth centuries or* those who thought and acted in their name *never forgot that the king is the head of the feudal hierarchy even when they were not in a position to gain from their feudal superiority the advantages which potentially it offered*" (p. 310–11). *The idea that the inhabitants of the kingdom were subjects* " *slowly re-emerged* ". *Saint Louis even considered that* " *the king had the right to impose his will on everybody because it was obviously in accordance with the* general interest " (p. 308) [1]

The victory over disorder, selfishness, feuds, and private wars and over the excessive independence of the urban communities—which had been promoted in the first place—had been all but completed by the end of Saint Louis' reign as much by legal and administrative means as by force. The feudal edifice was sapped by the work of ants.[2] *There can be no question of summarizing here that slow and complex evolution: it is necessary, however, to insist on the parallels and differences which it presented in France and England.*

"*A prince cannot govern without the assent of his loyal followers.*"[3] *The* Curia, *the Court, an indeterminate institution which, in principle, was the same in both countries is the beginning. It is a Council sometimes restricted, sometimes expanded, which advanced centralization and the division of functions at the same time. All the great organs of the State— administration, justice, finance—are to be found there in embryo* (p. 244).[4] *In the development of an officialdom, the sheriff in England and the Bailiff or seneschal in France, agents of the king and delegates of the Curia, played a part of primary importance and comprised the real basis of government.*[5]

---

[1] On the latent conflict between the dual principles of monarchy and feudalism, see pp. 325–6.
[2] See pp. 290–1, 293, 302, 313.
[3] C. Petit-Dutaillis, *The King of England and his Parliaments in the Middle Ages*, p. 18, reprinted from the *Revue Historique*, 1927, vol. cliv; cf. in this vol. pp. 131, 182–3, 352.
[4] pp. 137, 139–144, 242–7, 252–8.
[5] On the sheriff, see pp. 126–8; on the bailiff, pp. 184–6, 247–8; on the officials in general, pp. 241, 352, 377, 379.

PREFACE

The "political society" which foreshadowed the State appeared quickly in England, earlier than in France. Ch. Petit-Dutaillis has shown this and explained it clearly.[1] The Norman Conquest found " strong local institutions" which could provide an able prince with the means of action. By a fusion of Anglo-Saxon and Norman elements William and his successors established " the strongest and most experienced government" existing in Europe at the time. " It revived Carolingian practices and, at the same time, by the accuracy of its machinery the roughness of its manners and its appearance inevitably calls to mind the Roman State, or, if you prefer it, the State of to-day." [2] But the Church and Nobility of England took advantage of favourable circumstances to subject the monarchy to a "tragic" crisis. Throughout, however, the latter remained powerful and we are mistaken in believing that the rule of parliament dates from that period. In a convincing interpretation of the revolutions of the thirteenth century both here and elsewhere, Ch. Petit-Dutaillis has proved that the Great Charter was " essentially a victory of the feudal reaction over the progress of an advancing royal administration and an arbitrary system of finance ".[3] By the same stroke the middle class achieved a political advance but neither a declaration of rights nor the establishment of a constitutional regime. " The Great Charter has retained a sentimental force which even to-day is not yet extinct. . . . But no permanent system had been created to control the monarchy and prevent abuses" (pp. 370–1).

The French monarchy grew strong more slowly but without the same vital crises ; under Louis IX it had achieved an authority and a prestige which was dependent on the king's personality—with his position came the definitive creation of the " religion of the monarchy ".

At this point we must insist, with the support of our colleague, on the part played by individuals. He has written somewhere in relation to the constitutional history of England in the Middle Ages: " A false estimation of this history will be made by anyone who neglects the psychological data.

---

[1] See pp. 36, 39, 45, 46, 47, 51.
[2] See pp. 374, 376.
[3] Article cited p. 10. Cf. in this volume, pp. 36, 339, 341, 343–4, 347, 372, on the character and results of the successive crises of the thirteenth century which are vigorously summarized here.

PREFACE

There is no reason, because we are dealing with the history of institutions, to fail to depict the men. If we do not succeed in creating a life-like model of the past, the dangers of empty hypothesis multiply indefinitely." [1] To create a life-like model of the past, to recreate the moral atmosphere (p. 373), to represent adequately mental states (p. 355) has been the task—or the natural tendency—of our colleague. In this book, of which we have emphasized the sociological importance, appear in the light of reality the actions of those individuals who have stimulated or, for the moment, hindered the development of institutions and administrative, financial, and judicial progress (p. 377) who, in a word, have made history.

A work has recently appeared in Germany under the striking title of " Menschen die Geschichte machten " [2] which poses, without, however, giving it adequate treatment, one of the most important problems of historical synthesis.[3] In what does the " collective consciousness " of which our sociologists talk consist? It undoubtedly shows itself in the " crowd psychology ".[4] That is, however, a rare condition—arising particularly from a certain degree of social organization—and, even when it is produced, not all the individuals appear to be conscious of those needs to the same degree or equally affected by those sentiments which are agitating the group. In this book, we can see at work, with varying effectiveness, personalities of widely varying status and nature. There are the great ministers, clerical and lay,[5] whose ability and devotion contributed very largely to the advance of the monarchy : there are equally the humbler collaborators

---

[1] Pamphlet quoted p. 5.

[2] *Viertausend Jahre Weltgeschichte in Zeit- und Lebensbildern*, a collective work published by P. R. Rohden, 2nd ed., two vols. 8vo, Vienna, Seidel and Sons. In spite of several pages of introduction by Fr. Meinecke—on the relations of individuality to the historical medium—this gallery of " famous " men with widely varying claims to fame, of all ages and all countries, pass in rapid, almost cinematographic review, and if it is not lacking in interest it is lacking in any explanatory value. Philippe Augustus, Saint-Louis are treated by W. Kienast (Berlin), vol. i, pp. 451–8 ; Charles of Anjou by E. Sthamer (Berlin), pp. 494–7 ; William the Conqueror by M. Weinbaum (Berlin), pp. 395–9 ; Henry II by A. Cartellieri (Jena), pp. 429–435.

[3] See *Synthèse en histoire*, pp. 166–221, and in the *Evolution of Humanity*, General Introduction, p. xiv, vol. xi, p. xxxviii, vol. xxix, p. xvii. Cf. Individuality in the Publications of the Centre International de Synthèse.

[4] On " crowd psychology " (état de foule), see *Synthèse en histoire*, pp. 104–7. Cf. in the same publication " The Crowd " (La Foule) (appearing shortly).

[5] " Ecclesiastical dignities offered to the villein's son the opportunity of exercising an influence of primary importance in politics. In the Middle Ages it was the means by which mental ability took its due," p. 79, cf. p. 119.

PREFACE

in the work of economic and political organization, all the new class of officials, lawyers, financiers, bailiffs, holders of various offices, all the " royal agents," [1] *but, well to the fore also, there are individual kings and their personal genius.*[2] *If the early Capetians—with " their changing passions, their infantile fickleness, their boorish ruses, and their inability to follow a consistent line of conduct "* [3] *" were unable consciously to pursue any end ", in that more happy series—Philip Augustus, Louis VIII, Blanche of Castile, and Louis IX—the monarchy was represented for almost a century " by kings and a queen regent who were of very different temperaments but all equally endowed and able who had all consecrated their lives to the realization of their dreams of glory or active holiness."* [4]

We shall find striking portraits within these pages in great numbers. Frequently a few words, two or three epithets are sufficient to bring the person again to life mentally and even in the flesh.[5] *" Men change " and it frequently happens that the development of character is noted; " At this point," says Ch. Petit-Dutaillis about Philip Augustus, " we cannot draw a portrait of this great king which would be valid for his whole reign." (p. 180). Philip in fact changed a great deal during the forty-three years of a troubled reign. In adolescence, " this ' ill-kempt' youth nervous, emotional, subject to sickly fears and hallucinations, nevertheless loved action and hunting and gave little care to his studies. . . . His mother Adelaide of Champagne had given him her intelligence and her love of glory and power." Action, the Crusade, and his journeyings matured him quickly. He returned from Syria " physically worn out, bald, lame, and neurotic", but his " moral strength " gave no signs of breaking (p. 181). Once he was cured " of the neurasthenia he had contracted in the East " he achieved the height of his activity. Then " his energy, stubborn in the accomplishment of his plans, was moderated only by his supple mind and a political wisdom which rarely made a mistake. The springs of his will were bent to an immense ambition " (p. 214): he was obsessed by the*

---

[1] pp. 294, 301, 310, 379. [2] p. 179; cf. p. 235.
[3] p. 22; cf. p. 84.
[4] p. 377; cf. p. 288. For the House of Anjou in the Twelfth century, see pp. 100, 114, 132.
[5] William the Bastard at 38 years of age. "This big, bald man with an athlete's arm and a harsh face, whose cold anger roused fear, loved nothing but politics, war, and the chase. He was austere and chaste, and his character, taciturn, deliberate, and obstinate" (p. 56).

dream of uniting the crowns of France and England—who was the obstacle to this? A " maniac ", a " half madman ". John Lackland presented all the symptoms of a disease well known to-day, the periodic psychosis or cyclothymia.¹ What a striking contrast to the portrait of Philip Augustus is provided by this prince burdened with serious hereditary disabilities, unstable and irresponsible, incapable of finishing what he had started!

How many other people will similarly achieve the proportions of life for the readers of this masterly book?² Above all, surely, Saint Louis the " good king " who tried " to establish order and justice on earth and to lead his subjects to the heavens " (p. 426), the great king who, in spite of his " pitying heart " and his exalted devotion, had been brought up in a school of action and had a " firm will " and knew how to " speak very sharply even to bishops ".³ The figure of the man who made the monarchy loved among the French and France honoured throughout the world appears here delicately shaded.⁴ Thorough knowledge blossoms into very sound psychology.

As we have said elsewhere, art is neither essential to history nor useless. It should not be sought after but achieved. It is displayed here equally in the magnificent clarity of explanations and in the penetrating incision of the analyses of character.

HENRI BERR.

[1] In relation to John Lackland and other men of the period, Ch. Petit-Dutaillis in the pamphlet we have quoted, makes this remark : " We must examine, in the uncertain light that is provided for us, what was the temperament and even the physical condition of these men. I believe that in doing this we shall make some startling discoveries " (p. 6). On John Lackland, see pp. 215, 217, 327, below. At the recent Congress of Historical Sciences at Warsaw, Dr. Laignel Lavastine communicated a paper on the cyclothymia of Danton—on these questions see Aug. Brachet, *La Pathologie mentale des rois de France* ; A. Luchaire, " *La Pathologie des Capétiens* " in the *Journal des Savants*, January, 1904 ; Dr. Cabanès, *L'Histoire eclairée par la clinique* (full bibliography).

[2] pp. 24, Robert the Pious ; 76, Philip I ; 77, Louis the Fat ; 106, 180, Louis VII and Eleanor of Aquitaine (the " tireless ", 213, the " energetic " 221, the " imperious " Eleanor 260) ; 299 Alphonse de Poitiers ; 270-1, 311 Charles of Anjou. 100, Geoffrey Plantegenet ; 109-110, 157, Henry II, the " lawyer King " 165 and Richard Cœur de Lion ; 85, Gregory VII ; 208-9 Innocent III ; 207 the Emperor Henry VI ; 78, Suger ; 94, Etienne de Garlande ; 119-120 John of Salisbury ; 146 Thomas Beckett ; 343, 363, 367-8, Simon de Montfort ; 364 Stephen Langton.

[3] pp. 260, 261-2. On the admirable energy with which Louis IX was concerned with business until his last moments, see in the *Mélanges Jorga*, pp. 139, 146, L. Bréhier, " Une ambassade byzantine au camp de Saint Louis devant Tunis."

[4] See pp. 260, 272, 275, 288, 312, 318-19, 322-5, 378.

THE FEUDAL MONARCHY IN FRANCE AND ENGLAND FROM THE TENTH TO THE THIRTEENTH CENTURY

INTRODUCTION

THE object of this book is to show how the monarchy was preserved and developed, in France and England, in a period when the reorganization of political society into seignorial and feudal forms seemed to be condemning it to destruction. We have not sought to trace once more all the political history of France and England from the tenth to the thirteenth century; in an epoch when the annals of the royal house, at least in France, are often more scanty and less interesting than those of some Duchy or County, we have, nevertheless, devoted our attention to them alone. The causes, material and moral, for its weakness in the time of an Edward the Confessor or a Hugh Capet, the conditions which have enabled it to persist and expand, the machinery it has established, profiting by the very principles of Feudalism itself, the failure of the attempts made in England to impose upon it an aristocratic control, these are the problems we have tried to explain.

Feudalism in the West was born spontaneously under a diversity of forms.[1] It appeared, above all, in those areas where anarchy had produced the system of lordship. The springs of the new social order grew swollen in the disorder and misery of the tenth century and burst forth with an irresistible force offering to men some means of continued existence. But Feudalism was not a temporary expedient: it had had a long life. During the centuries that we are studying, above all during the twelfth and thirteenth, its sentimental inspiration was extremely powerful. Personal devotion, loyalty, the vassals' spirit of sacrifice, the suzerain's patronage, were the deep and lasting foundations of this organization

[1] Remember that the establishment of a truly feudal regime was only slowly achieved during the course of the period we are here studying. See further, pp. 13 and 82 below.

which was replacing the state in decline. Seignorial exploitation of the land, municipal liberties won by a mercantile class which, in some cases, made a " collective lord " of the greater men of the town assured this new society of an adequate and rapidly advancing economic life. Finally the jurists found means to co-ordinate and systematize the practices of the administration. At the end of the period we are reviewing, Beaumanoir's *Coutumes de Beauvaisis*, to speak of France alone, express a doctrine making the maintenance of civilization dependent on a respect for the mutual obligations which bind lord and vassal, the observance of the traditional customs of old and the new laws made in the feudal court. To read them it might be supposed that the idea of the State was obscured in men's minds for long years to come. And yet, Saint Louis could command obedience even to the extent of forbidding the wearing of arms and, according to Beaumanoir himself, could issue general ordinances. In England, for a century already, the monarchy had been provided with all the instruments of government and the barons had been unsuccessful in their attempts to prevent its progress. This simultaneous growth of two political systems, one of which was beginning to strangle the other, was due to such matters of fact as the conquest of England by the Normans, the victories of Philip Augustus, and the genius of individual statesmen; but at the same time reasons of a spiritual character also played their part. In the first place, in proportion as the feudal regime became systematized, logic demanded a recognition that the pyramid had a summit; the hierarchy ends in the monarch whom Beaumanoir calls sovereign over all: the kings will turn to the development of this principle and sooner or later will reap all its consequences. The Feudal System includes a king.

On the other hand the Church, that is to say the thinkers and writers, the preachers and teachers, who made up a large part of the personnel of the royal administration and councils —the Church preserved and developed the political doctrines of classical authors, the fathers and the theoreticians of the Carolingian age. It was essential for it to have a public authority which could help it in its work of salvation. Monarchy would not be necessary if man were virtuous; but to help the priest to destroy the tyranny of sin there

INTRODUCTION

must be kings. The experience of past centuries had gone to prove this fact. Custom and the mutual obligations of lord and man could not replace the state. This inability to guarantee an assured and permanent society had been clearly shown. From the feudal regime emerged war, brigandage, the brutal satisfaction of passions, and the ruin of souls. As a result, the Church believed in the divine mission of kings and taught its belief.

The attention it had devoted to inventing consecration, the consecration oath, the royal healing powers, and in helping to build administrative institutions was repaid, at the end of the period we are going to study, by the appearance of St. Louis. In the thirteenth century the monarchy in France and England was a powerful force in a feudal order which it began, more or less consciously, to destroy. It was equipped with officials, an army, finances, a system of justice and of police. It was popular: the mystery of kingship had been created. We shall examine under what conditions and by what men.

BOOK ONE

THE MONARCHY IN FRANCE AND ENGLAND FROM THE END OF THE TENTH CENTURY TO THE CREATION OF THE ANGEVIN EMPIRE

CHAPTER I

CHARACTERISTICS OF THE PRIMITIVE CAPETIAN MONARCHY

I

THE EVENTS OF 987

TO study the development of the French monarchy in the framework of Feudalism, we will take up our position at its traditional starting point, the accession of Hugh Capet in 987. This is not due to any inability to suggest good reasons for choosing some other. Ever since the end of the ninth century the transformation of political society by the system of homage, by infeudation, and the excessive weakening of the royal power had been an accomplished fact. Moreover, since that period the ancestors of Hugh Capet had held the throne alternately with the Carolingians: Hugh was the fourth of his family to assume the crown and the pretended change of dynasty in 987 is only a legal convention, an invention of historians to make classification more easy. It would be quite possible, therefore, to start at an earlier date. We could equally well select one more recent and ignore the reigns of Hugh Capet (987–996), Robert the Pious (996–1031), and Henry I (1031–1060) for during this three-quarters of a century the nature of the royal power, its instruments, and its sphere of authority, even its political exterior, did not differ from those of the later Carolingians. It was only in the time of Philip I (1060–1108) that the first outlines of a less nebulous French monarchy were drafted and that the conquest of England by the Duke of Normandy created a new problem.

But when we have taken all this into account, the year 987 is the best starting point we can find. After that date, as a matter of fact, the customary method of election did not give the throne to the Carolingian family and the Capetians succeeded from father to son. Finally, the survival of the institutions of the period of Carolingian decline almost to the time of Philip I will provide a useful introduction to the study of the political advances achieved under the Capetians.

It is not necessary, for the treatment of our subject, to analyse how Hugh Capet achieved the crown.[1] We shall confine ourselves, in these early pages, to a definition of what the kingdom of France and the monarchy were in the reigns of Hugh, Robert, and Henry I.

II

THE KINGDOM OF FRANCE

When the powerlessness of the early Capetians is fully realized one is apt to ask if, in reality, there was, at that time, " a kingdom of France." Was the " kingdom of France " anything more than a myth fostered in the mind of the king, his ministers, and a few churchmen ? To contemporary eyes, the only geographical reality contained in the word France was the region bounded by the Seine, the Meuse, and the Scheldt ; France was being narrowed down more and more to a point where it signified only the northern part of the diocese of Paris. If a man said " I am going to France ", he meant that he was going into this area.[2]

In spite of the weakness of the kings, in spite of the ambiguity of the title France,[3] we can admit that there was a kingdom of France not only in the formulas of chanceries but in the opinions and speech of the people.[4] There was a kingdom of France in distinction to the Empire and the Christian and Moslem principalities of Spain.[5]

The Capets were Kings of France because they were

---

[1] Cf. the classical treatment of Luchaire ((**CDXL**, I, introd.) on the coup of 987 and the origins of the Capetian family : F. Lot (**CDXXXI**, bk. ii, and app. xi).

[2] Bibliography in **CLXXVII**, 209, n. 1. See particularly **CDXXIX**, 1-28 ; **DXXI**, chap. iii ; **CDXXXII**, 187, n. 4 ; **CDLXIV**, i, 29-36.

[3] This ambiguity was already in existence in the time of the Franks. See **CCCLXXXVIII**, 337 ff.

[4] The formula of royal charters is " Regnum Francorum ". As early as the texts of the tenth century we find " Regnum Franciae " ; we should speak in the vernacular of the King of France and not the King of the Franks (**CCCXVI**, 320). As for the so-called Duchy of France, it did not exist in the Carolingian period ; there was only a *Dux Francorum*, a sort of viceroy.

[5] Cf. **CDLXXX**, 240.

THE KINGDOM OF FRANCE IN 987.

maintained by a strong popular tradition created by the Carolingians ; a study of the final clauses of charters shows that they were recognized as such to the most distant southern frontiers at least *de iure* if not *de facto*.[1]

There was, then, in the eyes of contemporaries, a King of France and a kingdom of France. What were the frontiers of that kingdom ? The kingdom of the last Carolingians and the early Capetians had an eastern boundary very different from the frontiers of to-day : starting from the Scheldt and taking in the region of Waes and Ghent, it roughly followed the river giving Tournai and Valenciennes to France, Cambrai to the Empire. From the sources of the Scheldt, it ran from west to east as far as the Meuse on the near side of Hainault and Mauberge which were subject to the Empire. Then it veered south dividing Champagne from Lorraine and the Duchy of Burgundy from the County (Franche Comté) extending approximately along the course of the Saone. For the sake of simplicity we can say that henceforward it followed the Rhone though, in fact, the regions of Lyons, Forez, Vienne, and Viviers were outside France. To the south, on the other hand, the frontier of the kingdom went beyond the Pyrenees from the Diocese of Urgel to that of Barcelona and Borel, Count of Barcelona, called in the help of his distant overlord, Hugh Capet, against the Arabs.[2]

So Capetian France was equivalent to neither Roman Gaul nor the France of to-day. The Treaty of Verdun had taken from the kings of " Western France " the traditional frontiers of Gaul, a numerous latinized population speaking a Roman dialect, and the most important of the great junctions on the Roman road system, Arles, Lyons, Treves, Metz, and a ready access to the Mediterranean.

A day would come when the recovery of the frontier of Gaul would appear to the kings of France a permanent objective in their policy. They would find in the uncertainties of the frontiers of the Middle Ages sometimes a check, sometimes an opportunity. There was no longer any distinct conception in men's minds. The idea of lordship had displaced that of the State. Were there any visible signs of the limits of

---

[1] **CCXXXIX** ; **CDXXXI**, 292 ; **CDXXXIII**, 121.
[2] **CDXXVI**, pl. xi ; **CDXXVII**, 215 ff. ; **CDXXVIII**, 19–20, and the works quoted after that. On the Empire and the Middle Kingdom in the eleventh century, see p. 83.

PRIMITIVE CAPETIAN MONARCHY

the kingdom? We doubt it very much. The Celts had marked the division of their territories by religious monuments and the Romans recognized the borders of cities, cantons, and villages, by means of boundary stones, inscriptions, ditches, etc.[1] It is only natural that in a period when the Roman Empire was co-extensive with the civilized world the only signs of external frontiers were the military defence works built against the Barbarians.[2]

We have good reason to believe that things were different in the Middle Ages but the evidence is scanty. Slowly, it would seem, boundary stones were set up along the Meuse.[3] In Argonne, near Luzy, the priest set up a stone cross in the fifteenth century to show that the territories of the Empire began there.[4] But, during the period we are studying here, the only marks of frontiers, as far as we know, were those in the interior of France, for instance between Artois and the neighbouring areas or between the royal demesne and the Anglo-Norman territory.[5] As a result, there were inevitably disputed strips [6] and groups of people did not know whether they were subjects of the Empire or of France.[7] When the matter came up for discussion, texts, Carolingian charters, chronicles, and compilations like that of Vincent of Beauvais were produced but their value as proof was often very small. When Philip the Bel demanded the overlordship of the Ostrevent, a region which was really a part of France but had been attached since the Treaty of Verdun to Hainault, a county of the Empire, both sides did everything possible to find proofs to support their respective contentions.[8] The Count of Hainault, forced to render homage to the King of France, protested to the Pope. The Ostrevent, he wrote to him, belongs to the King of Germany, " and possibly that appears fully in the registers and chronicles of the Roman Curia by whose authority, we understand, the division between the two kingdoms was made."[9] But this hope was vain.

[1] See the chapter of Albert Grenier in **CCXXXVII**, vol. v, chap. v.
[2] See the article " Limes " in the *Real Encyclopädie of Pauly and Wissowa*.
[3] **DCLXXXIII**, 27, n. 2.   [4] **CCXXVII**, 9.
[5] **CCXI**, vol. i, 52, 64, and Nachträge, 134–5 ; vol. iii, 120 ; vol. iv, i, 40. For the rest, the extent of the administrative boundaries of Medieval France was as vague as the frontiers : **CCLXXVI**, 18–20 ; **CCLXXV**, 50.
[6] **CCXCII**, 164–5 ; **CDXXXIV**, 5 f. ; **DVI**, 374 ; **DCVI**, 3–4 ; **DLXXIV**.
[7] **CCCLXXXIV**, i, 8.
[8] **DCLIV**, 316 ff. ; **CCXLIII**, 241 ff. ; **CCXLIV**, pref. and *passim*.
[9] **XXXVI**, 39.

In fact we should compare this quotation with a letter from Pope Clement V to Saint Louis where he states that no one in Rome had any exact information about the Franco-German frontier : " We do not find it determined in any document ; although for a long time we have dared to say that, in certain places, it was fixed by rivers, by ecclesiastical provinces, or by dioceses, we cannot clearly demark it ; we are in complete ignorance." [1]

The best way was to question the natives ; but it was only possible to ask them to what jurisdictions they were subject, which was a question of justice and lordship, not of sovereignty, and the arguments were of a feudal not a national character. The feudal idea was comparatively clear but the idea of State, of state frontiers, or nationality was shrouded in haze. Are we justified in using the light shed by the former to dispel the obscurity which surrounds the latter ? Clearly not, for lordship and sovereignty have never been the same thing. It was quite possible to be the vassal of the king without being his subject and everybody fully accepted this fact. We are not trying to make clear the significance of the term " subject ". There were magnates with territories on both sides of the frontier [2] such as the Count of Flanders, of Chalon, or of Mâcon, the Lord of Beaujeu, the Abbot of Beaulieu, the Count of Valentinois, and even the Count of Toulouse who did homage to the Emperor for the County of Provence ; but, a feature that is even more significant, there were lords of the Empire who were vassals of other lords of the Empire for lands held within the kingdom of France which were not liberties ; the Count of Bar held the fief of Hans near to Sainte Menehould of the Bishop of Verdun [3] ; and, conversely, there were lords of France, vassals of the Emperor for lands held in the kingdom of France ; for a century the Counts of Champagne were vassals of the Hohenstaufen for three of their French territories.[4] From the time when Count Henry rendered homage for them to Frederick Barbarossa, the King of France had no feudal rights over them but he was still their king. Moreover he was lord in the fief of Bar le duc after 1301 but he was not king at that date and Joan of Arc was

[1] LXXII, iv, n. 5439.   [2] CCCLXXXIV, i, Einleitung.
[3] Ibid., 23.   [4] Ibid., i, 15 ff.

born in the fief of Bar in a district of Domremy which, as a fief of Charles VII, was subject to a bailiwick of Champagne and, as Imperial territory, to a bailiwick of Bar.[1]

In this particular case, the king's party would work to confuse enfeoffment and sovereignty. At other times they would make every effort to distinguish them.

III

The Diversity of France in the Eleventh Century—The Great Lordships

Within this frontier there was a complete lack of uniformity. It was not the feudal regime alone which gave an impression of anarchy in a survey of France, for this regime was incomplete and still in the throes of definition, its centrifugal force was not yet fully developed. The hereditary principle of enfeoffment was not generally recognized and the king maintained his right to resume lands which he had granted as a "beneficiary gift". Everything tended to produce infinite variety—language, customs, and private law. Six centuries of great movements of peoples had destroyed, directly or indirectly, the unity of Roman Gaul.

In spite of the great powers of absorption and survival which the Latin language has shown [2] a German dialect was spoken in Flanders and as far south as the district of Boulogne; in Bayeux Scandinavian was spoken, the Celts driven out of Great Britain by the Anglo-Saxons had reintroduced their language into the Armorican peninsular which was beginning to be called "Little Britain"; finally the Gascons in the sixth century had invaded the region between the Pyrenees and the Garonne and established, at least in the mountain country, the Basque language. On some of the frontiers of the kingdom, groups speaking foreign tongues had thus established themselves, peoples totally uncultured and barbarous, over whom the Church could only establish its civilizing influence after a long time.

As for the Romance speaking districts, even there many

---

[1] DI, first part.   [2] CCIII, 81–116.

dialects were spoken.¹ As the distance from the Alps and Mediterranean increased, so did the lapse from the original forms of the Latin language but the differences were more marked towards the North than towards the West. South of a somewhat sinuous line from near the mouths of the Gironde to near Annonay there existed a group of idioms marked by the preservation of the Latin tonic " a " which formed what the people of the south themselves called the lingua Romana and of which philologists to-day abusively speak as Provençal. It has been essential for us to insist on the transitions, the unnoticed graduations, the overlapping which existed, but, in fact, our divisions have not been contrary to historical reality.

In those regions where there was the most faithful adherence to low Latin, there was also a system of custom permeated with principles of Roman Law,² ways of life and dress, and a particular mentality which astonished and naturally scandalized the people of the North.³

Great as the diversity of France in the eleventh century undoubtedly was, it would be false to consider it as a simple mosaic of minute lordships. The great obstacle to the maintenance of the royal power was precisely that above the kaleidoscope of petty fiefs and allods there were, particularly in France, principalities, dynasties of dukes and counts frequently established by Carolingian ministers of old and often more powerful than the royal house.

In fact they showed such independence and were such a menace to the royal power that many authorities have found reason to question whether they were legally subject to it.

One of them has suggested that in the eleventh century the Capetian is merely the chief of an " ethnic grouping " with the same title as the other great lords of Gauls; that the " princes " were his " peers " and did not render homage to him; that he only enjoyed some form of pre-eminence among them.⁴ But our documents do not allow us to say

---

¹ See the résumé given in **CCI**, i, 296 ff.
² See the map of written law which corresponds in the main to the philological map in **DCLXXIV**, at the end of vol. ii, or in J. Brissaud, *Cours d'histoire du droit français*, vol. i, 1904, p. 152.
³ **XCVIII**, 89.
⁴ **CCLXXXVIII**, especially vols iii and iv, cf. **CCCXLIV**, 275–281. **CDXXXIII**; **CCLXXII**, 159 ff., 347 ff.

that the region between Lorraine and the Loire formed a separate " ethnic grouping " while they justify the opinion that the great barons considered themselves as the kings' " men " : the Count of Flanders, the Duke of Burgundy, the Duke of Aquitaine, the Count of Blois and Chartres, the Duke of Normandy himself performed host service on several occasions and frequently journeyed to Rheims to be present at the consecration.

It is important that we should exaggerate nothing and maintain the reserve which the scanty nature of the documents and considerations of probability demand. As a personal opinion, we do not believe that the oath of homage and fidelity was regularly renewed at each accession in the royal house or the princely dynasties. But when circumstance made it possible no one refused to render homage.

Who were these great princely dynasties ? We must speak of them in detail for they were not all in the same relationship to the Capetians. This fact is easily deduced on first principles by a glance at the map and the mountains which separate the basin of the Loire and the Seine from Aquitaine and Languedoc, all but invincible obstacles in a period when the king had neither an administration nor an army of his own and when only at rare intervals did he embark on the adventure of making a long journey himself.

In the South and Centre, the lords of Catalonia and Roussillon, of Languedoc, of Toulouse, of Gascony, Poitou, and the Central Plateau grouped themselves fairly readily round the Counts of Barcelona, Rouergue, Toulouse, and Gascony and the Duke of Aquitaine. The last mentioned, with his capital at Poitiers, styled himself " Duke of all the monarchy of Aquitaine ".

This monarchy of Aquitaine comprised all the centre of Gaul from Berry, Bourbonnais, and Auvergne to the shore of Vendée and Saintonge. William the Great (V) held magnificent courts and exchanged embassies with the kings of the Iberian Peninsula, of England and with the Emperor. He had married the daughter of the Duke of Gascony and in 1030, shortly after his death, the two duchies became united into an immense principality. The people from the North who travelled in this area gained the impression that he was completely independent of the King of France. It was an

Aquitainian chronicler, Ademar of Chabannes, who invented about 1130 the famous dialogue between the associated kings, Hugh Capet and Robert the Pious and Audebert of Perigord : " Who made you a Count ? " " Who made you Kings ? " It is highly unlikely that the dialogue ever took place,[1] but it is not, by any means, fantastic. The princes of the South had no connections with the early Capetians unless they had a personal sympathy for them or thought their friendship worth winning. Robert was a friend of William the Great who, like himself, was pious and an amateur collector of manuscripts and he travelled to Toulouse to hold a court but, after his reign, the bonds between the royal house and the southern principalities grew weaker and weaker : each tended to ignore the other.[2]

North of the Loire in the area where they were themselves established, seeking to maintain and extend their influence, the early Capetians found dangerous rivals. The Counts of Flanders, Baldwin IV and V, the Dukes of Normandy Eudo I and II, Counts of Blois, Tours, and Chartres and the terrible Black Fulk, Count of Anjou, were insatiably seeking new conquests. If we were writing a history of France we could not avoid returning at this point to the annals of these four great houses, showing the Count of Flanders consistently seeking to carve out a Netherlands kingdom for himself, defying the Emperors ; the Duke of Normandy and the Count of Anjou bickering over the possession of Maine and the overlordship of Brittany sought after quite as eagerly by the reigning Count of Blois ; Eudo II of Blois grasping at Champagne and endeavouring for his own benefit to re-establish Lotharingia, and to reign over Lorraine, the kingdom of Arles and Italy. Their mutual rivalries saved the monarchy as surely as their unity could have destroyed it. The powerful house of Blois made an unsuccessful attempt to dethrone both Hugh Capet and Henry I. Their fickle and uncertain policy enabled the first three Capetians to keep their domains generally intact from their rapacious vassals and it was only rarely that they allowed themselves to be drawn into their quarrels. Moreover for sixty years the

---

[1] **CDXXXII**, 353–4.
[2] **DXXI**, 271–299 ; **CDXXXII**, 199–215 ; **CDXXXIII**, chaps. iii–iv ; **CCLXXXVIII**, iv, 519 ff.

Capetians were supported by the powerful dukes of Normandy. This tradition of alliance between the monarchy and the Duchy of Normandy was abruptly broken off by Henry I who was naturally combative and worked for ten years to build up a coalition against William the Bastard. At Varaville in 1058, he was decisively defeated and when he died two years later the royal power was weaker than ever in relation to the four princely dynasties of northern France.[1]

In this way a ring of powerful principalities had been built up from the Pyrenees to Flanders encircling the region around Paris and Orleans to which the royal power was restricted. In addition the king had to make allowance for other neighbours who, though less powerful, menaced his security at certain periods. The Counts of Amiens, Vermandois, Soissons, Corbeil, Melun, Sens, and many others fall into this category. Their counties encroached further and further on the Capetians' domains and often formed enclaves within it. The advances in military architecture during the eleventh century made these petty counts and the lords of even less importance who swarmed in the country around Paris more and more dangerous. This was the period during which the strong halls with wooden keeps were giving way to well built stone castles from which they could ignore the King of France even in the centre of his own demesne.[2]

IV

THE ROYAL DEMESNE

The royal demesne was the aggregate of territories in which the king exercised on his own behalf the privileges of baron, or independent lord, and of justice; this last was the most important for it offered him an opportunity for constant intervention and endowed him with a reality of power. This at least is the definition to which a study of the documents leads but they do not express in it any formula; the word " demesne " does not even appear in

---

[1] **CDXXXII**, chaps. v and vi; **DXXI**, 209–245; **DCIX**, 48 ff.; **CCCXXXIX**, chaps. i and ii; **CDXL**, ii, 205 ff.; **CDXVIII**.
[2] **DXXI**, 209; **CDXXXII**, 190; **CDXXVIII**, 45–7.

them.[1] Once this definition has been made it must be immediately corrected by a realization that the demesne was neither uniform, compact, nor even continuous. In one place he possessed personal property bringing in the revenues of land—villages or part villages with fields or else meadows, vineyards, woodland, fishponds, mills, or even the village church in the material implication of the term, with the lands and dues which pertained to it or else a town or even houses or a crenellated tower in the town.

For instance when Sens was annexed to the royal demesne part of it belonged to the king and part was left for the archbishop. In other cases, the king could not use the revenues to his own advantage but he had the " administration ", that is to say he retained all, or almost all, the rights of lordship; possibly, he only retained the rights and profits of justice.

It is not possible to draft an accurate map of the royal demesne for there is no text which describes its extent under the early Capetians. The only royal property which the Carolingians had bequeathed to the new dynasty was a few palaces. Hugh Capet had endowed himself with the regions around Paris and Orleans, the districts of Étampes, Poissy, and Senlis, and, in addition to this fairly compact block, several scattered holdings and the port of Montreuil through which alone the monarchy had access by the sea.

His brother Henry held the Duchy of Burgundy and, when he died in 1002 leaving no heir, King Robert, who possessed both ambitions and the energy necessary to realize them, succeeded in gaining the inheritance for himself. The acquisition was not so much important because of the new resources it placed at the disposal of the crown, for the Duke of Burgundy was not a landowner of outstanding importance, as because on this side the royal demesne would have reached the frontiers of the kingdom breaking the circle of feudal principalities. But Henry I was forced to give up the Duchy and invest his rebel brother with it. The annexation of the district of Sénon to the demesne was a very inadequate compensation. The monarchy had been advancing consider-

---

[1] The Carolingian term *fisc* soon fell into disuse. Later, in some documents, we find the word *potestas*. The use of the word *dominicum* is still rare in the time of Philip Augustus.

ably till the reign of Robert but it now seemed condemned to stagnation.[1]

There was one important legacy, of both material and moral value, which the Carolingians had bequeathed to the new dynasty. This was the royal power over the Gallican Church.

V

THE EARLY CAPETIANS AND THE CHURCH

The Church which had seen the disappearance from France of Roman and Imperial government and had been forced to exist on terms with lay lordships could not altogether isolate itself from the political and social order or the habits of life of the feudal aristocracy any more than it can to-day from the republican and democratic forms of government with which, in certain countries, it is essentially bound up. But, in the eleventh century, it was, much more than to-day, a world to itself. If, when we speak of the Church, we mean all the hierarchy of prelates and clerks, secular and regular, who were heart and soul devoted to the Christian ideal, if we can ignore the brutal pugnacity and the frequent dissolute excesses which were found within it at this time, it is true to say that it viewed with great regret the welter of anarchy and disorder and that it considered as dearly bought the independence which in some respects it gained from them. It preserved as its political ideal the memory of the Christian Roman Empire. This was not only because it needed peace for the salvation of souls; in spite of its violent internal disruptions the Church had a sense of unity and hierarchical authority. With the failure of Imperial Rome, the Gallican Church looked more and more towards Pontifical Rome.

The amazing success of the False Decretals [2] for a hundred and fifty years showed quite clearly its desire to establish on an ancient tradition the government of Christendom by the Holy See. Nevertheless, it preserved also its enthusiasm

[1] **CDXXXII**, 187-9; **DXXI**, 86 ff., 206-7, 246 ff.; **CCXCII**, 123 ff.; **CDLXXXVI**, chap. v.
[2] Summary bibliography in **CDXXXII**, 361 ff., and in **CCLXXIX**, 166, note 116.

for royalty and, throughout the Middle Ages, maintained the Carolingian doctrine of the two powers. The divine mission of the Holy See and the monarchy were the basis of all its political doctrine. Even at the time when their authority was weakest, that is to say during the period we are dealing with in this chapter, the Pope and the French king found champions in the clergy. The reform of the monasteries, which was initiated in the tenth century and vigorously carried through in the eleventh by the Abbots of Cluny and other churchmen, resulted in the triumph of this theory; for the monasteries could only regain their dignity, independence, and wealth and avoid the brutal domination of the nobles and the unreasonable demands of the bishop by gaining the support of the monarchy and the Holy See.

The kings of France had, for five centuries, been tying the bonds between themselves and the Church. The Merovingians and Carolingians had enriched and protected it almost consistently. In Hugh Capet and Robert the Pious it found zealous advocates of ecclesiastical reform. On the day of their coronation oath, the Capetians were ready to make a speech in which their duties to the Church were almost the sole issue. In return the Church granted money to the crown, sent its knights and tenants to serve in the royal army, and provided experienced counsellors for the court. This was not all. Within the royal demesne and in many dioceses outside, it was subjected by the right of regale to the will, almost the whim, of the king. In the South, in Britanny and Normandy, the nomination of bishops fell to the Capetians but in the ecclesiastical provinces of Rheims, Sens, Tours, and in the centre of France four archbishoprics and twenty bishoprics were at the disposal of the king.[1] What does this mean? On the death of the holder the king disposed of the temporalities of the see as their landlord, he nominated to the vacant benefices (right of regale), he enjoyed and abused the right of spoils which gave him the right to seize the moveable property of the dead man and, after a delay that was frequently excessively prolonged, he imposed his candidate—a personal friend, a relation, or a clerk of the Royal Court. The canons of the cathedral who actually elected the bishop by agreement with certain nobles of the

[1] **CDXXXII**, 216 ff.

PRIMITIVE CAPETIAN MONARCHY 21

diocese were rarely moved to protest and the bishops of the province were usually equally submissive in electing their metropolitan. Unless the Pope took up the cause of some defeated candidate the episcopal or archiepiscopal cross remained in the hands of the royal favourite.[1] To a lesser degree the king possessed abbeys often important and wealthy which were counted as part of his " fisc ", as part of his demesne. Some of these were royal houses founded by the Carolingians or Merovingians or else added to the fisc by Hugh Capet in 987; others the Capetians had gained by granting them immunities, exempting them from the exactions of the counts who had encroached on them. We have mapped out the abbeys and collegiate foundations, whose existence in the time of Hugh Capet we may assume, from the extremely scanty evidence available. Of an approximate total of 527 he was patron of about thirty-two and he shared the patronage of sixteen with the bishop or some noble.

Twenty-six of them were situated in the province of Sens principally in the neighbourhood of Paris and Orleans, fifteen in the province of Rheims, four in the province and diocese of Tours, two (possibly four) in Lyons, one (possibly three) in Bourges.[2] The king was himself abbot of Saint Martin de Tours, Saint Denis, Saint-Germain-des-Prés, and Saint Corneille de Compiègne.[3] In the other royal monasteries he imposed abbots of his own choice as far as the Cluniac reforms still allowed and in any case he was able to use the resources of the abbey very extensively.

Even his most powerful subject could not dispose of so many bishoprics and abbeys or command such observation points beyond his own demesne as the king could. In this respect the early Capetians had no challenge to their supremacy but, as we shall see, though the bishoprics and monasteries of the South, the West, and of Normandy fell to the king, he could not count confidently on the obedience

---

[1] These questions have been studied in detail in **DXXII**, 17 ff., and **CCCLXIX**.
[2] **CDXXXII**, app. xiv.
[3] Hence the nickname Capet or Chapet (clad in ecclesiastical cloak). This name was given in the eleventh century to the father of Hugh the King. It was not applied to him until the twelfth century. The name "Capetian" seems to have been invented by the English Chronicler Raoul de Disci. **CDXXXII**, app. vi.

and the consistent fidelity even of those within the demesne. We must always remember, even while we show the extent of the relations between the early Capetians and the Church, that they could demand only a tardy obedience and a grudging respect. The Emperor presents a striking contrast for he maintained a rigid control over all the clergy of Germany. This is the reason why there was an investiture controversy in Germany but not in France.

The narrow limits of this book do not allow us to trace again the story of the relations between Hugh and Robert and the Church.[1] It is, however, an exceedingly interesting story.

In the first place it shows clearly that the early Capetians had no conscious objective and provides us with many examples of their fickle passions, their childish versatility, their peasant like tricks, their complete inability to follow any political line, or even to be faithful to their allies. In opposition to them was only a divided clergy. At the famous Council of St. Bâsle summoned by Hugh to pass judgment on a traitor, the Archbishop Arnoul, who had handed Rheims over to his enemies, the king could count on the assent of several bishops. Later on Robert even found an archbishop to celebrate a marriage which, according to canon law, was an incestuous union. Nevertheless many prelates were not prepared to obey and the two incidents—the deposition of Arnoul and the marriage of Robert—ended in reverses for the King of France. Even those bishops who, at St. Bâsle, upheld the theory of the supremacy of the Council were not inspired by any spirit of nationalism. They demanded something very different—the right of the theologians of the district to direct its spiritual affairs, particularly when the Pope was worthless as was the case at the time that the Council met. The French monarchy was not yet able to use the clergy to achieve its own ends. In the time of Hugh and Robert it was still only a question of an alliance (and strained by frequent disagreements at that) comparable to that between two partners who have need of each other's assistance but whose interests are quite distinct and whose ultimate ambitions are almost diametrically opposed.

---

[1] See its excellent treatment by F. Lot, **CDXXXII**, chap. ii–iv; **DXXI**, 41 ff.

VI

THE SACRED CHARACTER OF THE MONARCHY AND ITS POPULAR BACKING

It was to the Church, however, that the French monarchy owed its spiritual character, its religious basis which was one of the causes of its survival amongst principalities jealous of its success or indifferent to its failure. The traditions of the sacred character of the monarchy, derived from Biblical, Roman, and German sources alike which had almost died out in the Merovingian era, were revived for the benefit of Pepin and Charlemagne and since that date had grown stronger and more definite. When Charles the Bald was anointed by the Archbishop of Sens in 848 he had received from him the crown and sceptre and from that time the consecration ceremony was immutably determined. The unction, a ceremony of Biblical origin, was particularly important. The king was anointed on the head and various parts of his body and was entitled to the Chrism, a mixture of oil and balsam. By right of this he could claim all the privileges of a bishop. Further popular belief mantained that the Chrism in the coronation vial at Rheims had been brought to Saint Remy by a dove for the baptism of Clovis. This legend increased the prestige of the kings of France and of Rheims very greatly and in the eleventh century the latter became fixed as the place of coronation.[1]

The document which has come down to us on the coronation of Philip I [2] when he was associated with his father in the kingship in 1059 bears all the marks of authenticity and shows very clearly the predominantly religious and ecclesiastical character of the ceremony which bound the new king to the Church for ever. The Archbishop of Rheims called on him to repeat the following formula :—

" I Philip, by the grace of God soon to be King of France, on the day of my ordination promise, in the sight of God and his Saints, that I will maintain inviolate for everyone of you and for all the

---

[1] **CLXXIX**, bk. i, chap. ii ; bk. ii, chap. ii ; app. iii.
[2] H. F., xi, 32. This document was drawn up at a later date during the first quarter of the twelfth century (Prou., **CIII**, p. xxiv, and n. 2). Hans Schreuer has published again the *Ordines ad consecrandum regem* of the thirteenth century with a minute study **DXCIX, DC, DCI**. Cf. Lot, *Derniers Carolingiens*, 1891, pp. 212-13.

churches under your charge their canonical privileges, their legal rights and their security in Justice; that, with the help of God, I will defend you to the utmost as a king must defend every bishop and church in the kingdom committed to him. Further I promise to the people over whom I am given authority that I will use it solely in the execution of the laws which are their right."[1]

This constitutes an important treaty for both parties. The Church gains solemn guarantees and can claim the power of making kings: The king henceforward " rules other mortals by Divine Grace ".[2] The unction places him outside the world of men, apart. Humble folk realizing the sacred character of the king can find no distinction between him and the bishop. When the Chancery of Louis VII declared that kings and priests are associated by the unction of the Holy Chrism it fell but little short of those cleric and lay subjects who regarded the king as a priest. The enlightened clergy grew angry at the loquacious ignorance which could believe that coronation conferred sacerdotal powers, but bishops and even popes spread the confusion, encouraging kings to consider themselves as " Holy ".[3] Naturally no French noble apart from the king, not even the powerful Duke of Normandy, enjoyed this exultation resulting from the ritual formality of the coronation ceremony. The king alone was consecrated with the unction.

The further recognition of the miraculous powers of the kingship was only a short advance probably made in the reign of Robert the Pious. This brutal and sensuous monarch sought absolution for all his excesses in the fervour of his devotions; he gained a reputation as a scholar and a theologian and loved to pass his time in the company of clerks singing hymns with them or to " take his place in the episcopal synods directing and discussing ecclesiastical affairs ". He was merciless to heretics, an ardent patron of monastic reform and of the Gilds for Promoting the Peace of God, welcoming everything which the Church welcomed.

His panegyrist, the monk Helgaud, tells how he cured the sick with the sign of the cross and in this way, with the pious complicity of churchmen, the legend of the royal healing power became established. At the beginning of the

---

[1] That is to say the administration of custom.
[2] Formula of a charter of Robert: **DXXI**, 146.
[3] See the documents cited in **CLXXIX**, 73 ff., 120 ff., 186 ff.

PRIMITIVE CAPETIAN MONARCHY

next century the tradition assumed its particular and limited form—the king, by touching for the king's evil, became the curer of the scrofula.[1]

Here we have reached the point where popular support for the monarchy was reinforced by the theoretical conception of the Church on the two powers, the secular arm, the responsibilities and rights of kingship. The Church presented the king to the congregation which acclaimed him in the cathedral of Rheims as sovereign by Divine Right, absolute, responsible to God alone, charged with the sacred duty of defending the Church, administering good justice, and defending customary rights, peace, and the frontiers of the kingdom; the clerks of the royal courts never drew up a charter without reminding all of the divine mission of the monarchy.

They advised the sick to come to him for alleviation and fostered around him an atmosphere of religiosity.[2] But the bishops, chancellors, and councillors of the curia were not the only forces creating this mystery of kingship. There was also a strong popular tradition along all the main pilgrim routes and around the holy places where crowds gathered and a common tradition, a national life, was being built up; poets, inside the Church and without, were singing the praises of "Gentle France" and her former glories and of the time when Charlemagne had conquered all the West. If we turn again to the *Chanson de Roland* to understand how it had the strength to live on, we shall perhaps gain a true idea of the monarchy in the eleventh century.[3]

The exact date and place of the "story which Turold tells" is of little significance to us. The story, written in the reign of Philip I or Charles the Fat in "France" or Normandy, can safely be used as an index of the position of the monarchy in France in the reign of Henry and Robert. It reveals a state of mind among the people which none of the early Capetians was in a position to create for himself, which went beyond their weak and inadequate personalities and had roots embedded in the distant past.

---

[1] **CLXXIX**, bk. i, chap. i; **DXXI**, 34 ff., 169 ff., bk. iii, chap. iv.
[2] **CDXL**, i, 40 ff.
[3] **XXI**, 10, 12–14, 42, 184–6, 190, 216, 300 etc. Cf. **CLXII**, particularly the conclusions of vols. i and iv; iv, 437 ff.; iii, 185 ff.; **CCCVI**, 79 ff.; **DIII**, 345 ff. and the additional notes 544; **CCCLXI**.

It shows, above all, that the ideal of national unity had not been completely forgotten in the eleventh century and that when a poet spoke of the Empire, a unity stretching far beyond the narrow confines of the Capetian kingship, he was generally understood. Turold and his predecessors reminded their audiences that Charlemagne had conquered Italy, that his councillors had included Germans as well as Bretons and even attributed to him an expedition to England. Through all this the focus of national life remains " Gentle France ", the country with kindly skies where the folk are sober and well advised. There Charlemagne loved best to live and, when he sought the advice of his barons, " he valued most the opinions of the French." It is easy to visualize him there and who can fail to recognize him ? " In the shade of a pine, close beside a sweet briar, a throne of pure gold is arranged ; upon it sits the man who rules our gentle France, his beard is snow white, his head wreathed in flowers, his body speaks of perfect fitness, his face of mighty pride."

Two hundred years have passed since his birth ; with bent head he sits and ponders ; his speech is never hasty and it is his custom to speak in a leisurely fashion ; he knows how best to lead discussion in his assemblies and his reproof for the idle chatterer is sharp. This wise and sober monarch is respectful towards women and deals gently with them, for he has a tender heart ; in the terrible moment when he finds Roland once more, to find him dead, he faints away. Before all else he was a servant of God ; after capturing Sarogosa he ordered all the pagans to be taken to be baptized and if any man refused to comply he ordered him away to be hung, burnt, or to execution. He passed his life in war on the Infidels and God gave him no time for rest ; his life was one of trouble and difficulty, but he had the protection of God who sent angels to talk with him, to preserve him, and encourage him in the day of battle. On his behalf miracles could be achieved—the course of the sun was stayed ; the Great Emperor himself had sacerdotal powers and authority for the remission of sins.

Such was the myth of kingship which was fostered and developed by churchmen and poets.

VII

ELECTIVE MONARCHY—ASSOCIATION IN THE THRONE

Since the deposition of the Carolingian Charles the Fat in 887 the principle of elective monarchy [1] had triumphed once or twice during the tenth century over the tradition of hereditary succession. Eudo, Robert, Raoul, and Hugh Capet had become kings by election. The men who chose Hugh Capet in 987 had no intention of establishing a new dynasty and the right by which the Capets ascended the throne was the right of election, a principle clearly enunciated by the clergy and welcomed by the baronage. The coronation ceremony in the eleventh century gave only the sanction of ritual to this doctrine. The Archbishop of Rheims " chose the king " in accordance with the agreement previously arrived at by the great men of the kingdom before anointing and crowning him, and the subjects who thronged the cathedral, greater and lesser nobility alike, gave their consent by acclamation. Theoretically the unanimous choice of the whole kingdom was necessary for the election but, in fact, once the will of those who were of decisive importance was made clear, the approbation of others was merely a matter of form. Nevertheless the conventions of the chancery attached considerable importance to it; the first year of the reign only began on the day of consecration and this rule, closely related to the theory of election, was to last for two centuries.[2]

In fact, then, this Capetian kingship whose supernatural character we have been illustrating was, at the same time, elective. To the modern mind that may present a strange contradiction but contemporaries found no cause for surprise. The very fact that the kingship was so closely comparable to the priesthood justified its non-hereditary character. How could churchmen deny the divine nature of an institution because it was elective? Even bishops and popes were appointed by election. The monk Richer attributes to the Archbishop Adalbéron a speech to the nobles in 987 which

---

[1] On all this question, see **CDXL**, I, bk. i, chap. ii; **DCLXIV**, ii, 46 ff., and the works of Hans Schreuer, particularly **DXCIX**.

[2] It has been clearly shown (**DXVII**, intro., p. xii) that the transmission of the royal power from the death of the father only began in 1223.

does not exactly represent the ideas of Adalbéron but it is quite in accordance with the principles of the Church. " The kingdom," he says, " has never made its choice by hereditary right. No one should be advanced to the throne who is not outstanding for intelligence and sobriety as well as for a noble physique strengthened by the true faith and capable of great souled justice."[1] The best man must reign and, we may add, he must be chosen by the " best " men.

This was the theory of the Church without modification or limitation.[2] Once he had been elected by a universal acclamation, which, in fact, represented the assent of a few individuals, and consecrated, he became king by the Grace of God commanding the implicit obedience of all.[3]

This doctrine of the Church was equally acceptable to the instinctive anarchy of the nobility. The election of the king seemed quite natural to a baronage which regarded it as no more than an individual contract.

And so the only means that the Capetians could use to ensure that the crown stayed within their family was to provide for the election and coronation of their heir during their own lifetime. For three hundred years they were fortunate enough to have sons and practised a system of association in the monarchy until the period when Philip Augustus felt that he had good reason to believe that he was strong enough to neglect the precaution. In 987 there was a very recent precedent to hand. The Caroling Lothair distrusted the ambitions of his brother, and in 979 he had associated his son Louis V in the throne and had him consecrated.[4] When Hugh Capet was elected and enthroned he immediately demanded that the greater nobility should allow him to share his throne with his son Robert. This roused some opposition from Archbishop Adalbéron, and the expedition which Hugh was about to make against the Saracens in Spain was used as the main argument. In no other way could a peaceful succession to the throne be guaranteed in case of disaster. On Christmas Day of the same

---

[1] **CXI**, bk. iv, chap. xi, p. 132.
[2] **CCLXXX**, 357 ff.; **DCLXIII**, 35 ff.
[3] See the theories of Abbon de Fleury on the omnipotence of the elected king in his *Collectio Canonum* dedicated to the kings Hugh and Robert; i, 478–480.
[4] **CDXXXI**, 108–9.

PRIMITIVE CAPETIAN MONARCHY 29

year, Robert was crowned in the cathedral of Orleans, but we have no evidence to show whether he was anointed at the same time. Father and son reigned jointly without any division of territories or titles and without discord until Hugh expressed his opposition to the marriage of Robert and Bertha.[1]

After the death of his father Robert reigned as sole monarch for twenty years but after his repudiation of Bertha his private life was greatly disturbed by the evil intrigues of his wife Constance. In an age when manners were rude and passions strong, shrews were not infrequent and this one caused an amazing state of terror in the royal household. " When she promises evil there is certainly no reason to doubt her word," writes Fulbert, Bishop of Chartres. In 1017 she demanded the consecration of her son Hugh and overrode all the objections of the nobles who said they could not see what useful purpose would be served.

Once he was king, Hugh fled from his mother's ill treatment to live a life of plunder and die at the age of eighteen. Then Robert called together his bishops and barons to bestow the crown on his second son Henry but Constance pressed the claim of her own preference, the third. The principle of primogeniture had not yet been established in deciding the succession.[2]

The suggestion made the bishops and barons very uneasy, for many reasons of widely differing character they would have preferred to avoid the issue. It was a strange and ominous thing " to make a man king while his father was still alive ". The powerful Duke of Aquitaine stayed away from Court in his anxiety not to estrange either king or queen. Bishop Fulbert came to Court to speak in favour of the elder son and a year later Henry was consecrated at Rheims. Nevertheless Fulbert did not dare to be present at the coronation for fear of Constance's wrath. Her hatred of the young king was only intensified and, after the death of Robert the Pious, she used every means in her power to dethrone him. This was one occasion which showed how a premature coronation might guarantee an orderly succession. Not only was Henry I able to maintain his own position but

[1] **DXXI**, 40, 49, 141, 142 ; **CDXXXI**, 216, 241–2 ; **CCCLV**, 290 ff.
[2] This was undisputed after the twelfth century.

in 1059 he secured the consecration of his son Philip. In spite of the troubles which accompanied almost every accession, the system of association in the throne assured the continuance of the dynasty.

The young king was first " designated " and then solemnly crowned by the Church. The profession, read by Philip in the ritual of 1059,[1] which has been transcribed above is followed by a declaration by the Archbishop of Rheims of the rights of his Church to chose the king and consecrate him in his office. His father gave his consent next and the Archbishop proclaimed his election by the acclamation of those present. Finally he proceeded to the consecration itself.[2]

When his father died the young king had himself crowned a second time and in fact he received the crown again every time he held a formal assembly, a Curia Coronata, but he was only consecrated once.

In this way the coronation of the young king designate brought about the return to the hereditary principle to the advantage of the house of Capet which was their only major political victory in the eleventh century. It was at one and the same time a victory for the family prestige and the principle of monarchy, for the bishops and barons who were not yet in antagonism to the king did not dare to neglect being present at the ceremony. For this one day there was a return to the time of which the poets spoke when the baronage of " Gentle France " all came together around the Emperor.

VIII

The Court

The early Capetians had neither the wish nor the ability to change the traditions of the Carolingian Court, either in theory or practice, in the routine of everyday life, or the pageantry of days of festival. Their court is a shrivelled and foreshortened reflection of the palace whose ideal form was

---

[1] DXXI, 71-83; CDXL, i, 79-81; DCIX, 45 ff.
[2] CCXCII, 2-4.

sketched by Hincmar long ago.[1] The life of the king continued to be nomadic because he had to take advantage of the resources of all his demesne in turn and his right to hospitality without overburdening any one district. He occupied the ancient palaces of the Carolings in Francia and built several new ones. Robert, for example, rebuilt the palace of La Cité in Paris. Paris, however, is not yet the most important of the royal towns, Orleans is the " King's principal residence ". The Capetians journeyed from palace to palace, from abbey to abbey, with their household, their records, and their seal and, wherever they were, there was the " Court ", the centre of monarchy, the centre of monarchial administration we would have said if that had been anything but embryonic.

The queen consort and the queen mother whose political activities are frequently apparent, and the sons and brothers of the king, all take part in the work of government—a part that is frequently productive of dissatisfaction and disorder. Their services are all the more embarrassing because he has no force of officers carefully chosen and trained in the execution of the royal commands. We have very little knowledge of the " *domestici* ", that official nucleus which consisted of both ministers, secretaries, and councillors, who travelled with the king and those bishops and nobles who came to court and were retained there for some long time on account of a desire to avoid dangerous and tedious journeys as much as possible. Fulbert of Chartres must be numbered among these. Even from his episcopal see he sent advice to Robert the Pious.[2] Among these " *domestici* " was an undefined group who at a later period would be called the chief officers of the crown and their position was very vague. Their names appear among the witnesses of charters together with those of barons or bishops. The complete lack of any unity among these signatures undoubtedly reflects the prevailing disorder and uncertainty. At court, as in the administration of the royal demesnes, the Carolingian order was crumbling and the Capetian system was not yet established.

At the important festivals, and from time to time as

---

[1] For all the next passage see **CDXXXII**, passim ; **DXXI**, bk. ii, chap. iv ; **CDXL**, vol. i ; **CDLXXXVI**, chap. iii.
[2] **XLIV**, 454, 457–460, 470, etc.

necessary, the king summoned a "full court" to meet, including the barons and bishops either of a certain region or possibly of the whole kingdom. Although we know very little of the *placita* and *conventus* of the tenth century we can easily believe that this was nothing new. As a result of the weakness of the monarchy, however, the full court of the Capetians was even farther from our idea of a representative political assembly than a similar gathering under the Carolingians, for the king invited whomever he pleased and the magnates, living a long way from court, did not inconvenience themselves to attend. Even on the occasion of a particularly solemn reunion such as a consecration there was never a full attendance of the nobility or even of the episcopacy.

The assembly did not meet to legislate, for there were no laws common to the whole kingdom ; neither did it meet to raise finance for the crown, for there was no taxation and the king had to depend on the revenues of his demesnes and the regalian rights. Then surely, at least, it met to assist the king in maintaining peace and doing justice ! That is the ambitious claim of the theorist Abbon. " Since it is the duty of the king to understand thoroughly what is going on all over the kingdom," he writes, " it is surely essential for him to seek the advice and the agreement of the leading men of the realm both spiritual and temporal." He can only attack evil with their " co-operation and advice ".[1] This celebrated text seems hardly less an expression of the ideal, or at least the obsolete, than the one in which Richer describes Hugh Capet as " making decrees and putting laws into execution in accordance with royal custom." It is true that barons and bishops assisted the king in judging certain important cases but when a magnate such as the Count of Anjou or Chartres refused to appear to answer a charge the king could do nothing to punish his contumacy.

Even if the first summons was obeyed and condemnation followed it was always possible to withdraw from court and defend the rights to privileges by force of arms. The king can be in fact the fount of justice only when, through the strength of his army or the power of his baronage, he can execute the sentences of his court. At this period he was dependent on the services of the feudal host to conduct a

[1] I, 478.

PRIMITIVE CAPETIAN MONARCHY

campaign or to carry out a simple matter of police work. He was forced to bargain for that service with his vassals and its regular performance was by no means certain.

The general courts were summoned by the first three Capetians very largely to gain support for the ambitious foreign policy on which they had embarked.[1] They sought to be recognized among the sovereigns of Europe. They exchanged embassies with the eastern Emperor and the kings of England and promised assistance to the Spanish Christians. Henry I married a Russian, the daughter of the Grand Duke of Kiev; his father, Robert the Pious, had met the Emperor Henry II, the Holy, at Ivois and Mouzon from 6th–11th August, 1023, at a highly ostentatious and ceremonious gathering of prelates and nobles where they had talked of ecclesiastical reform and the establishment of the Peace of God throughout Christianity.

A permanent alliance with the emperors of Germany remained however an idle dream. During the eleventh century the Capetians began to demand the return of Lorraine, but the emperors so far from receiving this suggestion sympathetically were seeking to add the rest of the Middle Kingdom established by the Treaty of Verdun to their domains. Robert the Pious and his son Henry I for their part envisaged, at certain periods, a policy of eastward expansion based on the dukes of Lorraine and other faithful vassals. Robert tried to prevent the extension of imperial suzerainty to the Rhone but the mad expansion policy of Eudo II, Count of Blois and Chartres, in rebellion against the King of France and at war with the Emperor resulted in the loss of the kingdom of Burgundy; from the district around Mâcon to the Mediterranean, from the valley of the Aoste to Forez, the whole of south-eastern Gaul was reunited to the Empire though only by an extremely loose bond (1033–4). Conrad, who also succeeded in becoming King of Italy, founded the German hegemony in Europe, the anarchy of the French princes reduced the Capetians to impotence.[2]

The early kings of the new dynasty were, then, in every respect comparable to the Carolingians.[3] They had exceedingly

---

[1] **DXXI**, bk. iii, chap. v; **CDXL**, ii, 215–241; **CLXXXIII**, 19 ff.; **CCIV**, 13 ff.; **DXXXVII**, 1st part, chaps. iii–v.
[2] To avoid any exaggeration on this point, see **DCLXXXIII**, 21–2.
[3] **CDXL**, vol. i, 37–9; vol. ii, 205–6, 252–3; **CCCXXXIV**, iv, 103–7.

high ideas of the authority which they believed they held of God. So far from devoting themselves to the modest policy of newcomers, they developed all the pretensions of legitimate sovereigns, the successors of Charlemagne in the kingdom of the West. Nevertheless, the first of them, Hugh Capet, had no easy task to maintain his position. With the passage of time they became even more threatened within their own demesnes by robber lords who began to build impregnable castles; Robert and Henry I instead of devoting their energies to the creation of an administration which met their needs and a small reliable force which could make them masters in their own house took up projects out of all relation to their means of realizing them.

To gain an adequate idea of the monarchy at this period we need only consider the fact that in spite of its weakness, it excited only very rarely a spirit of irony among its contemporaries. They took advantage of its weakness but they did not despise it. We have said what were the sources, ecclesiastical and popular, of its prestige. Even the barons recognized that it constituted a superior power of a different character to their own as long as it was prepared to be exploited by them. This is revealed very clearly in a curious document which has come down to us, the letter written to King Robert by Eudo II, the Count of Chartres.[1] The king was seeking to take some of his territories into his own hands and Eudo in the midst of an armed defence of his rights wrote a letter of protest to Robert. Why did the king, without giving him a chance to state his case, seek to deprive him of a fief of which he had previously recognized his legitimate possession by hereditary right? Eudo had served him "in his palace, in his wars, and on his journeys", and even if he had displayed some impatience and committed some imprudent acts when the king had sought to dispossess him, that was only to be expected. Punning on the term "honour" which applied to a group of fiefs at that period Eudo declared that he cannot live "dishonoured". He asked nothing better than to be reconciled with Robert whose benevolent regard he craved, believing that the king had been led astray by "false council". "This discord, my lord,

---

[1] CCCXLII, 287 ff.; cf. DXXI, 239–243; CDXXXII, app. xi; CDXXXIII, 163–4.

PRIMITIVE CAPETIAN MONARCHY

will destroy your office *root and branch, justice and peace alike*, and I therefore beg and implore that clemency which is natural to you ... permission to become reconciled with you *either by the mediation of your ministers or of the princes*."

This letter, in a tone that is at the same time humble and insolent, portrays exactly the attitude of the *principes Galliae* to the first Capetian monarch and their ideas of the nature of the *Curia Regis*. In a period when the thoughts of princes and their advisers were equally lacking in polish and boldness, when considerations of reason or ordinary common sense were outweighed by the violence of passions, or the memories of precedents of the routine of an obsolete past, it was by no means easy for the kings of France to find the appropriate direction for their policy. The very prestige which they enjoyed lessened still further their range of vision, while the dangers of their situation were growing more intense.

After the death of Henry I a new threat developed. In 1066 a great event took place which changed the course of the history of western Europe when the Duke of Normandy became King of England.

CHAPTER II

THE ANGLO-SAXON MONARCHY. THE DUCHY OF NORMANDY

I

The Primitive Social Elements of England

ABOUT the end of the thirteenth century, there were some very striking resemblances between the institutions of monarchy and the theory and practice of royal power in the France of Philip the Bel and the England of Edward I. It was merely a point at which two systems met. They had not pursued a parallel development before and, subsequently, their histories were widely different. Only in a study of their sources can the explanation of these divergencies be found.

In the eleventh century and still, to a large extent, in the twelfth, the kingdom of France was only a mass of independent principalities surrounding the royal demesne united by little but theory. There was no reason, before the reign of Philip Augustus, to believe that the Capetian monarchy had the power to become oppressive. The relations between those who exercised the remains of public authority were focused in feudal homage and the administration was on the verge of anarchy.

There was no political society comparable to the one that was forming in England. We must realize clearly that there is no basis for the belief that the English nobility deliberately and consciously established parliamentary liberties for they were activated, throughout the Middle Ages, by the spirit of Feudalism; it would be equally untrue to suggest that there was anything approaching the modern parliament in the thirteenth century. Nevertheless there was a social structure with its skeleton in every district from a very early date, popular courts, and a tradition of paying central taxes which provided a vague national unity, the basis on which the Crown could build the state at a later date and also the nucleus of a resistance to the undue growth of its power.

THE ANGLO-SAXON MONARCHY

In this sense we can speak of a political society and try to establish its origins.

To appreciate the position we must remember that the kingdom of England during the Anglo-Saxon and Norman periods was not much more than a quarter of the size of modern France. It included neither Ireland, which remained independent till the reign of Henry II, nor Wales, conquered only in the reign of Edward I, nor Scotland which was not united until a much later date, the accession of James I. It was a very much easier task to unify the lands from Northumberland to the Channel than from Flanders to the Pyrenees.

Many invaders had conquered this small tract of land.[1] The Celts had succeeded the prehistoric peoples and after them the Gaels and the Brythons. For almost four hundred years Britain was patrolled by Roman legions. They finally departed during the fifth century, leaving a free entry for German invaders; the leaders of the Anglo-Saxon bands established petty kingdoms under conditions of which we have little evidence and it has been said with some justification that the first page of English history is blank.[2] The Germanization of the country was completed and reinforced by the arrivals from Denmark, Norway, and even Sweden at the beginning of the eighth century. The Scandinavians colonized the north and east of England which Alfred the Great abandoned to them by the Treaty of Wedmore (878) in the same way as they colonized " Normandy " when it was given up to them by Charles the Simple. During the first part of the eleventh century the Danes conquered all of England.[3] Finally in 1066 it was invaded, for the last time, by the Normans under William the Conqueror with many recruits from Flanders, Picardy, and the Armorican peninsula of Britanny.

All the race groups that we have mentioned were to be found in France also and formed the basis of the French population but the character and relative importance of the

---

[1] See particularly **CLXI, DLXIII**; for the general history of England before the Norman Conquest there are good summaries in **CCCLIX** and in C.M.H., vols. i–iii.

[2] **CCXVII**, 1 ff.; **CDXXXV**, 19; **CDXXX**.

[3] We shall not deal here with the Scandinavian occupation in spite of its interest to the legal historian. See **DCLVIII**, 4–11, and a summing up in **DCXV**, 173–7.

invasions was very different in the two countries. The most important factor was that the Romanization, which was extremely thorough in Gaul, was very weak and superficial in Britain.[1] This essential contrast cannot be overemphasized, although certain English archæologists, proud of the discovery of interesting Roman remains, have tried to dispute it.

All the great English historians belong to the " German School " and they have good reason. The Roman School advance the evidence of Roman tombs and some hundreds of villas discovered in the south-eastern plain, fortifications, such as the wall of Hadrian, roads, and inscriptions.[2] The Roman legions and the merchants who went with them could obviously not be there for three centuries without leaving some traces of their occupation; in a distant and fogbound country, the conquerors would not fail to introduce some elements of Latin comfort or the gaiety of the decorative art of the south to relieve their homesickness. There were even great estates run on Roman lines and from London, the foundations of which are lost in the mist of pre-Celtic Antiquity, a network of roads spread out along which many towns sprang up.

Nevertheless Roman Government was confined to the plain and even there large areas remained uncultivated while the Government seems to have been almost exclusively military in character. The tombs are soldiers' tombs, the roads were military roads, and trade developed there to supply the needs of the high command; the so-called Roman houses were built on a pre-Roman plan. Lastly, and most important, the great works of Latin civilization, moral and intellectual, which transformed Gaul, only touched the fringe of Britain. The Britons did not learn Latin except in the towns; Christianization was too superficial to resist the German invasions; with the exception of some advances in agricultural method, rural life remained the same as before the Conquest.

Thus Celtic elements were not so completely suppressed as they were in France and they retained a fundamental

---

[1] This question is still hotly debated. See DVIII, 321–6; F. J. Haverfield (CCCLIV, CCCLIII, 265 ff., etc.) exaggerates the Roman influences. Cf. CCCXX, 1 ff., particularly DCLIX, bk. i, chap. ii.

[2] On the position of contemporary research, see CCXV (includes bibliography). Cf. CCXX, third part, chap. x.

importance in the political and social history of the country. The Romans doubtless changed little in the Celtic village community.¹ As far as we can judge from the Gaelic laws of a later period, private ownership of property only developed very slowly among the Britons. An extensive agriculture with a cumbersome and costly outfit of tools was quite alien to their mode of life.

At certain intervals the soil was redistributed, by drawing or by lot, among the members of an association which provided and manned a large plough drawn by four or eight oxen. In origin it was a clan association between people who believed themselves descended from a common ancestor,² but at some date which we cannot fix, the clan gave place to a contractual association governed by its own rules, general meetings, and elected officers. The Roman idea of the city state did not become established in Britain or rather it did not triumph over the spirit of rural co-operation. This organization of local life, embryonic though it must have been in the Anglo-Saxon period, was a phenomenon of very great importance, a distant but essential origin of the English political system.³

The Anglo-Saxon invasions undoubtedly involved a good deal of brutality and many Britons were driven into Wales, Cornwall, and Armorica. Nevertheless many remained in England and the union of the conquerors with the British women assured the survival of the Celtic elements and the village community.⁴ Anglo-Saxon society at the beginning of the seventh century is known to us by an admirable series of legislative texts in the common tongue which English and German scholarship have made understandable to us, and by the Latin charters of gifts to the Church.⁵

These texts do not remove every obscurity but thanks to their continuity they allow us to trace their very complex evolution. With the passage of centuries, Anglo-Saxon

---

¹ The strange theory of Seebohm (**DCIV**, chap. x) is no longer held.
² The laws and civilization of the Anglo-Saxons themselves have been dominated by the spirit of the clan and the family, little favourable to the progress of monarchy, and traces remained even after the Norman Conquest. See **DCV**, particularly p. 508.
³ **DCLIX**, bks. i and ii, and p. 365. Cf. the reservation of Maitland, **CDLIV**, 20–21.
⁴ **DCVIII**, 376 ; **DLXIII**, 108–110.
⁵ **LXXIV**, **CCXXXV**, 418 ff. ; Gross, *Sources and Literature of English History*, second edition, 1915, 36–7.

society was profoundly modified but now, at the beginning of its history, we need only remark one striking and permanent feature—the existence, in addition to the slaves, of an important class of free men who were both agriculturists and warriors who took over the old British villages and adopted their collective practices and regulations, frequently forming free communities recognizing no lord. Even at the date when William the Conqueror had Domesday Book drawn up there were still communities of this kind in existence. Even in those districts which fell under the domination of a lord the old Celtic rural settlement remained the basic social unit. The towns were unimportant, inhabited mainly by agricultural workers: it was the villages —the townships—which became the nucleus of the parish when Christianity was once more established in England, and of the legal and fiscal administration as the organization of the state developed. It was on the basis of their representatives, for instance, that an inquest was conducted to which each sent its reeve, priest, and four of the principal inhabitants.[1]

The representatives of the townships appeared in the Hundred courts and the Shire courts. The Hundred is a judiciary district found in all constitutions of Germanic origin (it corresponds to the pagus of Tacitus), holding monthly courts for dealing with robbers and bandits.[2] The development of seignorial justice and the organization of the royal court lessened its importance considerably but the Germanic Hundred, which disappeared very quickly in Gaul, has lasted down to the present day in England as a geographical subdivision.[3] After the Norman conquest the Hundred court appears again, generally transformed into a seignorial court. The Hundred like the township is one of the sources of local political activity in England. The Shire,[4] to be renamed County by the Normans, was a larger territorial unit. Originally it is found in only one of the Anglo-Saxon kingdoms—Wessex—but its value as an instrument of

---

[1] **DCLVIII**, 390 ff.; **CDLIV**, 340, 356; the accounts of Stubbs, **DCXXVII**, i, 97 ff., 105, 111 ff., are still valuable.
[2] **DCXXVII**, i, 118 ff.; **DCLVIII**, 96–107. Cf. **CCXVIII**, 239–248.
[3] England is divided into 729 *hundreds* or (in the area of Scandinavian colonization) *wapentakes*. See the table in **DCXXVII**, i, 123.
[4] **DCXXVII**, i, 129 ff.; **DCLVIII**, 90–6; **CCXVIII**, chap. viii.

monarchical authority led to its introduction into other kingdoms and the establishment of thirty-nine counties which still exist. The Shire court met twice a year to deal with judical business.

The strength of local life did not hinder the development of unity. There was an English state the moment that William the Conqueror arrived with his warriors. The ambition and energy of certain Anglo-Saxon chieftains and above all, the determined will of churchmen had built up a unified England.

When the Germans invaded Gaul they found powerful bishops some of whom were to become, at a later date, territorial magnates with titles of count or duke. When they came to Britain they found no parallel situation. The Christian Church which Gildas portrayed in the middle of the sixth century was in a most wretched condition. The British had relapsed into paganism and the conversion of the Anglo-Saxon proceeded slowly and was not even begun until 597 (the mission of Augustine). At the end of the seventh century an Asiatic Greek, Theodore, Archbishop of Tarsus, received from the Holy See the task of organizing the new Church. This remarkable man established the moral unity of England at a time when it was divided between rival and warring monarchies. He effected a new division of dioceses and gave the primacy to the Archbishop of Canterbury. He demanded the regular holding of councils and, in addition to the regional conclaves, established a system of meetings near London, almost every year, to which all the bishops came. The Church was in fact a national Church providing the people with a uniform religious tradition and an intellectual and artistic civilization. The Archbishop of Canterbury might come from Wessex or Mercia and a Kentish cleric became a bishop of East Anglia.

Although these prelates had no lay titles their role in political life was no less important than that of their Continental peers. On the contrary their culture, their habit of discussing in council, and publishing canons, made them, just as in Gaul, the political instructors of the lay magnates. They took their seat in the Shire court as the vicar did in the Hundred when a unified monarchy was established. The Primate Archbishop of Canterbury became its supreme adviser and kept that pre-eminence for many centuries. At times he took the place of the king as president of the meeting of Wise Men. In a charter of 812 they speak of the "wise men of the king and archbishop". In this country where every Latin influence had been stamped out, the Christian Church brought the Latin spirit, the appreciation of an abstract right (law), and the idea of national unity and the State.[1]

II

THE ANGLO-SAXON MONARCHY

It was only in the ninth century that monarchical unity was achieved. The Anglo-Saxon chieftains had established many kingdoms but no federation had grown up.[2] They fought bitterly against each other and against the Danes. Finally in the ninth century the kingdom of Wessex brought unity. For a century and a half the king of the English was a powerful sovereign during a period when the Carolingian Empire was falling to pieces. The reigns of Egbert, Alfred the Great, Athelstan, and Edgar were glorious and the last two assumed the styles of Basileus, Cæsar, Imperator Augustus.[3]

The great struggles undertaken for hegemony over one of the kingdoms or for the expulsion of the Danes together with the influence of the Church explains how the chieftains of Anglo-Saxon lands became real kings and were able to organize their power in a country where the memories and experiences of Roman rule had been obliterated.[4] They had to create an administration, finances, and an army. At the beginning of the tenth century England was divided into shires. The shire was governed by a war lord comparable to a Carolingian count, the ealdorman, and by the sheriff, an officer responsible for superintending and checking the revenues of the king.[5]

---

[1] **DCXXVII**, i, chap. viii; **CCCLXV**; **CDXX**, 3-4, 30-33.
[2] The word *Heptarchy* means nothing. It only indicates that there were seven kingdoms more important than the others.
[3] **CCCLIX**, chap. vi ff.; **DXXVII**.
[4] **DCXXVII**, i, 221 ff.
[5] **CCXVIII**, chap. v and viii; **CDLXXXIV**, i ff.

THE ANGLO-SAXON MONARCHY 43

The most remarkable of these revenues was the Danegeld, a tax levied throughout England for defence against the Danes. In addition, the population was under obligation to maintain roads and bridges and to keep itself trained as an armed militia in case of invasion. This national army, in which all classes were mixed up in an ill equipped rabble, was obviously inadequate and it was necessary to make use of mercenaries. As a result the practice of " host service " grew up comparable to the feudal service of the Continent.[1]

The character of this monarchy which arose from the stress of war was exceedingly complex. From one point of view it was very much like the Carolingian monarchy (and, hence, the primitive Capetian monarchy); it had borrowed from that source rites which would enhance its prestige. In other respects it was still profoundly Germanic. Though the king had pompous titles and a sacred person he was no despot and his power was limited.

We cannot say without doubt that he was always elected, since the practice of associating the royal heir on the throne had not been neglected by the Anglo-Saxon kings. Nevertheless it was the custom to make a formal acceptance of the new king and this continued in certain cases after the Norman Conquest. After the formality of election the king was consecrated. A pontifical probably dating from the eleventh century describes the ceremony. The king was crowned with a helmet and annointed. The influence of Carolingian rites is obvious. Then the Anglo-Saxon king pronounced an oath absolutely parallel to the oath of the French kings. He promised to maintain the Church and all his people in peace, to put down rapine and injustice, to be just but merciful in all his judgments. Sometimes he was required to pledge himself; in 1014 Ethelred had to guarantee reforms. Once the consecration was finished the Anglo-Saxon king was regarded as a superior being whom it was a duty to love and serve. The laws of Ethelred imposed obedience to the king as a religious duty. The Danish conquerors preserved this tradition. The first article of the laws of Canute says: " Above all our subjects must always love and adore one God alone, join together in observance to the Christian faith and show loyal devotion to the King Canute." It would be

[1] **DCLVIII**, first essay, 14 ff.

easy to borrow analogous passages from the Carolingian capitularies.¹

But even after he had been sanctified by consecration the king was subject to restriction. The Anglo-Saxon Church was not servile or even indulgent towards him and the Church took considerable part in the deposition of certain monarchs. Finally, there were occasions when the king undoubtedly had to make allowance for the assembly of wise men—the Witena Gemot.²

This title does not appear either in the laws which the assembly issued or in the charters. The author of *Annales Anglo Saxones* uses it in the eleventh century and this determines its place in the development of history. The editors of Latin charters make use of the term *synodus, concilium, conventus,* but in the texts in the common tongue from the eighth to the twelfth century we find the word " *Wita* " (those who know, the wise), used to refer to those who take part in the meeting of the Gemot.

Authentic documents on the Witena Gemot begin in the seventh century but there is good reason to believe that even before the missions of Augustine and Theodore and the participation of the Christian clergy in the government every petty kingdom had its Witena Gemot which had developed from the rude *concilium* described by Tacitus in the Germania. When the kingdom of Wessex succeeded in unifying England its Gemot became the national assembly. It obviously could not include all the freemen who had usually been present at the Gemots of the smaller kingdoms but it maintained, to some degree, its old Germanic character. These old usages do not appear to have been challenged and interrupted by Roman influences as they were in Gaul. We have seen that there were many parallels between the Anglo-Saxon and French systems, but the Assembly probably played a more considerable part in Anglo-Saxon history chiefly because it was a more regular and continuous part. However it is still a subject of doubt and controversy.

Like the Carolingians and early Capetians, the Anglo-Saxon

---

¹ DCXXVII, i, 173 ff., 221 ff.; CLXXIX, 73, 464–7. Cf. CCXVIII, 356 ff.
² The most complete study is the one made by F. Liebermann, CDXX ; DCXXVII, i, 154–181; cf. CCXVIII, chap. ix, and Excursus iv ; CCXXXV, 428–9.

THE ANGLO-SAXON MONARCHY 45

monarch was surrounded by *ministri*—permanent advisers—his relatives, including the women of the family, his officers, the warrior nobles attached to his person, and clerics : at least one bishop lived at court with him and the Archbishop of Canterbury was, as we have already said, a sort of chief minister. This permanent entourage authorized the acts of the executive—royal letters (writs). Its importance grew with the passage of time and the growing importance of French and Norman institutions. Around this nucleus of councillors the other wise men gathered when the king called a meeting. They had no representative character any more than in Gaul. The king invited to his presence the Churchmen, leaders of the army (ealdormen), warrior nobles (thanes), whom he considered it would be possible and useful to bring together or whom tradition demanded that he should summon.

They were not very concerned to obey or many in number and a hunting box or the hall of a royal village would accommodate them all. An assembly totalling a hundred people like that of November, 931, which included the Archbishops of Canterbury and York, two French princes visiting the court, seventeen bishops, five abbots, fifteen ealdormen, and fifty-nine ministri was considerably above the average of about thirty persons. It was only on rare occasions that clerks trained in law or officers from the localities took part in the debates or, when the Gemot met in London, representatives of the townsmen. Even more rarely was the meeting a mobilization of the army though this was the case in 1051 when the warriors were called on to ratify the banishing of Godwin. In general it was an aristocratic assembly whose discussions were led by the churchmen but its national character was very clearly marked by the fact that the laws on which it agreed were published in the vernacular, an unprecedented feature in the legislation of the Germanic peoples.

The Witena Gemot seems to have met fairly regularly at least once a year, usually on the occasion of one of the great feasts, Easter, Whitsun, or Christmas. The early Capetians adopted the same practice.

The scantiness of sources has driven scholars seeking to describe the powers of the Witena Gemot to add up all the information provided by four centuries of its history. It is quite clear that we must distrust such a fallacious method for none of the meetings of which we have any knowledge could have fully discharged all those functions. It is certain that sometimes the king carried through on his own authority acts for which at other times he demanded the approval of his councillors. With this reservation we must admit that they dealt with all sorts of matters. They published religious prescripts and ecclesiastical rules—for Church and State were closely linked and the men of the period did not distinguish, even a learned man as Alfred the Great, between a council and a National Assembly. They made laws and repealed them: Alfred declared that only the Witan could abolish laws. They dispensed justice concurrently with the royal councillors who were evidently normally the highest court of appeal. They were consulted about taxation though our evidence does not justify saying that this assent was essential. We have altogether seven decisions of the Witan authorizing the levy of the Danegeld and we see that they refused to sanction it in 1051.

It is impossible to define their administrative competence more closely but they have a part in the appointment of ealdormen and a great part of the documents which throw light on their functions for us consists of grants of royal land to which they have given their assent. Above all, there were disagreements and violent quarrels between king and Witan. It would be a mistake to imagine that this primitive assembly, dating from the period of barbarism, possessed the characteristics of an organ of modern constitutionalism. There were no established safeguards, no regulation of the date of its meetings or of the people invited to be present, no provisions for minuted records or for carrying a vote against the royal will. We have no example of a law that was created in opposition to the King's wish. Above all he could dismiss it at will and gave it no supervisory powers during the intervals between sessions. If he wished, he merely sought the advice of his ministers in place of calling the Witan together. In short the " Assembly of the Wise " was not an independent institution capable of a sustained and regular constitutional opposition. In many respects it was essentially

THE ANGLO-SAXON MONARCHY

comparable, as we have said above, to the assemblies of the Carolingians and Capetians.

Nevertheless it seems to have limited somewhat the authority of the crown even apart from moments of crisis when it relieved England of an unsatisfactory monarch. The formula " I and all of us ", which appears at the beginning of legislation is a fair representation of the position. The Witena Gemot certainly contributed to the establishment of a political society in England. It provided a forum for the discussion of matters of common interest for people from all quarters of the realm, an occasion when boorish thanes were called on to listen to churchmen and try to comprehend points of law.

At the end of the period the Witena Gemot was in decline and frequently its assent was not invited to alienations of royal demesne. This is not an index of the growing powers of the monarch but rather the reverse. The realization that his power was weakening drove him, as it had driven the Carolingians in France, to adopt remedies more disastrous than the disease. He created clients by dispersing his resources and tried in this way to increase the numbers of his thanes.

As early as the tenth century, Edward the Elder (899–925) had suggested to the Witan that they should themselves enter his retinue. There was reason to wonder whether the Assembly of the Wise and the monarchy itself were on the way to losing their national character. There were no reasons why England should escape a development that was general in that period. Centrifugal forces were threatening unity and the royal authority and the division between the powerful and the weak (among free men) was becoming increasingly marked. The Scandinavian invasions in England had the same effect as the Norman raids on France; they gave the force of a revolution to the military organization and social distinctions created by the possession of extremely costly weapons, the mobilization of the people under the banner of a local magnate or the erection of a stronghold for the lord in which the local population could find refuge.

III

ANGLO-SAXON SOCIETY AT THE PERIOD OF THE NORMAN CONQUEST

There is no more illuminating document than Domesday Book [1] for gaining an appreciation of the changes which had been caused or more clearly revealed by the last Scandinavian invasions. This great survey records the findings of an inquest demanded by the first of the Anglo-Norman kings in 1085.

Domesday Book is a source not only for the policy of William the Conqueror but for the condition of England at the time of his arrival, for its condition could not be totally changed in the course of twenty years and, moreover, the frequent mention of "the time of King Edward" shows us that the picture provided is intended to represent the period of the reign of Edward the Confessor.

William the Conqueror intended to continue the levy of Danegeld but he wished to assess it equitably and projected a survey of the realm which would show the number of taxable units and the value of the income of each. He was equally anxious to know of whom each piece of territory was held so that he could define the political and administrative responsibilities of his tenants. This was the origin of the book. As a result, its interpretation is extremely difficult for those who are seeking information on the condition of the population, for definitions are framed from the angle of raising taxation and this fiscal return cannot be used as a review of social conditions. Moreover, the Norman clerks who prepared the Latin version have not always translated English technical terms or have been satisfied with very vague equivalents; above all they have completely omitted certain areas with a particular fiscal administration and Domesday Book is not altogether exhaustive. Nevertheless, with all its limitations it is an unparalleled document of extremely great value; there is nothing to compare with it in France, for instance, where no authority existed capable of commissioning its compilation.

Attempts have been made to base population figures on

---

[1] See **CDLIV**, 1 ff. Domesday = "*dies iudicii*," day of judgment.

THE ANGLO-SAXON MONARCHY 49

Domesday.[1] No exact computation is possible but there is sufficient authority to say that the most numerous class, amounting to perhaps two-thirds of the population, was that of free peasant farmers termed by the Norman editors, villains, bordars, cottars.[2]

The villains had a high wergild rated at two hundred pennies, the price of thirty oxen, and many owned their own plots of land but most of them also held lands for which they owed some moderate rent to the lord who, in many cases, had jurisdiction over them. The free small cultivators, the characteristic group in the society, remained the principal element in the population but they were already being subjected to the system of lordship. Their development could only be hastened if the word villain in Norman England became very quickly applied to the agriculturists in a status of serfdom and not as in France to those who were free.[3]

Above these free peasants, Domesday tells us of a class of farmers higher in status but barely a fifth of their numbers, socmen, freemen, etc., terms which overlap one another but are applicable to the same social condition. If they owe services to the lord they are light labour dues such as a number of hours of work at harvest time or even merely " soc ", the duty of suit in the court of justice; some of them held their land without rendering any service to the lord, others commended themselves to a lord without holding any land from him and their own holding remained completely free.[4] Finally, Domesday includes several thousand prelates, chiefs of noble families who are either Norman conquerors or thanes of the former regime whose dispossession receives special mention or who have been received into favour. The greater part of this landed aristocracy consisted of landlords who had rendered homage to the great magnates lay and ecclesiastical. Even in the Anglo-Saxon period these great magnates were

---

[1] **CCLXXVIII**, ii, 511–14. Cf. **CCCXVII**, 103; **DLV**, i, 512; **CDLIV**, 17 ff. In general the people named are the heads of households but sometimes it is possible to estimate the number of women and children.

[2] According to Ellis, *op. cit.*, Domesday Book enumerates 108,407 villains 82,119 bordars, 6,803 *cottars* or *coscets*, and only 25,156 *serfs* who are in general all but slaves. On Anglo-Saxon serfdom, see **CDLIV**, 26 ff.

[3] **CDLIV**, 36–66; **DCLXII**, 89 ff., 205 ff.; **DCLIX**, 332 ff.; **DCLVIII**, 446 ff.

[4] **CDLIV**, 66–79, 103–7 *et passim*; **DCLIX**, 340–3; **DCLVIII**, 431–446; **DLXXXV**, 30–4.

few in number and could dispose of very few considerable fortunes. Godwin and Harold on the eve of the Conquest had immense demesnes. They were subject only to the king who formed the apex of the pyramid of commendation.[1] What was the origin of commendation among the Anglo-Saxons ? It had general causes which were to be found also in primitive Gaul and others which were particularly English. The most pressing reason was obviously the need for protection, above all in the courts of justice. Some of the Anglo-Saxon laws do not give us ground for saying with confidence that impartiality was always assured. They explain why it was advisable to seek powerful support. In addition the Crown, lacking any organized police, regarded commendation as a means of introducing some measure of order and authority in a society where violence was habitual; it regarded a man without a lord as a source of danger. Above all there was a need for soldiers and taxes especially during the period of the Danish invasions. As the basis for a dependable army, it encouraged the formation of groups of warriors round a powerful lord; military tenure was not yet established but it was not far off. The lord's hall was adopted as the centre for the payment of Danegeld; even for the most peaceful inhabitants of the village the lord became a chief who must be visited and to whom it gradually became customary to commend oneself and swear fidelity.

As time passed, the monarchy showed increasing favour towards the nobility which was entrusted with the collection of taxation and the defence of the country. They made it responsible also for the maintenance of the public peace, increased their powers of jurisdiction, and allowed the old Hundred court to become a court of seignorial justice. They divested themselves of rights, revenues, and even territories in their favour.[2]

When the Normans arrived in England they found, therefore, a society which, in some respects, resembled French society in the eleventh century [3]—relations between man and man of a hierarchical character; an embryonic

---

[1] CDLIV, 161 ff.; DCLVIII, 403 ff.
[2] CDLIV, 69–76 and 163 ff. (cf. the criticism of Round in *V.C.H., Worcestershire*, i, 250–1); DCLIX, 212 ff.; DCLVIII, first essay; DCXXVII, i, chap. vii.
[3] CDLIV, 154 ff.; DCLIX, 293 ff.

seignorial regime; a nobility with military duties; a monarchy which had the glories of a great past and the consecration of the Church but had become weak and had surrendered its rights creating intermediaries between itself and its subjects in the hope of resisting the advance of anarchy and foreign invaders. It would not be difficult for the Normans to establish in such a country the rule of the military fief and the manor.

But, nevertheless, Anglo-Saxon society with its numerous small landowners and its system of commendation (still loose and vague) presented certain original features which retained their significance. In this country where there was no special legal terminology to differentiate the status of demesnes, there was still a system of tenures though not a feudal system in the sense that the term possessed in France. It was the monarchy which was to use the instrument of Feudalism for its own ends. In spite of its alien origin it was to be helped in its task by the memories of a national monarchy which had been able, with the support of the Church, to create a national state, and a legislation, an administration, and a general system of taxation with the assistance of the Assembly of the Wise. The embryo of a political society already existed in England. It was not now to be infected with the germs of anarchy for there was in Normandy a powerful principate capable of organization.

IV

The Duchy of Normandy c. 1066

The early history of Normandy is extremely obscure; charters are rare before the eleventh century and chronicles are meagre and of doubtful authenticity. The establishment of the Norwegian, Danish, and Swedish hordes in the valley of the lower Seine, the Bessin, and the Cotentin and the agreement made between Rollo and Charles the Simple are scarcely known except through their consequences.[1] The Pagan pirates who, in the ninth century, had ravaged

---

[1] **DXLVI**; **DXLVII**; **CCCL**, 4 ff., 241 ff.; **CDXXXIII**, 177 ff.

Gaul, terrifying peasants and clergy alike, and contributed to checking the Carolingian renaissance became, during the tenth and eleventh century, landowners fully qualified to get the best returns from their lands. They supported the growth of an extremely powerful regional Church and a brilliant monastic civilization; above all they accepted the authority of a powerful duke. We have no evidence of the causes and methods of this transition.

It is quite clear that the invaders had great energy, intelligence, and practical ability and a series of remarkable dukes. Moreover these changes were not sudden. The Normans of the Bessin and Cotentin retained for a long time their Scandinavian language and accepted the domination of the prince very reluctantly.[1] William the Bastard himself was expelled by them during his youth and was forced to seek the alliance of the King of France to conquer them. Towards the middle of the eleventh century, however, the power of the " Duke by the Grace of God " was firmly established and only the title of king was lacking to the man who " held the monarchy of Normandy ".[2]

The Norman monarchy, in its country of origin as later in England, gained its power from the feudal ideas and governmental principles which were developed there in their strictest form.

In Normandy, sooner than elsewhere, the political system of Feudalism established itself and worked out a logical definition.[3] Sooner than elsewhere, allods largely or even entirely disappeared, fiefs became hereditary, and even in the clerical holdings subinfeudation established itself.

Earlier than elsewhere fiefs were charged with an exactly fixed military service and the rights of relief and subjected, in case of minorities, to a rigorous right of wardship. Even before the King of France, in his own demesne, the duke forbade the building of castles or fortifications without his permission, and William the Bastard even destroyed those which had been built during his minority There has been a tendency to attribute to the dukes even greater powers.

---

[1] **D**; **CCC**, i, chap. iv, ii, chap. viii, iii, chap. xii; **CCCXCII**; **DXLVII**, 292 ff.; **CDXLV**, 53 ff.

[2] On the "kingdom of Normandy", see **DCL**, 26 ff.; **DXLVII**, 367 ff.

[3] **CCLXXXVIII**, iii, 88 ff. For all that follows **CCCL**, chap. i; **DXLII**, chap. iii; **DCL**; **CCXXIX**, chap. 2; **CLXXX**, 3-42.

It has been maintained that he had no mesne vassals, all the nobles holding directly from him, and that he retained in his own hands the monopoly of justice in important cases but recent work has refuted these exaggerations. Sub-infeudation was usual and was taken into account by the duke himself imposing the duty of host service on his barons ; the number of mesne tenants who should accompany each was fixed usually at five or a multiple of five. The barons had major powers of justice and held pleas at which they could inflict death or mutilation. Nevertheless the famous peace of the Duke of Normandy, which chroniclers mentioned in admiration, was not absolute but in relation to a particularly violent moral standard.[1] The right of vengeance, blood feuds, and private wars was only abolished by such regulations as the Truce of God, which the Church imposed with the support of the duke and a series of particular laws which the latter strove to extend. It was forbidden to attack anyone working on the land or travelling at his lord's summons ; to carry arms in a forest, to seek vengeance on an adversary in war arrayed with banner and horn to rally supporters, to take prisoner, etc.[2] The important fact is that the duke has the power necessary to enforce respect for his rules. Nowhere else was there the same suppression of brigandage. Respect for the ducal peace was maintained by the sheriff's officials who had no counterpart in the royal demesne before the institution of bailiffs. They were not merely agents in the demesne responsible for collecting the lord's revenue and holding a local court; even in the territories of counts there were sheriffs who administered a district comparable in extent with a small English county and maintained permanent communication with the ducal *Curia*.

The ducal court, about which we have very little information, bore a very strong resemblance to the Capetian court. The same officers were there, the same shifting personnel of bishops and barons, and it had the same atmosphere and characteristics.

Under the guise of a solemn assembly which it assumed from time to time it seemed to be sometimes a meeting of

---

[1] On the probable Scandinavian origin of the Norman peace, **DCLXXXII**, cf. **DXLII**, 93 ff.

[2] *Consuetudines et Justiciae*, published in **CCCL**, 281 ff.

judges, warriors, and political councillors; sometimes a sort of semi-council of exactly the same character as the court of Robert the Pious. It was in such circumstances that in 1080, in the mixed assembly of Lillebonne, William, in the presence of his vassals lay and ecclesiastical, established the already traditional customs concerning the jurisdiction of the Church.

Within his duchy, William was in effect master of his clergy quite as much or even more than a Capet in the dioceses subject to the Crown. Not only did his court regulate the extent of ecclesiastical jurisdiction but, if a sentence of the Church seemed too light, the duke intervened. He gave full protection to the riches of the monasteries and cathedrals and in effect nominated the bishops and the principal abbots. However, he did not abuse his power to impose unworthy candidates; he found, in the higher clergy, political advisers from whom he demanded wisdom and experience, he supported the plans for reform to which the great councillor of the Holy See, Hildebrand, later Gregory VII, was devoting his attention and in return the Holy See was prepared to support his greatest ambition.

The Capetians, in the eleventh century, lacked a dependable army and finance. Doubtless at this period the Duke of Normandy had not a very experienced financial administration but he had the monopoly of coinage in his duchy, and he had control of a considerable supply of bullion. Further, he had an excellent corps of archers and the best cavalry in Europe. No other country possessed warriors as disciplined or as active. The adventurous spirit of the vikings was handed down to their descendants and the dukes had a difficult task in preventing undue emigration to countries where fighting was going on—Spain, Italy, and the East. The comment made by William about Baudri, son of Nicholas, would have been true of many Norman knights, " I have deprived him of all his lands as the penalty for going to Spain without my permission. . . . I don't think a better knight is to be found in arms but he is unreliable and wasteful and spends his time running from one country to another."

Such was the principality, small but by no means negligible, which dispatched the new invaders of England. The explanation of why they were able to dominate the Anglo-Saxon kingdom so easily and reshape its constitution must be sought in the results of the policy of William the Bastard and his predecessors in the duchy and the youthful vigour and daring of the Normans. One example [1] illustrates very clearly both their swashbuckling heroism and their political spirit and had been well considered by William the Bastard. During the forty years which preceded the conquest of England, little bands of Normans had settled in Southern Italy living on their profits as mercenaries or acts of brigandage and then establishing small principalities. Their victory over the troops of the Holy See in 1053 demonstrated their strength very clearly but their leaders were too well advised to remain at enmity with the Pope. Robert Guiscard, the Crafty, did homage to the pope as " Duke, by the Grace of God and St. Peter, of Apulia and Calabria and, with their aid, of Sicily ". This was in 1059, seven years before William the Conqueror landed in England with a banner blessed by the Pope.

Here in Southern Italy and Sicily where Latins, Greeks, and Moslems formed a heterogeneous mass of the superimposed religions and traditions of Rome, Byzantium, and the East, the Normans were to establish the state which, in the middle of the twelfth century, was the richest and strongest in Western Europe. It is more than probable that they introduced into the two Sicilies the same principles of authority as the dukes of Normandy had established in their duchy, and subsequently applied to England. Wherever they went the Normans carried some idea of government, and, in addition, there is evidence that from the north of Europe to the south they kept up communications with one another. From each realm they borrowed the administrative forms it had evolved. In a society of brutal and simple knights, the Normans were not content to use their swords best, they also theorized. Already they had a legal outlook which at this period was the endowment of a people qualified for dominion.

[1] **CCXIX**, 1st and 3rd parts ; **CCCXLIX**, chap. viii.

CHAPTER III

THE FOUNDATION OF THE ANGLO-NORMAN MONARCHY

I

The Conquest

IN 1066[1] the founder of the modern English monarchy, William the Bastard, was 38 years old.[2] He was a stout, bald man with the strong arms of an athlete and a stern face, terrible in its cold rage, who loved nothing but politics, war, and the chase.[3] His life was disciplined and chaste, his character taciturn, deliberate, and stubborn, and he was capable of working silently for a long time in the execution of a plan he had formed and waiting for his opportunity. His early life had been harsh and insecure but from the age of 20 he ruled Normandy without rival. He had snatched the rich countryside of Maine from the powerful Angevin dynasty but his principal anxiety was to secure the English inheritance. There can be little doubt that he had been preparing its annexation for a long time. Many incidents in English politics from 1042–1066 are obscure and inexplicable if we hesitate, as most historians do, to assume this secret preparation but, once admitted, everything is explained.

The powerful Anglo-Danish dynasty founded by Sweyn and his son, Canute the Great, had been meteoric ; in thirty years its force had burnt itself out.[4] Harthacnut, an epileptic destined for an early death, consented to the association on the throne of the legitimate heir of the Anglo-Saxon kings

---

[1] On all that follows the extremely tendencious exposition of E. A. Freeman, **CCC**, vols. i–iii, must be read with caution. For a summary treatment which can be recommended, see **CCCLIX**, chap. xxv, xxvi.
[2] **DXLVIII**, 1st series, 73 ff.
[3] Compare the scribe who continues the Anglo-Saxon chronicle who lived at his court, **CXXV**, i, 219–221.
[4] **CDIII**.

THE ANGLO-NORMAN MONARCHY   57

who had been brought up at the Norman court.¹ It was not long before Harthacnut died (8th June, 1042), and Edward became an easy prey for William the Bastard; a man of extreme piety in temperament, so weakly that he passed his married life in celibacy, the Confessor, though revered as a saint, was negligible as a king. He was generally under the influence of Continental advisers and during his reign the court acquired an administrative personnel of Normans with a system of offices all but parallel to those of France.² Already Normans of noble birth were beginning to settle and build castles, arousing the discontent of the population by their exorbitant violence. Norman clerics were beginning to monopolize the bishoprics and even the archbishopric of Canterbury was given to Robert Champart who had just given up the cross of the Abbot of Jumièges, the famous monastery which the dukes had protected and enriched. Here, surely, appears the hand of William. He was already beginning to control the English Church by his tools and supporters. Above all, the brother-in-law of Edward, Eustace, count of Boulogne, the most overbearing and most hated of the foreign intruders,³ was a friend and accomplice of the Duke of Normandy. At any rate he was to be his lieutenant at Hastings. There seems little reason to doubt that already these foreigners were working on behalf of William the Bastard.

The aristocracy, however, the powerful ealdormen to whom the later Anglo-Saxon and Danish kings had entrusted groups of counties, could not be left out of account. There was good reason for asking whether England was going to disintegrate once more, whether the three kingdoms of the past, Northumbria, Wessex, and Mercia, were to be revived or even whether one of the ealdormen would be able to maintain unity for his own advantage. The man who has been portrayed as the leader of the Anglo-Saxon nation against

---

[1] The three families of Edward the Confessor, William, and Harthacnut were related by the two marriages of Emma of Normandy. A daughter of Duke Richard II and sister of Duke Robert the Devil (William's father), she had married the Anglo-Saxon King Ethelred (dethroned by Sweyn in 1013) and Canute the Great. Edward was one of the children of her first marriage, and thus William's cousin. Harthacnut was the son of Canute and Emma.

[2] **DLXXXVIII**, 90-2; **CDIV**, 193 ff.

[3] Welisce men; foreigners (**CXXV**, i, 173 and glossary).

the Normans, Godwin, ruled Wessex as ealdorman and, with his two sons, held half the kingdom in his grasp. He was English but owed his power to Canute and was looked on rather as a Dane. He played almost the same role in relation to Edward as the dukes of France, ancestors of the Capetians, to the Carolingians. There is no doubt that he sought to bring the Crown into his family which means that he was implacably opposed to Norman influence.

The inevitable conflict broke out in 1051. Edwin invited Godwin to punish the people of Dover who had refused to entertain Eustace and had killed some of his retinue; Godwin, unwilling to comply and threatened with a trial for treason, fled into exile with his sons. Immediately afterwards William paid his cousin Edward a visit which has always been a matter of mystery. Norman chroniclers all tell us that on some unspecified occasion Edward promised the Duke of Normandy the succession to the Crown and it is very probable that William forced the promise from him in 1051.

The success however was premature; Robert Champart and his underlings had not sufficient weight to fight Godwin and his sons who returned to England next year, regained their power, and expelled the Normans. After the death of Godwin, 1053, his son Harold was, for the remainder of Edward's reign, the real master of England. He installed in the See of Canterbury a man he could trust, the Bishop Stigand, but he gave William an opportunity because when he journeyed to Italy to receive the pallium from the Holy See he acknowledged Benedict X who had been deposed as an Antipope. Moreover, in extremely mysterious circumstances, Harold fell into the hands of William during a trip to France, a victim of his own imprudence and possibly of a carefully laid plot. We know that William made him take solemn vows on consecrated relics by which Harold undoubtedly swore that he would not seek the English Crown.[1]

William had only to await the death of Edward the Confessor which occurred on 5th January, 1066. Harold was not concerned about his oath and immediately had himself recognized as king by a small group of magnates. For all these events we have an extremely convincing piece

[1] See the different versions in **CCXCII**, 198–201.

THE ANGLO-NORMAN MONARCHY 59

of evidence, the famous embroidery, "the Bayeux tapestry,"[1] which is of contemporary date. As soon as he has shown us the new king of England seated on his throne, the artist pictures an "English ship sailing for Duke William's land" carrying the news to him. Subsequently the tapestry shows us woodmen cutting down trees to build the Norman fleet. Then the launching and equipment of the ships. William,[2] had neither as many vassals nor as many subjects as his adversary and when he revealed his plans at the Assembly of Lillebonne his barons were reduced to an amazed silence and could offer no constructive advice. He approached them individually with promise of magnificent spoils and all the chivalry of Normandy prepared to follow. Finally, he addressed an invitation to the adventurers who existed everywhere at this period and bands of Flemings, Picards, and Bretons joined him. Chroniclers tell us that he assembled an army of sixty thousand men, fitted out three thousand ships. These are stereotyped figures which medieval annalists always introduce. According to a more reliable authority, seven hundred ships carried William's army which amounted to something between five and ten thousand men, an army which was a considerable size for that period.

There is no doubt that the one which Harold could field against him was smaller for it had been materially weakened by the great effort it had been called upon to make against another invasion. William landed at Pevensey on 28th September, 1066. On the 20th the King of Norway, Harold Hardrada, accompanied by the brother and rival of the King of England, Tostig, had landed his army on the Yorkshire coast. The coincidence was so obviously fortunate for William that it is difficult not to imagine some collusion. The scheming Tostig had made offers to William which it was impossible for him to refuse.

Caught between two invading armies, Harold would be destroyed and his conquerors would divide the spoils. William's hopes were more than justified. Harold made a forced march to York at the head of an army which he had

---

[1] On this embroidery, certainly executed very shortly after the Conquest, see particularly **CDXVI**; **DXLVIII**, first series, 51 ff.
[2] On the Conquest, see **CCC**, iii, chap. xiii–xvi; **DCXVII**, résumé of the chroniclers in **CCXCII**, 201 ff.: on the retinue of William **CCCIX**, 83–97; **CCXLIX**; **CCLXXIV**; **DXLIX**, app. i.

mobilized in the South to resist the Normans. After an extremely violent battle the King of Norway and Tostig were defeated and killed (25th September, 1066). William was rid of embarrassing rivals and at the same time the resistance to his disembarkation was removed. While the English army was resting at York after its severe ordeal, William landed without any difficulties on the Sussex coast. The battle which decided the fate of England was staged on the 14th October, a little to the north of Hastings.[1] The heroic death of Harold deprived the English of their only leader. William, with his customary energy, took advantage of a somewhat doubtful victory and the divisions among his adversaries. He brought with him a banner which had received the papal blessing and the English Church, which might have resisted the invasion, yielded. The Witena Gemot, under the leadership of the Archbishop of York, recognized William as lawful king and crowned him at Westminster with the customary ceremonial. He swore to govern equitably and to defend the churches and their ministers. He did not base his claim on conquest but on his relationship to Edward the Confessor and the customary election.[2]

II

THE EARLY ANGLO-NORMAN KINGS AND ANGLO-NORMAN INSTITUTIONS (1066–1135).

The century of Anglo-Norman history which began with the election of William as king and was closed by the accession of Henry II (Plantagenet) saw many disturbances. Nevertheless it would not be true to assess it as, on the whole, a period of destruction. On the contrary it laid the foundations of medieval England with its contented populace, its social system, and its strong monarchy.

Native resistance lasted for five years.[3] Deprived of any co-ordinated leadership it became merely a series of local

---

[1] See particularly, **DLXXVII**, 61–77.
[2] **DCXXVII**, i, 319. On the question of elective monarchy, see p. 43 above, and Bk. II, chap. i, § 4 below.
[3] The political history of the reigns of William I, William II (Rufus), and Henry I (Beauclerc) is dealt with in **CCC**, vols. iv and v ; **CCCI**.

THE ANGLO-NORMAN MONARCHY 61

risings which William ruthlessly crushed. The revolts of the French barons, dissatisfied with their share of the booty and anxious to lighten the royal yoke, were much more serious and imperilled the new dynasty. The question of the government of Normandy added to the difficulties of the Crown and the Capetians, suzerains of the duchy, tried to fish in the troubled waters. The Anglo-Norman monarchy succeeded in achieving equilibrium but only after oscillating violently between anarchy and an irresponsible tyranny. William I had known how to achieve and maintain it and when his two sons succeeded him, the first, the brutal William Rufus (1087–1100), did not live long enough to compromise the development of his father's work and the second, Henry I (Beauclerc, 1100–1135), was endowed with remarkable political ability and able to consolidate its position for a considerable period. Treatment of the period of anarchy which followed the death of Henry will be reserved for a later chapter. Here we shall only deal in outline with the work of the first three Norman kings as a whole and cannot hope to assess in detail the contribution of each one of them. The constitutional history of the reign of Henry I alone, which one scholar has found justification for calling the most absorbing chapter in English history, demands considerable attention.

The social and political upheaval which accompanied the birth of the Anglo-Norman monarchy was naturally not the abrupt work of a consciously revolutionary determination. Led by circumstances to represent himself as the heir of Edward, continuing the traditions of his reign and faced by considerable difficulties, William the Conqueror made concessions, accepting English law and institutions which were in part at least new to him, but he also introduced certain Norman characteristics.[1]

His primary concern was to make certain provision for an army and finances for the establishment of peace and order. We shall see that he loaded his followers with property and introduced into England the feudal host-service according to Norman usage, but the Anglo-Saxon fyrd, the mass levy of the people which reminded him of his full levy of Norman vassals, proved a valuable institution which he preserved.

---

[1] Stubbs remains the principal authority for all that follows: **DCXXVII**, i, chap. ix–xi, 306–541. Cf. **CCCXVII**, 94 ff.

His son, William Rufus, knew occasions when, attacked by the Norman baronage, he owed his preservation to the English fyrd:[1] in 1086 at the Moot of Salisbury all the free tenants, whether of knightly rank or not, whether English or French, who were subject to the obligation to serve the king in case of emergency, came to take their oath to William as his lieges, to swear to defend him against all comers. This oath of allegiance rendered to the king by all his free subjects is an index of the immense difference between the Anglo-Norman and Capetian monarchies. Some historians have seen in this event the definitive introduction of Feudalism into England. This theory takes no notice of the feudal tendencies which existed in Anglo-Saxon society and leads to false analogies with the feudal regime which in fact existed on the Continent. By the Oath of Salisbury, the king established his power independent of the hierarchy of vassals while at the same time determined to gain all the support possible from the Feudal System. He upheld the Anglo-Saxon and Danish tradition, itself very similar to the Carolingian tradition which had died out in France, but there is every reason to believe that the clergy preserved in their libraries a copy of the capitularies by the side of the Anglo-Saxon laws. This is not the only occasion on which we shall compare Anglo-Norman institutions with French law and practice.

William retained a considerable share of the confiscated lands in his own hands. The income of the agricultural holdings enumerated in Domesday Book amounts altogether to about seventy-three thousand pounds; the Conqueror retained about a seventh of this landed wealth.

Territories realizing eleven thousand pounds a year, scattered more or less throughout the length of England, made up the royal demesne. From this source William received more than twice the income of Edward the Confessor. Subsequently he increased it further by confiscation after the revolt of the Norman barons in 1076.[2] In addition to the rents of the demesne he possessed the Feudal profits (aid, relief, wardships, marriage), the fruits of justice and the various contributions of the town communities, the Jews and, incidentally, the Church—all dues which the king had been

---

[1] Henry I began to use Flemish mercenaries. **CCCLXXXIV**, i, 47 ff., 59 ff.
[2] Corbett, in *C.M.H.*, v, 507 ff.

accustomed to receive as the Duke of Normandy and which the King of France levied in the territories which were subject to him.

The distinctive feature of Anglo-Norman finance was the coincidence, which proved somewhat burdensome for their subjects, of the levies customary in Normandy and the old war tax established for the defence of England against the Danes—the Danegeld. As we have already remarked, it was to assist the regular levy of the Danegeld that Domesday Book was compiled.

The financial administration was consolidated in the same way. The sheriff who raised the Danegeld and farmed the revenues of the shire was preserved; the Normans, employing their customary terminology called him Vicomte just as the shire became the county.[1] It is the institutions of Household, Treasury, and Exchequer which give us the most remarkable example of the amalgamation of Norman and Anglo-Saxon institutions. The dukes of Normandy and the Anglo-Saxon kings, like the Carolingian monarchs, stored their valuables in their bedchamber of which the wardrobe formed an important part. The keeper of the Chamber and the chamberlains were personal servants who travelled with their master on his progresses and were responsible for the custody and transport of his purse, jewels, and records. This was the constitution of the household which is described to us, as it existed at the time of Henry I, in an invaluable little treatise the *Constitutio domus regis*. From the earliest days of the Conquest, the Public Treasury was separated from the Chamber and fixed at Winchester, an old royal city: the Chamber only kept a chest for the personal expenses of the king.[2] But the Treasury at Winchester did not have or did not retain for any considerable period the duty of checking the sheriffs' accounts, the control of which was entrusted to a section of the Curia Regis and carried out by a method of counters on a squared table called the *Exchequer*; its results were inscribed in a parchment roll known at a later date as the *Pipe Roll*. The roll for the year 1129–1130 is extant. In this fashion, at a very early date, apart from both the Chamber and the Treasury at Winchester, was created the Exchequer—the *Curia Regis ad Scaccarium*.

[1] **CDLXXXIV**, chap. i–ii.   [2] **DCXL**, i, 67–96.

They carried on there the Anglo-Saxon custom of melting and weighing the coins which the sheriffs presented. Whether the system of auditing by counters had been adopted in Normandy before its introduction into England we have no means of saying, but it is certain that the Exchequer system only existed in Normandy and the countries conquered by the Normans.[1]

Thus William the Conqueror and his sons, in their efforts to strengthen their defence against their enemies and to build up financial reserves, discovered in England, and carefully preserved, principles of a sort of national army and public taxation and traditions of financial administration which only required their attention and improvement. Similarly, the Norman monarchs found in the country they had conquered admirable instruments for watching their people, for fixing collective responsibilities, and determining those causes which it appeared best not to hand over to feudal and seignorial jurisdiction, above all for keeping in contact with their subjects and asking them for information and even, if necessary, sacrifices in the county court (shire moot, or more simply shire) and the hundred court. They were preserved and it is impossible to lay too much emphasis on that fact. These local assemblies, which were always a burden to the inhabitants and would gladly have been allowed to become obsolete, gave its peculiar character to the constitution and political development of England. Documents on the work of these courts and their relations with the central administration [2] are very few, but the letter addressed by the Conqueror to Archbishop Lanfranc, the Bishop of Coutances and the Count of Mortain on the rights of the Church of Ely is one of the most interesting documents in English history.

> I summon and bid you to assemble once more all the shires (all those present at the county court) which were present at the proceedings about the possessions of the church of Ely just before the recent voyage of my wife to Normandy. Those of my barons who are competent to take a place there and were present at the previous proceedings and hold lands of the Church should be present with the shires. From the assembly (*in unum congregatis*) proceed to elect a group of Englishmen who know of the situation of this Church's territories at the time of King Edward's death and can give their evidence under oath.

[1] See the *Studies* of Petit-Dutaillis and Lefebvre, **DXX**, i and iii ; or in **DCXXVII**, i, 804 ff. ; and iii, 732 ff. **DLXXVIII, XXXIII, DXXXIII**, etc. (bibliography in the notes to our studies).
[2] They have been cited in **DCXXVII**, i, 479–480 notes.

THE ANGLO-NORMAN MONARCHY 65

The king's policy towards the natives, the system of inquest and jury, the summons of members of the shire court to the royal court are brilliantly illuminated by this document. What was William's policy towards the Witan once it had elected him king ? Would he seek to preserve this established institution which he had been able to use very well to his own advantage or would he seek to replace it by a feudal curia of the French type ? The question is irrelevant. At this period men were moved by necessities and acted in accordance with the tendencies directing society rather than with theoretical principles. It was generally agreed that a monarch could neither dispense law nor administer his realm without the advice of his supporters. The feeling and ideas which gave rise to the feudal regime of France and, even more important, the Anglo-Saxon system of commendation alike would not accept the idea of monarchy without some limitation.

Practically speaking, a man only rendered obedience to his lord on the basis of a personal contract ; those who were directly subject to a prince were in duty bound to reach agreement with him and to assist him in making judgment or decisions if he called on them and this duty of advice easily led them to formulating the ideas of a corresponding right, for we must never overlook the spirit of independence and pride which animated the companions of a king. It finds reflection in epics better than in chronicles or annals. In short, no king, French or English, could fail to summon his court ; it was an essential institution, though, as yet, undefined, changing in appearance, and very different from county to county, for nowhere had it yet evolved any rigid forms. The court of the Anglo-Norman kings therefore continued at the same time to be the Witan and the Norman *Curia*. The English certainly considered its members as the successors of the *Witan* and they were often referred to under that name or as the *Sapientes*.[1]

The Anglo-Norman court, like the Anglo-Saxon Witan[2] varied in numbers, formality, and composition. The numbers

---

[1] See the documents quoted in **CDXX**, 75 ff.
[2] Our treatment might well be developed, modified, and restrained by a few question marks. However we have not sufficient space in this volume to give reasons for our decisions. Cf. Gneist, **CCCXVII**, 201 ff. ; Stubbs, **DCXXVII**, i, 443 ff.; and the conciliatory thesis of Liebermann, **CDXX**, 75 ff.

of relatives of the king, friends, servants, churchmen, lay magnates, and casual workers was never constant. The king invited whom he wished and the only difference, in fact, that we need remark is that owing to his increased power the king was able, even more than before, to dispense with the assent of the Assembly and, on the other hand, that the word Curia was more comprehensive than the Anglo-Saxon term. It became applied not only to these special meetings but, equally, to the permanent council of the king—the statesmen, lawyers,[1] and financiers, who helped him in the everyday tasks of government. The Norman clerks gave the same meaning to Curia and Consilium and used them without distinction.

So far we have found a fusion of institutions and interesting developments rather than innovations.

In two spheres, however, the Conqueror and his advisers achieved revolutionary work of the highest importance. Territorial power had been transferred to the Norman lords and the transference was accompanied by the establishment of a tenurial system; the government of the national church was transferred to Norman prelates, a transference which was accompanied by the creation of ecclesiastical tribunals. In spite of the influences which drew England towards a social and territorial system comparable to that of the Continent, there remained many proprietors in 1066 who were either free or subject only to very light and undefined obligations. In Normandy the French seigniorial regime was a little more developed than in the rest of the kingdom but otherwise presented no special characteristics. At the end of the eleventh century Anglo-Saxon society bore absolutely no resemblance to either of the societies from which it had arisen. The catastrophe of the Conquest, the interaction of two peoples, and the ability of a strong monarchy served by remarkable advisers had remodelled it and given to it a legal foundation that was quite original. The vocabulary of social obligations was not the same as across the Channel.[2] *Vassal* was a word

---

[1] In the Norman period the royal court was not so overloaded with business. William I had very largely handed over the rights of justice to the barons and the Church (see **DCLVIII**, 110 ff.) and the pleas reserved to the king were still dealt with in the county courts except when a baron or an important issue was involved. The institution of itinerant justices would seem to date back, however, to the reign of Henry I. See **DXXXII**, i, 109; cf. Bk. ii, Chap. II, below.   [2] **CDLIV**, 152; **DXXXII**, i, 234 ff., 297.

THE ANGLO-NORMAN MONARCHY 67

rarely used but tenens (tenant) is frequently met. A *tenens in capite* (tenant in chief) was a man who held his land of the king without any intermediary whether he was a powerful baron or a simple farmer of the demesne. All the subjects of the king rich or poor, free or bond, were tenants with the exception of the proletariat and outcasts of town and country ; everyone held a tenure of the king or of an intermediary and, ultimately, everyone held, directly or indirectly, of the king. This systematization, clearly the work of Norman lawyers, is the key to the condition of the people in medieval England and produced political consequences of considerable importance.[1]

The origins of this remarkable constitution lie in the transference of lands after the conquest. The general truth of that fact has been challenged in vain. Although the dispossession almost certainly took place by degrees, there is equally little doubt that finally the majority of the English had lost their lands.[2] The most unfortunate victims were the numerous Anglo-Saxon small farmers of free status whose lands were given to Norman warriors without any compensation. They were classed as " villains ", a term which implied personal liberty but now they became tenants bound, both personally and in their holdings, to the lord and sank to the lowest depths of the social scale alongside the serfs of Anglo-Saxon society. They were still called villains but the word which in Capetian France continued to denote free peasants gained a new meaning in England after its conquest by the Normans and villainage became the type of servile tenure.[3] This process had an equally severe effect on many socmen.

Out of nine hundred socmen in the County of Cambridge, seven hundred had lost their liberty and become serfs by the twelfth century.[4] This upheaval, which not only ruined the great native families to the benefit of the conquerors but degraded the middle class of the rural areas, led to the formation

---

[1] **CDLIV**, 151 ff. ; **DXXXII**, i, 232, 296, 356, 407 ; **DCLIX**, 293 ff. ; my study of the general position in **DXX**, i, 52 ff., or in **DCXXVII**, i, 810 ff.

[2] The most masterly studies on this difficult question are by Round in *V.H.* See my note and the bibliography in **DXX**, i, 21, n. 2, or in **DCXXVII**, i, 783, n. i.

[3] On villainage before and after the Conquest, **DCLXII**, 43 ff., 89 ff., 127 ff., 218 ff. ; **DCLIX**, 296 ff., 339 ff. ; **CDLIV**, 38 ff., 60 ff. ; my study on the origin of the manor in **DXX**, i, i ff., or in **DCXXVII**, i, 782 ff., and pp. 50–1 above.

[4] **CDLIV**, 62–3 ; **DCXXVII**, i, 785. On socmen see p. 49 above.

in England of a seigniorial regime comparable to that of Normandy, the regime of the manor,[1] and it was William's followers above all who gained by the change. Nevertheless not all the distinctive features of Anglo-Saxon agrarian society were obliterated. Manorial organization did not destroy the community spirit and agricultural co-operation but rather, as a result of contact with Norman influences, the traditions of solidarity were strengthened.[2] The English peasants had quite as clear a view of their interests as the Normans and knew how to act together.

Moreover not all the small free cultivators of native origin were reduced to servitude nor all the great landlords to an end of misery and despair, only they were not willingly left in possession of their previous possessions. For instance, Oda of Winchester had been able to convey an impression of loyalty and was given territories equivalent to those he lost.[3] What was the legal status of these free Anglo-Saxons whose hierarchy had been so complex in the reign of the Confessor ? How did they stand in relation to the invaders—powerful barons, knights, mesne tenants, nobles, and even commoners who had come from the Continent knowing nothing of the structure of English society ? The lawyers of the Curia would be involved in tremendous difficulties if so many different elements had to be fused in the same furnace. The tremendous heterogeneous mass of free tenants of the king, freeholders, emerged from the fusion. The necessity for the king to have obedient subjects and to be able to choose the best and to make use of them led him, as we have seen, to demand a personal oath from all freemen. Those who could not offer it to him in person discharged the summons in the county court between the hands of the sheriff. This common obligation to swear fidelity to the king and to serve him with arms and advice created a very large class of subjects socially unequal but equal before the law. Free villagers, townsmen, and warriors holding a free tenure all enjoyed the same right and had the advantage of the common law. The English nobility was only distinguished in this mass by the will of the king who as we shall see granted special military tenures and needed administrative officials.

[1] DCLIX, 299 ff.; description of the manor in DCLXII, 314 ff.
[2] CCXLVIII, 137 ff., 251.
[3] DLXXXI, 427–8.

At the end of the eleventh century, it was the English nobles who were the closest followers of the Conqueror and were honoured by the monarchy with particular responsibilities and privileges but they did not enjoy any particular personal law. Before the *Common Law*, they were *freeholders*.[1] *Freeholders* who held no military tenure, whether farmers or townsmen, could be summoned to service with the fyrd in case of national emergency and formed part of the county court and juries; they formed a numerous and compact element in society; they were called *socagers* in memory of the socmen.[2] Those who held a military tenure " a fief of arms " owed host service of forty days according to Continental usage.[3] The need for several thousand warriors well equipped and ready at the first sign of danger[4] had led to the imposition of compulsory service (*servicium debitum*) on the barons and bishops, each of whom had to supply from ten to thirty knights, sometimes sixty or even a hundred. The primary military tenures, created by the king himself, were those of the great tenants in chief. They, in turn, established, in their holdings, mesne fiefs of arms to maintain a certain number of knights. This number often exceeded the quota which the king demanded for host service, for private war was not unknown in England and the barons needed warriors.

In this way, the extremely important class of knights was formed which fairly quickly freed themselves from the responsibility of military service in person but remained the leading figures in the English counties and were one day to represent the country in the House of Commons.[5]

For a long time it has been maintained that the class of barons was composed of those knights who held military fiefs directly of the king but we must finally discredit the theory. Tenure *per baroniam* had not necessarily a military character and, at least in the eleventh and twelfth centuries, there were barons who did not hold directly of the king.[6] The barons seem to have originated from the men in whom William the Conqueror had confidence and to whom he

[1] DXXXII, i, 408–9.
[2] DXXXII, i, 291 ff.; DCXXVII, i, 676–7, 815.
[3] This problem has been finally settled by Round, DLXXXV, 225 ff., the same author, DLXXXVI, 103 ff., and DLXXXIII, i, 250–1, etc. See my study, DCXXVII, i, 814–823.
[4] Five thousand, DLXXXV, 264–5, 292.
[5] DXXXII, i, 411–12.   [6] DCXXIX, 14 ff.; 182 ff.; CCXXIII, 161–9.

entrusted public duties or, to a greater or less degree, judiciary powers.[1] The most important among them, the *majores* (such as the Montgomeries, Beaumonts, Lacys, Bigots, Giffards, Varennes, Mandevilles, Briouses, Mortimers, and the brothers and relatives of the king), were powerful lords well endowed with possessions, dignities, and privileges but they also played a part in the government of England. It was they who provided the sheriffs, the chief officers of the court, and, above all, the counts.

The dignity of count was hereditary, but it was conferred on each holder of the title by the king who entrusted to him " the sword of the count ". Until the death of the prudent William the Conqueror the number of English counts was very small; later they were frequently the leaders of the baronial opposition, but, even so, they were very different from the great counts of France, sovereigns in their own territories like those of Blois, Anjou, Flanders, Toulouse or even a Count of Boulogne or Armagnac. In the first place, they held a royal office and though it was an honorary one they often combined it with that of sheriff, in which case they administered the county in the name of the king; secondly, the manors on whose revenues they were dependent were almost always scattered and their demesne rarely coincided with their county.[2]

The fact that in general there were no large compact fiefs in England has attracted some attention and the credit for this very wise dispensation has been given to the political genius of William. It was obviously in accordance with the royal interests, but, in many cases, it simply arose from the fact that a certain follower of the Conqueror had received *en bloc* the property of an Anglo-Saxon lord and that it was already dispersed. A careful study of Domesday does not justify us in attributing to the Conqueror a deliberate and consistent policy in distributing holdings.[3] We should add that the dispersion of property was in the Middle Ages [4] a rule so general that princes and powerful nobles of the period spent

[1] **DLXI**, 161-199.; **CDLXXXIV**, 75.
[2] **DCXXVII**, i, 437, ff. We must make an exception for the Palatine counts in the frontier regions (Durham, Chester, Lancaster), who were sovereign in their domains; **CDI**, 31 ff.
[3] See Round's studies: **DLXXX**, 353; **DLXXXI**, 421-2; **DLXXXII**, 277; cf. **DCXVI**, 305; **CCLXXXV**, pref., p. v.
[4] Particularly in Normandy; cf. **DCL**, 49 ff.

a great deal of their time in trying to draw together the parts of their demesne.

Mingled with the free lay tenures were the alms tenures (*en frank almoin*) so called because the possessions of the Church were freed in theory from all temporal services and only paid their benefactor by their prayers. The most characteristic feature of this tenure is that it was only subject to ecclesiastical tribunals.[1]

William the Conqueror had introduced far reaching modifications into the existence of the Church of England.[2]

He was distrustful of the native clergy and contemptuous of their abilities and, as a general policy, installed Normans as bishops and abbots. His appointments were made in a high handed manner and his disregard for freedom of election constituted an ominous and dangerous precedent. His son, William Rufus, was to show no scruples about simony. The Conqueror, however, was austere and devout and his desire was only to purify the English Church in which he had the assistance of one of the greatest prelates of the age, the Italian Lanfranc, Abbot of St. Étienne de Caen, whom he made Archbishop of Canterbury. Under his guidance he applied the ideas of Gregory VII in relation to ecclesiastical jurisdictions and put an end to the confusion of powers which existed in the Anglo-Saxon period. Church tribunals were established to give judgment according to Canon Law in all causes which were subject to ecclesiastical jurisdiction, because of the people concerned or the issues involved.[3]

So far from isolating the English clergy in its own tasks, this important reform gave it a position of first rate social importance. The development of the study of Canon and Roman Law trained the clergy, teaching them to give their thought a logical direction, and formed a class of jurists who applied their intelligence equally to problems of the Common Law. The shapeless mass of native custom with its traces of Norman influences was illuminated and codified by them

---

[1] **DXXXII**, i, 240 ff. According to calculations on the basis of Domesday, the English Church was endowed with manors bringing in a total of £19,200, while the landed income of the 170 baronies amounted to £30,350.

[2] On all that follows, see **DCXXVII**, i, 346 ff.; **CLXXX**, 79 ff.; **DCXVIII**, chaps. i–vi.

[3] Most probably from April, 1072. See **LXXIV**, iii, 274–5; **DCLXIX**, 399–400.

and found its expression in the Common Law. Above all, the Church, led by the powerful Archbishop of Canterbury, who was normally the Crown's chief adviser, continued to occupy a political position of prime importance, to furnish administrators, and to give practical direction to the discussions of the Court, whatever its particular interest or constitution. It possessed everything which the world of laymen lacked as the basis for a political society; its life was systematically organized, it had established methods for the election of representatives, for the conduct of meetings, for preserving written records of discussion, for the formulation of decisions. As in France, it was destined to be the tutor.

As a result of the power of the Norman kings, however, it was not so consistent an ally as the French Church was to the Capets, but occasionally figured among the opposition. Beyond the petty personal ambitions which inspired the barons, the Archbishop of Canterbury was concerned to maintain his independence as Primate against a monarchy that was often tyrannical. He was the leader of the spiritual life of the nation and in direct communication with the leader of Christendom. This responsibility developed the idea of opposition on matters of principle and soon the greater part of the higher English clergy adopted the same idea of their duties. In the period we have been considering, the only definite example we can mention of their resistance to the king in the full meetings of the Curia is the incident of Anselm, Archbishop of Canterbury. Rufus, a soldier of extreme coarseness, had no understanding of the character or motives of the theologian and was unwise enough to become involved in a quarrel with him. As he had not yet decided to recognize Urban as pope, he forbade Anselm to make the customary journey to Rome to receive the pallium and Anselm refused to obey. The matter was raised at the Magnum Concilium, which met at the royal castle of Rockingham in 1095. The king and some of his personal friends remained in a room while the tenants in chief, lay and ecclesiastical, and the other people summoned met in the chapel. The bishops were those whom the Conqueror and his son had appointed and therefore, owing all to the monarchy, they hesitated at this issue. William de Saint Calais, Bishop of

THE ANGLO-NORMAN MONARCHY 73

Durham, ran backwards and forwards between the royal presence and the chapel, seeking some means of securing the submission of the Primate. Anselm was accused " of having made Urban, Bishop of Ostia, pope in the kingdom of England without the authorization of the king ". At the end of the first day's sessions, the Bishop of Durham called on him " to reinvest the king with the Imperial dignity he had robbed him of " and Anselm declared that he would only answer at the Court of Rome. Next day the bishops maintained their servile attitude and William de Saint Calais spoke of banishing Anselm from the kingdom. But the barons had at last realized that they must not let the king humiliate a tenant in chief, and the irritation which the brutal despotism of the king had caused them suddenly crystallized round the primate's wrongs and they declared in his favour. The king, in a furious temper, threatened them. " No one can be loyal to me who chooses to support him." They replied " He is not our Lord but our Archbishop ; the direction of religion in this kingdom is in his hands and no one has suggested that he is not discharging his responsibilities ". The king took fright and yielded the point, but he opened a new quarrel on a question of taxation and Anselm went into exile.[1]

On the 2nd August, 1100, William Rufus was killed by an assassin and Henry I (Beauclerc) unexpectedly succeeded to the crown.[2] His first concern was to conciliate the clergy and on 5th August, when he was hastily crowned before his elder brother Robert, Duke of Normandy, could enforce his rights, he agreed to take the oath of the Anglo-Saxon kings and recalled Anselm. He wrote to him, " Elected with the consent of God, by the clergy and people of England and already in your absence (though I could not wish it) consecrated king, I require you as my father and father of all the English people to come as quickly as possible to advise and guide me. . . ." It is true that William Rufus on his accession had made the same promises and addressed the same protestations to Lanfranc. It is equally true that Henry was almost immediately to enter into a new conflict with Anselm who had returned from Rome with ideas more uncompromising

---

[1] DCXVIII, chap. v ; CXLIV, 23, and the note.
[2] XVII, intro., p. vii ff. On the reign of Henry I, see DCXXVII, i, 371-388 ; DCXVIII, chap. vi ; CXLI, chap. vi–viii ; CCXXXVI, chap. iv.

than ever, but their long disagreement, which ended in compromise, was not marred by the brutal violence of the investiture controversy between the Empire and the Holy See. The attitude of Henry I, like that of William the Conqueror and, at a later date, Henry II, created a tradition of religious policy for the medieval English monarchy. The king wished to remain master but he sought to rely on the clergy rather than to tame it and allow it to become a political force.

To illustrate the stage of the development of English monarchy at the beginning of the twelfth century we could not find a better conclusion to our chapter than an analysis of the manifesto which Henry Beauclerc published on the same day, the 5th of August, when he suddenly succeeded to the throne. It has been called " the first Charter of English liberties ", one of those formulas which distort historical truth. We will steer clear of titles and look at the text.

This famous charter is only signed by three bishops and half a dozen canons.[1] It begins with general guarantees to the Church whose independence both material and spiritual had been destroyed by William Rufus. Henry I undertook never to take advantage of the death of a bishop or abbot to seil the lands of the bishopric or abbey. William had used the same despotic power in the case of the lay baronage. Henry promised not to resume the possessions of barons dying intestate, not to marry widows and heirs by force, and not to demand excessive fines and reliefs. It has been argued that this charter was simply a contract between the king and the feudal magnates of England.[2] It is true that Henry reserves his rights of " forest "[3] which, we can well imagine, was a concession snatched from the barons by negotiation but the charter is addressed " to all his faithful subjects " and he promises the people of England that " the law of King Edward " i.e. custom, for which the barons had no respect, should be maintained. In his statement of motives, which is completely in accordance with the theories of the Church

---

[1] According to the texts of it which we possess, it is subscribed by three bishops, with a variant for the name of one of them, by the counts of Warwick and Northampton, and by four or six barons. One text edited by Lieberman, however, adds. ". . . and many others." (**CDXXI**, 40–1. Cf. **LXXIV**, i, 521–3, and iii, 282 ; **DLXIX**, 321–331.)

[2] This is the opinion of G. B. Adams, **CXLIV**, 27.

[3] See Bk. Two, Chap. II, § IV, below.

THE ANGLO-NORMAN MONARCHY 75

on the duties of kings, he says that "the kingdom has been oppressed by unjust exactions" but that he is bound by his subjection to God and love of his subjects. Above all, there is no sign of any exchange of promises between kings and barons, no guarantees of execution are specified. In our opinion, the declaration was primarily inspired by the three or four bishops who were with him at the time and both the idea and the form of this venerable precedent were due to the Church.

The characteristic of the so-called "Charters of English Liberties" of the twelfth and thirteenth centuries is already clearly marked—it is not the expression of constitutional formulas but a renunciation of the abuses of the preceding reign. Even the Great Charter itself will have this significance when properly appreciated.

We can see also, in Henry's manifesto, that the native population has not been forgotten and that the Norman kings considered it good policy to place some dependence on them.

This was another service that the Church had rendered to the Norman monarchy. From the first days of the new order, it had worked for a fusion of conquerors and conquered into a society in which were only Christians. In similar fashion, across the Channel also, it was building a homogeneous society.[1] So far, however, from seeking unity for the benefit of the monarchy, the nation only found unity and its clear manifestation in reaction against the excesses of royal power. Its achievement, either on this side of the Channel or the other, was not the work of a day.

[1] **DII**, 68-74.

CHAPTER IV

THE CAPETIAN MONARCHY AND ITS DOMAINAL POLICY
(1060–1152)

I

The Kings of France and their Advisers

While the Anglo-Norman monarchy was being evolved and struggling for control of all power in the tumult of conquest and civil wars, the Capetian dynasty was succeeding in losing the nominal prestige and the general powers which it had inherited from the Carolingians. The century which elapsed between the accession of Philip I (1060) and the death of Louis VII and the foundation of the Angevin Empire was one of great events, great conflicts, and great innovations. The Capetian monarchs took little or no part in them and could merely watch their development either owing to weakness or because they had to fight, even in the Île de France, against brigandage.

The valour and energy vainly expended by Philip's father, Henry I (1031–1060),[1] show clearly that the winds were unfavourable and that it was no time to make for the open sea. The unbelievable apathy of Philip I who reigned forty-eight years (1060–1108) put the monarchy back a long way.[2] A fat man, gluttonous and sensual, he soon lost any fitness in the pleasures of feasting and debauch. Sufficiently intelligent to bear full responsibility for his inertia, he has been described by Orderic Vital and the author of the *Miracles de Saint Benoit* as " lazy and incompetent in war . . . dulled by his masses of flesh and too occupied in eating and sleeping to fight ". After repudiating his wife, Bertha of Holland, he had a companion worthy of his attentions in Bertrade de Montfort whom he carried away from her husband Fulk of Anjou ; a bishop celebrated their marriage and in the course

---

[1] **DCIX**, 47 ff. ; **CDXLV**, 161 ff.
[2] **CCXCII**, 32 ff. passim ; **CXCIV**, 213–18.

of a good dinner she was able to reconcile her two husbands. For the rest of his reign, Philip was dominated by this astute and cynical woman to such an extent that, to please her, he made the vain request that the King of England should retain in captivity the son of his first marriage, Louis the Fat, and then the rumour gained currency that Bertrade was trying to poison her stepson. Philip, however, appeared to have no intention of breaking the tradition of association in the throne [1] and feeling himself growing more and more incompetent he relinquished part of his power to his heir at least after 1101 and the latter undertook several great attacks on the robber barons. Louis [2] was afflicted with the same disease of fatness as his father and mother, Bertha; in the later years of his personal reign (1108–1137) he was frequently reduced to inactivity but until almost the end of his life he showed remarkable energy as a warrior. This human giant with a pale complexion had some attractive qualities. He was gallant, genial, and somewhat ingenuous even, as his adviser Suger admits, being rated as " simple " by some.[3] In his premature old age, he appears to have considered that he had let many opportunities slip.[4] At least he had some realization of his duties as a king and bestowed many valuable sword blows. His son, Louis VII, whom he associated on the throne in 1131,[5] did not possess his active character and very quickly fell under the domination of priests; his long reign (1137–1180) bears no sign of a statesman's direction.

These three men as a result of their weakness or the simplicity of their intellect were subject to the influence of those around them—their wives, the barons and prelates who thronged the Court, and the minor officers equally with the most important.

The queen was " queen by the Grace of God " crowned and consecrated and shared the prerogatives of monarchy. We have already seen the dominating position held by a Bertrade, and Adelaide de Maurienne played a similar role. She could boast of giving Louis VI a family of nine children and, after the death of her husband, she fought with Suger for a short time for a position of power. Eleanor of Aquitaine would

[1] The question is obscure. Cf. Luchaire, **CDXLIX**, 19 ff., 45 ff.; **CDXLIV**, intro., p. xxi et seq. and app. iii; and Fliche, **CCXCII**, 78 ff.
[2] **CDXLIV**, p. xi ff.; **CDXLV**, 311 ff.; **CXCIV**, 219 ff.
[3] **CXXXV**, 9.   [4] **CXXXV**, 123.   [5] **CCCLVIII**, 4–5.

probably have played an equally important part in our history had she remained the wife of Louis VII. The influence of these three queens was clearly of considerable importance. What part was played by Baldwin of Flanders to whom Henry I had entrusted the guardianship of Philip?[1] He appears to have used the regency merely for his personal advantage. We know very little of most of the highly born people who appeared at Court but we can state that they watched with very ill grace the establishment of the influence of councillors originating from the lesser nobility or of plebian stock. Even Suger, himself, was not entirely protected against these intrigues and jealousy.

Suger, who was of plebian origin, is the only outstanding personality among the royal advisers of the period. He has won a well earned celebrity in French history—although it is difficult to reconstruct all the stages in his career as adviser to Louis VI and VII—in spite of the possibility of frequent wrong estimations of his character.[2] He was primarily a churchman, devoted to the monarchy because he saw it as the champion of the Church.

If he became devoted to Louis VI it was because he saw that, even before his accession, he was reviving traditions that had lapsed into oblivion. " Illustrious and courageous defender of his father's kingdom," writes Suger in his *Vie de Louis le Gros*. " He looked after the needs of the churches, guarded the security of priests, working men and the poor, duties which for a long time no one had discharged." After the death of Philip I, Louis the Fat could not renounce his habit of defending the churches, of looking after the poor and unfortunate and giving his attention to the preservation of peace and the defence of the realm.[3] This is the reason why Suger, who had been elected Abbot of Saint Denis, 1122, put his very considerable administrative ability at the disposal of the Crown about this time when it began to recognize the responsibilities of its coronation oath. He was only small and frail but he had a concise and practical mind and was untiring. He divided his time between his abbey, which he

---

[1] The question of the regency from the eleventh to the twelfth century has been cleared up by M. F. Oliver-Martin. See **CDLXIII**, 12 ff.

[2] **CCXIV,** ; **DCXXVII,** 52 ff.; **CDXLIV,** p. lvii ff.; **CDXLVI,** 20 ff. The act in which the king calls Suger " my friend and faithful counsellor ", dates only from 1124. **CDXLIV,** n. 348. Cf. **CCXIV,** 20. [3] **CXXXV,** 9 and 41.

THE CAPETIAN MONARCHY, 1060–1152

reformed and enriched, providing it with a magnificent basilica, and politics. At both St. Denis and the Court he showed keen attention to his work and a spirit of equity and moderation. He was devoted to the ideal of Christian unity and shrank from the fanatical reforming zeal of St. Bernard, only turning to asceticism very late in his career. For the same reason he could only envisage war against brigands or pagans. He maintained friendly relations with Henry I, Beauclerc, for whom he had a profound admiration, and even hoped to reconcile Louis VII with Thibaud of Champagne of whom he should have been extremely suspicious. When Louis VII set out for the Holy Land he left the regency principally in the hands of this monk of obscure birth. This was Suger's opportunity to show his value (1147–9).

He administered the royal demesne most carefully, forwarded the necessary resources to his master, built up reserves, and maintained public order. These long absences in the East were a source of considerable danger to the monarchy. When Louis returned he found the old Abbot of St. Denis overburdened with the responsibility. He had been forced to put down the king's own brother who had been pushed towards the throne by dissatisfied elements. Only shortly afterwards he died (13th January, 1151). In his last letter to the king he wrote " Love the Church of God, care for the fatherless and widows. This is my advice to you ".[1] He was only repeating the Church's regular admonitions to the monarchy. New complications were about to arise with which Suger's pupil was to find himself unable to cope.

The close relationship of the Abbot of St. Denis with two kings and the accession to the regency of this monk of doubtful origin had excited more jealousy than surprise. Ecclesiastical dignities offered to the villain's son the opportunity of exercising an influence of primary importance in politics. In the Middle Ages it was the means by which mental ability took its due. The new factor, or rather the one we must consider as new, is the administrative and governmental importance assumed by the " Palais ", i.e. the retinue and servants of the king. This and the freeing of the demesne are the principal characteristics of the history of the French monarchy in the period we are studying.

[1] CXXXIV, 281.

80 MONARCHY IN FRANCE AND ENGLAND

The eleventh century Capetians, including Philip I during the first part of his reign, lived like the Carolingians surrounded by clergy and household officials, calling the chief nobles and bishops together at frequent intervals to take their advice and settle cases with their assistance.[1] Personally I can find no grounds for the belief that the household officials who represented institutions of Merovingian origin had disappeared by the time of Hugh Capet and Robert in spite of the silence of the texts which are so inadequate that they are no evidence. If we find the chief ministers among the witnesses to the charters of Henry I we have little ground for believing that his predecessors in the interval had lacked their assistance.[2] He needed the services of a seneschal, a constable, and a butler to arrange the royal progresses, administer the royal household, prepare accommodation, and take charge of supplies; a chamberlain and staff to look after the royal chamber and the other institutions attached to it containing his clothes, furs, arms, jewels, and the treasure which was always kept near his person; a chancellor and his clerks to draft, seal, and dispatch letters and charters; chaplains for his religious services. These personal servants were able to play a decisive role on certain occasions as we have seen,[3] but towards the middle of the reign of Philip I a change began which was of considerable advantage to them. Full meetings of the Council became less frequent and the permanent members of the palace became almost exclusively responsible for political decisions, royal grants of privilege, and the determination of legal proceedings. They became the signatories and witnesses of royal charters; after 1085 the counts' signatures grew less regular and finally disappeared while those of the simple knights of the palace increased; the signatures of the great officers—seneschal, constable, butler, chamberlain—were, until that date, scattered among the others, but now they formed a separate group. Finally, in two acts of 1106 and 1107, they appear alone, preceded by the formula which was to have an historic importance, " In the presence of those of

---

[1] **CCXCII**, bk. ii, chap. i.
[2] See **CXXX**, p. 15; Fliche, **CCXCII**, 113, 119–120, conjectures that " under Hugh Capet and Robert the Pious the chancellor alone existed." Pfister, **DXXI**, 147, is unwilling to commit himself.
[3] List of chief officers in **CIII**, p. cxxxvi ff., and in **CDXLIV**, app. v.

our household whose names and signs are appended below . . ."¹

The chancellor's signature, which even at this date was often missing, became more and more frequent and a regular feature of formal enactments of the twelfth and thirteenth century. This change in royal diplomatic is clear evidence of an abrupt departure from the political ideas of the Carolingians.

II

POLITICAL CONSTRICTION: THE LIBERATION OF THE DEMESNE

How are we to interpret this development and what were its causes? We have been told "the monarchy was consolidating itself". That is apparent but it is equally clear that it had drifted into its position and not arrived as a result of a definite decision. We can hardly number the somnolent Philip I among those who plan a programme and proceed to put it into execution. He allowed his life to pass indifferently and let slip the occasions when he could have gathered the dukes and counts to his assistance. The most natural occasions at that period were those of war. In the early part of his reign, particularly in 1071, Philip did not fail to exact host service. The only meeting during his reign, at which any considerable number of counts was present, was in 1077 at the time when William the Conqueror, after his vain attempt to establish a suzerainty over Brittany (siege of Dol, October, 1076), was forced to capitulate and make his peace with Philip. The Count of Poitiers, in particular, went to considerable inconvenience to be present at this meeting at Orleans and seemed prepared to support the king against William the Conqueror but subsequently Philip made no further effort to put himself at the head of the nobility in an effort to disperse the Anglo-Norman danger, although he could easily have taken advantage of the intrigues and ambition of Robert Curthose, the Conqueror's son, the brother of William Rufus and Henry I. Philip and his son, Louis the Fat, lost the best possible opportunity of separating Normandy and England. Philip thoroughly understood the policy to be

¹ CIII, p. cxxxvi ff.; DXI, 106–7.

adopted but it demanded careful negotiations, stimulating the distrust of the counts of Flanders and Anjou, to build up a feudal coalition against this Anglo-Norman king whose pretentions were so disquieting. The apathy of the king was too great to tackle these tasks.[1]

On almost every occasion he showed the same carelessness in matters of internal politics. He did not even demand that his major vassals should do homage. Royal justice was only exercised in the demesne or when one of the parties concerned were domiciled in it. He could have done good service to the cause of public peace by giving his support, as William did, to the efforts of the Holy See to win respect for the Truce of God and the Peace of God but he gave the matter no attention.[2] We need not say that his legislative work, like that of his predecessors, was nil. Of the 172 authentic charters which are the sum of his extant enactments, 170 are entirely concerned with questions of routine—grants to churches or settling questions concerning them. Only one records a changed obedience of the baronage to the Crown.[3] No one came to court and, as a consequence, his retinue monopolized the position of adviser to the Crown. We have been told that this evolution was favourable to the interests of king and kingdom but I have not been convinced of it. In a period when the full consequences of the French feudal regime, which was still undefined and in process of formation in the time of Hugh and Robert the Pious, were appearing in hereditary fiefs [4] and the independence of feudal governors, the king could only re-establish his authority by forming the closest links with his vassals and taking every advantage of his supreme position as suzerain. Barely a century later the Crown itself realized this. On one point alone Philip displayed some foresight; he gave some attention to extending the demesne and succeeded in his object stimulated by his need of money. His scanty resources do not justify the scandals of his conduct but they explain [4] them in part. He stands convicted,

[1] **CCXCII**, 269 ff.   [2] **CCXCII**, 166 ff., 248 ff., 499 ff.
[3] The king freed a serf belonging to Fulk Count of Anjou, at his request in 1069 (**CIII**, n. xli, p. 118), cf. the acts of Robert the Pious in **DXXI**, p. lxii–lxxxvi, and Henry I, **CXXX**.
[4] Hereditary fiefs are presented as a general phenomenon in the systematic little treaty written between 1095 and 1136, which begins the famous Lombard section of *Libri Feudorum I*, I, i. The *Libri* are published at the end of the older edition of the *Corpus Juris Civilis*.

THE CAPETIAN MONARCHY, 1060–1152

literally, of brigandage and shamelessly accepted simony as customary.

He indulged in such doubtful practices without hesitation but he realized that an adequate landed income was more dependable. He brought off some lucky annexations which proved as important politically as financially. He took advantage of the family quarrels which were dividing his barons to gain the cession of the Gatinais in 1068 and Corbie in 1071. The Gatinais formed a corridor between two fragments of the royal demesne, the districts around Sens and Orleans,[1] and Corbie was an invaluable position on the Somme. After the death of his father-in-law, Raoul de Vermandois (1074), he seized the French Vexin which added the course of the Epte to the demesne as the Franco-Norman border. We should note that all these conquests were made before he reached the age of thirty; in the latter part of his reign the only accession was the sale, by a noble who wanted money to go to the Holy Land, of Bourges and his "septaine", i.e. his judiciary district. In this way the monarch acquired an enclave to the south of the Loire.[2] On the other hand, after his vain attempt to capture the castle of Puiset, he allowed the chatelains Hugh de Puiset, Bouchard de Montmorency, the savage Thomas de Marle, and others, to subject churches, abbeys, towns, and the countryside to a reign of terror. The monarchy abandoned its position as protector.[3]

The real achievement of Louis VI from the time when he was associated on the throne was to answer the appeals of the oppressed inhabitants of the royal demesne. For thirty-four years (1101–1135) he fought courageously against the brigands of the Île de France, the Laonnais, the Orleannais, and even sometimes the Bourbonnais and Auvergne. He burnt or destroyed their keeps; he freed the bishoprics and abbeys, offered the peasants some security, re-established communications between Paris and the Loire, consolidated the demesne by confiscation or purchase and the construction of royal fortresses.[4] He could not do more, his father's inheritance was too clumsy and he had not sufficient ability. He did not appreciate the importance of the social and economic movement which was developing at that time. The

---

[1] **DL,** 177–190. [2] **CCXCII,** 138 ff.; **CDXXVIII,** 70 ff.
[3] **CDXLIV,** p. lxv ff. [4] **CDXLIV,** p. lxvii ff.; **CDXLV,** 314 ff.

first revolutions in the towns took place in the reign of his father who paid them no attention. In his relations with the communal movement, he adopted a policy of immediate profits ; the legend that he was responsible for the emancipation of the bourgeoise has for a long time been discredited.[1]

In general he lived in his demesne fully occupied in the struggle against the squires, driven to defend even the great offices of his court against the encroachments of the minor nobility. The major barons did not attend the infrequent formal meetings which the king summoned ; only the prelates who willingly accepted royal authority attended.[2] It is true that Louis succeeded in securing recognition of a count of his choice, William Clito, by the Flemish nobility after the assassination of Count Charles the Good and was able to punish those responsible, but his man was badly chosen and his intervention ended in a humiliation made inevitable by the drunken brutality of William Clito. The townsmen of Bruges, in revolt against William, were summoned by Louis VI to submit. They wrote to remind him " that the king of France has no right in this election of a count of Flanders " and he was obliged to recognize Thierry d'Alsace [3] the candidate of the Flemish people. Louis had endeavoured to establish William Clito, who was a nephew of Henry Beauclerc, King of England, as Duke of Normandy but Henry was stronger than his opponents in every respect and the decisive battle of Brémule (1119) was a disaster.[4] The only occasion when Louis the Fat was able to appear as King of France answering the menace of invasion at the head of his baronage was a very fleeting one but it must not be forgotten. In 1124 the King of Germany, Henry V, felt that he had found an opportunity to take his revenge for the exceedingly valuable support that Louis had given to the Pope. He summoned Louis who was at war with Theobold, Count of Blois, to make peace with his vassal to which, according to an English raconteur of historical anecdotes, Walter Map, Louis VI replied " Bah German ! " The German summoned his feudal army and announced his attention of destroying Rheims. The king paid a visit to St. Denis to place on the altar the oriflamme which he was

---

[1] **CDXL**, vol. ii, 117 ff. ; **CDXLV**, 328–9.   [2] **CDXLIV**, p. xlii ff.
[3] **XLV**, 24 ff., 151–3 ; **CDXLIV**, pp. xcv–ciii.
[4] **CDXLIV**, pp. cxiv–cxvi.

THE CAPETIAN MONARCHY, 1060-1152

entitled to bear as Count of Vexin and a vassal of the abbey and he presented to St. Denis the profits of the fair of Lendit.

At Rheims there gathered around him all the forces which the nobles clerical and lay had had time to mobilize; the Count of Blois himself had conformed to feudal rules and sent troops. Henry V accepted the result as a foregone conclusion and did not advance beyond Metz.[1] Obviously, in such circumstances, the King of France was a suzerain entitled to the service of all his vassals but it is interesting to note that he could count on it in fact if the kingdom was threatened and that there remained some feelings of unity. The mobilization of the host in 1124 is one of those events which shows us that history is more complex and exhaustive than a historian can realize or depict. That was merely an isolated episode but nevertheless the reign of Louis closed with an appearance of diplomatic triumph which actually had fatal consequences. On the death of William X, Duke or Count of Aquitaine, his daughter and heiress, Eleanor, with the assent of the clergy of Aquitaine, married the heir to the throne who on 1st August of the same year succeeded his father as Louis VII.[2] His seal shows him as a crowned king with his sceptre in his hand and on the counter seal he is represented as a duke with baronial insignia mounted on a galloping horse; Aquitaine remained a principality. It was not to maintain its independence for long but it was the King of England who benefited. For the effective annexation of Aquitaine, the monarchy had to accomplish a hard task. It had to destroy the feudal aristocracy of Poitou which separated them and expel the English from France. Louis VII was not equal to such a task.

III

Gregorian Reform: The Popes in France

To gain a correct idea of what the Capetian monarchy was in this period, we must deal also with its attitude to the problem of religion and to the sudden emergence of an important new power, the restored Papacy.

[1] **LXXXII**, 217, n. 391; **CDXLIV**, n. 348, 349, 358; **CDLXXI**, 273-9; **CDLXXX**, 238 ff. [2] **CCCLVIII**, 1-16.

Severely shaken, in the tenth century, by the Norman invasions and the disorder and violence of a time of stress, the Church had succeeded, in the eleventh century, in reconstituting its material prosperity. The magnificent outcrop of Romanesque architecture is a witness which has retained nearly all its force until the present day. The lay nobility and the kings—even a Philip I—loaded the French Church with gifts and privileges for fear of Hell. But when Philip ascended the throne, it had scarcely begun the repair of its moral ruins. The evil was general throughout Christendom and sprang everywhere from the same social and political causes. The disappearance of the Carolingian Empire had brought no new freedom to the Church. In Germany it had been suffering from Imperial oppression since the days of Otto the Great.

In France and in every country where the power of the monarchy was disintegrating, the lay princes—kings, dukes, and counts—were imposing their feudal suzerainty on abbots and bishops, particularly the latter. The right of election was destroyed by the nomination of official candidates and the insignia of abbeys and bishoprics were conferred on the friends or relations of the prince or even on those who had brought his benevolence.[1] In France, Philip I followed the example of his father, Henry I,[2] and indulged in simony without shame and his wife, Bertrade, paid her creditors by selling bishoprics to the highest bidders.[3] Yves de Chartres relates in a letter how the Abbot of Bourgueil repaired to court to receive the bishopric of Orleans which Bertrade had promised him but on arrival she had granted it to someone else who had been prepared to bid for it. "And when the abbot complained to the king about the treatment he had received, he replied ' Wait till we have made what we can out of him and then demand his expulsion and I will do as you wish '."[4]

The result was that abbeys, bishoprics, and even archbishoprics were to a large extent in the hands of prelates who had the morals of a dissolute squirearchy. In the reign

---

[1] **CCCLXIX**, 222 ff., 319 ff., 360 ff.; **CCXCI**, i, 18 ff.
[2] On the first Capetians, and particularly Henry I : **DCII**, vol. xlii, 258 ff.; **CCCLXIX**, 366, 439 ; **CCXCI**, i, 29, 103.
[3] **CCXCII**, 409 ff. ; for elections of the abbots, 490 ff. ; **DCII**, 271 ff.
[4] **LXII**, 98–9.

THE CAPETIAN MONARCHY, 1060-1152

of Philip I, the Bishop of Beauvais was an illiterate debauchee, the son of Philip's seneschal; Engeran, Bishop of Laon, took the dogmas of the Church as texts for witticisms; the Abbot of Saint Medard de Soissons, Pons, embezzled the property of the abbey; Yves, Abbot of St. Denis, had the people who protested about his orgies tortured; Manasses, Archbishop of Rheims, lived a life of coarse brutality, devoting more attention to hunting and brigandage than to the sacraments; Raoul II, Archbishop of Tours, was notorious for his original code of morals and the younger clergy composed songs on his relations with John his archdeacon whom he succeeded in promoting to a bishopric.[1] These notorious prelates in turn sold the ecclesiastical preferments of which they could dispose and there was no thought of demanding from curates or monks a chastity which they did not practise themselves. Simony and nicholaism [2] were ripe throughout the Church and the charge of being married was the least deplorable accusation which the more puritanical could levy against the country clergy. Pierre Damien has described the monastic sodomy of the eleventh century in his *Livre de Gomorrhe* with the precise detail which he felt essential to any successful attempt to root out such a common vice.[3]

However, a forceful current of reform which had monastic origins was already beginning to stir the world of the Church and cleanse it.[4] The order of Cluny which was one of the authors of this renaissance [5] was at the height of its prosperity during the reign of Philip I and the foundation of other orders with an extremely strict rule was developing. The most famous was that of Citeaux (1074) which was to make Saint Bernard immortal. The institutions of monasticism, founded on a communal life and a strict discipline, began to penetrate among the secular clergy who began to form colleges and establish themselves in the cathedrals under a regulated collective existence.[6] Finally, from the pontificates of

---

[1] **CCXCII**, 342-3, 417, 436, 441, 491-2.
[2] On the origin of the words which implies "licensed fornication", see **CCXCI**, i, 31, n. 2.
[3] **LXXXIX**, 162-190; cf. **CCXCI**, i, 175-264.
[4] This movement has been fully described by Fliche, **CCXCI**, i, 39 ff.
[5] The classic work on Cluny in the tenth and eleventh centuries is **DXCI**. The part of Cluny in the Reforms, a subject of heated controversy, seems to be fairly estimated in **CCCLXIX**, 374-5.
[6] **CCXCII**, 451 ff.

Leo IX (1049–1054) and, even more important, Gregory VII (1073–1085), the Holy See, emerging from the decadence in which it was sinking, as we have seen, in the time of Hugh Capet, took over the leadership of the religious revolution.[1] The Papacy considered, not without good reason, that the interference of the laity in the nomination of bishops was the principal source of the evil and that it was intolerable that a lay prince should "invest" the elected candidate: the investiture controversy had begun.

History has been justified in making Gregory VII the protagonist in this conflict but it has for a long time distorted his stature. He has been portrayed as an ambitious man greedy for power, a politician, an elaborator of theories of theocracy.[2] Scholars of the present generation have restored him and his work to true proportions.[3] He was neither an inventive genius nor a strict logician but a high souled believer convinced of the divine mission of the Holy See and determined to reform the Church, a man of consistent and practical character. He relied continually on precedent and tradition which he strengthened by commissioning the preparation of full collections of material on canonical history. Led astray by the ingenious theories of Peter Damien who urged the Holy See to rely on the temporal princes to govern the Church, he tried to reach agreement with them. In fact, he remained on good terms with William the Conqueror because, for all his tyranny, no one could complain of the bishops he chose but he could not work with either the Emperor, Henry IV, or the King of France, Philip I, whom he distrusted. Following an act of brigandage by the latter (he had caused a company of Italian merchants to be robbed), Gregory wrote on 10th September, 1074, to the French bishops that the cause of the decadence of the kingdom was the king himself. He was a "tyrant", that is to say a prince unworthy of his office; "he has defiled his whole reign with infamy and crime, he has encouraged his people in evil by the example of his deeds and morals."[4]

---

[1] CCXCI, i, 129 ff.
[2] See particularly the interesting but prejudiced work of Doellinger, CCLXII.
[3] The chief works are those of Paul Fournier, W. M. Peitz, and Fliche. See the bibliography in CCXCI, ii, 425 ff.
[4] CVIII, 130–1.

THE CAPETIAN MONARCHY, 1060–1152

The faults which he discovered in France and Germany soon led Gregory to the codification of the theories which he found in the Bulls of his predecessors and the False Decretals concerning the divine power of the Papacy. He formulated them very briefly as early as 1075 in twenty-seven articles which became famous under the title of the *Dictatus papae*[1] in which were made clear, for the first time, all the consequences of premises, which had, for a long time, been accepted. The Roman Church had been established by the only God and is infallible; the Pope can invalidate any decision and is subject to the judgment of no one. Without consulting a synod, he has full power to depose or absolve a bishop; he administers the Church and judges important cases. All princes kiss his feet in homage and, at his word, they are open to accusation by their subjects whom he can absolve from an oath of fidelity made to the unjust. He has the power of deposition over the Emperor.

In 1076–7 the Emperor Henry IV anticipated Gregory VII in a battle of depositions and thus the Pope was gradually driven towards the abandonment of the doctrine of the Divine Right of Monarchy. In 1081, forced to extremes, he cast off the traditional reserve which gave monarchy a sacred character and, after long consideration, published his opinions. At this moment a German army was marching into Italy to enthrone an antipope and he wrote to the Bishop of Metz: ... " who doesn't know that kings and generals (*duces*) originate among those who, unmindful of God, are driven by blind passion and intolerable presumption to lord it over other men their equals by force of arrogance, treachery, murder—in a word by every crime at the instigation of the Prince of this world—the Devil ? "[2]

Gregory's historical declaration was superficial and informal but it had, at least, the merit of striking an important blow at the principles of the Divine Right of Kings which the Church had generally considered justifiable or, more or less,

---

[1] CVIII, 201–8. On the canonical collections commissioned by Gregory VII as proofs for his " *dictatus* ", see, in particular, CCXCVIII and CCXCV. We have not been able to take advantage of volume ii of the *Histoire des Collections canoniques en Occident*, by P. Fournier and G. Le Bras, which has just been published.

[2] 15th March, 1081 ; CVIII, 552. On this letter, see CCIX, 94–8 ; CCXCI, ii, 389 ff.; and an article by Cauchie in the *Revue d'Histoire eccl.*, v, 1904, 588–597.

necessary to maintain. Gregory's eyes were opened by the brutal usurpation which threatened him and the mists of the scholastic theories of monarchy were blown aside.

It was not inevitable that this disillusionment should provoke the formulation of theocratic doctrines. Scholars have asked whether he was seeking to establish a political control over Christendom, a temporal monarchy of the pontificate, to which lay princes would be bound by homage, but the question was not one that really concerned him. His aim had been to stamp out simony and purify clerical morals. Everything else was subordinate to that.

The execution of his reforms led him, however, to a much more active intervention in the affairs of the Christian monarchies than his predecessors had attempted. He saw, from experience, that the Holy See could not rely on the temporal princes alone to cure such far reaching abuses or even wait for the active co-operation of the metropolitan archbishops who were often indifferent to reform. He came to the conclusion that it must maintain a direct supervision over bishops and monasteries, reserving or hearing on appeal the most important cases in the ecclesiastical courts.[1] The Holy See thus accepted an immense burden of daily administration. Personally inadequate to direct the moral and religious life of Christendom, Gregory transformed the legation which before his time had been only a temporary mission into a regular instrument of pontifical power.[2] The permanent legation was to have a considerable importance in the political history of Western Europe in the Middle Ages.

So, in the period during which Philip I, Louis VI, and Louis VII were reigning in France, the Holy See was re-establishing its authority. It found only one remedy for the abuses which kings tolerated or even profited by—the despotic government of the Church—and to this it added the claim to impose taxation. The Pope demanded the payment of Peter's Pence once more. We have already seen that almost all the royal dignity which the Capetians could boast was due to the French Church and the material and moral support it gave to the doctrine of the divine origin of monarchical power which Gregory VII was rejecting. The Pope assumed

---

[1] CCCLXIX, 476 ff.
[2] CCXCI, ii, 112 ff., 210 ff; CCXXXVIII, 33-84; DLXXV, 5 ff.

THE CAPETIAN MONARCHY, 1060–1152 91

the role, therefore, of a foreign king who was invading France and divesting the king of his prestige and his means of action alike.

It would have been possible for a St. Louis to have resisted the Holy See because he would have had the support of all those who contributed to the formation of public opinion but Philip I, who knocked down the mitre to the highest bidder and threw into prison a bishop who showed some independence, had no basis for a struggle against a Gregory VII or an Urban II and he did not trouble to establish one. He was sunk in a cynical indifference from which he was roused only by debauchery or vulgar intrigues, and he seemed to look for nothing except to gain time and disarm his opponents by his very inertia.[1] As soon as he was installed on the papal throne Gregory talked of deposing him and his marriage with Bertrade embroiled him with the Papacy for twelve years (1092–1104). During that period even the servility of the bishops could not prevent his being excommunicated three times. The popes, harassed by their opponents, developed, at this time, the habit of coming frequently to France and making fairly long stays there during which they took over the direction of important matters like the organization of the Crusade and the application of the Truce of God (Urban II at the Council of Clermont, 1095). Nothing betrayed the degradation of the monarchy more clearly than its silence and impotence at such times.

It was thus possible to realize the principal tasks of religious reform in France—the destruction of simony and nicholaism—during the long reign of Philip I, by the measures on which Gregory VII had decided, without any serious resistance by the House of Capet to the encroachment of the Holy See and its representatives. Hugh de Die, who was appointed legate in France and Burgundy on the 16th March, 1074, sought not only to reform the morals but to direct the whole religious life of the country and it was necessary on occasion for Gregory VII to moderate his energy, for his haughty tyranny was provoking anger and bad feeling.[2] We know him chiefly through an extraordinary letter which

---

[1] There is full detail and many references for what follows in **CCXCII**, bk. iv. Cf. **CDLXXIX**; **CCXXVIII**, chaps. xv, xxiii to xxvi.
[2] **DLXXV**.

the clergy of Cambrai wrote to those of Rheims in 1078 about "certain imposters", Hugh de Die and Hugh de Langres. These "Romans" were continually summoning councils, excommunicating the metropolitan, changing the bishops, interfering in everything and were even guilty of working to diminish the dignity of the crown.[1] By the end of Gregory's pontificate, Hugh de Die was at the same time legate, Archbishop of Lyons, and Primate of the provinces of Tours, Rouen, and Sens. The old-established primacy of the Archbishop of Sens over the Gauls and Germany was thus destroyed for the benefit of a prelate whose metropolitan see was in imperial territory. Urban II took over the policy of Gregory VII and succeeded in finally disintegrating the primacy of Sens.

The energy of Gregory VII and Urban II and their legates guaranteed the triumph of their ideas in France. The authority of bishops and archbishops, and "Gallican liberties" were threatened but simony, the source of the evils of the Church, had been almost entirely wiped out. To speak only of the royal bishoprics in the eleventh century, the Capetians had themselves nominated or even imposed their candidate; they invested him with the ring and the cross and authorized his consecration. By the end of the reign of Philip I, however, we can consider the investiture problem as settled in France. The king left to the chapters the election of the bishop, no longer "conferred the bishopric" with the ring and cross but invested the bishop elect with his regalian rights, demanding only an oath of fidelity. This was the obvious solution which the bishop Yves de Chartres applauded. The King of France retained considerable powers, the right to authorize the election and even to postpone it for some long time, the right to enjoy the regale and to confirm the election. In fact, the kings continued to interfere but the scandals of the reigns of Henry I and Philip I did not reappear. The Crown had given way to the Holy See.[2]

Even had Louis VI [3] any desire to work for the return of the old practices, it would have been risking his throne to

---

[1] H. F., vol. xiv, 778–780.
[2] **CCCLXIX**, 398 ff., 436 ff.; **DCII**, vol. xliii, 92 ff.
[3] Our interpretation will be very different from that of Luchaire, **CDXLIV**, intro., chap. vi and vii; **DCXLVII**, particularly i, 264 ff., interesting but hagiographical.

embroil himself with the Holy See and the reformers. Threatened even in his own demesne by feudal brigandage, he was more dependent than anyone on the material and financial resources of the Church and the goodwill of Rome and in fact he was assisted and even encouraged in his role as warrior by the Church and the papal legate. The tyrannical pretensions of the Emperor Henry V made good relations between Louis the Fat and the popes much easier, for they relied on him.

Four out of five visited France or stayed there either to find refuge from the threats of the Emperor, to negotiate with his ambassadors, or to hold councils and triumph over an antipope. We have seen how consistently Louis VI met the threats of Henry V; on several occasions he showed himself equally capable of defending royal interests against the Pope and winning concessions, but he was involved in the struggle between reformers and anti-reformers in the sphere of monarchical influence. The mistakes with which he has been charged were not always the result of " necessities of state " but were, too often, due to his failure to take a firm attitude towards his entourage.

The Church of France in the time of Louis VI was leading a more stormy life than ever. Abuse, excommunication, quarrels, and exile were regular weapons. Admittedly this was no new feature, for, throughout the Middle Ages, the differences of churchmen were as violent as those of the more extreme political parties of to-day but the zeal of the new apostle of reform, St. Bernard, gave conflicts both of doctrine and person an impassioned vehemence. Not only was the famous Abbot of Clairvaux able, in a very few years, to cover France with Cistercian monasteries subject to the harshest discipline but his extraordinary, almost diseased, energy affected every sphere of religious life in France and beyond. His prestige and determination were often valuable to the cause of Christian peace but through pæans and panegyrists we can discern a passionate and dogmatic character, hasty to attack and condemn, the temperament of the excited mystic. His interference in every matter of faith and discipline caused considerable anger even in the Roman Curia.

Louis VI did not allow St. Bernard, who had little influence at court, to become viceroy but he often paid attention to the reformers. He loaded the new orders with possessions, showing particular favour to the great theological school which was founded in his reign, the community of St. Victor de Paris. We see him forcing the monks to accept the rule of Cluny, the priests to abjure their concubines.[1] He could have anticipated the policy, which St. Louis adopted at a later date, of defending the interests of religion which stood, at that period, for spiritual interests and at the same time defending his own interests as king and judge if necessary, but (without speaking of Suger who was a moderate who tried to avoid such questions) he was dependent on officers and a chancery drawn from the clergy who were anxious to assure their own benefit. In listening to them, he threw away the advantages of the prestige to which his personal honesty and candour entitled him.

His chancellor, Étienne de Garland, was probably the instigator of the church scandals in which the monarchy became involved. Long before the great prelates of the Renaissance, this amazing adventurer brazenly accumulated benefices and offices and indulged in the most flagrant nepotism. He was Archdeacon of Notre Dame de Paris, Dean of St. Geneviève de Paris, Dean of Saint Samson and Saint Avit d'Orleans and, finally, Dean of the cathedral of Orleans. Louis VI allowed himself to be dominated by him and, in spite of the disfavour in which the queen and higher clergy held him, he managed to secure two of the five chief offices of the Crown—those of chancellor and seneschal. He was responsible, thus, at the same time, for the administration and the army while one of his brothers held another major office as butler. The reformers had prevented his becoming a bishop [2] and he began a merciless attack on them. The brutality with which Louis VI treated the most famous of his prelates like Yves de Chartres, the Archbishop of Tours, Hildebert de Lavardin, and the Bishop of Paris, Étienne de Senlis, must be attributed to Étienne de Garland

---

[1] The most characteristic of the somewhat rare instances of direct intervention by Louis VI is the Charter of Confirmation of the liberties of Saint Corneille de Compiègne (**CDXLIV**, n. 632); the king forbade priests to maintain concubines, but clerks who were not in orders were left free.

[2] See the invectives of Yves de Chartres and Saint Bernard against him (H. F., vol. xv, 110, 547), and the letter of Yves de Chartres to Étienne de Garlande, p. 166.

THE CAPETIAN MONARCHY, 1060–1152 95

and his friends. A palace revolution [1] interrupted his career for five years and threw him into opposition (1127–1132) but his influence over Louis VI was so great that the king pardoned him and reinstalled him as chancellor. His hand is clearly to be seen in the two tragedies which stained the end of the reign; in 1133, two reforming prelates, Archamband, sub-Dean of Sainte Croix d'Orleans, and Thomas, Prior of Saint Victor of Paris, were assassinated, the first by retainers of the Archdeacon Jean, clerk of Étienne de Garland, and the second by vassals of Étienne. The royal Court did all it could to shield the guilty [2] and this infamous epilogue marks the end of the relations between Louis VI and the Church.

Louis VII himself was rated as an opponent of religious reform at the beginning of his reign.[3] He dismissed Étienne de Garland but his Chancellor Cahour was equally insatiable and Louis VII was no stronger than his father. In addition, the young queen, Eleanor, who was merry and sensual, hated the austerity of the reformers. Cahour sought to secure installation as Archbishop of Bourges although a candidate had been elected by the canons with the approval of the Holy See. Thibaud of Champagne, a friend of the reformers, who had grounds for complaint at the king's treatment, joined in the quarrel which became serious and far reaching (1141–4).[4] An interdict was placed on the royal demesne. During an expedition of pillage and destruction into Champagne led by Louis VII, the tragedy of Vitry occurred. The church of Vitry was caught in the fire and hundreds of refugees perished there (January–March 1143). The young king was stricken with horror at his deed and received a nervous shock which seems to have transformed him. He could not bear the remorse for any long time. The insistent approaches of St. Bernard helped to break down his resistance and he submitted. From that time we can note the declining political influence of Eleanor; for the rest of his life, Louis was under the domination of priests and the Holy See. At Christmas, 1145, he took the Cross and the kingdom was more than ever subject to the two international authorities of the

---

[1] He thought that without consulting the king he could transfer his office of seneschal to his son-in-law.
[2] See the texts in **CDXLIV**, n. 505, 506, 518, 519, 531, 546.
[3] **CCCLVIII**, 17–54.
[4] **CCCLVIII**, 28–38; **CXLVII**, ii, 344 ff.; **DCXLVII**, ii, 183 ff.

pope and Saint Bernard. They arranged the details of the Crusade which Louis had decided to make and it was with *the consent of our lord the pope* that Louis, "after consulting archbishops, bishops, and the chief nobles," entrusted to Suger "the responsibility for the administration of the kingdom".[1] The result of all this was that during a century that was of decisive importance in the relations of Church and Monarchy and for religious life in Western Europe, the Capetians had no constructive or consistent policy but were generally swayed by their own greed or that of the people around them. In spite of vacillations and setbacks, the Holy See and the reforming clergy had a plan which they realized not without involving the status and machinery of the Capetian monarchy. It was they, often in opposition to the Crown, who preserved the moral heritage of Christianity in France.

In the period when the Normans were mastering Sicily and England, when the progress of the Feudal System and the growing importance of the bourgeoisie demanded a new policy, the Capetian monarchy confined its efforts to a few acquisitions of territory and police measures which it carried out with difficulty within its demesne. In the period of religious reforms and the investiture controversy, the period when the major dogmas of Christianity were being debated in France and Beranger of Tours, Roscelin de Compiègne, and Abelard were being condemned or exiled, when France was being covered with cathedrals and the first epics in the native language were being evolved along the pilgrim routes, the intellectual and moral influence of the Capetians was almost negligible. The important events which were taking place passed almost without comment; the chief intellects of the kingdom were the priests who regarded the dynasty as merely a weapon in intrigues of high policy. An urgent crisis was already brewing which would demand a king of supreme ability.

[1] Letter of Suger, 1149; **CXXXIV**, 256.

BOOK TWO

THE ANGEVIN EMPIRE AND THE CAPETIAN MONARCHY

CHAPTER I

FORMATION OF THE ANGEVIN EMPIRE. THE NEW MONARCHY: THE MEN AND THEIR IDEAS

I

THE HOUSE OF ANJOU. THE MARRIAGES OF THE PLANTEGENETS. THE REIGN OF STEPHEN AND THE ANARCHY IN ENGLAND

THE dynasty established by William the Conqueror was less fortunate than its Capetian contemporaries. It died out within seventy years through lack of a male heir in the direct line. After a period of anarchy during the nominal reign of the French baron, Stephen of Blois, it was replaced by the seignorial family, equally French in its origins, of the counts of Anjou.

This Angevin dynasty rose in the ninth century in an area which the Carolingians had disputed with the Breton and Norman bands. Its founders, Enjeuger, chatelaine in Touraine, and his son, Fulk the Red, who became Count of Anjou, had won their offices by resisting the invaders. At a later date when William the Bastard and his ancestors were building the Norman power, the terrible Fulk the Black and Geoffrey Martel were establishing the Angevin. They built impregnable castles and fought bloody battles with their equally war-like neighbours—the counts of Brittany, the counts of Blois, the dukes of Aquitaine, and the dukes of Normandy themselves. The House of Anjou annexed Touraine and Maine, established an administration and gained control over the clergy of the area. In the time of Philip I it was suffering the same eclipse as the House of Capet. We have seen how Count Fulk the Red shared his wife with Philip I whom he rivalled as a voluptuary and gourmand while he allowed feudal anarchy to canker his demesnes.[1] Then, at the time when

[1] **CCCXXXIX**, 1 ff.; **CDV**, chap. iv–vii; **CCXCII**, 223 ff.

Louis the Fat was re-establishing order in the possessions of the Crown, Fulk the Young and Geoffrey Plantegenet [1] were carrying out the same cleansing work in Anjou, reducing the baronage and razing dangerous castles.[2] Geoffrey was an attractive prince—educated, witty, and energetic—and, after the death of Henry I Beauclerc (1135) and Louis the Fat (1137), he became a leading figure. His abilities marked him out for a brilliant political career at the expense of his mediocre neighbours. Neither Louis VII, although he happened by a singular stroke of luck to become Duke of Aquitaine, nor Stephen, the new king of England, were able to check the advance of Geoffrey Plantegenet and his son, Henry.

The house of Anjou in the twelfth century was able to take advantage simultaneously of a dynasty of brilliant fighting and administrative leaders and the good fortune of a series of profitable marriage alliances. Geoffrey had been married in adolescence to the Empress Matilda, the widow of the Emperor Henry V and daughter of Henry I Beauclerc of England. Henry I had lost his son in the wreck of the White Ship and had taken considerable trouble to obtain from the barons and prelates of his realm an oath to accept Matilda as heir to the throne.

Nevertheless, when he died, Geoffrey and Matilda could not gain the succession ; the usurper, Stephen of Blois, son of a daughter of William the Conqueror, and a Norman baron as Count of Mortain, succeeded in his claim. He seized the royal treasury at Winchester, issued promises to prelates and barons [3] and had himself crowned almost conspiratorially on the 22nd December, 1135, by the Archbishop of Canterbury in the presence of two bishops, a handful of barons, and the citizens of London.[4] This inaugurated a crisis which has considerable interest as a constitutional study. It reminds us in some respects of the events of 1066 while others bear a strong resemblance to the coup of Henry I in 1100.

The Empress Matilda claimed the throne as the daughter of the dead king and the heir recognized by the baronage. She sent the Bishop of Angers to Rome to maintain her

---

[1] The nickname was doubtless due to the fact that, as a keen hunter, he loved gorse-covered country (**CCCXXI**, 6). We should not say " Plantagenet ".
[2] **CCXXI**, 4 ff. ; **DLXV**, ii, 12 ff.
[3] Stephen's first charter : **CXXXIII**, 142.
[4] **DCXXVII**, i, 389–391 ; **DLXXVI**, second part.

FORMATION OF THE ANGEVIN EMPIRE

claims at the Papal Court but he refused to give a judgement for her.[1] Stephen relied on the right of election, the agreements he had made with barons and clergy, and the support of the Church. It would be true to say that he was accepted as king " during good behaviour ",[2] that is to say as long as he offered no opposition to feudal and ecclesiastical reaction. A few months after his accession, he granted a Charter which quietened all the discontent caused by the violence of William Rufus or the energetic administration of Henry I. He gave up the new " forests ", a source of considerable profit; he promised to suppress the abuse of authority by sheriffs and " others " and undertook to return to established custom in the execution of justice. He thus gave up any claim to continuing the work of Henry I and his officers and itinerant justices. Most important, however, he made extremely important promises to the Church. He not only yielded to the bishops the advowsons of benefices and returned to the Church all that it had been robbed of since the days of William the Conqueror, but he did not exercise the right of regale while bishoprics and abbeys were vacant and he yielded to the Church the responsibility for punishing criminous clergy. His charter began: " I, Stephen, by the Grace of God and with the assent of the people, elected King of England, consecrated by William, Archbishop of Canterbury and Legate of the Holy Roman Church, confirmed by Innocent, Pontiff of the Holy Roman See, grant, in reverence and love of God, that Holy Church shall be free and I fully accord to it all the respect that is its due. . . . "[3] It has been said that Stephen did nothing by this but abandon excessive privileges. In fact, however, the whole policy of the Anglo-Norman kings was reversed and, in practice, it was even a great deal worse. Partly because he allowed the imposition of particular conditions, equally because he closed his eyes, the incompetent Stephen allowed the baronage to encroach on the military and administrative prerogatives of the Crown, to administer the justice reserved to the Crown, to coin money, to raise taxes, and to build castles

[1] **DLXXXVI**, 8 ff., 30, and app. B.
[2] **DLXXXVI**, 27.
[3] **XVII**, 8–10.
[4] For what follows, see **DCXXVII**, i, 394 ff.; **DLXXXVI, DLXXVI**, parts 3 and 4.

I. DESCENDANTS OF WILLIAM THE CONQUEROR (ORIGIN OF THE PLANTEGENETS)

William I the Conqueror = Matilda of Flanders

```
├── Robert Curthose Duke of Normandy from 1087–1106
│   └── William Clito ob. 1127.
├── WILLIAM II (RUFUS) King of England 1087–1100.
├── HENRY I (BEAUCLERC) King of England 1100–1135
│   └── MATILDA = (1) The Emperor Henry V; (2) Geoffrey Plantegenet, son of Fulk the Young Count of Anjou
│       └── HENRY II Son of Geoffrey and Matilda Duke of Normandy in 1149 King of England, 1154–1189.
├── Adela = Stephen Count of Blois
│   └── STEPHEN King of England 1135–1154.
├── Cécile Abbess of La Trinité of Caen.
└── Constance = Alain Count of Brittany.
```

[*page* 102

II. DESCENDANTS OF HENRY II PLANTEGENET AND ELEANOR OF AQUITAINE

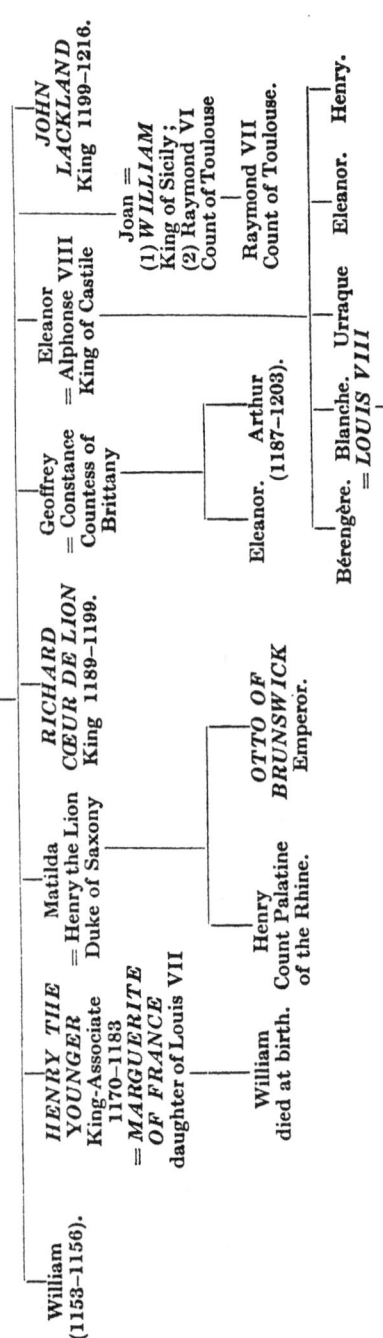

III. DESCENDANTS OF JOHN LACKLAND AND ISABEL OF ANGOULÊME

without licence. In a few years eleven hundred and fifteen had been built. It was in vain for him to authorize everything, to dissipate the income and the lands of the Crown to create supporters, or to take Flemish mercenaries into his pay; he was able neither to satisfy anybody nor to stem the tide. In 1139 under the impression that he was doing something energetic and useful he committed an irreparable mistake; the powerful Bishop of Salisbury, Roger, who, through his family, controlled the Chancery and Treasury, had built several castles without permission and Stephen cast him into prison. This precipitated his downfall. All the clergy turned against him and the royal bureaucracy was almost completely disorganized. The supporters of the Empress Matilda won a big victory at Lincoln (2nd February, 1141) and Matilda, in turn, was received at Winchester by the bishop, at that time a papal legate. The Bishop of Winchester was the brother of Stephen but Matilda promised to entrust the direction of the ecclesiastical policy of the kingdom to him and he undertook to be faithful to her " as long as she did not break the agreement ". After a secret consultation with the bishops, abbots, and archdeacons present at Winchester he formally received Matilda and conferred the office of governor upon her in the following terms :—

> God has exercised his judgement on my brother and allowed him to fall into the hands of powerful enemies without my knowledge. To prevent the collapse of the kingdom because of its lack of ruler, I, in virtue of my powers as legate, have invited you all to be present here. Yesterday the majority of the clergy of England who have the chief right in the election and ordination of the king discussed this matter in private. After invoking divine guidance, as we clearly must, we have chosen as Lady (domina) of England the daughter of a king who was peace loving, glorious, and prosperous, a king whose merits find no equal in our time and we promise her our loyalty and support.[1]

Matilda was then proclaimed as " Lady of England and Normandy " until she could be crowned queen but she was sullen, bad tempered, and clumsy and her husband, Geoffrey Plantegenet, was more than occupied by the Conquest of Normandy. The eastern section of southern England remained faithful to Stephen while in the West Matilda found support[2]

[1] Text in **CXXXIII**, 139. On the meaning of *domina* see **DLXXXVI**, 70 ff. Was *Dominus* the provisional title which the heir to the throne assumed before coronation ? Rossler, **DLXXVI**, 424 ff., has denied this.

[2] See the boundaries (which, however, were constantly changing) indicated in **CCXXXIV**, 631.

FORMATION OF THE ANGEVIN EMPIRE 105

but in North and South alike anarchy was supreme. A very interesting history has been written of the concessions which Geoffrey de Mandeville, one of the barons, was able to extort first from Stephen, then from Matilda, thus succeeding in creating a powerful independent lordship.[1]

Matilda retired in despair to live with her husband who had achieved his object and, on his death (1151), left his son, Henry, a principality consisting of Normandy,[2] Maine, Anjou, and Touraine which, it seemed possible, might be destined to continue independent of England. But Henry Plantegenet was a vigorous fighter and he undertook to reconquer the kingdom of his grandfather (Henry I). He disembarked, in January 1153, and Stephen who was old and worn out was ready to make peace by November.[3] Henry was recognized as heir to the throne and asked to share in the work of government. On the death of Stephen, in December, 1154, he became King of England. He was determined to restore the monarchy of William the Conqueror and Henry I which for sixty years had been maintained on " pacts " and legalized and organized anarchy, but Church and baronage had not forgotten the times of King Stephen and they looked for their return.

Two years previously Henry Plantegenet had married Eleanor, Duchess of Aquitaine. Since her time and particularly in the thirteenth century, Eleanor has had a terrible reputation[4] and historians and publicists have exaggerated her misconduct to an absurd degree, but there is good reason to believe that Louis VII had divorced her because of infidelity rather than because he was assailed with doubts of the validity of their marriage on ground of consanguinity.[5] The estimations made by William of Tyre and the author of the *Historia Pontificalis* of her conduct in the East during the Crusade agree with Suger's letter to the king asking him not to prolong his absence; concerning the queen, Suger urges the king to keep his bitterness in check until his return and

---

[1] **DLXXXVI**, 43 ff., 98 ff.
[2] Henry had been its duke since 1149; **DXXXIV**, 569 ff.
[3] **CVI**, n. 56, p. 61.
[4] **DCXLVI**, 408 ff.; **CCCLVIII**, 51 ff., 58 ff., 79 ff.; **CLXVIII**, 702 ff.
[5] In fact they were not related within the prohibited degrees; their common ancestor was Thibaud Towhead, Duke of Aquitaine, father-in-law of Hugh Capet, **DCXLVI**, 417, and n. 2.

then to make his decision.¹ In the autumn of 1149, husband and wife returned through Rome in a state of open antagonism and the Pope, Eugenius III, undertook to reconcile them. The extremely well informed author of the *Historia Pontificalis* tells us " The Pope forbade anyone henceforward to suggest that they were related ; he confirmed their marriage, under pain of anathema, in speech and writing and forbade anyone to listen to those who attacked it or to dissolve it on any grounds whatever. This command seemed to please the king greatly as he was passionately, almost childishly, attached to the queen. The Pope decorated a bed at his own expense with the most costly materials for their joint occupation. He used every day of this short respite in personal conversations trying to renew their affection. He honoured them with gifts and when they took leave of him he could not restrain his tears though he was a stern man ".² This is a curious piece of evidence of the constant interference of Catholic priests in the married life and psychology of Louis VII whom jealousy and religious scruples brought into an antagonism with his wife which was quickly dispelled by the suggestion of a simple passion and an authority he respected.

Eleanor returned from Rome pregnant but again she failed to give Louis VII the male heir he wanted. The wife who was able to present Henry II with five sons now gave birth to a second daughter and it was undoubtedly one of the considerations which enemies urged to stimulate the ill humour of Louis VII. After the death of the statesmanlike Suger on 13th January, 1151,³ they resumed the offensive. Eleanor, for her part, had no desire to remain married to a husband whom she accused of having the morals of a monk. During the year, Henry Plantegenet visited the court ; the athletic bearing of this young man who was ten years younger than herself made a deep impression on Eleanor.⁴ " Louis in a state of violent jealousy departed with her for Aquitaine, commanded the destruction of the fortifications he had put in hand, and withdrew his garrisons." ⁵ He had made up his

---

¹ **CXXXIV**, 260.
² **LX**, 537. The author of this fragment is the famous John of Salisbury, who lived on familiar terms with Eugene III.
³ **CCXIV**, 170 ff.
⁴ **LV**, i, 93 ; **LXXIX**, 237.   ⁵ **XXIII**, 135.

FORMATION OF THE ANGEVIN EMPIRE 107

mind to divorce her and at once began the evacuation of Aquitaine. Then, on the 21st March, 1152, a council met at Beaugency and announced the dissolution of the marriage on grounds of kinship. The Pope, possibly better informed of Eleanor's intentions than Louis, kept silent.

The hand of Eleanor was in such demand that she had to return to Aquitaine in secret at night to avoid the suitors who sought to win her. Evidently she already had some agreement with Henry Plantagenet for scarcely two months after, on the 18th of May, 1152, or thereabouts, they were married.[1] In vain Louis VII, who realized too late the danger, opposed the marriage[2] which made Henry even before he became King of England a more powerful vassal than his suzerain.

II

Henry II and Richard Cœur de Lion

When Henry II, Plantagenet, was crowned in London on the 19th December, 1154, he was not yet 22 years old. He granted his subjects the following charter:—

> Henry, by the Grace of God, King of England, Duke of Normandy and Aquitaine, Count of Anjou, to all his counts, barons and loyal subjects, French and English, greeting. Know that for the honour of God and Holy Church and the general benefit of the whole kingdom, I have granted and given and by this present charter confirmed to God and the Holy Church and to all my counts, barons and subjects, all the concessions and grants, liberties and free customs which King Henry my grandfather gave and granted them. I likewise remit and abolish for me and my heirs all the evil customs which he abolished and remitted. For this reason, I desire and unhesitatingly prescribe that Holy Church and all my counts, barons, and subjects shall have and hold freely, fully and in peace, all the customs and grants, liberties and free customs of me and my heirs, for them and their heirs as freely, fully and peaceably in every respect as the King Henry my grandfather granted, conceded and confirmed to them by his charter. Witness Richard de Lucé at Westminster.[3]

This Charter of Liberties, evidently drawn up by the Norman Richard de Lucé, one of the most remarkable of the ministers of Henry II, shows clearly, under its exterior

[1] DLXV, ii, 108 ff.
[2] CCCLVIII, 82.
[3] Latin text; XVII, 13–14.

of redundancy and verbiage what was the programme of the new monarchy. There is no question of election by clergy and people, of confirmation by the Holy See, or of renunciation of the work of Henry I. He abolishes or grants just those things which Henry I had abolished or granted. A veil of silence is cast over twenty years of anarchy and the reign of Henry I is continued. But now, for the first time, the king addresses his " French " and " English " subjects alike. Henry II is head of an Empire and from the moment of his accession he announces his intention of governing it all according to the same principles.

The pacification and reorganization of the kingdom of England alone was a mighty task. It would involve Henry II in the consolidation of his frontiers, reducing the King of Scotland and the Welsh chiefs to vassaldom and undertaking the conquest of Ireland. But Henry was primarily a French prince and he passed the greater part of his reign in his Continental possessions.[1] The possession of Aquitaine put the King of England in touch with the South for the first time. Henry II married two daughters to the kings of Castile and Sicily, made an alliance with the King of Aragon, tried to become master of the County of Toulouse, and to gain possession of Toulouse for one of his sons and possibly even thought of becoming emperor.

His son Richard was won over by the attractions of the Mediterranean and the East and for a considerable time acted as if he was master of Sicily, conquered Cyprus, and affected to regulate the succession in the kingdom of Jerusalem. After his unsuccessful Crusade, he dreamed of making a new start, delivering the Holy Land, and assuming the Imperial Crown in Constantinople.

The men who surveyed such wide prospects were made for vast enterprises. Henry II and his son Richard the Lionheart, in spite of their very different characters, were both ambitious and restless men.

One of the best of contemporary writers, Pierre de Blois,[2]

---

[1] The itinerary of Henry II has been established in detail in **CCLXXXIII**; a summary description in *C.M.H.*, vol. v, 554.

[2] See **CDXXXIX**, 371 ff. We are not ignorant of the doubts which have been cast on the letters of Pierre of Blois and a critical edition would be very valuable. See **CCXXV**, 43-60. Those which are transcribed are generally accepted as authentic and agree with what we know of Henry II.

has painted us an illuminating picture of Henry II whom he had studied at first hand.

He is, he tell us,[1] a reddish headed man of medium height; he has a square, leonine face and goggle eyes which are soft and gentle when he is good humoured but flash lightning when he is annoyed. His horseman's legs, broad chest, and athletic arms reveal him as a man who is strong, active, and daring. He takes no care of his hands and only wears gloves when hawking. His clothes and head-dress are becoming but never extravagant. He fights the obesity which threatens by sobriety and exercise and, thanks to walking and horsemanship, he preserves his youthful vigour and tires out his strongest companions. From morning to night he is engaged unceasingly on affairs of state. He never sits down except when he mounts his horse or takes a meal and he frequently rides in one day a journey four or five times the length of a normal day's ride. It is very difficult to find out where he is or what he will do during the day for he frequently changes his plans. The fidelity of his followers is subjected to severe tests for they are frequently forced to wander through unknown forests for three or four miles after nightfall before they find lodging in sordid hovels. Nevertheless, in this way, while other kings are resting in their palaces, he is able to take his enemies by surprise and off their guard and he inspects everything, taking particular care to judge those whom he has made judges of others. When he is not occupied with a bow or a sword he is at a council or reading. There is nobody more quick witted or eloquent and, when he can find freedom from his anxieties, he loves an argument with scholars. He is a great builder and whether he is building fortifications or enclosing hunting forests or fishponds, no one can equal his keenness and magnificence. His temperament is calm in danger and subdued in prosperity. He has a horror of bloodshed and regards peace as the greatest good a king can bestow on his people. He undertakes enormous tasks to maintain it and spends the large income he has built up for he would rather gain his end by financial than military pressure. This is his object in threatening the proud, humiliating the mighty, building castles, and making treaties and alliances. He is friendly and generous to his courtiers; the Church he enriches with gifts and keeps clear of simony. Once he has given his affection, it is only very great forces that will destroy it but once he takes a dislike to anyone he is equally loath to admit him to his confidence. To churchmen [2] who urge him to show mercy to his enemies he replies that his heart is neither sufficiently patient nor humble but in spite of the armed revolts which deserved disinheritance he has had neither the will nor the power to deprive his sons of their rights; his heart cannot take such a step.

The other writers of the period (particularly the novelette writer Walter Map who was one of the chaplains of Henry II)

[1] Letter lxvi in **XC**, i, 193 ff. I have abridged and rewritten the text, which is diffuse, and I have added certain traits borrowed from letter xiv, p. 50 ff., letter xli, p. 125, and the curious Dialogue with the Abbot of Bonneval (ibid., vol. iii, 289 ff.).

[2] I have quoted here the answers attributed to Henry by Pierre de Blois in the dialogue cited above.

and the excellent chroniclers of the end of the twelfth century in general confirm this description of his appearance and character which Pierre de Blois has given us though there were undoubtedly other traits which Pierre failed to notice.

Henry was extremely libidinous and did not deny himself his niece, a Breton girl who had been entrusted to him as a hostage,[1] or even his son Richard's fiancée, Adelaide, the daughter of Philip Augustus, for whose education he had assumed responsibility. Everyone who came near him remarked on his agitation, his inability to keep still, even in church, and his outbursts of temper. He had obviously inherited a nervous weakness which was a legacy from the eleventh century counts of Anjou, his ancestors, and which showed its full effects in the physical and moral constitution of John Lackland, his youngest son. But Walter Map, even while commenting on the sufferings inflicted on the Court by the impatience of this eternal wanderer, this restless monarch who did not hesitate to disturb half Christendom, admires his simplicity, affability, and intellectual gifts and makes a justifiable comment on the juridical and political bias of his mentality.[2] Henry II was one of the great kings of England and one of the founders of the monarchical system in Western Europe.

Richard the Lionheart is a less complex figure although he was quite capable, in general, of preserving his father's work.[3] Physically he resembled his father though somewhat slimmer; only at the end of his life, when worn out by excesses of every kind and an intermittent fever which he almost certainly contracted in the swamps of Poitou, he was less robust and began to put on weight but all his life he remained, like his father, active and restless. Henry II and Eleanor had bequeathed to him their passion and violence and though he could be generous and beneficial he was equally capable of vindictive cruelty. He developed an intense hatred for his father and did his best to kill him. He was subject to maniacal rage and the author of the *History of William the Marshal* portrays him heaping coarse insults on the papal legate and threatening him with physical violence.[4] This passion found full play in hunting and war which were his

---

[1] John of Salisbury, letter ccxlvi in **LXV**, ii, 142.
[2] **LXXIX**, 237 ff.   [3] **CCXII**, 131 ff.   [4] Line 11596 ff.

FORMATION OF THE ANGEVIN EMPIRE

favourite occupations. He despised peace for which his father made so many sacrifices and, on the battlefield, he rallied his men by the example of a bravery which has become proverbial; his nickname " Lionheart " appears in a contemporary account of his adventures in the Holy Land. Above all, this epic hero inherited southern tastes from his mother. He loved to show off in sumptuous apparel and to make a noise. He composed fluent poetry in French or Provençal. He was not deficient in a sense of order and administration, but he gave little attention to administration and juridical reforms. He was a mythical paladin and, in fact, his real life was quickly buried in a mass of legend.[1]

III

THE MINISTERS

During the reign of Richard Cœur de Lion, it was the secretaries and officials who preserved monarchical prerogative while the king spent his time seeking adventure. It was they who, under the directions of Henry II, had restored some measure of order and established his power throughout his immense empire. It has been suggested that Henry wished to be served only by English advisers and officials.[2] Such a mistake would invalidate our whole estimate of the character of these Angevin kings which was essentially cosmopolitan. Henry II read Latin and understood Provençal and Italian; he spoke French but knew no English.[3] He passed very little of his time in England and when he realized that he was surrounded by enemies he did not think of seeking asylum there but retired to his native province, Anjou, to die. His son Richard was at heart an Aquitanian and passed almost all his time on the Continent even when he was king. Even in the thirteenth century, John Lackland and Henry III surrounded themselves with Poitevins and even Flemings. Certainly among the host of officials, which had become so great that Peter de Blois compared it to a swarm of locusts,[4] there must have been many local officers who lived and died in their native country but Henry II meant to use each one

[1] DLIII, 130–155; DV, 362–8, 386–7.
[2] CDLXXXVIII, i, 417.   [3] LXXIX, 237.   [4] Ep. xcv in XC, i, 298.

as he thought best and send the most capable where he needed them. The inconsistent diplomatic of his Chancery marks simultaneously the diversity and the unity of his Empire. On occasions, he addressed letters to his loyal subjects or officers of a particular country but very frequently he addressed them " to his faithful subjects of France and England " or " to all his officers throughout England, Normandy, Anjou, Touraine, and Aquitaine " which means not only that all owe him obedience but that some of them were being continuously transferred to all parts of the Empire in his service. His ministers crossed and recrossed the sea just as the bullion of his treasury did. French and English are mingled in the lists of barons or officials who witnessed his acts or judged in the assizes which he established to reconcile Norman and English interests.[1] The Chancellors of Henry II were Thomas Becket, a Norman; Raoul de Wanneville, who had previously been sacristan of the church of Rouen and left the Chancery for the episcopal throne of Lisieux; finally Geoffrey, a natural son of the king: Henry II gave him with this office dignities and castles on both sides of the Channel. The Chancellor of Richard Cœur de Lion was a Norman clerk, William Longchamp; another Norman, Richard de Lucé, gained fame as Chief Justice and administrator and on several occasions he governed England during the absence of Henry II. On the other hand, the Exchequer and Treasury of Normandy were put in order by Richard d'Ilchester, an Englishman, who seems to have been the best financier of the era, with Richard Fitz Neal the author of the *Dialogue of the Exchequer*. However, it is frequently very difficult to decide whether a certain man is Norman rather than English. Walter, who is generally known as Walter of Coutances and who had studied at the University of Paris before becoming one of the principal officials of the English Chancery, was born in Cornwall. He was successively Bishop of Lincoln and Archbishop of Rouen. Ranulf Glanville, who was a sort of viceroy at the end of the reign of Henry II, was undoubtedly of Norman stock transplanted to England.[2]

---

[1] See the Recueil des Actes (**CVI**), and the *Introduction* of Delisle, 208 ff.; **CCCL**, 181.

[2] On all these people see the Introduction and notes to **CVI**, the articles of the *N.B.*, and **CCLXXXIII**.

FORMATION OF THE ANGEVIN EMPIRE 113

Henry II and Richard Cœur de Lion had good lay servants among their English sheriffs, the viscounts and seneschals in France, and their chief military officers, like the loyal and devoted William the Marshal, but the people who reformed the Chancery, Exchequer and Courts of Justice or maintained their good traditions were clerks; the king paid them with bishoprics and they did not look after their posts any the worse. In the reign of Richard, the "royal court" was often composed of a dozen people among whom were nine clerks or prelates in process of becoming bishops. This combination of spiritual and secular functions aroused many keen critics but they made the relations between Church and State much easier, and, in any case, it gave the monarchy an opportunity for progress and a new life. The lay world at this date was sunk in routine; it was in the Church that political intelligence arose and the spirit of administrative and judicial organization. It was through the Canon Law, thanks to its methods and system of expression, that Roman Law, developed at Bologna, exercised its influence in the kingdom of Henry II. It was the churchmen, Norman or English, who created judicial interpretations, introduced the habit of reasoned argument and the idea of system in the law; on this evidence, they can claim responsibility for the Common Law of England. The Assizes and Constitutions of Henry II, which remind us so much of the capitularies of the Carolingians, were possibly only like them as a result of family characteristics inherited through the ecclesiastical canons.[1]

IV

Different Conceptions of the Monarchy. The Ideas of Lawyers, Church, and Nobility

If we are to show the innovations of Henry's reign, we must record that around the king there gathered a group of canonists who stayed at Court for long periods and met there men of letters and polemists like Peter de Blois or Walter Map and chroniclers like Gervais of Canterbury or

---

[1] DXXXII, i, p. xxxii ff.; DCXXVII, i, 757.

Roger de Hoveden. These literary figures were brought into continual contact with the specialists of the Chancery, the Exchequer, and the Royal Courts, hammered out principles in argument with them, wrote treatises on law or administration, political theses and chronicles, and became as competent to discharge public offices as to hold ecclesiastical dignities. From the point of view of intellectual temper and profitable innovation, as in many other respects, the Court of Henry II was almost a century in advance of the Capetian court. Nevertheless, the enthusiasm of these men for the monarchy varied and they maintained the right of free criticism and if we were forced, on the basis of their writings and actions, to define the English monarchy of the period in two words—to say whether it was a feudal monarchy or not—we should be in danger of a clash between contradictory texts. We must always remember that not all of them had the same idea of the nature of the royal power.

We will try to illustrate how their ideas agreed and in what respects they differed. What was the theory of the Court lawyers? What were the theories of the Church? What did the barons, whom the king summoned to court, think on those occasions when they thought at all?

The permanent advisers who were perpetually working to extend the royal prerogative envisaged no limits to it whatever. At a later date Glanville quoted the Institutes "Quod principi placuit legis habet vigorem". Already Henry's Treasurer in his *Dialogue of the Exchequer*, a technical work on the public finances, was formulating a similar doctrine but for purely personal reasons. Kings, he says, must be able to spend lavishly on the preservation of their kingdom and their ministers must keep a very careful check on the finances; it is by no means unconstitutional to find churchmen among these ministers even acting as Treasurer, for the service of a prince was service to a power established by God. All power comes from God; that is the doctrine of the Church but Fitz Neal emphasizes this in an explicit confession of faith:—

> It is possible that kings will not examine law but will be guided merely by local custom on the impulses of their own hearts or will even act on a purely arbitrary decision. Whatever they do is no matter for discussion or condemnation by their inferiors for their

hearts and their impulses are in the hand of God and the fate of those who have been made responsible for subjects depends on divine and not on human judgment.[1]

Thus to destroy the arguments used against clerical functionaries, Fitz Neal reached a theory of royal absolutism and completely ignored the limits which the Church had set to the divine right of kings. He was not alone in perverting ecclesiastical doctrines in this way. John of Salisbury provides us with evidence that the worst flatterers of Henry II were among the bishops. It was one of the Court priests who, in the reign of Henry I, had advised the King of England to exercise the prestige of the Capetians.[2] By the time of Henry II the tradition was so firmly established that Peter de Blois, who had little inclination to flatter, accepted it and saw in it a reason to justify the clerical functionaries. " I must admit that it is holy work to help the Lord King for he is a saint and the Christ of the Lord and the royal unction which he has received has not been in vain and, if anyone is unaware or doubtful of its power, it is made fully evident in the disappearance of the inguinal plague and the cure of scrofula." [3]

The Royal Chancery gave official expression to these pretensions. The formula " King by the Grace of God ", fortuitous during the century which followed the Conquest, became regular in the diplomatic of Henry II and his successors from the beginning of the year 1173 and it has been pointed out that the assumption of divine right coincides with the period when Henry was doing penance in the cathedral of Avranches (27th September, 1172) for the murder of Thomas Becket. From that time, the Chancery rigorously formulated this pretension of the crown in the subscription to its edicts.[4]

Nevertheless, the Church, and, on its example, lay subjects maintained the doctrine of the elective monarchy. That was the real doctrine of the Church which does not exclude the idea that the royal power, like all power in general, comes from God. We have seen that Stephen humbly admitted that he owed the crown to his election by clergy and people, to consecration by the Archbishop of Canterbury, and even to

---

[1] **XXXIII**, 55. [2] **CLXXIX**, 41 ff., 83–4.
[3] Ep. cl in **XC**, ii, 82–3. [4] **CVI**, intro. by Delisle, 12 ff.

the confirmation of the Holy See. In 1141, his brother, the Bishop of Winchester and legate, abandoned his cause because he had been defeated and captured. The battle of Lincoln had been a sort of judicial duel and God had given the verdict in favour of Matilda. Yet Matilda, Lady of England, was not consecrated as queen and this is significant of the confusion and incoherence of ideas and theories which beset England.

At the accession of Henry II the opposite procedure triumphed. There was no consultation by clergy and barons, and Henry II who had already begun to re-establish order in England seized power with a firm hand. By virtue of the right of succession and the pact he had made with Stephen " he took his hereditary kingdom with the acclamation of all ",[1] and " was elected by all "[2] and, as we have seen, did not trouble to mention the election by acclamation in his charter ; above all there was no delay before his consecration. It appeared as if the Church was going to renounce the right, which it had claimed, to consult and weigh the merits of the candidate for the throne either alone or with the barons.

Henry II would never have recognized the right either in regard to himself or his heirs. He adopted the means, used by the Capetians, to avoid succession crises and to establish the principle of primogeniture—the system of association in the crown. Henry II adopted it under circumstances which clearly revealed the conflict of ideas between monarchy and Church on the subject. In 1155, at a big gathering of barons, he secured the recognition of his eldest son as his successor and in 1170, when the king was at open war with the Archbishop of Canterbury and Thomas Becket was an exile in France, he held a formal Court in London and secured the coronation of Henry the Younger who was not yet sixteen years old and had not been dubbed a knight. The coronation was entrusted to the Archbishop of York and took place in the presence of eleven English or Norman bishops who did not dare to disobey the king. The Pope put up a vain opposition to a coronation for which the Archbishop of Canterbury was not responsible, in violation of his prerogatives. No alterations were made in the form of the oath although the Holy See had

[1] LV, 151.   [2] CXVI, i, 289–290.

FORMATION OF THE ANGEVIN EMPIRE 117

demanded that the prince should swear henceforward to preserve the rights and liberties of the Church and of the Church of Canterbury in particular.[1] In short the coronation of Henry the Younger appeared to be a victory for the monarchy over the Church but it was a short-lived victory.

Events proved that Henry II had made a mistake and that association in the throne could put a dangerous weapon in the hands of a rebellious son. Henry the Younger considered himself, by virtue of his anointment, a king equal to his father and sought an ally in the Church and Papacy against the man who had had him crowned despite the opposition of the Holy See.[2] After the premature death of Henry the Younger, the king abandoned the practice of association and to the end of his life refused to allow Richard Cœur de Lion to demand from the barons a recognition of his hereditary rights.[3]

The Church and baronage accepted Richard as king without opposition. He was very much feared and very popular at the same time but his consecration was celebrated with an extraordinary pomp and the Church multiplied the ceremonial and formalities so much that the ritual established at that date was henceforward a traditional rule.[4] The Church, in form at least, was revenged. She achieved a very much more serious revenge when, in 1199, a wound received in battle carried Richard off without warning.[5] Who would be king ? It seemed that Richard's associates had sworn on his death bed to recognize his brother John, the youngest of Henry's sons [6] but the treasonable and fickle character of this young man had rendered him suspect. A possible rival was his nephew Arthur, the son of Geoffrey of Brittany, the fourth son of Henry II, but Arthur had been brought up at the Court of Philip Augustus. The Archbishop of Canterbury, Hubert Walter, was in Normandy at the time and the author of the *History of William the Marshal* records the discussion

---

[1] **DLIV**, 6, 114–120 ; **CCCLX**, 5 ff.
[2] See the letter of Henry the Younger to the papal legates ; **CVI**, intro., 250–1.
[3] **DCXXVII**, i, 594.
[4] **DLXXVIII**, chap. ix.
[5] On the accession of John, Miss K. Norgate (**CDLXXXIX**, 56 ff.) has not said the last word. Cf. **DCXXVII**, i, 617 ff. ; **DXLII**, 193–5.
[6] **CXVIII**, vol. iv, 83.

between the Archbishop and the Marshal.¹ " We must arrange the election quickly," said the latter, " who are we going to make king, sir ? " The archbishop replied " By right we must crown Arthur." William opposed this idea ; Arthur was in the hands of the King of France and did not love the English. Hubert Walter accepted his opinion, crossed the Channel, and, not without difficulty, secured the support of the English barons while those on the banks of the Loire and in Brittany recognized Arthur. The Archbishop of Canterbury took advantage of these favourable circumstances to make a formal assertion of the doctrine of an elective monarchy. On the arrival of John in London, " Archbishops, bishops, counts, barons, and all who were to be present at the coronation came together and the Archbishop stood up in the midst of the meeting and expressed his opinions in these terms :—

> Listen everybody. Your political ability tells you that no one can succeed a man as king before he has at least been unanimously chosen by the community of the kingdom, after the invocation of the grace of the Holy Spirit, for his excellent character which clearly marks him out as a worthy successor of Saul, the first consecrated king, whom the Lord proposed to his people although he was not a king's son or even of royal stock ; after him David, son of Jesse, was king. The former was chosen on account of his strength and ability as king, the latter on account of his holiness and humility. . . . If some one of the stock of the dead king is more outstanding than the others, it is possible to agree on his election more easily and more promptly. All this can be said of the illustrious Count John who is present here, the brother of our most illustrious king, Richard, now dead without any heir to succeed him. John has foresight, ability, and manifest nobility and, after invoking the Grace of the Holy Spirit, we are unanimous in electing him as much for his merits as for his royal blood.

" Those present had confidence in the wisdom of the archbishop and understood that he had reasons for his action and, choosing John as king, cried out ' Long live King John ! ' " ²

This story which is found only in Matthew Paris has been considered suspect. It is certainly marked by the lack of precision and confused impression of this loquacious

---

¹ Line 11844 ff. The author has a natural tendency to exaggerate the importance of William, but he expresses ideas which were evidently those of his times, and that is their interest for us. The order of succession to the throne was not fixed, and priests and barons interfered on every possible occasion.
² **CXXXIII**, 265–6.

FORMATION OF THE ANGEVIN EMPIRE 119

chronicler; it is impossible to see whether " the unanimous election " took place before or after the archbishop's speech; but there is reason to believe that the general substance of Hubert Walter's remarks is authentic. They are natural in his mouth and have a double advantage for the peace of the kingdom. They finally dispose of the claims of Arthur's supporters by basing John's rights on election and they reinforce the new king's coronation oath by a moral obligation.[1]

Thus, at the end of the period we are studying, the Church had succeeded in gaining public acceptance for its theory of the monarchy which neither Henry II nor his advisers would have admitted. The doctrine had theological and moral foundations which it is easy to trace, for in the time of Henry II, a theological moralist, John of Salisbury, had given it full exposition.

In the Western Church of the twelfth century, a Church so rich in educated and intelligent clerks and brave and sincere men, John of Salisbury is particularly arresting.[2] Born in England, but really a cosmopolitan like King Henry II himself, John of Salisbury studied in the famous schools of Paris and Chartres and gained an intimate knowledge of Italy, the Roman Curia, and the public affairs of Western Europe. About 1148 he became secretary to the Archbishop of Canterbury, Theobald, and his independent spirit displeased Henry so much that he was deprived of his prebends. So when he wrote the *Policraticus* in 1159, a work which he dedicated to his friend Thomas Becket, he was personally a victim of " tyranny ". When Becket became archbishop in 1161 he gave him a position close to his own person. Through good fortune and bad alike, John remained, on principle, faithful to his friend though openly condemning his pride and violent temper. He ended his life as Bishop of Chartres.

His *Policraticus, sive de nugis curialium et vestigiis philosophorum*[3] is a doctrinal work which contains a very general description of the life of the Court and its dangers and above all political theories and moral considerations on how to assure happiness and salvation. It is the first book of the Middle Ages

[1] DXV, 42–3.   [2] DXXXV, 176 ff.; CCLVI, 308 ff.; CCCXXXI.
[3] LXVI; important quotations in CCIX, vol. iii, 137–145.

in which a political philosophy is systematically expounded in an orderly and coherent fashion. The author, among his ethical arguments and quotations from Scripture and the classical authors, makes rare allusions to contemporary monarchical and social institutions. But the *Policraticus* is an extremely precious exposition of the doctrine of the Church in its purest form on human governments and the relations of the two powers—even more precious because John of Salisbury has a judicial air and no fanaticism; he is an exceptionally well balanced moralist rather than a polemist.

In formulating his ideas, he has recourse to an analogy, which was already hackneyed in his day, between the body politic and a living body whose vigour depends on the good condition of all the organs and their harmony. The feet are the workers in the fields and the city; the hands are the army; the stomach, always inclined to fill to the point of indigestion and to cause trouble throughout the rest of the body, is the administration of the finances; the head is the prince and the heart is the "Senate", that is to say the officials and advisers who surround him. But the soul is religion which must inspire the movements of the body politic; it is the clergy whose impulsions must be obeyed.

The theory of monarchy which forms the centre of John of Salisbury's system is extremely interesting. A monarch does not seem to him to be indispensable.[1] He would be useless if man could live without committing serious offences, but a strong king is essential to maintain respect for the divine law. This function gives him a sacred character: he is the image of God on earth and the crime of *lèse-majesté* deserves death. But John of Salisbury takes good care to make the civil power equal to the ecclesiastical. Between these two there is no common standard and the first is dominated by the second. If the prince possesses the temporal sword it is because he received it from the hand of the Church who gave it to him because it cannot wield a sword of blood. "The prince, therefore, is a minister of the priesthood. He exercises that part of a saint's duties which is not fitting for the hands of the saints." That is the origin of a theory of the succession to the throne which we know very well. The

---

[1] This is, in general, the doctrine of the Church at this period; cf. **DXXXV**, 198 ff.

FORMATION OF THE ANGEVIN EMPIRE 121

principle of hereditary rule should be respected when it is customary in the country concerned. Hereditary right does not provide an absolute title but if the prince whom it designates follows the ways of the Lord or does not stray from them in any important respect, he should be elected. Who will elect him ? John of Salisbury is embarrassed by this question and makes only vague and contradictory suggestions which, nevertheless, accord with the shadowy ideas of his contemporaries on this subject. He speaks in a convincing manner of the " reasonable prayers of faithful subjects " and he does not consider that clerical mediation will be necessary in every case though he obviously inclines to the belief that the Church's nominee will be the best.

Up to this point the ideas of John of Salisbury are in complete agreement with those current in France as expressed by Abbon in the tenth century, Yves de Chartres and Suger in the eleventh and twelfth, and, above all, the formulas of Capetian diplomata. The Capetian monarchy is a power established by God to preserve spiritual and temporal property and Louis the Fat assumed the " sword of the Church " when he undertook the punishment of the wicked. Yves de Chartres expressed it " A king is consecrated with a good title if the kingdom belongs to him by hereditary right and he has been elected with the common consent of bishops and barons ".[1]

But in England this theory was to form part of a hypothesis of intolerant tyranny which never arose in France. Memories of the reign of William Rufus or even some of the acts of Henry II, which had no parallel in France, inevitably forced on the English cleric the consideration of the question of an abuse of power. The brutality of the emperors towards the Church and the Holy See probably affected John of Salisbury even more. Whatever its origin, a theory of tyrannicide found a place in his fully developed political doctrines. As long as a king did no more than oppress his subjects, John counselled patience and resignation but if he began to sin against God or to attempt the destruction of religion he must be deposed or even killed, for God must be put before man whoever the man. There is no doubt that the author had not considered the possible applications of this doctrine. There is no suggestion in his correspondence that

[1] LXII, 144.

Henry II or even the tyrant Barbarossa, whom he fiercely hated, deserved to be killed. In writing the *Policraticus* he had been carried away by his logical spirit, dominated by his memory of the Bible, and the Classics.[1] Nevertheless, the ecclesiastical doctrine of deposition and regicide, however reluctant its expression, was not to be forgotten and, at a later date, the English assumed the responsibility for its application.

We must understand quite clearly that John of Salisbury and his twelfth century contemporaries had no idea of a " community of the kingdom " which could get rid of a bad king through its representatives. He specified quite clearly that there is no representative of the community but the king himself and he is all powerful. Deposition can only be an act of the Church in defence of religion and tyrannicide the deed of an individual as Judith beheaded Holophernes.

John of Salisbury has no general idea of a contract between king and nation or of a body politic existing apart from the king; he does not conceive of public institutions which can limit the royal power and prevent its abuse. " Everything must be decided," he says, " by the discretions of the prince alone." This is equally the doctrine of the *Dialogue of the Exchequer*. In his theory of royal prerogative he makes no clear distinction between the lawyers and the bishops of the Court, whose servility, however, he reproaches, except in one respect : the king has no right to dominate the clergy, neither to intervene in canonical elections nor to take into his own hands the property or the jurisdiction of the Church. In a word, John of Salisbury understands liberty only as the liberties of the Church. In that alone is he interested. In his eyes, a king who respects the independence and privileges of the clergy can be allowed a free hand in everything else and his subjects must submit. It is an extremely narrow point of view but it must be understood before it is possible to appreciate the political ideas of the time and the basis of the great movements of the thirteenth century.

The ecclesiastical conception of the monarchy might have developed considerable practical importance from the time of Henry II onwards if it had been adopted by the

[1] Cf. **CCXXX**, chap. vii. *Tyrannicide avant Jean Petit.*

baronage. I am not speaking of the bourgeoisie which in the twelfth century was even less important in England than in France but a nobility imbued with the " clerical " spirit and dominated, intellectually and morally, by the clergy could have provided an alliance of considerable danger to the monarchy. But only on rare occasions did nobility and clergy reach mutual agreement. They were often in conflict and always distrusted each other and had scarcely an idea in common. A noble might suffer an access of piety and make some sacrifice of pride or wealth to avoid Purgatory but he despised clerks as much as merchants and had no interest in theories of divine right. He considered the king nothing but a suzerain who should be a valiant fighter providing lavish spoils of war. The noble's ambition was to find adventure and the good prince was the one who gave him opportunity for it. Stephen, however, although he allowed the expansion of feudal independence, was despised as a " king who can neither take nor give, neither win nor lose, who is good for nothing ".[1] Henry II, who forbade tournaments and preferred diplomacy to war, gained little popularity but the " young king " Henry, son of Henry II, and his brother Richard were brilliant knights errant beloved of the knights. There was a moral code which bound the nobility in their relations with the monarchy but it was the feudal code, respect for a sworn oath. The most significant document from this point of view is the *History of William the Marshal*. It was undoubtedly written by a herald and is saturated in the feudal spirit. William the Marshal had a reputation as the most loyal of the servants of Henry II, Richard, and John and his conduct was based on the principle of observance of homage. This explains why he first served the young King Henry against his father Henry II, then Henry II against Richard Cœur de Lion, then Richard against John Lackland, and finally John against the rebellious barons, not because kings represented God on earth but because he had sworn homage to them. He received from John Lackland permission to do homage to Philip Augustus to preserve his Norman possessions and subsequently, in spite of John's threats, he refused to go into battle against Philip Augustus. Such was the feudal spirit and the idea of his duties which a loyal noble could obtain.

[1] LVIII, iii, 12.

Many others less scrupulous were guided only by their interests and their passions. It is certainly true that when they banded together against Henry II they were stimulated by the threat to their independence but it was only at a much later date and in a very halting and hesitating fashion that the English nobility developed a real political spirit.

Meanwhile the monarchy was able to reap its harvest.

CHAPTER II

ADMINISTRATION AND LEGISLATION IN ENGLAND, 1154–1204

I

THE PACIFICATION OF THE KINGDOM

WHEN Stephen recognized Henry Plantegenet as his heir and signed the Treaty of Wallingford,[1] England was in a sad state of disorder and exhaustion. Obedience was rendered only to the lord of the nearest castle. The sheriffs whom Stephen had retained only collected scanty revenues and did not always pay those into the Exchequer.[2] Stephen agreed with his heir to resume the demesnes and revenues of the crown which he had alienated, to destroy the " adulterine castles " which had been built without licence, to send the Flemish mercenaries home, to appoint honest sheriffs capable of restoring order in each county, and to strike good coinage. He was also bound to restore to his subjects the possessions they had enjoyed in the time of Henry I and to give security to the clergy and the working class. He had scarcely the means and no time to fulfil this programme and it was Henry II who, after his accession, carried it out with remarkable energy and promptness. The resumption of the royal castles was achieved only at the cost of severe fighting but, within a year, England was nearly pacified.[3] Obviously a civil war that had dragged on so long and been marked by such atrocities left its scars; on the one side, was the economic ruin which prompted Henry II to avoid large-scale wars; on the other, the strengthening of the dangerous elements in society and an aggravation of immoral and violent habits which were certainly the primary cause (although no one seems to have realized it) of the reforms in the system of police and justice.

[1] See the text in **DCXXVII**, i, 406 ff. notes.
[2] **CCXXXIV**, 630 ff.; cf. **DLXXXVI**, 99–100; **DCXLV**, 127–8; **CDLXXXIV**, 105–7.
[3] **DXCII**, chap. ii; **CDLXXXVIII**, i, 427 ff.

II
Local and Central Administration

The kingdom needed peace; the monarchy needed to build up its resources, to revive its power in the corners of the realm and to use for that purpose the old local institutions, the hundred court and the shire court.

For these essential tasks, there was nobody more useful to the Plantegenets than the sheriff. In the time of Henry II, the sheriff had been transformed by the energy and will power of the king into an official almost of the modern type. There is, in fact, nothing more interesting than the study of the evolution of this office from the Anglo-Saxon period, made possible by modern research. Its history helps us to appreciate the transition of the monarchy from Feudalism to centralism.[1]

At the end of the Anglo-Saxon period, the sheriff (shire-reeve, the bailiff of the county) is a big local landlord who administers the royal revenues; above all, however, he is the agent of the great magnate, the ealdorman, who governed one or more shires. After the Norman Conquest, the sheriff, called in official texts and chronicles " vicecomes ", but considerably more powerful than the Norman viscount, is essentially a royal officer almost invariably appointed by the king himself. Already he is the agent of the executive power. Nevertheless, the office tends to become hereditary in certain important families. The sheriff is a feudary who frequently abuses his position. Henry I, whose strong policy foreshadowed that of Henry II in many respects, entrusted the office as far as possible to men on whom he could rely and the members of the Curia kept an eye on them.

At the beginning of his reign, Henry II was dependent on the support of certain big families and was forced to entrust many sheriffdoms to barons, lay or ecclesiastical. During his long absence in Normandy, 1166–1170, these magnates and their agents abused their powers enormously; they made arbitrary arrests and filled their pockets by every possible means. On his return, Henry II made his itinerant judges responsible for a comprehensive inquiry similar to that which Saint Louis had to set on foot. All those convicted of peculation, including the judges of the Church, but particularly

[1] **CDLXXXIV**; DLXXXIV, 481 ff.

ADMINISTRATION AND LEGISLATION 127

the sheriffs, were sued [1] and the sheriffs were degraded in a body. After that, in spite of some fluctuations marking the rise and fall of the royal power, the sheriffs were obedient and responsible officials drawn from the middle classes. They, nevertheless, still exercised some considerable power.

In each county, the sheriff or sheriffs (for there were sometimes two or three) were the collectors of the royal revenues. They drew from the farm of the demesne a profit which must have been considerable for they frequently bought the office at a good price. They had many further functions. They maintained the public peace, arrested criminals, prepared the work of the travelling justices, and carried out their sentences. The sheriff himself judged cases of robbery, assault, and wounding in the ordinary sessions of the shire court. He furnished the royal castles and was frequently the chatelain: he was in charge of the big administrative inquiries: he published and carried out the king's orders and acted as his political agent, keeping the towns and clergy in check. In spite of the diminution in his power which the establishment of the itinerant justices occasioned, his authority increased with that of the Crown. After 1170 his office was, in fact, a delegation of the Royal Court; very frequently, indeed, he had held some office at Court, possibly, for example, in the Exchequer.

Beyond the sheriffs, who formed the bond between central government and the old local institutions of shire and hundred, the king's servants residing at the Court established the tradition of the monarchical bureaucracy and, after the disappearance of Henry II, carried on his work. From the Curia Regis in England there grew in an unevenly developing process an administration and a political parliament. At the time of Henry II and his sons, Parliament was only embryonic but the administration had been born and specialized functions were growing up much earlier than in France.

The character of the Court, however, was not changing. It remained feudal or, in some respects, prefeudal and recalled the Court of the Norman dukes, the Court and Witena Gemot of the Anglo-Saxon kings, and the palace of the Carolingians simultaneously. Among the throng of lackeys, servants, mountebanks, quacks, and sharpers which Peter de Blois

[1] **CXXXIII**, 175 ff.; **DLXXVIII**, 125 ff.

has described for us,¹ it was always possible to pick out the relatives and personal friends of the king, his household officials, the men who had special knowledge of the administrative departments and the Courts; they formed the smaller Curia. When the lay and ecclesiastical vassals, in varying numbers, came to fulfil their duty of help and advice they formed, with the permanent attendants of the king, the Curia in its wider character. All the functions of the Court could be exercised by either of these gatherings.²

A General Court, on certain occasions, could count its attendance in thousands like the great assemblies held by Charlemagne before his military campaigns. This was the character of the assembly of "counts, barons, and knights of the kingdom" at Winchester in 1177 when Henry II was envisaging an expedition to France.³ Most common, however, is a "*Concilium*", a "*colloquium*" of the chief barons and prelates and members of the Court which the King of England, like the Capetians in France, summoned at need. Above all it was a feudal Court⁴ but, by virtue of his royal prerogative, the prince could invite whoever be wished.⁵ These gatherings attended to all sorts of business and no exact distinction can be drawn between their competence and that of the more restricted Curia. They judged the important indictments for treason, the cases which affected public order, but the king retained his prerogative of justice. They gave their consent to the great administrative reforms, their advice on questions of peace and war, on alliances and royal marriages but it was quite possible that they would not be consulted.

In 1191 the assembly of barons and prelates enjoyed, as a result of immediate circumstances, a political role which must be assessed without either exaggeration or depreciation. Its intervention was apparently of a revolutionary character for no regular convocation anticipated the meeting; it was obviously due to the intrigues of John Lackland, the young brother of King Richard, and not to the initiative of the baronage lay and clerical. Richard was, at the time, in the Holy Land and his faithful Chancellor, William Longchamp,

---

[1] Ep. **XIV**; **XC**, i, 50.
[2] **CCCXXXVII**, chap. v–x; **CLII**, 3–4; **DXXXII**, i, 153.
[3] **XVIII**, i, 178.
[4] *Constitutions of Clarendon*, chap. xi, in **CXXXIII**, 166.
[5] **CXLIV**, 57 ff. **CDXX**, 78 ff.

ADMINISTRATION AND LEGISLATION 129

was exercising some sort of regency. His pride and greed were stimulating discontent among the nobility and the royal officials alike. John Lackland decided to overthrow him as an opportunity to fish in troubled waters and the barons met in London at his instigation where the citizens rose demanding the right to establish a commune. John counted on the men of London to advance his cause. The meeting of barons and prelates, reinforced by the citizens of the capital, gave John honorary title of regent " summus rector totius regni " but at the same time accepted the Archbishop of Rouen as Chief Justiciar according to letters of nomination received from Richard. It was the Archbishop of Rouen who, basing his power on the authority of Queen Eleanor, really took over the government. William Longchamp was forced to leave England and the baronial assembly had succeeded in transferring the power and thus preventing a Civil War. Evidently the baronage was led by people of intelligence and ability who knew how to safeguard the interests of the absent king and the peace of the kingdom even while turning to the magnates for support. In such hands, John Lackland could only keep quiet.[1] From the part played by the prerogative in matters of taxation, the feudal character of the "*colloquium*" appears very clearly. Consent to taxation, in the modern sense of the word, did not exist. Medieval custom demanded that vassals should provide their suzerain with assistance, including pecuniary aid, as he needed it. The levy of the Danegeld which continued to be paid until 1163 had accustomed the English to the idea of a general contribution which had no equivalent in France. The king published, either in general assemblies or in the shire courts, the amount he needed and, according to our very indefinite texts, men then " gave " or he " took " or he " decided what each would give him ". There are a few examples of refusals but they are individual refusals deprecated by churchmen : we know of no instance of collective refusal.

In 1163 Henry II claimed to include in his accounts, as income due to the king, an indemnity to be paid to the sheriff in each county as the price of his services. At the meeting at Woodstock, the Archbishop of Canterbury,

[1] **DCXXVII**, i, 601–4.

Thomas Becket, declared that under those conditions he would not pay any longer.¹ (This is the first incident in a conflict which was only ended by the assassination of the archbishop, seven years later.)

In 1198 at the Oxford meeting a more characteristic thing happened; Roger de Hoveden, itinerant justice and chronicler, tells the story as follows:—

> King Richard made the demand through Hubert, Archbishop of Canterbury, Chief Justiciar at that time, that his subjects of the kingdom of England should provide three hundred knights to serve with him for a year or should give him enough money to maintain three hundred knights for a year at the rate of three English pennies per day for each knight. *When all the others were ready to make the grant, not daring to resist the king's will*, Hugh, Bishop of Lincoln, a zealous servant of God who took no part in evil deeds, alone replied that *so far as he was concerned* he could not agree to the king's request, for in course of time it would result in damage to his church and his successors would say: "Our fathers have eaten sour grapes and the teeth of the children are set on edge." ²

The bishop's opposition was based on the fact that knights were wanted for service outside England and, acting on his example, the Bishop of Salisbury, in his turn, refused. The Chief Justiciar did not press the point but declared the meeting ended and wrote to the king that he had failed.³ As far as we can see, there was no vote and the refusals given were those of individuals.⁴

Henry II called together many General Courts precisely because he had no reason to fear organized opposition. It was his means of maintaining contact with his nobility, testing their feelings, and organizing support among them. They showed no political consciousness which was likely to cause him anxiety; very rarely the assembly took the initiative over some reform. We are lucky to be able to instance the Assize of Measures published by King Richard " on the demand and advice of his bishops and all the barons ".⁵

Henry II and Richard did not come into conflict with the traditions of a permanent and organized royal court for it did not yet exist but they had relatives and trusted friends

---

¹ **DCXXVII**, i, 561–2. In spite of the coincidence of dates it is doubtful whether he was dealing with a transformation of the Danegeld. See **DLXXXV**, 497 ff.
² **CXXXIII**, 248.   ³ Text of the life of Saint Hugh in **CXXXIII**, 249.
⁴ **DLXXXV**, 528 ff.   ⁵ **DCXXVII** i 684–8.

ADMINISTRATION AND LEGISLATION 131

near at hand. Before her violent quarrels with her husband, Eleanor had an important place at court and dispatched orders " by letter of the king from Overseas " and brought trials to an end; during the interregnum of 1189, during the captivity of Richard, and at the accession of John Lackland she played her part in the government.[1] Henry the Younger, as king-associate, adequately fulfilled the office of regent during his father's absences. John Lackland might have played the same part during the reign of his brother Richard but he only understood how to be a rebel.[2] Beside the royal family, the most influential people were the Chancellor, the Treasurer, and, above all, the Chief Justiciar who became, in the twelfth century, a sort of Prime Minister. We shall have to speak of them again; their offices were usually purchased. As for the hereditary offices of Norman origin to which we find parallels at the Court of Louis VII, they were held by the chief barons though, owing to the King's distrust, they were left no real power.[3] Finally we often find mention in the chronicles or in the lists of witnesses to royal deeds of *familiares, aulici, consiliarii* of extremely diverse social conditions—bishops, barons, clerks, knights. In 1166, in a letter to the Pope, the clerks of the province of Canterbury talk of the " faithful and intimate subjects who are particularly engaged on the secret business of the king and whose hands direct the royal councils and the affairs of the kingdom ". In practice, then, there was a Council formed of people in whom Henry II had confidence and who, during the reign of the absentee Richard, knew how to maintain their position: they were either magnates fulfilling their feudal obligation to advise or Court officials. It would be a mistake, however, to see in it a rigid and permanent organization. This was but one aspect of the Curia. Only in the thirteenth century did the Royal Council begin to take institutional shape; at the same time the constitutional question of the choice of advisers came up for discussion; in the twelfth century it had not been raised.[4]

There is no specialization of duties except for the Chancery, the administration of the finances, and of justice.

---

[1] CVI, intro., 173–4; DCXXVII, i, 673–4.
[2] DCXXVII, i, 603, 673–4.
[3] DCXXVII, i, 419 ff. Mrs. Doris M. Stenton has produced an excellent study of the office of Chief Justiciar in *C.M.H.*, v, 574–9.
[4] CLII, 1 ff.

132   THE ANGEVIN EMPIRE

The Chancellor, Keeper of the Great Seal, and, if we may use the term, "Editor in chief" of the royal deeds became a person of considerable importance; more and more he is the chief legal adviser of the sovereign. In origin, he was merely an officer of the Household.[1] The Chancery, equally, is still a department of the Household and remains, like the Chancellor, migratory. Henry II was continually on the move and, apart from the permanent establishment of such administrative centres as Westminster in England and Caen, Rouen, or Angers on the Continent, where there was a regular staff, clerks travelled with the king and drew up, at need, letters and writs in the towns, villages, hunting boxes, or abbeys through which he was passing. In spite of this dispersion, Henry's Chancery obeys standard rules; the make up[2] is remarkable for its accuracy, clarity, and precision at a period when the style of Capetian charters is still rambling and diffuse. The clerks of the Plantegenets had no time to engage in preambles or to embellish their work with rhetorical flourishes. Every day they had to draw up an enormous number of deeds and particularly of financial and judicial writs. We can be sure of that although to-day we have only an infinitesimal fraction extant of the deeds of Henry II. The preservation of archives was still open to many improvements but the officials of the Exchequer, since the reign of Henry I, had adopted the principle of enrolment, that is the system of transcribing the sheriff's accounts on to parchment rolls. We have an almost complete series of these Pipe Rolls for the reign of Henry II. In the reign of Richard and, in particular, at the beginning of John's reign important reforms were made in the Chancery. For charters, letters patent, letters close, the cases settled in Court, the affairs of Normandy, etc., they began to make a collection of copies which were preserved and which the passage of time has not destroyed. These Rolls constitute the richest and most continuous series of ancient archives to be found in Europe.[3]

The royal Court considered as a financial tribune, "The

---

[1] **DCXL**, i, 15–16, 122–139.
[2] Already notable in the time of Henry I; see the writs of that king edited in **CCCL**, app. F, n. 4, 5, etc.
[3] **CVI**, intro., p. 1 ff., 61 and n. 3, 151, 161, 166, 193–6; **CCCXCIV**, chap. v. Bibliography in Gross, Sources, §§ 6 and 12.

ADMINISTRATION AND LEGISLATION

Court of the king sitting at the Exchequer," had achieved an equally high degree of organization.[1] It is known to us through the *Dialogue of the Exchequer* which the Treasurer, Richard Fitz Neal, composed at the end of the reign of Henry II.[2] It is a dialogue between the author and a member of the Exchequer who has sat there for a long time without understanding all the mysteries and asks for an explanation. The author distinguishes between the Lower Exchequer "*Inferius Scaccarium*", which is a Treasury, and the Upper Exchequer, "*Superius Scaccarium*," which is an Audit Department. Twice a year—at Easter and Michælmas—the sheriffs of the counties came to submit their accounts to the Upper Exchequer and pay into the Lower.[3] The older of these two sections was the Treasury, the principal agents of which were the Treasurer and his clerk and the two Chamberlains of the Exchequer with the assistance of two knights. They were responsible for preserving Domesday Book, the Pipe Rolls,[4] and the wooden tallies on which were notched and marked the sums received : in addition they had charge of the treasure chest. As a general rule they demanded payment of the sheriffs in good money ; the amount tendered was melted and assayed. The Treasurer and the Chamberlains of the Lower Exchequer also figured in the Upper Exchequer but this exceedingly formal Department of Audit included also the Chief Justiciar, the Chancellor, the Constable, the Marshall, and all those sent there by the will of the king chosen from among " the most important and prudent subjects of the realm ". The members of the Upper Exchequer were called Barons of the Exchequer. Technical experts and important personalities of the royal household and the baronage clerical and lay were assembled there together to inspire a salutary fear in the sheriffs and, in fact, they succeeded in terrifying them. The specialists alone, however, served any useful purpose and there is entertaining proof of that in

---

[1] We have seen already (Bk. One, Chap. III, § II) how the Exchequer came out of the Household and was distinguished from it. It retained its private chest—the wardrobe, for the development of which see Bk. Three, Chap. IV below.   [2] **XXXIII** ; **DLXVII**, 336–340.

[3] The exposition of the *Dialogus* is a little too theoretical. The sheriffs came to account with this regularity only from twenty-four out of thirty-nine counties. See **CDLXXII**, 483.

[4] It seems that Pipe Roll merely means roll composed of membranes of parchment (pipes) sewn together end to end. **DLVII**, 329 ff., 749.

F

the argument between the two characters introduced in the *Dialogue of the Exchequer* :

"Why don't you teach the others your knowledge of the Exchequer ? "

" But, my dear brother, you have been sitting at the Exchequer for a long time now and nothing escapes you for you are too scrupulous."

" But just as those who walk in the dark and feel with their hands often knock themselves, many are sitting there who look and see nothing and listen and hear nothing."

" Why do you speak so disrespectfully ? "[1]

The technicians and accountants sat round or near to a table ten feet long and five feet wide covered with a squared black cloth, the divisions of which looked like the pigeon holes of an Exchequer. They used counters for the addition; and, according to the position they occupied, they could represent one penny or ten thousand pounds.[2]

Besides this audit, the Upper Exchequer was responsible for drawing up the Pipe Roll and, in addition, it established itself as a court of justice as need arose to settle disputed points. In addition to these different aspects the Exchequer possessed the mobility of the royal Court since there was no rigid separation from it. It was normally held at Winchester or London but could meet anywhere else.

It was not only during the sessions of the Exchequer, however, that the royal Court established itself as a tribunal. One of its principal occupations throughout the year was to do justice either at a common centre like Westminster or by an itinerant delegation.

Before the reign of Henry II the vast majority of cases were dealt with either in seignorial courts or in the old local courts of shire and hundred. The seignorial courts did not merely judge the petty matters affecting the use of the demesne but all civil cases concerned with tenures ; in a word, the protection of property was entirely in the lord's hands. On the other hand, the shire court was dominated by the magnates of the district and the hundred court had frequently fallen at an early date under seignorial control. It was a court of criminal justice in which the lord exercised his " franchisal " jurisdiction.[3] In spite of the judiciary powers invested in the sheriffs and the appointment of

[1] **XXXIII**, 59.
[2] See the diagram reproduced in **XXXIII**, 46.
[3] **CLI**, 1–8 ; **CXL**, 151–178.

certain judges working on the spot under conditions of which we know nothing,[1] the great part of local justice slipped out of the king's hands. In short, it was either popular or feudal. At the centre, the Curia, like the Court of the Anglo-Saxon kings, judged issues which affected the interests of the monarchy and heard appeals: it was a feudal court, like that of the ancient Norman dukes, which settled differences between barons. Sometimes it assumed an extremely solemn form, at others it consisted only of a group of competent lawyers whose work is already visible in the reign of Henry I.[2] In short, it was extremely reminiscent of the Capetian Curia in its judicial aspect.

At the beginning of the reign of Henry II, as the result of an extraordinary legal revolution that we shall deal with later, it provided a powerful instrument of monarchical progress: instead of being an extraordinary tribunal with very little business, it became a normal court for the whole kingdom. For that purpose, it was necessary to organize the delegation of business and to dispatch *missi*: there were precedents for this among Carolingians, Anglo-Saxons, and Normans alike but it was probably Henry II who systematized the circuits. England was patrolled by personal friends of the king among whom we find Richard de Lucé, Thomas Beckett, Glanville, the Chronicler Roger de Hoveden, and the story-teller Walter Map. The editors of the Pipe Roll of 1176 gave them the title of "*justitiarii itinerantes*" which has had a long history subsequently. From this date of 1176, the institution is fixed and there are circuits almost every year. The kingdom is divided into regions (six for example in 1176) and each region is dealt with by a group of judges. The travelling justices were engaged on all sorts of business but chiefly " pleas of the Crown ", which particularly concerned the king and the good government of the realm. It was the king's Court on its travels but they only made use of the meetings of the shire courts. When they were presiding in the shire court it became the king's Court and twelve loyal men from each town were summoned to these extraordinary sessions.[3]

[1] Unpublished documents used by Mrs. Stenton in *C.M.H.*, vol. v, 584.
[2] **DXXXII**, i, 109–110; **DCXXVII**, i, 473.
[3] **CXXXIII**, 167 ff., 251–7; **DCXXVII**, i, 723 ff.; **DXXXII**, i, 155 ff., 170; **DLXVII**, 167–171; **CCVII**, 16 ff.; **DCXIV**, p. xvii ff.

This systematization of the missions is an important innovation but some considerable reform was brought about at the centre also. From 1178 onwards, we can trace the beginnings of the organization of a "*Capitalis curia regis*" (this is the term used by Glanville) distinct from the feudal *concilia* (for it did not include any barons) and from the Exchequer. If consisted of five experienced lawyers—two clerics and three laymen—who did justice in the king's name. Very soon it became known as the King's Bench. The King's Bench was at the disposition of the sovereign who could decide to take it with him on progress. John Lackland frequently did this and, as a result, a division occurred. The Chief Justiciar remained at Westminster with a separate group of judges and this duplicate Bench became the Court of Common Pleas.[1]

This extraordinary development of the royal courts in England was parallel to that of legislation and the law. In fifty years the most rapid revolution which Western Europe witnessed throughout the Middle Ages was accomplished in the development of centralization and uniformity under the monarchy. Whereas, previously, the royal judges had taken cognizance only of those cases which affected their master, the public order or the people immediately dependent on the Crown, the new legislation gave them jurisdiction over a wide variety of cases. The victory was all the more important because it was a definitive one. In the thirteenth century, in spite of the slight setback marked by the Great Charter, the rising tide of royal justice continued to overwhelm seignorial jurisdictions. There only remained a few islets.[2]

In short, the king considered that "liberties" existed only by his grant, that justice could be administered only as the delegation of his authority and that he had the right to resume alienated powers. But at the same time, by the institution of the jury, Henry II established throughout the country for many centuries the spirit of decentralization and self government.

---

[1] Text of the Gesta Henrici Secundi in **CXXXIII**, 155; **DCXXVII**, i, 719 ff.; **CDLVI**, pp. xi–xvii; **DXXXII**, i, 153–4, 169 ff.; **CXLIV**, 136–143; **CXL**, 214 ff.
[2] **CLI**, 6.

III

LEGISLATION. THE ASSIZES. THE JURY

Thanks to Henry II who, we are told, was capable of legal innovation [1] and his advisers who understood the principles of Roman Law and knew its technicalities [2] the English monarchy was the only lay power in Western Europe to establish a common law by the beginning of the thirteenth century. In France and Germany local custom still prevailed. The characteristic of royal justice in England was that it held local custom as of little account and that through its system of assizes and writs it established a procedure and a jurisprudence of general application which was, on the whole, favourable to a free middle class and hostile to the seignorial spirit.[3]

We might well add " hostile to the clerical spirit " for Henry II sought to limit ecclesiastical jurisdiction and to make certain that criminous clerks were punished. The constitutions of Clarendon formed an important and significant part of his legislation. He suffered a partial check on that issue, however, and the question is so closely bound up with his conflict with the Primate, Thomas Becket, that it is best to deal with it separately. Apart from the Constitutions of Clarendon, the legislative documents of Henry's reign are called Assizes, a word which also means " a session of the court " or " a jury which inquires and decides a question of fact " or even " an action where the procedure of assizes is employed ".[4] The texts of the Assize of Clarendon (1166), the Assize of Northampton (1176), the Assize of Arms (1181), and the Assize of the Forest (1184) have been preserved for us.[5] Like the Carolingian capitularies which were, for the most part, a kind of circular sent out to the " missi " to assist them in deciding difficult cases, the Assizes in most of their provisions were practical rules to put into operation rather than laws. The assizes of *Novel Disseisin* (? 1166),

---

[1] **LXXXIX**, 237.
[2] **CDLXX**, 374 and note ; **DXXXII**, i, 160 ff.
[3] Vinogradoff (**DCLXI**, 195-8) has raised objections to these opinions which, I think, have little weight. It is certainly true that the claims of custom are put forward in the Great Charter, but as a line of reaction against the advance of the royal power.
[4] **CCCLXXVIII**, 48, n. 3.   [5] **CXXXIII**, 170 ff.

the *Grand Assize* (1179), the *Assize of Mort d'Ancestor* (? 1176), and of *Dernier Presentement* which we know only through the commentaries of Glanville must have been of a similar character. We shall have to speak of the Assizes of Arms and of the Forest later. The Assizes of Clarendon and of Northampton were primarily important police regulations issued to deal with the brigands who were still abundant in 1166 and were revived by the civil war of 1173. Henceforward no privilege could give malefactors impunity. More important in legal history are those of which our knowledge is derived through Glanville. They were not without precedent. They were based on the procedure already adopted in the time of Henry I and Stephen but they systematically replaced the rule of violence by the reign of law and they gave complainants an opportunity to avoid the delays and the barbarous procedure of feudal justice. However, they were not aimed directly at the destruction of feudal justice. They offered to everybody a quick and rational procedure by which the nobility itself could frequently profit. Their intention was to protect possession as distinct from proprietorship. One could not be disseised of possessions without process of law even if the possessor's title was not above suspicion. For example, after " Mort d'Ancestor ", the dead man's heir could not be disseised by violence of his ancestor's possessions. If a lord considered his rights better than those of the dead man and took possession of the inheritance, a jury of neighbours would be required to say whether the dead man held the tenure at the time of his death and whether the man disseised is his rightful heir; if these are agreed, the heir would resume possession pending judgment. An even more severe blow was directed against the baronage by the Grand Assize of 1179; it roused no resistance although it attacked their very right to do justice: no sentence of disseisin could be pronounced in a case concerning a free tenure unless the trial had been authorized by a royal writ; on the other hand, the defender in such a case could always refuse the judicial duel (a very unpopular Norman practice introduced after the Conquest) and even demand to be tried by the royal judges if he was justiciable in a feudal court.[1]

[1] DXXXII, i, 136 ff.; CCCLXXVIII, 48 ff.; DLXXIX, 268-9.

ADMINISTRATION AND LEGISLATION 139

The jury, to which it was possible to have recourse to avoid the duel, was a group of neighbours called together by a public officer to answer some question on oath and state the truth concerning it.[1] It was an institution of Frankish origin; the Frankish kings employed the jury to discover criminals and false officials; William the Conqueror introduced the jury to England and used it in the compilation of Domesday Book,[2] but before the reign of Henry II it had been more frequently used for administrative purposes than judicial.[3] Henry II did not cease to use it for obtaining information but he must have the credit for making it a smoothly working judicial institution. In cases of Novel Disseisin the jury answered on questions of fact but the plaintiffs were allowed to declare acceptance of their verdict. In this way, trial by jury was introduced. Finally, in each county twelve men from every hundred and four from each village were required to lay information against murderers and robbers before the itinerant justices; the sheriffs were instructed to make equal use of the jury of presentment to learn what crimes had been committed. The jury of presentment of the hundred, chosen by the sheriff in the time of Henry II, was recruited by election from the end of the twelfth century. The method of election was a complicated one inspired by an ecclesiastical usage (the method of compromise): there was always considerable distrust of any simple system of election in the Middle Ages. The chief men of the county, probably those who were present in court, elected four knights who, in turn, chose two " loyal knights " for each hundred. These two loyal knights with ten others whom they chose themselves comprised the jury of the hundred. If knights were not available, free men might be chosen.[4]

In using the elected jury in this way the English kings were sowing the seeds of a representative system in their

---

[1] For all that follows, see the classical work of H. Brunner, **CC**, 127 ff.; **DXXXII**, i, 138 ff.; **DCXXVII**, i, 728 ff.; and above all, J. B. Thayer, **DCXXXV**, chap. ii.
[2] The accusing jury of twelve thanes existed, however, ever since the Scandinavian invasions, in the counties most affected by Scandinavian influences, the Danelaw.
[3] See the examples of administrative inquiries before Henry II, and during his reign, quoted by Haskins, **CCCL**, 234 ff.
[4] Instructions of 1194; **CXXXIII**, 252.

140 THE ANGEVIN EMPIRE

counties. We shall meet the jury again when we come to speak of taxation.

IV

THE REVENUES OF THE MONARCHY

When we consider the fruits of the royal demesne or the other revenues paid into the Treasury we are struck by the extent of the rights which the English monarchy assumed for itself; it is on this side that it undeniably oversteps the boundaries of Feudalism.[1]

Like the Capetians, the Plantegenets were expected to draw their normal revenues from their demesne. It was farmed out to the sheriffs just as the demesne of the Capetians was to the Provosts.[2] But in England there was an exorbitant privilege attached to the rights and revenues of the demesne in " The Forest " which was of Frankish and Norman origin. The forest, said the author of the *Dialogue of the Exchequer*, consists of certain hunting preserves which the king has built up for himself in the well wooded counties; he goes there to forget his anxieties in enjoyment of the rest and freedom of nature.

Offences against the forest were outside the jurisdiction of the ordinary courts; the special Forest Laws were based

---

[1] Stubbs's exposition has become out of date, **DCXXVII**, i, 461 ff., 690 ff. The most important financial documents are the Pipe Rolls (see above). At the present time, unfortunately, they have been published only in part, and even those which have appeared have not been made the subject of any profound studies. The work of Sir J. H. Ramsay, **DLVI**, must be used with caution (see **CCLXXXVII**, 48 ff.). The extant accounts, even when minutely studied, do not provide a total of the resources—they are not budgets. The king possessed a Household Chest in the king's chamber (*in camera regis*) for which we have no accounts. In our opinion, it is impossible to make a precise estimate of the financial resources that Henry II, Richard, or John could dispose of, and even more to attempt any comparison with those of their Capetian contemporaries. We can say, however, that all the facts we possess and the comments made by contemporaries show that they were much richer than the kings of France. We cannot accept the contrary conclusions of F. Lot, **CDXXXVI**, 185 ff. See our c.r. criticism of this work in B.E.C., 1933.

[2] **DCXLV**, 117–149; **DVII**, 13 ff.; **CDLXXXIV**, 124 ff. Turner has given figures county by county from the fifth to the fifteenth year of Henry II. Parow has studied his sixteenth year in particular, and established the total of all the revenues drawn from England: £23,535 16s. 10d. sterling, of which £13,425 19s. 7d. were paid into the Treasury, and the rest spent on the spot. Of this £23,535 16s. 10d., £10,529 17s. 4d. came from four of the counties (**DVII**, 48–9). The pound sterling was four times the value of the pound tournois (**CCLIX**, 333).

ADMINISTRATION AND LEGISLATION 141

" not on the Common Law of the kingdom but on the will of the prince and so we say that their consequences may not be absolutely just but they are just according to the Law of the Forest ".[1] The forest chiefly consisted of woodland but it also included heathland and pasture, and even arable country and villages not only on the royal demesne but in tenures held by subjects, even important lords. In the twelfth century, only six out of thirty-nine counties did not contain some forest land and Essex, which was certainly exceptional, was completely under Forest Law. In these extensive preserves game swarmed and the forest dweller, whether he was peasant, knight, or churchman, was not only forbidden to interfere with the beasts, he dare not touch the greenery which fed and sheltered them. Fines and extra rents were constantly being extorted. In his Assize of the Forest for which he gained baronial acceptance in 1184, Henry II re-established the ancient regulations in all their force :—

> No one shall fail in his obligations to the king for his game of his forests in any respect. Henceforward if any man is convicted of having failed, the king will have full justice of him as it was in the time of the king his grandfather. . . . Let his foresters take care that the trees be not destroyed in the forest by knights and others who have woods within the king's forest ; if any are destroyed take careful note to whom they belong so that the fine is levied on them and their lands and not on others. . . . The king forbids any man to have bows, arrows, or dogs in his forests at least without surety. Henceforward he forbids hunting by night within his forest or without in those places where his big game is to be found and where it is usually left in peace, under penalty of a year's imprisonment and composition and redemption at the king's will." [2]

The forest is, at the same time, an expression of the king's pleasure and a financial instrument. It provides the king not only with tyrannical pleasures but also with arbitrary revenues.

It is not subject to the custom of the kingdom but is the refuge of despotic power.

The rights which the Plantegenets enjoyed as suzerains were much more fruitful than a Louis VII or even a Philip Augustus could command because they were more severe and the power of the monarchy had practically no limits but

[1] **XXXIII**, 105.
[2] **CXXXIII**, 186–8.
[3] **CDXXII, CXXVII** ; my studies, **DXVIII** and **DXX**, vol. ii, p. 147 ff. (or **DCXXVII**, ii, 757 ff.).

those of the kingdom. Escheats, that is to say the forfeited property that reverted to the Crown, provided the Treasury with considerable resources. Glanville informs us that the heir to a barony in chief paid a relief " at the kings will ". The nobility and churches suffered from abuses of the right of wardship : widow and daughters not yet of age from abuses of the right of marriage. The barons complained that the king monopolized the Jews and reserved for himself the right to part of their inheritance.[1] The feudal aid due on three occasions (sovereign's ransom, knighting of his eldest son, and marriage of his eldest daughter) became, on occasions, a crushing burden. To ransom their captive King Richard, his subjects had to pay a quarter of their movable goods.[2] Finally, the regularity of the sessions of the Exchequer and the circuits of the itinerant justices, the extension of the pleas of the Crown, and the procedure of assize gave royal justice a fiscal importance it had never possessed before.

When we seek to measure the forces of expansion and resistance in the Angevin empire, obviously we must remember that Normandy and the other fiefs held of the King of France were not only sources of expense for the Plantegenets but also of revenue. Normandy, in particular, provided them with important receipts which they used not only on local defences but to meet any pressing need of the moment. Bullion was frequently shipped across the Channel. The Capetians possessed nothing outside the boundaries of their kingdom comparable to the demesnes and extremely valuable rights which the King of England enjoyed in France.

In particular, however, it is the early development of taxation in England which deserves our attention. The expansion of the administration, the expenses of an imperialist policy, and also the Exchequer's difficulty in collecting debts forced the Plantegenets to seek other sources beyond their demesnes and their feudal rights. They levied " customs " on trade in the ports and markets [3] and none of them showed any hesitation in imposing frequent direct taxes either of lands or movables which, under one form or another, fell on all classes of the nation—clergy, nobility, free tenants,

---

[1] **DXXXII**, i, 468 ff. ; **CCCLXVII**, chap. iii–vi.
[2] **CDLXXIV**, 346.
[3] **CCCXXXVIII**, i, 57 ff. ; **CCCXVIII**, chap. i.

ADMINISTRATION AND LEGISLATION 143

and towns.[1] The old Danegeld which was farmed out to the sheriff and profited scarcely anybody but him was suppressed by Henry II and replaced by more productive taxes. All the forms of imposition used in the thirteenth century can be found already in the twelfth; sometimes one was employed, sometimes another. It was not Henry II who invented scutage, the tax on knights' fees in place of military service, for we have an example of its use by Henry I but he used it seven times to provide mercenaries who were more dependable and manageable in time of war than the feudal levies. Then he exempted from military service those of whom he demanded scutage. It was usually imposed at the rate of two marks per knight's fee.[2] Richard Cœur de Lion invented a land tax on holdings of all sorts called "carucage" or "hidage", because English land was divided into carucates or hides. Finally, this period provides instances of taxes on movable goods levied for the needs of the Holy Land.

These extraordinary aids, it is true, were only remotely akin to modern taxation. They were based on the principle of the help which a man owed to his lord in cases of emergency and, consequently, were not imposed annually or even regularly extended to include all his subjects. Frequently they spared the royal demesne and the goods of the clergy which the king could reach by other means, tallaging the inhabitants of the demesne and demanding gifts from the clergy. The chroniclers have exaggerated the burden they imposed. Gervais of Canterbury, for instance, suggests that the great scutage of 1159 raised £180,000; but the sum received from scutage at the rate of two marks a fief was, at most, £2,240. On the other hand, in the assessment and distribution of the tax, the royal agents used liberal methods: they arranged circuits (which frequently coincided with those of the itinerant justices) to consult the people concerned, collected their returns, and even made use of the jury. The taxation, nevertheless, grew heavier and heavier and the feudal fiction of assistance given to a suzerain was inadequate justification for financial policy more and more arbitrary and exacting.[3]

[1] **CDLXXIV**, 5 ff., 346 ff.; **DCXX**, 466 ff.
[2] There is a complete literature on this obscure question of scutage. See, in particular, **CLIII**, chap. i–iii; **DLXXXV**, 262 ff.
[3] On the needs and expedients of Richard Cœur de Lion, see **DCXIII**; **CCXI**, ii, 89–91; iii, 101, 179 ff.

Conflict was brewing and no one thought of preventing it by the creation of methods adapted to the new circumstances.

V

Army and Navy

We have seen that William the Conqueror, to establish his power and his military forces in particular, fused Anglo-Saxon, Danish, Carolingian, and Norman traditions. He had retained the fyrd, the Anglo-Saxon national army, and introduced Norman feudal service. The Norman kings had also made use of mercenaries. These principles and practices had become thoroughly degenerate during Stephen's reign and led to disorder and anarchy. Henry II reconstituted the royal army by stages.

His predecessors had negotiated with the counts of Flanders to obtain knights and sergeants. The numerous families of the petty Flemish nobility provided excellent soldiers who were hardy and gallant but ruthless pillagers. Henry II on his accession cleared the kingdom of them. In need of mercenaries for his wars in France, in 1163 he concluded agreements with the Flemish barons and gave them fees in money on condition of homage. They undertook to provide a knight's service at the rate of three marks a year. He also concluded a recruiting treaty with the Count of Hainault who became his vassal on condition of the payment of 100 marks a year.[1] For his Crusade in the Holy Land Richard enrolled knights and sergeants drawn from every country of Western Europe and men of Wales, Brabant, Flanders, and Navarre fought by his side in his French wars. John Lackland made use of mercenaries and abused their potentialities.[2]

Henry II had the wisdom to rely on his knights and the fyrd to maintain or restore order in England. As a result of the big inquests he made in England in 1166 and in 1172 in Normandy he fixed anew the number of knights that each tenant in chief owed him. The rate of scutage when he demanded it from his barons was based on the same

---

[1] CCCLXXXIV, i, 68–71, 76.
[2] DCXXVII, i, 703–4; CCCXII, 131 ff.; CCCXI, 421 ff.

ADMINISTRATION AND LEGISLATION 145

assessment.[1] Finally, in 1181, by his famous Assize of Arms he reconstituted the fyrd. This curious ordinance bears a very close resemblance to the capitularies of Charlemagne on military service by free men. All subjects of noble and free status must possess military equipment and swear to maintain it at the king's service. Whoever holds a knight's fief must have as many coats of mail, helmets, bucklers, and lances as he has fiefs; the free layman who possesses sixteen marks' rent must possess the same equipment as the knight; the one with ten marks must have a coat of mail, an iron helmet, and a lance; other freemen a padded coat, an iron helmet, and a lance. The export of arms is forbidden and the itinerant justices are made responsible for drawing up lists of freemen in their classes by inquest of a jury and receiving the oath of arms.[2]

The same assize forbids the export of ships or of wood that can be used in their construction. This is one of our oldest texts about English maritime legislation the origins of which are shrouded in obscurity by legend. The early Plantegenets certainly needed to make sure of having some rapid and dependable means of communication with Normandy and Richard Cœur de Lion assembled an imposing fleet for his Crusade.[3] From the time of Henry II, the Federation of the Cinque Ports (originally Hastings, Sandwich, Dover, Romney, Hythe) undertook, in return for its privileges, to provide ships in time of war.[4]

VI

THE KING AND HIS ENGLISH SUBJECTS. THE CONFLICTS

What was the reaction of the English to the attacks of this powerful monarchy with its efficient servants and its extensive resources which was attempting to restore public peace and the prerogatives of the Norman monarchy which

---

[1] **DLXXXV**, 236 ff.; **DXLII**, 482–520; **DXLI**, 89–93; **CCCL**, 161. Comparison with the Sicilian *Catalogus baronum*, **CCCXLVIII**, 655 ff.
[2] Text in **CXXXIII**, 183 ff.
[3] **CCXI**, ii, 99, 125.
[4] See my notes in **DXVII**, 96 n. 1, and in **DCXXVII**, i, 842 n. 2; **CLIV**, 732–3; **DCXX**, 459–461.

had disappeared during Stephen's period of anarchy and even seeking to establish a new law and oblige all subjects to recognize royal justice? Did it provoke conflicts?

They had occurred and sometimes in a very serious form particularly during the reign of Henry II but reaction and conflict had produced each other in succession and had done little to damage the achievements we have just been surveying. Unity among the aggrieved holders of privileges was only achieved at the period of the Great Charter. Under Henry II there developed an antagonism between the king and the Archbishop of Canterbury and later a feudal rising which proved less serious in England than on the Continent. The towns and London in particular did not demand serious attention from the monarchy till the end of our period.

The story of Thomas Beckett need not be repeated here; its importance for us lies in the light it throws on the relations between Church and State in England at that period. We shall see that Becket by no means personified the Church or even the English clergy. An unbalanced and spiteful prelate, impatient of every restraint, he came into collision with a king jealous of his authority who was not able to maintain his customary prudent and farsighted approach. In a field in which peace had throughout only been maintained by supple and discreet diplomacy two overbearing men were brought abruptly face to face. Neither of them presented his case well, but our interest, in this book, is to see what was the basis of the question and how it was solved.

Thomas Becket had previously been Chancellor and the king's friend and Henry II, believing that he could rely on him, had secured his election as Archbishop of Canterbury (1162). Thomas had been an irreproachable priest but he made a hateful primate, a troublesome and aggressive lord in his temporalities, and an intractable subject. He had already alienated one group among the bishops and the baronage and Henry II was already thoroughly annoyed by his attitude when the publication of the Constitutions of Clarendon brought them into open hostility.[1]

The record which we possess of the meeting held at

---

[1] The conflict is well dealt with in **CCCLXVI**, chap. v and vi; **CXCVII**, chap. xiii; **DCXVIII**, chap. ix and x; **CXLI**, chap. xiii and xiv; **CCXXXVI**, chap. vii.

ADMINISTRATION AND LEGISLATION

Clarendon (January 1164) and the text of the Constitutions show us clearly how the question was raised.[1] The king's advisers, Richard de Lucé and Jocelin de Bailleul, who had drafted the text did not claim to be introducing any innovations. They began as follows :—

> ... In the presence of the king we have made record and recognition of a certain part of the customs, liberties and dignities of the king's ancestors, namely of King Henry I and others which should be observed and maintained in the kingdom. And on account of the disagreements and dissensions which have arisen between the clergy on the one hand and the Justices of the Lord the King and the barons of the realm about these customs and dignities, this recognition was made in the presence of the archbishops, bishops, and clergy and the counts, barons, and magnates of the realm.

In fact he was seeking in general to effect a restoration, and to check the advances at the expense of the State made by the Church and the Holy See and to destroy them whether they had been achieved as a result of the anarchy of Stephen's reign or of the new Canon Law. The English Church at the time of William the Conqueror, William Rufus, and Henry I was submissive; he sought now to reduce it to submission again. The king found that certain prelates now stood for political independence forgetting that they had duties as barons. They failed to make an appearance at Court and departed to the Continent to cabal with people of suspect loyalty. The regalian rights were challenged; the election of bishops and abbots were not always carried through according to the king's will and the elected candidate secured consecration before doing him homage. The king also received with some satisfaction the personal complaints of the barons —the power of excommunication was used prematurely and improperly; the Church robbed the lord of his peasants by conferring ordination on them without his consent; it challenged the rights of patrons who were entitled to appoint incumbents to churches. Above all, however, the encroachments of the ecclesiastical courts,[2] which William the Conqueror had imprudently established, menaced lay society and thwarted the re-establishment of public security. The Church courts claimed to be the only judges of criminous clerks and murderers were sentenced only to degradation;

---
[1] **CXXXIII**, 161 ff.
[2] On the powers of ecclesiastical courts in England : **DXXXII**, i, 124 ff.; **CCCVIII**, vol. ii, chap. v.

they controlled trials for debt on the pretext that the debtor had sworn an oath to his creditor; the archdeacons who were proverbial for their greed summoned laymen before their courts at random to inflict unjust fines. Conflicts between lay and ecclesiastical courts were all the more numerous because there was frequent litigation over the origin and character of tenures; thus, a case about a lay tenure was claimed by the church court on the grounds that it was "in free alms"[1] and they would not admit the right of the royal courts to determine this point of fact.

The Constitution of Clarendon sought to remedy such abuses and avoid conflicts. They compelled prelates to fulfil the obligations of loyal barons and they limited the rights of the ecclesiastical courts, but they were framed with moderation and provided for the liberal use of juries to settle cases; they laid it down, for instance, that the archdeacon should not be deprived of any of his just rights and that if he was concerned with land recognized by a jury in the royal court as a tenure in free alms the cases should be concluded in the Church court.[2] Similarly the king promised to check any magnates of the realm who refused to acknowledge ecclesiastical jurisdiction in cases which concerned them or their retainers. Six out of sixteen articles were subsequently declared by the Pope to be quite acceptable, including the one which made the ordination of peasant's sons dependent on the previous consent of his lord and the one which compelled the archdeacons to accept a jury of presentment when they wished to summon laymen.

Others, however, were in conflict with the letter or, at least, the spirit of the Canon Law as it was then taught, particularly the one forbidding appeals to the Pope without the king's permission and two others which we must quote in their context:—

> In case of the vacancy of an archbishopric, bishopric, abbey, or priory in the king's patronage ... when the time comes to make provision to the church, the lord king should instruct the principal dignitaries of that church and the election should take place *in the lord king's chapel* with the consent of the king and the advice of the people he has summoned for the purpose. And there the elected candidate shall do homage and swear fidelity to the lord king as

[1] See p. 71 f. above.
[2] CCCLXXXV, 1-11.

ADMINISTRATION AND LEGISLATION 149

his liege lord on his life, limbs, and his worldy honour, saving his order,[1] before being consecrated.

Clerics accused of some crime having been summoned by the king's judge shall come to his court to answer there the charges which the royal court considers they should answer there and to the ecclesiastical court to answer the charges which they should answer there so that the royal judge will be able to see how the matter is being treated in the Court of Holy Church. And if the clerk is convicted or has confessed, the Church should protect him no longer.

This famous clause about criminous clergy was too concise and badly drafted and it raised many difficulties in interpretation.[2] It seems to us that the lay court would have the first dealings with the matter and that the clerk would have to answer there for offences which were within the competence of the church courts. From there it would be sent to the Church court where, if the offences had been proved, the trial would be carried out in the presence of a representative of the royal judge ; if he was found guilty and degraded, the lay court would condemn him to the temporal punishment he deserved and the sentence would be carried out.

Because of the enormous number of crimes committed by clerks at that time, the solution was reasonable as many of the English bishops thought, but Becket, after some hesitation, rejected it, repeating the words of the prophet Nahum " God does not punish twice ". Henceforward he opposed it with the obstinacy of a man who has found a slogan and refused to accept the Constitutions of Clarendon. Henry II employed devious methods to force him to resign. He heaped penalties on him and accused him of misappropriating the royal revenues when he was Chancellor ; finally, he secured his condemnation by the Court as a traitor and perjurer. Deserted by the bishops, who were satisfied to stay away from the trial, Becket fled to France. That was the only means open to a man who declared that the spiritual is infinitely superior to the temporal power. He relied on the King of France who supported him as far as his scanty means allowed. He was also counting on the Pope, Alexander III, but he was involved in his quarrel with Frederick Barbarossa and was himself in exile at the Court of Louis VII and could not afford to break with the powerful Henry II. For six years, the adversaries cast vain insults at one another. Becket

---

[1] i.e. saving what the divine law enjoins on the clergy.
[2] CDLV, 224 ff. ; DXXXII, i, 447 ff. ; CCCVIII, ii, 97 ff.

excommunicated the English bishops and Henry's advisers without daring to excommunicate the king.¹ The Pope's delays involved the king and the archbishop in such an embarrassing situation that the enemies reached a sort of truce. Becket returned to England in 1170 with no intention of yielding and we know how he was assassinated by four knights of the king's household. Henry II had not given instructions for the murder but, by his own confession, he had unwittingly encouraged his followers to it by his complaints against the archbishop.² At Avranches on 21st May, 1172 he submitted to a humiliating penitence.

This crime which had been promoted by zeal for the monarchy did not heighten the tension between Church and State. On the contrary, Henry II was now forced to make concessions and the Church was quite ready to express satisfaction. Freedom to appeal to the Holy See was recognized and criminous clerks, except in cases of high treason or crimes against the Forest Laws, were not subject to royal justice. The Church courts retained their competence not only in the affairs which were purely ecclesiastical and those which related to tenures of free alms but in the correction of sin (adultery, usury, etc.) and on questions of marriages, wills, and promises on oath ; the extent of Church jurisdiction was therefore, as on the Continent, very considerable. The appointment of beneficiaries by the patrons of churches, however, remained a temporal right and this principle, which was peculiar to England, was to involve important consequences at a later date. Finally Henry II and his sons retained control of episcopal and abbatial elections which only became free once more at the time of the Great Charter.

Among a small implacable section of the English clergy there remained a leavening of bitterness against the monarchy. They preserved their admiration for the holy martyr, Thomas Becket, and also for those who had offered him asylum— and they thus formed the nucleus of an English party supporting the Capetians in reaction against the tyranny of the Plantegenets. The great majority of the Clergy, however, showed no lasting hostility to the king because of the brutality

---

¹ There is a detailed account of Becket's stay in France in **CDXIX**, i, chap. xx–xxiii ; ii, chap. i–xvii.
² *De reconciliatione regis* in **CXVII**, vii, 514–15 ; **CCCXXXV**, 182–191.

ADMINISTRATION AND LEGISLATION 151

he had shown but remained faithful to Henry II and Richard and continued to furnish the Crown with advisers and officials.

Nevertheless this great struggle had not left the position of the monarchy unaffected.[1] In the Middle Ages, a king who was forced to do penitence could expect little good of his subjects for his authority was primarily based on the fear he inspired. Now, even in England, the great feudal lords had little love for Henry II. He was not ostentatious or vainly extravagant. He used his money for purposes of administration or corruption and kept the best hunting lands for himself when they were in the demesnes of his barons. He preferred diplomacy to war and took little pleasure in tournaments. The author of the *History of William the Marshal* says that in his time England was not a good place to live in except for the lesser country gentry. For the life of the chivalry and tournaments, one had to go to Normandy or Brittany.[2] There is little to suggest that the English nobility was very quick to feel the crushing weight of taxation but they were extremely dissatisfied by the encroachments of royal justice and the sheriffs whom the king no longer appointed from among the barons were frequently very ungraciously received when they came to enforce their claims to apprehend fugitives even within the castles. In short, there was general regret for the good regime of King Stephen and, in the year which followed the king's humiliation at Avranches, there was a growing belief that the time had come to shake off this yoke.

The royal prestige was so great and its administration already so strong that the rebellion would probably not have been very serious if its centre had not been in the royal family itself. It was Henry's sons and his wife Eleanor who were the principal promoters of the coalition of 1173 which set fire to the whole of the Angevin Empire and the danger was greater on the Continent than in England.[3] The counts of Leicester, Chester, and Norfolk and the Bishop of Durham had control of formidable castles in the centre and north of the island [4] and their rebellion had the support of

---

[1] On all that follows, see **DCXXVII**, i, 577–617 ; **CDLXXXVIII**, ii, chap. iv ; **DXCII**, chap. vii.
[2] **LVIII**, i, 56–7, lines 1532–1545.
[3] **DLXV**, ii, 165 ff. ; **CCCLX**, 21–49.
[4] Map of the Castles in **CDLXXXVIII**, ii, 149.

the King of Scotland, but they found no support among the rest of the population which is a fact of some significance. The severe administration which Henry II had instituted was satisfactory to almost all the clergy, to the smaller country gentry, to the free tenants, and to the citizens of the towns; led by the parvenu barons and the royal officials they conducted a good campaign in Henry's absence and forced the great Anglo-Norman counts to yield. Henry II, a conqueror on the Continent, showed his generosity when he returned to Britain and pardoned them. The family feuds and revolts which darkened the last year of his life only disturbed his French possessions.

During Richard's reign, part of the nobility accompanied him to the Holy Land and in spite of his mistakes and the treachery of his younger brother, John Lackland, he was able to spend almost his whole reign out of the kingdom without compromising the authority of the Crown. Peace was maintained during his absence by extremely crude police methods [1] and when John ascended the throne he had strong support.

We have just seen that Henry II in 1173–4 had fully tested the loyalty of the mercantile classes. We may wonder what he considered the political role of the English towns to be at this period. Could they give or had they given the Angevin kings the support which, as we shall see, the French communes had given to Philip Augustus?

The fact that in the thirteenth century the Plantegenets considered it an easy matter to summon representatives of the towns to certain " parlements " of the Court must not mislead us. We must not imagine that, apart from London, there were at that time important towns with extensive franchises enjoying the status of royal vassals. They were small semi-rural concentrations.[2] In spite of their commercial relations with Normandy, Poitou, and Flanders and the undoubted influence of Continental municipal customs on their own [3] they had followed only at a great distance and in a very hesitating fashion the twelfth century emancipation movement of the French towns. London alone

[1] **CXXXIII**, 257–8 (Royal edict of 1195). Cf. **DXLIII**, 110–16.
[2] The population of the largest, except for London, scarcely exceeded five thousand inhabitants (**CCCXXIV**, i, 73, n. 4).
[3] **DLXXVIII**, 245 ff.; **CLVIII**, 1st article, 73 ff.; **DCXXIX**, 60 ff.

was a great centre though extremely incongruous and cosmopolitan,[1] alone able to make an attempt to model itself on the French Communes. Its chief men were occasionally referred to as " great barons of the city ".[2] As one legate remarked, they were so to speak Magnates of the Realm.[3] They were discontented and the monarchy was forced to make concessions. Henry I had granted them the right to hold the farm of the City and the whole County of Middlesex directly and to elect their own sheriff. They took part in the election of Stephen and bound themselves under oath to drive out Matilda. They were held closely in check by Henry II but they took advantage of the absence of Richard and the conflict between William Longchamp and John Lackland to form themselves into a commune in 1191 and elect a mayor. Some of the citizens did not hesitate to say that their mayor was the only king they knew. On his return, Richard abolished the commune but allowed them to retain their mayor.[4] In the other towns,[5] the Plantegenets sold for ready cash judicial, commercial, and financial privileges,[6] in particular the right of collecting and paying directly into the Exchequer the " farm of the borough "[7] but they rarely allowed them to have elected officers. Henry II considered the grant of charters merely a means of enriching his revenues and, in fact, as a result he did nothing but confirm liberties previously granted by Henry I. Richard was rather more liberal largely because he was in more urgent need of money. Not until the reign of John Lackland, however, can we distinguish a policy favourable, at least

[1] On London in the twelfth century, see **CDXCIX**, chap. vii–ix.
[2] **DLXXVIII**, 252 ff.
[3] **LIV**, ii, 576.
[4] **DLXXXVI**, app. P. ; **DLXXVIII**; my study of London in **DCXXVII**, i, 846 ff. ; **XIV**, 481 ff. ; **DCLXXV**, chap. i–iv.
[5] Not only to the towns on the royal demesnes, but to those under seigniorial jurisdiction. Certain liberties were obtainable only from the king or with his authorization. Seigniorial towns frequently obtained charters simultaneously from their lord and the king. The charters of Leicester provide a typical example ; see **XV**, and the intro. p. xv ff.
[6] It is impossible to go into details here. See the bibliography in **DCXXVII**, i, 824–860, and iii, 648, 656 ; C.M.H., vi, 886–7, 898 ; Gross, Sources, §§ 24, 57. The reader will find a judicious selection of charters in **CCCXXIV**, vol. ii, in **CXXXIII**, and systematically classified texts with an important introduction in **XI**.
[7] On the *firma burgi* and the meaning of *liber burgus*, "borough," see **CCCXXIV**, i, 5 ff.; **DXXXII**, i, 634 ff.; **CDLIV**, 173–4; **DCXXIX**, 62; **DCXXVIII**, 821 ff.

intermittently, to the development of municipal liberties. It was on his accession and during the grave crisis of his reign—in 1204–5 and 1215–16—that John granted the majority of the sixty-one charters enrolled on the Charter Rolls. It was undoubtedly a fiscal expedient but it was also a means of securing allies. Two-thirds of these deeds are dated in 1199, 1200, or 1201.[1] At the same period, with an intention we shall emphasize later, John was multiplying his concessions to the towns of Normandy and Poitou. We must collate these facts to find their real significance: it is one of many proofs that the history of England at this period should never have been separated, as it has been by many scholars, from the history of the Angevin Empire.

[1] CLV, 102–3.

CHAPTER III

THE PLANTEGENETS' POLICY OF OVERLORDSHIP. THE CONTINENTAL POSSESSIONS

I

IRELAND, SCOTLAND, WALES

THE Norman and Angevin kings were the heirs of the Anglo-Saxon monarchy and had not given up any of their claims. Ethelred had formerly adopted the style of "Sovereign of the English race and King of all the Island of Britain and the neighbouring isles ". This was a nominal sovereignty about which Henry need have troubled little, especially when he had to maintain the huge structure of his French fiefs. He was not without justification for some anxiety lest he was going to see the adventurers of the Scottish borders and the petty Celtic kings of Wales invade his frontiers but he even launched an attack on Ireland from which he had nothing to fear and we are apparently driven to the conclusion that he had deliberately set out to establish throughout the British Isles his feudal supremacy at least.[1]

After 1155 the thoughts of Henry were turned on the conquest of Ireland. It is not easy to gather a correct impression of the place which Ireland occupied in Christian civilization at that time. The prejudices of certain scholars are likely to do little but lead the reader astray.[2] One thing seems certain—that the country was a prey to clan feuds and that only its poverty saved it from total conquest. Its petty kings were powerless to establish order and they had neither a disciplined army nor castles to defend their possessions against an invasion. The Roman Church hated the Celtic Church on account of its traditions of independence and because the most pious of the Irish clerks and monks

[1] On the whole of this question, see **DCXXVII**, i, 664-670.
[2] **CCCLXXIX**, i, p. xi.

called for radical reform in their vows. There is no cause for surprise, therefore, that Henry II considered the occupation of Ireland an easy matter and, according to John of Salisbury, obtained from the Pope Hadrian a Bull conferring Ireland on him by a hereditary title. He stayed in the island for a period of six months (1171-2), received the homage of numerous chiefs, and a decision was made to reform the Church, but, after his departure, no serious attempt was made to consolidate the conquest and John Lackland, created lord of the country by his father, succeeded in endangering it by his unheard of conduct.[1]

The mountaineers of Scotland and Wales would not allow themselves to remain subject for any length of time. They had taken advantage of Stephen's weakness. Henry II had demanded the restitution of the territories occupied by the King of Scotland and after the rising of 1173-4, in which William the Lion, the king, had been imprudent enough to take part, he occupied Edinburgh and several other places with garrisons and demanded homage from William for all his kingdom. But the feudal bonds which he wished to retie remained very slack and for four centuries Scotland was to remain a menace: it possessed a spirit of independence which led it into an alliance with France. The practical result of the action of Henry II was that the counties in the north of the kingdom which Scotland had been on the point of annexing were, henceforward, securely attached to England.[2] Henry made three expeditions under difficult conditions into Wales and he had to be satisfied with a suzerainty which troubled the two native kings very little. The Welsh were awaiting an opportunity to take up arms again and the folly of John provided them with it. The conquest of this wild country was not to be achieved until Edward I and then not without difficulty.[3]

All these wars to render Ireland, Wales, and Scotland subject to him date from the first half of Henry's reign. Subsequently other anxieties absorbed him and we must look elsewhere to assess the greatness of his reign.

[1] **CLXIII**, 41 ff. with the bibliography; **DLXXVIII**, n. vii and viii; **CDXCIV**, i, chap. iv, viii, ix; and ii, chap. xvi.
[2] **CXCIX**, i, bk. ii, chap. ii; **CDI**, 29.
[3] **CDXXIII**, ii, chaps. xiii-xvi; **DLXIV**, chap. vii; **CDLXXXIII**, chap. l.

THE PLANTEGENET'S POLICY

II

THE CONTINENTAL POSSESSIONS

Henry II and Richard Cœur de Lion had the cosmopolitan political ideas, tastes, and instincts of an emperor rather than of a king and this is the justification for the expression " Angevin Empire " which modern historians have invented. In any case, Henry II and Richard were more French than English. During a reign of thirty-four years and a half, Henry did not pass thirteen in England. He spent long periods on the Continent sometimes two years, four years, or even longer (at the beginning of his reign ; August, 1158–January, 1163 ; March, 1166–March, 1170).[1] As for Richard, he only made a few short visits to his English subjects.

The reason was that, as we have seen, the Plantegenets held the western half of France in fee. They held almost all the Channel coast, almost all the Atlantic seaboard: no mountain barriers cut up their possessions ; from Rouen, Caen, or Mans warriors, merchants, and pilgrims found their way towards the great commercial and religious centre of Tours and, from there, to Angers, Nantes, or even towards Poitiers, Bordeaux, and the Pyrenees.[2] Finally the rights in the County of Toulouse which Henry and Richard derived from Eleanor encouraged them to hope that one day they would reach the Mediterranean. The French demesnes from which their family originated were their special care but they could not maintain them without constant watch on their vassals and officials, stamping out rebellions, resisting the Capetians. The task was rendered more complicated because from Normandy to Aquitaine the demesnes of the Angevin dynasty varied constantly

We shall attempt here some description of their administration. A complete description has never been made doubtless because research has not yet produced all the materials necessary for a synthesis. Noteworthy pieces of work which, however, have not thoroughly illuminated the questions, give us an opportunity to describe Norman institutions, but for Anjou, Brittany under the Plantegenets, or Aquitaine we have very little precise information and the sources themselves are very scanty.

[1] See p. 108 above. [2] **DXLII**, 14.

THE ANGEVIN EMPIRE

A general survey cannot be attempted. Henry II, a great legislator in England, did not attempt to coordinate the laws and administration of his Continental possessions. It is absurd to say [1] that he sought to make Brittany an English province. We cannot argue from the subsidies of 1166 and 1184 for the defence of the Holy Land or the Saladin Tithe of 1188 [2] imposed on all subjects, for these were obligations of a religious character which naturally had a general or even international character. The inquiries which Henry II instituted to gain a knowledge of local customs shows that he had every intention of respecting them as far as he considered possible.[3] It is not that he was precluded from imposing his decisions on a general scale. He gave the Assize of Arms of 1181 [4] the force of law in his overseas possessions and he introduced, even into Normandy and Brittany, the Angevin practice of divided succession which prevented subinfeudation in cases of division.[5] He thus departed somewhat from the advice his father had given him not to introduce into Anjou the customs of Normandy or England and vice versa.[6] On the occasion of a petition addressed to him by the religious community of Grammont he decided that his subjects could not be forced to provide sureties to their lords " above all in his *potestas* namely in Normandy, Aquitaine, Anjou, and Brittany ".[7] On the other hand we have seen how his officials were to some extent transferable from one country to another and that Henry made changes primarily based on the needs of the administration and the capabilities of his servants but he certainly never thought of a systematic unification which everyone advised him against. Even if that had been his ambition, he could never have achieved it ; he did not possess the same means of action throughout his *potestas*. Normandy, which was very different from the other Continental possessions, alone had a strongly centralized administration. In Brittany or Aquitaine, for example, there was no question of introducing similar institutions, the power of the Plantegenets must be wielded there very prudently by other means.

---

[1] As de la Borderie has done : **CCCXCI**, iii, 273.
[2] **CCXI**, ii, 7, 55, 58 ff.   [3] **DXLII**, 24, 25.
[4] **XVIII**, i, 269–270. On this assize see p. 145 above.
[5] **DXLII**, 68, 98 ff.
[6] **LXIV**, 224.   [7] **CVI**, iii, 63–4, n. 507.

THE PLANTEGENET'S POLICY

Within the *potestas* we can distinguish three groups: Normandy, Brittany and the Loire country, and Aquitaine.

III

NORMANDY

Normandy and England in the twelfth century had very close affinities—political, social, and intellectual. They were much more alike than Normandy and Aquitaine.[1]

The administration in the two countries had developed according to the same tendencies in the hands of men who, frequently, started their career in one and finished in the other. After the long troubles in the Duchy which followed the death of William the Conqueror,[2] Henry I had re-established unity and order and built up a strong administration. It was the work of a long time and absorbed a great deal of his activity. He had revoked the alienation of demesne, probably created the Exchequer which we, subsequently, find in operation, organized a group of judges who went on circuit, utilized the system of sworn inquests, and inaugurated legal procedure which Henry II elaborated and which was formulated by Glanville.[3] Normandy fell into anarchy again during Stephen's reign.[4] We have seen that it was Matilda's husband, Geoffrey Plantegenet, who took up Henry's work and consolidated it; he assumed the title of duke in 1144 and in 1149 he handed a pacified Normandy back to his son Henry who governed it with the assistance of Matilda.[5] Henry II achieved in Normandy a work of some magnitude, comparable to that which has made his name immortal in England. Richard and John altered nothing but they took full advantage of the institutions and resources he had built up.

During the second half of the twelfth century, the ducal Court functioned like the king's Court in England or France sometimes as a formal assembly [6] sometimes as an administration. The officials were very numerous. Some of them acted

[1] CCCI, 190–3. [2] CCXXXII, chap. iii, v, vi.
[3] CCCL, 85 ff. [4] LXXXVI, v, 56 ff.; CCXXII, 41 ff.
[5] CCCL, 128 ff.; CCXXI, 49 ff. See p. 105 above.
[6] These assemblies have none of the characteristics of a regional parliament. The king and duke consults his loyal subjects, who are present, but he has his own way and he frequently asks their advice on extremely general questions not specifically concerned with Normandy.

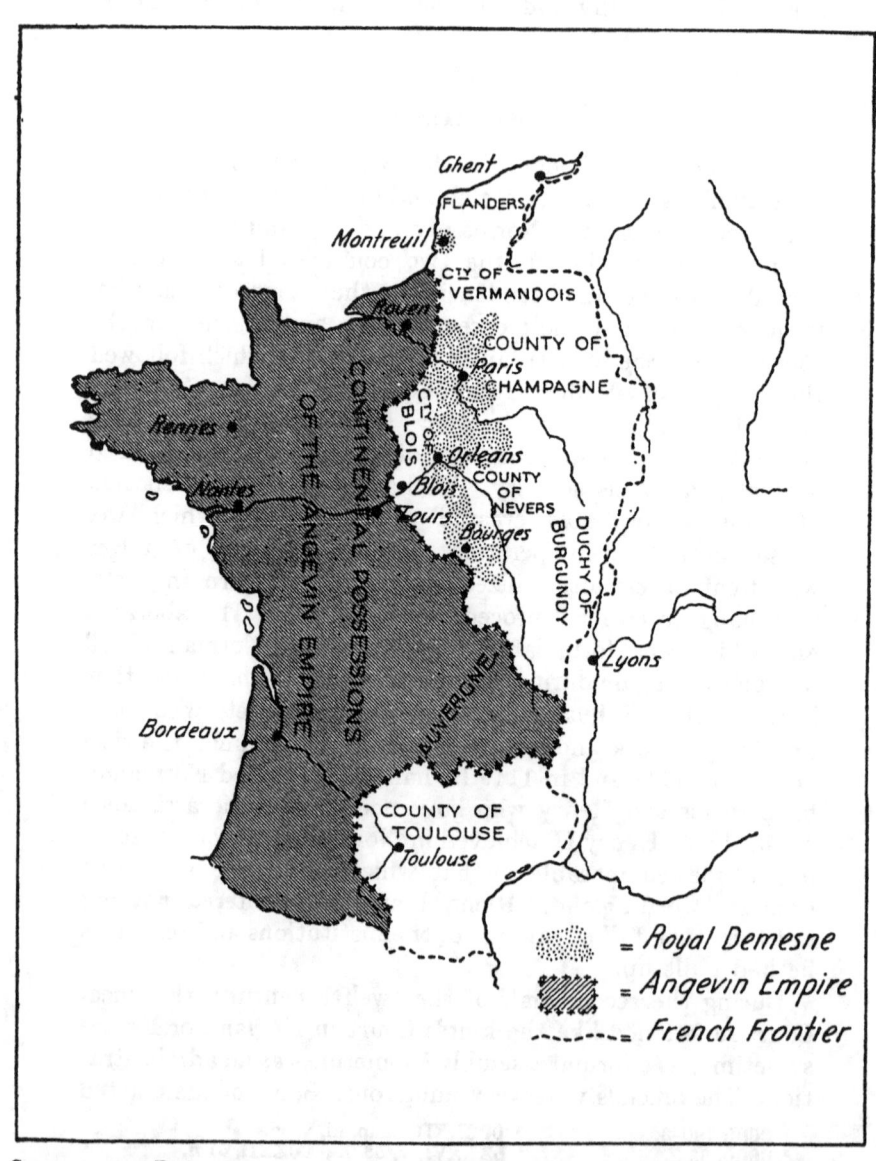

Continental Possessions of the Angevin Empire and the Capetian Demesne in the reign of Louis VII.

THE PLANTEGENET'S POLICY 161

in Normandy and in England without distinction. The Chancery, for instance, which travelled with the king, was a common service most often under the direction of a Norman.

There were, however, great officials particularly for Normandy—a butler, a constable, and a grand seneschal.[1] According to the Great Customal of Normandy the last named looked after the lands and hunting country of the prince, visited every part of the duchy once every three years, and was concerned with the preservation of custom and the peace. He received the complaints of the people, ordered inquiries, and saw that no crime went unpunished.[2] At the same time he was the fount of justice. Sometimes he might be a lord, at others a churchman like Rotrou de Warwick, Bishop of Evreux, or Richard d'Ilchester, Bishop of Winchester. The longest tenure of the office was that of William Fitz Ralph (1178-1200). He was, indeed, a viceroy, a tireless inspector, and legislator. He had been an itinerant justice and sheriff in England.[3] After him, in four years, John Lackland nominated three seneschals in succession. Philip Augustus even more distrustful was to suppress the office. The only position in Normandy comparable to it was that of Constable which the lords of Hommet held as an hereditary fief. The defection of William du Hommet in 1204 was to be one of the chief causes of the success of Philip Augustus.[4]

Local administration prior to the Plantegenets was primarily in the hands of some twenty viscounts who were frequently hereditary.[5] Henry II decided that they could not help him in the work of reorganizing the demesne which he was engaged on throughout his reign. He carried through a reform which had been foreshadowed by Henry I and Geoffrey.[6] At the same time that he was proceeding with inquiries for the resumption of lands and income which had been alienated[7] he appointed new agents of justice and administration called bailiffs[8]; the term was no more precise than our expression " trusted servant " and was often

---

[1] **DCL**, 102-3, 109 ff., 143 ff.
[2] **XXVIII**, ii, 12-15.
[3] **CLIX**, **CCLI**, x, 266-7; **CVI**, intro., 421, 445, 455 ff., 476 ff., 481 ff.; **DCL**, 155 ff.; **DXLII**, 69-71; **CCCL**, 183-4.
[4] **CVI**, vol. ii, n. 549; intro. 429-430, 485; **DXLII**, 255 ff.
[5] **CCLI**, x, 263 ff.; **CVI**, intro., 212 ff.; **DCL**, 99-100; **DXLII**, 62 ff.
[6] **DXLII**, 66-7; **CCCL**, 151-2; **DCL**, 98 ff.
[7] **CCCL**, 159-160; **DXLII**, 71.
[8] Already in a charter, 1151-3; **CVI**, i, 49 n., 43.

used to designate subordinate officers. Both the word and the office were to have a conspicuous history; the Norman bailiff and the English sheriff were the prototypes of the Capetian bailiff. The origins of the Norman bailiffs are extremely obscure because we cannot discover the exact meanings of the words used in charters and probably the clerks who drafted them would find difficulty in giving a precise definition. In any case, documents of 1172 prove that, at that date, there were bailiwicks referred to by the name of the officers who administered them; for example, the north of the Cotentin is the bailiwick of Osbert de la Heuse and Pont Audemer is the centre of the jurisdiction of William de Maupalu.[1] That designation of the area by the name of its official is one of the characteristics of French and Norman bailiwicks of the early period.[2]

We should like to be able, for the sake of clarity, to say that the bailiff replaced the viscount and that, henceforward, it was he who held the castle, did justice, and collected the revenues and we have some examples of it. But the officers of bailiff, viscount, castellan, provost could exist side by side, be added to one another, and duplicate themselves. In the Bessin, we see an hereditary viscount, a castellan, a bailiff, and two provosts. In the Vau de Vire, there were two bailiffs at once, a viscount, and a provost.[3] Such a confusion must not be considered something extraordinary for the Middle Ages. Officers duplicated rather than replaced one another.

The functions of these officers, new or old, was fiscal and judiciary. Finance and justice in Normandy was based on old and well established foundations which Henry II had only to strengthen. We have only fragmentary, though very important, documents on Norman finances in the twelfth century.[4] The innumerable writs of authority without which no payment could be made have almost all perished and so have the texts of inquiries conducted to re-establish royal rights. The material which we possess seems to show that the

[1] **DCX**, pp. xxxiii–xxxiv; **CVI**, intro., 409, 490–1; **DXLII**, 72–3.
[2] There was nothing in France comparable to the old traditional and permanent division into shires which existed in England. The Carolingian county had not persisted as an administrative unit. Hence the vagueness of the early bailiwicks (**DXLII**, 34–5, 50–1).
[3] **DXLII**, 103 ff.
[4] On all that follows, see **CCLI, CCCL**, 159–160; **DXLII**, 64–5, 75–9.

THE PLANTEGENET'S POLICY 163

ducal demesnes, which were very important at the time of William the Conqueror, had been pillaged, usurped, and whittled away during the civil wars of the twelfth century and the great rebellion of 1173-4. What was left did not bring in more than 12,000 marks. We have seen that the Capetian demesne consisted of scattered rights and possessions and the ducal demesnes in Normandy were very similar. For instance, in the diocese of Rouen, the towns of Rouen, Dieppe, Arques, Lyons, Lillebonne, Montivilliers, Fécamp, and Blosseville had the duke as their lord; that is to say, there were properties and rights which he had not alienated and that, in some parts, his farmers could raise quit rents on the houses; in the viscounty of Avranches, a fragment on the conditions of the domanial rights tells us that the City and Tower of Avranches and the meadows and chestnut grove of the town belonged to Henry's demesnes.[1] The king had extensive forests rigorously patrolled for the sake of his game. The fines and compositions arising from ducal justice and the profits on the English and Angevin money which was in circulation in the duchy [2] and the commercial and fishing rights were, however, the most important resources. Finally, in cases of particular emergency, the king could levy extraordinary taxation, feudal aids, and scutages. In short, the Duchy constituted a source of finance of considerable importance for the Plantegenets all the more since money was becoming abundant and inconvenient payments in kind had for a long time been almost obsolete. Richard and John took undue advantages of these resources: we should almost be justified in saying that they drained Normandy of its strength.

The financial administration bore many close resemblances to that of England; it had shown parallel developments in the two countries.[3] The Court of the king-duke when concerned with financial business is generally called "*Curia domini regis ad scaccarium*"[4] the king's Court sitting at the Exchequer. The Exchequer was at Caen where the treasure was kept and, as in England, it had two sessions a year at

---

[1] CVI, intro., 345 ff.
[2] Details in CCLI, x, 193 ff.
[3] CCLI, CVI, intro., 333 ff.; CCCL, 159-160, 174 ff.; DXLII, 64 ff., 73 ff.; DCL, 116 ff., 163.
[4] CCCII, 683.

Easter and Michaelmas under the direction of the seneschal of Normandy and the treasurer. Besides the important individuals who were known as Barons of the Exchequer there were, at the time of Henry I, Justiciars who were the technical officials. Under Henry II there were still barons but the title did not necessarily imply magnates; it was assumed by the specialists, and the bishops who appear at the Exchequer at Caen at the end of the reign are veteran officials rewarded with benefices. The system of accounting was the same, in principle, as in England but the existence side by side of farmers, old and new, viscounts, provosts, bailiffs, who like the sheriffs across the Channel were responsible for collecting the moneys and rendering account made the Norman Roll of the Exchequer much more complicated. It was the task of the Exchequer to receive and check the revenues and subsidies, to judge matters of dispute, and to audit the accounts. When the bishop Richard d'Ilchester, an official of the English Exchequer, became Seneschal of Normandy in 1176, the Norman Exchequer received a considerable stimulus. The farms were revised and many arrears were realized dating back, in some cases, twenty years. In short the Anglo-Norman financial administration was alike on both sides of the Channel in its methods, its competence, and the relative abundance of the resources with which it provided the sovereign.

The title of Exchequer was frequently given in Plantegenet Normandy to the ducal Court considered not as a Chamber of Account but as a Court. In the twelfth century the Court of Justice was called the Exchequer if it sat at Caen in the Exchequer chamber. It was a question of location. The Court of the king duke, in any case, was not divided into strictly specialized divisions and the same people might well be concerned with both justice and the finances. Fiscal controversy, moreover, provides a link between the two administrations. The Court of Justice, however, did not sit only at Caen; it was essentially itinerant. The Great Seneschal, the Constable of Normandy, and the bishops had, on these occasions, the title of "justices" and presided at "plenary assizes" with the assistance of "men of importance" and legal specialists.[1] They judged issues concerning lords,

---

[1] See the lists in **CVI**, particularly intro., 347, 349, and vol. ii, n. 647.

THE PLANTEGENET'S POLICY 165

abbeys, and matters which affected the king. Once or twice a year, in each viscounty, a less important assize was held, which, however, was just as much a session of the Court, for minor cases. There was a local session held once a month by the viscount or bailiff. Finally, the lords, lay and ecclesiastical, had not lost their rights of justice. Some of them even continued to judge murders, highway crimes, offences against the coinage, and other important cases constituting the " pleas of the sword " but this was rare and the higher justice was almost always reserved for the ducal judges. We can see that the administration of justice in Normandy and England shows, in many respects, similar characteristics. Even the terms *justiciœ itinerantes* and *assisœ* are common to the two countries.[1]

This is equally true of procedure. Its development was parallel in the two countries. The sworn inquest and the deposition of witnesses were Carolingian usages which the Church had preserved in the break-up of the tenth century. They can be found before the time of Henry II in England and Normandy alike. In particular, Henry I had made use of them to determine the possessions of the Bishop of Bayeux. It seems probable that they were introduced into England by William the Conqueror for primarily fiscal purposes such as the collection of the data for Domesday Book; he also brought with him the barbarous system of the judicial duel which roused much dissatisfaction among the English. The lawyer king, Henry II, earned the glory of generalizing the system of juries. By a letter from the Chancery (the writ of English law) Norman plaintiffs could take advantage of the " recognizance " or local inquest in place of trial by judiciary duel or by the oaths of witnesses in support of the suitor. However, the court could refuse an inquest when the papers of the case provided sufficient information. Here is the record of an assize held at Caen in 1185 : it has a quite modern atmosphere : it is concerned with a case over the right to present to a benefice and the judges are seated round the Exchequer table.

Ralph Fitz Eudo has produced a writ (which he has obtained) from the lord the king to the Assize at Caen to William Fitz Ralph,

[1] CCCL, 164 ff., 178 ff.; DCL, 112 ff., 164 ff., 220 ff., 231 ff.; **DXLII**, 79 ff.; CCXXI, 128–130. Cf. the disputed theories of CCCII, 684 ff., and CCCXLVI, 43 ff.

at that time Seneschal of Normandy, and to the other justices holding assize at that time. By which writ the lord the king orders recognizance to be made by verdict of loyal subjects to discover who presented the last beneficiary, now dead, to the church of Carpiquet. On this the dispute arose between the Abbess of (Holy Trinity of) Caen and Ralph Fitz Eudo. The abbess has said that the church of Holy Trinity has held the right since its foundation by gift of King William and Queen Matilda and that it has been confirmed to the abbey by the charter of King William and of King Henry son of the Empress Matilda. After hearing the matters, the barons of the Exchequer, William Fitz Ralph and the other justices of the lord the king, in the Exchequer, have considered that there is no need to make recognizance and that the abbess should not be called to plead about this church which was confirmed to the abbey by charters of the lords of Normandy. Therefore Ralph Fitz Eudo has been nonsuited in his claim against the abbey for this church by judgment of the barons of the Exchequer in the Exchequer in the presence of William Fitz Ralph.[1] . . . (twenty-four names follow.)

We have seen the system of the writ, the inquest, and possessory actions to prevent evictions by force in use in England but it is almost certain that the normal use of the inquest in cases concerning property or possession began in Normandy in consequence of an assize or law due to Geoffrey Plantegenet. Henry II ensured the systematic extension of the procedure first in Normandy and then, some years later, in England. Normandy, however, did not maintain its pre-eminence for the full development of the jury was confined to England.[2]

Even when we have taken full account of the reserves which made the persistence of Anglo-Saxon institutions in England of such great importance, Normandy remained, at that period, the basis of the English monarchy and of its expansion on the Continent. The Plantegenets were as powerful there as across the Channel; they imposed a minutely regulated feudal military service and they possessed castles of tremendous strength which they continued to build. The coronation oath of the duke, corresponding to the consecration oath in England, did not impose any practical restraint on the power of Henry II. Above all there was not so much an Anglo-Norman patriotism as an Anglo-Norman hostility to France.

It is true that Normandy had not the strong unity which it had in the time of William the Conqueror and its character

[1] CVI, ii, 647.
[2] XXVIII, ii, p. cxiv, clvii ; DCL, 194 ff. ; DXLII, 86-93 ; and, particularly, CCCL, 149 ff., 196 ff.

THE PLANTEGENET'S POLICY

was complicated by the existence of very divergent interests, but the policy of Louis VI, Louis VII, and Philip Augustus contained little to attract the Norman to the Capetian cause. Norman literature of the period reflects only contempt; the French are constant subjects of mockery as poverty-stricken and mean. For instance, Wace in one section of his *History of the Normans* composed in 1174 after the attempt of Louis VII to take possession of Rouen writes that the French are false and treacherous, covetous and greedy, always seeking to dispossess the Normans. King Henry must be on his guard against them. But the Normans are quite capable of keeping them in check by the mighty blows they strike at them and King Henry is so wise, so brave, and so powerful that he can make Louis and his men tremble.[1]

IV

Anjou, Touraine, and Maine

Anjou, Touraine, and Maine did not cause Henry II such constant anxiety as Normandy, which was always threatened by the Capetians; they did not provide him with either the same resources or the same models of justice and administration. Anjou was not as advanced as Normandy either from the point of view of justice and procedure or of the editing of deeds or of executive and fiscal organization. The Loire countries were administered by provosts, local seneschals, and bailiffs in the primitive sense of the term, subordinate officials who, by 1190, had no functions in common with the Norman or Capetian bailiffs. The most original institution was that of Seneschal of Anjou, an important official who generally presided in the count's court at Angers in place of the king count.[2] Almost throughout his reign, Henry II was content to leave the office in the hands of a local noble, Stephen de Marsai. There is a charter which contains an account of what he understood as his duties. A local lord,

---

[1] **DIV**, 44 ff. Cf. the map of Normandy given in **DXXXIX**, ann. 1906, p. 633 ff., and **CCCXLIX**, chap. vi.
[2] **CVI**, i, n. 37, 118, 131; ii, n. 684, etc.; and intro., 220, 378; **CLX**, 1st part, ii, 10 ff. and *passim*; **CCCL**, 123 ff., 136 ff., 146, 230 ff.; **DXLII**, 37-9; **CCXXI**, 97 ff., 108 ff.

Hamelin, had wronged the monks of Marmoutiers who complained to the king. Stephen de Marsai somewhat reluctantly summoned the guilty party who refused to appear.

> Because of Hamelin's noble status, I did not take any notice of his injustice to the monks whereupon the monks told the lord the king that for justice I could never be found but that for injustice I was always available. Learning this, the king became extremely angry with me and did not hesitate to make the most violent threats. I left him in fear and summoned Hamelin.[1]

The monks gained their case but Stephen remained a somewhat unreliable official. On the accession of Richard he pretended that the treasury at Chinon was empty. Richard threw him into prison and made him disgorge.[2]

At times of emergency, the kings of England, lacking a stable administration, were forced to entrust the Loire provinces to a sort of viceroy. During the great feudal revolt of 1173–4, Henry gave charge of Anjou and Maine to his faithful follower Maurice de Craon.[3] In 1200, John Lackland, in a fit of uneasiness, created a hereditary dapiferate for William des Roches who was at the same time Seneschal of Anjou, Maine, and Touraine.[4]

The Angevin kings thus provided a baron with the dangerous weapon which they had used themselves against the Capetians for, by right of their position as counts of Anjou, they claimed to exercise the office of Seneschal of France by hereditary title and thus to destroy the long standing rights of the French kings in the churches of Tours like St. Martin and St. Julian. To maintain this claim, Henry II commissioned his retainer, Hugh de Cleefs, to compose a "Treatise on the Mayoralty and Seneschalship of France" in which it is extremely difficult to distinguish exactly the genuine from the false.[5]

It was probably in 1158 that Henry II produced this strange document. He raised the matter to provide himself with a title which he lacked for seizing Brittany. Louis VII, a man of little subtlety, allowed himself to be persuaded.

---

[1] **CVI**, i, n. 200 ; cf. the intro., 459 ff.
[2] **LVIII**, i, 331 ff., line 9177 ff.
[3] **CXCVIII**, i, 82.
[4] **CCLXVII**, vol. xxxii, 104–5 ; **CCLXXXII**.
[5] Texts in **CVI**, n. 87 ; **CCCXLVI**, 63–8. Cf. **CDXLI**, 1–38 ; **CLXVI**, 252–260.

Henry II entered Brittany as Seneschal of the King of France, he forced the Count Conan to resign the County of Nantes and, some years later, completed the conquest by marrying his son Geoffrey to Constance the daughter of Conan.[1] Of this marriage came Arthur the rival and victim of John Lackland. As long as he lived, Henry remained master of Brittany; he put down anarchy and kept peace for the lesser men and he was probably the creator of the eight bailiwicks administered by seneschals. He introduced the principle of Norman law into the law of Brittany and one of the chief landmarks in Breton law, the Assize of Count Geoffrey, bears the name of his son. He forbade the division of baronies and knights' fees.[2] On the whole, it was during the short period of Plantegenet rule that Brittany was brought into the orbit of western civilization.

V

Aquitaine

The government of Aquitaine was a difficult and thankless task for Henry and his sons; in fact, it is not until the thirteenth century that we can say the country possesses an English administration. In the twelfth century, Aquitaine continued to present a picture of feudal anarchy comparable to that which had existed throughout France in the time of Hugh Capet. The reign of William VIII, Eleanor's father, had been nothing but a succession of deeds of violence, brigandage, and petty wars which were always welcome to the duke though he was not always victorious.[3] That is the reason why, having no male heir, he had entrusted his daughter Eleanor to the king Louis the Fat to avoid the disintegration of his duchy already shorn of many of its dependencies during the two previous centuries.

After his marriage with Eleanor, Louis VII was quite incapable of keeping a hold on the reins. His officials could not keep order and it was only with great difficulty that

---

[1] CCCLVIII, 68 ff.; CCCXCI, iii, 271 ff.; CCXXII, chap. ii.
[2] LV, i, 146–7; CVI, intro., 220, 413, 479, 487; DXXVI, 117 ff., CCV, 55 ff.; CDXCIII, p. vii ff., 22 ff.; CCXI, i, 232–3.
[3] DLXV, ii, 1 ff.

they raised any income now and again.¹ What were the feudal ties which bound the Gascon and Poitevin nobility to the Duke ? Historians have rarely defined them either owing to lack of illustrative texts or because the bonds remained extremely indeterminate. The Count of Angoulême claimed for the majority of his fiefs to owe homage only to the King of France.² Even minor lordlings, the "bachelors" of Poitou, refused feudal duties to the Plantegenets.³ In general their oaths were of little practical value and the disloyalty of the Poitevin nobles was proverbial. "An extremely warlike country of uncertain loyalty" said William the Breton⁴ at a later date. Neither the clergy, although loaded with gifts, nor the towns offered any stable support.

The only policy to follow, therefore, was to maintain and extend the ducal demesne, to hold strong castles to make traffic possible and uphold the prestige of the sovereign, to put officials in those positions from which finance could be raised, and to entrust the general supervision of the country to a few dependable men. That is what Henry II did. His original demesne consisted of the provostships of Poitiers, Niort, Benon, La Rochelle, St. Jean-d'Angely, Fontenay-le-Comte, and several scattered holdings.⁵ He bought the country of La March for fifteen thousand pounds and during his reign and his sons' the County of Angoulême, the Viscounty of Limoges, and the County of Périgord were occupied at different times and these ancient dependencies of Aquitaine Berry, Auvergne, Toulousain, were the subject of disputes with the Capetians. The rich county of Angoulême with its rich countryside, its strong castles, and its main routes from Paris to Bordeaux was a particularly valuable prey. John Lackland lost control of it in 1200 when he signed the peace of Goulet with Philip Augustus but he recovered it shortly afterwards on his marriage to Isabel, the heir to the county.

This policy could be maintained only at the price of incessant war and it demanded the almost constant presence of the king or some members of his family. Richard Cœur de Lion passed a great part of his life between the Loire

---

¹ See, in particular, a letter from the Seneschal William de Mauzé to Suger : H.F., xv, 486.
² CLXXXIV, 1 ff.   ³ DLXV, ii, 369, 385.
⁴ LVII, 282, line 24.   ⁵ DXLII, 42.

THE PLANTEGENET'S POLICY 171

and the Pyrenees both as Duke of Aquitaine during his father's lifetime and during his own reign. Eleanor, who only died in 1204 full of years but still vigorous and alert, played an important part in the history of Aquitaine on several occasions. She was mistress of the county in her own right and it was under her direction that her young son Richard enjoyed the ducal prerogatives from 1169 onwards. Eleanor settled herself in the palace at Poitiers and would have remained there if she had not rashly taken part in stirring up the great revolt of 1173 against her husband who held her in captivity for twelve years until 1185 when he made use of her to recover Aquitaine from Richard who was in revolt. On the accession of John she did homage in person to Philip Augustus for the Duchy of Aquitaine.

She made a long progress through the country and it was thanks to her that her son, whose enemies were rallying to Arthur's cause,[1] did not lose Aquitaine.

Even more than in Normandy the essential weapon of domination was the château. Since the service of Guard and Host could not be regularly exacted, bands of mercenaries like that of the famous Mercadier[2] were made responsible for holding the fortified places at considerable expense to the local population. Above the castelans was the seneschal. The creation of this important office appears to have been the work of Eleanor's father, William VIII, who borrowed the idea from his neighbour the Count of Anjou. Nobles of the district held the title at first. One of them, Ralph de Faie, Eleanor's uncle, was excommunicated for his exactions at the expense of the Church. Subsequently, Henry II tried to secure the discharge of the office by an Englishman, the Count of Salisbury, to whom he gave very extensive powers. An important Poitevin noble, Hugh de Lusignan, killed the Englishman with a lance thrust in 1168 and Henry returned to the practice of appointing a local man. Richard Cœur de Lion seems to have been more fortunate in his administration; he was not lacking in political intelligence and immediately on his accession he appointed as seneschal an old servant who had given frequent proof of bravery and ability—Pierre Bertin, previously Provost of Benon: Pierre

[1] **DLXV**, ii, 148 ff., 316–17, 333 ff., 350 ff.; **CDXXIV**, 24.
[2] **CCCXI**, 421 ff.

Bertin suppressed revolt without ceremony and thanks to him the Plantegenets retained Poitou while Richard was absent on his Eastern adventures. Pierre Bertin had charge only of Poitou; Gascony formed a second seneschalship entrusted to the loyal Geoffrey de la Celle. John was not able to maintain this organization. From the time when he received the duchy from his mother's hands confusion and intolerance marked the administration of Aquitaine. During the first three years of his reign, he had sometimes two seneschalships sometimes only one; sometimes they were left in the hands of dependable men French or English, at others they were abandoned to local barons or mercenary leaders.[1] Fear of seeing Poitou take up Arthur's cause appeared to have sent John mad. Happily for him the Poitevins were no more anxious to accept the domination of the King of France than his and they only sought their independence.

VI

Relations of the Plantegenets with the Nobility, Clergy, and Towns of the Continental Possessions

The administration of the Plantegenets, able in Normandy still amorphous in Aquitaine, seemed rigorous to the nobility.[2] In Normandy they had, for a long time, been controlled and the Feudal System functioned extremely logically entirely to the advantage of the suzerain but the Norman barons were held in check by fear alone as the rising of 1173 clearly shows. Outbursts of loyalist enthusiasm stimulated by the bravery and generosity of Richard Cœur de Lion and examples of unshakable allegiance like that of William the Marshal are sufficient to prove nothing more than a sincere attachment. Even in Normandy many nobles were in need and ready to support the highest bidder. In Anjou, Henry II could only make sure of his possession of the country in the early part of his reign at the price of a war against his own brother Geoffrey aided by a powerful Poitevin baron, the Viscount of Thouars.[3] In the south-western area the typical

---

[1] **CVI**, intro., 220, 369, 411, 416; **DLXV**, ii, 14, 136, 204, 263, 279, 300–1, 312, 317, 349, 368 ff., 389 ff., 415; **DXLII**, 39–41.
[2] **DXLII**, 52 ff.; **DXXXIX**, ann. 1906, pp. 636–7; **CCXXII**, 57 ff.
[3] **DLXV**, ii, 112 ff., 139, 147; **CCCLVIII**, 94–6.

THE PLANTEGENET'S POLICY 173

baronial figure at this period is Bertrand de Born, the warrior poet, an insufferable bully who found pleasure in nothing but slaughter and arson; this monomaniac has been represented as a southern patriot seeking to defend his " nationality " but he showed no reluctance to change sides when his love of battle or self interest recommended it.[1] The energy of Henry II during the early years of his reign was largely engaged in suppressing feudal risings in Poitou. The counts of Angoulême, La Marche, and Périgord, the viscounts of Thouars and Limoges, the lords of Saintonge and, south of the Garonne, the Count of Bigorre were violent enemies. In 1173-4, with the assistance of Eleanor and the king's sons, they found allies in every part of his dominions and all but overthrew him.[2] After that heated incident Richard became for several years his father's faithful lieutenant and passed his time in fighting and ravaging the country. He formed in Poitou an association of knights, the Pacifiques, to exterminate the brigands. After becoming king, Richard, after his Eastern crusade, returned to Poitou to end his life of battles. Covertly encouraged by Philip Augustus, the Poitevin barons remained throughout the enemies of the Plantegenets.[3]

The brutality of Richard did not find any more docile victims in the Bretons. In 1196 he attempted to force them to give up to him his nephew Arthur. They refused and appealed to the King of France. Richard subjected Brittany to widespread devastation which had no result except to exasperate the population, and the Bishop of Vannes who had charge of Arthur gave him up to Philip Augustus.[4] When Richard died before the castle of Chalus, the nobility of Brittany, of the Loire Valley, and northern Poitou recognized Arthur as their lord.

In principle the cause of the Clergy was inseparable from that of the prince; it was the Archbishop of Rouen who girded on the new Duke of Normandy the sword of the duchy; the new Duke of Aquitaine was proclaimed Abbot of Saint Hilary de Poitiers and went to the cathedral of

---

[1] **CCXXIV**, 97-105. Cf. his "sirventes" with translation in **CXCIII**.
[2] See p. 151 above.
[3] **DLXV**, ii, 134 ff., 173 ff., 202 ff.; **CDXXIV**, 17 ff.; **CLXXXIV**, 5 ff.; **CCXI**, i, 212 ff., 271 ff.; iii, 17, 75 ff., and *passim*.
[4] **CCXI**, iii, 127 ff.

Limoges to receive the ring of St. Valery among the customary acclamations. The majority of the charters of the Plantegenets concerned with their overseas possessions are grants and confirmations of privileges of all sorts in favour of the churches.[1] In return, in almost every case, they claimed the right to secure the appointment of prelates acceptable to them and exacted the regale. In the two lines, from William the Conqueror to Geoffrey Plantagenet, their ancestors had bequeathed them a tradition of authority which they maintained in spite of the progress of the Papacy and the development of the Gregorian spirit. Henry II and Richard refused entry to their dominions to the papal legates, resisted the encroachments arising from the new Canon Law, maintained their right to intervene in elections even in important semi-independent fiefs like the Viscounty of Limoges.[2]

In Normandy, in spite of this tyranny, the Norman bishops displayed a loyalty to the Plantegenets which only the extravagance of John Lackland could shake.[3] In Aquitaine and Poitou, on the other hand, the clergy resisted in the first place because the general powers of the Plantegenets were not firmly established and also because Louis VI forfeited the authority of the prince in part in order that the Church should favour the marriage of his son with Eleanor. He had yielded to the Archbishop of Bordeaux and to the bishops of Poitiers, Perigueux, Angoulême, Saintes, and Agen " entire canonical freedom in the election of bishops and abbots without obligations of homage, oath, or faith ".[4] As a consequence, the Archbishop of Bordeaux, Geoffrey du Lauroux, considered himself an independent lord and claimed to reign over the Bordelais. Henry II and Richard frequently succeeded, however, in dominating the elections and getting their candidates accepted. But there were, particularly at Bordeaux, Limoges, Poitiers, conflict, violence, and brutal expulsions. John Lackland, on Eleanor's advice, made up his mind to put himself under the protection of the Archbishop of Bordeaux, Helie de Malmort. Although in general

---

[1] **CVI** and intro., 152. Catalogue of Richard's deeds in **CCXI**, ii and iii, appendices.
[2] **CCCLXIX**, 455 ff.; **CLXXX**, 310 ff.; **CCCL**, 153–4, 170–3; **DCL**, 79, 82 ff.; **CCXXI**, 163 ff.
[3] **CDXCVI**, 16 ff.
[4] Text quoted in **CCCLVIII**, 9, n. 2.

THE PLANTEGENET'S POLICY 175

he had little to recommend him, he was faithful to John and helped to preserve Aquitaine for him.[1]

Between the Plantegenets and the burgesses of their Continental possession there was no open alliance. Even in Normandy they measured their concessions very narrowly. They established communes primarily to provide soldiers.[2]

For a long time the English kings had been thinking of granting special liberties to the towns which, by their position, commanded the entrance into Normandy and were grouped round a castle. Verneuil, built on the frontier by Henry I,[3] due one day to repulse the attacks of Philip Augustus, so decisively fell into this category and so did Breteuil an important stronghold, established by William the Conqueror, the customs of which were a model for the lords who founded towns in the Welsh marches.[4] The case of Rouen, however, is typical as an example of Plantegenet policy in this matter. It received valuable privileges of a judicial, financial, and economic character without the right of self government by charters of Henry I, Geoffrey, and Henry Plantegenet. About 1170 it assumed the title of *Commune* and its *Établissements*, so famous in the history of urban liberties, were drawn up.[5] But, so far as Rouen is concerned, the title of commune is somewhat mistaken. The prince retained the higher justice, chose the mayor from a list presented to him, and controlled the municipal administration. On the other side, the population were subject to very severe military obligations. The mayor was chief of the militia and when, on the king's order, he summoned the men of the commune and led them to the Host no one dare fail to attend.

> If the commune has to go outside the country by command of the king or his justiciar, the mayor and aldermen shall decide who are responsible for guarding the city. Whoever is found in the city after the hour of departure shall be arrested by those who have remained to guard the city and shall be at the mercy of the mayor and his aldermen for the destruction of his house or condemnation to a fine of a hundred sous if he has no house. If, when the commune is on the march, anyone departs without the permission of the mayor and aldermen he shall be in mercy.[6]

[1] **CCCLXIX**, 463 ff.; **DLXV**, ii, 97-8, 126 ff., 194 ff., 308 ff., 389, 431 ff.
[2] Cf. **CDXCVII**, 231 ff. S. R. Packard believes rather in fiscal motives. His argument does not seem to me entirely convincing.
[3] **CCCXIV**, i, 52.   [4] **CLVIII**, cf. **CLVI**, 646 ff.
[5] **DXLVIII**, 2nd series, 3 ff. Cf. **CCCXIV**, i, 24 ff.
[6] **CCCXIV**, ii, 37, § 28.

The *Établissements de Rouen* became a model charter. The Plantegenets assured its extension because it offered the double advantage of very strictly limited municipal liberties and guarantees for burgess military service. During the ten years which preceded the conquest of Normandy by Philip Augustus, charters of this type were granted to or imposed on Evreux, Bayeux, Alençon, Fécamp, Harfleur, Montivillier, Falaise. . . .[1] John Lackland specified in those which he granted in 1202 that he wanted the town concerned to have a commune so long as it pleased him and that it must immediately prepare resistance to the King of France.[2] It was in fact a burgess vassalage which was thus created and it might well involve mesne vassalage.

In Aquitaine, the Plantegenets met greater difficulties. The ducal towns directly administered by provosts or seneschals bore their extortions badly. Poitiers in the time of Louis VII had tried to throw off the yoke. Henry II in the period between 1173 and 1178, when feudal menaces forced him to make concessions, granted to this town and to La Rochelle charters as communes based on the liberties of Rouen. Eleanor and John generalized the system and Bayonne, Niort, Saintes, Saint-Jean-d'Angely, and the Île d'Oléron received charters generally modelled on those of Rouen and La Rochelle for the better defence, as it specifically stated, of the rights of the King of England and their own rights.[3] About the same period, Bordeaux which led a rather separate existence also became a commune governed by jurats but it enjoyed much greater independence.[4] As for Limoges and Angoulême their relations with Henry II were stormy; the burgesses were fighting for independence from their counts and it was only in 1204 that Angoulême after becoming a part of John's demesnes received the Charter of La Rochelle.[5]

The system of the *Établissements* of Rouen and La Rochelle, we must repeat, aimed at providing the King of

[1] **CCCXIV**, i, 47 ff.
[2] **CXXI**, 13*b* and 14*a*.
[3] **CII**, i, n. 27 and intro. by Boissonnade, p. xxxvi ff.; **CCCXIV**, i, 54 ff., 106 ff., 239 ff., 294 ff., 357 ff.; **XXXV**, n. 27, 28, 56, 57.
[4] **CCCLXXX**, 136 ff.; **CDXXIV**, 154 ff.
[5] **DLXV**, ii, 113 ff., 207 ff., 443–4; **CCCXIV**, i, 319 ff. In John's reign, Limoges, disputed between the King of England and the King of France, was almost independent—see **CCCXXII**, 71, 86–7.

THE PLANTEGENET'S POLICY 177

England with strong towns capably defended and a trained bourgeoisie ready to take part in a military expedition. The town was in the hands of a municipal aristocracy whose loyalty was capitalized. The reckoning was only correct in part, for the upper bourgeoisie were to show in the future that it was concerned only with its own interests.

VII

AMBITIONS IN THE MEDITERRANEAN

Henry II has been accused of aspiring to world domination. This ancient Roman dream was shared by many in the Middle Ages. In any case there is no doubt that Henry II had enormous ambitions. He wanted to extend his power to the shores of the Mediterranean and beyond the Alps.[1] We have seen his attempt to annex the County of Toulouse, an old dependency of Aquitaine, and his son Richard received the homage of Raymond VI. The alliance with the Count of Barcelona (1159), the marriage of one of Henry's daughters to the King of Castille (1170) and of Richard to Berengar of Navarre (1191), the projected union between John and the heiress of Savoy (1173), Richard's homage to the Emperor Henry VI for the kingdom of Arles and Burgundy (1193), his dominating attitude in Sicily (1190-1), the occupation of Cyprus (1191), the ambition which Richard cherished to lay his hands on the kingdom of Jerusalem and the Eastern Empire and secure his election as Emperor on the death of Henry VI, all these are plans, abortive schemes, which reveal a megalomania which surely contributed in large part to the exhaustion and disintegration of the Angevin Empire.[2] But if France had not possessed, during the storms of the end of the twelfth century, a man of the stature of Philip Augustus the Capetian monarchy, hemmed on all sides, would undoubtedly have succumbed.

[1] **CCX**, 269 ff. The thesis of F. Hardegen, **CCCXLVII**, according to which Henry II wished to displace the Emperor as Supreme in the West is extravagant. See the analysis of H. W. C. Davis in *E.H.R.*, 1906, 363-7.
[2] **CCXI**, i, 230 ff., 272 ff., 321 ; ii, 4, 131 ff., 187 ff., 260 ; iii, 41 ff., 73, 107, n. 3, 173–4, 213 ; **CCCLXXXIV**, i, 1 ff., 78 ff. ; **CDXXXIII**, 127 ff. ; **DXLII**, 129 ; **CDXLVI**, 33, 67.

The account we have given must lead, in effect, to the conclusion that the Norman kings had prepared and the first two Plantegenets realized the foundations of the strongest feudal monarchy Europe had ever seen. In some respects it even went outside the framework of feudalism and its principles and procedure were borrowed from the government of Charlemagne. To check its progress demanded an intensive and violent effort.

CHAPTER IV

RESISTANCE OF THE CAPETIANS TO THE ENGLISH HEGEMONY. PROGRESS OF THE FRENCH MONARCHY, 1152–1201

I

THE RESOURCES OF THE MONARCHY

FROM the divorce of Louis VII and Eleanor and the foundation of the Angevin Empire until the moment when Philip Augustus discovered the means of disinheriting John Lackland, three major facts dominate the history of the Capetian monarchy; its authority in the kingdom grows and it finds a new basis of support in the bourgeoisie; it was compelled to use almost all its resources, new and old alike, in a war of attrition against the Angevin dynasty; finally its ambition to settle this long-standing quarrel by victory, to live, and to grow brought it into conflict with the old traditional powers, the Empire and the Holy See who had little interest in the quarrels of the " petty kings " of the West and sought to re-establish peace between all Christians that it might involve them in a Crusade, in which the Capetians could do nothing but expend their resources in vain.

It is surprising that for half a century the Capetians were able to resist the Plantegenets. To the North, West, and South, the still scanty royal demesnes were threatened. We may well ask of what means and of what circumstances the feeble Louis VII and the young Philip Augustus had been able to take advantage.

The most important of the resources of the monarchy was the personal ability of the king. Louis VII, who was to be succeeded by a statesman of the first water, had himself been vigorous and warlike in his youth and, throughout his life, he remained capable of harshness and cruelty,[1] but the treason of Eleanor, whom he loved passionately, and the misfortunes of the Crusade increased his devotional tendencies and his submissive attitude to the church and

[1] **XLIII**, 588, 595.

deadened his faculty of judgment, decision, and perseverance. Ecclesiastical writers never cease praising his piety and humility and the simplicity of his life but they add that he easily made mistakes and, at times, was " almost silly ".[1] When he was only just 59 years old, at the beginning of 1179, he was stricken with a partial paralysis and henceforward he did nothing but live an invalid's life. On the 1st November steps were taken to consecrate his heir, Philip, who had just reached the age of 14: officially there were two kings ruling jointly and that, of course, was no innovation. In June, 1180, the advisers of the young Philip were afraid that advantage would be taken of the growing incapacity of the old king and Louis VII was deprived of the seal.[2]

Born at Paris on the 21st August, 1165, Philip was 15 years old when his father died on the 19th September, 1180.[3] It is impossible here to present a " portrait " of this great king which would be valid for his whole reign. Men change and the drama and experience of a life marked by important events modifies character and tempers ambition. Philip certainly changed greatly during the forty-three years of his troubled reign and even during the period which we are considering here. At the end of his life he was to be a good companion, careful, crafty, and somewhat cynical but at the period when, an immature youth, he was tossed from day to day through a political career full of pitfalls, this " ill-kempt boy ", nervous, emotional, and subject to sickly fears and hallucinations, loved action above all and hunting and cared little for study; it had not been possible even to teach him Latin.[4] His mother, Adela of Champagne, had given him her intelligence and her love of power and glory.[5] When he was barely 22 years old, the

---

[1] See the texts quoted by Alex. Cartellieri (**CCXI**), i, 2, and *Addit. et Correct.*, 131-2. Cartellieri, to whose monumental political history of the reign of Philip Augustus we shall have to make frequent reference, has given in the *R.H.* of 1891-3, for the first time, a French edition of book I. Our references will be to the German edition.

[2] **CCXI**, i, 29-90, apps. ii, v, and vii, and addit., 143; **CXCIV**, 227 ff.

[3] **CCXI**, i, 5. The surname Augustus was given to him by his biographer Rigord, who generally calls him simply Rex Philippus. We shall frequently do the same. Throughout the Middle Ages, the king's general surname was " the Conqueror ".

[4] **CDLXVIII**, 7; **CXCIV**, 247 ff.; **CDXLVI**, 283.

[5] **CCXI**, i, 3; **CXCIV**, 240-2.

RESISTANCE OF THE CAPETIANS

Count of Flanders said of him that he was prudent and strong in action and forgot neither good nor evil.[1]

The dangers he encountered during the early years of his reign and the complex intrigues which revealed humanity to him in its true light matured him very quickly. His "Will" of 1190 which he dictated at the age of 25 is the work of a judicious politician. Above all the Crusade and the experience of the world of the Mediterranean and the Orient did much to open out his spirit. I think that historians have not appreciated the primary importance, from this point of view, of the two months' journey which he made in Italy (October–December, 1191). He saw Rome and its monuments and learnt to understand the pontifical Curia which he tried, in vain, to win over to his side. He could appreciate its prudence and diplomacy and the difficulty of turning it to account. He saw great Italian Republics like Sienna and Milan where the burgesses were all powerful and, at Milan, he met the proud Emperor Henry VI in an interview.[2] But these years of intense schooling and the serious disease he caught in Sicily had sapped his nervous system. He returned to France physically worn out, bald, lame, neurotic, subject to furious rages and baseless anxieties. He seriously believed that Richard Cœur de Lion was seeking his assassination. This neurasthenic state was acute at the period when he married Isambour of Denmark in 1193; he was pale and trembling during the ceremony of the queen's coronation and unable to consummate the marriage.[3] However, his moral strength never broke down and there was no moment when Richard or John Lackland could find him at a loss.

Precocious though he was, it was clearly his relations and advisers who governed during the first four or five years of his reign. After the death of Suger (13th January, 1151)[4] and the retirement of the Templar Thierri Galeran about 1163,[5] no first class statesman was discovered in the retinue of Louis VII. We can believe that mediocrity had free play when we see the latter, as death approached, charging the vain and inconsistent Count of Flanders, Philip of Alsace,

---

[1] **CCXI**, i, 257.   [2] **CCXI**, ii, 246–257.
[3] Ibid., iii, 10, 19–20, 64 ff., 78 ; **CXCIV**, 253 ff. ; **CCXLII**, 180 ff.
[4] **CXXXVI**, intro., p. x.
[5] **CDXL**, ii, 324–6 (note on Thierri Galeran).

to watch over the young king. The count, surrounded by a brilliant chivalry, held the royal sword at the consecration ceremony and established himself as "Guardian" much to the annoyance of Adela and her brothers.[1]

The Champenois quickly retaliated. They had on their side an important ministerial family, the Cléments, who were minor lords of the Gâtinais and appear to have directed the administration during these critical years.[2] About 1184, this direction passed into the hands of "William of the white hands", Archbishop of Rheims and brother of Queen Adela.[3] During the Crusade he, together with the queen, acted as viceroy: Philip Augustus in his Will of 1190 particularly made him responsible for holding every four months audiences in Paris "to hear and decide petitions of men of the kingdom". This same text, in addition to the two regents, named Bernard, prior of Grandmont, Guillaume de Garlande, Pierre le Maréchal, the clerk Adam, and six burgesses of Paris; the personnel of the government was recruited at this period and for some time afterwards among the minor lords, clerks, and plebians of the Île de France and the district around Orléans. We know very little about them. We merely see that after Philip achieved manhood he knew how to take advantage of their ability and loyalty while always demanding to be kept in touch with affairs and consulted even when he was at a distance. The clerk Adam was his Receiver of Finances and the Prior Bernard his adviser on religious affairs.[4]

As for the five great offices which it would be dangerous to place in the hands of people who might overshadow the king, Philip Augustus left the Chancellorship vacant after 1185 and on the death of his uncle, Theobald of Blois, Seneschal of France, in 1191, he suppressed his office. In the others he placed dependable men drawn from the Beauvaisis district—minor counts of Beaumont and Clermont, Dreu de Mello, and the lords of Senlis.[5]

Around these people the "Kings Court" was grouped, sometimes including barons and prelates travelling through

---

[1] **CCXI**, i, 37 ff., and app. iii, 14 ff., **CCCLXXXIV**, i, 92 ff.
[2] **DLXVIII**, i, 187 ff.; **CCXI**, i, 13, and app. xi.
[3] **CDLXV**, **CCXI**, i, 140, and genealogical table n. 2.
[4] The chief text is the "Will" of 1190; **CIV**, n. 345.
[5] **XXXI**, intro., p. lxxxi ff.

RESISTANCE OF THE CAPETIANS

or summoned to a full meeting, sometimes reduced to the permanent bureaucracy. We have already described it [1]; it changed little during the course of the twelfth century; nothing here comparable to the amazing progress, administrative, financial, and judicial, across the Channel. France was two hundred years behind.

The development of the Curia Regis is marked, however, by three important features. First, important trials were heard there; bishops cited dukes and counts or even a commune in that court; thus, in 1153, the Bishop of Langres appeared there against the Duke of Burgundy; in 1165, the Abbot of Vezelay against the Count of Nevers; in 1190, the Bishop of Noyon against the burgesses of the town. On the other hand, we cannot dispute that the trials were prepared and conducted by professional lawyers like the *jurisperitus Mainerius* and as a result, in the presence of the barons, the delivery of judgment had to be specifically delegated to these specialists. We should add that the Palais de la Cité, in Paris, became the chief judicial centre.[2] Finally important sessions were frequently held [3] and under Louis VII they played a decisive political part either in the organization of the Crusade or in the conduct of the war with England. We must agree that the general ordinances which arose from these discussions, such as that of 1155 [4] for the establishment of peace for ten years to the profit of the Church and the people had no practical implications; only those which concerned the crusades were put into effect. Nevertheless, it is of some importance that the king obtained for his major enterprises as for the execution of his judicial sentences, the consent of his barons and bishops. He could do nothing without them.[5] Seeing the King Louis VII imprudently becoming involved in a war with Geoffrey Plantegenet, Suger wrote to him:—

"Wait until you have the opinions of your loyal bishops and barons who, in virtue of the loyalty they owe the kingdom and the crown, will help you with all their resources. in doing what they have suggested to you."

---

[1] See p. 30 ff. above.
[2] Texts in **LXXI**, 16 ff.; **CDXL**, i, bk. iii; **CIV**, n. 343, etc.
[3] On the obstruction caused in Paris by these meetings: **DXXIX**, i, 112.
[4] **LXXVI**, n. 342.
[5] **CDXL**, i, bk. iii, chap. i; **CCCIII**, **DCLXX**, 61 ff.

This text exactly expresses the advantages which the Capetians might gain from their feudal right of asking the advice of the barons. Louis VII and Philip Augustus undoubtedly drew their moral strength from the Church and the people, their consecration and monarchical tradition, but in respect to their baronage they owed it to their position as suzerains and we shall see Philip reaping decisive profits from his feudal prerogatives. The Curia by very reason of its feudal character became a powerful weapon in his hands.

As for material force, the king still drew upon it particularly in his demesnes. Louis VII had allowed Aquitaine to slip from his hands and gained no new territories. But Philip made up for lost time from the earliest years of his reign. Without mentioning the strongholds in Normandy and Berry which, as we shall see, he wrested from the Plantegenets, he acquired Artois in consequence of his marriage to Isabella of Hainault; the County of Amiens, Montdidier, Roye, and Peronne. Thus the royal castle of Montreuil-sur-Mer which had been isolated up to that time was connected with the demesne and the monarchy gained access to the Channel.[1]

Finally an innovation of capital importance was carried out in the administration of the demesne. For more than a century it had been governed and exploited by provosts who, in general, held their office as a fief and did their best to make it hereditary. They farmed the king's land, collected the revenues, arrested and judged law breakers, had charge of the royal tower in the town, and summoned the Host. Some of them were already affected by the aggressive and authoritative spirit of royal officials which gradually destroyed the feudal organization.[2] The provosts, however, were a greater liability than asset for their brutal and plundering methods, exhausted Church, burgesses, and peasants alike. Their management was frequently suspect and their turbulence a cause of anxiety to the royal councillors who made visits of inspection to the more distant provostships very rarely.[3]

Philip Augustus had decided to increase these inspections, to invite his advisers on their journeys to make prolonged stays in districts, to do justice and supervise the collection

---

[1] CDXXVIII, 95 ff.; CLXXXVII (cf. B.H.P., 1897); CCCXIII, 245 ff. For the acquisition of Montargis and Gien, see below.
[2] See, for example, the very curious deeds of 1146 in CCCXIV, ii, 72, 73.
[3] CCCXIX, 66 ff.; CDXL, i, 201, 214 ff.

of the revenues. In this way the institution was gradually created which was the most valuable instrument of the progress of the Capetian monarchy, *the institution of the bailiffs*.¹ It is impossible to fix the exact date of their creation particularly because the term " baillivus " was employed in the general sense of " agent " and was to keep that vague meaning for a long time. However, from 1184–1190 we have some fifteen letters from Philip to " his provosts and bailiffs " ² and we believe we are justified in thinking that he was concerned with bailiffs delegated from the Court to do justice ³ and supervise the provosts. All these letters are seeking protection for churches and abbeys and we may assume that one of the reasons for their creation had been the discontent of the clergy inadequately protected against brigandage and frequently plundered by the provosts. The decisive document, however, is the ordinance of 1190, the " Will " published by Philip before his departure for the Holy Land. It seems certain that the institution of bailiffs had acquired by that time a force and precision which it had not possessed before. In a certain number of territories, " distinguished by their own names," the king has established bailiffs. Every month they will hold an Assize at which plaintiffs will obtain justice without delay and the kings rights will be safeguarded ; the fines due to the king will be tabled in writing. At these sessions held in Paris each year by the regents, the bailiffs will report on the conditions of their area. In each provostship, they will appoint four experts whose advice they will always take ; there will be six at Paris. The provosts cannot be displaced by the bailiffs nor the bailiffs by the regents, except in particularly serious circumstances, except with the king's authorization.⁴

After Philip's return to France, from 1191–1201, we see bailiffs active at Orléans, Sens, Étampes, and, particularly, in the possessions newly acquired or threatened : in Artois, Vermandois, at Bourges and Gisors. They assume different

---

[1] There is no comprehensive work on the origin of the bailiffs. We are giving here a summary of our personal researches. Cf. CCII, chap. xxxv, CDX, 179 ff. ; CDXLVII, 544–6 ; CDXLVI, 236 ; CLXXXVI, 195 ff. ; DCXXXVIII, 11 ff. ; CDXCVIII, i, 1 ff. ; CDLX, 105 ff. ; CCLXXIX, 346–7.
[2] CIV, n. 108, 152–3, 215–16, 231, 244, 294, 310, 337, 339, 340, 348, 350, 352.
[3] In jurisditionibus vestris (n. 215). Cf. n. 287.
[4] CIV, n. 345. On the institution of four or six umpires, see what I have said in *Ann. de l'Est et du Nord*, 1905, pp. 282–3.

titles—bailiff, officer, assessor, justiciar, constable. They are knights belonging to the families which provided the monarchy with many administrators in the thirteenth century like the Bethisys and the La Chapelles.[1] Henceforward the tradition is established.

In our opinion, their creation was suggested to Philip Augustus and his advisers by the Anglo-Norman institutions.[2] There is evidence for this view. During the early years of his reign, Henry II adopted a friendly attitude towards the young king who was to entrap him so mercilessly on a future occasion. They had interviews and published a joint ordinance in 1184.[3] Henry's sons paid visits to the Court of France. Normandy, Anjou, and Aquitaine were administered by seneschals who were higher bailiffs responsible for supervising the local officials and this was well known to the Capetians. Louis VII had seneschals when he was Duke of Aquitaine.[4] The monthly assize is a Norman institution. But the Capetian bailiffs were even more comparable to the itinerant justices and the sheriffs of England whose functions they combined. Like the itinerant justices, they came from the Curia Regis; they were organized in colleges to do justice and uphold the prerogative and rights of the king. Like the sheriffs, they represented the king, received his instructions, supervised his finances, and gave him an account of what happened. The four men of the provostship are the four men who represent the town in the county court. Thus on a particular point we find substantiation for Ralph de Disci's[5] assertion that Philip imitated the administration of Henry II.

The principal task of the bailiffs became more and more to ensure honest financial management but they also had to find new sources of revenue. Louis VII comparing his modest life to that of the King of England said : " We French have only got bread and wine and a contented mind."[6] Philip Augustus, however, found this poverty intolerable and sought ways and means to escape from it.

---

[1] CIV, n. 385, 433–5, 437, 438, 471 ; CCXLV, Pref. 43, 49, 54, 76–7, 84, 89, 116, 183, 271.
[2] The countal bailiffs of Flanders were different in character ; see CDXCII, 17 ff.
[3] CIV, n. 123.
[4] See p. 169 above ; LXXVI, n. 163, 173 ; CCLXXIX, 346–7.
[5] XCVI, ii, 7–8.   [6] LXXIX, 225.

RESISTANCE OF THE CAPETIANS

The new conquests that were made increased in proportion the products of the demesne and income of all sorts, taxes in commutation of services which were generally farmed out to the provost. The right of lodging and purveyance, that is the right which the king had by established custom, particularly in certain church lands, to demand food and accommodation for himself and his followers when travelling began during this period to be bought up for a fixed annual tax. Tolls and rights against the Jews provided a considerable revenue. In addition there were the fines and profits of justice, the rights of the chancery, and the profits of the coinage.[1] These revenues were enjoyed by the chief barons in their territories as well as by Louis VII and Philip in the royal demesne. As patron of a considerable number of bishoprics and abbeys, however, outside the demesne the king possessed resources which were extra-feudal in character and, even before the reign of Philip Augustus, it would be incorrect to say that there were no monarchical elements in the Capetian finances. The regale collected during the vacancy of an episcopal or abbatial seat proved to be so vexatious that the Church began to demand subscriptions from its proceeds[2]; apart from the King of England, no one among the great vassals could draw on such extensive regalian rights. In virtue of this title and the prestige of the Crown Philip was able to demand large money gifts from the abbeys or even the acceptance of his coinage in their possessions.[3] Finally the king, as supreme suzerain, possessed, in theory, the right to demand relief on each change in the holder of a fief held directly of him. From the period we are now studying, Philip Augustus tried to enforce this right. In 1192, the circumstances being favourable, he demanded of the new Count of Flanders a relief of 5,000 marks of silver, troy weight, equal to a year's revenue of the fief, and from Renaud de Dammartin, whom he confirmed in possession of the County of Boulogne, a relief of £7,000 pounds arras. In 1199 the Count of Nevers paid a relief of 3,000 marks of silver, troy weight, and in 1200, by the Treaty of Goulet, John Lackland promised to pay a relief of 20,000 marks sterling.[4] It is very difficult

---

[1] CDXL, i, 88 ff.   [2] CIV, n. 88, 322.   [3] CIV, n. 36, 162.
[4] CCXI, iii, 10–11; iv, 1st part, 23, 41. The mark of Troyes, made famous by the development of the Champagne fairs, had been adopted by

particularly during our present period of financial upheavals to give an idea of the purchasing power of money in the Middle Ages. We can note, however, for purposes of comparison that three years previously Philip had promised the Consuls of Genoa 5,850 marks of silver for being carried by sea to the Holy Land with 650 knights, 1,300 squires, 1,300 horses, arms, baggage, and provisions.[1]

The king had also the right to levy aid in four instances (kings ransom, knighting his eldest son, marriage of his daughter, Crusade). This, in fact, was equivalent to a tax but the history of the aid for the Crusade in the time of Louis VII and Philip Augustus gives us no reason to believe that the period ended with the establishment of a royal taxation in France. Its history, which must be linked with that of the subsidies demanded of the three estates by Philip the Bel, remains, however, of great interest even more because the aid during the twelfth century had assumed an international character. At that point we must stop for the moment.

In 1146, at the solemn meeting at Vezelay, when Louis VII took the Cross, the idea of taxing all subjects who were not going on Crusade was adopted apparently on the suggestion of the churchmen, like Suger present.[2] Although Louis had promised [3] not to transform this into a permanent tax, its collection was badly organized and there arose complaints of spoliation of the poor and the churches. Subsequently, both in France and England, it became necessary to impose a general tax for a number of years to provide the Christians in the Holy Land with the means of resistance. Louis VII and Henry II tried to establish one in 1166.[4] We have the text of an Anglo-French ordinance of June, 1184, entitled " Provisions for the assistance of the land of Jerusalem approved by Philip King of France and Henry King of England by the common counsel of the bishops, counts, and barons of their dominions ". The tax, based on the value

---

the Monarchy. It weighed 244 gr., 753. A deed of Philip Augustus shows that in 1185 it was worth two pounds of Parisian money (**CIV**, n. 145). The mark sterling, used in Normandy, weighed 230 gr., 352. See **CCCXXVII**, 205, note 2, 232-3, 447-8 ; **CCCXXIX**, 1 ff. ; **CCLVIII**, 27 ff., 36 ff. ; **CCLIX**, 331-2.

[1] **CCXI**, ii, 120.
[2] **CLXXXIX**, 63-70 ; **CXCVI**, 69.
[3] Letters for the Bishop of Le Puy, 1146-7 ; **LXXVI**, n. 185.
[4] **CCXI**, ii, 7-9 ; **CDLI**, 1-2.

RESISTANCE OF THE CAPETIANS

of possessions, was to be collected in every English and French diocese by a Templar and a Hospitaller assisted in every parish by the incumbent and two loyal parishioners.[1] It is highly improbable that it was ever levied but that is not equally true of the famous " Saladin tithe " collected in favour of the Crusaders who were on the point of departing to recapture the kingdom of Jerusalem from Saladin. After January, 1188, the kings of France and England came to an agreement on the measures to be taken after consulting the barons and prelates of their realm.[2] The ordinance issued at Le Mans by Henry II after a meeting to which, for the first time, came barons and prelates from England and from the continental fiefs was followed in March by one issued by Philip Augustus.[3] The two texts throw light on each other. All clerks and laymen, nobles, burgesses, or peasants, who had not taken the Cross were commanded, under penalty of excommunication, to pay the tithe, that is a tenth of their movable goods and all their revenues for the year. Burgesses and peasants who had assumed the Cross were only exempt from the tithe if their decision was taken with the assent of their lord. The fruits of the tithe had to be paid to the lord of the land on which any contributories lived if he had taken the Cross (and if he had not, the money was doubtless to pass to the most immediate suzerain who had). According to Henry's ordinance the collection was carried out in each parish by the curate, the archpriest of the province, a Templar, a Hospitaller, a squire, and a clerk of the king and a squire and a clerk of the bishop. In case of dispute a sworn declaration was referred to seven influential men in France, four or six in England. The churchmen had secured a provision in France that they would deal only with their bishop who would pay the tithe to whoever should receive it.

These ordinances sought to provide lords going on crusade with the means of life and of maintaining their followers; they were not particularly favourable to the royal finances but they gave to Philip Augustus as to Louis VII an opportunity to legislate for the whole kingdom on the

---

[1] CIV, n. 123; LXXVIII, 240-2. W. E. Lunt has ignored the edition of H. F. Delaborde, which appeared six years before his own.
[2] CCXI, ii, 52 ff., where all the documents on the question, French and English, are brought together for the first time.
[3] CIV, n. 229.

pretext of serving the interests of Christ. The related ordinance of March, 1188, concerning the respite granted to debtors on Crusade and the suppression of interest which was published by Philip " on the advice of the archbishops, bishops and barons of the land " had an equally general character and the same sanction of a threat of excommunication.[1]

It was the Church which had thus provided the monarchy with the means to obey the Holy See and to provide for the expedition which no Christian soul could ignore. The Pope ordered the Bishops to display their generosity to stimulate their flocks by their example and to promote meetings.[2] Nevertheless, the discontent was tremendous and contemporary literature is full of complaints. There were obviously abuses and scandals; the poorer folk were spoiled and an Arnold of Guines publicly spent the money he was given on feasting while the Bishop of Durham bought expensive plate.[3] Above all, however, the Church feared the precedent. Eminent clerks like Pierre de Blois and the Abbot of St. Geneviève at Paris urged the clergy to disobey. Pierre de Blois considered it outrageous that " the champions of the Church despoil her instead of enriching her with the spoils of victory " and said that the King of France should ask nothing of the clergy but their prayers : " The payment of the tithe will become a general habit and the church will fall into a shameful servitude." [4] Henry II and Richard Cœur de Lion shut their ears to the complaints of the priests and demanded payment [5] but Philip had to yield. After a year, by agreement with his barons, he abolished the Saladin tithe. That is the most striking evidence of the power of the Church in France at that period. Here is the beginning of the ordinance of abolition agreed to at a meeting which met in Paris at the beginning of the year 1189 ; the King of France seemed to be doing public penitence there :—

> The tithe for the recovery of the Holy Land has been levied once. In order that that outrageous fact shall not be made a precedent, we have decided, on the demand of the churchmen and princes alike, by a law valid for ever, that no future exactions shall be made by reason of it or for any similar cause. Because it is a remedy which, devoutly carried through, may serve the salvation of faithful souls, it seems to us that God would be offended rather

[1] CIV, n. 228. [2] CCXI, ii, 51.
[3] CCXI, ii, 69 ff., 82–3.   [4] XC, i, letters 20, 112, 121.
[5] CCXI, ii, 62, 88 ; DLXXXIX, 447 ff.

than conciliated by a sacrifice offered to him at the price of the tears of widows and the poor. In order that neither we nor others shall ever make any similar attempt in future by royal authority and the public authority of the churchmen and princes of the kingdom we have decided that this present law prevents us on pain of damnation from venturing on such an attempt ; if by some rash audacity either we or another attempts it we decree that it shall be void. . . .¹

Before his departure, dictating his will, and foreseeing the possibility of his death in the Holy Land, he commended his heir Louis of France to his subjects so that, in case of need, they should aid him with their bodies and their property and to the churches so that they should secure for the son the assistance they had always provided for the father but he forbade them to pay any extraordinary taxation while he was, himself, in the Holy Land.²

Once again to be able to offer some resistance to Richard he mobilized all his resources, squeezed the churches and forced those who could not supply soldiers to pay taxes ; he plundered the abbeys in the Plantegenets' territories and in 1198, at the time when the fanatical Fulk de Neuilly was preaching against usurers, he gathered the fugitive Jews within his dominions fully realizing what profit he could extract from them.³ In his *Carolinus*, composed about this date, Gilles de Paris complains of the king's greed: " Oh France ! tortured by the agents of the royal fisc, you have had to bear harsh laws and terrible occasions." ⁴ However, Philip did not possess sufficient ingenuity even to establish a general tax like the English scutage or carucage and Richard maintained a superiority in resources which would have given him the opportunity, had he lived, to crush his rival.

What do we know of the administration of the finances of the Capetians from 1152 to 1201 ? The oldest account that we possess is a general account of receipts and expenses from All Saint's Day, 1202, to Ascension, 1203. It would be dangerous to take it as typical of the budget for the reign of Louis VII and the first twenty years of Philip's reign. There were

---

¹ CIV, n. 252. Cartellieri (CCXI, ii, 84) does not seem to have understood the character of that deed.
² CIV, n. 345 (June, 1190).
³ CCXI, iii, 92, 100, 183 ff. ; iv, 74–5.
⁴ H.F., xvii, 291. On the date of the *Carolinus*, see the note of Delaborde in the *Mélanges Châtelain*, 1910, pp. 195–203.

evidently important financial reforms right at the end of the twelfth century and, already in 1202–3, there appear certain receipts realized from the conquered Norman lands. We should be well advised not to make use of this account until a later chapter. We can only make use of a very few texts for the period with which we are concerned at the moment.[1] We know that the provosts anticipated these receipts and thus raised the money to maintain the fortified posts and pay the rents due to the king. One of them, Géraud de Poissy, who had made a false return had to pay an enormous fine in 1186 (11,000 silver marks, according to Rigord)[2] and was replaced. It was about this period that Philip instituted bailiffs. In his will he gives to six burgesses of Paris and his faithful subject Pierre le Marshal the responsibility for banking the moneys which were due at Paris at the three terms—1st October, 1st February, and the Ascension. He had also a number of portable money chests which for greater security Philip kept in different places.[3] He had one of them with him at Fréteval in 1194 and lost it. The real Treasury, however, was in the Temple in chests to which a Templar and the seven cashiers had each a key. In his will, Philip directed that, if he died during the Crusade, half of his treasure should be put in reserve, " for his son's needs " and the other half distributed among the Churches and the poor particularly in reparation of the damage done by his wars and the levy of the taxation. He evidently still regarded his Treasure as his personal property.[4]

However, he sought riches only as a means of defending the Crown. He certainly led a simple life, spent little, and made full use of his right to hospitality. He coveted money for the purpose of building fortresses on the frontier, undertaking the construction of machines of war, the effectiveness of which he rated very highly, and retaining soldiers.

The service of the feudal Host was uncertain, and Philip preferred a less precarious system.[5] Louis VII had employed mercenaries before him and at the beginning of his reign he employed Brabantine knights who were notorious pillagers

---

[1] For the reign of Louis VII, see **CDXL**, i, 129–131.
[2] **CXII**, 64, § 40. [3] **CCXI**, iii, 92. [4] **CIV**, n. 345.
[5] The question has been studied in **CLXXXVI**, 467 ff.; **CL**; and by me in B.E.C., 1915, 545 ff. It has been reviewed from the financial point of view in **CDXXXVI**, 15–20.

but brave and dependable. He also created military fiefs or money rents to make permanent provision for crossbowmen and archers. These measures, however, were inadequate. It would appear that Philip introduced new ideas and considered the systematic application of the Carolingian principle of imposing service on the whole population. By this step, he was adopting the English system. An English chronicler assures us that he published an ordinance modelled on the Assize of Arms of 1181.[1] We have no text of that ordinance but we can form some idea of it. Philip certainly never pretended to imitate the Assize of Arms. Henry II was sufficiently powerful to compel all the freemen of his kingdom to do military service and revive the Carolingian and the Anglo-Saxon traditions at the same time. But the King of France could address himself and, in fact, did address himself only to the abbeys dependent on him, to his communes, and the provosts of his demesnes. The "Prisée of Sergents" of 1194 proves this fact. Whenever it was necessary, Philip demanded from the ecclesiastical and lay communities, of which this "prisée" gives a list, either a certain contingent of sergeants whom they had to support or a tax in commutation of the duty: as in Normandy and England, the contingents were in multiples of five or ten and the effective unit consisted of ten men. Service was for three months. A foot sergeant demanded a pound a month for hire and, consequently, this rate was three pounds for those who preferred to pay the tax instead. This system allowed Philip to dispose of two thousand sergeants throughout the year, a number very different from the fantastic figures we find in the chroniclers. Armies and garrisons in the Middle Ages were very small.

II

ALLIES AND OPPONENTS

On several occasions we have glanced at the problem of estimating the amount of support which Louis VII and his son could depend on among the clergy, the lower classes, and

[1] **XVIII**, i, 270. On this Assize of Henry II, see p. 145 above. Cf. **CCCXXVI**, 227 ff. Guilhiermoz believes that the essential point of the ordinance of Philip Augustus was to fix the rate of revenue (undoubtedly £60) at which a noble had to arm a knight and carry a full equipment.

the nobility, within the demesne and without. We must now examine it more closely.

Conflicts between the monarchy and the clergy, frequently quite sharp during the early years of the reign of Louis VII,[1] were rare during the latter half of the twelfth century. Good relations were general. Louis VII was a saintly man who gave refuge to the two fugitives Thomas Becket and Alexander III at the risk of alienating Henry II and Frederick Barbarossa. Philip, not without considerable doubts, went to fight in the Holy Land and, at the beginning of his reign, he did nothing to check the persecution and burning of the Jews.[2] Reform of the Church was carried through; the principle of Canonical election had triumphed though without prejudice to the king's right of supervision.[3] This is precisely expressed by the following provision of Philip's will:—

> If it happens that an episcopal see or a royal abbey is vacant, we will that the Canons of the Church or the monks of the vacant monastery shall come before the queen and the archbishop (William of Champagne) as they have been used to come before us and demand of them a free election and we will that they shall grant it without any refusal. We warn the canons and monks to elect someone who will be pleasing to God and useful to the realm.[4]

The collection of the deeds of Louis VII and Philip Augustus very largely consists of letters by which the king interferes to re-establish peace and order in the churches and abbeys and particularly to defend them against lay feudation. Louis VII and his successor made important military expeditions, particularly into Auvergne, Burgundy, and Berry to punish the oppressors of the Church.[5] Through special letters of protection or patronage contracts (for the joint administration of ecclesiastical lands) they became patrons of churches situated outside the demesne. The bishop of Tournai carried this to its conclusion. The bishop of Tournai, exhausted by the turbulence of the burgesses, handed over the town and forty villages surrounding it to Philip in

---

[1] **CCCLXIX**, 442 ff.; **CCCLVIII**, 73 ff.
[2] **CCXI**, i, 58, 124; iii, 183. On his change of policy in respect of the Jews after 1198, see p. 191 above.
[3] **DLXXIII**, 165 ff.
[4] **CIV**, n. 345.
[5] **CDXL**, ii, 287 ff.; **CCXI**, i, 82 ff., ii, 343; **DCLXX**, 101-2.

1187.¹ It was an extremely valuable acquisition. Tournai was to remain for more than three centuries an integral part of the royal demesne. Finally, at Court the clergy was orderly and willing to be of service providing that their goods and property were respected; it provided the monarchy with councillors, administrators, historiographers who told of the miracles performed for the king's benefit. When Philip repudiated his second wife without any adequate reason, the bishops and abbots showed a disgusting complacency when they came together in Council. They were, as Rigord himself wrote, dogs who didn't know how to bark.²

The alliance of the Capetians and the clergy was of long standing. The great innovation at the end of the twelfth century was their alliance with the lower classes and particularly the burgesses.

The rural population, despised and terrorized by the nobility and slandered by minstrels, could hope for little relief or defence from the Church. The latter administered its wealth strictly, granted freedom to its serfs extremely reluctantly, and was powerless against feudal violence. The monarchy had the opportunity to root its popularity in the very heart of the country by protecting the peasants; a policy that would one day be adopted by St. Louis. During the period we are considering, it did not entirely neglect this source of prestige and profit.³ Its sanction had, at all periods, given a special validity to the enfranchisement of serfs in the kingdom. Louis VII declared, in a charter of 1152, "that it was a prerogative of the royal majesty to grant liberty to former serfs." He did not employ it often but he renounced his right of mortmain throughout the diocese of Orléans, characterizing it as extremely oppressive. It is very obviously in their interest, that Louis and his son established "new towns" (*Villeneuves*) where many serfs could establish themselves in the enjoyment of privileges which were frequently very extensive. The famous customs of Lorris granted by Louis VI were confirmed by the two kings and granted to many villages either in the royal demesne or in

---

¹ **CCCLVII**, 593–610; **CCXI**, i, 266 ff.
² **CXII**, 125, § 92.
³ See **CDXL**, ii, 117 ff.; **CLXXVIII**, 45 ff. Cf. a testimony of the brutality of Philip Augustus towards serfs: **CLXXVI**, 255, 259.

the ecclesiastical territories.[1] Many of the deeds of Philip Augustus in the first part of his reign have rural communities as their beneficiaries.[2] Most frequently, he is concerned with villages that the abbeys cannot guarantee against ravaging. The king takes them under his protection and attaches them to the Crown on condition of dues or is even accepted as co-lord ; he instals a provost in them.[3] It is a characteristic symptom of troubled times. The general insecurity is to the king's advantage for he is in a position to help the oppressed.

An alliance with the rich bourgeoisie which had been in existence for about a century offered even more direct advantages. It began to appear in the reign of Louis VII[4] who grants or confirms charters of franchises, encourages the formation of communes in the ecclesiastical demesnes, and the idea that ecclesiastical cities with communes are royal towns is expressly attributed to him. Frequently, however, he hesitates, wavers, and supports the Church against the bourgeoisie and he had no wish to establish communes in the royal demesne.[5] He seems to have experienced that horrified reaction that burgess independence stimulated in the Church. Philip Augustus's attitude was much more decided. In the first twenty years of his reign there are numerous charters confirming or increasing the privileges of the enfranchised towns in his demesne or outside.[6] The most striking fact, however, is his acceptance of communal independence. The measures which he took in favour of certain abbeys against their burgesses, or even the abolition of the Charter of Étampes[7] in the royal demesne are exceptional incidents ; between 1182 and 1188 he established communes at Chaumont, Pontoise, Poissy, Montreuil[8] and, outside his demesne, he re-established the commune of Sens[9] and confirmed the communes of Soissons, Noyon, Beauvais, and Dijon.[10] After annexing Artois, the Tournaisis,

---

[1] DLI.   [2] CIV, n. 51, 110, 129, 183, 197.
[3] Typical cases of Escurolles in Auvergne : CIV, n. 253. See also, n. 21, 61, 180, 188, 189, 232, 248.
[4] CDXL, ii, 179 ff. ; CDXXXVIII, 264 ff.
[5] Except Senlis (CCXC, 3).
[6] CIV, n. 10, 15, 19, 30, 40, 43, 46, 52, 73, 84, 168-9, etc.
[7] L, 36, n. 5.   [8] CIV, n. 59, 233, 234, 236.
[9] CIV, n. 280 ; CLXXXVIII, chap. vi.
[10] CIV, n. 35, 43, 53, 101, 210 ; CLXXXVIII, 119 ff., 362 ff. ; CDXI, 42 ff. ; CCCXC, 90 ff.

RESISTANCE OF THE CAPETIANS 197

and part of Vermandois, between 1188 and 1197, he confirmed or completed the charters of Tournai, Saint Riquier, Amiens, Hesdin, Arras, Saint Quentin, Montdidier, Bapaume, and Roye.[1] Many of the Charters of these communes show us clearly the motives which are activating him.[2] He declares that he is acting from love of the burgesses of the town and there is no doubt of his desire to satisfy that class as he feels that it would provide a dependable support. Moreover, he drew from the communes a rent in return for his concessions.[3] Above all, however, he realized that they were potential armies for his defence and imposed military duties on them. They formed a militia which undertook to be a very valuable weapon for the king. " Every time," says the charter of Tournai, " that we send for our service the sergeants of the communes, our subjects of Tournai shall send to our service 300 well equipped footmen if they are required by us or our successors ; if we are moving with our host towards the Arrouaise, the whole community of Tournai must come before us."[4] It has also been pointed out that the towns which Philip favoured with the grant of a charter and commune were almost all on the frontiers of the royal dominions. They were defensive posts and the militia provided a reserve of troops. In 1188 the commune of Mantes near to the Norman frontier checked the English and saved Paris.[5]

Paris had never had a charter as a commune and in the thirteenth century did not even possess a municipality in embryo. Roman Lutecium had become a rural borough by the beginning of the Carolingian period but, emerging from the purely agricultural era in the eleventh century, Paris assumed, during the course of the twelfth, the characteristics of a big city. Its relations with the kings Louis VII and Philip Augustus are remarkably significant and marked a stage in the development of the monarchy. We must pause over it for a moment.[6]

In spite of its dangerous proximity to the Norman frontier,

---

[1] **CIV**, n. 224, 271, 319, 408, 473 ; **XXXI**, n. 437, 441, 486, 510 ; **CCCLVII**, 602 ff. ; **CDLXVII**, 284 ff. ; **IX**, intro. by Giry, 22, 28 ff.
[2] **CDXXXVIII**, 280 ff.
[3] **CLXXXVIII**, 250, 265.
[4] **CIV**, n. 224. On the Arrouaise, see **CCXXVI**, ii, 81.
[5] **LVII**, bk. iii, line 327 ff. Cf. **CDXLVIII**, 159–166.
[6] See principally **DXXIX**, i ; **CCCXLIII**.

it was the capital of the kingdom. Its definite predominance was assured by its industrial and commercial development. The neighbourhood of the great and rich abbeys—Saint Denis with its Lendit fair (11th June) ; Saint Germain des Prés which also had its fair ; Saint Geneviève ; Saint Victor—had created industries. The powerful corporation of Marchands de l'Eau was in permanent communication with the merchants of Rouen and through them with the sea. Foreigners came in vast numbers ; Paris was a place of transit between the northern countries and the Champagne fairs on the one hand and Orléans and the South on the other. Business men and pilgrims rubbed shoulders and many settled there to be a source of the bourgeoisie together with the old population of serfs and landlords turned townsmen. Already it is becoming possible to distinguish the families which, at a later date, will form the municipal aristocracy. The isle of the city comprised only a small part of the capital of Louis VII and Philip. We can still distinguish some remains of the enclosure built on the right bank after 1190 if, after crossing the little square of the Louvre, we reach the rue Étienne Marcel and return by the rue des Francs-Bourgeois and the Charlemagne college ; on the left bank, where the enclosure was not built until 1209, the wall of Philip Augustus is actually visible behind the Henry IV college and in the neighbourhood of the Institute.[1] Although the houses were low, the gardens stinted, and the cultivated or even waste plots were numerous, it seems that the population was quite equal to that of a middle sized town of to-day. All the distinctive features of a capital were to be found there. The city was a religious and political centre. The official quarter, the Palais, was at its western end and was already the principal centre of the Curia Regis and the lawyers. At the other extremity, Notre Dame, the choir of which had been completed since the end of Louis's reign, raised its white mass amid a labyrinth of little streets. There, already, one could find the swarming crowd of teachers and students, French and foreign, so numerous that they could not find accommodation. On the other side of the Petit-Pont,

---

[1] **CCCXLIII**, 31 ff. Plans and designs and a tracing of Philip's enclosure in the volume of maps. It was along this wall that Philip Augustus built the first Louvre the remains of which can be found beneath the Cariatides room. It was a fortress.

RESISTANCE OF THE CAPETIANS 199

on the left bank, was the quarter where Latin was spoken. There were so many schools and such famous teachers that Philip Augustus granted them corporative privileges. The University of Paris was only to be recognized at a later date [1] but already its power existed. Around the Pont aux Changes, on the right bank, was the business quarter, with its changer's shops, luxury industries, victualling trade, markets, and its river port crowded with boats. Around the twelve gates of Paris there was a thickly populated and well cultivated suburb whose inhabitants for a distance of two leagues shared in some of the privileges and responsibilities of the Parisian burgesses. The capital was not entirely royal demesne. The Bishop of Paris, in particular, had extensive jurisdiction there. The rights of the king were entangled with those of other lords but there were complications which occurred in most towns. In this case, however, the king is clearly the principal lord just as the bishop is elsewhere. Paris is the king's town [2] and the author of the *Moniage* calls the latter " King of Paris ". Philip Augustus, continuing the work of his predecessors Louis VI and VII,[3] took considerable trouble to organize the trade of Paris,[4] set on foot considerable schemes to improve the sanitation of the city which was very necessary. By a piece of rare good fortune, Rigord has given us some details of one of the enterprises in which we can see the king and the bourgeoisie co-operating. In 1186, he tells us, Philip had returned to his palace in Paris after a victorious expedition in Burgundy :

> He was strolling in the great royal hall thinking over affairs of state and came to the Palace windows from where he often looked out on the River Seine as a diversion. The horse waggons, crossing the city and cutting up the mud, stirred up a stench which he couldn't stand and he decided on a difficult but necessary piece of work which his predecessors had not dared to initiate because of the crushing expense. He summoned the burgesses and the provost of the city and ordered by his royal authority that all the roads and streets of the city should be paved with strong, hard stone.[5]

---

[1] CCCXL, 134 ff.; CCCXLV, 220 ff.; DXLV, 26 ff.
[2] Well brought out by Monod ; CDLXXXI, 81 ff.
[3] CCCXLIII, 13 ff., 18 ff.; CCCLXIV, 2 ff.
[4] CIV, n. 31, 74, 426, etc.
[5] CXII, 53-4, § 37 ; cf. William the Breton, ibid., 184, § 33. Only the roads leading to the gates were paved.

Evidently on this occasion Philip Augustus made the aristocracy responsible for raising a special tax and administering its receipts [1]; from the beginning of his reign he had understood how to appreciate and make use of those Parisians who had made their fortunes in finance, commerce, or luxury industries like Theobald the Rich and Ébrouin the Changer who figure in the will of 1190. We have already said that while he was in the Holy Land, six Paris burgesses were ordered to assist in the administration not only of the capital but of the whole kingdom; it is " all my subjects of Paris " on whom he calls to guard his treasure for his son if he should die. During his absence, the six burgesses have the key to it and receive the taxes brought to Paris. Thus we find that the tradition of entrusting major financial responsibilities to the burgesses of Paris is already established.

Thus the monarchy had a new force at its disposal. It was a welcome reinforcement for it could not hope to find the baronage anything but a precarious and hesitating ally.

It had mastered only the small and middle nobility enfeoffed in the Île de France, Beauvaisis, or Orléans and the other districts where the king held his own demesne. It provided Philip, as we have seen, with his chief officials and many of his advisers. Even now they were supplying knights, lawyers, and diplomats, who foreshadowed the legal authorities of the later thirteenth century.[2] But what means could Louis VII or Philip Augustus employ to enforce obedience from their most important vassals?

Here we have reached the kernel of the subject of this work. We have seen that the king, by virtue of his consecration, enjoyed an external prestige of a feudal character reinforced by memories of the Bible, Antiquity, or Carolingian times but that noble society had scarcely any cohesion apart from the bond between lord and vassal. The fundamental truth which, we hope, will emerge from this book is that Philip Augustus and, up to a certain point, Saint Louis had accepted the ideas of their barons on the subject and that their position as supreme suzerain, more and more clearly defined and

---

[1] In 1214, he gave the Hanse a responsibility of this kind: **XXXI**, n. 1476; **CCCLXIV**, 12.

[2] See particularly the list of negotiations in **CCXI**, i, 238; iii, 97; iv, first part, 55, etc.

RESISTANCE OF THE CAPETIANS

applied, was the source of at least as much profit as their status as a consecrated king.

Philip, more definitely than any of his predecessors, established the principle that the feudal hierarchy culminates in the king who is nobody's vassal. In 1185, when he took possession of the County of Amiens a fief of the Church of Amiens, he bought from the church the right not to do homage to any one. He owed homage to the Lord of Orville for the castle of Beauquesne: in 1192 the fief was transformed into a manor which did not render homage. In 1193 he bought in from the Bishop of Thérouanne the homage due for the fief of Hesdin.[1] We may still ask whether he had succeeded in exercising all the rights of supreme suzerain, exacting homage and the services of Court, host, and aid which his vassals owed him. In fact, what did he achieve? We can guess the answer. Many centuries were necessary for the disappearance of the independence of the nobility and feudal anarchy. It would be interesting to collect here all the precise facts that we know for the end of the twelfth century. We shall have to be satisfied with some indicative examples.

It is remarkable that neither Henry II nor his sons Henry the Younger nor Richard Cœur de Lion cast off the homage which they owed to Louis VII and Philip Augustus for Normandy and Aquitaine[2]; it would have been wise to deprive the Capetians of their constitutional means of aggression. In fact, the vassal, more powerful than the suzerain, fulfilled none of the obligations created by homage. However, the vassalages of the English princes had not been a pure fiction. Henry II appears often to have been restrained by respect for the feudal bond. On the other hand Philip Augustus accepted the homage of Richard (in 1188) and John (in 1189) to weaken their father and at a later date John's homage against his brother Richard (1193). In the same way, he used his position as supreme suzerain to maintain centres of dissension in the Angevin Empire. The old Eleanor was so convinced of the danger of Capetian suzerainty that in 1199 after the death of Richard she hastened to do homage to Philip Augustus for Aquitaine and subsequently invest

---

[1] **CIV**, n. 139, 422, 445. Another example of 1204: **XXXI**, n. 879. The relief for the churches consisted in the abandonment of the right of hospitality.
[2] **CDXXXIII**, 80 ff., 204 ff.

John Lackland with it, who, as a result, was no longer the direct vassal of his enemy for this fief.¹

The Plantegenets against whom Louis VII and Philip Augustus had to maintain the independence even of their crown were not the only powerful vassals whom the king had to mistrust. Between the royal demesne and the Empire the great noble houses had an uncertain and frequently hostile attitude.

The principal baron of the area, the Count of Flanders, reigned over a warlike chivalry and rich and populous cities where the wool of the English sheep was woven.² He was a liege subject of the King of France but, for imperial Flanders, he was also a vassal of the Emperor. Finally, he held certain money rents in fief of the English king to whom he was bound by a pact of military service. The Flemings were usually considered hostile to France.³ We must add that Flanders included in its economic and often in its political orbit two principalities beyond the borders of Capetian France: Hainault and Brabant. A count of Flanders might seek to live in peace under the guarantees of the English alliance; or he might be anxious to intervene in French affairs and play the role of tutor to the monarchy as Baldwin V had done at the time of Philip I or finally he might be tempted to adopt a policy of aggrandizement and annexation. Between the three ideas, all more or less dangerous for the Capetians, the policy of the counts oscillated during the reigns of Louis VII and Philip Augustus. The Count Thierry of Alsace found it possible to be a liege subject of Louis VII and a pensioner of the King of England, to obey Louis's summons to the host and provide sergeants for Henry II.⁴ His son Philip of Alsace (1169–1191) was too vain and impulsive to walk the tight rope in this way. As we have seen, he took it into his head to become regent to the young Philip Augustus. As a means of ensuring his tractability, he arranged for him to marry his niece Isabella, a daughter of the Count of Hainault (1180). He died childless and promised to break up his possessions. After his death, Artois was to go to Isabella and her heirs and, consequently,

---

¹ **CCXI**, i, 293, 307, 315, iii, 32–3; **CDLXXXIX**, 22–3 **CDXXXIII**, 86.
² **DXXIII**, i, bk. ii.
³ **LVII**, 45, line 132. Texts quoted in **CCXI**, iii, 161, n. 1.
⁴ **CDXXXIII**, 17 ff.; **CCCLXXXIV**, i, 64 ff.

RESISTANCE OF THE CAPETIANS

to the Capetian dynasty while his sister and her husband, the Count of Hainault, would take over Flanders.[1] It was not long, however, before he was quarrelling with Philip Augustus and on two occasions he made a desperate attack on him in an attempt to build up an Anglo-Flemish-German coalition against the Capetians like that which, thirty years later, was to be defeated at Bouvines.[2]

Even in the intervals of reconciliation, Philip Augustus could expect nothing from such a vassal who in 1186, when war between the kings of England and France was in preparation, was providing both sides with troops.[3]

Philip of Alsace departed for the Holy Land with Philip Augustus and died before Acre in 1191. Baldwin of Hainault reunited the crowns of Hainault and Flanders; in the absence of the king, the regents of the kingdom had no wish to provoke the intervention of the Emperor and they were content to safeguard Artois and Vermandois. Baldwin, who had been antagonized by his son-in-law's temper, was a faithful vassal [4] but his son Baldwin IX returned to the English alliance in the hope of conquering Tournai and recovering Artois. Heavily subsidized by Richard Cœur de Lion he entered on a campaign in July, 1197. Philip Augustus had followed the feudal rules and several times made vain offers to the count to do justice by him in his Court. On this occasion, for the first time, we hear an offer of " judgment by peers ".[5] " Filled with a terrible fury " against a rebellious vassal, he invaded Flanders in so imprudent a manner that he was all but captured. Baldwin was still subject to scruples and did not dare to take his suzerain prisoner but he only accepted a truce. The death of Richard Cœur de Lion and John Lackland's reputation for duplicity finally decided him to make peace on the 2nd January, 1200, on conditions in general very advantageous for him. Philip Augustus had to abandon part of his demesne and direct suzerainties which he had recieved from his marriage with Isabella, particularly the towns of Aire and Saint Omer; the Count of Flanders

---

[1] **LI**, 129-130; **CCXI**, i, 48 ff., and app. iv; **DXVII**, 3 ff., 17. On the boundaries of Artois, see **CDII**, 192 ff.
[2] **CCXI**, i, 95 ff.; **CCCLXXXIV**, i, 103 ff.
[3] **CCCLXXXIV**, i, 125.
[4] **CCCLXXXVI**, chap. iii, p. 359 ff.
[5] **CXXXVIII**, i, 430.

continued to receive a pension from the King of England and so did his relations and his Chancellor.¹ It was necessary to wait for fifteen years and the great crisis of Bouvines before Flanders ceased to be a danger.

The house of Blois-Champagne, like that of Flanders, had direct contacts with the Empire. Louis VII had bound it to the Crown by marriages and honours ; of the four children of Theobald II (*ob.* 1152), the eldest, Henry the Liberal, Count of Champagne, married a daughter of the king ; Theobald, Count of Blois, also became the son-in-law of Louis VII and was Seneschal of France (from 1154 to 1191) ; William became Archbishop of Rheims in 1176 and was regent during the third Crusade ; finally, Adela married Louis VII himself and was the mother of Philip Augustus. Louis VII thus held in his hands a warp which the crown almost succeeded in weaving. The house of Champagne sought either to dominate the monarchy or to free themselves from it. The Seneschal Theobald in 1159 allied himself with the King of England and invaded the royal demesne. Henry the Liberal made responsible for negotiations with Barbarossa betrayed Louis just as badly ; he saw in the occasion an opportunity to change his suzerain and gain the same independence as the imperial princes of the other side of the Rhine and only failed by very little in making Champagne an Imperial fief as the result of agreements made by the Count in the king's name but without his knowledge.² The young Philip Augustus had violent conflicts with the house of Champagne who sided with their rival Philip of Alsace to make war on him. Richard Cœur de Lion on several occasions numbered a Count of Blois among his allies. Philip Augustus mastered this house only on the death of the young Count Theobald III : his widow Blanche of Navarre came and put herself under royal protection, gave up her castles to the king, and, henceforward, he was able to draw from Champagne important resources in men and money. This submission, however, which was one of the great events of the reign, did not take place till 1201.³

In the Duchy of Burgundy a family of Capetian origin

---

¹ **XXXI**, n. 579, 591 ; **CCXI**, iii, 5 ff. 147 ff., iv, first part, 12 ff., 34 ff., 85–6 ; **CCCLXXXIV**, i, 133 ff.

² Luchaire has dealt with these negotiations well : **CDXLVI**, 36 ff.

³ **CDXXXIII**, 172 ff. ; **CCXI**, i, 26 ff. ; iii, 186–7 ; iv, 1st part, 74–5 ; **CXLVII**, 1st part, 101 ff. ; **DX VII**, 88–9.

RESISTANCE OF THE CAPETIANS

reigned. They were inadequately endowed with personal demesne and money and were often reduced to doubtful expedients and plundering. The land primarily belonged to the bishops who were directly subject to the king and powerful abbeys protected by the Capetians.[1] In 1186 Philip, acting on a judgment of his Court, reduced the Duke Hugh to compensating the victims of his brigandage; Hugh had asked in vain for the protection of the king of the Romans; he subsequently remained a faithful vassal providing host service as called upon.[2] A powerful neighbouring lordship, that of Nevers-Auxerre, was likewise forced, on the occasion of discord with the churches, to recognize the royal supremacy of Louis VII.[3] Philip succeeded in subduing them by installing his cousin Pierre de Courtenay (1184) and then Hervé de Donzy (1199) as successive counts by the use of marriages; from this modest piece of brokerage the crown earned the lordship of Montargis which commanded the route from Paris to Bourges, the control of the castle of Gien which protected Orléans, and the liege homage of all the men of Hervé de Donzy.[4]

To the south of the royal demesne, there was no great lordship in Berry; Auvergne was divided between a count and a dauphin of Auvergne. These two holdings were claimed by the King of England as Duke of Aquitaine and their lords changed allegiance according to their immediate advantage. Louis VII and Philip Augustus established their authority there only slowly.[5]

The dynasty of the counts of Toulouse and the feudal nobility of Languedoc which had been, for a long time, completely isolated entered into fairly consistent relations with the Capetians after the Second Crusade. Relations between the men of the North and South were cemented in the Holy Land. Raymond V, Count of Toulouse, married the sister of Louis VII (1154) and, in the same year, Louis VII, who had set out on pilgrimage to St. James of Compostella,

---

[1] **DXIII**, ii and iii, particularly chapter xix; **CDXL**, ii, 286-8.
[2] **CCXI**, i, 195 ff.
[3] **CDXV**, i, chap. ix ff.; **CCLV**, 4; **CDXL**, i, 208, 279, ii, 98, 293.
[4] **XXXI**, n. 100 and 568; **CCXI**, i, 110 ff., 236; iii, 47-9; iv, 1st part, 22 ff.
[5] **CDXL**, ii, 292 ff.; **CCXI**, i, 83, 253 ff.; iii, 110, 145-6, 187; iv, 1st part, 20 ff.

made a visit to Languedoc. The southern nobility, anxious about the ambitions of the Plantegenets, preferred the more distant suzerainty of Louis VII and the pious king established a real popularity for himself in the South [1] but it was of no value to Louis or his son. The fickle Raymond V whom Louis had saved from an English invasion in 1159 acknowledged himself a liege vassal of Henry II in 1173 and Raymond VI, who had married an English princess, did homage to John Lackland in 1200.[2]

III

Attitude of the Emperors and the Popes

Beyond their own frontiers, Louis VII and Philip Augustus had no allies of any importance. Of the marriages which had allied them to foreign houses, only one, that between Philip Augustus and Isabella of Hainault, was any profit to the crown. As for the two powers with claims to world domain, the Empire and the Papacy, each of them was pursuing an ideal which could not be in accordance with the particular ideas of the kings of France.

The pontifical schism of 1159 and the new conflict between the Empire and the Holy See embarrassed Louis VII greatly, and embittered his relations with Frederick Barbarossa. The Pope Alexandra III was recognized by Louis VII and Henry II while Barbarossa supported his contemporary Victor IV.[3] He refused to negotiate with petty kings and sought to impose Victor IV on the Christian world. From 1162 to 1165, Alexander III, forced to flee from Italy and unable to demand asylum from the persecutor of Thomas Becket, lived in France. He established himself at Sens in the royal demesne. It has been suggested from a study of his correspondence [4] that he sought to rule for Louis VII and that it was for France a period of " theocratic government ". It is an assertion, however, which is very much exaggerated. The envoys of Saint Louis in the papal presence in 1247 were to declare that, during his stay in France, Alexander did not

---

[1] **DCXLVIII**, iv, note 53, pp. 230–1 ; **CDXL**, ii, 295 ff.
[2] **CCXI**, iv, 1st part, 54–5 ; **CDXXXIII**, 126 ff.
[3] **CCCLVIII**, 100 ff. [4] **IV**, 774 ff.

present to a single benefice.¹ But the alliance of Louis VII and Alexander III inevitably gained him the enmity of the powerful emperor and made the efforts of his ministers to win Imperial support against Henry II ineffective.² At the beginning of Philip's reign ³ an inhabitant of the border country, Sigebert de Gembloux, thought that the Germans wanted war with France. " See," he wrote in 1182, " how frequently the Germans seek opportunities of attacking the French; it is not justice but the spirit of violence, not equity but a desire to dominate and a thirst for pillage which calls them to arms." ⁴ The conflict between the Emperor and Henry the Lion, Duke of Saxony and leader of the Guelf faction, and the sentence of exile passed on Henry the Lion in 1180 brought the Emperor and the King of England into hostility, for the latter was Henry's father-in-law. Thus an Anglo-German alliance was avoided on the first occasion but Henry VI, the successor of Barbarossa, disturbed Philip Augustus again. He was a visionary, a megalomaniac, greedy for prestige. At first he was at enmity with Richard Cœur de Lion, another man of great ambitions, who had offended him by his display of power in Sicily at the time of the Third Crusade. Then, during Richard's captivity in Germany, he became reconciled with him and received his homage. Philip Augustus was distrustful and carefully followed the development of their relations. He had agents at the Imperial Court; he kept in his pay the Seneschal Marquard d'Annweiler and it was undoubtedly he who killed the project for an Anglo-German alliance. Henry VI died prematurely. A German historian had said in regretful tones that he would have been able to destroy the Capetian dynasty. Doubtless true but Henry VI had no desire to do so. The dream of his life had been to bring all the princes of Western Europe to recognize themselves as his vassals and to lead them to the Crusade under his banner.⁵

The Crusade was, naturally, the dominating idea also of the Holy See. In 1189–1190, the Pope Celestin III saw the

---

[1] Memoire published in **LXXX**, vi, 99–112, analysed in **CLXXII**, 275.
[2] **CCXI**, i, 17 ff.
[3] On the relations of Philip Augustus and the emperors, see **DXCV**; **CCXCVII**, 65 ff.; **CCXI**, i, 245 ff., and *passim*.
[4] Published in **CCXI**, i, app. xiii, p. 99.
[5] **DCXXXIX**, passim; **CCXI**, iii, 104 ff., 146–7, 165–6.

Emperor Barbarossa and the kings of France and England set off at last for the Holy Land. It was the culmination of a patient diplomacy but the Crusade failed and it immediately became a question of beginning it again. Subsequently, as before, the legates of the Pope were ceaselessly occupied in bringing about a reconciliation between the kings of France and England and they succeeded in getting treaties signed, but they held a position of neutrality between the two parties and neither of the two kings would have allowed the Pope to declare his rival in the right. During the twenty years between the death of Alexander III and the accession of Innocent III, the Papacy was neither very strong nor very respected. The Curia was regarded as poor, easily corrupted, and frequently uncertain of its own intentions.

Everything was changed in Germany and in the direction of the Christian world after the death of the Emperor Henry VI (September, 1197) and the accession of Pope Innocent III (January–February, 1198). The new pontif was an Italian of high birth, according to the standards of his age and, judged by his ability, a great theologian and lawyer, trained by the masters of Paris and Bologna in the sciences and dialectics. During his reign, the Papacy attained the height of its power.[1] The whole of Christianity was the object of his jealous and imperious attention and Rome became the diplomatic centre where the threads of world policy were tied and undone. The Carolingian idea of the single power to which the whole Christian world should be subject, foreshadowed, in the twelfth century, by the Staufen, was now to be upheld not by the Empire but by the Holy See even more clearly now than in the time of Gregory VII; for Innocent III based himself on the famous Decree of Gratian which had been drawn up in his beloved University of Bologna and considered that "God entrusted to Peter not only the government of the Universal Church but of the whole world". This was precisely the moment when the death of Henry VI plunged Germany into unbridled anarchy.

In spite of his protestations of affection for France and the Capetian monarchy, Innocent III was to be for Philip Augustus an opponent to be feared for he was extremely intelligent, a profound thinker, little subject to sentimental

[1] **CDXLII**, particularly i, 26 ff.; **CCXI**, iii, 166 ff.

RESISTANCE OF THE CAPETIANS

arguments, naturally using heinous methods, and rarely deceiving himself.[1] His theory that the Holy See must be the only judge of the major sins brought him into conflict, from the first, with Philip on several occasions. The king had repudiated and imprisoned his second wife, Isambour of Denmark,[2] after asking for a divorce from a Council of French bishops which had been a farce. In spite of Isambour's appeal to the Court of Rome, he had married a German, Agnès de Méran (1196). From his accession, Innocent commanded Philip to take back his legal wife and send away "the intruder". Agnès was undoubtedly the only person for whom the harsh Philip had any affection and he refused to leave her. Innocent III put part of France and " the lands which render obedience to the king " under interdict on 13th January, 1200.[3] In the dioceses of Paris, Senlis, Soissons, Amiens, and Arras the interdict was observed and the churches closed. Philip, in exasperation, drove out the bishops and canons who had obeyed the Pope. The Gallican Church and religious life in France received such a shock as a result that the two rivals grew anxious and became milder. The king consented to separate from Agnès and the Interdict was raised (September, 1200), but when the Council of Soissons, under the presidency of two legates, summoned Philip and Isambour to appear and sought to judge the fundamental issues, Philip seized Isambour under the eyes of the astonished cardinals and imprisoned her more straitly than ever (May, 1201). Innocent III kept his anger in check for the moment and, after the death of Agnès, even consented to legitimize the children she had had by Philip Augustus (2nd November, 1201).[4] These relations with Rome which caused very violent controversy among contemporaries become even more interesting when chronologically set in the matrix of general policy. Innocent, as his letters clearly show, would willingly have given up Isambour's cause on condition of compensation. He grew angry or gave way according to circumstances. The two objects on which he

---

[1] I have had occasion to show it : **DXV**, 32, 45–6, 105.
[2] Also called Ingeburge, Eremburge, Hildeburge, etc. (**CCXI**, iii, app. iv, pp. 236–7.) Isambour is the name she gives herself and she is given in Philip Augustus's will and is the one that should be used.
[3] **CCCLXXXVII**, 110–125.
[4] **CCXXXIII**, 39–180 ; **CCXI**, iii, 57, 129 ff., 167 ; iv, first part, 24 ff., 55 ff., 82 ff. ; **CCCX**, 3 ff., 93 ff.

was obstinately set were the Crusade, made difficult by the Anglo-French war, and the triumph of the Guelf faction in Germany. At the bottom of his heart, he was little concerned whether Philip had Isambour or Agnès at his side or whether he possessed the Norman Vexin or not.

From August, 1198, we find him telling Philip Augustus and Richard Cœur de Lion to make peace or, at least, a five years' truce for the recovery of the Holy Land. His legate, refusing to be put off by the brutality of Richard, succeeded in persuading him and it was thanks to his efforts that the truce of 1199 was concluded at a moment when Philip Augustus was at his last resources.[1] But, in the conflict between Guelf and Ghibelline, Innocent III was following a policy contrary to French interests. He had undertaken to be the guardian of Frederick II, the young son of Henry VI, but he only helped Sicily, and, through fear of seeing the power of the Hohenstaufen built up again, he sought the election of an emperor from the Guelfs. He announced his support, therefore, for Otto, Duke of Brunswick, a son of Henry the Lion, who was crowned emperor on the 12th July, 1198, while Philip Augustus on the 29th June made an alliance with Otto's rival, Philip of Swabia, the brother of Henry VI. Otto was through his mother a grandson of Henry II Plantegenet; he had been brought up in England, and his uncle, Richard Cœur de Lion, had given him the title of Duke of Aquitaine and entrusted to him the administration of Poitou.[2] Otto was to be one of the most serious enemies of Philip Augustus. The fate of the Capetian monarchy on several occasions was determined, or all but determined, by the combinations of Pope Innocent III.

IV

Conflicts with Henry II and Richard Cœur de Lion

In general, it was with inadequate resources and no external alliances that Louis VII and his son for half a century resisted

[1] CCXI, iii, 194 ff.
[2] CCXI, iii, 171 ff., 206; iv, 1st part, 66 ff., 80 ff.

RESISTANCE OF THE CAPETIANS

the powerful kings Henry II and Richard Cœur de Lion.[1] They owed their success primarily to their position as suzerain. Henry II who had a fairly noble character always retained some respect for the feudal bond. He had forced Eleanor's first husband to hand the Duchy of Aquitaine over to him, but when he sought to establish his suzerainty over Languedoc in 1159 and take possession of Toulouse, he did not dare to attack his lord and retired when Louis took possession of the town to defend it. Later, when Louis VII left the throne to a youth of 15 years of age, Henry II showed himself a magnanimous vassal and did not try to take advantage of the cabals and discords of the Court of France but played the role of a conciliator. Philip Augustus, on arrival at man's estate, did not consider it useful to remember the fact, and, once he was in a position to take the offensive, he found his position of suzerain merely a justification for his attack. By the use he made of legal claims he weakened his opponent and forced his other vassals to help fulfil his aims. One of Henry's sons, Geoffrey of Brittany, had died without an heir of age; another, Richard, had taken possession of the County of Poitou. In vain Philip demanded the wardship of Brittany and Richard's homage. On several occasions he summoned Henry II to his Court for a judgment of their differences, but the chief of the Angevin Empire could not consent to appear and the King of France was able to break off relations with a rebel as was customary (1187). Throughout his reign he coolly sought serviceable weapons against his opponents in the feudal law.

On the other hand Henry II was weakened by his quarrel with the English church, the insubordination of a section of his baronage, the difficulty of maintaining his authority throughout a vast Empire, and, finally, by complications and discord in his family. His daughter Mathilda had married Henry the Lion, leader of the Guelf party, and, as we have seen, the proscription of Henry the Lion led to a quarrel between Henry II and Frederick Barbarossa. It was, however, the hatred of his wife Eleanor and his sons, Henry the Younger, Richard, and Geoffrey of Brittany, which poisoned Henry's life and destroyed his courage and ambition. His son John,

---

[1] For all that follows, see **CCXI**, i–iv, 1st part; **CCCLVIII**; **CDLXXXVIII**. vol. i, chap. x, and vol. ii; **CDXCI**, books ii and iii; **DXLII**, 126 ff.

the last born, in whom he trusted blindly, finished by also betraying him.

About 1193 wars between Capetians and Plantegenets were frequent, but there was no apparent intention on either side to destroy and supplant their opponent. They fought for the suzerainty of Berry, Auvergne, and the County of Toulouse, which opened the way to the Mediterranean and the south, and, above all, for possession of the Norman Vexin at the gates of Paris. Louis VII was not able to take advantage of his opportunities even of the general revolt of 1173 which threatened the whole Augevin Empire but, from his twentieth year onwards, Philip Augustus was an opponent to be watched. He roused the treacherous ambitions of Henry's sons and the appetites of the Poitevin barons. In 1189 the founder of the Plantegenet dynasty, ill, deserted, and enclosed by the deadly animosity of his son Richard and Philip Augustus, submitted and accepted peace. He died two days later and thus the King of France obtained part of Berry and Auvergne.

Philip Augustus and the new King of England departed, on good terms, for the Holy Land to conquer the kingdom of Jerusalem from Saladin. But Philip whose status as suzerain and organizing ability should have assured the leading position in Syria found himself constantly thwarted and humiliated by his arrogant vassal. The death of the Count of Flanders which gave him hopes of increasing his demesne caused him to decide to return to France (July, 1191). When he learnt that Richard, also returning from the Holy Land, had been made prisoner by Duke Leopold of Austria [1] he wished to take advantage of his opportunity and his mind conceived the idea, which obsessed him for twenty years, of disinheriting the Plantegenets for the benefit of his own dynasty. In 1193 he married Isambour, sister of the King of Denmark, to provide himself at the same time with the claim on the Crown of England, which Canute the Great had substantiated in an earlier period, and the support of the Danish fleet for the conquest. The same year he formally announced to the Emperor Henry VI that he was renouncing Richard's homage and challenging him for disloyalty.

For fear of involving himself with the emperor he adopted a more modest project and undertook the conquest of

[1] DXCVIII, 268 ff.

RESISTANCE OF THE CAPETIANS

Normandy. But, on 4th February, 1194, Richard was freed. He was a warrior whose reputation was high and resources abundant. For five years the kings waged a fierce war which was interrupted only by truces or a precarious peace. In spite of all his courage Philip Augustus would have been destroyed if Pope Innocent III had not imposed a truce on the belligerents, who had forgotten the Holy Land, in 1199 and if Richard had not been killed a few weeks after at the siege of a castle in Limousin.

Philip Augustus hoped again for the dismemberment of the Angevin Empire. The barons of Brittany, Anjou, Touraine, and Maine supported, against John Lackland, the claims of the young Arthur, the son of Geoffrey of Brittany, who had been brought up at the Court of the King of France. But John was recognized as king in England and duke in Normandy; he was pushed and directed by his untiring mother, the old Queen Eleanor; he was well provided with money and servants. We have seen above how, at this time, Innocent III was preparing to lay the kingdom of France under Interdict. Philip decided to await a better occasion and a peace was concluded at Goulet near Gaillon on 22nd May, 1200.[1] John abandoned the district of Évreux, a part of the Norman Vexin, and Berry. His niece Blanche of Castile was to marry Louis, heir to the French crown. John did homage to Philip Augustus and paid the enormous relief of 20,000 marks sterling. This undoubtedly constituted a very large part of the war treasury which Philip Augustus was soon to use to disinherit John.

[1] **XXXI**, n. 604 ff.

CHAPTER V

THE VICTORY OF THE CAPETIANS

I

PHILIP AUGUSTUS AND JOHN LACKLAND

THE fundamental cause of the victory of the Capetians over the Plantegenets was the personal superiority of the kings of France, Philip Augustus, Louis VIII, and Saint Louis compared with John Lackland and Henry III.

During this period, Philip Augustus, cured of the neurasthenia which he had contracted in the East, freed from his terrible enemy Richard Cœur de Lion, and full of confidence in the future, achieved his greatest activity. It was during this period that the author of the *Chroncicle of Tours* was able to depict him as " a fine man, well proportioned in stature, with a smiling countenance, bald, a rubicund complexion, inclined to eat and drink well, sensual . . . farsighted, obstinate, rapid and prudent in judgment, fond of taking the advice of lesser people ".[1] Others tell us that his dress was simple, that he spoke with studied brevity, and knew how to make himself feared.[2] His energy, stubborn in the accomplishment of his plans, was moderated only by his supple spirit and a political wisdom that rarely made a mistake. The springs of his will were bent to an immense ambition. It was the period when poets and historians were giving the widest expansion to Carolingian legend and the Capetian dynasty, as a result of Philip's marriage to Isabella of Hainault who claimed to be descended from Charles of Lorraine, was seeking to find its connections with Charlemagne's line. In the last years of the twelfth century, Giles of Paris composed his *Carolinus* for Louis of France the son of Philip and Isabella and suggested his great ancestor as his model.[3] The positive and practical spirit of Philip

[1] **XXV**, 304.
[2] See the evidences brought together in **CCXI**, iv, 2nd part, 577 ff.
[3] **DXVII**, p. xxviii, 12-13.

VICTORY OF THE CAPETIANS

Augustus was not proof against the mirage-visions of a world Empire. His contemporary Gerald of Cambrie puts these words in his mouth, " Will God never be willing to give to me or another king of France the glory of restoring to the kingdom of France its ancient estate and the grandeur which it had in the time of Charles ? "[1] Another says that Philip " thought one man enough to govern the whole world."[2] It is highly unlikely that he thought of taking the Imperial Crown from Otto of Bunswick[3] but he was obsessed by the dream of uniting the Crowns of England and France.

Against him, to defend the Crown and the French fiefs of the Plantegenets, was a semi-madman. It is our opinion that John Lackland was subject to a mental disease well known to-day and described by modern psychiatrists as the periodical psychosis. It is surprising that modern historians have been able to estimate his character so wrongly and suggest for instance that he was a villain whose wickedness was cold and deliberate, who never allowed passion to guide him, and must, therefore, be regarded as all the more unpardonable. On the contrary John was unstable and irresponsible. He carried as well a heavy burden of unwelcome legacies from his father's family; among his Angevin ancestors were fools and madmen and the life of Fulk IV the Surly presents singular analogies to his.

John had fits of furious anger during which "his eyes darted flame and his face went livid ".[4] It was a weakness common to his times. He got this nervous weakness from his father Henry II and shared it with his brother Richard. Even more characteristic was his truly morbid incapacity to finish what he started and, at the beginning of his life, to stay on the side he had chosen. He betrayed everybody who tried to win his support—his father, his brother Richard, his allies, friends, and barons even when it was to his own interest to remain faithful to them.[5] With this instability went a boastful levity and a cynical frivolity which roused the indignation of the Churchmen. He was not even capable

---

[1] **XLIX**, 294.
[2] **LXI**, 426.
[3] According to English chroniclers (**XLVII**, 545 ; **XCVII**, 88), some German princes thought of electing him.
[4] **CX**, 408.
[5] See **CDLXXXIX**, *passim*.

of maintaining a decent attitude during such a ceremony as his ducal coronation at Rouen. His career in war and politics, however, provides us with the clearest information on his mental constitution. During the wars which Philip Augustus and his son waged against him, his conduct presents amazing alternations of the excitement and depression of disease. Gervais of Canterbury has clearly defined them; he shows him at the beginning of his reign taking vigorous action, then making himself a subject of laughter and gaining the name of " Soft Sword "; recovering himself and leading a victorious campaign to become once again, on receipt of the first bad news, feeble and cowardly; ultimately he earns a reputation for cruelty that none of his predecessors possessed to the same degree.[1] Even his enemies recognized his irresponsibility. William the Breton, the Chaplain of Philip Augustus, speaks of " the acts of fury which this unfortunate man *could not prevent himself committing* ".[2] He was regarded as possessed of a devil. The Englishman Roger of Wendover tells of the lazy life which John led while Philip was taking Normandy from him. John, he says, showed a smiling face as if everything was going well for him: one considered him " sent mad by witchcraft and sorcery ".[3]

We know that in the Middle Ages the mad were often believed to be possessed. All the symptoms we have enumerated are those of the periodic psychosis or cyclothymia. Philip Augustus had a madman as his rival.

II

THE DISINHERITANCE OF JOHN LACKLAND

The size and character of this book prevents us from dealing in detail with the description of the phases of the fall of the Angevin Empire but we must insist on the fact that, in origin, it was a feudal conflict. It was the appeal of the Poitevin barons which gave Philip Augustus the opportunity to summon the King of England to appear before his Court and a legal title to take away from him any of his French fiefs that he could conquer.

---

[1] **XLVIII**, 92–5.
[2] **LVII**, 177 (book vii, lines 19–20).
[3] **CXIX**, ii, 482.

VICTORY OF THE CAPETIANS 217

Now that Philip Augustus was in occupation of Berry, the Kings of England could rely on their communications between the northern part of the Angevin Empire and Aquitaine only when they could place implicit trust in the lords of La Marche, Angoumois, and Limousin. Henry II and Richard Cœur de Lion had been constantly at war with the counts of Angoulême and the viscounts of Limoges and had seized the County of La Marche which the House of Angoulême demanded should be returned. As an occasional ally they had a Poitevin house which had been made famous by the Crusades, the Lusignans, who also claimed the County of La Marche. The old Queen Eleanor and John Lackland recognized the claims of Hugh de Lusignan. Audemar, Viscount of Limoges, on the other hand, had gained support from Philip Augustus. In April, 1199, the three of them had signed a pact. " I have come to the lord the king," declares Audemar, " and I have come to an agreement with him on such terms that I will help him every day to the best of my ability, and I will not willingly desert him." Philip Augustus, for his part, promised to him " right by judgment of his court for the County of La Marche ".[1] Poitevin fickleness, however, had justifiably become proverbial. The houses of Angoulême and Lusignan were reconciled; Hugh the Brown of Lusignan, Count of La Marche, and Isabel, only daughter and heiress of the Count of Angoulême, exchanged promises of marriage " by personal vow ", which was preparatory to the nuptial benediction. Thus, at a later date, the House of Lusignan would reunite Angoumois and La Marche. John's advisers saw the danger and won over the changeable Count of Angoulême. Suddenly, taking advantage of the absence of Hugh the Brown and with the connivance of Audemar, John Lackland married the young Isabel on the 30th August, 1200; his father-in-law, as reward, was to receive the County of La Marche. In this way John secured the expected succession to the lordships which the Lusignans were reckoning to acquire. It was a good stroke of business [2] but it should have been completed and guaranteed by satisfying the Lusignans with

---

[1] **LXXII**, i, 201, n. 492-494; **XXXI**, p. 502.
[2] **CLXXXIV**, 4-12; **DXLII**, 208 ff.; **DLXV**, ii, 366, 376 ff.; **CCXI**, iv, 1st part, 3, 49 ff.

generous damages. They waited for them until Easter next year in vain and then, after addressing an appeal to the supreme suzerain, the King of France, they began to make war on John who confiscated their territories. Surrounded by young nobles who stimulated his vanity, John antagonized a section of the Poitevin baronage by his provocative actions. Philip Augustus, on the other hand, showed himself very prudent and maintained the unshakeable position his title as suzerain gave him. John did not follow his example or obey his summonses.[1] We cannot follow the details of this extremely interesting procedure here [2] but this is the summary drawn up by Philip Augustus for the use of the Holy See. We know this version, representing the point of view of the French Court, from the following letter which Innocent III sent to John Lackland.

> As you have taken away, without justice or reason, the castles and lands of men who consider them as his fief, Philip, as higher suzerain, driven by the complaints of the victims, has demanded, not once but many times, that you make reparation; you have promised but have done nothing and you have crushed the prostrate further. He has borne with you more than a year awaiting the satisfaction he has asked for. With the advice of his barons and subjects he has fixed a certain term for you to appear in his presence to do as the law demands without any withdrawal; although you are his liege subject, you have not appeared on the appointed day or sent any representative but have treated his summons with nothing but contempt. As a result, he has met you in person and warned you in his own words [3] for he does not wish to make war if you show yourself what you should be towards him. You have been unwilling to satisfy him. Then, although on the advice of his barons and subjects he had challenged you and started war against you, he has, nevertheless, sent four of his knights to find out whether you are willing to repair your faults against him; in case of refusal, he wants you to know that he will henceforward make alliance with all men wherever he can.[4]

---

[1] **DXLII**, 212 ff.; **CCXI**, iv, 1st part, 72 ff., 92 ff.

[2] It is known to us chiefly through William the Breton, Philip Augustus's chaplain: **LVII**, 155 ff. (bk. vi, line 104 ff.).

[3] If we refer to other sources, some of which have the authority of first-hand information, it makes it quite apparent that, to maintain his role of a conciliator, Philip Augustus colours the truth here. He must be speaking here of the conversation of 25th March, 1202; actually the two kings did not meet, and the conference was held between arbitrators; we know this from two of the people concerned and letters patent of John, dated 11th May (**DXV**, 8, n. 4). John was invited to give satisfaction or even give up the fiefs; on refusing he was summoned to appear before the Court of France on the 28th April.

[4] Letter of 31st October, 1203 II.F., vol. xix, 444–5 (**XCIII**, n. 2013). Cf. **DXLII**, 218 ff.

In these assertions of Philip Augustus, which are not entirely accurate or sincere, there is not, explicitly, the question of a judgment. Modern historians have thought that no sentence had been pronounced by the Court of France.[1] However, the challenge, mentioned in Innocent's letter, was the formal break which followed the condemnation of a guilty feudatory and, from the legal point of view, we can be certain that John had been condemned by the barons composing the Court of France on the 28th April, 1202. It is our opinion, however, that there was no formal sentence. In any case, it was clearly not written; the barons assented by acclamations to the proposals of the king of despoiling a rebel vassal.

An extremely well informed English chronicler has preserved a verbal tradition which is possibly expressed in too legalistic a form but provides us with the grounds and the basis of the decision taken. It tells us that :—

> The Court of France had met and judged that the King of England should be deprived of all the lands which he and his ancestors had held of the King of France up to that time because, for a long time, they had neglected to do the services due for those lands and, on practically no occasion, were they willing to comply with their lord's summons.[2]

Thus Philip had won a very easy acceptance by his barons of a confiscation based not on facts particularly relating to Poitou but on the refusal of a vassal's obedience from John and his ancestors. It was the best way to introduce, without any possible controversy, the question of the fief which was the chief object of Capetian ambition, Normandy.

In fact, for the moment, Philip's idea was to hold all that he could conquer of Normandy (he could not believe at that moment that the entire occupation would be possible) and to confer the other fiefs of the Plantegenets on Arthur who was affianced to his daughter, Marie of France. Arthur,

---

[1] **CDLXXXVII**, 53 ff.; **CDLXXXIX**, 83–4; **CCCXLVI**, 246 ff.

[2] **XCVII**, 135–6. Cf. **DXV**, 7 ff. It will be noticed that this text agrees with the only official act issued from the Capetian Chancery in which the condemnation of John is specifically mentioned. I am speaking of the mandate of Louis VIII in 1224, ordering the burgesses of Limoges to help him in the war he was about to undertake " to gain his rights " (**DXVII**, p. 516). The king says : " Know all of you that John, late King of England, by the common and unanimous judgment of the peers and other barons of France lost in law (*abjudicatus*), for ever, all the land which he held on this side of the English sea of our late dear father, Philip King of France, and that since then those possessions have belonged of right to our said father."

betraying the homage he had offered John, did homage to the King of France for Brittany, Anjou, Maine, Touraine, and Poitou (July, 1202),[1] and was entrusted with a campaign in Poitou while Philip began the conquest of Normandy. The coalition failed, however; by a stroke of good fortune, John captured Arthur and the Lusignans (1st August, 1202). Arthur was put in prison and, from the moment when he was taken to the Tower of Rouen, nobody knows what happened to him. About 1206, Philip and his court gave up hope that he was still living. Some years later, about 1210, the truth was revealed in detail thanks to the confession of William de Briouse, one of John's accomplices and the guardian of the young captive. On 3rd April, 1203, John had killed his nephew with his own hand because he was afraid of seeing him escape and become a strong claimant for the English throne. Subsequently, in 1216, when Louis of France invaded England at the invitation of the barons in rebellion against John, his agents tried to gain credence for the story that John Lackland had been "condemned to death by his peers in the Court of the King of France" as Arthur's murderer. It has been fully shown that this was a shameless lie.[2] The sentence of confiscation and the severance of the feudal bond between the two kings, pronounced on the 28th April, 1202, a year before the secret tragedy of Rouen, had been sufficient justification for the conquests of Philip Augustus. Feudal law allowed Philip to gain a sentence of disinheritance against his vassal; the feudal spirit which inspired both French and English nobility guaranteed his victory.

It was just at the moment when he invaded Normandy that many of his barons were setting off for the East; but the fourth Crusade, while robbing the king of many warriors, relieved him also of many disquieting vassals who might have thwarted his ambition, in particular Baldwin, Count of Flanders, who was to become Emperor of Constantinople. Those who remained showed themselves loyal. The Duke of Burgundy and Renaud of Dammartin, Count of Boulogne, then at the height of his favour, assisted Philip to conquer

---

[1] **LXXII**, i, 236, n. 647.
[2] On all these facts see **CLXV, DXV, DXLII**; Cartellieri (**CCXI**, iv, 1st part) has adopted Guilhiermoz's views (**CCCXXV**). Powicke who formerly defended them has ceased to support them (*C.M.H.*, vol. vi, 1929, pp. 249, 315, 320).

VICTORY OF THE CAPETIANS

the Loire lands. When Innocent III sent a legate to France to stop the hostilities which were on the point of breaking out, Philip called his magnates together on several occasions; the Duke of Burgundy, the Count of Boulogne, the countesses of Champagne, Blois, and St. Quentin, the counts of Sancerre, Nevers, Beaumont, Soissons, the Lord of Coucy, and Guy de Dampierre all promised him solemnly that they would not allow the Pope to force them into an alliance or a truce with the King of England [1] and Philip thereupon replied to the Pope that a feudal matter was no business of the Holy See.[2] The ecclesiastical barons, holders of the royal bishoprics, declared in turn that the king's cause seemed just to them. John Lackland, on the other hand, was deserted because he himself set the example of desertion. Irritated by the inaction of their lord who failed to fulfil his duty of protection, the barons and towns of Normandy renounced their allegiance to retain their fiefs or privileges. John with his immense resources lost the game because he had not won the hearts of his men; he could measure the worth of the poet's words:—

> It isn't the wealth of fur or ornament, of gold or silver, of forts or horses but the wealth of family and friends; a man's heart is worth all the gold of the realm.[3]

The reduction of Normandy took two years (June, 1202-June, 1204). Henry II and Richard who had, with good reason, considered it the richest jewel in their crown had built up defences and castles, permanent bands of hired knights, and mercenaries.[4] The incredible inertia of John gave Philip Augustus the richest country in the Angevin Empire, the most advanced in material, social, and intellectual, civilization in Western Christendom. Henceforward, the Capetian monarchy had established the security of their capital and become a maritime power while the English kings had lost their easy access to the West and the South.[5]

The feudal system being based only on the personal bond and the sworn faith carried, within itself, alongside the spirit of chivalry, a leaven of brutal anarchy and warrior barbarism which only a strong and constantly vigilant

---

[1] **XXXI**, n. 762, 770–780 (June–August, 1203).
[2] H.F., vol. xix, 441. On the interventions of Innocent III see **CCXI**, iv, 1st part, bk. ix.
[3] **CXX**, ii, 265.
[4] **DXLII**, chap. vii and viii.
[5] Ibid., 220 ff.; **CCXI**, iv, 1st part, 113–202.

monarchy could prevent from developing. This became very apparent during the thirteenth century to the south of the Loire, particularly after the death of Eleanor who died an octogenarian on 31st March, 1204, when disorder began to increase. Philip Augustus had, at first, taken advantage of the instability and inconstancy of the barons of the West. He had formed an alliance with two powerful seigniorial houses. He makes sure of the conquest of Anjou and Touraine; he had conferred the seneschalship on William des Roches who had previously betrayed him and, henceforward, remained faithful to him [1]; but Aimery of Thouars whom he made Seneschal of Poitou returned to John Lackland in 1206. Philip Augustus, in all, seized from the King of England not only Normandy and Maine but the lands on the Loire Basin and even Brittany which, at a later date, he entrusted to his cousin Pierre de Dreux, but he could not conquer Poitou which remained a cockpit of intermittent hostilities and feudal anarchy. It was Philip's successor, Louis VIII, who reduced Poitou in 1224 thanks to an alliance with Hugh de Lusignan, Count of La Marche; from that time the Capetians had in La Rochelle, Saint Jean d'Angély, and Niort, a port on the ocean and important commercial centres. Louis VIII left Poitou together with Auvergne as an appanage for his fourth son, Alphonse. When Alphonse, on reaching his majority, came to Poitou to receive the homage of his vassals (1241), the Poitevin barons tried to shake off the Capetian supremacy and called in the King of England, Henry III; the victories of Saint Louis at Taillebourg and Saintes brought Henry III to the decision to abandon Poitou and the Capetians finally established monarchy and order there.[2]

III

ANGLO-GERMAN COALITION. BOUVINES

We must return to Philip Augustus. In 1206 he concluded a truce with John Lackland but it was not observed. From time to time, John had bursts of activity and as he was

[1] **CCLXVII.**
[2] **CCXI**, iv, 1st part, bk. ix; **DLXV**, ii; **DXVII**, 224 ff.; **CLXX**, chap. iv and vii; **CLXXI**, 5–44; **CLXIV, CLXXXIV.**

VICTORY OF THE CAPETIANS 223

lacking neither in intelligence nor resources, Philip Augustus remained anxious and ready to fight. Warlike preparations, the strengthening of fortifications, underhand negotiations, attempts to seduce their opponent's barons, and finally the circumstances which favoured the formation of the two systems of antagonistic alliances in the West, all led to a general war. In fact, it was on the point of breaking out and was to have extremely important consequences. Empire and Papacy were to take part in this decisive conflict; France, England, and even Germany were to be involved and the course of their political history modified by it.

Philip Augustus and John Lackland sought allies everywhere.[1] Philip made agreements with the lords of the newly annexed districts, negotiated with the discontented barons of England or Gascony and the Welsh prince, Llewelyn ap Joverth while John maintained communications with Normandy and Poitou. Both sent ambassadors to the neighbouring countries on the frontiers of the Empire and even as far as Holland and Thuringia; the support they found there was far from reliable; the recantations of Henry I, Duke of Brabant, were typical. The decision which the two most powerful counts of North France, of Boulogne, and Flanders, took was more important.

Renaud de Dammartin belonged to a family of loyal châtelains of the Île de France; he had married the heiress to the County of Boulogne and had fiefs reaching to the frontiers of Britanny. Philip Augustus appreciated his understanding and ability and tried to strengthen his wavering loyalty by satisfying his ambition. Either as the result of wounded vanity or perhaps, because he thought Philip too weak to stand against the alliance of John and Otto of Brunswick, in 1211 Renaud entered into negotiations with the King of England and the Emperor. A sentence of the Court of France declared him a traitor and deprived him of his fiefs. He fled into exile On 3rd May, 1212, he did homage to John and, henceforward, he was to be the inspirer and organizer of the coalition against the King of France.[2]

Philip Augustus believed that he could rely on the Flemish alliance. Jeanne, the daughter and heiress of the late Count

---
[1] See particularly, **CCXI**, iv, 2nd part, bk. x.
[2] **CDLVIII**, and the supporting documents; **CCXI**, iv, bk. ix and x.

Baldwin IX, came to Paris to marry Ferrand, the son of the King of Portugal and a relation of Blanche of Castile (January, 1212). The Flemings, since the departure of their Count for the Crusade, had submitted to the protection of the King of France but the commercial classes, which had the strongest reasons for keeping on good terms with John, remained hostile, and it was necessary to take hostages in the towns; the nobilities accepted the pensions offered for lack of higher bids. The new count, a stranger in the country who was badly received, needed external support. Philip Augustus made the mistake of alienating him by taking away the two towns of Saint Omer and Aire. Ferrand was naturally loyal but his suzerain had done him wrong and refused any compensation. King John turned to his financial weapons to win over the count's advisers.[1]

In Germany, pounds sterling could work wonders. Otto of Brunswick, relieved of his rival Philip of Swabia (died by assassination in 1208), remained firmly attached to a lucrative alliance and became a disturbing enemy for France. He had quarrelled with the Pope, however, by reviving the policy of the Staufen and showing his ambition to reduce Italy. The Pope found himself forced to support against him " the child of Apulia ", Frederick II, the son of Henry VI, and to allow the formation of an alliance between the young leader of the Ghibelline party and Philip Augustus. On 19th November, 1212, Louis of France met Frederick at Vaucouleurs and they entered into mutual engagements. A certain number of German princes, convinced by the specious arguments of Philip Augustus, elected Frederick as king on 5th December. By the end of this critical year, two systems of alliances had been established in Western Europe.[2]

Innocent III had no objects but the interests of the Church and the triumph of Christ. He would have wished to make peace between the Christian princes but the complexity of the questions involved led him to adopt a contradictory policy and a dangerous route. Previously, he had tried to maintain the Angevin Empire and put a check to the conquests of Philip Augustus. The abominable persecution of the English Church, carried on by John, had forced him to depose the

[1] CDXCV, chap. i and ii; CCLIII; CCLIV, 314 ff.; CCXI, iv, 2nd part, bk. x.
[2] CCXI, bk. x; CCCLXXXIV, i, 195 ff.; DXVII, 31-2.

VICTORY OF THE CAPETIANS

King of England in the same way as he had deposed Otto. Philip Augustus was the only prince to whom he could appeal to reduce John. In January, 1213, the sentence of deposition was promulgated in France by the Holy See and the King of France and his subjects were instructed to take away John's crown for the remission of their sins. Louis VIII, who had married one of John's nieces, was to replace him on the English throne. Philip Augustus allowed himself to become a pawn for the Pope and assembled an army and a fleet. The legate, Pandulph, however, had been given instructions on the conditions under which John would receive pardon; he travelled to England and gained his submission. John consented to become the liege man of the Pope and Philip Augustus, on pain of excommunication, had to abandon the expedition he was preparing on the prompting of the Holy See.[1]

By this tortuous manœuvre, Innocent III had freed the English Church but he had unleashed war. Philip found himself threatened by an Anglo-Flemish-German coalition. Ferrand had refused host service for the expedition to England and now received John's emissaries. The King of France set out to ravage Flanders. In 1214 after losing a lot of time, the allies attacked him on both sides at once. John Lackland, himself, conducted the campaign in the West; taken with panic at the arrival of Louis of France he departed without giving battle (La Roche au Moine, 2nd July). In the North, the Germans with their emperor, the troops of the counts of Flanders and Boulogne, and an English detachment had met at Valenciennes to march on Paris. A decisive battle was fought in the marshy plain between Bouvines and Tournai. Tactical dispositions based on common sense were made by Guerin, the Bishop of Senlis, whose sound judgment and intelligent activity were marked in every sphere of politics. But the battles of those days were not a matter of science; there was a series of hand to hand encounters, of furious charges by heavily armed knights who tried to unhorse each other. Victory was won by sporting enthusiasm, personal bravery, endurance, and loyalty to the leaders. Philip Augustus though lacking a numerous army had a magnificent band of knights with him whose loyalty was assured. He fought

[1] **DXVII**, 30–8; **CCXI**, bk. xi. See Bk. Four, Chap. I below of this volume.

bravely himself and all but perished. His enemies did not work together very well; the feudal spirit weakened any coalition before it was put to the test. The Duke of Brabant who seems to have been bought by the King of France gave the first signal of disorder among the allies. The flight of the Emperor Otto and the capture of the other leaders made it irretrievable (27th July, 1214).[1]

The Capetian dynasty had never known such a triumph in battle. Bouvines simultaneously guaranteed its hegemony in France and the West.[2] In Germany the Guelf party gave up the fight and Frederick II entered on his imperial career. He remained in general friendly with the Capetians. Flanders, whose count was to remain a prisoner in the Louvre until 1227, passed under the strict surveillance of Philip Augustus.[3]

IV

Last Conflicts. Treaty of Paris

John returned to England crippled and less than a year later the barons dictated to him their conditions (Great Charter, 15th June, 1215). To get rid of a man who was incapable of keeping a promise it was necessary to turn to a foreigner and once more Louis of France received the offer of the English crown. But this time, Innocent III supported John who was a liege of the Holy See. Philip Augustus was distrustful of the fickleness of the English barons and the ability of the Roman Curia. He left his son to depart on his own and to assume full responsibility for the war. Louis was well received by the majority of the barons and bishops and the people of London, he confirmed the Charter and expected some great success to achieve his consecration as King of England. But he was excommunicated, as were all his supporters, and his forces were inadequate. The tyranny of the Plantegenets was forgotten by the English when they learned of the disappearance of John Lackland who had

---

[1] **CCXI**, bk. xi and xii; **CDXLVI**, 174–196; **DXVII**, 40–51; **DCVII**, 151.
[2] See the description of the victory festivals in **LVII**, bk. xii; **CCXIII**.
[3] **CCLIII**, 137 ff.; **CCXI**, iv, 2nd part, 491 ff.

VICTORY OF THE CAPETIANS

died of indigestion on 19th October, 1216. The new Pope, Honorius III, intervened warmly in favour of John's young son, Henry III, and Louis of France found himself being gradually deserted and had to give up his ambitions (Peace of Lambeth, 11th September, 1217). The war he had carried on and the ravages of John's mercenaries had at least ruined England and made her impotent. Philip Augustus was able to finish his busy life in peace, holding the prisoners of Bouvines in gaol, strengthening his fortifications, and keeping a watch on his nobility.[1]

He bequeathed to his son a crown with considerable prestige, an orderly kingdom, and a war treasury. Louis VIII (1223-6) had a cold and determined character, energetic and ambitious. Well supported by the remarkable woman he had married, he would undoubtedly have had a brilliant reign but he died prematurely after some fruitful expeditions in Poitou and the South. Blanche of Castile and Saint Louis preserved the conquests of Philip Augustus and Louis VIII. On two occasions, in 1230 and 1242, Henry III had dreams of conquest; but the two expeditions failed miserably.[2]

Henry III still possessed Guienne but he was no longer the vassal of the King of France for the sentence of 1202 had broken the feudal tie between Capetian and Plantegenets. Saint Louis and he, however, had married sisters. Attracted towards peace by family sympathies, his Christian sentiments, and, above all, by his dislike for any intrigue that was of doubtful character, Saint Louis proposed a compromise and the recognition of accomplished facts to his brother-in-law. Henry III, who had become very unpopular in England, finally yielded on the eve of a rising even more serious than that of 1215. The baronial party wanted an end to the conflict with France. The peace, concluded on 28th May, 1258, was published in Paris, 4th December, 1259. Henry III gave up Normandy, Maine Anjou, Touraine, and Poitou, and again became the liege of the King of France for the fiefs he retained.[3]

---

[1] **DXVII**, 1st part, chap. iii-ix. Subsequently, I have published an important text, **XLII**, and, in **DXV**, taken up again the question of the justification of Louis's claim to the English Crown. Cf. **CCXI**, iv, 2nd part, bk. xiii.
[2] See pp. 292-3.
[3] **CCCVII**; **CLXIX**, p. v ff.

IV. DESCENDANTS OF LOUIS VI AND LOUIS VII

Alliances with royal and seigniorial dynasties. Capetian Ecclesiastical dignitaries.

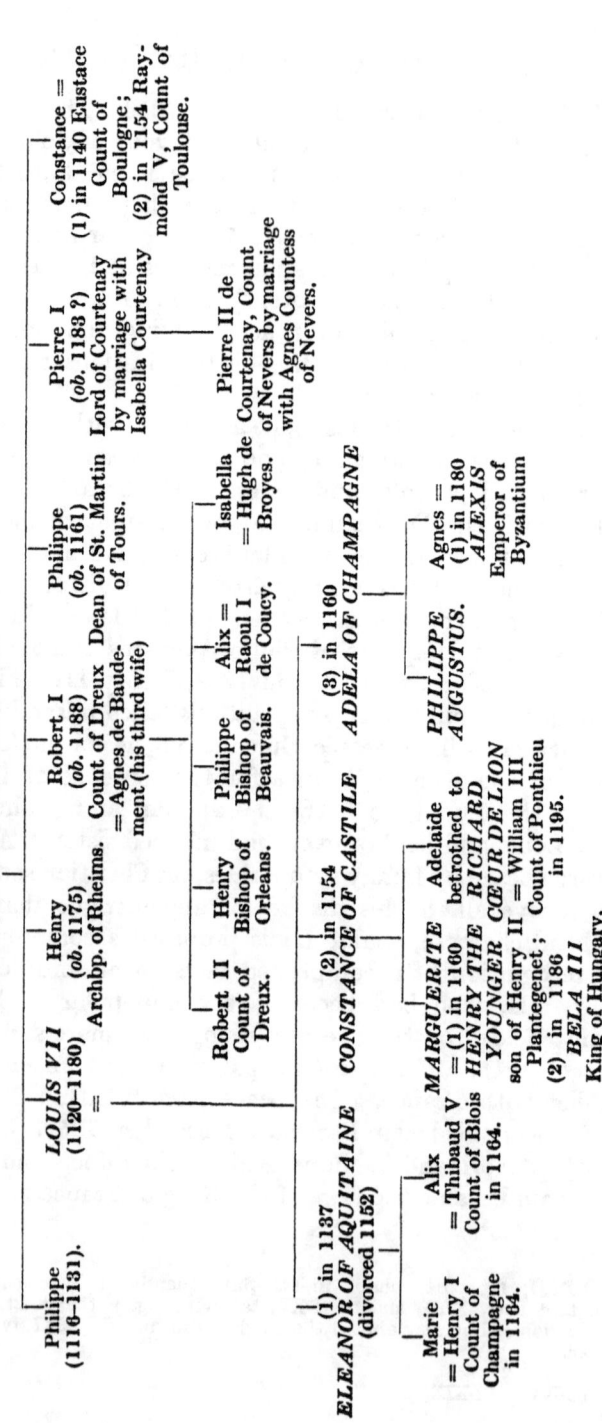

V. DESCENDANTS OF PHILIP AUGUSTUS, LOUIS VIII, AND SAINT LOUIS

Princes holding appanages. Alliances. Origin of Valois and Bourbons.

Philippe Augustus =
- (1) in 1180 **ISABELLA OF HAINAULT**
- (2) in 1193 **ISAMBOUR OF DENMARK** — Divorce not recognized by the Pope. No children.
- (3) in 1196 **AGNES DE MERAN** — children legitimized by Innocent III
- Morganatic union with "a maiden of Arras"
  - Pierre Charlot, Bishop of Noyon.

Children of Philippe Augustus:

- **LOUIS VIII** = **BLANCHE OF CASTILE** — 12 children; the following survived adolescence
- Philippe Hurepel, Count of Boulogne by marriage with the heiress to the county.
- Marie, betrothed to Arthur.

Children of Louis VIII and Blanche of Castile (the following survived adolescence):

- **LOUIS IX** = **MARGUERITE OF PROVENCE** — 12 children; the following survived adolescence
- Robert, Count of Artois by appanage.
- Alphonse, Count of Poitiers by appanage and Count of Toulouse by marriage with the daughter of Raymond VII.
- Isabella. Charles, Count of Anjou by appanage, Count of Provence by marriage with Beatrix of Provence and King of Sicily.

Children of Louis IX and Marguerite of Provence:

- Jean Tristan, Count of Nevers.
- Pierre, Count of Alençon.
- **PHILIPPE III The Bold** — Common ancestor of the last Capetians and the Valois.
- Robert, Count of Clermont = Beatrix de Bourbon. *Founder of the Bourbon dynasty.*
- Isabella = Thibaud V, Count of Champagne and King of Navarre.
- Blanche = Ferdinand of Castile.
- Marguerite = Jean, Duke of Brittany.
- Agnès = Robert II, Duke of Burgundy.

To those who deprecated the treaty, Louis said, " He was not my man and he has entered my homage."[1] Like the popes of the period, he saw in homage the guarantee of political and moral order. The first Hundred Years' War (1152–1259) finished thus in an act of loyalty by the standards of Feudalism. It laid the seeds for the second which was to be more incessant and more disastrous. In practice, the Treaty of Paris was not the clear and definitive agreement which the King of France would undoubtedly have liked. The situation of Aquitaine was so involved that the editor of the treaty had been forced to make allusions, exceptions, and reservations which, immediately after the death of Saint Louis, gave rise to incessant conflicts. Louis IX was activated by a love of peace and order; but his memory could not bind, in a later age, those agents of the King of France, the Parlement of Paris and local officials, to a renunciation of suzerainty or to see it abused nor the King of England to be a willing vassal. In feudal principles, Saint Louis believed he had found the means of assuring Christian peace. Philip Augustus had sought in it only a method of unlocking the vice which was cramping the Capetian monarchy and a justification for his conquests; it was he and not Saint Louis who established the tradition which statesmen of the *ancien régime* have consistently followed.

[1] See Joinville (**LXVIII**), §§ 65, 678–9.

BOOK THREE

THE APOGEE OF THE FEUDAL MONARCHY IN FRANCE AND THE ARISTOCRATIC REACTION IN ENGLAND

CHAPTER I

THE INSTITUTIONS OF THE CAPETIAN MONARCHY FROM THE CONQUEST OF NORMANDY TO THE DEATH OF ST. LOUIS

I

RESIDENCES AND HOMES OF THE KING. THE HOUSEHOLD

THE disinheritance of John Lackland marked a date of extreme importance in the history of the French monarchy the prestige and resources of which were suddenly doubled. The conquest of Normandy, in particular, had been of considerable importance. The royal demesne there was extensive and wealthy; the country was well administered, accustomed to obey, and furnished with a judicial and administrative bureaucracy, the traditions of which gradually penetrated Capetian methods of government. Henceforward, sheltered from the threat of an English invasion and adequately provided with money, the monarchy was able for seventy years to develop its machinery, regularly and without sudden changes, with the help of a personnel drawn from the ancient demesne not to speak of the traces of the influence of southern lawyers which can be found, at least, at the centre. The Capetian power was strengthening itself without emerging from its traditional setting, the feudal framework. It is a period which has a unity of its own, in which the essential traits can be distinguished which differentiate the medieval from the modern monarchy.

The traditional simplicity of the dynasty showed itself without any considerable modification in the daily life of Philip Augustus, Louis VIII, and Louis IX.[1] It was from Paris, " a historic town whose fame and glory has spread throughout the world,"[2] that royal acts were, as far as possible, issued from which we can surmise that it was the king's normal residence at this period. But Philip Augustus, particularly

[1] **CDXXXVI**, 132-3 ; **CLXX**, chap. vi.
[2] **LXXXIV**, 330.

towards the end of his life, made frequent stays in the forest districts where he had the opportunity to hunt, at St. Germain-en-Laye in particular, at Compiègne, or at Melun. He liked the Vexin and the neighbouring parts of Normandy, Mantes, Gisors, Anet, Pacy, Pont-de-l'Arche. Louis VIII had a preference for St. Germain, Louis IX for Vincennes. They adopted their predecessor's habits and, even in time of peace, frequently changed their quarters for two reasons : first, the right of hospitality, which they exercised particularly at the expense of the Church, allowed them to effect considerable economies on the maintenance of themselves and their followers [1] ; secondly, they wished to see things for themselves and be seen. It was not without some gain in prestige that Saint Louis, during the later years of his life, made several journeys through Normandy, visiting the poor, talking to the nobles, lay and ecclesiastical, and being formally received in every abbey from the Vexin to Mont Saint Michel.[2]

The king travelled with his full household or, at least, some part of it. It was an ancient institution of which, however, we have no details before the reign of Saint Louis.[3] The household, in the narrowest domestic sense of the term, consisted of six departments—the pantry, the butlery, the fruitery, the stable, and the chamber. The department or ministry (ministerium) which was in constant contact with the royal person and, alone, had a political importance was the chamber where clothes and valuables were kept ; the chamberlains gradually became people of primary importance. The offices of the chamber were situated in the Palais de la Cité and the Louvre. In the tower of the Louvre was the household chest where the king had under his control a treasury of precious metals and coined money.[4] The chamber was also responsible for the archives which, from the end of Saint Louis's reign onwards, were preserved in an annexe of the Sainte Chapelle. Gautier of Nemours, a chamberlain, and the Bishop Guérin had been the principal archivists of Philip Augustus. They had established what was known, at a later date, as the Trésor des Chartes which included original

---

[1] **DXVII**, 330.
[2] **XXXI**, p. ciii ff. ; Itinerary of Louis VIII in **DXVII**, 438 ff. ; **LXXVII**, 408 ff.
[3] **DCLXVII**, pp. lvii–lxi.
[4] **DXVII**, 374, 387 ff. ; **CCCXCIX**, 323 ff.

dispatches and registers. It consisted of the charters which seem to have had the greatest financial and administrative interest.[1] The register which Saint Louis took with him on the Crusade as a ready source of information was of this character. It is possible to-day for us to turn the leaves of this volume which Saint Louis handled.

II

THE COURT

The most important servants of the household had originally been the seneschal, the constable, the butler, and the chamberlain. In a decree of 1224, they are still called *ministeriales* of the king's household. They had become separated from their domestic duties and, like the Chancellor, developed into major officials of the Crown.

At the same time, the marshals, formerly in charge of the stables under the direction of the constable, had been raised to command of the army. These offices, by their historical development, were the concrete proof that the king's court, the centre of government, was nothing but an enlarged household, entertaining numerous guests permanent or in transit. Philip Augustus, from mistrust, suppressed the office of seneschal (1191), and left vacant that of chancellor (1185–1223). The latter was only restored for a short period (1223–7) for the benefit of the Bishop Guérin but the three other great offices were held in the thirteenth century by men who played an important part, such as the constables Dreu de Mello, Mathieu de Montmorency, Raoul de Nesle, the butlers Robert de Courtenay and Henry de Sully, the chamberlain Barthélemy de Roye, etc. Guérin (ob. 1227) and Barthélemy de Roye (ob. 1237 ?) were the principal advisers of the Crown until the time of their death. The great officials were the trusted ministers of the Crown without any very exact specialization of functions. For instance, the constable is not yet in charge of the army. Most of them belonged to the middle nobility of the royal demesne; Guérin was of humble birth.[2] The secondary offices were

---

[1] Studies of Delaborde, in **LXXII**, vol. v, p. 1 ff., xxii ff., and in **CIV**, intro.
[2] **XXXI**, intro., p. lxxviii ff.; **DCLXX** 38 ff.; **CCXI**, iv, 2nd part, 444, 588, etc.; **DXVII**, 334 ff.; **CLXXXVI**, 385 ff.; **DXI**, 155 ff., 509 ff.

still very largely monopolized by certain families such as the Clermonts who succeeded one another as marshals, the La Chapelles, the Tristans, and the Villebeons who were chamberlains. The principle of hereditary office, though constantly watched and restricted, still found expression in these able and devoted servants. Besides them, there were numerous petty nobles and "royal knights" who lived at Court and from whom were drawn diplomats, judges, councillors, and bailiffs; in this class fell the counts of Dreux, Sancerre, Saint Pol, the Beaumonts, Coucys, Beaujeus, Archambaud de Bourbon, the lawyer Pierre de Fontaines, Simon de Nesle who was Saint Louis's "lieutenant" in France during the king's last crusade, and the famous Sire de Joinville.[1]

The clerical element which had previously been preponderant still held an important place in the personnel of the Curia. In every branch we find *clerici domini Regis*. The people who probably did most, apart from the kings themselves, to impress on monarchical policy of the period its conservative and moderate character were the great churchmen who appear so often among the king's following: Pierre de Corbeil, Archbishop of Sens, who was, next to Bishop Guérin and Aimard, the commander of the Templars, one of the advisers who had most weight with Philip Augustus; the Archbishop of Rouen, Eudo Rigaud; the Bishop of Paris, William d'Auvergne; Guy Foulquoi (the future Pope Clement IV), Bishop of Le Puy. The Archbishop of Bourges and three bishops formed a sort of Council of Regency during the crusade in Egypt and Mathieu de Vendôme, Abbot of St. Denis, was the king's lieutenant, together with the Sire du Nesle, when Louis set out for Tunis.[2]

In spite of the liberty to elect their superiors which the three kings left to the chapters and convents, it is highly probable that some of these prelates owed their clerical dignities to the political administrative services they had rendered. The fact is indisputable in the case of Guérin. The Franciscan Eudo Rigaud had been the friend and

---

[1] **DCXII**; **CCLII**, 187 ff.; **DCLXX, CCXI, DXVII**, passim; **CLXX**, 52 ff.; **CCCXCIX**, 46 ff.

[2] Will and codicil of 1270; **LXXII**, iv, n. 5638, 5730, 5734; **CCXI**, iv, 2nd part, 591; **CCL**, 61 ff.; **CCXLV**, 312–13; **CCXCIII**, 40–1; **CLXXII**, 57 ff.; **CLXIX**, p. lxix; **DCLI**, chap. ix.

INSTITUTIONS OF CAPETIAN MONARCHY 237

adviser of Louis IX before being promoted to the see of Rouen. The alliance of Crown and Church, in spite of mutual dissatisfaction and controversies, was so close that the ecclesiastical electors had no objection to such candidates on principle. Further, Louis IX was so scrupulous on such matters that he was, we believe, the first Capetian to ask the Pope to give formal authorization to the royal clerks not to reside in the benefices in the king's gift which had been given to them as appointments.

This question of the remuneration of officials was still solved and was for a long time yet to be solved in the old way in the majority of cases. Many of them were lodged and fed at the expense of the household. Those who distinguished themselves were given a living if they were clerks, or, if they were laymen, a money fief for which they did homage or an annual rent levied on some provostship or on the chest of the chamber.[1] The system of wages, however, was already established.[2]

As in the past, the Court was expanded from time to time, and great meetings were arranged with the same functions and the same purely consultative character as of old. As previously they remained very irregular and very variable in the number and qualifications of those taking part. It would appear that during the reign of Saint Louis they became less frequent in France than in England where the king made frequent demands for money. The institution remained, however, far from moribund. The officials, the royal clerks and knights, and the permanent residents at the Court witnessed the arrival, on these occasions, of prelates, great lords, and even burgesses, all summoned to discharge their duty of giving counsel and all sitting down together.

It was particularly in view of the necessity of taking political decisions of major importance demanding a meeting of the barons that the largest assemblies were brought together; for example, in 1205, at Chinon, the barons were consulted by Philip Augustus on the unjust claims of the Pope; they pledged him to resistance and promised their support; in

---

[1] **XXXI** (numerous examples); **CDXXXVI**, 88–94.
[2] **LXXXI**, ii, lxxxix (1285), xcvii (1286), etc.; **CCCXCVIII**, 320, n. 4; **CXLVIII**, 94–5.

1213, at Soissons, and in 1216, at Melun, a decision was taken for an expedition to England ; during the three years of Louis VIII's reign, many political gatherings were held ; there were at least ten at which the war with England and the Albigensian Crusade came up for discussion.[1] In the reign of Saint Louis, in 1235, we see forty-one great lords and councillors " and other barons and knights ", in conclave with the king at St. Denis and drawing up a protest against the actions of the clergy which was sent to the Pope ; other great meetings were held about the matrimonial alliances which affected the dynasty or to decide to end by arbitration the quarrel between the House of Dampierre and the House of Avesnes or on the occasion of the peace with England and the homage to Louis IX rendered by Henry III, etc.[2]

Other " concilia " were concerned with legislation and administration. This was the character of the assembly at Villeneuve le Roi (1209) which accepted an ordinance concerning the division of fiefs [3] or those which Louis VIII held to reach agreement with his barons on the position of Jews in the kingdom, to fix his rights over certain land, to make a definite enactment on a claim against host service, to issue ordinances against the heretical and excommunicated subjects of the South.[4] " By common council of the barons " a new ordinance on the Jews was published in 1230.[5] But when he was concerned with financial problems, he turned most readily to the burgesses. Louis IX consulted them on many occasions on questions of currency : we have the name of three burgesses of Paris, three of Provins, two of Orléans, two of Sens, and two of Laon who took part, in this way, in the preparation of the ordinance of 1263.[6]

The chief business of the Court, throughout this period, was still to give judgment and in its plenary sessions it retained this right even after its judicial session, the Court in Parliament, has been organized. In the first place, the king in person was the chief justiciar. He could cast into

---

[1] Index Concil. Philippi Augusti, nn. 70, 79, 85, in **CCCIII**, 99 ff. ; Ass. du règne de Louis VIII, nn. 3, 6, 8, 12, 17, 18, 20, 22, 23, 24, in **DXVII**, 442 ff.
[2] **LXXII**, ii, n. 2404, 2335–2353, 2387–8, 3408–9 ; iii, n. 4192, 4566, etc.
[3] **CCCIII**, n. 72.
[4] **DXVII**, n. 2, 3, 9, 14, 22, 24, etc.
[5] **LXXII**, n. 2083.
[6] **LXXXVII**, i, 93–4.

INSTITUTIONS OF CAPETIAN MONARCHY 239

prison without any form of trial, he could condemn to death or he could pardon.[1] The sentences which Louis IX, in session under the oak of Vincennes, executed or had executed straightway by his personal advisers were neither legendary nor exceptional.[2] Finally, the king alone had power " to be judge and party to his own quarrel and those of others ",[3] but he delegated his powers of justice to whom he would.

Controversies which were somewhat complicated were frequently cut short by arbitration, sanctioned by a royal charter, or by mutual agreement reached in the presence of the king.[4] In cases of litigation, it might be the whole Court, reinforced with prelates and barons, whom the king invited to pronounce judgment or it might be a limited number of lawyers who knew what was already beginning to be called " the custom of the kingdom of France ".[5] It is not always easy, during the first half of the thirteenth century, to distinguish in the document between the two latter categories more so as they merge into each other by insensible gradations. Clearly, however, the king expected to consult his barons on a case which concerned the great feudal houses like that of the succession in Champagne (1216) and, with even greater reason, when he was concerned with a political verdict of condemnation. By way of example, since we are fortunate enough to possess the authentic text, we will quote here the sentence pronounced in June, 1230, " on the field, before Ancenis," on Pierre Mauclerc who was count of rather regent of Britanny pending his son's majority.

> We would have you know that, in the presence of our most beloved lord Louis, famous King of France, we have unanimously adjudged that Pierre, sometime Count of Brittany, because of the crimes he has committed against our lord the king which have in very large part been proved to us all has forfeited at the bar of justice his position in Brittany. All who by reason of that position have rendered him loyalty or homage are completely quit and absolved from that loyalty and that homage and are not bound to obey him or do anything for him on account of that position.

---

[1] See the case of Enguerran de Coucy below. Remission granted by Philip Augustus : **XXXI**, n. 1987.
[2] **LXVIII**, §§ 57–60, 115–18, and Eclaircissements, pp. 455–7.
[3] **XVI**, §§ 35. Cf. however, **LXXII**, iv, n. 3115.
[4] **DCLXX**, 90 ; **DXVII**, 353–5 ; **LXXII**, ii, nn. 2747, 2873, 2947, 3377, etc.
[5] Consuetudo Regni Franciae (**XXXI**, n. 1456). Cf. Guilhiermoz, in B.E.C., 1899, p. 54, n. 5. Some texts of judgments will be found in **II, LXXI, CIV**.

The deed is sealed with thirty seals, belonging to the Archbishop of Sens, the bishops of Chartres and Paris, the counts of Flanders, Champagne, Nevers, Blois, Chartres, and counts, viscounts, and lords who are known to us as supporters of Blanche of Castile and Louis IX and officials of the Crown. It is further indicated that "other barons and knights have taken part in the judgment".[1]

In certain cases we find mention, at this period, of the famous "Peers of France", whose early history has stimulated such a flow of ink.[2] In the Middle Ages, it was a principle of law that the nobility (and even the burgesses and, in certain countries, the villains) should be judged by their peers.[3] At the beginning of the thirteenth century, we can see, from an authentic text, that an important vassal of the King of France, the Count of Flanders, could already claim judgment by his peers.[4] But it was only when the Capetian monarchy had become a force to be respected, in the course of the thirteenth century, that the great lords of the kingdom, being justiciable before the Curia Regis in practice as well as in law, began to demand their rights, and in 1216, for the first time, we have, in a text, a sentence in which six peers of the realm are named: the peers of the realm, "namely, the Archbishop of Rheims, the bishops of Langres, Chalons-sur-Marne, Beauvais, and Noyon, and the Duke of Burgundy," judge the case of Erard de Brienne and the Countess of Champagne. Moreover they judged it together with "many other bishops and barons".[5] It was enough that the court should include "peers". We possess other official documents dating from the end of the reign of Philip Augustus, from the reign of Louis VIII and Saint Louis in which peers of the realm appear but none of them mention a "court of peers", nor even "twelve peers". The list of twelve peers (Archbishop Duke of Rheims, bishop dukes of Laon and Langres, bishop counts of Beauvais, Chalons-sur-Marne, and Noyon, dukes of Normandy, Aquitaine, Burgundy, counts of Flanders,

---

[1] **LXXII**, ii, n. 2056.
[2] See the analysis of texts in **DCLXIV**, iii, 301 ff.; **CCII**, i, 646 ff.; **DCLXX**, 77–88; **CCCXCVII**, 84–6; **CDXXXVII, CDXLIII, CDLIX, CCCIV, CCCXLVI**, 205 ff. On a recent work of M. de Valon, see B.E.C., 1932, pp. 155–7.
[3] **CCLXXIX**, 257–8.
[4] **CXXII**, 7.
[5] **LXXI**, n. xix.

INSTITUTIONS OF CAPETIAN MONARCHY 241

Champagne, Toulouse) given by the English chronicler Matthew de Paris[1] is a very old list which since the annexation of Normandy and the County of Toulouse to the royal demesne represents a tradition in part at least obsolete. The genuine texts relative to the period that we are considering now almost all fall between the years 1216 and 1237 and for the most part concern the relations between the Crown and the County of Flanders. They bear witness to the fact that the magnates saw some guarantee in judgment by their peers and that the king was seeking to limit his concessions. Since Bouvines Flanders had been under his yoke and that was the fief in which, of all the great fiefs, the custom of judgment by peers was most vital.[2] The Countess of Flanders claimed its benefits for fear of the king's servants.[3] In 1224, obviously at her prompting, the peers present demanded that the four great officers of the Crown should not sit with the eleven " peers of France " in judgment on an appeal brought against her by one of her vassals and they were dismissed.[4] In the same way, the king claimed to be able to make a distinction in cases where the ordinary jurisdiction is insufficient; in 1259 in a case about the ward of a church, he could not agree with the Archbishop of Rheims " to have his peers ".[5] However, he did not give the peers any predominance among his advisers on matters of government. In vain did supporters of the aristocracy like the poet Hue de la Ferté press the idea and it was in vain that the English and Germans claimed to recognize a political prerogative in the peers of France.[6] In short, the peerage has existed in the French kingdom since the thirteenth century but its ambitions were stillborn.

These represent the varying aspects of the political and judicial assemblies held between 1202 and 1270. They deserve the more careful attention of scholarship; they are clearly the embryo of the future States General. It would be equally possible to find the origin of the local and provincial assemblies of the fourteenth and fifteenth centuries, in gatherings like those of the knights of the French Vexin who,

---

[1] **LXXX**, v, 606-7.
[2] On the peers in the north of the kingdom see **CCCXXV**, 79 ff. and notes.
[3] **LXXII**, ii, n. 1831, 2583-4.
[4] **LXXI**, n. xxi. Cf. **DXVII**, 349.
[5] **LXXI**, n., xxxii, xxxii *bis*.
[6] **LXXXVIII**, 191-2; **LXXX**, v, 281, 482-3, 606; **LXXII**, ii, n. 3380.

in 1235, took an ordinance on feudal relief in their province into the presence of the bailiff, or of the nobles of Maine and Anjou who met for the same object in 1246 under the presidency of the king himself,[1] or the commissions of jurors which the ordinance of 1254 recommended bailiffs and seneschals to establish to advise on the export of foodstuffs.

But the monarchical administration based on specialization, the development of special competence and bureaucracy was growing and from it the new order in France was to arise.

III

MASTERS AND COUNCILLORS

During the reigns of Philip Augustus, Louis VIII, and Saint Louis, the word " *Consilium* " was applied to all kinds of meetings of the Court and the *Consiliarii Regis* [2] were men more concerned with justice than policy. We cannot yet see a separate council. As a result, the commission of lawyers and accountants emerges particularly at the end of the period. Their traditions were established and their methods of work improved.

Scholarship tends to place at an even later date the birth of a Parlement of Paris distinct from the Curia Regis. During the thirteenth century, the term "*parlement*" meaning " discussion " remained a vague word frequently referring to general sessions of the Court.[3] Applied to justice, it signified a special session of the Curia during which consideration was given to some previously prepared business. There was no Parlement, there were parlements which might be judiciary sessions three or four times a year and outside these sessions the Court was competent to give judgment. This remained so even under the sons of Philip the Bel.[4] Nevertheless, from the reign of Saint Louis, the improvements of the judicial machinery of the monarchy, which was already noticeable in the time of Philip Augustus and even under

---

[1] **LXXII**, ii, n. 2382, 3521. See also n. 2768, 3588 ; **XXX**, n. 425-6.
[2] See the interesting texts of 1234, in **CV**, n. 295, and of 1264 in **CXXIX**, ii, 269.
[3] **DLXVI**, 137 ff.
[4] **DCLII**, 74 ff. ; **DCLIII**, 60 ff.

Louis VII, became most marked and many innovations appear.[1] Accumulations of business was one of the principal reasons for the changes. The number of cases of first instance and on appeal was so great that the establishment of a permanent judicial personnel, excluding unqualified elements, became more and more essential. Under Saint Louis, some thirty people formed this personnel. Already they were called " Councillors " or " Masters "; one of them presided and pronounced the sentence: they sat at sessions known as " parlements " with other people whom there had been some reason to summon. For example, on 24th February, 1253, the Prior of Saint-Martin-des-Champs appeared before " the councillors of the King of France holding Parlement ": there were three professional magistrates, Geoffrey de la Chapelle, king's knight, who presided, Master Étienne de Montfort, Dean of Saint Aignan d'Orléans, and Master Eudo de Lorris, Dean of Angers; three royal clerks qualified as " masters "; the three bailiffs of Caen, Étampes, and Orléans (the bailiffs were often lawyers and rendered service in Court); the two Provosts of Paris who were concerned in the case; and, finally, the Archbishop of Bourges and the two bishops of Paris and Evreux summoned because a churchman was involved.[2] The case was heard in Paris " *in domo regia* ", undoubtedly in the chamber of pleas, of which Joinville tells us,[3] in the Palais de la Cité. The itinerant character of the commissions of royal judges was disappearing more and more: many reasons combined to make their settlement in Paris inevitable. It was impossible for the vast number of plaintiffs to follow the king's progress: on the other hand, under the influence of Norman methods, a written procedure was making rapid advances and the habit of preserving decrees on rolls and " registering " the most important of them began to grow up. Henceforward, a record office and a permanent situation were essential. This was the first step in the establishment of the Parlement of Paris. At present, it is still only one aspect of the Curia Regis but already the royal judges form a corps in almost permanent session in Paris, there are archives and registers in which are entered

---

[1] **CCCXCVII**; **CXLIX**, 67. It would not be out of place to instance a decree of 1228 which is characteristic of the previous period: **X**, 255–8.
[2] **LXXI**, n. xxiv.   [3] **LXVIII**, § 673.

244   APOGEE OF THE FEUDAL MONARCHY

the decisions which will form the basis for " precedent ".[1] The term " Chambre des Comptes " does not appear before the beginning of the fourteenth century. Nevertheless, the organization of the Curia Regis in session to receive the accounts submitted by the bailiffs and to prepare their estimates in advance is certainly more ancient than the judicial session " in parliament ". It appears already in a considerably advanced stage in the oldest account which the general destruction of financial documents of the period has left us—the General Account of 1202–3.[2] Thanks to the model provided by the financial administration of the Duchy of Normandy, there was a gradual improvement. The classification of receipts and expenses became clearer and more precise during the reign of Saint Louis [3]; but the reforms of the finances and the Treasury did not take place till the reigns of Philip the Fair and his sons. Throughout the period we are studying, the main features of the administration remained the same. The Treasury was in the Temple at Paris and remained there till 1295. The Templars were bankers to the king and the princes of the royal family. It was in the Temple that the money paid in by provosts and bailiffs was deposited. The household chest at the Louvre received the sums necessary for meeting the expenses of the household services and its curator had to justify his expenditure before the Treasurer of the Temple. These people, however, merely rendered simple accounts. The real financial agents of the monarchy were the bailiffs and provosts and the members of the Curia who directed and controlled them. When the Court was concerned with financial questions, it adopted the title " *Curia in compotis domini Regis* "; it met three times a year at the Temple to supervise receipts and expenditure with the help of the accounts of the bailiwicks and the estimates prepared by the specialists.[4]

This Curia Regis in which was embodied the nucleus of

---

[1] **LXXXV**, preface, p. lxxiv ff.; noticed by Grun in **II**, i, p. 1 ff.; **XXXII**, 305; **CVII**, 256–7, 267 ff.; **CCCXCVI**; **LXXI**, p. vi ff.

[2] Preserved by Brussel who has edited it in **CCII**, ii, p. cxxxix ff. Cf., **CDXXXVI**.

[3] Documents published by De Wailly and Delisle in H.F., xxi, 226 ff., and xxii, 565 ff.

[4] **CCL**; **CLXXXVI**, n. i–ii.

INSTITUTIONS OF CAPETIAN MONARCHY 245

all the great departments of state, had a high reputation for integrity. " From the King of France, or his Court," wrote the Bishop of Cahors in 1246, " comes nothing but what is just and equitable, lawful, and honest." [1] The barons recognized in the Court a royal power; in 1245 the new Countess of Flanders speaks of permission given her by the Court since the king is too ill for anyone to speak to him on business. She says, "He has granted us through his Court. . . ." [2] It was the Court, also, which governed when the king was absent and it was by commissions issuing from it that the demesne was administered.

IV

THE DEMESNE AND LOCAL ADMINISTRATION

Since 1202 the demesne [3] had been increased by the ducal demesne of Normandy which included about forty " cities " (centres of dioceses) or châtellanies; the demesne of the counts of Anjou with Angers, Tours, and le Mans; the demesne of the dukes of Aquitaine in Poitou and Saintonge with Poitiers and Saintes and, finally, by fiefs which had been confiscated from rebellious vassals, such as the County of Boulogne and Auvergne, or which had fallen to the king through lack of an heir or by negotiation, such as Eastern Vermandois with Saint Quentin, the counties of Valois, Clermont-en-Beauvaisis, Beaumont-sur-Oise, Alençon, the lordships of Nogent and Issoudun. If we add to these acquisitions those dating from the beginning of the reign,[4] we shall appreciate that Philip Augustus had increased by four times the royal demesne which was extended from the neighbourhood of Saint Omer as far as Saintonge. Louis VIII completed the annexation of Poitou and acquired the châtellanies of Saint Riquier and Doullens, the County of Perche, and, following the Crusade in the heretical districts

[1] **LXXII**, ii, n. 3543.
[2] **LXXII**, ii, n. 3323.
[3] On the demesne and the appanages: **CDXXVIII**, lectures vii–ix; **CCXI**, iv, 2nd part, 595–6; **DXVII**, 358–363; **CXCI**; **XXVII**, ii, intro.; **LXXV**; Du Cange on the word *apanare*.
[4] See p. 184 above.

of which we shall have to speak, the Seneschalship of Beaucaire and Carcassonne seized from the Count of Toulouse. In the reign of Louis IX, the County of Mâcon was acquired but most important was the conclusion of a series of treaties which simplified and clarified the relations of the king, his barons and the neighbouring kings: in 1229 treaty with the Count of Toulouse who, except for his capital and the Toulousain which he retained, yielded to the King of France his demesnes and his rights of suzerainty; in 1234 treaty with the Count of Brittany who handed over to the king the important fortified posts of Saint James of Beuvron and Bellême; in 1258-9 treaties with the King of Aragon who retained nothing in France but the suzerainty of Montpellier and with the King of England.[1]

It is true that in the time of Saint Louis the demesne had been seriously reduced by the custom, introduced by Louis VIII, of establishing important appanages for the younger sons of the king; by his will, he bequeathed Artois to his second son, Anjou and Maine to the third, Poitou and Auvergne to the fourth. If the holder of the appanage died without a direct heir his possessions returned to the Crown. Many of the predecessors of Louis VIII had enfeoffed their young sons in lordships. It was customary, in those areas where baronies were indivisible, for the elder son to give the younger a " means of life " *apanamentum*. It was not a " part of the inheritance " as Robert of Artois wrongly claimed.[2] In this way Louis VIII had alienated at least a third of his demesne " to prevent the growth of discord " among his sons. That is easily identifiable as a result of the ascendency undoubtedly exercised over him by his wife, Blanche of Castile. For a mother, even for a mother of her character, the desire to endow her children adequately and prevent jealousy could easily triumph over considerations of policy. Louis IX carried out his father's wishes but he only conferred very modest appanages on his own younger sons. Nevertheless, a dangerous precedent had been created;

[1] See p. 227 above.
[2] **LXXII**, ii, n. 2562; Robert of Artois declares that his brother, in accordance with the will of their father, has conferred Artois upon him *pro parte hereditatis*. Cf. the judgment of 1284 against Charles of Anjou, who claimed the heritage of Alphonse of Poitiers : *Regis fratres portionem certam bonorum patris . . . non possunt petere sed primogenitus quantum vult et quando vult eis confert* (**XXXII**, n. 537).

INSTITUTIONS OF CAPETIAN MONARCHY 247

the history of France in the fourteenth and fifteenth centuries was to show that the princely dynasties of the blood royal were as much a menace to the monarchy and unity as the others. In the thirteenth century, thanks to the firm stand of Louis IX and some lucky chances the dismemberment of the demesne between the king and his brothers was not serious. The tremendous appanage of Alphonse of Poitiers, to which was added the inheritance of his father-in-law the Count of Toulouse, was prudently administered and the way was prepared for assimilation to the royal demesne in regions which were not readily absorbable.

The administration of the royal demesne did not undergo any essential changes. The bailiffs retained their character of delegates of the Curia and they were not the only delegates of the Curia sent into the provinces. Some of its members took their seats on the Exchequer of Normandy; others were commissioned to receive submissions, oaths of loyalty, and guarantees, to arbitrate and hold administrative or judicial inquiries: the procedure of the inquest showed considerable development and provided the agents of the king with an opportunity, even outside of the demesne, to appear the defenders of truth, law, and the peace. The great inquests which Saint Louis set on foot, of which we shall speak again, have a special character but they are only the ideal form, the theoretical manifestation of a procedure which was one of the vehicles of monarchical progress.[1]

The bailiffs [2] were more permanent delegates than the others but, particularly during the first third of the thirteenth century, the institution retained its original character of a delegation sometimes individual and sometimes collective; even during the reign of Louis VIII and the Regency of Blanche of Castile, the bailiffs frequently formed commissions; there were two or three to hold judicial sessions and the bailiwicks were of varying extent but all were known as bailiffs. They were responsible for justice and administration, they received the revenues but they often returned to resume their place at Court. Subsequently, the bailiwick became

---

[1] **LXXII**, ii, n. 2004, 2071, 3102, 3231, 3608, etc.; **LXXXV**, i, 956 ff.; **DCLXX**, 91 ff.; **DXVII**, 371–2; **CDLXXV**, 464–5.
[2] **CCXLV**, preface, 15–385; **CDXLVII**, 545 ff., 587 ff.; **DXVII**, 363 ff.; **CLXXXVI**, 195 ff.; **DCLXXIII**, 3 ff.; **CDXXXVI**, 148 ff.; **CDLXXI**, chap. i.

a fixed district which had a local name and was administered by only one bailiff : for example, the bailiwicks of Vermandois reached this stage between 1234 and 1236. In the South after 1226 royal seneschalships were being created. The seneschals were bailiffs who, owing to their isolation, were more independent of the Curia. The bailiffs and seneschals were important people sometimes given, in documents, the title of "bailiff in chief", or "lieutenant of the king".[1] They administered, primarily, the lands belonging to the king and those over which he had rights, particularly the rights of higher justice; already, however, their activities were spreading beyond the demesne and they interfered as much as they could in the life of the neighbouring lordships or free towns.

There still remained seneschalships of a feudal character. William des Roches had been recognized by Philip Augustus as Seneschal in Anjou, Maine, and Touraine, and the Viscount of Thouars as Seneschal in Poitou and Aquitaine. Under this title they did liege homage and handled part of the revenues.[2] The real administration was in the hands of inferior seneschals or bailiffs. Philip Augustus had not intended to make anything but a temporary concession to the great lords whom there could be no question of transforming into officials. He hoped through them to gain a mastery over a local nobility which was far from reliable. The seneschalship of Anjou, after the death of William des Roches, passed to his brother-in-law and then to his daughter. Aimery of Thouars proved disloyal and lost the seneschalship of Poitou.[3] The duties of the grand seneschal of Normandy which, in this case, had been more than nominal, had been suppressed by Philip Augustus.[4]

V

THE KING'S REVENUES

One of the most important functions of the bailiffs and seneschals was to provide the king with money.

The revenues of the Crown had been considerably increased

[1] *Baillivi capitales:* **XXX**, n. 251 ; **LXXII**, ii, nn. 2022, 2025.
[2] **CDXLVII**, 550 ff.
[3] **DXVII**, 368–9 ; **CCXI**, iv, 1st part, 208–9 ; **LXXII**, ii, n. 1915, iii, n. 3628.
[4] **CLIX**, 10.

INSTITUTIONS OF CAPETIAN MONARCHY 249

since the conquests of Philip Augustus. It was not only that they took on a new character and regular public taxation was levied but the demesne had been extended as we have already seen and the king, now able to command some respect, was not only able to impose his will on towns and churches but to draw every possible advantage from feudal custom and his position as supreme suzerain.

The receipts from the provostships in the account of 1202 amount to £31,782 Parisian but by the middle of the thirteenth century they are in the neighbourhood of £50,000 Parisian.[1] Many of the revenues, however, particularly those of the forests and fishponds, were not received by the provosts and appear in the accounts under a different heading. In the General Account for Candlemas, 1227, which is devoted to the last of the three terms of the year 1226-7, each of the great forests brings in about £800. In 1202 the total product of the forests had been £7,080.[2] There had been a considerable geographical extension in the collection of certain dues formerly limited to the royal demesne or neighbouring ecclesiastical lordships. The *expleta*, that is the products of justice, the fines, were a case in point. In the account of 1202 they amounted to £5,310.[3] The dues of the Chancery[4] and the tax on franchises provide further examples: in 1225 the Canons of Orléans promised the king that they would pay him £200 if he would enfranchise their serfs of Étampes.

The old right of hospitality allowed the king, as in the past, to travel through the kingdom without any great expense. During the progress made by Louis VIII in 1223 it brought in £1,815 and, under this right, the Archbishop and people of Rheims paid the considerable expenses of the consecration.[5] But more and more it became fixed or even transformed itself into an annual tax of, for instance, £100.[6]

Apart from the dues which we have just enumerated, taxes and voluntary gifts imposed on individuals because

---

[1] **CDXXXVI**, 49; **CLXXXVI**, 59-60.
[2] **DXVII**, document in proof, n. 13; **CDXXXVI**, 55-6.
[3] **CDXXXVI**, 57-8.
[4] **CLXXXVI**, 378-9.
[5] **CCII**, i, chap. xxxviii; **LII**, 397 ff.
[6] **XXXI**, n. 1396; **DXVII**, 378; **LXXII**, iii, 3690, 4163, 4537, etc.

of their position or on communities, lay and ecclesiastical, became more and more productive. The former have a seigniorial or feudal character; the latter can be explained only by the prerogative of monarchy. Foreigners (aliens, Jews, Lombards) were only tolerated as long as they could be exploited. Aliens settled on the royal demesne and even on certain Church lands paid the king a special tax. Philip Augustus, after showing himself brutally fanatical towards the Jews,[1] adopted the policy of mulcting them regularly and their life was peaceful and prosperous in the royal demesne during the last years of his reign. Loans at interest or "usury" were tolerated. Louis VIII and IX showed themselves much more harsh; the one undoubtedly stimulated by greed and the influence of the barons, the other by hatred of the Jews. Louis VIII in agreement with twenty-four lords, lay and ecclesiastical, decided that debts belonging to Jews should not bear interest and should be repaid within three years to the lord of the lender. It is probable that the lenders rarely saw their money again. The "Summa Judaeorum" amounting to £8,682 Parisian which appears in the incomplete account for 1227 undoubtedly came from the levy, imposed by the king, on Jewish debts. This ordinance and the similar ordinances of Saint Louis were not enforced so far as the suppression of loans at interest was concerned but, henceforward, the royal agents treated the Jews of the demesne in a completely arbitrary manner and pillaged them shamelessly. In a royal mandate of 1246 to the seneschal of Carcassonne it is cynically said, "take as much as you can from those of our Jews who are in prison for we want control of their resources, *quia volumus habere de suo.*" The Lombard bankers were installed in Paris after 1224; each of them paid the king £2 10s. a year; they practised usury, like the Jews, and were not treated much better.[2]

The economic development which the population gained from several prosperous years of peace did not only lighten the incidence of taxes on industry and commerce. The towns

---

[1] On the Jews in France in the thirteenth century: **CXIII**, 211–224; **LXXXVII**, i, 53 ff., 85; **XXXVIII**, 9–11, 15, 440, 458, 460–2, 464, 743–8, etc.; **CDVI**, 233 ff.; **DXVII**, 414–17; **DLIX**; **CDLXXI**, app. ii; **LXX**, 130 ff.

[2] **DXXV**, i, 29–30; **DXVII**, 417–18; ordinance of 1269, in **LXXXVII**, i, 96.

INSTITUTIONS OF CAPETIAN MONARCHY

of the demesne and many episcopal towns were squeezed, particularly at the end of Saint Louis's reign. They were not only asked for aids on the four traditional occasions; they were arbitrarily required to make presents or loans which were not always repaid.[1] The king's exactions, particularly the rights of regale and relief which were received on the death of a prelate or baron, grew as his control extended to the remotest parts of the kingdom. In 1202–3, the regales brought Philip Augustus £4,956 Parisian; Rheims alone provided £2,829 although it was vacant only four months.[2] The king had good reason to delay for a long time the " leave to elect ". A certain number of bishops secured the suppression of the regale by paying an indemnity or an annual rent.[3] The " relief " of the fief [4] brought in considerable profits by this date in accordance with the extension of the royal authority. In 1212, Theobald, Count of Blois, a vassal of the Countess of Champagne paid £4,000 Parisian to the countess and £5,000 to the king; in 1219, the widow of the Count of Eu paid 15,000 marks of silver [5]; in 1239, Henry de Sully, whom the Countess of Dreux was to marry as her second husband paid £4,000 Parisian as a redemption for the County of Dreux; the same year, the new viscount of Châtellerault paid £1,500 Tournois [6]; the relief of the County of Ponthieu provided Saint Louis with £5,000 Parisian.[7]

Finally all subjects lay and ecclesiastical were subject willy nilly to *aids*. They contained the germs of the modern system of public taxation. Philip the Fair invented nothing, he merely developed an established procedure. The tax in lieu of military service—" aid of host," " host tallage "—which was probably introduced by Philip Augustus,[8] was paid by all those people or communities who did not wish to do personal service. They were rarely nobles but they included, in particular, abbeys, communes, the provostships of the demesne and the bishops; for instance, in 1226, the Bishop of Soissons paid £120 to avoid accompanying the king

[1] **CDXI**, Actual document, n. 47; **CCCXC**, 242–3. See below.
[2] **CDXXXVI**, 63–4.
[3] See below, Chap. II, § III.
[4] See the ordinances of Louis IX: **LXXXVII**, 55, 58.
[5] **XXXI**, n. 1398, 1402, 1920.
[6] **LXXII**, n. 2761, 2777.
[7] **CV**, n. 452–3.
[8] **CL**, 20 ff.; **CDXXXVI**, 59–60.

on his expedition against the heretics.¹ Finally, the feudal aids which had been so rare and so badly collected in the twelfth century were increasing not without rousing some protest. Saint Louis had levied twice for the Crusade, once for the marriage of his eldest daughter, once for the knighting of his eldest son, and even once for the extension of fief, in 1259, when the promises of subsidies made to Henry III obliged him to levy " the aid for the King of England's peace ".² The aids for the Crusade were particularly heavy. In 1248, Beauvais paid £1,750 to this, Compiègne and Senlis £1,250, and Soissons, a second account, £1,000.³ The Church paid the aid in the form of a tenth or a twentieth of their annual revenue when the defence of the faith was concerned, i.e. for the crusades against the Moslems or the Albigensian heretics or for the conquest of Sicily by Charles of Anjou. The king demanded a tenth which the Pope granted and the clergy paid not on their personal property but on the revenues of their ecclesiastical possessions. For example, in 1227, the Archbishop of Sens undertook on behalf of his province to give £1,500 a year for four years for the Albigensian business.⁴ Recalcitrants were punished with excommunication and distraint. Further the taxes levied on the authority of the Pope had an international character. The money might come from England, Spain, or the Empire and might be used to support a certain prince or knight who had taken the Cross as much as the King of France. It was in France, however, that the charges were greatest and it was primarily the king who benefited from the tenths and twentieths levied during the period. The Capetian monarchy had made some progress since the time when Philip Augustus had been forced abjectly to renounce the Saladin tithe.⁵

Monetary history, like the history of the aids, allows us to measure the progress of the royal power. Its fluctuations show equally the spirit which inspired a particular king and his advisers. In the twelfth century, currency was weak, unstable, and scanty.⁶ Philip Augustus and Louis VIII

¹ **DXVII**, 379.
² **CCVI**, 48–57 ; **CCCVII**, 64–5 ; **DCXIX**, 308 ff.
³ **CLXXXVIII**, 169.
⁴ **LXXII**, ii, n. 1930, 1942 ; **XXV**, 314.
⁵ **CXV**, 86, 88, etc. ; **CLXXII**, 189 ff. ; **CDXLVII**, 581–3.
⁶ On the debasement of the coinage under the early Capetians see **CCLVIII, CCLVII**.

INSTITUTIONS OF CAPETIAN MONARCHY

commenced a reorganization of the currency by making the system of Tours coinage general in all the newly annexed territories while the Paris coinage was retained in the ancient demesne. The pound Tournois was worth four-fifths of the Parisian pound. Louis VIII fixed the customs of the Parisian mints and for the future there was a true Capetian coinage, but there were even better things to come. Every lord, including the king, had the right to fix the currency of the coins he struck and to vary at will its relation to the pounds, shillings, and pence which comprised the money of accountant. On the other hand, he was trying to lower the value of the coins. It was essential that the king should abandon these vagaries, that the royal money should be stable and the best in France, that he should not make excessive profits out of the minting, and that the relations between the coins and the money of account and between gold and silver coinage should not be arbitrarily altered. This was the work of Saint Louis. He re-established the prestige of a good coinage. The value of gold pieces in his reign was $\frac{990}{1000}$ fine and of the silver ones $\frac{23}{24}$ fine. The gold crown of the Tournois coinage (about fifty-eight of these coins made up a gold mark) weighed a little more than 4 grammes and was worth twelve shillings and a half of the Tournois money of account. The tournois silver penny, at the rate of fifty-eight to a mark of silver, was worth one shilling Tournois. Innumerable silver and gold coins were set in circulation. This coinage of Saint Louis was accepted so confidently that it was possible without rousing any undue anger to restrict the currency of seigniorial monies in its favour. He provided that the royal money should be current throughout the realm and forbade the use of any other in districts where there was no seigniorial mint. As for claiming the sole right of striking coinage, or authorizing its issue, he had too much respect for the rights of his barons to entertain any such project. His officials who did not always obey his orders, frequently claimed to restrict somewhat unduly the currency of seigniorial coinage but the following generation was to see the introduction of many serious abuses and at that period there would be regretful memories of the time of the good money of Saint Louis.[1]

[1] **CCLI**, vol. x, 187–8 ; **XXX**, n. 350 ; **CCLIX**, 328 ff. ; **DCLXVIII**, pp. lxxvii–lxxxi ; **DXVII**, p. 381 ; **DLII**, 79–84 ; **CLXXIV**, ii, 147 ff., 225 ff.

Historians of the Capetian monarchy have forgotten to mention among its resources ransoms and the spoils of war. It was a source of such considerable profits that it gave rise to treaties. Thus when Louis VIII assisted the Countess of Flanders against her revolted subjects he was careful to reserve for himself half of ransoms, spoils captured in towns taken by assault, and sums paid on surrender.[1] The Crown sought to gain some benefit from its wars for they cost it very dear.

VI

THE EXPENDITURE. FINANCIAL BALANCE OF THE PERIOD

The bailiffs and provosts, after meeting on the spot local expenses such as the wages of the royal agents, rents, pious gifts, the upkeep of castles, bridges, roads, etc,[2] carried to Paris a surplus which, with the addition of some other receipts, was sufficient for the expenses of the household and the religious or political administration in time of peace. The daily style of living of the household, the wages in money or kind of the civil and military personnel of the Court, the gifts, alms, and festivals still retained a character of patriarchal moderation.[3] Louis IX, in his youth, was not an enemy of finery, he said to his friends, " You should dress yourself properly and cleanly and your wives will love you the better,"[4] but he deprecated untoward luxury and, at the end of his life, dressed himself as a priest. Philip Augustus and his closest descendants had not the same extravagant ideas which later made it necessary for the Valois to create new resources for themselves. Their only luxury was building but it was not devoted to palaces at that period. Philip Augustus was haunted to the end of his life by the fear of a revival of English power and he built many strong castles and fortified Paris and his chief towns.[5] Military architecture reached

---

[1] **DXVII**, 382–397 ; **CDXXXVI**, 73 ff.
[2] **CDXXXVI**, 83–128 ; **DCLXVII**, pp. lxviii–lxxiii ; **CDXLVII**, 584 ff.
[3] The expenses of the household are, nevertheless, very difficult to evaluate (**CDXXVI**, 131–3).
[4] **LXVIII**, §§ 25, 36, 94, 228.
[5] **CDXXXVI**, 117 ; **LVII**, 367, line 498 ff. ; **CDXLVI**, 248–9.

INSTITUTIONS OF CAPETIAN MONARCHY 255

heights which involved expenses which were obviously considerable. Even to-day such ruins as Gisors bear witness to that. The pious Louis IX was a great founder of churches and hospitals for his religious feelings determined him to assume responsibility for some of the expenditure on public assistance which, for many centuries, the Church alone had met. " Like the writer who has made his book and illuminated it in gold and blue, this king," said Joinville, " illuminated his kingdom with fine abbeys and many Houses of God." We no longer possess the famous hospital of the Quinze Vingts built near the Saint Honoré gate for three hundred blind people of Paris but we still have almost intact the beautiful Sainte Chapelle built to receive the Crown of Thorns.[1]

The expenses of the diplomatic system began to appear in the budget. Lacking permanent ambassadors, the king certainly hired agents in foreign countries through whom he gained information; he paid pensions to influential people (particularly in Germany) and sent very frequent missions specially to the Court of Rome, the political centre of Christian Europe. Similarly within the kingdom he guaranteed the loyalty of certain nobles by hard cash.[2]

The support of a small permanent army in time of peace was not a very heavy burden. The troop of knights, crossbowmen, horse or foot sergeants, and " gunners " which formed the military establishment was largely maintained by means of the lands and residences which the king granted to warriors of proved fidelity.[3] Garrisons, in time of peace, were disbanded or reduced to a few men.[4] In times of war he relied on the feudal and seigniorial levies we have already described. More and more, however, warriors both noble and base born were being recruited for wages. During the period of Philip Augustus's conquests, a famous band of scouts commanded by Cadoc appeared in the accounts for the year 1202 at £3,290 Parisian. There is little doubt that it consisted of three hundred foot sergeants each paid eight pence a day. According to the same account, a sapper received a shilling

---

[1] **LXVIII**, § 758 ; **LVI**, 86 ff. ; **CDXII**, 107 ff. ; **DCXI**, 119 ff.
[2] **XXXI**, intro., p. cxvi ; **DXVII**, 375 ; **DXV**, 40, n. 2.
[3] **XXXI**, n. 650, 693a, 817, 946a, 955, 1037, 1124, 1399, 2139, 2140.
[4] See a roll of about 1251 in **LXXII**, iv, *acta omissa*, n. 3973².

and a half (eighteen pence), a mechanic fifteen pence ; a crossbowman on foot one or two shillings ; a mounted crossbowman or sergeant three shillings. A knight's fee was about six shillings. All these soldiers were signed on at the last moment, sometimes along the route, merely for the number of days estimated as necessary to finish the expedition. In 1231 when she had to make war on the Count of Brittany, Blanche of Castile engaged Breton nobles for preference.[1]

The king's wars against his vassals during the period we are studying here were relatively short and more burden on the peasants whose holdings were ravaged than on the monarchy. The crusades were the ruinous adventure. The army assembled at Bourges in 1226 to exterminate the Albigensian heretics was undoubtedly the biggest that a Capetian monarch had ever commanded.[2] When Saint Louis set out on his disastrous expedition to Egypt he needed enormous sums for the transport of the crusaders in Italian boats, for the accumulation of the " mountains " of wheat and barley which Joinville saw heaped up in Cyprus, for the ransoms of the prisoners including the king himself, and, subsequently, to carry out the great works of fortification in Syria. When the king returned after six years of absence and incessant appeals for funds he still sent money and men to the Holy Land.[3] There was also the costly crusade for the conquest of the kingdom of Sicily, which the Pope entrusted to Charles of Anjou the king's brother.[4] Finally the preparations for the Tunisian crusade which was cut short by the king's death demanded an even greater effort.[5] All these extraordinary expenses, however, were met by ecclesiastical tithes, money wrung from the cities, from crusaders who wished to be relieved of their vows, and by all sorts of expedients. The administrative correspondence of Alphonse of Poitiers forms a supplement to the very scanty royal documents and shows us this prince, during the three years preceding the Tunisian crusade, alienating forests and dues, selling charters of liberties to the towns, letters of pardon to criminals, and finally ordering the arrest of all Jews and

---

[1] **CL**, 109–121 ; **CLXX**, 302 ff. ; **DCXXVI**, 318 ff.
[2] **DXVII**, 295.
[3] **LXVIII**, §§ 130–1 ; **DXCIV**, 254 ff. **CLXX**, 356 ff.
[4] **CCCLXXVI**, 536 ff.
[5] **LXXII** ; iv, numerous acts of the years 1268–1270 ; **CLXIX**, p. lv ff.

INSTITUTIONS OF CAPETIAN MONARCHY

the seizure of their goods in order to force them to redeem them.[1] By these means they succeeded with some difficulty, in spite of resistance and complaints, in collecting the necessary money and paying off more or less completely the Italian bankers who had made advances.

What, from the financial point of view, were the results of the reigns of Philip Augustus, Louis VIII, and Saint Louis ? We have no exact knowledge of the extent of the resources which each of these monarchs could command. The General Account of receipts and expenses from All Saints Day, 1202, to Ascension, 1203, which Brussel has preserved for us, alone includes the three terms at which the provosts and bailiffs came to make their accounts and there is reason to believe that certain receipts and expenses are not entered there at all. If we take into account only those which appear there, we see that, in this critical year when Philip Augustus was realizing all his resources, he had the disposal of £197,000 Parisian including £59,000 drawn from his war treasury.[2] After the annexations made at the expense of John Lackland the receipts were considerably increased and the king built up his reserves again. The pious legacies which Philip Augustus made in his will of 1222 to the King of Jerusalem and to the knightly orders sworn to defend the Holy Land, to those whom he feared he might have wronged, to the poor and the Church, and the considerably smaller amounts which he bequeathed to his family and suite amounted, in money and jewels, to £419,600 Parisian without allowing for a sum which was certainly considerable but for which we have no figures left to his successor for the defence of the realm.[3] It was the result of a prudent and economical administration and his consistent opposition to merely adventurous projects.

On the finances of Louis VIII, we have two documents, the first is his will, the legacies of which amount to £105,000, the remainder being left to his heir. Secondly the General Account of Candlemas, 1227, presented three months after his death of which we possess the totals : receipts £53,729 14s., expenditure of £37,480, a balance of £16,249 14s. and a surplus in the chest of £123,898 16s. The situation on the accession of Louis IX was, therefore, quite satisfactory.

[1] **CDLXXV**, 518 ; **LXX**.
[2] **CDXXXVI**, 131.
[3] **XXXI**, n. 2172 ; **CCXI**, iv, 2nd part, 558 ff., 566 ff.

It seems clear to us that although Saint Louis avoided extravagant expenditure he was not a prudent financier.[1] At the end of his reign he was exclusively occupied with the salvation of his soul, making restitutions, and preparing for the Crusade. The famous reform of the provostship of Paris, the character of which has been so badly appreciated for many years, shows us that payments by assignment on the provostship of Paris were continually increasing although the revenues remained stationary so that no one was willing to accept the farm of the provostship. It was necessary to put it in the charge of an official who would render accounts and the deficit had to made up by the Treasury.[2] In his will of 1270, made in Paris before his departure for Tunis, Saint Louis began by distributing a relatively moderate sum —about £20,000—between Queen Margaret, his wife, the religious foundations, the houses of God, the poor, and his servants. He declared that he did not know whether he left enough money to satisfy all these gifts but that did not prevent him subsequently bequeathing £10,000 to his daughter Agnes and the remainder to the royal heir. This document not only reveals a straightened treasury but also an indifference towards accuracy which, in its contempt for exact division, contrasts very strongly with the meticulous will drawn up during the same period by Alphonse of Poitiers.[3]

Nevertheless, the monarchy had an established administration and was provided with considerable resources. It was ready to act. In fact, during this period it was carving out at a very rapid rate the course of its development. Some part of its forces was employed, it is true, in the crusade against the Moslems but, from the crusade against the heretics, which, as we shall see, others had initiated and almost carried through, it was able to draw considerable profit.

[1] On the accounts of Saint Louis, cf. De Wailly in H.F., xxi, p. lxxiii ff.; **DXVII**, 384–5; **CLXXXVI**, 224 ff.
[2] **CLXXXVI**, 531 ff.
[3] **LXXII**, iv, 5368, 5712.

CHAPTER II

RELATIONS OF THE FRENCH KINGS WITH THE CHURCH AND THE HOLY SEE, 1202-1270. THE CRUSADES AGAINST THE ALBIGENSIANS AND IN THE EAST

I

The Principles of Royal Policy

"THE King of France" wrote the poet of the *Gestes de Louis VIII*, "is, at all times, the shield of Holy Church."[1] The kings of the period we are studying, Philip Augustus, Louis VIII, and Louis IX, to whom we must add Blanche of Castile, were faithful servants of the Catholic Church although they always fought against it for what they considered the rights of the temporal power. Even the most material of them, the least subject to mystical ecstasy, Philip Augustus, was a believer who had suffered for Christ in the Holy Land. There was united to this sincere faith a practical sense which led him to appreciate the value of the alliance between the monarchy and the Church. Contemporaries have called him "the very pious patron of clerks",[2] and have attributed these words on his death bed, " My son, I beg you to honour God and Holy Church as I have done. I have gained considerable profit from it and you equally will enjoy many advantages."[3] We cannot explain his religious policy better than by this quotation. To describe it in terms of the measures he had to take against over-ambitious bishops and to assess it as anticlerical is to do it some injustice.[4] As for Louis VIII he died during a crusade against the heretics. His wife, Blanche of Castile, who played a leading role in politics both as regent and queen mother, was austere in her devotion. She reconciled piety with a determined opposition towards bishops who displayed undue

---

[1] LXXXIV, lines 1009-1010.
[2] XXXIV, 400.
[3] DXVII, 406 ; CCXI, iv, 2nd part, 580-1.
[4] Cf. DXXVIII, I, 54.

independence.¹ From the beginning of this chapter, however, the figure who demands our chief attention is Louis IX. This saint went even farther than Philip Augustus in defence of the temporal power. It is essential to understand in what way and for what basic reasons this spirit of resistance, which we should be wrong to call " secular ", could be allied with the most ardent piety and the most devoted respect for the Church. Then we shall have really appreciated what was the religious policy of the Capetians at the apogee of the feudal monarchy.

Louis IX ² was the son of a father who had been nicknamed " The Lion " and his grandfathers, Philip Augustus and Alphonse the Noble, King of Castile, were men of valour. On the maternal side, he was the great-grandson of the Empress Eleanor and the great King of England, Henry II. Trained by his mother Blanche, he had been brought up in a school of activity. Personally, he was of a nervous, irascible temperament but he possessed a firm will. He was a brave knight and a king who could punish severely. He complained, like many mystics, that he had not the gift of tears, and, when he prayed, could not " water the dryness of his heart ". He was no bigot, had no love for fanatics, and was horrified by hypocrisy. His relations with his followers, as they are reported to us by his friend the Sire de Joinville, reveal his malicious gaiety. After his majority, he passed several years of brilliant youth and this fine knight won great admiration, " slender, tall stature, angelic countenance, and gracious figure." Joinville has told us how he hid from his mother to make love to his young wife, Margaret of Provence, but he was chaste and had an unsmirched soul. He had been brought up in the practices of an exalted devotion and he developed more and more rigorous habits of mortification. He was afraid of not loving his Saviour enough and not suffering enough for him. He deprived himself of earthly enjoyment, submitted to regular beatings with chains of iron, and attended the sick and the poor, preferably the most repulsive. Worn out by vigils and fasting and still infected by an ague he had caught in Saintonge during the war against

---

¹ **CLXX**, 100-2, 275-285 ; **DCLI**, 66 ff. On the regencies of Blanche of Castile see **CDLXIII**, chap. iii.

² I have chiefly used **LXVIII, LVI, CXXXII**. Cf. **CXCIV**, chap. xii ; De Wailly, *Eclaircissement*, i, in **LXVIII**.

RELATIONS WITH THE CHURCH

the English in 1242, he all but died in 1244. There is no doubt that the idea of approaching death contributed not a little to make him an ascetic.

Before he was forty, the gallant knight had became bald, bent, and sickly. He dressed himself now as a priest and the people of Paris called him Frater Ludovicus. His devotion always remained enlightened, however: his beliefs were founded on a thorough knowledge of Holy Scripture and, in place of the interminable masses which his cousin the King of England attended, he preferred long meditations, reading sacred texts, sermons, and discussions on morals with his followers.

For such a man who had been placed on a throne the essential obligation was to guide his subjects towards heaven and to assure the salvation of their souls. He believed that a consecrated king had a mission in this respect and this was obviously one of the reasons why he retained the crown in spite of his secret desire to abdicate.[1] He sought to fulfil all the promises he had made at his consecration. He believed that the unction he had received from the vial brought from heaven for the baptism of Clovis imposed on him very extensive obligations. He considered also, however, that it conferred rights upon him and a direct communication with God. On occasions of important decisions, if his conscience showed him clearly the course to pursue, he would listen to nobody. At such moments he believed himself inspired by God. As a result, in spite of his affectionate deference towards the Holy See and the clergy, in spite of the joy he experienced in travelling from monastery to monastery and dining in the monks' refectories,[2] he considered himself able to draw the limit between the spiritual and the temporal, to distinguish the prerogatives of the two powers which, to his mind, had been created to seek the same ends by different means, and to co-operate in bringing about the triumph of Christ. In his opinion it was possible for Pope and clergy to be mistaken and he had the right to say so and resist them. He was called on to speak very sharply to his bishops, to forbid a papal legate to interfere in certain matters,[3] and it was

[1] **LVI**, 50, 129–130, and **XLVI**, 7, are very definite on the desire to abdicate.
[2] **XXX**, 450–1, 543 ff., 749, etc., and the notes of Delisle ; **XXIV**, 454–5 ; **DXIV**, 586–9.
[3] **LXVIII**, §§ 673–5 ; **LXXII**, ii, n. 2415.

only at the end of his life that he displayed an excessive docility towards the Holy See. In short, in spite of considerable differences of personal temperament, these four sovereigns pursued the same religious policy differing only in minor details. Moreover all four of them, even including Philip Augustus,[1] were glorified by the Church.

II

SERVICES RENDERED BY THE CHURCH. ROYAL FAVOURS TO THE CHURCH

The exchange of services between the two powers was incessant. The bishops were more than ever charged with political or administrative responsibilities and many of the Court functionaries were clerks. The Church agreed, as in the past, to share certain demesnes with the king by means of partnership agreements. Philip Augustus, chiefly concerned not to weaken his position, made very few gifts to the chapters and convents but he confirmed their goods and privileges. Louis VIII and Louis IX heaped favours on them as the Trésor des Chartes and the Cartularies bear evidence. There was rarely need by now to protect them against feudal violence; but the king frequently gained lay lords when they gave up tithes usurped by their ancestors.[2]

The University of Paris, an important ecclesiastical foundation, subject to the pontifical authority, owed to Philip Augustus its independence of the provost of the capital. In 1200, even before it was a corporation or a legal personality possessing a seal, masters and scholars were recognized as justiciable only in the Church courts. In 1225 when the legate forbade the University to have a seal, provoked a riot of the scholars, and excommunicated twenty-four masters, Louis VIII interfered. It was not easy to show indulgence to the scholars' pranks and, at the same time, maintain good order. In 1229 Blanche of Castile agreed with the Bishop of Paris and the legate to deal with them severely: the University resisted and dispersed and, in the end, Blanche yielded.[3]

[1] **XCIV**, ii, n. 4542 (25th October, 1223).
[2] **XXX**, 780 and note.
[3] **XXXI**, 629; **CDL**, 89 ff.; **DXVII**, 289–290; **CLXX**, 132 ff., 204 ff.; **DLVIII**, i, chap. v; **CCCXL**.

RELATIONS WITH THE CHURCH

III

THE LIBERTIES OF THE CHURCH AND THE SUPREMACY OF THE CROWN

We should be making a very false characterization, however, of the relations between the monarchy and the world of the Church if we instanced only these mutual services and royal concessions. In other spheres, the king dominated the Church.

In the first place the king was the feudal chief of the ecclesiastical barons. Philip Augustus gained the homage of the bishops of Cahors, Limoges, and Clermont and thus won some support in the areas which were in dispute with his enemies.[1] He enforced a more and more exacting recognition of his prerogatives as suzerain. We have seen how after 1185 he had refused to do homage to the Bishop of Amiens. Till the end of his reign he continued negotiations for his release from homage in return for various concessions.[2] His successors demanded, as he had done, feudal services from the Church. On several occasions some of the bishops tried to refuse host service or at least the personal service which was distasteful to them. The king sometimes forced them to yield, sometimes to accept some agreement but he would not allow the matter to be settled by precedent: there are examples of this during each of the three reigns.[3] In the same way suit of Court had to be rendered by the bishop or his agent.[4] If it became necessary to enforce obedience the king would seize the revenues of the rebel. Philip Augustus considered that, for the defence of the realm, he could demand anything of the clergy and put forward a claim to build a fortress on episcopal land.[5] In a memorandum drawn up by Saint Louis's advisers and presented to the Pope in 1247 the theory is taken to its extreme: "The right of the king is that he can take as his own all the treasures of the churches and all their temporal goods to meet the necessities of himself and his realm."[6]

---

[1] **DCLXX**, 101 and notes.
[2] **XXXI**, 879–880, 1460, 2204. For Saint Louis: **LXXII**, iv, n. 5294.
[3] **XXXI**, n. 1393–5; **DCLXX**, 102; **CCXI**, iv, second part, 293–4; **DXVII**, 408–9; **LXXII**, ii, n. 2285.
[4] **LXXII**, ii, n. 2206 (ann. 1232).
[5] **XXXI**, n. 1803, 1830.
[6] Memorandum published in **LXXX**, vi, add., 99–112.

The rivalry between the two jurisdictions acquired an unprecedented importance : the progress of canon law and the tacit or overt support of the Holy See gave arms to the clergy and a long era of conflicts opened out. The bishops tried to withdraw themselves completely from the royal jurisdiction and, in their turn, Philip Augustus, Blanche of Castile, and Saint Louis maintained their right to summon them before their Court and do judgment on them when the case concerned temporal matters.[1]

On the other hand, the recognized right of the Church to judge not only in matters of faith, wills, and marriages but also of oaths was a source of grave abuse, for feudal loyalty was based on the oath. In general neither of the two powers allowed principles to hamper them and the king's ministers hesitated no more than the judges of the ecclesiastical courts about contravening them. The right of asylum, excommunication, prohibition of loans at interest, or Sunday trading, the punishment of clerks guilty of a capital crime were equally matters of controversy.

In 1205-6 the king held in Paris an assembly to discuss these questions and the *réponses* of the king and his barons sound an echo of the famous Constitutions of Clarendon. The line of conduct followed by the kings and their advisers at this period was consistently firm and reasonable and they no more accepted the encroachments of the Church than they tolerated the violence of local officials or of the communes.[2] But the problem was not settled. The lay power and the ecclesiastical remained on a war footing. In 1225 the Chronicler of Tours tells us :—

> The archbishops and bishops of France, in the presence of the legate, made insistent demands of the king and his barons for the right to judge, in cases concerning moveables, all men summoned before them by churchmen. They said that this jurisdiction was a right of the Gallican Church. He declared, with peremptory arguments, that this was an unreasonable demand since cases concerning moveables which were not claimed as being concerned with oaths, faith, wills, or marriage were purely lay matters with which the ecclesiastical tribunal had no concern. . . . Finally, by the interventions of Divine Grace and the legate, the parties left the matter undecided.[3]

[1] **XXXI**, n. 1241 ff., 2034 ; **DCLXX**, 103 ; **CLXX**, 101–2, etc.
[2] **XXXI**, n. 927–8, 1209, 1477, 1811, etc. ; **LXVIII**, §§ 61–4, 670–1 ; **CCXCVI**, 65 ff., 98 ; **CLXXXVIII**, 146.
[3] **XXV**, 309 ; **CCXCVI**, 99.

RELATIONS WITH THE CHURCH

Ten years later, the barons and councillors of the king at a meeting held at Saint-Denis discussed rebellions of churchmen against the king their patron. For instance, the Archbishop of Tours had forbidden the abbots and priors of his province to plead in cases concerned with temporal affairs in the Court of the king or a lord. The Archbishop of Rheims and the Bishop of Beauvais had refused to recognize the jurisdiction of the king's Court over the temporalities. Barons and councillors drew up and sent to the Pope a memorandum which has been preserved in the Trésor des Chartes [1]; the Pope is urged to watch over and safeguard the king, his barons, and the kingdom.

The reply of Pope Gregory IX was that the king and his barons were making attempts against the liberties of the Church.

The accession of Innocent IV [2] who was " to reign or rather to fight for eleven years six months and ten days " (1243–1254) led to a recrudescence of anti-clericalism. The hostility which he evoked by his animosity against the Emperor Frederick II was heightened by the imperial manifesto published in France and turned against the clergy who were, however, far from uncritical in their approval of the policy of Innocent IV. Frederick II wrote to the sovereigns of Europe in the early months of 1246 : " It has always been our settled intention to reduce clerks of every order, and particularly the higher ranks, to their position in the primitive Church to live as apostles and to imitate the humility of the Lord."

In the course of this same year a movement gradually developed in France against the " Liberties of the Church ". Finally, in November, the barons in their turn issued a manifesto which agreed remarkably with that of Frederick II : " the kingdom," they said, " was founded by warriors and not by clerks and it was to the wars of Charlemagne and other kings that the Church of France owed its existence, to the generosity of the nobles that it owed its castles. Humble at first but full of intrigue the clerks have finished by monopolizing the jurisdiction which belonged to the secular princes. These sons of serfs have reached a position where they judge free men by their laws. They must be reduced to the status

[1] LXXII, n. 2404 ; **CCXCVI**, 99-100.
[2] For all that follows see **CLXXII** ; **DXIII**, iv, 121 ff. ; **CCXCVI**, 100-7.

of the primitive Church. Henceforward, neither layman nor cleric may begin an action (except in cases of heresy, marriage, or usury) before the ecclesiastical courts on pain of confiscation and mutilation." As a result, the barons signed a treaty of alliance against the clergy to defend their rights and undertook to pay a levy of one-hundredth part of their annual revenues for the assistance of those who were threatened by the ecclesiastical authority.

Innocent IV immediately sent instructions to his legate in France. "These attacks," he wrote, "have been inspired in the French baronage by the Emperor, that enemy who is working for the overthrow of the faith." The legate was ordered to excommunicate the leaguers (*statutarii*) and all those who had accepted their statutes. The faith was certainly not the object of the attack for the four commissioners named by the leaguers—the Duke of Burgundy, the counts of Brittany, Angoulême, and Saint Paul—were pious men who had gone on crusade at the same time as Saint Louis. During Louis IX's stay in the Orient (1248–2254), since the most ardent barons had gone with him, the league gradually disintegrated. It had aroused, even in the towns, measures against the extension of ecclesiastical justice.

The king had not given his explicit support to this lay defence organization but he had not disavowed it and the original of the treaty of alliance of the *statutarii* exists in the Trésor des Chartes [1]; during his absence, although the regency was in the hands of the pious Blanche of Castile, the king's agents, particularly in the South, became aggressive and conflicts over jurisdiction became more numerous. It was only after the return of Louis IX that matters were settled.

In the history of the relations between the Capetian monarchy and the Church, the nomination of bishops and abbots was a serious matter and aroused even more controversy than the quarrels over jurisdictions. From the thirteenth century, the question began to be raised in three ways: the king wished to preserve his ancient prerogatives, the clergy their liberties, and the pretensions of the Holy See were growing. We must remember that the king had regalian rights in a great number of bishoprics and abbeys even outside his demesne.

[1] **LXXII**, ii, n. 3569.

The southern districts and Brittany, alone, were not within his grasp.[1] When an episcopal or abbatial seat was vacant the chapter or convent humbly sought permission from the king to proceed to an election; in the interval, the king enjoyed the revenues, nominated to vacant benefices, and only gave up the regale when he confirmed the election and the new dignitary tendered him an oath of loyalty. On the other hand, even in normal times, he had the presentation to a certain number of prebends in the churches. With these he could pay for services rendered and win himself supporters.

Philip Augustus, during the second part of his reign, made many concessions which can scarcely be explained except by his need of money or by political reasons the details of which have escaped us. Not only did he rarely refuse to grant freedom of election or to approve an election that had been made, not only did he re-establish in Normandy canonical election but he gave up the right of granting permission to elect in favour of the Chapter of Langres and he gave up his enjoyment of the regale during the vacancy of the see in this bishopric and also in Arras, Auxerre, Nevers, and Mâcon.[2] On the other hand, on three occasions, he allowed the Holy See to dispose of very important sees: Sens, Rheims, and Paris. Louis VIII, Blanche of Castile, and Louis IX maintained their rights in theory with possibly rather more determination than Philip.[3] The instructions to his mother left by Saint Louis on his departure for the Holy Land bear witness to this.[4] In practice, however, they showed themselves conciliatory and generous. The restoration of the revenues taken during the period of the regale became customary: Louis VIII granted this, in the newly annexed demesnes, for the sees of Angers, Le Mans, and Poitiers on condition that the new bishops swore fidelity within forty days. Examples are frequent during the reign of Saint Louis but the king kept his rights.[5] More surprising, at first glance, is the ease with which Blanche of Castile and Saint Louis allowed the violation of the freedom of canonical election by

[1] DCLXX, 98-9.
[2] XXXI, n. 791, 855, 1021a, 1102, 1115; CDXII *bis*, 108 ff. The date of some of these renunciations in return for finance corresponds to critical periods, for example, 1203-4.
[3] DXVII, 408 ff.; CLXXII, 373-4; DLXXIII, 168 ff.
[4] LXXXVII, i, 60.
[5] DXVII, 410; CLXXII, 41 ff., 374 ff.; CLXX, 407.

the Pope who appointed many bishops directly. Thus, in 1229, the Cardinal of Saint-Ange, the legate of Gregory IX, appointed the Bishop of Noyon.[1] Innocent IV agreed with the Archbishop of Rouen to raise to the see of Evreux the Dean of St. Martin of Tours and suggested for the see of Noyon the candidate who had received the support of a minority of the canons, Pierre Charlot. There is an explanation for all this, however; in 1229, Blanche of Castile could not thwart the legate who was supporting her against the rebel barons; the dean of St. Martin had been recommended to the Pope by Saint Louis and as for Pierre Charlot, he was a natural son of Philip Augustus.[2] We need not conclude from these last examples that Louis IX was a hypocrite. He would only give his support to worthy candidates and he lived in such close contact with the Church that his conscience could not allow him to abuse his position in such a case.

IV

Relations with the Holy See

The relations of the monarchy with the Holy See from 1202 to about 1260 were not as good as with the French clergy. Though there was no failure of professions of love and respect, the two powers came into conflict on many occasions. The long considered and obstinately developed policy of the Holy See could not be sidetracked. To guarantee the security of the Pope in Rome, to prevent the domination of the Emperor in Italy, to take advantage of every opportunity to subject the monarchs to the suzerainty of the Holy See, to maintain peace between Christians, to deliver the Holy Land, to exterminate heretics, in short, to establish under the direction of the Pope the Kingdom of God on earth—these were the items in the programme of Innocent III. We have seen that he was involved in almost perpetual conflict with Philip Augustus; the question of the repudiation of Isambour, serious as it was from the point of view of canon law, ended in compromise; but the external policy of Philip Augustus, the part played by Innocent III

[1] **LXXII**, ii, n. 1983.   [2] **CLXXII**, 39 ff.

RELATIONS WITH THE CHURCH

to force John Lackland to recognize him as suzerain, and the subsequent protection given to this English vassal, by the Holy See when the former was an enemy of the King of France gave rise to a permanent antagonism between the courts of Paris and Rome. Louis VIII did not really reach a reconciliation with Honorius III until he agreed to lead an army against the Albigensians.

The attitude of Saint Louis in the mortal combat between the Hohenstaufen and the Popes Gregory IX and Innocent IV was generous and loyal and, even if Charles of Anjou ended by taking advantage of the exhaustion of the two parties to win a kingdom for himself, it is impossible to doubt the disinterestedness of Louis IX. He maintained the prestige of the French Crown and when the French prelates, on their way to the Council of Rome, were captured at sea, he forced Frederick II to set them at liberty (1241). But he did not attempt to take advantage of circumstances to seize the kingdom of Arles or even Lyons, which he could easily have done, and he refused the imperial crown for his brother Robert of Artois. Like all the idealists of the Middle Ages, he considered that the Empire and the Holy See were both divine institutions and should not be subject to the greedy and vengeful spirit of man. When Innocent IV, whose position in Rome was very insecure, crossed the Alps and established himself at Lyons, the agents of the French king came to urge a policy of conciliation. Had not Frederick II offered to submit to the arbitration of the kings of France and England? Innocent IV refused all compromise and declared his opponent deprived of his dominions (1245). Louis IX held the balance equal; he continued to treat Frederick II in a friendly fashion, but two years later when he announced his intention of marching on Lyons, either to carry off the Pope, or, possibly, to stage a repetition of Canosa, the King of France let Innocent IV know that he would protect him against all violence and Frederick abandoned the project.[1]

In 1244 Saint Louis had taken the Cross and for some time he hoped for the co-operation of Pope and emperor in the expedition he was preparing. He probably did not realize that both sides were playing him false. Did he know that in

[1] **CLXXII**, chap. i, iv, vii; **CCCLXXVI**, p. cxxxix ff.; **CCXCVII**, 136 ff.; **CCCLXXXIX**, chap. i–v.

1246 the Pope gave secret orders for the preparations for the crusade, which had been started in Germany, to be broken off so that he could recruit supporters unhindered for his battle with the emperor or that Frederick II warned his friend, the Sultan of Egypt, that it was the intention of the King of France to stage his campaign in the Nile valley?[1] In any case, he ceased to count on the reconciliation of the two adversaries and set out for the East in 1248. He remained there six years.

During his absence Frederick II died (13th December, 1250), Innocent IV returned to Rome, and soon the cause of the Hohenstaufen was supported only by a bastard son of the dead emperor, Manfred, acting in the name of Conradin, Frederick's grandson. Manfred, with the support of an army of Saracens, expelled the Pope from the kingdom of Sicily. On his return from the East, Louis IX, considering Conradin as the legitimate heir, remained neutral at first but Manfred, a friend of the Moslems, inspired him with a violent antipathy. On the other hand, the idea of the crusade continued to obsess his mind and govern his policy. As the Holy See was occupied by men who knew how to handle him and win his support, his attitude gradually began to be modified.

In 1261 a Frenchman of energetic but stubborn character became Pope Urban IV; on his accession, he appointed three of Louis's advisers as cardinals, one of whom, Guy Foulquoi, an intimate friend of the king, was Urban's successor under the name of Clement IV (1265–8). During these pontificates there was a very close alliance between the Capetian monarchy and the Holy See. From the reign of Urban IV onwards, Louis IX had come to consider the question of Sicily as bound up with the pacification of Christianity and the deliverance of the Holy Land.[2]

One of the king's brothers, Charles, was marked out, by his character and history, to serve the ends of the Holy See. A man of olive complexion with a harsh and frowning countenance who looked more Castilian than French,[3] he had unbounded ambitions. His appanage of Anjou and Maine was of little interest to him; he dreamed of a

[1] **CLXXII**, 231–2, 354–5.
[2] **CCCLXXVI**, 293 ff., 401 ff.
[3] **CXCIV**, 376 ff.; **CCCLXXVI**, 410 ff.

RELATIONS WITH THE CHURCH

Mediterranean empire. Innocent IV had facilitated his marriage with Beatrice, Countess of Provence, in order to install in that imperial possession a man who could finally ruin the prestige which the Hohenstaufen had been able to retain there. The nobility and the free towns of the district were accustomed to having no master; Charles broke the resistance of the barons and secured the excommunication of Marseilles which was in revolt. Active and determined, with a delight in administration and bureaucracy, he imposed his authority by brute force. He took advantage of factions in Piedmont to extend his power over certain Italian lordships which were seeking protection against Genoa and Asti.[1] This was the man to whom Innocent IV and Urban IV, in succession, offered the kingdom of Sicily. Louis IX, who was held in high respect by his family, could have stopped it all by his veto. French knights and money, however, were essential for the defeat of Manfred and it was fairly easy to convince Louis that, in declaring Frederick II deprived of his fief in Sicily, the Pope had been exercising his right as suzerain and that consequently Conradin could not be heir to it. Other scruples, however, continued to worry him. Should he use the resources of France on the reconquest of Sicily when the Pope and Manfred could easily come to agreement and the most disturbing news was coming from the East? Charles of Anjou and the papal emissaries evidently knew how to show him that the essential condition for the success of the future crusade was that a dependable man should reign in Sicily which was a first class supply base for the crusaders. He allowed himself to be persuaded and assumed the responsibility for this great adventure which was to have so many consequences. He opened negotiations with Urban IV. The agreement of 15th August, 1264, was in part his work. He allowed his subjects to engage, in great numbers, in the service of Charles, and the Holy See to levy crushing taxes on the Church of France. Charles of Anjou, crowned King of Sicily at Saint Peter's in Rome on 6th January, 1266, conquered his kingdom in a month.[2] By the defeat and

---

[1] DCXXII, chap. i-xii; CCXCVII, 172 ff., 207 ff.; CCCLXXVI, 397 ff., 415 ff., 563 ff; CCCLXXXIX, chap. v-vi; CLXXXIX, chap. vi; CLXX, 357 ff.

[2] CLXXII, 396 ff.; CCCLXXVI, 370 ff.

merciless execution of Conradin, the triumph of the Holy See over the Hoheustaufen was established.

We have no knowledge of what Louis IX thought of the reign of terror by which his ruthless brother sought to assure his position. He was becoming more and more absorbed in his dreams and his last word was to be " O Jerusalem ! " He no longer thought of anything but winning martyrdom fighting the Moslems, or even Paradise converting them.

With the arrival of this period in his life, when the monarchy was quite definitely, in his opinion, only an instrument for the salvation of himself and others, there could be no question of conflict between the Holy See and Louis IX, but this had not always been so.

We must look back some years to the period when Louis IX privately disapproved of the refusal of the Papacy to come to any agreement with the Empire. He openly condemned the exactions and the abuse of power which resulted from the bellicose policy of Innocent IV and from which the French Church had to suffer. In 1246–7, the time at which the polemics between Innocent IV and Frederick II were at their height, the King of France expressed his dissatisfaction. He was himself very scrupulous in presentation to benefices, only gave those of which he had control to the most worthy, and avoided plurality. Innocent IV, however, maintained a Court of pomp and ceremony at Lyons and the mode of life of his following aroused some comment ; moreover, he was always in need of money to carry out his policy and he seriously annoyed both clergy and king by his demands. He claimed to have the gift of canonries, archdeaconries, archpriesthoods, deaconries, and curacies by apostolic " provision " for the benefit of the clerks who had served him or even who happened to be his clients or relations, whether they were French, Italians, or Spaniards, and without any obligation of residence. In fact the number which he granted them often made residence impossible. We can see from his registers, for example, that his chaplain, master Étienne, was provided with many canonries or prebends in different parts of France and a dozen Spanish benefices. The tax of a tenth agreed to by the French clergy for the royal crusade was raised by pontifical collectors, during the following five years from 1245 onwards, often in a most brutal fashion under threat of excommunication. The Holy See disposed of the money raised at its own discretion for the benefit of the crusaders whom it regarded with most favour. Further, it demanded money to meet its own needs. When apparently threatened in Lyons by Frederick II, Innocent IV sought to levy on the goods of the Church, particularly in Burgundy, a tax of a seventh and even a fifth of its revenues. Even further, he invited the French clergy to send him an army.[1]

There is no doubt that these abuses and arrogant pretensions aroused violent indignation in France. The Papacy, during its residence in Lyons, was extremely unpopular with all classes of French society. There was a continual demand to know why Innocent IV refused the offers of reconciliation and arbitration made by Frederick II and it was the most ardent supporters of the crusade who were embittered by his haughty obstinacy. They passed from hand to hand the letters of Frederick II " to all of the kingdom of France " (22nd September, 1245), in which he asked that Louis IX should arbitrate in the quarrel, promised to fulfil all the decisions of the French king and set out on crusade with him at once. In the thundering exordium of these letters we find an echo of the old quarrel between Innocent III and Philip Augustus :—

> We have good reason for thinking that the Roman pontiffs of the past and of the present have gravely injured us and the other kings, territorial princes, and nobles . . . in the fact that, against God and justice alike, they assume the power, the jurisdiction, and the authority to install, to dethrone, and to expel from their empire, their kingdoms, their principalities, and their lordships, kings, princes, and magnates in the temporal exercise against them of a temporal power, freeing their vassals from the oath by which they are bound to their lord and promulgating sentences of excommunication against the lords . . . and in the fact that if a quarrel arises between lords and their vassals, the said pontiffs, on the demand of one party alone, impose their temporal intervention and believe that their arbitration must be accepted. . . .[2]

We have seen how next year the French barons leagued themselves against the Church but their object was only to check the encroachments of ecclesiastical jurisdiction. To protest against the excessive power of the Holy See was the concern of the king and the French clergy themselves. In fact, on 2nd May, 1247, Ferry Paté, Marshal of France, one

[1] CLXXII, 267 ff. [2] LXXII, ii, n. 3380.

of the diplomats whom Louis loved to employ, arrived at Lyons with representatives of the bishops and the whole French clergy. He complained to Innocent IV of the abuses that we have mentioned above. Their grievances were detailed in a long memorandum which was presented to the Pope in June by an emissary of the king. It said that the king's patience was exhausted and that his barons, in an assembly recently held at Pontoise had upbraided him for, allowing the destruction of the kingdom. At that time when all the temporalities of the French Church should be at the King's disposal for the defence of the realm, the Pope claimed to use them for his own needs. As for benefices, he was distributing them to foreigners. " Things have reached such a pass that the bishops cannot provide for their well educated clerks or the worthy people in their diocese, and this is to the detriment of the king and all the nobles of the realm whose sons and friends, up till the present, have been provided for in the church." The wealth of the king was being carried abroad and religious worship was being undermined. The churches of France should have been able to help the king to carry out the crusade and still retain some resources for the defence of the kingdom. The Pope promised inquiries and made some small concessions but that was all.[1]

Historians have not yet determined with any exactness what was the policy followed by the successors of Innocent IV but certainly the financial demands of Rome remained heavy. The Italian bankers profited very much by making advances to the Pope and securing the excommunication of recalcitrants.[2] Meetings of the clergy to make some protest were held in Paris but Louis IX could say no more. He needed the money of the Church and the support of the Pope for the second crusade he was about to initiate and for the expedition of Charles of Anjou to Sicily. His correspondence with his friend Clement IV (1265-8), who had also been a clerk in the Parlement of Paris previously, reveals complete mutual confidence.[3] After the death of Clement, while the Holy See was vacant the cardinals sent to Louis IX, some weeks before his departure for Tunis, a long letter on the subject

---

[1] **CLXXII**, 82 ff., 189 ff., 267 ff.
[2] **CCCLXXVII**, 295 ff. ; **XXX**, 676-7.
[3] **LXXII**, iv, *passim*.

RELATIONS WITH THE CHURCH 275

of the union of the Greek and Latin churches by which they stimulated his zeal as the most Christian prince.[1] This affectionate alliance between the Holy See and the Capetian monarchy at the end of Saint Louis's reign prevents our admitting the authenticity of the "Pragmatic Sanction" dated March, 1269, by which the king appeared as commanding respect for the liberties of the churches of the kingdom and forbidding the imposition of taxes on them by the Roman Curia. However, there is no doubt of the spurious character of this document. It was forged during the fifteenth century by the advisers of Charles VII who wished to base their position on some precedent and invoke the religious policy of Saint Louis as a justification of their own.[2] They committed several blunders which reveal its falsity and, particularly, that of dating this Gallican manifesto in a period when there was a tacit compromise between the Crown and the Holy See at the expense of the French Church.

V

The Crusade against the Albigensians. The Inquisition

There was constant anxiety that Philip Augustus, Louis VIII, and Saint Louis should faithfully maintain the cause of the faith against false priests, blasphemous Christians, heretics, Jews, and pagans. They interfered in questions of discipline and concerned themselves with reforming the churches and monasteries where divine worship was neglected, and Saint Louis asked Pope Alexander IV that no one should prevent him dealing severely with married or criminal clerks.[3] Philip Augustus had blasphemers thrown into the water [4]; Saint Louis showed himself so harsh towards them that Clement IV interfered and advised the king to decide in consultation with his barons and prelates what temporal penalties should be inflicted on them "without going as far as mutilation or death".[5] Saint Louis tried, without any

---

[1] 15th May, 1270; **LXXII**, iv, n. 5691.
[2] **DCLXV**; **DXCVI**, 353–396.
[3] **XXXI**, n. 1028, 1486; **DXVIII**, 410; **LXXII**, iii, n. 4243, 4244 *bis*, 4578, 4580.
[4] **CXII**, § 5.
[5] **LXVIII**, § 685; **LVI**, 26–7; **LXXXVII**, i, 99; **LXXII**, iv, n. 5404.

great success, to convert the Jews. The rabbis tried in vain to defend the Talmud which the Pope had ordered to be destroyed; the pious king had every copy he could find burnt. He had no sympathy for the discussions between Christian and Hebrew theologians, which were then very fashionable, and he forbade laymen to take part in them fearing that they might be worsted; the only thing that a layman can do who hears the Christian laws being slandered by a Jew is to draw his sword and " plunge it in his stomach as far as it will go ".[1]

One of the great events of the period we are studying was the pursuit of heresy, the extermination of part of the population of the South, and the annexation of Languedoc and Toulousain to the royal demesne. To write the history of the Albigensian crusade would be to go beyond the scope of this book; we have only to examine the royal policy which was not at first involved in this bloodstained tragedy.

The name *Albigenses heretici* is given to the heretical Cathares (= Purs) by a contemporary, the famous author of the *Histoire Albigeoise*, Pierre des Vaux de Cernay, because Albi was undoubtedly one of the principal religious centres of his time. Catharism, however, extended not only throughout the south of France; it had followers in Lombardy and in the Slav countries of the Balkans, and was very probably of Oriental origin.[2] Many of its rites prove that it originated in a Christian heresy but its metaphysics and its morality set it apart as a religion nearer to the beliefs of Zoroastrianism than to the Christian faith. The Cathares admitted neither the resurrection of the body, Purgatory, nor Hell, and considered the terrestrial life, matter, the work of Satan. Among them, the " Perfect " practised chastity and abstinence and it was believed that after death, for which they were eager, their souls would return directly to God. They comprised, however, only a small minority which gained respect for their virtues, the love of the population for their good works, and led a religious life of great fervour. The mass of " Believers " or " Imperfects " were convinced that their souls would be saved after tests of metempsychosis and they

---

[1] **LXVIII**, §§ 51–3; **CDXXV**, particularly vol. i, 247 ff., 254 ff.; **DCLI**, 118 ff.; **CLXX**, 340–1.

[2] On the obscure question of the origins of Catharism, see the bibliographies and summaries given by F. Vernet and E. Vacandard in *D.Th.C.*, vols. ii and vii, articles " Cathares " and " Inquisition ".

RELATIONS WITH THE CHURCH

lived without fear. It is easy to understand that this religion, based on disgust with the material world, was of a sort to develop in the population easy morals and a merry character.

During the course of the twelfth century before the rise of Catharism, the Catholic clergy had been losing ground. They were recruiting to their ranks badly and with the utmost difficulty and they frequently led a scandalous life. In addition their wealth excited the covetous. The adherence of the upper nobility of the South to Catharism can undoubtedly be explained, in very large part, by a desire to secularize ecclesiastical possessions.[1]

The Holy See knew of all this but, for a long time, the fight against the emperors engaged all their energies. Innocent III was the first to deal with the matter systematically. He fumbled for a long while through lack of the necessary temporal support. He hoped to convert the Count of Toulouse, Raymond VI, who was one of the heads of Catharism but, tortuous and elusive, Raymond was able to evade his promises. The King of Aragon, Peter II, was not much more worthy of his confidence. There was no doubt about the orthodoxy of Philip Augustus who had already ordered the burning of the Cathares,[2] but to the ever more urgent invitations which the Pope sent him from 1204 onwards he replied by refusals or by demands that the Holy See could not accept. Master of Normandy, he feared an English revival and he wished to manœuvre in such a way that he did not compromise the defence of the kingdom and did not waste his resources of men and money. Later on the successes of Simon de Montfort were obviously disagreeable to him. He could not watch with satisfaction the formation in the South of a great Catholic principality possibly more dangerous for the monarchy than the dynasties of Toulouse and Foix. Raymond VI was the brother-in-law of John Lackland and Philip was, with some reason, suspicious of him but he had no desire to see the Count of Toulouse dispossessed unless it was in favour of the House of Capet. His natural mistrust,

---

[1] On the doctrine and its propagation, see, in addition to the articles of Vernet and Vacandard, **DXCVII** ; **CCCXXXII** ; **DCLVI** ; **CDXLII**, ii, chap. i ; **CXLV**, chap. ii–iii ; **CDLXXVII** ; **CCLX**, 294 ff.

[2] **LVII**, bk. i, l. 407 ff. In 1210, he was to order the burning of the heretic disciples of Amaury de Chartres (*Chronicle of Guillaume le Breton*, §§ 153–4).

the age he had reached, and the general circumstances decided him in favour of an almost complete neutrality. Events, as we shall see, proved him right in the end. He was to die too soon to pluck the fruits of his prudence but he lived long enough to see them ripening. In 1207 Innocent III abandoned the cautious policy of conversations and missions which had not succeeded and asked Philip Augustus to undertake the direction of a crusade. Philip demanded that the Pope should impose a truce on the King of England under the sanction of excommunication. If John Lackland withdrew from the war he had recommenced in Poitou it would be possible for the King of France to fall in with the wishes of the Holy See on condition that he could return to the North with his vassals if the truce was broken. He could only tax his demesne and the royal abbeys and he promised a contribution only if the nobles and prelates gave one also. Innocent III, however, was in violent conflict with John Lackland at this moment and could not impose a truce on him. Some weeks later, the legate Pierre de Castelnau was assassinated by a squire of Raymond VI and the crusade was decided (15th January, 1208). When Innocent III repeated his request, Philip maintained his conditions. At this moment, the theocratic doctrine and the doctrine of the lay power came into collision but the clash of theories had no great practical result. Innocent III claimed the right to summon Christians to the campaign for the extermination of heretics and to offer them the conquered territory as spoils : this was to be known in canon law as "the Exhibition of the Prize". Philip Augustus consulted the lawyers of his Court and wrote to the Pope :—

> Concerning the fact that you are offering the lands of the Count of Toulouse to those who occupy it, you should know that we have learnt from learned men and scholars that you have no right to act in this fashion until such time as the count has been condemned for heresy. Then, and only then, you can publish the judgment and instruct us to confiscate those lands since they are our fiefs. You have not yet informed us that, in your judgment, the Count is condemned.[1]

The crusaders began to march in June, 1209, and a war of massacres began. Simon de Montfort, a minor lord of the Paris region, showed such qualities as a captain and organizer that the legate Arnaud Amalric recognized in him the chief

[1] **XXXI**, p. 513; **DXXIV**, 37 ff.

RELATIONS WITH THE CHURCH

who was lacking. He was made Viscount of Beziers and Carcassonne " at the instance of the barons of God's army, the legates and the priests present " (August, 1209). Innocent III did not wish to be committed too far and had not given up hope of forcing Raymond VI to submission and preserving his principality for him. He did not like Simon de Montfort as he frequently showed him but the King of France continued to refuse his support and in the South, thrown into chaos by a war of atrocities, Simon de Montfort, relying on Arnaud Amalric, who had taken the Archbishopric of Narbonne for him, was the only man capable of re-establishing order and orthodoxy. We find him pursuing heresy even as far as Perigord, and even when Peter II of Aragon decided to give the Count of Toulouse the support which he owed him as his suzerain Simon remained the conqueror (Muret, 1213). Innocent III accepted the submission of Raymond in vain. At the Lateran Council the assembled prelates refused to follow the Pope's example; Raymond VI was declared dispossessed and exiled from his dominions; his only son, Raymond VII, could retain only those territories not conquered by the Crusaders, that is to say Beaucaire, Nimes, and, outside the kingdom, Provence. All the conquered lands were conferred on Simon de Montfort (Decree of 14th December, 1215).[1]

Philip Augustus, at this period, was bound by the promise he had made the English barons to help them to dethrone John and he nursed the chimera of an invasion of England. He had allowed his son to make a pious expedition to the South which profited nobody but Simon de Montfort,[2] and in 1216, at the meeting where Louis of France expounded his rights to the Crown of England and maintained his determination to enforce them, in opposition to the legate, Philip Augustus consented to receive the homage of Simon de Montfort for the Duchy of Narbonne, the County of Toulouse and the Viscounty of Beziers and Carcassonne (Melun, 24–25th April).[3] His son was threatened with excommunication and it was impossible to resist the legate on every point. However, he fully intended to make use of his rights as king and lord

[1] On the crusade under Innocent III: **XCI**, with valuable notes; **CDXLII**, ii, chap. ii ff.; **DCXLVIII**, vi; **CCXI**, iv, 2nd part, 264 ff.
[2] April–May, 1215; **DXVII**, 189 ff.
[3] **XXXI**, n. 1659; **DXVII**, 93 ff.; **CCXI**, iv, 2nd part, 522.

and many of his acts during this period show him using Simon de Montfort as a lieutenant of the monarchy in the South.[1]

The deposition of Raymond VI did not have the results which the authors of the decree of 1215 expected. He handed over the conduct of the affairs of the dynasty to his son who undertook to recover the lost possessions. At the voice of Raymond the Young the courage of the Cathares revived; Toulouse invited him. Simon de Montfort advanced rapidly, it was necessary to besiege Toulouse which resisted successfully and Simon was killed (25th June, 1218). Amaury, the son of Simon, did not possess his father's talents and the intervention of the King of France or a powerful prince became necessary: Philip Augustus was obliged to let the direction of the new campaign be taken by his son to prevent it being given to the Count of Champagne.[2]

Louis of France, with the personal assistance of the bishops of Senlis, Noyon, and Tournai, launched a campaign in the Agenais which Raymond the Young had just reconquered. Marmande was taken and destroyed: "All the burgesses were killed and their wives and children as well, all the inhabitants numbering about five thousand," as the historiographer Guillaume le Breton coldly tells us. Toulouse remained impregnable, however, and the sack of Marmande was useless. The barons did not want to continue the campaign and, at the end of three months, Amaury was left to depend on his own forces. At the moment when Philip Augustus died, Amaury had lost nearly all his father's conquests. The "Perfects" emerged from the mountains and forests where they had taken refuge, began preaching again, and reopened their schools.[3]

It was Louis VIII who finally engaged the monarchy on the mission which Philip Augustus had refused to undertake. In spite of his uncertain health he was a bellicose man and a very fervent Catholic. The Pope Honorius III hesitated for some time doubtful whether to sacrifice the new Count Raymond VII but, as frequently happened, the legate who represented him in France had fewer scruples than he had.

[1] DXVII, 189, n. 1.
[2] DCXLVIII, vi, 485 ff.; CCXI, iv, 2nd part, 541 ff.
[3] DXVII, 197 ff.

RELATIONS WITH THE CHURCH

The legate Romain, Cardinal of Saint Ange, was an imperious and energetic man who certainly, for several years, played an important role in Capetian policy. At the Council of Bourges (30th November, 1225) he secured the rejection of the offer of submission made by Raymond VII and at the Assembly of Paris (28th January, 1226) he excommunicated the count and transferred his territories to the king. Finally, Amaury de Montfort yielded all his rights to Louis VIII.

The Crusade was short and decisive. The prestige of the monarchy was already so high that protestations of enthusiasm for orthodoxy and the monarchy commenced even before Louis VIII arrived in the South. The southern clergy, or rather, I should say, the bishops and abbots recently invested who were men trusted by the Holy See or those who thought it best to bury their past, travelled about the region receiving submissions. The king had issued an ordinance condemning known heretics to the stake and their protectors to civil death (April, 1226). The monarchy officially adopted the cruel custom which the crusaders of 1209 had introduced into the South and which it had itself been applying in the North for a long time without the sanction of any definite ordinance. It was the "first French law which sanctioned the punishment of heresy by death by fire".[1] Finally, the strength of the royal army was shown in the capture of the strong town of Avignon which had refused to allow the crusaders to pass. By sentence of the legate the walls of the town were razed although they were on imperial territory. That provides a very characteristic testimony of the power which the popes assumed over heretical territories. The lands of Raymond VII on the left bank of the Rhône were occupied in the name of the Holy See by the king's forces who remained in Provence until 1234. This helps us to understand the panic which seized the nobility and towns of Languedoc on the king's arrival. His expedition was a military procession. "The whole region trembled and from every quarter delegates arrived at the king's camp." At a meeting held at Pamiers (October, 1226) it was decided in principle that all fiefs and demesne confiscated or to be confiscated from the heretics belonged of right to the king. Toulouse still held out but royal seneschals were installed in Beaucaire and Carcassonne.[2]

[1] **CCCLVI**, 595 ff.   [2] **DXVII**, chap. iv–v ; **DXXIV**, 68 ff.

The premature death of Louis VIII only delayed Raymond's submission for a few years. After the systematic devastation of the Toulousain by the royal troops, he was obliged to accept the very harsh terms imposed by the legate; the king permanently retained the seneschalships of Beaucaire-Nîmes and Carcassonne-Beziers. The count retained only the Toulousain, Agenais, Rouergue, Quercy, and the north of Albigeois (Treaty of Paris, 1229). Personally inclined to a kindly and tolerant policy, he was, henceforward, watched by the bishops and legates and as soon as he showed any signs of lukewarmness he was excommunicated. In 1233 he was forced to publish the statutes against heresy and to allow the organization of the Inquisition in his dominions in the same way as in the new royal seneschalships. A pitiless and incessant persecution eradicated Catharism. Even more characteristic than the examinations and treaties that have come down to us was the poem which the Dominican Izarn composed on his debate with the heretic bishop Sicart de Figueiras: "Look," says the inquisitor, "at the ravenous fire which is consuming your fellows. Tell me in a word or two, will you burn in the fire or join with us?"[1]

In practice the heretics had only the choice between conversion, death or flight. Tolerant Catholics were persecuted. Many families were decimated and ruined. Following the attempt of Raymond Trancavel of Carcassonne who tried to resume possession of his inheritance (1240), the Inquisitors redoubled their zeal and thus provoked a revolt which involved almost all the South. Two of them were massacred at Avignonet not far from Toulouse. Raymond was in communication with the enemies of the King of France and believed the moment had come to take his revenge. He threw off his mask and seized Narbonne and Beziers at the moment when his ally Henry III had just disembarked at Royan to reconquer Saintonge and Poitou. But the victory of Louis IX over the English at Saintes demoralized the men of the South. Threatened by a new crusade which would deprive him of all his possessions, on 20th October, 1242, Raymond VII sent to Louis IX and Blanche of Castile supplicatory letters. He obtained peace on condition that he destroyed heresy

[1] **XXIX**, 233 ff.

in his dominions. The last castles which were the usual retreats of the heretics were not slow to fall. Raymond VII, henceforward faithful to his promise, worked zealously. In the year of his death (1249) he ordered the burning near Agen of eighty Cathares who had confessed their errors and whom an Inquisitor was willing to let live. After his death, the king's brother, Alphonse de Poitiers, who married the daughter of Raymond VII and took possession of Toulouse, showed himself less barbarous but he maintained his position by persecutions, the profits of which the king left to him. The rest of the native nobility was ruined. Catharism had been able to develop in the twelfth century owing to the support of the aristocracy and the absence of repression: reduced to nothing but a heresy of the poor and surrounded by inquisitors it gradually disappeared. Under the Valois, there is scarcely any trace of it to be found.[1]

The only thing that remained was the Inquisition for which Saint Louis was directly responsible. It was thanks to his active support that the popes Gregory IX and Innocent IV were able to establish the Inquisition in France at a time when, in most European countries, the secular clergy refused the co-operation of the Dominicans and rejected the terrible means they had been led to take to crush the heroic resistance of the "Perfects"—secret inquiry, secret trial, repeated and captious questioning, torture to enforce a confession and the names of accomplices.

We can fix the year 1233 as the date of the organization of the Inquisition in France. The persecution extended practically throughout the kingdom. Louis IX and his mother paid the expenses of the Inquisitors and gave them a guard responsible for their protection. The secular clergy, at the instance of the Pope and king, abandoned their established prerogative of persecution. The blindness of Saint Louis is well shown by the credit he gave to brother Robert le Petit, a converted Cathare, called, for this reason, the Bulgarian (Bulgar = Cathare). Protected by royal sergeants and encouraged by Gregory IX between 1233 and 1239, this Inquisitor covered Burgundy, Champagne, and Flanders with martyr's stakes.

---

[1] **LXXII**, ii, n. 1992, 2234, 2995, etc.; **CDVII**, bk. ii, chap. i; **CLXX**, chap. ii, iii, v, vii; **CDLXXVI**, 448 ff.; **CDLXXI**, 154 ff., and app. i; **DCLV**, 57 ff.

When the persecutors against Catharism flagged for lack of Cathares, the procedure of the Inquisition remained. It was to have a fateful influence on criminal law in France.[1]

VI

Saint Louis's Crusades against the Moslems

The history of the religious policy of the French kings from the beginning of the thirteenth century to 1270 is very closely bound up with the history of the Crusades. One of the grievances of the Holy See against Philip Augustus and Louis VIII was that they devoted their attention to destroying the Angevin Empire instead of thinking about the deliverance of the Holy Land and remained deaf to all appeals from Rome. This was undoubtedly one of the reasons why those kings who wanted to safeguard their reputation as "Bucklers of the Church" considered their close alliance with the French clergy so necessary and made them so many concessions. With Saint Louis, on the other hand, the idea of freeing the Holy Land quickly became the dominating idea of Capetian policy. In contrast to a king of England who gave the Pope nothing but empty promises, a Frederick II who had friendships with Moslems, or even an Innocent IV who reached the point, as we have already said, of forbidding the preparations for the crusade in Germany,[2] Saint Louis represents the survival of the ardent crusader of earlier ages who is active in the cause and ready to die for it. After him, men made ambitious projects but few sacrifices.

The Mongol invasion which had destroyed the empire of the Kharismian Turks in Asia and showed itself momentarily as far as the shores of the Adriatic had set in motion dangerous forces[3]; in September, 1244, bands of Turks, flying before the Mongols, had taken possession of Jerusalem. Frederick II

---

[1] **CDVII**, i, chap. vii ff.; **XXXVII**; **CCLXV**; **CCLXIV**; **XIX**, i, intro., p. xliv ff.; **DCXXXI**; **CDLXXVIII**; article "Inquisition" (with bibliography) in *D.Th.C.*; **CCCXXXIII**, chap. iii; **CCXCIX**; **CCCLI**, 437 ff., 631 ff.; **CLXXIII**, chap. ii.

[2] Cf. the severe words on the Court of Rome and the "disloyal people there" which Joinville attributes to the legate Eudo of Châteauroux, Saint Louis's companion in the East: **LXVIII**, § 611; **CLXXXII**, 220 ff.

[3] See **DCXXV**, 322 ff.

RELATIONS WITH THE CHURCH

had only recently recovered the Holy City as a result of his negotiations with his friend Malek-el-Khamil, the Sultan of Egypt. Now, however, he could attend to nothing but defending himself against Innocent IV who was seeking his destruction. When the news of the fall of Jerusalem reached France Saint Louis was in the grip of an attack of malaria and generally believed to be on the point of death. He had scarcely recovered the use of speech when he took the vow to go on crusade.

The history of Saint Louis's crusades concerns our subject only indirectly. It is sufficient to recall what prestige they brought the Capetian monarchy even in Asia and Africa at a time when knightly heroism brought more glory than did ability. Saint Louis decided to attack the Sultan of Egypt in his own dominions, not without good reason, for the kingdom of Jerusalem could only be re-established and its security assured if the power of the sultan was destroyed. The expedition was carefully prepared at enormous expense; it was at that period that Aigues-Mortes was created. In spite of the recent Crusade of Jean de Brienne in Egypt, however, there was no detailed information available on the character of the Nile. The royal army arrived before the mouth of Damietta on 5th June, 1249, only a few days before the beginning of the floods and it had to wait six months for them to subside. Damietta had been taken but stores were running low and indiscipline in the army was growing. The march on Cairo was a disaster. The Crusaders, decimated by scurvy and dysentery and harassed by the Saracens, suffered terribly. It was necessary to retreat and finally the army and the king himself were captured. On the point of death, Saint Louis was cured by an Arab doctor but the emirs treated him most brutally. Under threat of death he refused to yield the fortified places of Syria. He freed what remained of his army on conditions of ransom and himself by giving up Damietta. He passed into Syria and there engaged in strengthening the fortifications. Even the news of his mother's death, which was the greatest loss of his life, did not make him decide to return (27th November, 1252). At this period he again opened negotiations with the Grand Khan of the Mongols which he had ingenuously started some years before with the idea of bringing these pagans over to Christianity. On the second occasion, as on the first, he received only an isolent invitation to make his submission. Finally, as a result of the urgent appeals of his loyal subjects, he re-embarked for France (24th April, 1254), after a four year stay in Asia, leaving in the East the reputation of a saint.[1]

All the efforts and sacrifices had been in vain. After the departure of Saint Louis, the Mongols and Moslems quarrelled over Syria.[2] The King of France, from 1267 onwards, made new preparations to deliver the Holy Land but, at the last moment, in circumstances which have remained mysterious, his objective changed.[3] Did Charles of Anjou, established in Sicily, persuade his brother that in the ancient province of proconsular Africa he could relight the great flame of Christianity which had burned there of old ?

The certain thing is that Louis IX, who ceased to see things clearly when he was concerned with the propagation of the faith, believed that the Emir of Tunis was prepared to become a convert. If El Mostanssir obstinately clung to his errors a conquered Tunisia would at least provide immense resources for a new expedition to Egypt. On 1st July, 1270, Louis embarked " to root out completely from Africa the errors of the Saracen infidels ".[4] He was so weakened by illness and mortification that he could not keep his seat on a horse. He had scarcely arrived in Africa when he died, as he wished, a martyr. On his return, throughout the journey of his mortal remains, miracles were reported in increasing numbers.[5]

The period of history that we are studying in this book ends with the canonization of the king. The French monarchy had never enjoyed such an exalted place in the moral sphere but it had also made immense advances in the political arena.

In a previous chapter, we have already seen how within half a century, by the development of established institutions

---

[1] See, in particular, the admirable account of Joinville, **LXVIII**, and the explanation, xvi of the editor; **LVI**; **CXXIV**, 428–432; **LXVII**; **DCLXXII**, i; **CCLXXXVI**, i; **CCXLI**; **CCCXCIII**, 231 ff.; **DCXXV**, 325–331; **CDLXVI**.
[2] **DLXXI**, 365 ff.; **CXCV**, 228 ff.; **DCXXV**, 332–343.
[3] **CDXIII**, v, 9 ff., 79 ff., 123 ff.; **DCXXIII**, particularly p. 308 ff.; **CLXIX**, p. vii ff.; xlvii ff.
[4] Letter of King Philip the Bold : **XXX**, n. 801.
[5] **XCV**, 68 ff.

and traditions, the monarchy established itself with an administration, a judiciary, and finances. It would have been very surprising if, before this moral and material advance of the monarchy, the independence of the nobility and the free towns had remained intact. In practice, in spite of the respect of a Saint Louis for the rights of others, an era of decline was setting in for them. It is this which we have still to examine.

CHAPTER III

HEGEMONY OF THE CAPETIAN MONARCHY IN FRANCE. PRESTIGE IN THE WEST, 1202–1270

I

THE ANARCHY

THANKS to energetic monarchs and their reliable ministers the Capetian monarchy during the first two-thirds of the thirteenth century had brought off a difficult coup. To the benefit of French unity and civilization throughout its widely extended demesnes and even beyond, it had won acceptance for the principles of peace and order. Their bailiffs and seneschals had, on occasion, committed abuses which it had been necessary to stamp out but many of them had been excellent administrators. Good or bad they had won respect for the name of the king and worked, in co-operation with the lawyers of the Curia Regis, to draw from the feudal position of the king as overlord all the advantages which custom and its interpretation allowed. Saint Louis, inspired by a religious appreciation of his duties and a certainty of his rights as a consecrated king, had gone even farther. Full of horror and disgust at the internal wars in which he had taken part during his mother's regency he was not satisfied with a vigorous check on feudal rebellions. He dared to publish and put into effect an ordinance forbidding personal revenge and the wearing of arms. He was the first to strike a blow at the communal separatism which was one of the roots of disorder and his equitable administration was successful in bringing about the assimilation of the newly annexed territories. He said that war between Christians was a sin and put his theory into practice. He was chosen as arbitrator by the nobles who quarrelled among themselves, by foreign magnates, and by the English at war with their king. He gave his dynasty a glory which was to last for many centuries. The present chapter will be devoted to a study of these facts.

Anarchy and violence had so deeply saturated the life of society that the success of monarchical authority was difficult and, in part at least, ephemeral. The Middle Ages had been an era of brutality. The nobility considered war as a normal condition of existence for a man of noble birth and peace as a necessary breathing space rendered bearable by blood-stained tournaments and savage hunting parties. War was the natural method of avenging an injury, of winning an inheritance or a wife, a source of pillage and pleasure, or even a method of support for an aggrieved lord or vassal. The more and more precise rules of feudal law were broken when they seemed likely to check or modify violence. Apart from that, even if they formed a close bond between lord and vassals, they took no account of the relations between the vassals of the same lord. Lateral obligations could scarcely find existence except within the State. At the beginning of the thirteenth century, this anarchy seemed irremediable, for the French baron was master in his own house. He knew no bond to the king except the feudal oath: he paid no taxation except in the particular cases we have analysed. He didn't allow the royal officers to enter his dominions. He struck his own money and could exclude the royal coinage. Within his barony, he legislated and granted charters and communes, he administered and did justice and exercised the seigniorial rights which were often harsh and oppressive. It was not only the dukes and great counts who enjoyed this independence. There were numerous châtelains whom none of their neighbours " dare resist ".[1]

It was not only the king's duty, in virtue of his oath, to protect the oppressed and the victims of feudal anarchy but he also had to defend his own position against it for at any moment a suzerain might be defied by his vassal and the king was not secure from the withdrawal of homage. It is true that a king in the thirteenth century was not assailed with immediate and humiliating dangers as Louis VI had been. Throughout almost all his demesne and generally throughout the northern and western parts of his kingdom he felt himself in comparative security but the spirit of feudal independence might break out anywhere even within the

[1] Case of the châtelain of St. Omer about 1200 : **CCCXV**, 96 ; on all this question see **CDL**, chap. viii, ix ; **CDXLVII**, 219 ff. ; **DCLXX**, 106–7, 109–110.

royal family. We have seen how until 1214 Philip Augustus was frequently betrayed by his vassals and a coalition built up by a man whom he had loaded with wealth almost destroyed his dynasty. Right at the end of his reign he again suspected certain barons of conspiracy.[1] Until the period when Saint Louis set out for Egypt, taking the most belligerent of his barons, the unsettled and warlike temper of the nobility was to cause the monarchy great anxiety. The turbulence of the other social classes, clerks and commoners of town and countryside, did not present a direct menace to the royal authority but it contributed to the general disorder. An extremely important document like the Register of the Visits which the Archbishop of Rouen, Eudo Rigaud, the friend of Saint Louis, made to his parishes shows that the lower clergy were themselves much too coarse to be able to influence men to respect one another. Christianity had but a weak grip on men's souls whatever their rank in society. In addition, the Church was being destroyed from within by furious hatreds which were given open expression of a character that it is impossible for us to imagine since the Reformation and the development of free thought has given an open expression to the opposition and forced the orthodox to mask their disagreements. Injuries, assaults, and bloodshed between clerks were not rare. The Church frequently became involved in violent conflicts with the bourgeoisie of the towns and ill treated its serfs. Tonsured vagabonds and criminals were numerous.[2] Although such theoreticians as Beaumanoir reserved the right of war to the nobles, the commons also practised the old custom of vengeance and small-scale wars developed between different families as the result of some assassination, particularly in the north or east of the kingdom. These feuds were only extenuated by truces and the assurances which custom imposed until the moment when a formal " peace to factions " ended the vendetta.[3]

In the towns, disorder was complicated by the grave

[1] XCVII, 195.
[2] LXIX; CCXLVII, 480–1; CDL, 41, 51 ff., 146 ff., 198 ff., 255 ff.; CDLXII, 38 ff.; CCLXI, 2nd part, chap. iii and iv.
[3] XVI, ii, 356 ff., §§ 1671–2, 1691; CDXXXVIII, 208 ff. For Burgundy see DCXLIX, 104 ff. For the North, CLXV, 202 ff. and *passim*; CCLXXXI, 417 ff.; CCLXVIII, 3 ff., 45 ff., 130 ff., 212 ff.; DXVI, 46 and n. 2, 221–4. For English Guienne, C, n. 504–6.

dissensions arising between rich and poor. The greater burgesses monopolized municipal office, governed the free towns to their own advantages, and oppressed the lower order until their egotism stimulated revolt in addition to the wars which they were frequently carrying on with the lord of the district or equivocal communications with the king's enemies.[1]

The victory of the monarchy over anarchy was almost complete by the end of Saint Louis's reign. It had been achieved by force and by judicial and administrative action.

II

MILITARY REPRESSION

We have seen that Philip Augustus possessed a well organized and dependable army which gave him the means to destroy the feudal coalition of 1214 in spite of the powerful support given by the emperor and the King of England, and to continue the struggle which he had started at the beginning of his reign against the lords, great and small alike, who robbed merchants and pillaged the churches. One of his biggest successes was the submission of Auvergne; the count, Guy II, was a shameless brigand; in 1213 the castle of Tournoël which was reckoned to be impregnable was captured by the royal troops who found an enormous booty stolen from the churches. It was all restored and a " constable of the king in Auvergne " maintained order there henceforward.[2]

The dangers of 1214 appeared again during the minority of Louis IX. The emperor, on this occasion, was not concerned. Frederick II owed his position to the Capetians and circumstances did not allow ingratitude but the young King of England, Henry III, dreamt of revenge and went to the support of the rebel barons. On the death of Louis VIII, the loyal monarchists immediately feared " the disloyalty of the traitors ".[3] The somewhat rough firmness of the queen regent, Blanche of Castile, gave the barons no opportunity of taking

---

[1] **XVI**, ii, 267 ff., §§ 1520 ff.; **CDXXXVIII**, 206 ff.; **CCCXV**, 159 ff., 316 ff.; **CCCXXXVI**, 87 ff.
[2] **CCXI**, iv, 2nd part, 393; **LXXII**, ii, n. 2485 (1237).
[3] **CXXVIII**, 124–131. Cf. **DXVII**, 323 ff.

advantage of the minority of Louis IX unless they found some excuse for taking up arms. They could not contest the validity of the oral testament [1] by which Louis VIII had decided that his children and kingdom should be entrusted to the guardianship of Blanche. Louis VIII had exercised a right conferred on him by a monarchical custom that was already of long standing. They claimed, however, that his choice was bad, declaring that "it was not a woman's business" to govern such an important thing as the kingdom of France. They reproached Blanche with bringing her son up to hate his barons and with surrounding him with clerks. The regency should be given to the barons, to the peers, not to a foreigner who sent the king's wealth to Spain instead of distributing it to the French.[2]

During the winter of 1226–7 a coalition began to form itself. In 1230, when the territories of the Count of Champagne, who had become an ally of the regent,[3] were ravaged by the confederates and the King of England disembarked at St. Malo with a strong force, there was every reason to expect the rapid collapse of the monarchy. The danger was avoided by the courage and ability of the regent and her advisers. It had, in fact, been lessened by the mediocrity and fickleness of the barons. Their puppet, Philip Hurepel, the king's uncle, was an incapable leader. Blanche's most dangerous opponent was another prince of the royal family, Pierre de Dreux, who was later nicknamed Mauclerc.[4] He held the county or duchy of Brittany as the guardian of his son, a minor, and was by no means satisfied with this temporary power. A rough and ambitious man he did not hesitate at open treason and transferred his homage and the fief of Brittany to the King of England. When the latter failed to send any assistance, Pierre de Dreux withdrew his homage and submitted (1234). The fomentors of the regent's trouble had, all in turn, disappeared or were on the point of disappearing.[5]

[1] **CDLXIII**, 48 ff.   [2] **CLXX**, 64 ff., 108–110.
[3] On their relations see **DCLXXI**, p. xv ff.
[4] **DXXVIII**, i, 48–9.
[5] **CLXX**, chap. ii–v ; **CLXXI**. In the same year, 1234, Louis IX reached his twentieth year. Should we say he became a major ? Philip Augustus had been considered such at the age of 14. In fact, it is impossible to say what date marked the end of the regency of Blanche of Castile. Until her death she reigned jointly with her son.

HEGEMONY OF CAPETIAN MONARCHY 293

A last explosion of feudal discontent developed between 1240 and 1243. We have seen how, at that period, the Albigensians, driven to despair by persecution, were raising their heads once more and that there were armed struggles in Languedoc (1240). The following year, the king's brother, Alphonse, was invested with his appanage and came to Poitou to receive the homage of his vassals. Hugh de Lusignan, Count of La Marche, the most powerful of them, however, had married Isabelle d'Angoulême, the mother of Henry III, King of England. In her infancy, we must remember, Isabelle had been Hugh's fiancée: John Lackland had married her and thus provoked the Poitevin barons to appeal to Philip Augustus. A proud and violent woman, she had no wish that her husband should do homage to the new Count of Poitiers. Stunned by a conjugal ultimatum the somewhat comic secret of which has been revealed to us by a contemporary,[1] Hugh de Lusignan resigned himself to plotting a conspiracy. The Poitevin barons who had been among the chief sources of the troubles of the regency asked nothing better than to join in some agitation. They held meetings, first among themselves, then with the barons and mayors of the big towns of Gascony. The " French ", they protested, want to reduce us to slavery: we should do better to come to an agreement with the King of England who is a long way off and has no designs upon our goods. Henry III promised to come in person to his mother's support. The King of Aragon, Lord of Montpellier, and the Count of Toulouse took a part in the game but the French king's army in the spring of 1242 lost no time in taking possession of the Poitevin strongholds; Henry III only brought three hundred knights over from England. Face to face with Louis IX on the bridge of Taillebourg he did not dare to risk a battle and retired within the walls of Saintes. On the next day when English and Gascons had made a sortie he gave the signal for flight. He returned to England with one more defeat on his record. The Poitevins submitted and the Count of Toulouse, as we have seen, was forced to do the same.[2]

Against the armed insurrection of the baronage the kings had known how to defend themselves. More remarkable

[1] **LXXIII**, 513 ff.
[2] **CLXX**, 342 ff.; **CLXIV**, 289 ff.

and a greater innovation was the legal and administrative struggle they waged against anarchy.

III

Administrative Action. Bailiffs and Seneschals

In this activity of the monarchy we must distinguish between the part played by the local officials, seneschals, bailiffs, and subordinate officers acting far from their master's eye, and the king himself governing his Court. The local officials worked stubbornly for the development of the royal authority and they secured universal respect for it. In many cases the re-establishment of order was due to their energy [1]; frequently, also, they had an audacious attitude towards the nobility, an aggressive policy which did not always win the approval of the Crown. Some of them (the provosts (*viguiers*) and farmers in the South, the provosts in the north) still bought their offices and had a personal interest in being extortionate and in rounding off the royal demesne; all wished to play important parts. Some of them had even come to consider themselves independent authorities and, if they had not been checked in time, they would have reconstituted, particularly in the South, a feudal hierarchy of officials.

We have practically none of the archives of bailiwicks and seneschalships left but we have some of the complaints addressed to the king about the conduct of his officials and important remnants of the inquiries which Saint Louis commanded. To these we must add the documents about the appanage of Alphonse de Poitiers. What do we learn from these texts? [2] For the northern and western parts of the demesne we know very little of the encroachments of bailiffs, seneschals, provosts, and subordinate officers at the expense of the lay and ecclesiastical nobility and the communes. It is certain, however, that they were not merely satisfied to apply the royal ordinances and the sentences of the Curia. They tried to extend their judicial competence at the expense

---

[1] Cf. for example, **DCLVII** documents cited 3 and 4, p. 203 ff.
[2] **XXXVIII**; **XXVII**. Cf. **CCCXCV**; **DCLXXIII**, chap. vii; **CDLXXV**; **CDLXXI**; **DLX**, vol. ii, bk. ii, chap. ii.

of the neighbouring lords. The Bishop of Orleans, for example, sent to Louis IX in 1245 a long list of grievances against the bailiff and he was primarily concerned with controversies over jurisdiction.¹ About 1257, the Countess of La Marche carried her complaints to Alphonse of Poitiers; the Seneschal of Poitou and his officials extorted money from the countess's men, encroached on her jurisdiction, summoned and arrested in a completely arbitrary manner.² Gonthier, châtelain of Laon about 1248, worked to increase the number of men subject to the king to the disadvantage of the nobles.³ As for the complaints presented by lesser men to the inquisitors sent out by Saint Louis, they are concerned with the thefts of the sergeants, the chicaneries of foresters and beadles, and the exactions of provosts anxious to get the utmost profit from their farm. This provost or that sergeant, we are told, arrests at random and the accused have to bribe him. Fines mounted up and were by no means bound by custom and they were increased further if it appeared that the victim had the means to pay more. The methods used to enforce their payment were barbarous in the extreme. The prisons were rough and confessions were obtained by torture. Taxes were continually increasing, peasants who were quite willing to fulfil their host service were obliged to pay the substitute tax, etc. Joinville, whose lordship was situated in Champagne, found a plausible excuse for not going on crusade a second time alleging that he had to defend his lieges. They had been "destroyed and impoverished" by the agents of the King of France and the Count of Champagne while he was in Egypt with the king.⁴ The bailiffs themselves, in spite of their prestige, did not entirely avoid accusations. Some of them, like Matthew de Beaune in Vermandois, seem to have been the subject of unjust complaint by the people over whom they had authority; on examination, the mass of grievances disappears,⁵ but, in Artois, Nevelon the Marshal left the reputation of a terrible man.⁶ After the Conquest of Normandy, Philip Augustus needed a man of some energy and he entrusted the bailiwick of Pont Audemer to a celebrated

¹ LXXII, ii, n. 3338. ² XCII, 509 ff.
³ XXXVIII, 260–9. ⁴ LXVIII, § 735.
⁵ XXXVIII, 318*–19*, proof n. 152; DCLXXIII, 165–7.
⁶ DXVII, 215–16.

mercenary leader, Lambert Cadoc ; it would be vain to expect much delicacy of him ; he pocketed £14,200 belonging to the king, and Philip Augustus, " enraged with him," cast him into prison. He did not emerge till 1227.[1] That, however, was exceptional. In general the bailiffs were faithful servants and the only reproach against them is undue zeal for the monarchy. Depredation and pillage were the work of provosts and sergeants of all ranks.

In the southern demesnes, annexed after the Albigensian crusade, and in the lands which Alphonse of Poitiers inherited from his father-in-law, the Count of Toulouse, abuses were certainly more serious. There were already seneschalships in the County of Toulouse at the period when the counts were independent and these powerful lords let their officials rob all at will. It was traditional. The seneschals and their lieutenants, the provosts (viguiers), who were established by Louis VIII and IX, were nobles and councillors from the North. They were not paid sufficient and they lived too far from Paris to be kept under any close surveillance. They adopted evil habits. Their provost, generally known as " *bailes* " (farmers), were local men who were not much better. The old abuses that the inhabitants suffered were now aggravated by the persecution of heretics, which gave an air of legality to their usurpations, and the determination of the royal agents to ruin the privileges of lords and cities alike even outside the royal demesne and even beyond the frontier of the kingdom. Under the pretexts of restoring order and defending the king's rights, the seneschals of Saint Louis destroyed numerous castles, prevented the exercise of other jurisdictions, enforced within the barons' demesnes ordinances which were applicable to the royal demesne and carried out themselves the regulation of the highways there, doing everything in their power to make the lands of the king coterminous with their seneschalships. The Albigensian crusade which had ruined so many families in the South had left in existence in the Gévaudan and Velay a nobility of needy minor barons, little but brigands, grouped around two powerful houses which had renounced the heresy, the Pelest, and the Lords of Anduze. The seneschals of Beaucaire

[1] **XXX**, n. 118–19, 132, 247, 363, etc. ; **LXXII**, ii, n. 1937–8 ; **CCXLV**, 130 ff. ; **DXIX**, 115.

carried on a bitter struggle with this nobility of the Cevennes, they destroyed the prestige of the Pelets and dispossessed to a considerable extent the Lord of Anduze. They even penetrated into the Vivarais which was imperial territory where they made annexations and summoned the Bishop of Viviers to their court. In the seneschalship of Carcassonne, a noble lady who refused to give up her rights of " haute justice ", was threatened with the fire and the Bishop of Lodève found himself deprived of his power to receive homage on the king's behalf and his rights of " haute justice ". At Beaucaire the consulate was suppressed.

The excesses of which the royal officers in the North and West were accused were multiplied in the South by the distance of the king and the absence of any effective control. The seneschals levied tallages contrary to all custom, set ransoms on the whole population of a town on the occasion of a murder, usurped private estates, and made requisitions without payment. Some of them adopted the methods of a Turkish pasha and brooked no resistance. If anyone was so ill advised as to say " The seneschals protect robbers ", or " The seneschals will soon be recalled ", he became liable to a heavy fine. The provosts and farmers were even more unpopular because they were natives and their frequently humble origins were well known.[1] The provosts followed the example set by the seneschals or even refused to obey them. One of them, accused of arbitrary imprisonment, replied that he had to get money out of those who had it for he had bought his office at a high price. The farmers' stole provisions, imposed undue services for their own advantage and overwhelmed the lesser men with annoyances, injuries, and unbearable humiliations. Their victims frequently preferred to flee the country.

Information of these things reached the royal court from time to time and there was a perfect willingness to repress them severely but it was not always respected or obeyed. The Seneschal William des Ormes having overtaxed the men of Roujan received an appeal to the king from them. He cast the protestants into prison. Pierre d'Athies who governed the seneschalship of Beaucaire by methods of terror (1239–1241) said, " I would gladly give a hundred marks to hear no more

[1] Curious complaints of the inhabitants of Beziers in L, n. 36, pp. 89–91.

of this talk about the king and queen," and to one of his victims who appealed to the king he replied, " Go and ——." He persecuted the Lady of Alais who obtained royal letters which he declared that he would not carry out.

It was under these conditions that the king decided, in 1247, to establish commissions of inquiry.

IV

Inquests and Ordinances

In fact, Saint Louis was disturbed in his conscience by thoughts of the iniquities which were being committed. Could he leave them unreformed on the eve of his departure on crusade ? Could he leave his subjects at the mercy of men who seemed to be guaranteed impunity by tradition ? His character made one decision inevitable but there is reason to believe that he was encouraged to take action by the churchmen who had such frequent cause to complain of his officials and even by his advisers who regarded the seneschals with some bitterness because of their independence. Further, it had been customary for the Capetians to send representatives of their Court on circuit but the measures taken had an entirely new character. It was no longer a question, as previously, of the delegates working in the king's interests ; on the contrary, it was their task to collect all the grievances against the monarchy which were brought forward and to satisfy them. The commissioners' task, the king declared in his letters of January, 1247, " will be to receive in writing and examine all the complaints which can justifiably be brought *against us and our ancestors* as well as statements concerning the injustice and exactions of which our bailiffs, provosts, foresters, sergeants, and the subordinates have been guilty." On the other hand one circuit was not sufficient and, on his return from Palestine, Saint Louis organized them every year. Since the inquiries were pious in intention and their object was to repair faults that had occurred, the commissioners were almost always churchmen, particularly Franciscans, at the beginning almost without exception. He gradually introduced among them some of the councillors of his court who presided over the commissions because it was found that the clergy had little experience and often allowed themselves to be deceived. Until the end of his reign, however, people considered the inquisitors' circuits as designed to do " justice to all, poor and rich alike ". After the death of Saint Louis, the character of these missions was completely changed and their only object was to extort money from the subjects.¹

Alphonse of Poitiers, who administered his appanage by the same machinery as the king his demesnes, also ordered inquests into the excesses of his officials but owing to his somewhat distrustful and peremptory nature he allowed them much less freedom, and his Court which, like that of the king, was held in Paris examined in general the demands recorded by the mission.² The royal inquisitors, on the other hand, had most extensive powers for dealing with grievances which had been established. They heard plaintiffs patiently, solemnly recorded the futile complaints of old women, questioned the local arbitrators, and, if there was need, commanded restitution to be made.³ The king so far from opposing them was overburdened with scruples. He was disturbed by the fact that in the restitution of goods unjustly acquired, particularly the goods of Jews, it was not always possible to discover the rightful owners and he sought the Church's authority to use the money on works of piety.⁴

The administrative result of the inquests was the publication of the great ordinances of 1254 and 1256 on the duties of bailiffs, seneschals, and provosts.⁵ Alphonse of Poitiers acting, as always, along the same lines as his brother published similar decrees for his demesnes.⁶ The bailiff or seneschal entering on his duties must swear in public to do justice truly, to respect local customs, to preserve the king's rights, to accept no bribes and offer none to the councillors of the royal court. There followed a series of regulations which frequently seemed to be inspired by the Roman legislation

---

[1] See the Preambles to the Inquests, **XXXVIII**, 253*a*, 259*b*, 301, etc.; **LVI**, 150-1 ; **CDLXXI**, 39 ff. ; **CCCXCV**, 1-4.
[2] **CDLXXV**, 506 ff.
[3] See, in particular, **LXXII**, vol. iii, nn. 4202, 4269, 4272, 4278, 4320, etc.
[4] Ibid., nn. 4404, 4502, 4508, 4510-4536, 4541-8 ; **XXX**, n. 622.
[5] **LXXXVII**, i, 65-81.
[6] **CDLXXV**, 481 ff. ; **CXCI**, 145-150.

on provincial governors,¹ in particular, the obligation to remain fifty days in his former office when a bailiff was moved elsewhere so that anyone he had wronged could seek remedy of him. Bailiffs and seneschals were forbidden to marry or to acquire land within their district without permission. They could not levy taxes which were not sanctioned by custom or, by craft or terror, extort money payments or make use of torture when the accused had little support. They had to check debauchery and gaming and set an example themselves. Finally, as we have seen, they had to call together meetings of arbitrators to consult them on the advisability of exporting wine and corn. That was not a new thing. In the South, at least, a system of consultations was quite usual. They were not by any means concerned with the creation of a small-scale parlement. In this particular case, the king wished to prevent his officials from forbidding export unseasonably so that they could sell licences to the merchants.² These assemblies did not exist everywhere but some of them were probably the origin of the provincial estates.³

These ordinances were not fully applied nor for long periods at a time but, at least in their administrative clauses, which the royal commissioners could watch in practice, they were useful and contributed to the good name of the monarchy. It was certainly a happy attempt to reduce the local officials to their duties again and to make the moderating and equitable influence of the Curia generally felt. In the South the results were very noticeable. The seneschals were left in office only for short periods—a year or two or four at the most—and they were frequently sent instructions. Appeals to the Curia grew in number and led to revisions of judgments. Even locally, the seneschal lost part of his judicial power which was given to a superior judge (*judex major*).⁴ Alphonse of Poitiers, for his part, abolished the abuses of his agents and forbade his farmers to inflict fines. Established in Paris, like his brother, he governed from afar but he liked to be fully informed and kept up an enormous correspondence; in spite of his greed, delays, and cavilling over details he contributed

---

[1] DCLXIV, iii, 263–4.
[2] CDLXXV, 508 ff.; CCLXIII, 127 ff.; CDLXXI, 49.
[3] DCLXXIII, 143–4.
[4] CDLXXI, 34 ff., 66–7, 89, 103 ff.

to the return of prosperity and peace in the South so depopulated and impoverished by religious wars.[1] From its experiences gained during three-quarters of a century the Court retained its distrust of bailiffs and seneschals and already the decline of their great powers was becoming apparent. However, they had undertaken and were to continue the work of weakening rival powers. Saint Louis himself so respectful of the rights of others took advantage, wherever possible, of the work of these ants which were gnawing away the feudal structure.

V

The King Overlord

Beyond the local officials, there was the king and his Court. What policy were they following ? What were their means of action ? What was the extent of their claims ?

Philip Augustus had been an adaptable man with few scruples ; Louis VIII and Blanche of Castile somewhat harsh and severe. Saint Louis bequeathed to his heir this maxim : " Maintain an honesty that you never compromise whatever may happen,"[2] but he had no intention of yielding any of the rights of the crown. All these princes, in varying degrees, felt very keenly that there was " only one king in France and, above all, they wanted to gain from their prerogative as " *dominus superior*", of "supreme suzerain", every advantage which it implied. The monarchy remained feudal but now it was a source of strength for them, for a suzerain who had money, an extensive demesne, a stable army, could demand a great deal in vassal service. A powerful feudal king should be ready to fix in writing, if necessary as a result of inquests, all the obligations of his vassals. That is what Henry II had done in England and what Philip Augustus did during the second part of his reign. The register of the Trésor des Chartes commenced by his vice-chancellor Guérin in 1220 contains transcriptions of 132 inquests made between 1195 and 1220 " on the order of our lord the king on various

[1] **CDLXXV**, 476 ff. ; **XXVII**, vol. ii, intro., p. lxvii ff. ; **CLXXXII**, 108 ff.
[2] **XXXIX**, 258.

subjects"; many are concerned with the rights of the king over certain territories in the way of justice, revenues, regale, hunting, etc.[1] From the same period date the feudal statistics which modern scholarship has, if not studied, at least prepared for study and baptized as the *Scripta de feodis*.[2] It is a series of inquiries, incomplete and somewhat incoherent, answered by the principal bailiffs of Philip Augustus on the feudal obligations of the nobles of their district. It also includes an enumeration of the bishoprics of the demesne and the duties of hospitality and host service which some of them owe, a list of the castles and fortresses of the king, a list of dukes and counts (to the number of thirty-two), a list of barons, that is to say lords who although of lower rank have sovereign rights (numbering sixty), of seventy-five châtelains, of thirty-nine communes, of the knights banneret, of knights with an income of £60, widows possessing a lordship, and finally the list of sergeants, horses, and carts which are due to the king in time of war. This great statistical undertaking, which was evidently suggested by the Anglo-Norman inquests, shows an interest in detailed information which the Capetian monarchy had not displayed before.

The most important thing for a feudal lord was to have the highest possible number of dependable vassals, to gain liege homages, to secure the immediate dependence of the sub-vassals, and to prevent vassals becoming under-vassals. In this respect the king had to adopt the same policy as a duke or a count; at the beginning of the system of vassalage, a Carolingian sovereign could depend on the loyalty of all his subjects and, in the thirteenth century, the conception of the " subject " was only just beginning to emerge again and an under-vassal would only serve the king on the order of his immediate lord or by virtue of special arrangements. Philip Augustus, Louis VIII, and Saint Louis increased considerably the number of their direct vassals throughout the southern part of the kingdom even outside the demesnes they annexed. The Count of Perigord (1204 and 1212), the Bishop of Limoges (1204), the Viscount of Turenne (1212),

---

[1] LXXXV, i, 956 ff. On the registers of the Trésor des Chartes before the death of Saint Louis see XXXI, intro., p. xxvi ff., and the Studies of H. F. Delaborde: CCXL, LXXII, vol. v, intro., and CIV, intro.
[2] CXXVI, 605-723,

and a number of lords who had to clear themselves of the suspicion of heresy[1] fell into this category. Saint Louis bought of Thibaud of Champagne, in 1234, for £40,000 Tournois the suzerainty of the counties of Chartres, Blois, and Sancerre and of the viscounty of Châteaudun which ceased to be fiefs of Champagne.[2] In Flanders, the kings continued to pay pensions, money fees, to the vassals of the count to secure their liege homage.[3] On the Rhône frontier several imperial territories, particularly parts of the County of Valentinois, became fiefs of the King of France.[4] Philip Augustus took advantage of circumstances and went so far as to demand, by an indirect method, an oath of fidelity from all the vassals of the Duke of Brittany. In fact, when Pierre de Dreux received the duchy from him, he not only offered him liege homage but took the following engagement: " I will receive the homage and loyalty of the Bretons only in accordance with loyalty to my lord the King of France in such fashion that if I do not serve him well and faithfully, they shall assist the said king against me until he has the satisfaction he requires."[5] A danger threatened the suzerain of a fief divided between several heirs; one of them received the homage of the others and became their immediate lord. Philip Augustus, in 1209, in agreement with a certain number of barons, published an ordinance prescribing that in such a case all the heirs " shall hold in chief and without an intermediary " of the lord of whom the fief was previously held.[6]

Feudal loyalties were so uncertain that the kings sought some means of guaranteeing them. We see, around Philip Augustus, " sworn knights."[7] They had, undoubtedly, taken a special oath; this was a very ancient custom. The same king tried to make use also of the threat of ecclesiastical censure.[8] Above all, however, he used the method of feudal sureties and it proved so effective that we find it constantly in use throughout the thirteenth century.[9] When a vassal

---

[1] **XXXI**, nn. 821–2, 875, 1409, 1401.
[2] **LXXII**, ii, n. 2310; **DCLXVI**, 224.
[3] **LXXII**, ii, n. 2959.
[4] **CDXXVIII**, 114–15.
[5] 27th January, 1213; **LXXII**, i, n. 1033.
[6] **XXXI**, n. 1136. On this policy of the kings, see also **LXXII**, ii, n. 1959.
[7] **XLII**, 111.   [8] **XXXI**, nn. 498, 500.
[9] **XXXVI**, n. 15, p. 55, example of 1292.

made a promise, pact, or agreement with the king, if he took charge of a fortress or if he had merely become suspect, the king demanded of the lords over whom he had authority that they should provide him with warranty or even the vassal concerned had to find sureties for himself among his relations and friends. The guarantors promised the king to assist him if necessary against a disloyal subject or to pay him a certain sum of money; in certain cases, the king could confiscate the goods of the lord standing surety. Examples are innumerable. In 1212 many lords of the Angevin area promised Philip Augustus to pay him a thousand pounds if Amauri de Craon refused to give up the stronghold of Chantocé [1] at the first demand. In 1230, Dauphin, Count of Auvergne, and his grandson, Robert, made peace with the king and did him homage. Five lords gave him security for their promise to recognize the authority of the Curia Regis if the case arose. In 1231 Foulque Pesnel became security for the loyalty of his nephew, the Lord of Fougères; if the latter broke his engagement the king could seize as forfeit all that Foulque Pesnel held of him.[2] The count and countesses who governed Flanders in succession after the period when Ferrand became suspect to Philip Augustus were surrounded with a network of securities demanded of the lords and towns of the district (1212, 1217, 1226, 1237, 1245, etc.); for example, when the Countess of Flanders married Thomas of Savoy in 1237 the representatives of Saint Louis received the guarantee of twenty-four lords and forty-eight towns.[3] Finally, we must note that it was impossible to escape the obligation. In 1235 Hugh IV Duke of Burgundy refused to stand surety for Thibaud, Count of Champagne, who seemed to be preparing some treason. Louis IX forced Hugh IV to make due apology and write to him in the following terms: " I have apologized to my very dear lord Louis, illustrious King of France, to do his will to the extent of five thousand marks of silver, because I was not willing to guarantee the loyalty of Thibaud, Count of Champagne, as he required." The duchess-mother of Burgundy and five of the vassals of the duke had to become security in turn for the payment

[1] **XXXI**, nn. 1339–1348. Other examples, **DCLXX**, 116 and note, 117.
[2] **LXXII**, ii, nn. 2038, 2129. See also nn. 2090–2126, 2741, 2799–2803, etc.
[3] Ibid., n. 2585 ff.

of these five thousand marks. If the case had arisen and the payment had not been made Hugh himself would have been held as a hostage in Paris or the king would even have occupied all the fief that the duke held of him. The letter finished with an obligation of loyalty and obedience to the king.[1]

This systematic use of guarantees, to which historians have not paid sufficient attention, was certainly one of the most powerful means by which the progress of the Capetian monarchy in the thirteenth century was achieved. The customs regulating feudal succession gave the king an opportunity to gain considerable advantages, strategical and territorial from his rights as suzerain. In place of the right of relief demanded of the chief heir, the suzerain could, by agreement with him, obtain some territory.[2] In cases of collateral succession, Philip Augustus frequently used or abused his authority to buy all or part of the inheritance.[3] When a fief held directly of the king passed to the widow of a lord or the heir was a minor, the Crown exercised its right of seizure without scruple from the time of Philip Augustus. When Raoul d'Exoudun, Count of Eu by right of his wife and a supporter of the English party,[4] died without an heir Philip Augustus demanded of his widow considerable cessions of territory and a relief of five thousand marks of silver. He placed one of his bailiffs in the county as a coadministrator until the sum was paid and forbade all new fortification.[5] Naturally the widow had always to swear to the king not to remarry without his consent and, if she had a daughter, to take a like engagement on her behalf.[6] Philip Augustus levied a handsome brokerage when he secured wealthy marriages for his friends[7] and reserved the most profitable unions for his relations. It was in this way that Pierre de Dreux came to marry the heiress to the County of Brittany, Philip Hurepel the heiress to the County of Boulogne, Alphonse de Poitiers the heiress to the County of

[1] Ibid., n. 2365.
[2] For example, Nogent l'Erembert in 1219; **XXXI**, n. 1891; cf. **DCLXX**, 121–2.
[3] Counties of Clermont-en-Beauvaisis, Alençon, Beaumont-sur-Oise: **DCLXX**, 122; **CDXIV**, 61 ff.
[4] Act of Philip Augustus edited in **CCXI**, iv, 2nd part, 644.
[5] **LXXII**, i, n. 1360; cf. **CCXI**, iv, 2nd part, 547–8; **CCXLVI**, 549.
[6] **LXXII**, ii, nn. 2027, 2335, 2353, 2378, etc.
[7] Acquisition of Montargis, Gien, Pont-Saint-Maxence; **DCLXX**, 121.

Toulouse. In all three cases lordships were involved which no man was in a position to defend. For the same reason, the County of Champagne fell to the guardianship of Philip Augustus who protected the countess regent effectively but treated Champagne as an annex of the royal demesne during the minority of Thibaud.[1] During the century which followed Bouvines the County of Flanders was kept closely subjected; the captivity of the defeated of Bouvines, Ferrand, the appearance of an imposter, the "false Baldwin" who claimed to be the old Count Baldwin, finally the release of Ferrand bought at a high price put the Countess Jeanne at the mercy of Philip Augustus, Louis VIII, and Blanche of Castile; subsequently the famous quarrel between the Countess Margaret's children gave Saint Louis a fine opportunity.[2] Feudal custom allowed for division and exchanges. Philip Augustus took advantage of this to secure places which commanded the frontiers of the demesne or the main routes and to take over some of the strongest fortified castles of the period.[3] He often imposed on his vassals the obligation to surrender a certain castle to him at the first summons.[4]

The vassal owed his suzerain military service and service at court. We have already seen how these feudal obligations developed in the thirteenth century. Forty days' host service, though irritating and inadequate, provided the king with a powerful force. This was very clearly seen in 1230 when the English invasion gave the regent an opportunity to summon and use in her service vassals who were at the height of a revolt.[5] The duty of aid and council at Court allowed Philip Augustus and his successors to rely on the baronage to guarantee their policy.[6] That was the ultimate source of the king's power to issue general ordinances which were not merely Utopian proclamations. In the thirteenth century ordinances agreed to by their vassals were a means of government used equally, we must point out, by the dukes and

---

[1] **CXLVII**, iv, part 1; **DCLXX**, 108–9, 115; **CCXI**, iv, 2nd part, 291–3, 334–5.
[2] **CCCLXXXIII**, vols. i, ii, bks. viii, ix; **DCLXXXI**, i, 402–9; **DXVII**, 396–402. See below.
[3] **DCLXX**, 119–120, 122–3; **DXVII**, 321.
[4] For example, **XXXI**, nn. 1840, 2191, 2225, etc.
[5] **CLXX**, 173–4, 177.
[6] For example in 1203: **XXXI**, n. 762, 770–780.

greater counts within their lordships [1]; the king, however, was supreme and he was to succeed in making ordinances for the whole kingdom.

The question is sufficiently important for us to note some of the stages. The articles of 1205–6 limiting ecclesiastical jurisdictions were drawn up " By agreement between the king and his barons " [2]; the ordinance of 1209 quoted above concerning suzerainty over fiefs divided between several heirs bears the following subscription : " Philip, king, Eudo, Duke of Bourgogne, Hervé, Count of Nevers, Renaud, Count of Boulogne, Gaucher, Count of St. Pol, Guy de Dampierre, and many other magnates of the realm of France have unanimously agreed and have established by their public assent that from 1st May onwards, this will govern all cases of feudal tenures ..." [3] In particular, however, there are successive ordinances concerning the Jews and regulating or forbidding usury which allow us to measure the progress of the royal power in the matter of general legislation during the reigns of Philip Augustus, Louis VIII, and Louis IX. Philip Augustus made ordinances only for the Jews of his *potestas*, his demesne,[4] or he made an agreement on this matter with the Countess of Champagne and the Sire de Dampierre which was binding only on the parties immediately concerned.[5] Louis VIII, in 1223, went very much farther. He secured the oaths of eleven dukes and counts and thirteen other lords to an ordinance which he had made in agreement with them in relation to an important financial agreement, " None of us shall receive nor hold the Jews of another," to which was added, " this stipulation applies to those who have sworn to establish it and to those who have not." The Count of Champagne had not been present at the meeting of 1223 and the king, Louis VIII, demanded a promise to respect the said clause. If he had refused the twenty-four signatories of the ordinance would have assisted the king to coerce him. The other clauses, however, were only obligatory in the demesnes of the king and those who had sworn to maintain them.[6] Finally, in 1230, in the regency of Blanche of Castile, the king published an ordinance forbidding usury in general

---

[1] CCLV, 41–2 ; LXXXIII, i, 914.
[2] XXXI, n. 928.
[3] Ibid., n. 1136.
[4] Ann. 1219 : ibid., n. 1872.
[5] Ann. 1206 : n. 1003.
[6] DXVII, 414–17, 426–7.

and the retention of Jews belonging to another lord. Twenty-one barons had subscribed or sealed it in some form or other. They were bound to enforce the observance of the ordinance in its entirety within their dominions and to assist in coercing those barons who did not wish to observe the statutes in question.[1] These texts show clearly the transition between the dominical or Utopian ordinances of Louis VII on the one hand and, on the other, the generally applicable ordinances of the second half of the thirteenth century. These generally applicable ordinances appear quite clearly at the end of the personal reign of Saint Louis without even a mention of baronial consent : he, himself, is the origin of the prohibition of private wars throughout the kingdom as we shall see below or of the ordinance that his moneys shall be current in all parts and that, throughout his realm, certain coins shall have a certain value, and that money counterfeiting the royal coinage should be pierced and confiscated even in the territories of lords " who have their own money ".[2] Saint Louis considered, on such questions, that the king had the right to impose his will because it was in obvious agreement with the general interest. Beaumanoir, some years later, interpreted his idea very well when he said that the king could make what ordinances he liked that were for the common good.[3] The idea contains elements of both Roman and religious theories but their application was only possible because the predecessors of Saint Louis had been able gradually to extend the effective area of their edicts thanks to the system of feudal conferences.

We have already shown by what machinery the royal justice was exercised and how a Parlement of Paris gradually emerged from the Curia. This development of monarchical justice during the reign of Philip Augustus, Louis VIII, and Saint Louis had had important consequences. One of the most serious of the barons' obligations in the opinion of these

---

[1] **LXXII**, n. 2083.
[2] **LXXXVII**, i, 84, 93–5. Ordinances of Philip Augustus and Saint Louis for the punishment of blasphemers throughout the kingdom (**LVII**, bk. i, l. 395 ff. ; **LXXXVII**, i, 99–102); they have a religious character which relates them to the ordinances concerning heretics and the crusades. They were not, in our opinion, the means by which the kings achieved general legislative power.
[3] **XVI**, ii, 1512–13. The first draft dates from 1280–3.

three kings was to answer summonses "*stare in Curia*".[1] It is true that the barons for their part had the right to claim judgment by their peers but in practice this principle frequently failed. From the beginning of the thirteenth century the competence of the royal court, largely composed of lawyers, to judge the differences of the barons was no longer questioned.[2] During the reign of Saint Louis the king's moral prestige and the high reputation of the parlement led to a rapid increase in cases and arbitration. By the end of the period the king's justice was invoked in the farthest corners of the kingdom.[3] Henry III himself, in a controversy with a powerful Gascon vassal, accepted an arbitral judgment in the court of France, pronounced, moreover, by his sister-in-law the Queen Margaret.[4]

Feudal justice, in France for the first time, received severe blows not only from the position of the royal bailiffs and seneschals but also from that of the Curia Regis. It was certainly restricted, not, it is true, altogether in the manner in which it is frequently said to have been. There is frequent talk of " royal causes ", of the " alien bourgeoisie ", and of the suppression of the judicial duel as powerful weapons in the hands of the members of the Curia. But the so-called royal causes were not regarded as an offensive innovation.[5] In the towns outside the demesne there were " royal burgesses " and " royal proctors " who could demand his justice unless they had been caught red-handed. The Count of Joigny was even imprisoned in the Châtelet on Saint Louis's orders for having imprisoned one of these " royal burgesses " and left him to die in prison.[6] They were not, however, very numerous and the Parlement of Paris does not often appear to have been concerned on their behalf.[7] As for the judicial duel it was, at the same time, a method of proof and a means of appeal; the plaintiff could challenge his adversary for a false oath or his judge for false judgment.[8] The custom had been prohibited by the Church many times, particularly by

---

[1] See, for example, **LXXII**, ii, nn. 1946, 2010.
[2] **DCLXX**, 80–90; **DXVII**, 351–6.
[3] **LXXI**, nn. 23 to 61 and the bibliography, p. xxv ff.
[4] **LXXII**, iv, n. 4917. On arbitration in the thirteenth century : **CCXCIV**, 33 ff.
[5] **DXII**, 317 ff.   [6] **LVI**, 148.   [7] **CCXVI**, 27 ff.
[8] **DCXXXIII**, 91 ff., 124 ff.

the Lateran Council in 1215, and it was abolished by the scrupulous Louis IX in 1258, but only in the demesne and before the royal judges.[1] Saint Louis was anxious to deal with the method of proof and the means of appeal at the same time. He ordered the use of " witnesses or charters as proofs ", and an appeal to Parlement in case of a false judgment. This celebrated ordinance which his successor, however, allowed to fall into disuse,[2] respected the independence of the lords with rights of justice who drew considerable financial profits from the practice of the duel. It harmed feudal justice only indirectly by its support for the " appelation ", which we usually call the appeal. This procedure of appeal had arisen quite naturally out of the feudal custom which, in a part of France at least, allowed for recourse to the lord immediately superior. The suppression of the judicial duel within the demesne popularized it even outside ; with a choice between two procedures leading to the same object, people of good faith and good sense became more and more ready to use the appeal rather than a remedy of pagan origin which the Church had deprecated as frequently being fatal to the innocent. On the other hand, the procedure of Inquest which was henceforward the normal usage made appeals easier and more certain by making it possible to reconsider the business on the spot by delegates of the Curia.[3] Appeals became more and more numerous.[4] Since the king was " suzerain over all ", the supremacy of the Parlement of Paris which was to prove of primary importance for the development of the monarchy was established to a very considerable extent on feudal principles.

VI

The King above Feudalism

This, however, was not all. The Capetians of the eleventh and twelfth centuries or those who theorized and acted in

---

[1] Text and commentary in **XL**, i, 487 ff., and Intro., 265 ff. ; **LXXXVII**, i, 86–93. Cf. **DCXXXII**, 163–174 ; **CCCXXX**, 111 ff. ; **CCVIII**, 623 ff. ; **CCLXXIX**, 279, 407.
[2] **DCXXXIII**, 92 ; **CCCXCVIII**, 200.
[3] **DCLXX**, 93.
[4] On their character, see **CCCXXVIII**, 50, note 3.

their name had never forgotten that the king was above
Feudalism even when they were not in a position to reap from
their feudal supremacy the advantages which, potentially,
it offered. Even more did the Capetians of the thirteenth
century seek, and find it possible, to realize their consecration
oaths, to stretch their arms beyond feudal bounds, to protect
the weak wherever they were to be found in the kingdom.
We have seen that they had the power to suppress anarchy
and brigandage by force of arms. By legal methods they had
also suppressed violence and injustice. Saint Louis's remark
that "there is only one king in France", has a very considerable meaning and from the end of Philip Augustus's
reign represented the real position. The idea that the
inhabitants of the realm were their subjects which, for a
long time, had been submerged slowly regained its prominence.
It was the duty of these subjects to obey and the members
of the royal family were the first subjects. At a correct
estimation, the submission of the king's relations was one
of the most characteristic events of the period. No longer do
we find sons, brothers, or the wife of the king putting up
serious opposition to his plans. Thanks to the growth of the
royal authority, Philip Augustus had been able to dispense
with the practice of associating his heir presumptive in the
throne while the latter, except in certain very rare cases
(and even then it may have been in connivance with the king),
had been a tool in the king's hands; he held of his mother
the lordship of Artois but he did not even hold the title of
count and was simply called "the eldest son of the King of
France".[1] Louis IX had frequently found it necessary to
reprove his brother Charles of Anjou who had a violent and
tyrannical character and he never allowed him to infringe the
moral rules which he had imposed on himself. He had forced
him to pay his debts, to give up lands which he had seized
unjustly, and even to give up dicing.[2] A day was to come when
the princes of the royal house, too generously endowed,
would be terrible rivals for the king but in the thirteenth
century the custom of appanages did not produce these
effects. The most dangerous resistance that Saint Louis
met with among his closest relatives was not from brothers

[1] **DXVII**, 1st part, chap. xi.
[2] **LVI**, 140–2; **LXVIII**, § 405.

but from his wife Margaret of Provence who was haughty and daring and claimed to pursue her own line of policy.¹ Eleanor, the wife of the King of England, was Margaret's sister; to her husband's misfortune, she had filled her court with Provençal friends and relations. Margaret, who might have done a great deal of damage, was reduced to kicking against the goad and she trembled in the presence of her " lord ".² Blanche of Castile, for example, had taught her son to suppress violence even when the guilty parties were churchmen.³ Louis IX, though brave and frequently very severe, had such a horror of brutality that he tried to eradicate the custom of tournaments.⁴ He particularly commended his son to maintain " a pitying heart " for all the suffering.⁵ He was not satisfied with doing justice to all who appealed to him for it but he refused to let the nobles abuse their judicial rights and this was an innovation. Thus Anseau de Garlande, a lord of the Île de France, put the sons of a creditor in prison to hold them as hostages. When he refused to release them, Louis ordered his incarceration.⁶ Gautier de Ligne had ordered the execution of one of his men without trial; the king put him in mercy and forced him to pay a fine.⁷ Enguerran de Coucy, one of the most famous lords of the kingdom, had had three young nobles hung on a charge of poaching in his forest. Louis IX came to the unheard decision that Enguerran should be put to death and it was only with the greatest difficulty that a less rigorous punishment was substituted—a huge fine of £12,000 Parisian for the succour of the Holy Land and the loss of " haute justice " over the woods and fish ponds of the lordship, etc.⁸ In general Louis IX thought little of this kind of interference and was anxious that justice should be equal for all. He would not even allow that a convicted gentleman should be executed in secret. All justice must be carried out " throughout the whole kingdom, publicly and before the people ".⁹

¹ CCCLII, 7.
² LXVIII, §§ 594, 631, etc.; LXXII, ii, nn. 2908-9; CXC, 417 ff.; CCXCVII, 229 ff.
³ CLXX, 410-11; CLXXVI, 224 ff.
⁴ CCCXCVIII, 195-6.   ⁵ XXXIX, 257.
⁶ LXXII, iii, n. 4659.   ⁷ LXXII, ii, n. 2850.
⁸ LVI, 136 ff.; CDXIII, iv, 180 ff.; DCXXXIV (unfinished).
⁹ LVI, 140 ff.

The great task which the monarchy could carry out only after a battle of several centuries was to stamp out the barbarous belief, as old as the world itself, in the legitimate character of the right of vengeance. Quite naturally, from one end of the social scale to the other, there was a feeling that two systems of justice existed side by side—that which could be sought from a judiciary and that which could be taken for oneself for the honour of the individual or of the family. It was the old germanic feud. There was no difference in character between the vendetta which caused these families of common people to take up arms against one another and the private feudal war. If we may believe Beaumanoir, Philip Augustus had protected those relations who saw no difference against the danger of an unforeseen attack; they could be only attacked after forty days (*quarantine-le-roi*). After this delay they had to be prepared to defend themselves or to have sought the protection of a truce or a guarantee.[1] At first, Saint Louis tried to discourage feuds by interference. They generally ended in a reconciliation (*paix à parties*) and a pilgrimage overseas imposed on the murderers: if the king did not consider the penalty sufficiently severe he increased it.[2] On departing for the crusades he sent his bailiffs the following circular:—

> We order and instruct you that, in all cases of wars and feuds within your bailiwick, you take and give, on our behalf, just truces that do right to all. These truces should last five years beginning from the next Nativity of Saint John the Baptist and do not wait until the parties call you in.[3]

Later, on his return from the crusade, he decided to take a measure which aroused great anger. We have not got the text of his ordinance but we know that he forbade private wars and the carrying of arms throughout the kingdom and that it was made about January, 1258. In fact, on this date he wrote to his loyal subjects of the diocese of Le Puy "Know that, after due consultation, we have forbidden in our kingdom all wars, ravaging, and disturbances of the work of the land".[4]

The fragments of the Inquests which we still possess prove to us that the royal officials enforced the ordinance, sought

---

[1] **XVI**, ii, p. 372, § 1702.   [2] **LVI**, 146–7.
[3] **CCXLV**, p. 303*, Proof n. 118.   [4] **LXXXVII**, i, 84; **DXII**, 149 ff.

to prevent squires travelling with arms, and arrested peasants who possessed sharpened knives ; these texts show us equally that these restrictions were complained of as a tremendous abuse.¹ Alphonse of Poitiers supported his brothers and, for example, condemned the son of the Count de Rodez and the sons of the Lord of Canilhac to a fine of £400 for carrying arms.² The higher justiciaries had the right to judge offences of this kind but it seemed quite clear that the king intended this ordinance to be applied generally. If that had been systematically carried out,³ the social history of France would have been very different.

VII

The Attempt to Subject the Towns

During the first quarter of the thirteenth century the development of the communes continued under the same conditions as at the end of the twelfth with the open favour of the monarchy. From 1205–1224 Philip Augustus and Louis VIII granted or confirmed communes in the newly annexed territories in the north-east, Normandy, Poitou, and Saintonge.⁴ Their object was always to secure a well defended stronghold and a well trained burgess militia. Philip Augustus also confirmed communal charters granted by his lords ⁵ and already the idea was growing that the king is the natural lord of the communes of the kingdom.

Certain liberties, particularly of an economic character were granted by these two kings to towns without a commune. As we have seen, the capital fell into this category. The powerful " House of the Water Merchants " of Paris was

---

¹ **CCCXCV**, 10 ff. Cf. the affairs of Boson de Bourdeille (1267–8), in **LXXXV**, i, 286, and **LXXII**, iv, nn. 5308, 5314, 5318, 5335–7.
² **LXXII**, iv, n. 4981.
³ Even during the reign of Saint Louis the system of guarantees, truces, and peaces continued to be applied (**CCLXIX**, 332). From the reign of his successor we see once more " many private wars within the demesne and outside " (**CCCXCVIII**, 200–1). Louis X granted formal recognition to the right of the nobles of Burgundy to wage private wars : **DCXLIX**, 120 ; **CCLXX**, 1st art., 261 ; 2nd art., 249–251.
⁴ **XXXI**, nn. 921, 1029, 1030, 1116, 1194, 1366, 1444, 1574 ; nn. 804, 903 ; **DXVII**, 420–1 ; **CDXXXVIII**, 279 ff.
⁵ For example, Poix, in Picardy, in 1208 (**XXXI**, n. 1108a).

granted new commercial and judicial privileges; gradually, during the course of the thirteenth century, it was to become a sort of municipality and after 1263 the provost of the merchants and the four aldermen appear.[1] The merchants native and foreign alike were always in danger of being robbed, particularly those who frequented the fairs of Champagne and they welcomed the effective protection of Philip Augustus.[2] In short, before the personal reign of Saint Louis, the alliance between the Crown and the rich bourgeoisie was stronger than ever. The towns of the North, almost without exception, provided dependable support for Philip Augustus in 1214 and for Blanche of Castile during her regency.[3]

During the reign of Louis IX a considerable change was brought about. The bourgeoisie continued to grow richer and the corporative system stronger. It was at this period that Étienne Boileau drew up in Paris his famous Livre des Métiers.[4] But the tyranny which the rich inflicted on the poor and the financial disorder in some towns [5] led Saint Louis to adopt a new policy. Urban independence which profited the oligarchy alone did not appear to him to be one of the rights which must, necessarily, be respected. Louis IX still confirmed some old charters but he only created one new commune, that of Aigues Mortes (1246) a naval and commercial base established in a barren region because of the Crusade.[6] Obviously the idea of the commune, the bourgeois lordship in alliance with the monarchy had had its day. The time was not distant when Beaumanoir was to compare the communes to a " precocious child " who must be guided and protected and recommends the lords of the towns and the bailiffs to keep an eye on the municipal administration and settle discord between rich and poor. In addition, charters and privileges must be respected.[7] In those words Beaumanoir formulates principles which he had seen Saint Louis apply. In the South this monarch worked for the maintenance or re-establishment of municipal franchises when his commissioners had revealed the extent of his seneschals' abuses

[1] **CCCLXIV**, 10–22.
[2] **XXXI**, nn. 1148, 1181, 1958, etc.
[3] **LXXII**, ii, nn. 1976², and 1979¹ to ³⁵.
[4] **XLI** ; **CCLXXXIV**, 5 *et passim*.
[5] See, in particular, **CCXC**, 37–8 ; **CLXXXVIII**, 160 ff.
[6] **CDLXXI**, 269 ff.
[7] **XVI**, ii, cap. 50.

of power. In 1254 he granted charters to Beaucaire and Nimes and in the latter town the consulate was re-established.¹ But that was not done " to help the precocious child " which was troublesome and improvident. He tried to reduce to administrative and financial dependence those towns in which he could take most direct action. In 1260 at least thirty-five towns possessing communes were required to produce their accounts for the year 1259 before two " masters " of the Curia Regis. Those documents are still extant in the Trésor des Chartes. They were towns from the region of Paris and the North-East, chiefly belonging to the demesne but including, also, episcopal cities such as Beauvais and Noyon.² In 1262, Saint Louis ordained that the communes of " France " and Normandy should not only present their accounts each year in Paris on 17th November, but that previously, on the 29th October, their town council should be appointed anew. These two ordinances, which were applicable only in a restricted area, became obsolete from the reign of Saint Louis's son.³

The king undoubtedly intended to use such measures to fight against the oligarchical spirit of the towns and to oblige the corporation to administer on sound lines, and the richer inhabitants to cease falsifying their incomes and to pay taxes according to their wealth. They also gave his councillors, who, during the second part of his reign, had to find enormous sums of money, an opportunity to estimate the resources of the towns more accurately and to extort money from them with a full knowledge of their circumstances. Further the deficits revealed in the accounts of 1260 were in many cases due to the demands of the crown. At the end of Saint Louis's reign, the bourgeoisie was heavily exploited and it was not only the Jews who were the object of financial oppression. This is how, on the 7th April, 1260, the municipality of Noyon explains " why the town of Noyon has fallen unto such heavy debt."

> When the king went abroad we gave him fifteen hundred pounds and while he was away the queen informed us that he was in need

---

[1] CDLXXV, 554 ff. ; CDLXXI, 247 ff.
[2] LXXII, iii, nn. 4583, 4591–9, 4609–4614, 4618, 4621, 4625, 4627–4636, 4643–5, 4654–5, 4662 ; CCLXXIII ; CCLXXI ; CLXXXI ; CCLXVI, 178 and note 1 ; IX, nn. 72, 80, 84, 86, and intro., pp. xcvii, cxiii ff. ; CCCXC, 236 ff.
[3] L, nn. 33 and 34, pp. 85–8 ; CLXXXVI, i, 102 ff. ; CCCXIV, i, 35.

of money and we gave him five hundred pounds. And when the king returned we lent him six hundred pounds. We have only received one hundred pounds back and we gave him the rest. And when the king made his peace with the King of England we gave him twelve hundred. And each year we owe the king two hundred pounds Tournois for the commune we hold of him and every year our presents to visitors cost us at least a hundred pounds or more. And when the Count of Anjou was in Hainault,[1] we were told that he needed wine and we sent him ten casks which cost us a hundred pound in all. Afterwards he let us know that he needed sergeants to maintain his honour and we sent him five hundred which cost us five hundred pounds or more. . . . And when the count was at Saint Quentin, he sent for the Commune of Noyon and it went there to preserve his person and that cost us at least six hundred pounds . . . and all this the town of Noyon did for the count in honour of the king. After the departure of the army we received information that the count needed money and would become infamous if we did not help him; we lent him twelve hundred pounds and released him of three hundred to have his acknowledgment of the nine hundred pounds.[2]

Noyon however was not a royal town and the bishop's authority, at this period, did nothing but increase. But the inhabitants inevitably opposed the king to the bishop: they said that " they held their commune of the king " and demanded to be judged by the Parlement of Paris.[3] At Beauvais, where there was another commune founded previously in opposition to the bishop, the position was pretty much the same. At the beginning of St. Louis's reign, when the " great " and " lesser " citizens could not reach any agreement on the choice of a mayor, Blanche of Castile wished to re-establish order and imposed a foreign mayor on the city. People and bishop united against her. The young king entered the city and punished the burgesses (1233). The bishop, enraged at the intervention, vainly cast an interdict on the province of Rheims. This was the beginning of monarchical supervision.[4] It meant a considerable financial loss to the town. Many other examples could be given of the intervention of the king and his agents in towns outside the demesne.[5] We should also be able to describe the relations

[1] In 1253, in the absence of Saint Louis, the Countess of Flanders had begged for royal help against Jean d'Avesnes, and Charles of Anjou had reduced Hainault.
[2] **CDXI.** Document cited 47. See also **CCCXC,** 244 ff.
[3] **CDXI,** 103 (year 1265).
[4] **CCCXC,** 69–77.
[5] Cahors: **CCLXIII,** 127 ff.; Limoges: **LXXII,** ii, n. 1960; Chablis: ibid., n. 2016; Montpellier, **CDLXXI,** 183 ff.

of Alphonse de Poitiers with the towns of his appanage, his oppressive administration, his financial demands, and his differences with the town of Toulouse.[1] In general, the bourgeoisie lost, in part, its independence and had to submit to growing demands for money and the protection of the Capet was of benefit to the whole population of the towns and the general prosperity increased. A number of " new towns " were founded within the kingdom at that time which is evidence of economic progress and the attraction of urban life.[2]

We know little of the relations of the monarchy with the peasants and the rural communities in the thirteenth century. It appears that the monarchy had a conservative policy in this respect while, nevertheless, interfering in their affairs, particularly in questions of common pastures and customary rights.[3] Rents, military charges, and tallages were increased [4] but the peasants obtained the tremendous benefit of security. The better police, the suppression of seignorial brigandage, gave the population of the countryside an ease which they had not known since time immemorial. For the peasants, the thirteenth century was a period of material and moral uplift and, for the French land, an era of great clearances of rising values, and, we may well believe, of demographic increase. The spirit of order and authority which inspired the monarchy was certainly the chief factor in this renaissance.

Naturally this period of prosperity was one of numerous enfranchisements of the serfs. They obtained their liberty in the royal demesnes or elsewhere wherever they were rich enough to buy it. Saint Louis was the first king to practise collective manumissions granted, in return for a certain percentage of the goods of each, to villages peopled by serfs : a hundred villages and several thousand households received this boon from him which brought immediate gain to the Exchequer.[5]

The enfranchisement of serfs, in spite of the fine formulas of the royal writs, was nothing but a fiscal expedient but, by his desire for peace and justice, Saint Louis procured the

[1] **CDLXXV**, 554 ff. ; **CXCI**, 504 ff.
[2] **CCCXV**, 72–3 ; **CXCI**, 512 ff. ; **CDLXXV**, 566 ff.
[3] **CDLXXI**, chap. v.
[4] Innumerable complaints on this subject among the inquests of Saint Louis.
[5] **CLXXVIII**, 60 ff. ; **CCXLVIII**, 390 ff. ; **DCIII**, 36 ff. ; **CDIX**, 172 ff.

monarchy a popularity in the countryside which it had probably never had before. Of this we have had very striking proof. In 1251, when the royal disasters in Egypt became known, the shepherds and churls, the " pastoral people ", rose throughout the north-east of the kingdom at the call of a visionary to rejoin the king. Blanche of Castile encouraged them, believing that these unfortunate people, more loyal than the clerks and nobles, were really going to deliver her son. They had no resources, however, and turned to pillage. The " Crusade of the Shepherds " finished badly. It has remained justly famous as a symptom of the love of the lower orders of France for the good king.[1] " Everyone loves him " wrote his chaplain, Guibert de Tournai.[2]

VIII

The Assimilation of the Annexed Territories

About 1270, in the north and south of the kingdom alike, the same spectacle is presented of a monarchy commanding general respect. Apart from the Duke of Aquitaine, the King of England, a distant vassal who nursed the bitterness of defeat, there was no one to fear among the great feudal nobility. The demesnes of the Capetians themselves stretched from the bailiwick of Artois to the seneschalship of Carcassonne. The subjection of the dominions annexed since 1202 had been completed if we allow for the divergencies that remained even under the regime of an absolute monarchy.

This rapid assimilation is the most striking evidence of the advance in the royal power in the thirteenth century and in the Capetian methods of government. There we must halt for a moment. The order we have followed has led us to speak already of the Capetian administration in the Albigensian south. It has necessarily been treated in close relation to the policy followed by the royal officials and the great reforms suggested by the inquests. We shall not return to that subject. It will be sufficient here to take a characteristic type of territory seized from foreign lordship in which

[1] **DLXXII**, 290 ff.
[2] **XXVI**, 501 ; letter of the Abbé of Troarn in **XXX**, n. 803.

success was difficult for reasons entirely different from those in the South : Normandy. At the same time it is a good example of direct action taken by the kings themselves and their personal followers. It throws into relief the whole policy of Philip Augustus, Louis VIII, and Saint Louis. The admirable works of Leopold Delisle, in particular his *Cartulaire Normand*, his *Recueil des Jugements de l'Echiquier* and his editions of the *Querimoniae Normannorum* of 1247 allow us to sketch at least an outline.[1]

In the first place the kings had to make their conquest secure against a return to the offensive and to prevent a possible alliance between the baronage and towns of Normandy and the King of England. Strategic points were kept under supervision and the fortresses held by dependable men. The Church alone had permission to retain its possessions across the Channel. The towns and nobility were forbidden to maintain communications with England except by special authority. The Normans who had gone over to England at the time of the Conquest were warned to return and present themselves at Philip's Court before Christmas, 1204; those who appeared after that date would lose their possessions as well as all those who subsequently returned to England or came under suspicion of communication with the enemy. These commands were very strictly carried out and were only modified by a few judgments of the Exchequer and decisions of Saint Louis where mistakes had to be rectified. The English lords lost their Norman possessions; those who at first succeeded in maintaining simultaneous homage to both kings, in 1244, were ordered to make their choice by Saint Louis. Thanks to these confiscations, Philip Augustus was able to enrich the ducal demesne and introduce new families of whose loyalty he had adequate knowledge. In this way officials, knights, and even humble sergeants of the king received lands and founded Norman families.

For the rest, the King of France proposed to govern Normandy and exploit it as " King Henry and Richard " had done. (He never spoke of John who was regarded as a usurper and had, moreover, left very bad memories.) His officials conducted inquests " so that the county should be treated as in the past." In 1207 the canons of Rouen, giving

---

[1] Here we are summarizing our memoire : **DXIX**.

an account of a visit which Philip Augustus's councillors had paid them, wrote: " They came on the king's behalf and told us that he wanted full observance of the rights and liberties of the Norman churches as elsewhere and has asked us to demand nothing that we did not have in the time of King Henry, King Richard, and the Lord King of France."

The only major administrative change was the suppression of the office of seneschal of Normandy and the appointment of chief bailiffs, " *baillivi capitales*," who were, in fact, the king's lieutenants and were chosen from among the most important members of the Court. The Exchequer (the ducal court) with its judicial and financial functions was preserved. It continued to give judgment and that was where the bailiffs of Normandy came to render their accounts. Far from lessening the importance of this provincial Court the royal officials took lessons from it in law and administration. But, at the same time, they watched it carefully. The most important of the king's advisers during the first third of the century, such as Guérin, the Bishop of Senlis, and the Chamberlain, Barthélemy de Roye, were regular attendants at sessions of the Exchequer.

Beyond that, the Court of France, *Curia Gallicana*, gave direct attention to certain questions and became the supreme court for Normandy as for the other countries subject to the king.

The important thing was to conciliate the Norman population which was intelligent, distrustful, and very much attached to its own interests and the independence which the Anglo-Norman kings had granted. The kings gave personal attention to this task. There was not a year between 1204 and the death of Philip Augustus when the prince did not make a stay at Pacy, Pont de l'Arche, Gisors, or Vernon. During the later years of his reign, Saint Louis made many progresses through Normandy in spite of the breakdown in his health. It was easy for the kings to go there and they saw important advantages in personally controlling the actions of the officials they sent there. That their administration was good is proved by the inquests themselves which contain very few grievances against the bailiffs. The earliest of them were energetic men who commanded obedience. In the time of Philip Augustus, his chaplain William the Breton tells us that

Normandy was " loyal or even very loyal if only they had been willing to spare the king their abusive outbursts ". We know that the town of Breteuil was punished for an unfortunate remark of its mayor. The Normans grumbled but the total number who helped the English during their expeditions in France in 1214 or 1230 was very small. It was very soon possible to relax the initial severity. The local nobility accepted their feudal obligations and provided the crown with the warriors it demanded. The lower classes severed their connection with England very quickly and very thoroughly. The bourgeoisie of the towns after a difficult break in the commercial relations with England found new openings by turning towards the French markets and seeking the royal favours which were generously granted to them. Finally, the churches and abbeys were treated with a respect they had not always enjoyed in the time of the English kings. They were loaded with gifts and privileges and became attached to the Capetians by bonds which became more and more cordial and sincere.

It has been said that Normandy at this period remained suspected and unfortunate, but the weight of documentary evidence decisively disproves this assertion. Normandy, which had never belonged to the Capetians and had been the cradle of the glorious conquerors of England, was, in general, very quickly and very securely attached to the demesne. The mistakes of the later Plantegenets, the community of language and civilization which bound the country to France, the positive and practical spirit of the Normans, and, equally, the firmness and wisdom of the Capetian administration, the spirit of charity, justice, and peace which made Saint Louis an object of affection and admiration are sufficient to explain this fact.

IX

Prestige of the Capetian Monarchy about 1270. Peace and Arbitration

Saint Louis's external position at the end of his reign was no less strong. It is almost possible to say France's position, for French civilization during the Middle Ages had never attained and was never to attain again to such a degree of prosperous expansion and celebrity. During that period great artists were bringing the so-called " Gothic " style to a point of perfection that their successors could not surpass : throughout the West architects were imitating French models. The most celebrated work in our ancient literature, the *Roman de la Rose*, dates from this period. French prose was in process of creation : Primat in his *Grandes Chroniques de France*, which the king commissioned from him,[1] gives a charming example of it. The pleasant language of our writers appeared to neighbouring peoples most delightful of all. The monarchy contributed, by its wisdom and the greatness of its political ideals, to this splendid development and its prestige profited by it. Matthew de Paris calls the King of France " The king of mortal kings ".[2] Who, in fact, could question his pre-eminence ? The King of England ended a reign in which he had known nothing but defeats in a quarrel with his barons : his only victory, that of Evesham, had been won in civil war. His foreign policy had been as sterile as it was ruinous. His son Edmund had failed to win the kingdom of the Two Sicilies and his brother Richard of Cornwall had lost Germany. The thirteenth century was a period of glorious conquests and expansion for the kingdoms of Castile and Aragon but, at the period when Saint Louis's life ended, his contemporary, Alphonse X of Castile, an adventurous blunderer, was likewise wasting his time in canvassing for the Imperial Crown, and the Mediterranean expansion of Aragon had scarcely begun. In Germany and Italy, Frederick II, one of the most amazing minds of his time, had tried to revive the glory of the Empire and had won the implacable hatred of the Papacy. After his death (1250) the prestige of the Emperor was destroyed for a long time. Germany was only saved from chaos by disintegration. Its expansive forces could be seen only in the Slav countries of the Baltic and Central Europe. The Papacy itself, after its hard-won victory over the last of the Hohenstaufen, suffered an eclipse. At the time of Saint Louis's Tunisian crusade, the Holy See was vacant (1268–1271) since the cardinals had been unable to agree on the election of a successor to Clement IV. In Italy the only great power was the kingdom

[1] **LIII**, i, Introduction.   [2] **LXXX**, v, 480.

of the Two Sicilies which belonged to Saint Louis's brother, Charles of Anjou.

An ambitious policy might have taken advantage of the favourable circumstances and the reputation of the dynasty. There have been braggarts to reproach Louis IX for his lack of initiative. We have seen that a certain party at Court were opposed to making peace with England. Even among the people there were individuals who reproached the king with being too much of a priest but Saint Louis followed his own path more concerned with Heaven than the earth. He respected the rights of others and hated war; not because he was afraid to die—he gave full proof of the contrary—but because war made men sin and sent many unfortunates to purgatory. It is good only when it is directed against the enemies of Christ. That is the basis of his pacifism. He knew how to defend his kingdom when attacked because it was essential to defend his rights. He was full of sympathy for the poor during war time and urged that they should be spared, but, above all, he had a horror of the sins of war. That is shown us by one particularly admirable page of the *Enseignements* which he wrote himself for his son Philip the Bold :—

> I advise you to take care, as far as your power allows, that you don't make war on Christians and, if anyone does you wrong, make as many attempts as you can to find out whether you can recover your rights in any other way before you make war and do your utmost to avoid the sins that arise from war. Take care that you have been well advised before you act in any warlike manner, that your cause is thoroughly reasonable, and that you have duly summoned the wrongdoer and waited as long as you should.[1]

It was in this spirit that he concluded treaties with his neighbours and undertook to act as an arbitrator in Europe during the years following his return from Syria. Almost at the same time he was negotiating with the King of England and the King of Aragon to fix the rights of each and to end the ambiguities that lead to conflict. For a long time the kings of Aragon had been claiming patronage over the " occitanien populations " and a suzerainty over Languedoc. By the Treaty of Corbeil (11th May, 1258), King Jaime renounced them, preserving only the lordship of Montpellier. Louis IX, in turn, abandoned the rights which the successors

[1] **XXXIX**, 259–260. Cf. **CCCLXXXII**, 63–4.

of the Carolingians had retained over Catalonia and Roussillon. As a pledge of this important modification of the frontier, a marriage united the heir to the throne, Philip the Bold, and Isabella of Aragon.[1] About the same time the Franco-Castilian alliance initiated by the marriage of Louis VIII was strengthened by matrimonial negotiations. Louis IX did not, for one moment, think of uniting the two kingdoms; he was only anxious that the friendship of the two sovereigns should assure peace in the West. Finally, in 1266, his daughter married the heir to Castile.[2] The minstrel Sordel wrote that the King of France lost Castile by his foolishness.[3]

At the end of his reign the attention of Louis IX was equally engaged in attempts to bring pacification between Christians. In 1246 he imposed a reconciliation, as arbitrator, on the sons whom Margaret, Countess of Flanders and Hainault, had had of her two marriages. He gave to William de Dampierre, a son of the second marriage, the inheritance of Flanders and to John d'Avesnes, a son of the first, that of Hainault. In addition Charles of Anjou was put in possession of Hainault by the Countess Margaret and retained the suzerainty, a source of future claims by the King of France on imperial lands. (Agreement of Peronne, 24th September, 1256.[4]) Louis IX was also arbitrator between the King of Navarre and the Duke of Brittany, between the Count of Bar and his neighbours the Count of Luxembourg and the Duke of Lorraine. In the kingdom of Arles and Vienne where it would have been so easy to take advantage of imperial decadence it was still in the capacity of arbitrator that he interfered between the Count of Burgundy and the Count of Chalon, between the dauphin Guigues and his neighbours the Duke of Savoy and Charles of Anjou, between the inhabitants of Lyons and the canons of the cathedral church. The king sent experienced councillors like Pierre the Chambellan who settled the matter in his name. Joinville tells us that when someone advised him to let all these people fight it out he replied that God had said " Blessed are the peacemakers ".[5]

When the English barons and Henry III in the midst of a bitter quarrel made him the judge of the validity of the

[1] CDXXVIII, 138-9.   [2] CCXXXI, 1 ff.   [3] CI, 93.
[4] CCLXXVII, chap. vii, xiv; Examples, n. 97 and 211.
[5] LXVIII, §§ 680-4; CLXIX, pp. xxvii-xlv; CCCXXIII, 370 ff.; CCCLXXXIV, ii, 173 ff.; CCXCVII, 210 ff.

Provisions of Oxford which had been broken by the Pope, Saint Louis asked for the documents, which are still extant in the Trésor des Chartes, to be sent and went to Amiens to meet the two parties. On 23rd January, 1264, he announced the annulment of the *Provisions of Oxford.* The *Mise of Amiens* is very clearly marked by the political ideas of Saint Louis.

They were not unknown in England or, at least, they were believed to be known. Evidently the barons deluded themselves when they agreed to accept the King of France as arbitrator. They knew he had a scrupulous respect for the rights of others; they thought that, in his opinion as in theirs, the barons' duty of council was not merely an obligation of the vassal to his suzerain but was also a right of the nobility, a privilege of their class. Saint Louis, however, with the best faith in the world was of a different opinion. In some respects his political ideal was contained within the framework of Feudalism: in others it went beyond it. Louis would not admit that a consecrated king should regard his power as limited by a council. That was a realm of ideas where he was groping in the dark. In England and in France, monarchical and feudal state, the conception of the kingly divine right and of the king as suzerain governing with his barons existed together and remained irreconcilable. After we have studied the development of the monarchy in France, without losing sight of this duality of principles, we shall grasp it even better in seeking the real character of the conflicts between King John and his son and their barons.

CHAPTER IV

THE ARISTOCRATIC REACTION IN ENGLAND. THE GREAT CHARTER AND THE BARONS' WAR

I

THE CHURCH AND BARONS AGAINST JOHN LACKLAND

THE political conflicts of the reign of John Lackland (1199–1216) and Henry III (1216–1272) form one of the most important, most complicated, and most controversial chapters in the history of England. We cannot hope to deal with all their vicissitudes here. We are only interested in placing the advantages won by the opposition in their proper perspective. Their character has been misrepresented by English historians of the Victorian age but their modern successors have cleared the way for an objective synthesis.

In the first place we must summarize the facts and analyse such major documents as **Magna Carta**; in our final pages we shall deal with the interpretations which recent work has suggested.

Henry II and Richard Cœur de Lion bequeathed to John Lackland an undisputed power. In fifteen years John was able to let the Angevin Empire fall to pieces and find himself expelled from his capital by his own barons who had rallied to the support of a foreigner: he died an outlaw in his own kingdom. He carried the burden of the undue ambitions of his dynasty and we have seen that he had neither the ability nor the strength to uphold it. No one could rely on him. Sometimes excited, at others depressed, he could not even depend on himself.

During the early years of his reign there was nothing to suggest that it would end in civil war.[1] The royal officials maintained and perfected the administrative and fiscal

[1] **DCXXVII**, i, 620 ff.

machine.¹ The discontent caused by their demands and the failures in France was not very keen. The loss of Normandy and the territories along the Loire did not seriously affect the prestige of the monarchy. The general opinion was that it was a purely personal matter which concerned the king alone and it was for him to get anxious. The government was in the hands of an experienced statesman, the Archbishop Hubert Walter, who had forced his services on the new king who was afraid of him. Everything changed at his death (13th July, 1205). The old queen, Eleanor of Aquitaine, whose judgment was so keen, had died on 31st March, 1204. The impulsive wilfulness and the sickly instability of John had no longer any counterpoise and the tragedy of the reign began immediately over the pastoral succession to Hubert Walter.²

The Archbishop of Canterbury was subject to canonical election by the monks of Christ Church. They were worldly monks who wanted an archbishop who would not ask too much. John Lackland, for his part, sought to fill the see of Canterbury this time with a servant of established docility. Innocent III, however, was unwilling to accept either of the two candidates and the monks of Canterbury had to elect a man of his choice, an English cardinal who was teaching theology at Rome, Stephen Langton. John refused to ratify his election or to admit him to his kingdom.

Conflicts between princes and the Church about elections were frequent in the West and the Pope generally succeeded in securing a triumph for his ideas by his diplomacy. John Lackland, however, was now surrounded by Poitevins and Tourangeaux who had swarmed into England after the loss of the Loire territories and won his favour. Such a man was Peter des Roches recently made Bishop of Winchester, typical of the Court bishops ready to do everything to preserve their master's favour.³ The exasperation of John, heightened by

---

[1] **CDLXXIV**, chap. ii, iii; **CCCLXXIV**, p. 244 ff. N. S. B. Gras, **CCCXVIII**, 221-2, has published a summary account of a fifteenth on all merchandise imported and exported, one of the chief financial innovations of the period. In two years it produced £5,000 sterling. On the extortions of the itinerant judges in the thirteenth and fourteenth centuries, see **CLXXXV**, 64, and *passim.*

[2] On this conflict and the interdict: **DXLV**, chap. i–iv; **CDLXXXIX**, 118 ff. For the previous conflicts between Innocent III and the English monarchy, see **CCCXXXV**, chap. iii, iv.

[3] **DLXV**, ii, 392, 423, n. 3; **LVIII**, iii, 188–9, note by P. Meyer.

ARISTOCRATIC REACTION IN ENGLAND 329

the play of foreign favourites on his vanity, and the proud and haughty character of Stephen Langton prevented any compromise. Finally England was put under interdict by the Holy See (24th March, 1208) and in the following year the king was excommunicated.

The interdict lasted six years. The royal authority was still so strong in England that John was able to command the obedience of his clerical officials who had been terrorized by the punishment inflicted on one of their colleagues and to impose his will on the English Church completely.[1]

The bishops alone, with the exception of two courtier prelates, left the kingdom to escape submission. All the property of the Church was confiscated and the clergy lived on allocations. A schism could have been achieved in time if John had not lost his head. He assumed the habits of a despot, allowed his officials to abuse their power more than ever, and personally offended some of his barons. Philip Augustus watched events carefully. He gladly responded to the overtures made to him. One of the richest lords of the London area, Robert Fitz Walter, fled to France in 1212[2] and finally, in 1213, Philip Augustus accepted the Pope's offer when he deposed John Lackland and invited the King of France to take possession of the vacant realm. John ran a great risk of being dethroned but he was advised that Innocent III despite his obligations to Philip Augustus was ready to pardon him on condition of a complete humiliation. He accordingly humiliated himself and, on 16th May, 1213, he agreed to pay the Holy See an annual tribute of a thousand marks sterling as the dues of a vassal for the kingdoms of England and Ireland. Here is the beginning of the Deed of Submission addressed to all the faithful in Christ :—

> We will that you all should know by this charter bearing our seal that as we have committed many sins against God and our mother Holy Church and consequently we are wanting in divine mercy and can only offer God and the Church the satisfaction that is their due by the humiliation of us and our kingdom ... of our good and free will and by the common counsel of our barons, we offer and yield freely to God and his Holy Apostles Peter and Paul, to the Holy Roman Church, our mother, and to the lord Pope Innocent and his Catholic successors, all the kingdom of

---

[1] It is well known that " English Church " like " Gallican Church " meant, at the period, " the Church of the Realm ".
[2] **CXIX**, ii, 534–5, 540 ; vi, 33–4 ; viii, 396 ff.; **DLXXXVII**, 707–711.

England and the kingdom of Ireland with all their rights and appurtenances for the remission of all our sins and those of our people, alike of the living and the dead ; and, henceforward, receiving and holding these kingdoms as vassal of God and the Holy Church, in the presence of the mediator Pandulph, subdeacon and companion of the Lord Pope, we have done and sworn loyalty to the Lord Pope Innocent and his Catholic successors and to the Church and we will do liege homage to the Lord Pope in his presence if we can come into his presence ; and we will bind our successors and lawful heirs in perpetuity in like manner to render an oath of loyalty without modification and to acknowledge their homage to the sovereign pontiff of that time and to the Roman Church.[1]

Thus John did an act of penitence for all his faults and for those of his race. But, like Henry II after the murder of Becket previously, he had got himself out of a bad position. The majority of his subjects showed themselves very glad to see the end of a long crisis which unsettled the faithful and had turned the English Church upside down. The feudal bond contained no element of humiliation and consequently few people realized the importance of this submission to the Holy See.[2] Had John Lackland seen in it a means of gaining a patronage which the growing opposition of the baronage would render very useful ? Was his action prompted by momentary discouragement or by craft ? We do not know but, in any case, he all but succeeded in re-establishing his tyrannical authority.

It was the Archbishop Stephen Langton, who, by his tenacity and apt judgment, stabilized and organized the wavering opposition. Established in the See of Canterbury, he intended to play the traditional role of the English primate and set the king on the right road again.[3] Without any great hope of gaining his ends, for he distrusted John Lackland, having been made responsible for absolving him from the excommunication, he demanded an oath to give everyone his rights. John swore everything that was asked of him but thought of nothing but his revenge. He was unable to draw his barons into the expedition he wanted to make to punish Philip Augustus. They claimed that they did not owe him host service outside of the realm. His anger turned against them

---

[1] **CXXII**, i, 1st part, 111.
[2] **CXIX**, ii, 550 ; **VII**, 275–6 ; **XIII**, 210–11.
[3] **DXLV**, 78, 106 ff. ; **CDLXXXIX**, 188 ff.

and he tried to reduce them by force. It was in these circumstances that, on 25th August, 1213, Stephen Langton brought together a considerable number of barons and prelates at the church of St. Paul's in London and asked them to swear to fight to obtain the liberties formulated in a charter the text of which was read and explained to them. It is probable that this text is the one which scholars have called " An Unknown Charter of English liberties " which, for reasons about which we can only make hypotheses, is preserved in the French Trésor des Chartes. It is a shapeless draft, hastily drawn up and undoubtedly representing concessions wrung from John some time previously which he refused to uphold. The text opens with a reproduction of the Charter of Henry I. Stephen Langton had good reason for basing himself on this famous charter in which Henry declared " First, for the freedom of God's Holy Church ". Next come some dozen articles on the maintenance of rights and customs in matters of justice, relief and wardship of fiefs, the jointure and dowry of widows, marriage of heiresses, debts of minors, military service in France, scutage : the Forest Laws are to be modified. It is a very interesting draft, for the provisions are taken from it and developed later in the Baron's Petition of 1215 and the Great Charter. We can note that it is scarcely concerned with anything but concessions to the nobility, and even in the Great Charter they remained the essential feature.[1]

For two years the conflict was postponed. The Pope had sent a new legate for " the reconciliation of the king and the kingdom ".[2] The clergy was fully occupied in obtaining the indemnities which were due to them and in reorganizing religious life. The barons awaited the result of the coalition formed between John Lackland, the Emperor Otto, and the Count of Flanders to partition France.

The defeats of the allied armies at Roche-au-Moine and Bouvines (2nd and 27th July, 1214), and the irritation produced by the order for the levy of a very heavy scutage on the fiefs of those barons who had refused to follow John

---

[1] **LXXII**, i, nn. 34, 1153. Bibliography on the " Unknown Charter " in my study : **DCXXVII**, i, 869 ff. In addition : **DLXX**, 449-458, and, particularly, **DXLV**, 113-120.

[2] **CIX**, 274-289.

to France [1] finally decided the discontented elements to take action against a king who was both discredited and incorrigible. The northern barons, the Noroys, had given the signal for resistance by refusing to go on the French campaign but the most ardent were the young barons of the Eastern Counties, particularly Essex, almost all of whom had personal grievances against the king.[2] On 21st November, 1214, John had granted freedom of canonical election [3] but Stephen Langton knew very well that if he dissociated the cause of the Church from the nobility he could not rely on the king's word. Finally, the Londoners were ready to open their gates to the barons. Innocent III interfered in vain. In vain, the king to gain the advantages granted to Crusaders promised to go to the Holy Land. After presenting the demands which John rejected " in a fury ", the barons withdrew their homage. John found his loyal subjects leaving him and his officials ceasing to function. As in 1213 he had no alternative but to yield.[4]

The two parties met on 15th June, 1215, on the plain of Runnymede near Windsor. On the same day he attached his seal to the document entitled *Capitula que barones petunt*, that is to say the Barons' Petition which already contained most of the essential articles of the Great Charter. Then negotiations began. On the one side were the two archbishops of Canterbury and Dublin who played the role of mediators—master Pandulph, the Pope's envoy, the Count of Salisbury, the king's natural brother, William the Marshal, the Counts of Varenne and Arundel, and lay and clerical councillors ; on the other, " all the English nobility." [5] It was undoubtedly on the 19th June, in spite of its official date of the 15th, that the Great Charter was concluded and sealed [6] after negotiations which are clearly reflected in the differences between the Charter and the Petition.

---

[1] **CDLXXIV**, 112–13.
[2] **DLXXXVII**, 710 ; **DXLV**, app. v.
[3] **CXXXIII**, 283–4.
[4] For all these events the principal source is **CXIX**, ii, 582–8. See **CDLXXXIX**, 206 ff. ; **CCCLXXXI**, 31 ff.
[5] **CXIX**, 588–9.
[6] On these dates : **CCCLXXXI**, 37–41. On the publication : **DXXXVI**, 449 ff.

II

The Great Charter

Magna Carta[1] is a "concession" by the king, made "by inspiration of God for the salvation of his soul and the souls of all his ancestors and heirs, for the honour of God and the exaltation of Holy Church, and for the betterment of his kingdom," on the advice of the archbishops of Canterbury and Dublin, Master Pandulph and a certain number of councillors who are named. It is "primarily" a concession made "to God" in favour of the Anglican Church. It is "also" a "concession of liberties to all free men of the realm and their heirs in perpetuity".

By the first article the king granted "the English Church should be free, enjoy its full rights and its liberties inviolate" and, in particular, "that liberty which is considered the greatest and the most necessary for the English Church, freedom of elections." Article 42 concerning freedom to leave the kingdom involved for the clergy the extremely important right to go to Rome without the king's permission.

The counts, barons, and other tenants in chief (direct vassals) whose demands were given first place after those of the Church secured[2] that their ancient rights should be respected in questions of military service, feudal succession, wardship, marriage, debts, etc. The king could only demand the military service that was normally due. On the death of a noble, he was only to receive the "ancient relief" of a hundred pounds for a barony, a hundred shillings or more for a knight's fee. He could not demand wardships if he had no right to them. He was to cease any action likely to damage the property of a minor who was his ward or any wrong to widows. He was not to force them to remarry: he could not suggest husbands for heiresses unless they were of their own rank. He could not take from the goods of a vassal living or dead, testate or intestate, any more than was essential to meet the debts of the Treasury. Minors and widows were to be protected against Jews and other usurers. Barons who

---

[1] I am following the text edited by Bémont, **XVII**, 26-39. Compare Mackechnie's important commentary, **CCCLXXXI**. On the origin of the term Great Charter (in opposition to the Charter of the Forests): **DCLXXVI**, 472-5.

[2] Articles 2-11, 16, 26, 27, 32, 46.

had established abbeys were to have the custody of them during vacancies. The lands of a felon were to be given up to the lord of the fief after a year and a day.

The rural middle class, by which I mean the knights who held their lands of a baron and those free tenants who did not hold a military fief, were not forgotten in the Great Charter for the barons were ultimately dependent on their support against John Lackland. It was thus that the nobles, holding baronies which had fallen into commission, or the free tenants, who were being made subject to military charges for which there was no justification or to the right of wardship, won their security. It is laid down that the king will not give his favourites authority to levy arbitrary aids on their free men. Finally, at the end of the Charter, it says that all the customs and liberties which the king has just granted to his subjects shall be observed by all the laymen and clergy of the realm in their relations with their own men.[1]

The principal clause relating to the privileges of the bourgeoisie is extremely general and purely conservative.

> That the city of London shall have all its ancient liberties by land as by water. Further we will and grant that all other cities, boroughs, towns, and ports shall have all their liberties and free customs.[2]

As for the articles confirming the uniformity of weights and measures throughout the kingdom and guaranteeing free progress, without arbitrary taxation, to foreign merchants they are obviously dictated not by the interests of English manufacturers and merchants but of the consumers.[3]

The other stipulations which are generally represented as the most important, although they do not appear at the head of the Charter, are not specially concerned with any particular class of the nation but are rules of administration and government.

Firstly, the king will nominate as judges, constables, sheriffs, or bailiffs only men who understand the law well and fully intend to observe it "[4]; it was only under that condition that he retained the right to appoint men who

---

[1] Arts. 15, 16, 27, 37, 43, 60, etc.
[2] Art. 13.   [3] Arts. 35 and 41.
[4] Art. 45.

were natives of his French fiefs. It is specified that certain officials who have served as sheriffs, châtelains, or foresters who are designated by name and " all their like " shall never again perform public duties : they are chiefly Tourangeaux.[1]

The officials must not tyrannize the population, make requisitions without paying for them, prevent the free navigation of the rivers, nor increase the number of preserved fisheries nor force knights to pay money for castle ward if they are willing to perform the service in person.[2] The recently created " forests " will be abolished and the officials are to create no new ones.[3] Subjects who live outside their boundaries are secured against the justiciars of the forests exceeding their powers.[4] The bad customs of the forest are to be abolished.[5] The " forest " was such an important subject that, two years later, it was to be the object of a special charter.[6]

One of the most characteristic sections of the Great Charter are the articles concerning royal justice. The king not only had to promise to restore the sums he had extorted as fines and the goods he had seized arbitrarily [7] but securities were taken for the observance of custom and sometimes of a custom prior to the juridical reforms of Henry II.

The very old principle of judgment by peers was invoked to prevent arbitrary decisions and violence.

> No free man shall be taken or imprisoned, disseised of his goods, or declared outlaw or exiled or harmed in any way and we will not advance against him or send anyone against him except by the loyal judgment of his peers according to the law of the land.[8]

We can see by the articles which follow [9] that *Judicium parium* had a very wide meaning and that, for example, wrongs done to the Welsh or Scotch—for this Charter for the re-establishment of peace is concerned with them also—could be dealt with according to the judgment of the Welsh or Scotch. By the same extensive meaning for " law of the

---

[1] Art. 50. [2] Arts. 28–31, 33, 47.
[3] Arts. 47–8. [4] Art. 44.
[5] Art. 48. On Art. 23, cf. **CCCLXXXI**.
[6] 6th November, 1217 : **CXXXIII**, 344–8. Cf. my study of the forest : **DCXXVII**, ii, 790 ff.
[7] Arts. 52 and 55.
[8] Art. 39 ; **DCLX**, 78–95 ; **DXLIII**, 96 ff. ; **DCLXI**, 201 ff.
[9] Arts. 56, 59.

land ", questions concerning Welsh tenements were settled according to their native land.

The return to custom was marked also in the precautions taken to prevent fantastic and ruinous fines and illegal confiscations.[1] When the maintenance of certain juridical innovations is provided for it is because they provide securities which the English value, such as the procedure of assizes held in the county court by two royal judges with the assistance of four elected knights to protect subjects against the violence of their lords or their neighbours.[2] The judicial duel, formerly introduced to England by the Normans, lost considerably in importance by the development of the new law and was obviously unpopular.[3] But the procedure of writs, *brefs*, which was the origin of this new law based on reason was not always favoured by the Great Charter: the barons demanded that cognizance of proprietary actions between their tenants should be yielded to them.[4]

For the administration of justice the authors of the Charter show their mistrust of the local officials, sheriffs, and others [5] and their confidence in the lawyers of the Curia Regis: the circuits of the itinerant justices are evidently regarded with favour: the more important cases, "the pleas of the Crown," can be judged in the counties only by them. They demand, however, that the central court shall not follow the king in his wanderings when it is concerned with civil actions, common pleas. There were plaintiffs who had been ruined in following the king and his court on their travels. This is the point of Article 17: "That the common pleas shall not follow the Court but be held in some fixed place."

Among the financial and political clauses of the Charter there are none more famous than those which regulate the summons of *magna concilia* and " consent to taxation ". For the moment we will confine ourselves to quoting their texts :—

> Article 12.—That no scutage or aid shall be established in our realm save by the common council of our realm unless it is to pay our ransom, to knight our eldest son, or to marry our eldest daughter

---

[1] Arts. 20–2.　　　　　[2] Arts. 18–19.
[3] Arts. 36 and 54 are directed against it.
[4] Art. 34 on the writ Praecipe. Art. 40 forbids the sale of writs, and seems designed to prevent their multiplication.
[5] Arts. 24–5, 38.

once and in these cases the aid shall be reasonable ; that it shall be the same for the aids of the city of London.¹

Article 14.—And to secure the common council of the realm on the establishment of an aid other than in the aforesaid three cases or on the subject of the establishment of scutage we will summon the archbishops, bishops, abbots, counts, and higher barons individually by our letters and, in addition, we will summon collectively, through our sheriffs and bailiffs, all those who hold of us in chief for a certain day and place with at least forty days' notice. And in all letters of summons we will state the reason and, once such a summons has been sent, on the appointed day we will deal with the business according to the advice of those who are present although all those summoned may not have arrived.

Finally the king promised remission and pardon for all the failures of his subjects " since the time of the discord ".² He found himself signing away all means of imposing his arbitrary will for he had to surrender hostages and the charters of enlistment which he had demanded and to send his mercenaries out of the kingdom at once.³ In return he accepted the perpetual control of the barons. By an unprecedented innovation the barons elected twenty-five of their number who were responsible for ensuring the observance of the peace and the liberties that had been granted. In case of any infraction by the king or one of his officers, if reparation was not made within forty days, the twenty-five " with the people of all the county will take measures against us and will apply pressure by every available means, seizing our castles, lands, possessions and other methods they can employ, saving our person and that of the queen and our children, until reparation has been done to their satisfaction ". All the population of the county were to swear obedience to the twenty-five under such circumstances. If the twenty-five were not unanimous they would take a majority decision.⁴

It is highly probable that neither side had any illusions about the extent to which this " peace " was likely to be observed. The barons remained in arms in the neighbourhood of London. The twenty-five showed themselves stern and implacable ⁵ : Stephen Langton, the supporter of a conciliatory policy, lost all influence and was disgraced.⁶ John,

¹ Thus London is considered as a feudal person. See **CXLIII**, 705–6 ; cf. **CCCLXXXI**, 234–8.
² Art. 62.   ³ Arts. 49, 51, 58, 59.   ⁴ Art. 61.
⁵ See, in particular, **XIII**, 222 ff. ; **LIX**, 151.
⁶ **VI**, 45 ; **LXXXI**, 326–7 ; Bull of Suspension in **CXXII**, i, 1st part, 139.

full of bitterness, wavered between discouragement and the preparation of a sly revenge. He had sworn to ask no one to do anything which might be a revocation of his concessions ".[1] Almost immediately he sent messages to Rome and, by a Bull of 24th August, Innocent III squashed the Great Charter " as a disgraceful, shameful, illegal, and iniquitous agreement ". It was offensive to the Holy See, for the Pope in his position of Overlord (*ratione dominii*) should have been made judge of their differences ; it was derogatory to the rights and honour of the king ; it covered the English people with shame and gravely imperilled " the whole of Christ's work ".[2] A few weeks later the Lateran Council was to open. We can explain the irrational violence of Innocent III by the fever of theocratic exaltation which was consuming him. He died in the following year (16th July, 1216) without having been able to prevent Louis of France from responding to the appeal of the English barons in revolt.[3] His successor, the old Honorius III, was pacific and prudent. After John's death, with the assistance of another veteran, William the Marshal,[4] he was able to save the Plantegenet dynasty. On 12th November, 1216, the Great Charter was confirmed in the majority of its provisions by the new king of England, the infant Henry III, " on the advice of Galon, cardinal, priest by the title of St. Martin, legate of the apostolic see," who, in the absence of the royal seal attached his alongside William Marshal's.[5] By the pressure he exercised on the English clergy, the barons, and, finally, on Philip Augustus, who gave no support to his son, Honorius III succeeded in disorganizing the League which the tyrannical obstinacy of John Lackland and Innocent III had gone to build up and drive to extremes. The Peace of Lambeth (11th September, 1217) received the legate's seal.[6] Henry III could say, at a later date, in a conversation that Bishop Robert Grossetete has preserved for us, " At a time when we were an orphan and a minor, when our subjects were not only alienated from us but were organized against us, it

---

[1] See Great Charter, Art. 61.
[2] **XVII**, 41–4. Cf. **CXLII**, 26–45 (very unconvincing).
[3] See above. [4] **CCCLXXIII**, p. 53 ff.
[5] **CXXXIII**, 336–9. Differences from the text of 1215 : **CCCLXXXI**, 139 ff.
[6] H.F., vol. xvii, 111–12.

was our mother, the Roman Church, which brought this realm once more under our authority which consecrated us as king, crowned us, and placed us on the throne."[1]

III

Progress of the Opposition under Henry III

The fight for the Great Charter was over. Whatever we think of this celebrated episode—and we shall see what reservations must be suggested to an interpretation that has been for a long time accepted—it weakened the autocratic monarchy founded by Henry II and his sons and provided a focus for the opposition. Conflicts were to continue, however, throughout the reign of Henry III. The period of his minority was, for a long time, very disturbed.[2] The Civil War had created habits of disorder and brigandage. Spirits were embittered and no one showed any readiness to support the king's advisers; a very long time was necessary before order was re-established. The financial surplus which had for a long time helped John to maintain his power had given place to a deficit. How would Henry III govern on reaching his majority? In spite of everything he could count on the loyalty of his subjects. A careful choice of his friends and ministers was all that was needed to assure him a tranquil reign during which he could satisfy in peace his tastes as an amateur of refinement[3] more capable of judging a work of art than leading an army, but he did not know how to make himself loved either by the English Church, which never found him a dependable protector, or by the warriors whom he led only to pitiful defeats. Very devout and obsessed by the memory of the years of his youth, throughout his life he remained the pupil of the Holy See. Above all he earned reproaches because he trusted no one but his immediate circle of relations and favourites.[4] Three great series of facts explain the revolution which ended his reign; the abuses committed by his foreign advisers, the attempts of the Holy

---

[1] **CXIV**, n. 117.
[2] See **DCXLIV**; **CDXC**, chap. ii–v. Good summaries in **DCXLII**, 14 ff.; **CCXXXVI**, chap. xvi.
[3] **CCCLXX**, 33–41.　　　　　[4] **DCXL**, i, 286, 294.

See in collusion with him to enslave and exploit the English Church, and, finally, the continual failures of his foreign policy.

A number of successive waves filled the court of Henry III with foreigners with whetted teeth. At the beginning of his personal reign, the barons got rid, as quickly as possible, of John's ancient favourite, the Bishop Peter des Roches and his nephew Peter de Rivaux who was a profiteer and also an unconciliatory administrator very antagonistic to other profiteers.[1] In 1236, however, the young king married Saint Louis's sister-in-law, Eleanor of Provence, an extravagant and imperious wife who brought with her a whole host of Provençals and Savoyards who quickly gained an ascendancy justified in some cases by their intellectual ability.[2] The Lusignans were much worse. Four half-brothers of the king on his mother's side, they had come from Poitou after the discomfiture of their father, Hugh de Lusignan, and Isabella d'Angoulême.[3] They, more than any others, seized public duties, lands, and feudal profits which were at the king's disposition and ecclesiastical benifices and made provision for relations and suitors. From 1240 onwards, the Household, the new administrative centre, which became, at such times of crisis, a veritable ministry, was dominated by foreigners. The Wardrobe of the Household was filled with alien clerks.[4]

The legates and nuncios of the Pope were no less detested. During the minority of Henry III the Holy See had developed the habit of governing England. At first it had acted with a moderation and a wisdom that had produced good results.[5] From that, however, it had been only a step to exploiting the country when it needed money and benefices to grant, and when the struggle between the Popes and the Hohenstaufen broke out anew that step was taken.

His foreign favourites and the Holy See imposed on Henry III a foreign policy which was barren and ruinous. The Poitevins urged him to reclaim his lost French fiefs and to revive an obsolete policy of imperialism. He was

---

[1] DCXL, i, 216 ff. ; CDLXXIII, 111 ff.
[2] CDLXXXV, chap. i–viii ; DCXL, i, 261 ff.
[3] Married John Lackland as her first husband. See p. 293 above.
[4] DCXL, i, 20, 240–2, 260, 263–4.
[5] See CXXIX, i *passim*, and the editor's preface, p. xx ff.

particularly concerned about the recovery of Poitou which Louis VIII had conquered (1224) by taking advantage of the anarchy then ruling in England. The expeditions of 1230 and 1242, as we have seen, were disastrous. Henry III did not even succeed in re-establishing order in Gascony. His greatest mistake, however, was to yield to the desire of the Holy See and accept the Crown of Sicily in 1254 for his son Edmund. On this occasion he was even foolish enough to guarantee the Pope's debts which amounted to 135,000 marks. His brother, Richard of Cornwall, succeeded in compromising him by accepting the imperial crown (17th May, 1257).[1]

The natural corollary of this bad policy was financial difficulties[2] which were the more serious because the English clergy were being drained by the Pope. The demands of the monarchy and Holy See, sometimes separate, sometimes combined, quickly became intolerable. Economic changes added to the limitations imposed on the royal despotism by the Great Charter, which were, in part at least, observed, had lessened the profits of the demesne and the income from casual sources. This falling off must have been balanced by the creation of a system of annual taxation just as the enormous development of the duties of the Roman Curia must have led the Holy See to impose regular contributions on the ecclesiastical benefices of all Christendom but they clung to the old formula of the aid granted in the case of emergency and, being irregular, it always seemed oppressive.

For a long time the clergy yielded. It negotiated with the agents of Henry III about " gifts " and the pope sent nuncios to tap their money and to ask for benefices.[3] Innocent IV irritated the clergy by asking for enormous subsidies for purely political ends, for neither in England nor in France was his hatred for the Hohenstaufen shared. From 1244, the opposition of the English Church to the Holy See commenced to assume violent forms. In the following year a papal nuncio had to re-embark secretly in fear of his life.

As for the barons, even before Henry III attained his majority they had obtained in practice that taxation should

[1] **CLXVII**, 129 ff.; **DLXII**, 20–7.
[2] **DCLXXX**, 710–11; **CDLXXIV**, 282, 345, 369–370; **DCXL**, i, 268–278; **DCLXXIX**, 179 ff.
[3] **VI**, 182, 197, 214, etc., and Preface, p. xx; in particular, **CDLI**.

always be agreed to although they did not always demand the insertion of any clause about consent in the new editions of the Great Charter (1216, 1217, 1225). The idea of a Council of barons and prelates helping the king to govern appeared in a comparatively short time (1237). In particular, the nobility wanted to have some supervision over the appointment of the great officials whom the king claimed to choose and dismiss at will. From 1242, since agreement could not be achieved, the barons only granted the aids which were demanded by custom and refused to pay any voluntary subsidies. In their opinion, Henry III had either to be satisfied with his revenues or submit to their control: the idea of a permanent Council gradually took form.[1]

It was under these conditions that the crisis opened.

IV

The Revolution. Government by Council. Provisions of Oxford and Westminster

The revolution of 1258–1265 was comparable in its development to that of 1215–17 but it disturbed England even more deeply and over a longer period.

At the time when *Parlement*—a word which for some years had been coming into use in place of *Magnum Concilium, Colloquium,* or *Generale Colloquium*[2]—met first at London (2nd April, 1258), and then at Oxford (11th June), the patience of the English was exhausted. They were dissatisfied with the king who glutted his favourites and subjected his policy to the fatal caprices of the Pope; they were enraged by the greed and threats of the Holy See and, finally, reduced to desperation by a year of bad weather and famine. The king presented to Parliament an unheard-of demand by the Holy See for the raising of a tax equal to a third of all goods moveable and immoveable. The barons

---

[1] **CDLXXIV**, chap. v–viii; **CLII**, 26–30; **CLXVII**, chap. v; **DCXVIII**, chap. xii–xiii.

[2] **CXXXIII**, 319 ff.; **DLXVI**, 137–149. The first official use of the word Parlement was in the Close Roll of 1242, and in the Memoranda Rolls of the Exchequer of 1248.

formed a league and appeared in military array at Westminster. In spite of the violent resistance of the Lusignans, the king yielded and his uterine brothers had to leave England immediately.[1]

One of the leaders of the opposition was Simon de Montfort, a son of the famous conqueror of the Albigensian heretics. By right of his grandmother Count of Leicester and Court of Bigorre in France, he was a powerful lord and had married King Henry's sister. He had reached the fifties without tempering his passionate character. Like his father he was, from one angle, a complete adventurer, from another, a Christian fanatic. He was moved to action under the simultaneous influence of a singular greed for gain, a boundless ambition, bitter hatreds, and his whole outlook. He distrusted his brother-in-law who had formerly entrusted him with the thankless task of administering Gascony and re-establishing order there and had given him no support (1248-1254).[2] He had had furious quarrels with the king and one of the Lusignans and the English had forgotten that he also was a foreigner seeing in him only a party leader. By his side stood the chiefs of the great feudal families such as the Bigods, Bohuns, Mortimers, and, above all, the Clares, Counts of Gloucester; Richard de Clare and his son, Gilbert, after him were to play the chief parts with the exception of Simon himself, although they did not always remain faithful to the policy of the Count of Leicester. If the barons had remained united, the king, deserted by the nobility and with very little support, would never have been able to get the better of them.

The revolution began in a wave of enthusiasm. We have affecting evidence for this in a letter from a court official which must be dated at the end of July, 1258, at the moment when the committees for reform and government were being set up. The barons and the king himself, he writes, have agreed that public offices should only be occupied by the English and that the emissaries of Rome and the foreign merchants and bankers shall be reduced to their proper position. Alienations of the demesne, the king's household, custody of the castles, all were to be revised. " The barons

[1] **CLXVII**, chap. v; **DCXLII**, 98 ff.; **DCXXVII**, ii, 86 ff.
[2] **CLXVII**, chap. i-iv; **CDLXI**, chap. viii; **CDXXIV**, 30-44.

have a great and difficult task which cannot be carried out easily or quickly. They are proceeding without caution, *ferociter*. May the results be good!"[1]

From the beginning the barons had demanded the formation of a Committee of Twenty-Four, chosen half by them and half by the king, for " the reformation and amendment of the estate of the realm ". The somewhat confused text which modern historians call the " Provisions of Oxford " consists of memoranda drafted either at the beginning or during the course of the work of this committee.[2] Their labours lasted two months (May–June, 1258). It was decided that the king should govern with a Privy Council of fifteen people and that was the principal point for the reformers. According to a method that was generally favoured by the men of the Middle Ages who distrusted direct suffrage and sought for some way of creating electors responsible for what they did, this Council of Fifteen would be chosen by four electors whom the Twenty-Four would appoint in their turn. Parlement was to sit three times a year but to lessen its cost it would normally consist of only twelve people nominated by the general assembly.[3]

The Archbishop of Canterbury, Boniface of Savoy, the Bishop of Worcester, twelve barons, and a single councillor who was loyally devoted to the royal prerogative composed the Committee of Fifteen which was the principal channel of the reforms and undoubtedly governed England for fifteen months (July, 1258–October, 1259). All important official acts mention the participation of the Fifteen. They directed foreign policy, dealt with the affairs of Gascony, stopped the invasions of the Welsh, carried on negotiations with Scotland and the Holy See, and finally decided on the peace with France. The real author, on the English side, of the Treaty of Paris of 1259 was Simon de Montfort. The whole administration was under their control. There was a moderate purge of the personnel but the bureaucratic system was hardly modified at all. The great offices were not entrusted to powerful lords who could abuse their position: they worked on the principle that the holders retained their

---

[1] V, 443–5. [2] CXXXIII, 378–384; CCCLXXII, 188–200.
[3] On the composition of the committees, see Stubbs's useful table: DCXXVII, ii, 97, and Tout's reflections, DCXLII, 99–100, 103.

position for quite a short time, three years at most and rendered accounts. The Council of Fifteen reserved to itself the right to nominate certain officials, the control of important letters and the great seal, authorization for the payment of debts, supervision of the Exchequer and Treasury, and permission to fortify.[1]

The local administration had been the subject of considerable complaint. The châtelains were replaced and a general inquest, comparable to the one Saint Louis had conducted in France a few years previously, was entrusted to the newly appointed justiciar, Hugh Bigod. Like Saint Louis's inquest, the main object was to redress wrongs suffered by subjects in the past or present at the hands of prevaricating or tyrannical officials. In England, however, they were based on the solid local mechanism of the county court; four elected knights prepared the work in each county and received complaints. In addition grievances could be presented direct to the justiciar. A study has recently been made of a local inquest and the extant rolls of the circuit which Hugh Bigod undertook in 1258–9. The facts revealed are quite comparable to those we have suggested for France; deceit and trickery by sheriffs and lower officers —money extorted for sheltering the guilty, delivery of prisoners, justice rushed through or deferred, excessive fines, undue requisitions and taxes, frauds at the expense of the royal demesne; sometimes serious matters and cases of cruelty.[2]

Without awaiting the results of this inquiry, which was never completed, the office of sheriff was reformed. In a petition which the barons presented to the king at the beginning of the crisis, they had indicated that the sheriffs abused their power to levy fines and that the system of farming the counties led to oppression of the people.[3] It was decided that the sheriffs should be appointed by the king " on the advice and suggestion of the magnates " that they should enter their obligations under oath, that they should be well paid and only hold their office one year. The rate of the farms was revised.[4]

[1] Apart from the works already mentioned see, particularly, **DXLIV**, 119 ff.; **DCXL**, i, 295 ff.; **CCCLXXI**, 5 ff.   [2] **CCCLXXI**, 15 ff.
[3] **CXXXIII**, 375, art. 16.   [4] **CCCLXXI**, 20–1, 51; **CDLXXXIV**, 169 ff.

The English wanted even more. The proclamations of the Reformers and the visitations of Hugh Bigod set in motion a class whose desires and grievances found only rare occasion for expression—the small free tenants, called, in Normandy, the vavasseurs, to whom were joined the middle bourgeoisie. They aimed at controlling the sheriffs through their own elected representatives. On the other hand, the great barons held complexes of lordships, " honours," the " franchises " of which were very extensive. The judges on circuit had received many complaints against the seigniorial officials and did not know how to respect the " franchises " as they should without forgetting the promise to do justice on all oppressors.[1]

The demands of the middle classes, particularly concerning the abuses they suffered in the great baronies, opened the second act of the drama. Simon de Montfort completely accepted the first idea and reproved the selfishness of certain important lords who were not willing to sacrifice their privileges. He obtained an Ordinance of the Council published on 28th March, 1259, by which the barons undertook to put their territories under the general authority of the inquest and the reforms carried out by the royal judges.[2] Under the increasingly active insistence of the rival middle class which adopted the title of the " community of the bachelors of England "[3] new Provisions were published at Westminster in October which completed the series of legislative and constitutional acts which we might call the system of the Provisions of Oxford. The Provisions of Westminster increased the powers of the Council of Fifteen and the Commission of Twelve, added councillors to the judges on circuit to receive complaints, and laid it down that the king should always have around him two or three councillors who were " lesser men " and not of the greater barons. In each county four knights were to supervise the conduct of the sheriffs; further they would choose them and it was one of the four knights who

---

[1] **CCCLXXI**, 20, 56, 60–1, 106–121, 147–9.
[2] **CCCLXXI**, 83–6, 137–142; **CLXVII**, 169 ff.; **DXLIV**, 126–7.
[3] See p. 370 below. The meaning of this term is obscure. It undoubtedly includes those free tenants who had a large enough revenue to rank as knights as well as young knights who have, as yet, no fief. The word is sometimes applied also to knights who form part of the king's household, or that of one of the great barons: see **DCXLI**, 89 ff.; **CCCLXXI**, 126–137; my note in **DCXXVII**, ii, 95; **DXLIV**, 129; **DXXXIX**, 42, note.

would generally be chosen by his colleagues. Finally seigniorial officials were justiciable before the itinerant judges ; the procedure used in the baronial courts was revised.[1]

V

THE BARONS' WAR AND THE PROTECTORATE OF SIMON DE MONTFORT

This great revolutionary effort which was so favourable to the middle classes cut the baronial party in two. Some of them remained faithful to Simon de Montfort : others drew nearer to the king again. Henry III, with good reason, shook off his torpor. He made a long stay in France (14th November, 1259–23rd April, 1260) on the occasion of the Peace Treaty. It is hardly possible to doubt that he discussed his position at length with his brother-in-law. Saint Louis, however, was antagonistic to the ideas which inspired Simon de Montfort. He believed in the sanctity of the monarchical prerogative. When Henry returned to England armed with £12,500 Tournois which Saint Louis had given him he undertook to get rid of the Council and officials which had been imposed on him. His resolution still wavered frequently but it was increasingly strengthened by the jealousies which divided his opponents and the lassitude they had fallen into.[2] He was not slow to find a secure foundation in his son Edward, the future great king Edward I. The young prince was ready to accept reforms and he did the monarchy good service by not establishing himself among the old courtier circles but founding a new party which attracted both those whom Simon de Montfort had alienated and those who sought immediate advantages, particularly the barons of the Welsh marches who were anxious to secure the king's support against Llewellyn.[3]

The arbitration of Saint Louis (Mise of Amiens, 23rd January, 1264), favourable to Henry III, confirmed the two successive annulments of the Provisions which he had gained

[1] CXXXIII, 389–394 ; CCCLXXI, 50, 86–100, 123 ff., 139 ff. ; DXLIV, 119 ff.
[2] CLXVII, chap. vi, vii ; DXLIV, 132–4 ; CLII, 32 ; DCXL, i, 299 ff.
[3] DCXLIII, 77 ff.

from the Holy See.¹ But the Mise of Amiens was not accepted by the masses of the population whom the royal officials had oppressed for such a long time. The tradesmen, particularly of London, the sailors of the Cinque Ports, and the rural middle classes now made up the opposition. A civil war broke out marked by a vigorous effort by the people of London. These lesser folk could have done nothing if the Count of Leicester, indignant at the " perjured fickleness " of the barons, had not assumed the leadership of them, with the support of his five sons. He won a great victory, south of London, at Lewes (14th May, 1264). Henry III was taken prisoner together with his brother Richard of Cornwall.² Then Simon de Montfort's dictatorship began and with it the series of revolutionary crises which have so frequently broken the course of the history of the English monarchy. After the capture of Henry III, we were to see Edward II, Richard II, Henry VI, Edward V deposed and put to death in their prisons, Richard III lose his life and throne at the same moment, Jane Grey beheaded after reigning a matter of weeks, Charles I beheaded, James II dethroned. We are justified in setting the events of 1264 in this perspective. It would be impossible to imagine those tragic years adequately without recalling the violence of the passions which have so frequently activated the English; even in the thirteenth century this people was marked by some of the most characteristic of its national features.

For fifteen months Simon de Montfort exercised a protectorate. After appointing to all the important posts administrators of his own choosing, he summoned a Parliament in which, by the side of the magnates and prelates, appeared " four loyal and trustworthy knights for each county elected by the assembly of that county ". This meeting was held at London about 24th June, 1264, and approved the Constitution, " the system of government of the lord king and the kingdom " required by Simon. Henry III until the end of his life was to remain under ward. The government passed to a council of nine people chosen by three electors—Simon de Montfort, the new Count of Gloucester Gilbert de Clare, and the Bishop of Chichester. In practice, Simon de Montfort, with the simple

[1] CXXXIII, 395–7; CLXVII, 206–7.
[2] CLXVII, 209–214; CCCLXXI, 276, 281–6.

title of Seneschal of England,[1] was dictator. He could rely on the support of the middle classes alone and he was anxious that that, at least, should find some formal expression. He summoned, therefore, the Parlement of 20th January, 1265, the first to see lords, knights of the shires, and burgesses sitting together. It was a Parlement of Supporters; Simon had summoned only five counties and eighteen barons on whom he could rely. The clergy, on the other hand, which was very largely favourable, furnished twelve bishops, fifty-five abbots, and twenty-six priors. The sheriffs were " to cause to come " two knights for each county chosen among " the most loyal, upright, and trustworthy " and the " cities of York and Lincoln and the other boroughs of England " were to send two citizens or burgesses equally chosen.[2]

Neither this Parliament nor the one which followed it and was held under ordinary forms secured a general pacification. The royalists would not accept the protectorate of Simon de Montfort and the young Gilbert de Clare himself reproached his colleague for his arrogance and his greedy harshness. The barons of the Welsh marches remained in arms. The queen, in France, prepared troops for an invasion. The papal envoys threatened the clergy. The Guardians of the Peace (*custodes pacis*), who had been established in each county, could not guarantee order. Recent research in judicial records has shown that Simon only maintained his position by terror and never succeeded in securing regular financial resources. He sent agents into the counties who levied subscriptions and favoured the formation of bands of supporters. The manors of the relations and officials of Henry III were systematically pillaged, either by the lesser people of the neighbourhood or by the castle garrisons. The sailors of the turbulent Confederation of the Cinque Ports turned pirate and swarmed in the Channel.[3]

The escape of Prince Edward, who had been held as hostage, was the signal for the downfall. The young Gilbert de Clare joined Edward after gaining a promise that the monarchy would be inspired by the spirit of the Provisions of Oxford. Edward led a decisive campaign vigorously. Simon de

[1] CCCXLVI, 121, 124–5.
[2] Documents on Simon's administration in CXXXIII, 397–407. See CLXVII, 214 ff.; CLII, 32–4; DCXL, i, 309–312; DIX, 56 ff.
[3] CCCLXXI, 223–239, 286–293; CLXVII, 232 ff.; DCXLII, 123 ff.

Montfort was defeated and killed at Evesham (4th August, 1265). The full fury of their hatred was let loose and the dictator's corpse was dismembered and thrown to the beasts.

The royalists in turn claimed the spoils of the conquered and threw themselves on the manors of Simon's supporters, granting themselves many of them by royal gift.[1] Documents which have recently come to light confirm a page written by Thomas Wykes, the most intelligent chronicler of the period, who shows us that " after their unexpected but triumphal victory at Evesham the king and his supporters so far from becoming more prudent became more stupid and, in their exultation, completely forgot all preparations for the future ", distributing at random the goods of the vanquished.[2]

This policy prolonged the disorders. The " disinherited " continued the war and England fell into chaos. The Pope Clement IV, a friend of Saint Louis, was of the opinion that Henry and his family were on the verge of destruction and, with them, " the noble fief of the Roman Church " ; his legate, the Cardinal Ottoboni, finally obtained signatures to a pact, the " Dictum de Kenilworth ". Gilbert de Clare, disgusted by the king's attitude, demanded its execution and prepared to enforce his demands by arms. The " disinherited " were authorized to buy their lands back from the new possessors at a rate which would be justly fixed proportionate to their guilt. In 1267 the civil war ended at last leaving England exhausted. The monarchy, impoverished and lacking any means of action, plunged into lethargy until Edward re-aroused it. The only one apparently to gain from the struggle was Llewellyn who was more powerful and independent than ever in Wales.[3]

VI

Character and Results of these Crises

What was the real significance of these movements of the thirteenth century and what was their outcome ?

[1] **CLXVII**, 238 ff. ; **CCCLXXI**, 149–167, 172–3.
[2] **CXXXVII**, 183–4.
[3] **CCCLXXI**, 167–221, 249, 258–262 ; **CDLXXII**, 489 ff. ; **DCXL**, i, 313–17 ; **DCXLIII**, 119–136.

The clashes between the two kings and their opponents were violent because neither John nor Henry III were ready to make any concession. The results of the conflicts were scanty because the English were still far from the idea of a constitutional government.

As we have said, the loss of the French fiefs had not lessened the royal power in England. It limited the field of action of the king's agents but it concentrated their activities which had been much too widely distributed. They did not cease to be hard working and enterprising. The great part of the reigns of John and Henry III formed a period of financial and administrative novelties. Westminster had decidedly become the centre of the state. The Exchequer sat there permanently with its special personnel, its seal, and, at an early date, its chancellor, with control over the principal Royal Treasury. The Exchequer was the great administrative power supervising all the services, the management of the sheriffs, and ordering inquests. It was in constant communication with the departments of justice which also looked after the king's interests developing the new procedure of writs and perfecting the national—*common*—law. This judicial body, which in the time of Henry III included eminent men such as Bracton, had not yet assumed its definitive form. Bracton gives us the best description of it when he says[1] that there are general and permanent chief judges in the king's presence, *a latere regis*, that is to say travelling round with him, and the " other permanent judges " staying " in a fixed place " at Westminster. The former judged *coram rege*, in the king's presence so called, and gave special attention to the big criminal trials, cases which affected the king or the great barons and cases called out of other courts; they formed a picked body of lawyers who decided difficult cases, interpreting and creating the law; the second group comprised the Court of Common Pleas. Finally alongside these official departments was one on which the Chancery was still dependent which, owing to its domestic and indefinite character, gave the king a means of avoiding, at need, the control even of his own officials. This we have already seen was the Household. To provide for links with the local administration the itinerant justices were retained who

[1] **XX**, vol. ii, 307 ff.

were sent from the Curia to preside in the shire courts and supervise the sheriffs as necessary. Thus the king possessed a fairly strong governmental machine which kept its course in spite of squalls. He could almost always have at his service men of his own choice; moreover, even if his officials had an independent character, they were constantly working for his greatness and for the destruction of rival powers.[1]

Of the old Curia Regis there remained the Council and the Great Council of tenants in chief. The *Consilium* and the *Magnum Concilium*, as the words themselves suggest, were the two forms of the Curia which was contracted or expanded according to circumstances, the king's will, or certain customs. There was no council in the modern sense of the term; the king consulted, as in the past, people who happened to be with him and whom he could trust. During the minority of Henry III, these *consiliarii* had played an important part and the barons had been able to prove that it was possible to govern a kingdom by a Council but it remained a changing and moving body of nobles and officials and not an organ with differentiated functions. There were no committees, no proper means of carrying out its decisions; the " system of Oxford ", alone, established a real Council for a few years in 1258.[2] Equally there was no Parliament in the modern sense of the term; the word appeared in official documents in 1242 as synonymous with *Magnum Concilium* just as it appeared in France about the same time as a designation of the judicial session of the Curia Regis. The frequent use of this new term changed nothing in fact. The English Parliament of the thirteenth century was essentially the Assembly of Magnates who, in virtue of their feudal obligations, owed their royal lord the benefits of their experience just as they owed him the help of their arms and their purse. They gave advice on political and, very often, on judicial affairs, for the king by no means conferred a monopoly on the professional judges. Surrounded by his barons, he remained the fount of justice. Bracton suggested that complicated cases should be remitted to them and that is why, for a long time, Parliament had an essentially judicial

[1] See particularly, **DCXL**, i, 12 ff., 23 ff., 97, 151 ff., 201–5, 240–1, 256 ff., 285 ff.; **CDLXXIII**, 111 ff.; **CLXVII**, 137–143; **CCVII**, 19 ff.; **CDLXXXIV**, chap. vi–ix.

[2] **CLII**, 16–68; **DCXL**, i, 10–12.

ARISTOCRATIC REACTION IN ENGLAND 353

character. The Parliament was still the old Curia in an extended form. The old institution of the Curia lived on on both sides of the Channel and, in principle, it was the same in both places.

Further, the king, in England as in France, could bring to his Court whomever he wished. Already in the twelfth century knights were being summoned, for example four for each county, to inform the Court on judicial matters. In the thirteenth century, the king occasionally saw the advantage of not being satisfied merely with the advice of his barons. Royalists and the king's opponents each tried, in times of crisis, to base their position on the support of the middle classes and thus precedents were established without anyone realizing their importance. One of the most ancient texts is the writ of 7th November, 1213: John was preparing for war with France and he summoned an Assembly in which the elements of the lesser nobility could balance the barons whom he distrusted. The king wrote to the sheriffs of all the counties :—

> We command you to cause to come to Oxford in arms, on the 15th of November, all the knights of your bailiwick who have already been summoned and similarly the barons personally without arms. And see that, on the same date, four trustworthy knights come there from your county to talk with us on the affairs of our realm.[1]

Under Henry III many summonses to knights of the shires can be recorded, particularly in 1227 and in 1254. There are also, from the reign of John, examples of the limited summons of burgesses. We have seen that Simon de Montfort called knights and burgesses in to his support. Henry III, though freed from Simon de Montfort, still considered it useful in 1267 to send for "the most prudent men of the realm, great and small". In 1268 he summoned to Parliament the representatives of twenty-seven cities. In 1254 he had specified that the two "loyal and prudent knights" coming from each county should be elected in the county court [2] but, in general, it was the sheriff who chose we cannot say these "deputies" but these attorneys of the middle classes. They have been represented as the origin of the House of Commons. It is a question of valuation, however. It would be possible to see in the burgess assemblies called together

[1] **CXXXIII**, 282; **CDXVII**, 85 ff.   [2] **CXXXIII**, 366.

by Saint Louis to examine " currency questions " the germ of the assemblies of the Third Estate. But we must fully realize that the custom of demanding the attendance of " trustworthy people " of the middle classes at Court was already old, that the Parliament called together by Simon de Montfort had been an expedient, and that no one realized at the time that a new institution was being born. For a long time it had appeared quite natural to appeal in certain cases to people who could provide valuable information and who could usefully be told about " affairs of state ". That was a very old tradition in the West. No one thought, however, of the regular representation of counties and boroughs or of parliamentary control.[1]

The only obstacle which hindered the king and his officials was, as in France, feudal custom and, in particular, the custom of consent to the aid.

Had the lawyers who surrounded the king at least some idea that the rights of the monarchy were limited and that there were rules to which they were subject ? In a confused fashion this idea already existed and we find it expressed, towards the middle of the thirteenth century, in the works of the royal judge Bracton. The law makes the king, he wrote, and there is no king where despotism rules and not the law. As the minister and vicar of God, the king can do in his dominions nothing but what is right. The dictum " What pleases the prince has the force of law " cannot raise objections, for " what pleases the prince " does not mean what can be taken with impunity by the king's will but what is done to establish the right and *has been duly decided* after considera- tion, the king giving the support of his authority to the advice of his " magistrates ". Moreover, Bracton says further : although the English laws are not written they are laws all the same for everything that has been properly decided and approved by the advice and consent of the magnates on the king's authority has the force of law.

Thus the king must respect the law and he can make new laws only on the advice of the magnates and men of experience whom he consults. Nobody, however, can be above the king.

---

[1] **DIX**, 1–83, 259–260 ; **DX**, 1–70, 223–4 ; **DXXX**, *passim* ; **CCCLXVIII**, intro. ; **CXLIV**, *passim* ; **DCLXXVII**, 735 ff. ; **DLXVI** ; **DXCIII**, 580–5. Summary and bibliography in **DCXXVII**, iii, 725 ff., or **DXX**, 348 ff.

ARISTOCRATIC REACTION IN ENGLAND

" He has no peer, no equal, no superior," save God. No one can force him to correct an injustice, they can only beg him to do so and, if he refuses, God alone can punish him. No one can abolish, discuss, or interpret the Charters which he has given and, if there is any doubt, he alone can provide the interpretation. He alone has the power to pronounce the law, just as the punishment of certain crimes and the maintenance of the public peace are his prerogatives and can be transferred to others only by express delegation.[1]

I do not know whether the historians of law and political doctrines have seen very clearly when they have interpreted these texts. It seems to me that they must be compared with those in which Bracton says that (in judicial matters) the king's Court alone can settle doubtful cases in which there is no guide to be found in precedent. We must imagine the state of mind of a proud official and then perhaps the basis of his thought will be clear. The law and even the king are abstractions for him. The thing which, for him, is real and living is the Court, of which he is part, either filled with barons or reduced to a council of " prudent men " experts in their duties. The king, the magnates who owe him their help, and the officials who serve him form a bloc. It is a useful theory which allows the men of the Exchequer and the judges *a latere regis* to govern while appealing sometimes to the theological argument of the king as God's servant and without peer, sometimes to the argument of the consent of the magnates and opposing, as necessary, in certain particular cases the king to the magnates and the magnates to the king.

In the same way, at the present day, a Director of the Ministry will speak sometimes of the law, or of the Council of State, sometimes of the will of Parliament, according to the needs of the case. The contradictions do not worry Bracton and his like; they are useful to them for doing what they want. Moreover this Machiavellianism is possibly entirely unconscious.

Naturally the kings took from these theories whatever suited them according to their temperament or according to the suggestions of their favourites and flatterers. In

[1] **XX**, ii, 19, 33, 305 ff., etc.; fragments of Bracton in **CXXXIII**, 412–13; **CDLIII**, 30–3. Cf. **CCCLXVIII**, 101–3 (Note: the fundamental law in Bracton); **CCCLXII**, ii, 252–4; **CCIX**, 34–40, 66–73.

certain periods of crisis they were even encouraged in their preference for absolutism by the highest moral power in Christendom, the Holy See, which was badly informed on English institutions, and the temper of the English and subordinated its whole policy to the objects it was pursuing—a crusade or the struggle against the Hohenstaufen.

John Lackland adopted the policy of an avowed tyrant. When the barons' petition was presented to him in 1215, based on the customs which he had incessantly broken, he exclaimed "Why don't the barons demand my kingdom as well as these scandalous claims?"[1] He yielded only at the point of the sword. By wishing to control him through a committee the barons aroused his impatience once again and he preferred to run the risks of a war. He was the first monarch to carry on his seal the title "King of England"; his ancestors had taken the title of King of the English.[2] Even during his struggle with the Pope he was on the look out for theological arguments to justify his mad despotism. A certain Alexandre Le Maçon gained his favour by providing him with them :—

> "This pseudo-theologian," says Roger of Wendover, "urged him to cruelties by his infamous preaching. He told him, in effect, that the general misery of England was not the fault of the king but arose from the dissoluteness of his subjects. He even assured him that, as king, he was the whip of God's fury, that the prince is established to rule his people with a rod of iron, to break all his subjects like the potter's clay, and to put manacles of iron on his nobility."[3]

Henry III had an equable temperament and in 1258 he accepted an oligarchic government for some time but finally his favourites got the better of his compliancy and ranged him against his barons. The tone of "The King's Grievances against his Council", a text dating from about 1261, which has recently been recovered is very curious. It contains the complaints of the king and of the dismissed officials. The king complains of being in tutelage. He cannot tolerate the members of his Council saying "We want this to be so . . ." without even giving their reasons when these people have done him homage and sworn fidelity. Formerly the king relied on the Exchequer administered by experienced and

---

[1] CXIX, ii, 586.   [2] DCXXVII, i, 663.
[3] CXIX, ii, 527. Cf. DXXXVIII, 246–260.

ARISTOCRATIC REACTION IN ENGLAND

trustworthy people but now it has been filled with new and servile officials who are *disciples where they ought to be masters*.[1]

What were the ambitions or achievements of the opposition against these monarchs and these royal officials who sought to be masters ?

In the first place, can we believe in the existence of a great current of public opinion, an " English nation ", as Stubbs says,[2] "led by events to a conscious unity and a personality " ? Historians of the Victorian age have thought that in the reign of John Lackland they could see a nation united in opposition to the king. Modern scholars, even those least disposed to paradox, have reached the conclusion that we must give up this idea. It is not that England at the beginning of the thirteenth century does not present a spectacle very different from the France of that period still lacking unity or uniformity. England was small and possessed a strong government, conditions which were favourable to unity. Local customs still survived but alongside them had grown up a common law which the royal lawyers were ceaselessly enriching.[3] Norman conquerors and Saxon conquered of earlier days had been fused into one people whom bilingualism seems to have worried little. Upper society spoke French but a faulty French which began to provoke the scorn of our ancestors [4]; the middle and lower classes spoke English and it was in English that Henry III published his adhesion to the Provisions of Oxford in 1258 [5]; the two tongues had not yet interpenetrated to form modern English but educated people knew both and also learnt Latin.[6] It is already possible to speak of an English nation. The extremely varying interests, however, and, above all, the absence of any analytical conception of the State and public liberty, the idea that monarchical government is the personal affair of the monarch, the idea that the feudal duty of Council is the only limit on his responsibility, and finally the idea that, in practice, the only defence against his despotism was the

---

[1] **LXIII**, 564 ff. Cf. **CLII**, 24.
[2] **DCXXVII**, i, 761. The same ideas appear in **CXCII**, 55–60.
[3] Bracton in **CXXXIII**, 412.
[4] **XCIX**, 279 ff.
[5] **CXXXIII**, 387–8 ; **CCCLXIII**, ii, 117–19.
[6] The English boast of knowing three languages : *Gens nostra tribus pollet idiomatibus erudita, scilicet latino, gallico et anglico* (**LXXX**, ii, 560–1).

maintenance of certain customs, by the preservation or winning of particular franchises for a certain social group, these formed an almost insurmountable obstacle to the development of a political spirit.[1] So far from leading the resistance of the English people, the barons set an example of division and political incapacity. They had the reputation of never being able to reach any agreement. The regent William the Marshall on his death-bed in 1219 was frightened of arousing jealousies by nominating his successor and finally left the little king Henry in the care of God and the legate for " there is no country where people are so divided in heart as in England ".[2] John Lackland had succeeded in uniting the barons in opposition after long years of tyranny but their party was only based on the aggregate of their personal grievances. The chronicler who has given the best accout of their rising shows us the motives of their irritation and there is little trace of political opposition :—

> There were, at that time, many nobles in England whose wives and daughters had been subjected to the King's violence, others who had been ruined by undue demands, some of whose relatives had been exiles and their possessions confiscated so that the king had as many enemies as barons.[3]

Other contemporaries speak of his preference for foreigners, his favours to the mercenaries who led him on to barbarities, his disinheritance of minors, and his seizures of babies as hostages.[4] All these allegations are in detail and it would be quite possible to quote the names of the barons whom John had dishonoured or ruined and who had fought against him.[5]

They embarked on it without any plan but the suppression of the abuse from which they were suffering most keenly. The text of the Great Charter proves very clearly that they had no thought of establishing a constitutional regime based on national unity but only of securing observance of the customs which they had secured. As the chronicler of Coggeshall says, they wanted to make an end of " the evil customs which the king's father and brother had established and the abuses which King John had added to them ".[6]

---

[1] We must not overestimate the value of public opinion, of the *commune consilium regni* in the thirteenth century. See below.
[2] **LVIII**, lines 18041-3. Cf. vol. iii, pp. 254-5.
[3] **CXIX**, ii, 535. [4] **XIII**, 232; Poem inserted in **XXII**, 118.
[5] **DXLV**, app. v; Powicke, *John*, in *C.M.H.*, vi, 243-4.
[6] **XCVII**, 170.

ARISTOCRATIC REACTION IN ENGLAND 359

Their ideal was in the past. Their inability to invent a new public law is marked in the measures they took to ensure the execution of this " peace " : the Committee of Twenty-Five, charged with organizing an armed revolt in cases of any omission, was a purely feudal idea. The Great Charter is absolutely saturated in the same spirit. Its essential character is the restoration of the ancient feudal law which had for a long time been undermined by the lawyers of the Curia and the royal officials and violently destroyed by John Lackland. It was certainly in this way that it was understood by contemporaries. Robert de Bethune, a French friend of John, had a minstrel of whom he commissioned a history of the Kings of England. He analysed the Great Charter in this way : the king was forced to promise not to " disparage " heiresses, to lessen rights of relief, to abandon the severe laws which protected his forest rights, and to surrender the rights of " haute justice " to the lords.[1] The biographer of William the Marshal says similarly " that the barons came to the King *for their liberties* ".[2] Those articles of the Great Charter which are not concerned with these " liberties " almost all contain benefits or securities for the nobility. For example, the clause which prevents the royal officials confiscating, on pretext of a fine, the tools which are essential for a serf to work and live [3] has been instanced as a proof that the rights of the whole people were defended against the king by the barons. The Great Charter, however, is concerned only with the seigniorial serfs and not with royal. It protects their property because it is their lord's property. The more exact drafts used in the confirmations of the Charter prove this conclusively.

The articles concerning scutage and the aid and the interpretation formerly [4] given to them deserve particular attention ; nothing shows better how easily it is possible to make a serious mistake when texts are taken in isolation and no serious attempt is made to examine the meaning of the words. We have given above a literal translation. John had raised the rate of scutage, i.e. the tax in lieu of military service and, by the addition of supplementary " fines ",

---

[1] **LIX**, 145–6, 149–150. [2] **LVIII**, lines 15038–9.
[3] Art. 20. Cf. **DCXXX**, 720 ff.
[4] See, particularly, **DCXXVII**, i, 641–2 ; **CXLVI**, 16–17 ; **CDVIII**, 285–7 ; etc.

he had made it a means of unlimited extortion. On the other hand, on the pretext of the " aid " due to a lord from his men, he had demanded what were, in fact, taxes. Everyone remembered that in 1207 following the refusal of his demand for a thirteenth on the revenues of clergy and laymen he had seized the property of the Archbishop of York, sold that of the Abbey of Furness, and imposed a heavy fine on the Abbot of Selby. Under these conditions, what was the barons' demand in their petition of 1215 ? That, apart from the three customary aids (ransom, knighting of son, marriage of daughter) which should, moreover, remain reasonable, the king should not establish any scutage or aid except by " the common council of the realm ", that is to say on the advice and with the consent of his subjects.[1] It was a vague formula in which it is impossible to see anything other than the desire to secure respect for the old rules of feudal right of which we have spoken so often ; the vassal must help his lord when in distress but that " aid " he gives after being consulted. That is all that the barons demanded.[2]

As for article 14 of the Charter concerning the procedure to be followed for the general assembly which will give its consent, *it does not exist in the barons' petition*. And who has inserted it here ? The normal procedure for the convocation has been remembered and an addition has been made that even if all the people summoned do not come its discussions will, nevertheless, be binding. Who is prepared to say that that paragraph, added after the negotiations between the mandatories of the barons and the king's agents, does not reflect the latter's desires ? He wanted to put an end to the individual strife of the prelates and barons who, not having appeared and not having personally consented to the aid, refused to pay it. Thus this article which has been put to the credit of the barons *was directed against them*. In the confirmation of 1216 it disappeared together with clause 12 concerning consent to the levy of a scutage or an aid. At the end of the Charter of 1216 it is said that it was one of those " chapters contained in the previous charter which appeared very important but doubtful " and that it had

---

[1] On the meaning of *commune consilium regni* : **DCLXXVIII**, 5 ff.
[2] *Capitula quae barones petunt*, art. 32 ; **XVII**, p. 19. Cf. art. 12 of the Great Charter. See the translation of arts. 12, 14.

pleased "the prelates and magnates to defer them" until the king had taken more adequate counsel.[1] In the confirmation of 1217 and in that of 1225 which constitutes the definitive text they merely say " Scutage will be taken in future as it was customary to take it in the time of King Henry our grandfather ".[2]

In emergency, therefore, scutage might be levied without previous consent ; beyond that, as its importance grew less and less, the concession of the return to ancient custom retained, in fact, little interest. If the English of that period had had the political spirit they are credited with they would have organized a detailed machinery of consent to extraordinary taxation which the king could raise proportionally on incomes and landed property. Neither side had any clear idea of how to solve the problem. Article 14 of the Great Charter was no solution. It spoke of the summons of all the tenants in chief which, in practice, was impossible. No one could seriously consider the frequent assembly of such a throng in which all the minor direct vassals of the king would rub shoulders with the barons. The royal agents certainly meant to persist in their somewhat unscrupulous habits. They continued to summon whom they would and, if the summons did not reach all those entitled to it, the consent of the assembly would still be secured. There was no idea of organizing a system of representation. That would be achieved only slowly and piecemeal under the influence of the much more intelligent practices of the church [3] and still without affecting the lords' privilege to be invited individually. Finally, let us note that, even if article 14 had been upheld, a decision of the *Magnum Concilium* bound only those vassals, lay and ecclesiastical, who held fiefs of the king which were subject to host service. The churchmen who were not involved in military service did not take part in the *Magnum Concilium* and gave nothing but gifts. In the same way, subjects living on the royal demesne did not pay the taxes agreed to by the assembly but were subject to tallages fixed according to the estimates of the royal councillors. Our modern theories of taxation agree in no

[1] **CXXXIII**, 339, art. 42. On the confirmations see **DCXXXVI**, 4 ff.
[2] Charter of 1217, art. 44 (**CXXXIII**, 343) ; 1225, art. 37 (**XVII**, 57).
[3] On the idea of representation in the Church and its development in England : **CLVII**, 7 ff., 13 ff., 30 ff. ; **DXLV**, 157-9.

respect with the ideas which the social structure of the thirteenth century imposed and we must not allow ourselves to be misled by certain formulas of charters which seem to imply the consent of " all the inhabitants of the realm ".[1]

In the reign of Henry III the *Magnum Concilium* assumed a new importance in financial history. The principles of consent to the aid did not change, however. Henry III, being weaker than his predecessors while nevertheless being greatly in need of money, was forced to respect the custom and never dispense with the consent of the *Magnum Concilium* to the levy of an extraordinary aid. The barons took advantage of the weakness and mistakes of the king to discuss and negotiate and secure the redress of their grievances and did not always grant what he had asked. This had rarely happened previously and it is impossible to deny that progress was being made. But the habit of partial consultations and, conversely, the idea that each baron agreed for his own lordship lived on.[2] For instance, in 1220 the barons of Yorkshire had not been summoned to the general assembly and were unwilling to pay the carucage it had agreed to but the sheriff wrote to Hubert de Burgh " Some of them have told me that if, on his arrival in York, the king summons the magnates and puts forward his demands they will agree and see that the aid is paid ".[3] The barons did not perceive that the only serious guarantee against arbitrary taxation is a general summons, a consent given by a collective gathering as large and as powerful as possible and that the demand for that must never be dropped. The king's agents saw very well that it was in their interests to break up the consultations. In France the system of provincial assemblies was to be one of the factors in an absolute monarchy. It was not established in England but it was not far off.

During the great crisis of Henry III's reign, the barons did not think of creating a parliamentary system but seized the administration and government as " councillors " invoking the feudal principle that the vassal owes council to his lord. We have seen that by " advising the king " they meant

[1] Cf. **CCCLXXXI**, 232 ff.; **CDLXXIV**, 9–10, 86–9, 340–3, 357–369, 388–9.
[2] **CDLXXIV**, 367, 371, 385–392.
[3] **CXXIX**, i, n. 130, p. 151; **CDLXXIV**, 129 ff.

reigning with him. To Henry's complaints they replied that they had no wish to lessen his dignity or his power and that they would willingly obey him when " he gave good orders " but it was necessary for them to deal with matters outside his purview to ensure order. If they made any mistake and appointed unworthy officials let some one point it out to them by inquest and they would make their errors good.[1]

The theory of the king advised by his barons might, it is true, have led to England being governed by the mass of tenants in chief. It is the idea which is expressed in a curious political poem of the times.

> From all that has been said it may appear evident that it becomes a king to see together with his nobles what things are convenient for the government of the kingdom and what are expedient for the preservation of peace ; and that the king have natives for his companions, not foreigners nor favourites for his councillors or the great nobles of his kingdom who supplant others and abolish good customs.[2]

This author was dreaming of an England governed by a vast House of Lords but the barons who made the revolution of 1258 considered that the assembly of a great number of magnates could produce nothing but disorder and anarchy and they had no desire to increase the prerogatives of Parliament. We have seen how they replaced it by a commission of twelve members working in co-operation with the Council of Fifteen. The oligarchy they installed in power was very limited.

Beyond that they had no idea how to defend it for any length of time against selfish passions or to preserve it from jealousy and controversy. They were frightened for its privileges and gradually it wore out and fell into dissolution. One great baron alone had upheld the idea that a king like Henry III was incapable of governing and must be kept in tutelage, one alone had been consistently revolutionary and died for his ideas. That was Simon de Montfort. Simon, however, did not truly represent the English aristocracy at this period ; this is proved by the fact that Gilbert de Clare, the noblest of the English barons, had betrayed him and contributed to his destruction.[3] Simon appears as the

---

[1] **LXIII**, 564–571.
[2] The Battle of Lewes in **CXXXIX**, lines 952–8, p. 120.
[3] On the interested motives of Gilbert de Clare, see **CCCLXX**, 25 ff. Simon de Montfort himself was not altogether free from personal calculations.

great adventurer, the forlorn hope who dares everything. Above all, however, he must be seen in the image of his father, the Christian fanatic. The key to his life and character is to be found in his relations with the English Church of his times; it was simultaneously his guide and his disciple.

The English Church which, at the end of the Middle Ages, was in such a sorry state, in the thirteenth century was still at the height of its power and social influence. After undergoing the exacting tests of persecution and interdict, it was revived and rejuvenated by the arrival of the mendicant monks, the friars. The first Dominicans landed in 1221, the first Franciscans in 1224. In a few years the English towns, crowded, sordid, infected with epidemics, and ill-served with clergy had one or two establishments of mendicants who guaranteed worship, preaching, education, and the care of the sick. The friars, whatever the name of their order, revivified this whole generation of Englishmen and brought them their work, their joy, and their disinterestedness, the charity of Saint Francis, a more noble conception of life, the taste of concerted action, and sacrifice.[1] Thanks to them and also to such great prelates as Stephen Langton, Edmund Rich, and Robert Grossetete the church became, under Henry III, the centre of the national life, the inspiration of the resistance to all oppression.

We have seen what an important part the Primate Langton had played at the end of John's reign. He had turned the barons towards the demand for a Charter: without him England would have fallen into anarchy. He had had the idea of concerted action. The place reserved for the liberties of the Church in this " peace " between the king and his barons is a sufficient revelation of his influence and his political ability. He was a moderate and prudent man: he did not approve of the violent attitude of the Twenty-Five and had no wish to force a rupture with the Pope. Conciliation, however, was impossible.[2] After his departure, twelve bishops out of fifteen braved pontifical excommunication and sided with Louis of France.[3] That was the origin of heavy misfortunes for the English Church; once the

---

[1] **DCXXIV**, chap. iii. Critical bibliography in A. G. Little, *A Guide to Franciscan Studies*, London, 1920.
[2] **DXLV**, chap. v.   [3] **DXVII**, 121-3.

French had gone, it was severely punished by the legate, and the Holy See thus developed a despotic attitude; encouraged by the weakness and collusion of Henry III it considered England as a province to be exploited.

For many years the English Church more or less defended itself against the demands of the king and Popes. The king asked for money and wanted to appoint his foreign favourites and, in accordance with the tradition of the dynasty, those officials who had served him well to bishoprics; the Pope, on the pretext that England was his fief, claimed to provide his Italian clientele with good benefices without, however, obliging them to take up residence or carry out their sacerdotal obligations. In 1241 the legate demanded three hundred benefices for Italians at one time. This despotism affected secular interests as well for there were many benefices which had lay lords as patrons who had the right of nomination. In 1231 a young knight whose rights were attacked in this way established a league which gained the support of nobles, ecclesiastics, and even royal councillors. The property of the Italian beneficiaries was pillaged, their granges were burnt, or their corn even given to the poor. The demand was raised for the expulsion of all beneficed foreigners from England. The Pope demanded measures against it and the chief victim was no less a person than the justiciar Hubert de Burgh who was arrested and imprisoned.[1] The English church found, however, even within itself leaders who would organize resistance. After the death of Stephen Langton (1228) it again found courageous primates. Edmund Rich was an ascetic far removed from worldly ambitions but on his accession in 1234 he succeeded for a moment by the threat of excommunication in freeing the Court of the Poitevin favourites. The Archbishop Boniface, although a "Savoyard", prevented the judge Robert Passelew from obtaining a bishopric on the grounds of his ignorance of theology. Many bishops and abbots took a direct part in the revolution: besides the archbishop, the bishops of London, Worcester, and Salisbury appear in the commission of 1258. We have already seen that the revolutionary Parliament of 1265 included many more prelates than barons. After his victory, Henry III proceeded against eight bishops for their actions

[1] **CDLII**, 183 ff.

and abbots of important monasteries like Bury St. Edmunds had to pay heavy fines.[1]

To gain some idea of the attitude of the higher clergy we must not rely on the diatribes of certain monastic chroniclers such as the annalist of Margan who regards the claims of the monarchy as "diabolical"[2] or Matthew de Paris whose coarse attacks on the Roman Curia anticipate the antipapist declarations of the sixteenth century. This hatred of the king or Pope was not general. If we refer to the writings of Stephen Langton or Robert Grossetete, Bishop of Lincoln,[3] or to the actual facts we shall understand that the English prelates submitted to papal decisions when they thought them just and well-considered and did not haggle over the price of their support when they believed him to be in danger. Similarly they felt they must help the king when the community was imperilled. But they claimed to judge each case, to remain free to grant or to refuse, and to have securities. The king should have good councillors and take their advice and observe the Great Charter, while those who gave him their money would demand the enjoyment of the liberties it included. Similarly the Pope had no right to demand subsidies from the clergy to make war on Frederick II who had not been condemned for heresies by judgment of the Church. Finally, canonical elections and the prerogatives of patrons of the churches must be upheld. On this point Robert Grossetete set an example of unshakeable firmness and carried the polemic on the higher plane of the interests of religion. In 1250 he went to Lyons and read, before the Pope and cardinals, a deed which has remained famous. He describes in it the evils caused by the insatiable greed of the Curia; he showed how spiritual life was affected by the grant of benefices to men who did not or could not fulfil their duties. He says boldly:—

> The source of all the evil is the Roman Church because by its dispensations, provisions, and collations it appoints in full daylight men like those I have described who are not shepherds of men but their destroyers. It abandons to the jaws of death thousands of souls when, for each one of them, the son of God was willing to be condemned to the most shameful of deaths. . . . The pastoral duties do not consist in merely administering the sacraments, repeating

---

[1] **CCCV**; **DCXVIII**, chap. xii; **CCCLXXI**, 293–7, 303–6.
[2] "Annales de Margan" in *Annales Monastici*, ed. Luard, i, 8.
[3] See **DXLV**, chap. iv–vi; **DCXXIV**, *passim*.

the canonical hours, and celebrating masses—although even these tasks are rarely carried out by mercenaries—but in teaching the living truth, in condemning and, if necessary, punishing vice and these are things which mercenaries do not often dare to deal with. They include also feeding the hungry, giving drink to the thirsty, clothing the naked, welcoming travellers, visiting the sick and the prisoners especially those who live in the parish and have rights in the endowment of the Church. These duties cannot be fulfilled by deputies or hirelings who receive of the church only the bare necessities of life. . . . If a zealous bishop takes the care of souls away from those who are not fit to hold it he has to suffer intolerable vexations particularly if those whom he has set aside have access to men who occupy state offices or dignities.[1]

These grievances of Robert Grossetete are the more interesting because they supply a clue to the fundamental preoccupations of Simon de Montfort. In fact, the Bishop of Lincoln together with Adam de Marsh and other Franciscans of the same circle was, for long years, the intimate friend of Simon.[2] He died before the revolution but he had had time to shape Simon's mind. The fearless bishop who, when braving excommunication by refusing a prebend to a nephew of Innocent IV, wrote to the Pope's representative " As an obedient son, I disobey, I oppose the demand and I revolt "[3] would not agree that the despotism of either king or Pope was lawful. He had written for the Count of Leicester a book on *The Principles of Monarchy and Tyranny*. Undoubtedly, Simon found in this book, which is lost to-day, the rules of his political thought. Grossetete had no precise ideas, however, on better methods of civil government; his ideal was beyond this world. The important thing for him was that the Church should be free so that it could attend to the salvation of souls. The Bishop of Lincoln and the Franciscans who surrounded Simon de Montfort offered him as the goal of his activity " the work of salvation which must be carried out in the kingdom of England ".[4] Simon was not a great statesman; even the idea of the councils organized in 1258 does not appear to have belonged to him but he was an apostle. He sought to destroy the monarchical despotism that the Plantegenets had created and he accepted as his task a job which was bound up with

---

[1] DCXXIV, 285–8.
[2] For all that follows : CLXVII, 39–48 ; DCXXIV, 269–275 and *passim*.
[3] Letter 128 in CXIV, 436–7.
[4] Letter of Adam de Marsh, n. 143, in III, p. 274.

that of the ecclesiastical reformers, for the whole policy of Henry III during the last twenty years of his life was a policy of enslavement to the Holy See. Simon's contemporaries regarded him as a martyr and a saint. "We believe," said the annalist of Waverley, "that he achieved a glorious martyrdom for the peace of the world, the restoration of the kingdom, and our mother, the Church." [1]

It is vain therefore to inquire into whether the Count of Leicester was "the founder of the House of Commons". Never for a moment did he imagine what the English Parliament might become some centuries later. When he called together the meeting of 1265 he summoned those who had shown sympathy for his efforts, laymen or clergy. If the majority of the barons had not abandoned his cause he would not have sought any other support. The fact that, according to certain precedents, he summoned four knights from each shire and that he had the idea of inviting the burgesses as well, surely completes our picture of him and finally distinguishes him from the self-centred and fickle baronage which had so quickly become frightened of doing too much. Primarily, however, it is a matter of general interest rather than purely biographical for it shows that the social condition of England invited Simon to take this step, it reveals the extent of the revolutionary feeling. Simon de Montfort had only to discover and utilize a very far-reaching movement which was seeking a leader.

We know very little of the history of the minor English nobility and the history of the towns has not received very much attention. Nevertheless we can say that the thirteenth century was a period of important changes for the class of knights and "bachelors". The feudal bonds between the knights and the great barons had been weakened at the same time as the administration of the monarchy was being perfected and the sphere of royal justice extended. This growth of the royal power did not, in any way, harm the public work of the lesser nobility; on the contrary,[2] the juries or commissions of knights—to prepare the business of justice, to assist the administration, to hold inquests, to carry information to the Curia Regis, to present the complaints of the county to the sheriff, to fix and collect extraordinary taxation

[1] **VII**, 365; **DXC**, 283-384.   [2] **CD**, 177 ff.

ARISTOCRATIC REACTION IN ENGLAND

—had never been more numerous.[1] This strengthening of the powers of the shire and hundred courts and of the local commissions is the most important feature which distinguishes English society in the Middle Ages. The burgesses of the towns played and were, for a long time, to play a less important part than the minor nobility of the countryside in public life. The city of London alone was comparable to the great towns of the Continent. It had a mayor and elected aldermen, it nominated its own sheriff and levied its taxes itself. It played a turbulent and not unimportant part in political movements.[2] The other towns were semi-agricultural boroughs. However, the thirteenth century was a period of economic prosperity and political progress for them. Most of them belonged to the royal demesne; John had given or sold more than seventy municipal charters and in Henry III's reign a number of towns gained the confirmation or grant of the right to freedom from the financial control of the sheriff and to elect their reeve (bailiff) and mayor. Moreover, just as on the Continent, the development of the towns produced violent social conflicts.[3]

In short, during the first half of the thirteenth century there had been a political advance of the middle classes but the more or less conscious aspirations for independence had not had any general consequences. Their interests were opposed to those of the upper nobility and they had made no great effort to help them defend feudal custom against the monarchy. Evidently they feared seigniorial tyranny as much as or more than royal.[4] They had not made any considerable demands in 1215 and their place in Magna Carta is not one of great importance. The barons, however, needed their support and had been obliged to respect the liberties they demanded. With the permanent exception of London, they had done little during the crisis and their inertia had enabled John to avoid complete defeat. Finally, during the revolution of 1258–1267, they had shown their bitterness against the barons even more than against the king.

---

[1] See the inquest mandates, the writs for the levy of subsidies, the summons of knights, etc., edited in **CXXXIII**, 303, 348, 351–366.
[2] **DCLXXV**, chap. v–x.
[3] **XII**, intro., p. liv ff. See also p. 154 above.
[4] On the claims of certain barons to sovereign jurisdiction, see **CCCLXX**, 23 ff.

There is a very curious page in the *Annals of Burton* which describes for us the demonstration of 13th October, 1259, which forced the barons to publish the provisions of Westminster.

> The community of bachelors[1] of England pointed out to the Lord Edward, the king's son, and the other sworn members of the Council at Oxford that the lord king had completely carried out all that the barons had imposed on him and that the barons themselves had done none of the things they promised for the public good, except what was to their personal advantage and the king's loss.[2]

But the alliance which Simon initiated with the middle class came to nothing. The " bachelors " and bigger burgesses were quickly outstripped by more popular elements and the revolution which had begun as an aristocratic reform finished not by the accession to political power of the middle classes organized round a Protector but by risings and brigandage among the peasantry and smaller artisans frequently led by starving priests and nomadic preachers.[3]

The different social classes, separated by deep divisions, had not known how to build a united front against the monarchy. The fight had been started without sufficient political preparation. The Great Charter was to restore many customs and guarantees which the Plantegenets had destroyed. In its 1225 edition it remained the evidence of a successful reaction against the royal despotism. It contained nothing but practical provisions saturated with the spirit of Feudalism and was accompanied by no declaration of rights. Its acceptance, nevertheless, by all the parties in England showed that, according to the distinctions dear to English theologians, there was no need for the king to be a tyrant. Above all it remained a storehouse of public rights, an arsenal in which the opposition could find arms, in which, at a later date, it would be possible to discover principles of which John Lackland's contemporaries had never thought. The false interpretations of some of these articles were not without their influence on the development of English liberties. The Great Charter has retained a sentimental

---

[1] See p. 346 above for the meaning of the word bachelor. Here the word community means simply the whole body.
[2] V, 471.
[3] CCCLXXI, part ii, chap. iii.

ARISTOCRATIC REACTION IN ENGLAND

force which, even to-day, is not yet extinct.[1] The Provisions of Oxford and Westminster renewed and completed part of the prescriptions of the Great Charter; these dispositions maintaining feudal franchises, and the guarantees against certain administrative abuses and improving procedure were incorporated in a statute which the king granted in 1267, the Statute of Marlborough.

No permanent system had been created, however, to control the monarchy and prevent abuses. Parliament remained little more than the old feudal assembly which the king summoned at will, inviting whomever he pleased. The attempt at an aristocratic council had been a complete failure. The great struggles of the fourteenth century were still to be waged between monarchy and nobility on this ill-chosen battle ground. Above all, the claims of the Holy See which affected the political and moral life of the country so closely had not been broken; religious conflicts were to grow even more bitter until the day when the king himself became Pope in England and thus consolidated his despotism.

[1] See my study in **DCXXVII**, i, 879 ff. Cf. **CCCLXXV**; **DXXXI**, 33 ff.; **DXXXII**, i, 171-2; **CCCLXXXI**, 120 ff.; **DXLV**, 122; **CDLVII**, p. xx.
[2] **CXXXI**, i, 19-25; **DCXXVII**, ii, 115; **CCCLXXI**, 142-3.

CONCLUSION

THE history of the monarchy in France under the first nine Capetians has been presented in this volume on the same scale as the history of the English monarchy. The reader has undoubtedly found a justification for this in the facts recorded. Throughout this period the lives of the two countries were bound up closely together. From the Conquest of 1066 the kings of England were of Norman and Angevin origin, they spoke French and almost all of them passed some part of their reign in France. Henry II and his sons ruled an empire that stretched from Scotland to the Pyrenees. The great problem for the kings of France had been how to resist their advance. Finally, it is easy to see legislative and administrative forms being borrowed from the opposite sides of the Channel. We have, no doubt, thrown a little more light on the history of the two peoples by the order we have adopted.

If we compare the evolution of the two monarchies, the differences strike us. Neither the point of departure nor the ground covered were the same but the atmosphere in which they developed was the same and hence the striking resemblances.

A continual effort of the imagination is necessary to re-create this atmosphere. In the present age the movements of humanity are dominated by the triumph of the scientific spirit, the development of production and demand, the conflict between democracy and capitalism, and the pressure of nationalist ambitions. How is it possible easily to appreciate the extent to which France and England from the tenth to the thirteenth century were completely saturated with the spirit of religion and Feudalism? It was on this moral plane, so different from our own, that the monarchy was reborn, developed, and fought its struggles. It found there both support and opposition. The Church which exalted the Crown sought to make it serve its own ends. The feudal spirit carried within itself the germ of anarchistic violence. The kings, however, exploited to the full the alliance they had established with the Church and, at the same time, they found it to their advantage to possess, by feudal custom, defined rights, to have loyal followers bound by oath, and they drew advantages of increasing value from their legal position as overlords. The political and administrative Curia, the finances, the army, interference in seigniorial justice and general legislation—these institutions and practices were rooted in the feudal law just as the consecration granted by the Church was the source of the special prestige which the king enjoyed. There was no question, however, of abusing his growing power. Church or nobility would never tolerate a " tyrant ". Both considered that the king was bound by contracts— the obligations of the lord to his man and the oath taken at his consecration. The king was the guardian of custom and had to uphold it at least to the extent that it could be modified only after the deliberation of his court. He had to win respect for the divine law and take care of the Church. He had to give true justice. If his obligations as suzerain were not fulfilled, conflict would result.

In fact there had been conflict in England. The participation of the English Church in the struggle against the king had given it a somewhat elevated character, a constitutional character we would say if it was not for fear of creating false ideas. In France the alliance of Crown and Church was not broken. The progress of the royal power had caused violent uprisings but they were incoherent and had no important results.

The stages are worthy of a short review. On the eve of the Norman Conquest, England was only just emerging from its isolation. A Celtic country which had never been thoroughly Romanized, it had received during the intervening centuries Anglo-Saxon and Scandinavian contributions which had become engrafted. There were strong local institutions— hundred, wapentake, shire, sheriff—the traces of which exist even to-day and which remained important throughout the Middle Ages. The Anglo-Saxon monarchy, however, had become incapable of defending itself and its fate reminds us of that of the Carolingians. The system of " commendation " had done nothing but ruin its authority. Its weakness, the energy and ability of William the Conqueror, and the political spirit and bold genius of the Norman people explain the revolution of 1066—one of the most fundamental changes that any country has ever undergone. William based his power on his alliance with the Church and the system of military fiefs and he governed with the help of certain Anglo-Saxon and Norman institutions which he had amalgamated in his strong hand. It had been necessary for him to reward the adventurers who had joined his expedition, to carry through an immense transfer of land, and condemn a section of the native population to a condition of misery. The new nobility built up from his companions was violent and was frequently to show resistance but this was of no importance for he had founded the State. The reign of the brutal William Rufus did not last long enough to endanger his work. In the following century, two great men, Henry Beauclerc and Henry II, with the service of a remarkable body of lawyers and financiers completed it. The strongest and wisest government in Europe was founded. It revived Carolingian practices and, at the same time, in the precision of its machinery, and the harshness of its style and manners it reminds us of the Roman or, possibly, even the contemporary state. The Angevin Empire, built up on marriages, in the time of Richard Cœur de Lion threatened even the existence of the Capetian monarchy.

The premature death of Richard and the incipient madness of John Lackland postponed, for more than a century, the threat of an absorption of France by the English monarchy. John was foolish enough to fall out with the Church and the nobility at the same time. He saved his dynasty by becoming reconciled to the Pope.

Innocent III who also "thought in feudal terms" and conceived the political supremacy of Saint Peter's successor as a suzerainty, made England a fief of the Holy See. This entry of the Papacy was not a happy omen for peace in England. It did not prevent the union of the English church and the nobility against the tyranny nor the active feudal reaction expressed in the Great Charter and its confirmations. During the reign of Henry III, who remained, throughout his life, a devoted son of the Holy See, the exorbitant demands of the Roman Curia were one of the principal causes of the long trouble which ended in civil war and the dictatorship of

CONCLUSION

Simon de Montfort. In spite of the gravity of this tragic crisis, the English monarchy was still standing at the end of the period we have been studying and the institutions with which it had been endowed by the great kings of the eleventh and twelfth centuries were so stable and so thoroughly based on the old local customs of *self government* that a very few years were sufficient for Edward I to restore it to full strength.

Serious doubts, however, still survived. The Great Charter was supposed to check the encroachments of the monarchy; its maintenance in full in the form in which it had been confirmed in 1225 was irreconcilable with the policy followed by the king and his officials. On the other hand, the royal finances, the army, decisions for peace or war, even the exercise of justice in important cases were dependent on the co-operation of his loyal subjects : there was no regulation of their participation, however. The word parlement was scarcely born and the institution was still in infancy. We have had to speak of it on very few occasions and then chiefly to warn the reader against anticipating later developments. The barons of Henry III did nothing to organize the representation of the nation. Their object was to establish a governing council to remedy the incapacity of the reigning prince. Finally, even the principle of the succession to the throne was not fixed. The last time it had been discussed, on the death of Richard Cœur de Lion, the English Church had supported the proclamation of the principle of election. The practice of association on the throne which Henry II had tried had proved itself dangerous in practice and it had been abandoned. On John's death, the question of a regency was raised. It had been solved at best by an excellent expedient but no regulation had been made for future application. For all these reasons to which we must add the misfortune of incompetent and disreputable kings, the rapid decline of the English Church in the fourteenth century, and the extreme violence of a passionate nation, we can understand that the rebellions against John Lackland and Henry III did nothing except inaugurate a long era of tragedy for the monarchy.

The history of the royal power in France from 987 to 1270 is less stormy. Its progress began late and in an obscure and hesitating manner. The only time when the pace was at all forced was during the reigns of Philip Augustus and Louis VIII. From 987, the Capetian dynasty had finally replaced the Carolingians and they retained the throne thanks to the fertility of the queens and the custom of association on the throne which made the principle of election a vain formality; it was a doubtful expedient, however, and Philip Augustus was warned by the revolt of Henry the Younger in England and abolished it. Thus hereditary succession in the direct line on the basis of primogeniture became the established custom. The question of a regency in the case of the minority and absence of the king was settled by the king himself before his death or departure. It might lead to trouble and disturbances but it would not involve revolution. The individuality of the kingdom remained unassailed: thanks to favourable circumstances, even the creation of appanages for the younger princes had no fatal results. In short, the continuity of the royal power and the unity of the monarchy were assured. But if we cease to take this legal viewpoint, we may find the reality very different.

The first Capetians were shadowy figures like the majority of their Robertian ancestors and the Carolingians of the tenth century. Monarchical institutions had given way. There was not, as in England, a local framework of assemblies like the shire and hundred courts which could, one day, provide an able king with the means of action. Everything was in dissolution. The seigniorial regime was the only social bond. France was dismembered and the regional spirit became so strong that it was to survive even the seigniorial regime. For the moment, the monarchy continued to languish with inadequate resources and obsolete pretensions. Without the support of the Church, it seemed as if it might become extinct and scarcely anyone notice it. The Church assigned to Robert the Pious the gift of curing the sick; it preserved memories of the glory of the Carolingians, of a France united under the sceptre of a mighty emperor but, in the period when the *Chanson de Roland* was written, the monarchy was becoming less and less effective, was shrivelling and falling to sleep. The great lords even gave up the habit of coming to the king's Court.

A new era began only with Louis VI. Threatened even within his narrow demesne by bandit nobles, he passed his time in fighting them. At this period they talk of a *Rex Francorum* in Gaul. A striking testimony, his vassals formed up under the banner of St. Denis to stop the Emperor Henry V on the frontier. After him, the undistinguished Louis VII found no suitable occasion to annex Aquitaine permanently to the demesne, but once the impetus was given advance did not completely stop. The Curia began to organize itself, to judge important cases, and with Suger that line of great servants of the Capetian monarchy appears in full view which, with the aid of some of the kings, achieved all that was done.

Finally, the King of France goes beyond his demesne. Louis appeared in Languedoc and even went on crusade. But beside Henry II, who reigned at Rouen, Nantes, Poitiers, Bordeaux, and Bayonne, or even beside the rich count of Flanders, Louis VII is yet only an insignificant individual and the general ordinances which he ventures to publish remain platonic demonstrations of good will.

Philip Augustus, Louis VIII, Blanche of Castille, and Saint Louis lifted the monarchy out of this rut. At that period she had an opportunity, which was not to recur, to be represented, for almost a century, by kings and a regent who differed widely in their temperament but were all gifted and courageous and had devoted their lives to the realization of dreams of glory or practical godliness. From them really dates the history of the French monarchy. The historical importance of a Saint Louis is symbolized in the fertility of his marriage with Margaret of Provence: all the kings of France until the nineteenth century were descendants of his sons.

These four princes found their support in the Church, in a loyal and well rewarded lesser nobility, and in a bourgeoisie which, behind the city walls, had organized the only self-government existing in France. Around the king developed and worked a whole new class of officials, lay and clerical, comparable to those who had established the greatness of the Norman and Angevin monarchy in the twelfth century. The administrative, financial, and legal advances were made parallel with the annexations to the demesne; the creation of bailiffs, the appearance in the heart of the Curia of a Parlement of Paris which very quickly fixed and emphasized the old traditions and made itself the determined defender of the Crown were events as important as the collapse of the Angevin Empire and the great Albigensian nobility. These great changes were not achieved without shocks. From the coalition of 1214 to the coalition of 1241-2 the monarchy had faced serious threats; as in England, but without the support of the Churchmen and without any other programme than a division of the spoils, the autocracy had tried to make it retreat and had failed. They could produce no sound justification and they had not thought of drawing up a Great Charter. Their rights were not openly violated as in England. To secure themselves financial and military resources as much as to carry through the conquest and seizure of some part of John Lackland's inheritance or to subject Flanders, Philip Augustus and his successors based their position primarily on feudal custom.

How could the French monarchy, thus limited by respect for custom, continue its advance ? The infiltration of Roman Law, which was already being taught at the University of Paris, was to change the conservative spirit of the Curia. Already, however, before the invasion of the southern lawyers, Saint Louis without any political design and in complete innocence of heart had provided the monarchy with a source of strength which neither his predecessors nor the powerful kings of England had been able to tap. By the interpretation he had given to his royal mission, for which he had won acceptance, he had opened, to his dynasty, an indefinite career. No reign was more decisive than this. The principle that the king is in direct communication with God, can dispense with council when he feels himself inspired, can make " provisions for the common good ", and must be obeyed as a mandatory of God, the principle, in a word, of monarchy by divine right, was clearly enunciated in France by Saint Louis who secured its acceptance by his scruples and virtues. His dynasty was to apply it and abuse it in application. He used it, himself, in an attempt to establish order and justice on earth and to lead his subjects towards heaven. He had been brought up by priests and a very pious mother and his morals were those of a Christian not those of a statesman which Philip Augustus and his successors had practised. His godliness, his pity for Christian sufferings, his righteousness, and his readiness to rectify wrongs gave the Capetian monarchy within France and beyond a prestige which it never lost. When he died on African soil, he was praised throughout Christendom. A service for Saint Louis composed in the fourteenth century summarizes all that the Church, which had already canonized him, said of him and of what he had done for the Church and for France :—

> Happy the realm whose king is farsighted, peaceful, pious, and modest and fearless in misfortune. Such was Saint Louis. . . . King, you have made France live in peace and you have based your throne on justice. . . . By this king the Church had been exalted and France is now honoured.[1]

It is natural that the clergy should have spread the fame of this saint who was the perfect fruit of ecclesiastical education. Here is evidence from a source other than the Church and of greater importance in the historian's eyes: from the north of the kingdom to the south, at the news of his death, the bards and the troubadours expressed a sorrow which was the feeling of the lay populace, even national in extent, overriding the bounds of the loyalty of vassals, for Louis was not mourned merely by his men whose loyal lord he had been but by every Frenchman even the most humble. The author of the *Regrès du roy Loeys* [2] writes " The good King Loeys ! You have held the land—to the profit of barons and lesser men alike. ...To whom can poor folk appeal in future—when the good king is dead, who can love them as well ? " The hope of finding a protector in the king was not, however, to perish. The people became patient as though they were awaiting the reincarnation of Saint Louis.

The religion of the monarchy was created. To make it omnipotent was the task of the king's people, lawyers, financiers, bailiffs, and office holders great and small alike.

---

[1] The complete text should be read ; it has been published by L. Delisle : *Les heures de Blanche de France, Duchesse de Orleans*, in B.E.C., 1905, p. 489 ff.

[2] De Villeneuve-Trans, *Hist. de Saint Louis*, vol. iii, 1839, illustrative examples, p. 673 ff.

LIST OF REFERENCES

The list that follows is simply a concordance between the numbers we have used and the documents and works that we have considered it necessary to cite. It cannot pretend to be a bibliography. Such a bibliography can be found, for England, in the second edition of *Sources and Literature of English History to about 1485*, by Charles Gross. There is, for France, no equivalent to this repertory which is an excellent work although it stops about 1910. The subject we have been treating has stimulated a number of works. For the early Capetians, to the time of Philip Augustus exclusive, the essential work has been done. The description of monarchical institutions to the time of Philip Augustus could be fairly rapidly achieved by the publication of his deeds. On the other hand, the reign of Saint Louis will, for a long time, offer a profitable field for study. As for the history of the royal power in England during the twelfth and thirteenth centuries, it is far from exhausted because of the admirable preservation of English archives. A general direction will be found in the articles which M. Halphen and M. Petit-Dutaillis have published in the *R.S.H.* (*La France sous les premiers Capetiens* by L. Halphen, in vol. xiv, 1907; *Histoire Politique de l'Angleterre au Moyen Age*, vols. viii–ix, 1904); for recent publications, reference can be made to the bulletin of the *Revue Historique* and the very valuable bibliographies of the *Cambridge Medieval History*.

LIST OF ABBREVIATIONS USED

I. NATIONAL COLLECTIONS

Bibliothèque de l'École des Hautes-Études	B.E.H.E.
Bibliothèque de l'Histoire de Paris	B.H.P.
Classiques français du moyen âge, published under the direction of MARIO ROQUES	C.F.M.A.
Chartes et diplômes, published by l'Académie des Inscriptions	Ch.et D.
Classiques de l'Histoire de France au Moyen âge, published under the direction of L. HALPHEN	Cl.H.F.
Collection de textes pour servir à l'étude et à l'enseignement de l'Histoire	C.T.E.H.
Collection des documents inédits de l'Histoire de France	D.I.
Historiens de France	H.F.
Harvard Historical Studies	H.H.S.
Historische Studien veröffentlicht von E. EBERING	H.S.E.
Collection des Inventaires et Documents	I.D.
Jahrbucher der deutschen Geschichte	J.D.G.
Monumenta Germaniae	M.G.
Migne, Patrologie latine	M.P.L.

REFERENCES

Oxford Studies in Social and Legal History	O.S.
Rerum britannicarum Scriptores	R.S.
Publications de la Société de l'Histoire de France	S.H.F.
Yale historical publications	Y.H.P.

II. Reviews, Publications of Academies and Learned Societies

American Historical Review	A.H.R.
Académie des Inscriptions et Belles-Lettres. (C.R. = Comptes rendus)	A.I.
Annales du Midi	A.M.
Académie des Sciences Morales et Politiques	A.S.M.
Bulletin de la Commission royale d'Histoire de Belgique	B.C.H.B.
Bibliothèque de l'École des Chartes	B.E.C.
Bulletin historique et philologique du Comité des travaux historiques	B.H.P.
English Historical Review	E.H.R.
History (Revue anglaise)	Hi.
Moyen Âge	M.A.
Nouvelle Revue historique de Droit (ou : Revue hist. de Droit)	N.R.H.D.
Proceedings of the British Academy	P.B.A.
Romania	R.
Revue belge de Philologie et d'Histoire	R.B.P.
Revue des Études Juives	R.E.J.
Revue historique	R.H.
Revue des Questions historiques	R.Q.H.
Revue de Synthèse historique	R.S.H.
Speculum (Medieval Academy of America, Harvard University)	S.
Société des Antiquaires de France	S.A.F.
Société des Antiquaires de Normandie	S.A.N.
Société des Antiquaires de la Picardie	S.A.P.
Société d'Histoire du Droit	S.H.D.
Société de l'Histoire de Normandie	S.H.N.
Société de l'Histoire de Paris	S.H.P.
Transactions of the Royal Historical Society	T.R.H.S.
Zeitschrift für Kirchengeschichte	Z.K.

III. Collected Studies and Volumes of Collective Works

Cambridge Medieval History	C.M.H.
Dictionnaire de Theologie Catholique, published by Vacant, Mangenot et Amann, Paris, 1899, ff.	D.Th.C.
Magna Carta Commemoration Essays, 1917 (Published by the Royal Historical Society)	M.C.C.E.
Mélanges d'Histoire offerts à M. Charles Bémont, 1913	Mél.B.
Mélanges Fitting, 1907	Mél.F.
Mélanges d'Histoire offerts à M. Ferdinand Lot, Paris, 1925	Mél.F.L.
Études d'histoire du Moyen âge dédiées a Gabriel Monod, Paris, 1896	Mél.G.M.
Haskins Anniversary Essays, Boston, 1929	Mél.H.

REFERENCES

Mélanges d'Histoire offerts à Henri Pirenne, Bruxelles, 1926, 2 vol.	Mél.P.
Essays presented to R. L. Poole, 1927	Mél.Poole
Mélanges offerts à M. Gustave Schlumberger, Paris, 1924, 2 vol.	Mél.Schl.
Essays in Medieval History presented to Th. F. Tout, Manchester, 1925	Mél.Tout
National Biography	N.B.
Victoria History of the counties of England, Westminster, 1900, ff.	V.H.

SOURCES QUOTED

ABBON DE FLEURY, *Collectio Canonum*, M.P.L., cxxxix, 1853	I
Actes du Parlement de Paris, publ. by BOUTARIC, Paris, 1863–7, 2 vol. (I.D.)	II
ADAM DE MARSH, *Adae de Marisco Epistolae*, ed. J. S. BREWER, in vol. ii of *Monumenta Franciscana*, London, 1858 (R.S., No. 4)	III
Alexandre III, Lettres, H.F., xv	IV
Annales de Burton, dans *Annales Monastici*, éd. LUARD, I., Londres, 1864 (R.S., No. 36)	V
Annales de Dunstaple, ibid., iii, 1866	VI
Annales de Waverley, ibid., ii, 1865	VII
Annales de Worcester (*Annales de Wigornia*), ibid., iv, 1869	VIII
Archives anciennes de la ville de Saint-Quentin, publ. by EMMANUEL LEMAIRE, 1888, t. i	IX
Arrêt inédit de la Cour du Roi (1228), publ. by G. RITTER, M.A., xxiv, 1911	X
BALLARD (AD.), *British Borough Charters, 1042–1216*, Cambridge, 1913	XI
—— and TAIT (J.), *British Borough Charters, 1216–1307*, Cambridge, 1923	XII
BARNWELL (CHANOINE DE), Chronique, ed. W. STUBBS, in t. ii of *Memoriale fratris Walteri de Coventria*, Londres, 1873, (R.S., No. 58)	XIII
BATESON (MARY), *A London Municipal Collection of the reign of John*, E.H.R., 1902	XIV
—— *Records of the Borough of Leicester* (1103–1327), Londres, 1899	XV
BEAUMANOIR (PHILIPPE DE), *Coutumes de Beauvaisis*, ed. AM. SALMON, Paris, 1899–1900, 2 vol. (C.T.E.H.)	XVI
BÉMONT (CHARLES), *Chartes des libertés anglaises* (1100–1305), Paris, 1892 (C.T.E.H.)	XVII
BENOIT DE PETERBOROUGH, *Gesta regis Henrici, Secundi*, ed. W. STUBBS, London, 1867, 2 vol. (R.S., No. 49)	XVIII
BERNARD GUI, *Manuel de l'Inquisiteur*, ed. G. MOLLAT, Paris, 1926, t. i (Cl.H.F.)	XIX
BRACTON, *De legibus et consuetudinibus Angliae libri quinque*, ed. G. E. WOODBIN, Yale University Press, vol. ii, 1922	XX
Chanson de Roland, publ. and trans. by J. BEDIER, Paris, 1922, 3ᵉ éd.	XXI

Chronica de Mailros, ed. J. Stevenson, Edinburgh, 1835 (Ballantyne Club) . . . . **XXII**

Chronicon Turonense magnum, ed. André Salmon, in Recueil des Chroniques de Touraine, Paris, 1854 (Public. de la Soc. Archéol., de Touraine) . . **XXIII**

Chronique du Bec (E chronico monasterii Beccensis), H.F., xxiii . . . . **XXIV**

Chronique du chanoine de Tours (Ex chronica Turonensi auctore anonymo S. Martini Turonensis canonico), H.F., xviii . . . . **XXV**

Conseils sur les devoirs des rois adressés à saint Louis par Guibert de Tournai, publ. by Kervyn de Lettenhove (Bull. Acad. Royale de Belgique, xx, 1re partie, 1853) . . . . . **XXVI**

Correspondance administrative d'Alphonse de Poitiers, publ. by Aug. Molinier, Paris, 1894–1900, 2 vol. (D.I.) . . . . **XXVII**

Coutumiers de Normandie, publ. by E. J. Tardif, Rouen et Paris, 1881–1903, 2 tomes en 3 vol. (S.H.N.) . . . . **XXVIII**

Débat d'Izarn et de Sicart de Figueiras, publ. by Paul Meyer (Ann. Bull. S.H.F., 1879) . . **XXIX**

Delisle (Leopold), *Cartulaire normand de Philippe Auguste, Louis VIII, saint Louis et Philippe le Hardi*, Caen, 1852 (S.A.N., Memoires, xvi, ou 2e série, vi) . . . . **XXX**

—— *Essai de restitution d'un volume des Olim*, in Actes du Parlement de Paris, i, 1863 . . . **XXXI**

—— *Catalogue des Actes de Philippe Auguste*, Paris, 1856 . . . . **XXXII**

De Necessariis observantiis Scaccarii Dialogus, ed. A. Hughes, C. G. Crump, et C. Johnson, Oxford, 1902 . . . . **XXXIII**

Dialogue entre Philippe Auguste et Pierre le Chantre (publ. by L. de Raynal), B.E.C., ii, 1840–1. . **XXXIV**

Dillay (Madeleine), *Les chartes de franchise du Poitou*, Caen, 1927 (S.H.D.) . . . **XXXV**

Documents inédits relatifs aux relations du Hainaut et de la France de 1280 à 1297, publ. by Ét. Delcambre, B.C.H.B., xcii, 1928 . . . **XXXVI**

Documents pour servir à l'histoire de l'Inquisition dans le Languedoc, publ. by C. Douais, Paris, 1900, 2 vol. (S.H.F.) . . . . . . **XXXVII**

Enquêtes administratives du règne de saint Louis, publ. by L. Delisle, H.F., xxiv, 1904 . . **XXXVIII**

Enseignements de saint Louis à son fils, texte primitif, publ. by H. Delaborde, B.E.C., 1912. . . **XXXIX**

Établissements de saint Louis, ed. Paul Viollet, t. i, 1881 (S.H.F.) . . . . . . **XL**

Étienne Boileau, *Le livre des métiers*, ed. Lespinasse et Bonnardot, Paris, 1880 . . . **XLI**

Fragment de l'histoire de Philippe Auguste, roy de France, 1214–16, publ. by Ch. Petit-Dutaillis, B.E.C., 1926 . . . . **XLII**

REFERENCES

Fragment inédit de la Vie de Louis VII, prepared by Suger, éd. Jules Lair, B.E.C., 1873 . . . **XLIII**
Fulbert de Chartres, *Lettres*, H.F., x . . . **XLIV**
Galbert de Bruges, *Histoire du meurtre de Charles le Bon, comte de Flandre*, éd. H. Pirenne, Paris, 1891 (C.T.E.H.) . . . . . **XLV**
Geoffroi de Beaulieu, *Vita Sancti Ludovici*, H.F., xx . . . . **XLVI**
Gervais de Cantorbery, *Chronique* in *Opera*, ed. Stubbs, t. i, London, 1879 (R.S., No. 73) . . **XLVII**
—— *Gesta regum*, ibid., ii . . . **XLVIII**
Giraud de Cambrie, *De principis instructione liber*, ed. G. F. Warner, dans *Giraldi Cambrensis opera*, viii, London, 1891 (R.S., No. 21) . . . **XLIX**
Giry (Arthur), *Documents sur les relations de la Royauté avec les villes en France de 1180 à 1314*, Paris, 1885 (C.T.E.H.) . . . . . . **L**
Gislebert de Mons, *Chronique*, éd. Léon Vanderkindere, Brussels, 1904 (Commiss. roy. d'hist., textes) . . . . **LI**
Gesta quae Ludovicus IX cepit (1254–69), H.F. xxi . **LII**
Grandes chroniques de France, publ. by Jules Viard, i, 1920 (S.H.F.) . . . . . . **LIII**
Guillaume de Malmesbury, *Historia novella*, in *Œuvres*, ed. Stubbs, ii, London, 1889 (R.S., No. 90) **LIV**
Guillaume de Newburgh, *Historia rerum anglicarum* in *Chronicles of the Reigns of Stephen*, etc., ed. R. Howlett, London, 1884–5, 2 vol. (R.S. No. 82) **LV**
Guillaume de Saint-Pathus, confesseur de la reine Marguerite, *Vie de saint Louis*, ed. H. F. Delaborde, Paris, 1899 (C.T.E.H.) . . . **LVI**
Guillaume le Breton, *Philippide* in *Œuvres de Rigord et de Guillaume le Breton*, ed. H. F. Delaborde, t. ii, 1885 (S.H.F.)—*Chronique*, ibid., t. i (cf. **CXII**) **LVII**
Histoire de Guillaume le Marechal, éd. Paul Meyer, Paris, 1891–1901, 3 vol. (S.H.F.) . . . **LVIII**
Histoire des ducs de Normandie et des rois d'Angleterre, publ. by Fr. Michel, Paris, 1840 (S.H.F.) . . **LIX**
Historia Pontificalis, éd. W. Arndt, M.G., *Scriptores*, xx **LX**
Historia regum Francorum ab origine gentis ad annum 1214, H.F., xvii . . . . . **LXI**
Ive de Chartres, *Lettres*, H.F., xv . . . **LXII**
Jacob (E. F.), *The complaints of Henry III against baronial council in 1261*, E.H.R., 1926 . . **LXIII**
Jean de Marmoutier, *Historia Gaufredi, ducis Normannorum*, in *Chronique des comtes d'Anjou et des seigneurs d'Amboise*, éd. L. Halphen et R. Poupardin, Paris, 1913 (C.T.E.H.) . . . **LXIV**
Jean Sarasin, *Lettre à Nicolas Arrode*, éd. A. L. Foulet, Paris, 1924 (C.F.M.A.) . . . . **LXV**
John of Salisbury, *Joannis Saresberiensis opera omnia*, ed. J. A. Giles, Oxford, 1848, 5 vol. . . . **LXVI**
—— *Joannis Saresberiensis Policratici libri* viii, ed. C. C. J. Webb, Oxford, 1909, 2 vol. . . **LXVII**

JOINVILLE (JEAN SIRE DE), *Histoire de saint Louis*, ed. et trans. par N. DE WAILLY, Paris, 1874, 2ᵉ édit. (ed. in 4°) LXVIII
Journal des visites pastorales d'Eude Rigaud, archevêque de Rouen, 1248–1269, éd. BONNIN, Rouen, 1852 . LXIX
JUSSELIN (M.), *Documents financiers concernant les mesures prises par Alphonse de Poitiers contre les Juifs (1268–9)*, B.E.C., 1907 LXX
LANGLOIS (CH. V.), *Textes relatifs à l'histoire du Parlement de Paris*, Paris, 1888 (C.T.F.H.) . . . LXXI
Layettes du Trésor des Chartes, ed. TEULET, J. DE LABORDE, E. BERGER, H. F. DELABORDE, Paris, 1863–1909, 5 vol. (I.D.) LXXII
Lettre inédite adressée à la reine Blanche par un habitant de la Rochelle, publ. by L. DELISLE, B.E.C., 1856 . LXXIII
LIEBERMANN (F.), *Gesetze der Angelsachsen*, Halle, 1898–1916, 3 vol. LXXIV
LOISNE (COMTE DE), *Catalogue des Actes de Robert Iᵉʳ, comte d'Artois*, B.H.P., 1919 LXXV
LUCHAIRE (ACH.), *Études sur les actes de Louis VII*, Paris, 1885 LXXVI
Ludovici noni mansiones et itinera, H.F., xxi . . LXXVII
LUNT (W. E.), *The text of the Ordinance of 1184 concerning an aid for the Holy Land*, E.H.R., 1922 . LXXVIII
MAP (GAUTIER or WALTER), *De nugis curialium*, ed. M. R. JAMES, Oxford, 1914 (Anecdota Oxoniensia, Medieval Series) LXXIX
MATTHEW DE PARIS, *Chronica majora*, éd. H. R. LUARD, London, 7 vol. (R.S., No. 57) LXXX
—— *Vie d'Étienne de Langton*, dans *Ungedruckte anglonormannische Geschichtsquellen*, éd. F. LIEBERGMANN, Strasbourg, 1879 LXXXI
Monuments historiques, cartons des Rois, publ. by JULES TARDIF, Paris, 1866. (I.D.) . . . LXXXII
MORICE (DOM), *Preuves de l'Histoire de Bretagne*, 3 vol., Paris, 1742–1746 LXXXIII
NICOLAS DE BRAI, *Gesta Ludovici Octavi*, H.F., xvii . LXXXIV
Olim (Les) ou registres des arrêts rendus par la Cour du roi, publ. by BEUGNOT, Paris, 1839, t. i (D.I.) . LXXXV
ORDERIC VITAL éd. AUGUSTE LE PREVOST, t. v, Paris, 1855 (S.H.F.) LXXXVI
Ordonnances des rois de France de la troisième race, Paris, 1723–1849 LXXXVII
PARIS (PAULIN), *Le Romancero françois*, Paris, 1833 . LXXXVIII
PIERRE DAMIEN, *Liber Gomorrhianus*, M.P.L., cxlv, 1853 LXXXIX
PIERRE DE BLOIS, *Petri Blesemsis archidiaconi opera omnia*, publ. by J. A. GILES, Oxford, 1846–1847, 4 vol. XC
PIERRE DES VAUX DE CERNAY, *Historia Albigensis*, pub. by P. GUEBIN et E. LYON, Paris, 1926–1930, 2 vol. (S.H.F.) XCI
Plaintes de la comtesse de la Marche contre Thibaud de Neuvi, Sénéchal du Poitou, publ. by ANT. THOMAS, B.E.C., 1907 XCII

REFERENCES

POTTHAST, *Regesta pontificum Romanorum*, Berlin, 1874–5, 2 vol.	XCIII
PRESSUTTI (P.), *Regesta Honorii papae III*, Rome, 1888–1895, 2 vol.	XCIV
PRIMAT, *Chronique*, trans. by JEAN DU VIGNAY, H.F., t. xxiii	XCV
RADULFUS DE DICETO (RAOUL DE DISCI, or DE DISS), *Opera historica*, ed. STUBBS, London, 1876 (R.S., No. 68)	XCVI
RAOUL DE COGGESHALE, *Chronicon anglicanum*, ed. J. STEVENSON, London, 1875 (R.S., No. 66)	XCVII
RAOUL GLABER, *Histoires*, ed. MAURICE PROU, Paris, 1886 (C.T.E.H.)	XCVIII
RAYNAUD (GASTON), *Nouvelle Charte de la Pais aus Englois*, R., xiv, 1885	XCIX
Recogniciones feodorum in Aquitania. Recueil d'actes relatifs à l'administration des rois d'Angleterre en Guyenne au XIIIe siècle, éd. CH. BÉMONT, Paris, 1914 (D.I.)	C
Recueil d'anciens textes bas-latins, provençaux et français, publ. by PAUL MEYER, 1re partie, Paris, 1874	CI
Recueil de documents concernant la commune de Poitiers, publ. by E. AUDOUIN, i, 1923 (Arch. hist. du Poitou, xliv)	CII
Recueil des actes de Philippe Ier, roi de France, publ. by MAURICE PROU, Paris, 1908 (Ch.etD.)	CIII
Recueil des actes de Philippe Auguste, roi de France, publ. by H. F. DELABORDE, under the direction of ELIE BERGER, i (1179–1194), Paris, 1916 (Ch.etD.)	CIV
Recueil des actes des comtes de Pontieu (1026–1279), publ. by CLOVIS BRUNEL, Paris, 1930 (D.I.).	CV
Recueil des actes de Henri II roi d'Angleterre et duc de Normandie concernant les provinces françaises et les affaires de France, publ. by L. DELISLE et E. BERGER, Paris, 1909–1930, 3 vol. (Ch. et D.)	CVI
Recueil des jugements de l'Echiquier de Normandie au XIIIe siecle, publ. by L. DELISLE, followed by a *Memoire sur les anciennes collections de ces jugements*, Paris, 1864 (Extr. du t. xx, 2e p. des Notices et extraits des manuscrits, et du t. xxiv, 2e p. des Mem. de l'A. I)	CVII
Register Gregors VII, ed. ERICH CASPAR, M.G. Epistolae Selectae, ii, 1920–3	CVIII
Relazione (La Prima) del Cardinale Nicolo de Romanis sulla sua legatione in Inghilterra, publ. by ANGELO MERCATI, Mél. Poole.	CIX
RICHARD DE DEVIZES, " *De rebus gestis Ricardi Primi*," ed. R. HOWLETT, in *Chronicles of the reigns of Stephen, Henry II, and Richard I*, t. iii, London, 1886 (R.S., No. 82)	CX
RICHER, *Richeri Historiarum libri III*, in usum Scholarum, éd. G. WAITZ, Hanovre, 1877	CXI

388 REFERENCES

Rigord, "*Chronique*," éd. H. F. Delabordde, in *Œuvres de Rigord et de Guillaume le Breton*, t. i, Paris, 1882 (S.H.F.) CXII
Robert (Ulysse), *Catalogue d'actes relatifs aux Juifs pendant le Moyen âge*, R.E.J., iii, 1881 . . . CXIII
Robert Grosseteste, *Roberti Grosseteste episcopi quondam Lincolniensis Epistolae*, publ. by Luard, London, 1861 (R.S., No. 25) CXIV
Robert Mignon, *Inventaire d'anciens comptes royaux*, publ. by Ch. V. Langlois, Paris, 1899. (H.F., Documents financiers) CXV
Robert du Mont or de Torigni, *Chronique*, publ. by L. Delisle, Rouen, 1872–3, 2 vol. (S.H.N.) . CXVI
Robertson (J. C.), *Materials for the history of Thomas Becket*, London, 1875–1885, 7 vol. (R.S., No. 67.) CXVII
Roger de Hoveden, *Chronique*, ed. W. Stubbs, London, 1868–1871, 4 vol. (R.S., No. 51) . . CXVIII
Roger de Wendover, *Chronique*, contained in the *Chronica majora* of Matthew de Paris ; see Matthew de Paris CXIX
Romans de Garin le Loherain, éd. P. Paris, ii, 1835 . CXX
Rotuli Litterarum patentium, ed. Th. Duffus Hardy, London, 1835 CXXI
Rymer, *Foedera*, vol. i, 1st part, London, 1816 (ed. by the Record Commission) CXXII
Saint Bernard, *Lettres*, H.F., xv CXXIII
Sancti Ludovici regis Epistolae de captione et liberatione sua, in André Duchesne, *Historiae Francorum scriptores*, t. v, Paris, 1649 CXXIV
Saxon chronicles (Two of the parallel), ed. Ch. Plummer, Oxford, 1892–9, 2 vol. CXXV
Scripta de Feodis ad regem spectantibus, H.F., xxiii . CXXVI
Select pleas of the Forest, ed. G. J. Turner, London, 1901 (Selden Society) CXXVII
Sermon en vers de Robert Saincereau, H.F., xxiii . CXXVIII
Shirley (W. W.), *Royal and other historical letters illustrative of the reign of Henry III*, London, 1862–6, 2 vol. (R.S., No. 27) CXXIX
Soehnée (F.), *Catalogue des actes de Henri Ier*, Paris, 1907, (B.E.H.E., fasc. 161) CXXX
Statutes of the realm, London, 1810, vol. i (Record Commission) CXXXI
Stilting, *De Sancto Ludovico Francorum rege commentarius praevius*, Acta Sanctorum, mensis augustus, t. v CXXXII
Stubbs (W.), *Select Charters and other illustrations of English constitutional history*, 9th edit., revised by H. W. C. Davis, Oxford, 1921 CXXXIII
Suger, *Vie de Louis le Gros*, ed. Aug. Molinier, Paris, 1887 (C.T.E.H.) CXXXIV
—— *Oeuvres*, ed. Lecoy de la Marche, Paris, 1867 (S.H.F.) CXXXV
—— *Vie de Louis le Gros*, ed. and trans. by H. Waquet, Paris, 1929 (Cl.H.F.) CXXXVI

REFERENCES

THOMAS WYKES, *Chronique*, in *Annales Monastici*, ed. LUARD, vol. iv, London, 1869 (R.S., No. 36)	CXXXVII
VARIN, *Archives administratives de la ville de Reims*, Paris, 1839–1848, 3 books in 5 vol. (D.I.)	CXXXVIII
WRIGHT (TH.), *Political Songs of England*, London, 1839 (Camden Society)	CXXXIX

WORKS QUOTED

ADAMS (G. B.), *Council and Courts in Anglo-Norman England*, New Haven, 1926 (Y.H.P.)	CXL
—— *History of England from the Norman Conquest to the death of John*, London, 1905 (The Political History of England, ed. by W. HUNT and R. L. POOLE, vol. ii)	CXLI
—— *Innocent III and the Great Charter*, M.C.C.E.	CXLII
—— *London and the Commune*, E.H.R., 1904	CXLIII
—— *The Origin of the English Constitution*, New Haven, 1912 (Y.H.P.)	CXLIV
ALPHANDERY (P.), *Les idées morales chez les hétérodoxes latins au début du XIIIe siècle*, Paris, 1903 (B.E.H.E., Sect. des Sc. relig. fasc. 16)	CXLV
ANSON (W. R.), *Loi et pratique constitutionnelles de l'Angleterre*, trans. GANDILHON, Paris, 1903	CXLVI
ARBOIS DE JUBAINVILLE (H. D'), *Histoire des ducs et des comtes de Champagne*, Paris, 1859–1869, 8 vol.	CXLVII
AUBERT (F.), *Histoire du parlement de Paris*, Paris, 1894, t. i	CXLVIII
AUBERT (F.), *Nouvelles recherches sur le Parlement de Paris, période d'organisation*, N.R.H.D., xl, 1916 (1re article)	CXLIX
AUDOUIN (EDOUARD), *Essai sur l'armée royale au temps de Philippe Auguste*, Paris, 1913	CL
AULT (WARREN O.), *Private jurisdiction in England*, New Haven, 1923 (Y.H.P.)	CLI
BALDWIN (J. F.), *The King's Council in England during the Middle Ages*, Oxford, 1913	CLII
—— *Scutage and Knight Service in England*, Chicago, 1897	CLIII
BALLARD (AD.), *The cinque Ports under Henry II*, E.H.R., 1909	CLIV
——*The English Boroughs in the Reign of John*, E.H.R., 1899	CLV
——*The Law of Breteuil*, E.H.R., 1915	CLVI
BARKER (E.), *The Dominican order and convocation*, Oxford, 1913	CLVII
BATESON (MARY), *The Laws of Breteuil*, E.H.R., 1900 et 1901	CLVIII
BEAUREPAIRE (CH. DE), *La sénéchaussée de Normandie*, Précis de l'Acad. des Sc., Rouen, 1883	CLIX
BEAUTEMPS-BEAUPRÉ, *Coutumes et institutions de l'Anjou et du Maine*, 1re partie, ii, Paris, 1878	CLX
BEDDOE (JOHN), *The races of Britain*, Bristol, 1885	CLXI

BÉDIER (JOSEPH), *Les légendes épiques, recherches sur la formation des chansons de geste*, Paris, 1908–1912, 4 vol. CLXII
BÉMONT (CH.) *La Bulle* Laudabiliter, Mél.F.L. . CLXIII
—— *La campagne de Poitou, 1242–3, Taillebourg et Saintes*, A.M., t. v, 1893 . . . CLXIV
—— *De la condamnation de Jean sans Terre par la cour des pairs de France en 1202*, R.H., t. xxxii, 1886 CLXV
—— *Hughes de Clers et le " de Senescalcia Franciae "* Mél. G.M. CLXVI
—— *Simon de Montfort, Earl of Leicester*, new edition, translated by E. F. JACOB, Oxford, 1930 . CLXVII
BERGER (ÉLIE), *Les Aventures de la reine Aliénor, histoire et légende*, Comptes rendus, A.I., 1906 . CLXVIII
—— *Les dernières années de saint Louis* (Intro. to. vol. iv of *Layettes du Trésor des Chartes*, 1902) . CLXIX
—— *Histoire de Blanche de Castille, reine de France* (Thèse, Paris, 1895) CLXX
—— *Les préparatifs d'une invasion Anglaise et la descente de Henri III en Bretagne, 1229–1230.* B.E.C., 1893 CLXXI
—— *Saint Louis et Innocent IV*, Paris, 1893 . CLXXII
BEUZART (P.), *Les hérésies pendant le Moyen âge et la Réforme dans la region de Douai, d'Arras et du pays de l'Alleu*, Paris, 1912 CLXXIII
BLANCHET (ADRIEN) et DIEUDONNÉ (A.), *Manuel de numismatique française*, ii, Paris, 1916. . CLXXIV
BLED, (ABBÉ O.), *La zoene ou la composition pour homicide à Saint-Omer*, Mém. Soc. Antiq. de la Morinie, xix, 1884–1885 CLXXV
BLOCH (MARC), *Blanche de Castille et les serfs du chapitre de Paris*, Mém. S.H.P., xxxviii, 1911 . CLXXVI
—— *L'Île de France (les pays autour de Paris)*, R.S.H., October, 1912 CLXXVII
—— *Rois et serfs, un chapitre d'histoire capétienne* (Thèse), Paris, 1920 CLXXVIII
—— *Les rois thaumaturges*, Strasburg, 1924 (Public. de la Fac. des Lettres) CLXXIX
BOEHMER (H.), *Kirche und Staat in England und in der Normandie in XI und XII Jahrhundert*, Leipzig, 1899 CLXXX
BOISLISLE (DE), *Une liquidation communale sous Philippe le Hardi*, Ann. Bull, S.H.F., 1872 . CLXXXI
BOISSONNADE (P.), *Histoire du Poitou*, Paris, 1915 CLXXXII
—— *Du nouveau sur la Chanson de Roland*, Paris, 1923 CLXXXIII
—— *Quomodo comites Engolismenses erga reges Angliae et Franciae se gesserint (1152–1328)*, Angoulême 1893 CLXXXIV
BOLLAND (W. C.), *The general Eyre*, Cambridge, 1922 . CLXXXV
BORRELLI DE SERRES, *Recherches sur divers services publics du XIIIᵉ au XVIIᵉ siècle. Notices relatives au XIIIᵉ siècle*, Paris, 1895 . CLXXXVI
—— *La réunion des provinces septentrionales à la Couronne par Philippe Auguste*, Paris, 1899. (Cf. B.H.P., 1897.) CLXXXVII

REFERENCES

Bourgin (G.), *La commune de Soissons et le groupe communal soissonnais*, Paris, 1908. (B.E.H.E., fasc. 167.) . . . . **CLXXXVIII**
Bourrilly (V. L.), *Étude sur l'histoire, politique de la commune de Marseille, des origines à la victoire de Charles d'Anjou*, Aix, 1926 . . . . **CLXXXIX**
Boutaric (Edgard), *Marguerite de Provence, son caractère, son rôle politique*, R.Q.H., iii, 1867. . **CXC**
—— *Saint Louis et Alphonse de Poitiers*, Paris, 1870 . **CXCI**
Boutmy (E.), *Développement de la constitution et de la société politique en Angleterre*, Paris, 1912, 6e éd. **CXCII**
Boysson (R. de), *Études sur Bertrand de Born, sa vie, ses œuvres et son siècle*, Paris, 1902 . . **CXCIII**
Brachet (Auguste), *Pathologie mentale des rois de France*, Paris, 1903 . . . . . **CXCIV**
Brehier (Louis), *L'Église et l'Orient au Moyen âge. Les Croisades*, Paris, 1921, 4e edition . . **CXCV**
Bridrey (Em.), *La condition juridique des Croisés et le privilege de croix* (Thèse), Paris, 1900 . . **CXCVI**
Brooke (Z. N.), *The English Church and the Papacy from the Conquest to the reign of John*, Cambridge, 1931 . **CXCVII**
Broussillion (Bertrand de), *La Maison de Craon*, t. i (1050–1373), Paris, 1893 . . . . **CXCVIII**
Brown (P. Hume), *History of Scotland*, i, Cambridge, 1902 **CXCIX**
Brunner (H.), *Die Entstehung der Schwurgerichte*, Berlin, 1872 . . . . **CC**
Brunot (F.), *Histoire de la langue française des origines à 1900*, i, Paris, 1905 . . . . . **CCI**
Brussel, *Nouvel examen de l'usage général des fiefs en France*, Paris, 1750, 2 vol. . . . . **CCII**
Budinszky (Alexander), *Die Ausbreitung der lateinischen Sprache über Italien und die Provinzen*, Berlin, 1881 . . . . **CCIII**
Caix de Saint-Aymour (De), *Anne de Russie, reine de France et comtesse de Vallois au XIe siècle*, Paris, 1896, 2e édit. . . . . . . **CCIV**
Calan (Ch. de la Lande de), *Mélanges historiques*, Première série, Paris-Vannes, 1908 . . . **CCV**
Callery (Alph.), *Histoire du pouvoir royal d'imposer depuis la féodalité jusqu'au règne de Charles V*, Bruxelles, 1879 . . . . . . **CCVI**
Cam (Miss H. M.), *Studies in the Hundred Rolls, some aspects of thirteenth century administration*, Oxford, 1921 (O.S., vol. vi) . . . . . **CCVII**
Canel (A.), " *Le combat judiciaire en Normandie*," Mém. S.A.N., t. xxii . . . . . **CCVIII**
Carlyle (A. J.), " *Political theory, from the tenth century to the thirteenth*," London, 1915 (vol. iii of History of medieval political theory in the West). . **CCIX**
Cartellieri (Alexander), *Die Machtstellung Heinrichs II von England*, Neue Heidelberger Jahrbucher, viii, 1898 . . . . . **CCX**
—— *Philippe II, August, König von Frankreich*, Leipzig, 1899–1922, 5 vol. (Cf. R. H., xlvii, 1891 ; lii, liii, 1893 ; liv, 1894.) . . . . **CCXI**

REFERENCES

CARTELLIERI (ALEXANDER), "Richard Löwenherz" (in *Probleme der Englischen Sprache und Kultur, Festschrift für Johannes Hoops zum 60 Geburtstage*, 1925) CCXII
—— *Die Schlacht bei Bouvines in Rahmen der europaischen Politik*, Leipzig, 1914 . . . CCXIII
CARTELLIERI (OTTO), *Abt Suger von Saint-Denis*, Berlin, 1898 (H.S.E., xi) CCXIV
CARY (M.), *La Grande-Bretagne romaine, nouvelles fouilles et recherches*, R. H. clix, 1928 . . CCXV
CHABRUN (CÉSAR), *Les bourgeois du roi*, Paris, 1908 . CCXVI
CHADWICK (H. M.), *The origin of the English Nation*, Cambridge, 1907 CCXVII
—— *Studies on Anglo-Saxon Institutions*, Cambridge, 1905 CCXVIII
CHALANDON (F.), *Histoire de la domination normande en Italie et en Sicile*, Paris, 1907 . . . CCXIX
CHAPOT (VICTOR), " *Le monde romain,*" Paris, 1927, (*Evolution de l'Humanité*, vol. 22.) . . CCXX
CHARTROU (JOSÈPHE), *L'Anjou de 1109 à 1151, Foulque de Jerusalem et Geoffroi Plantagenet* (Thèse), Paris, 1928 CCXXI
CHESNEL (P.), *Le Cotentin et l'Avranchin sous les ducs de Normandie*, Caen, 1912 . . . CCXXII
CHEW (HELENA M.), *The ecclesiastical tenants in chief and writs of military summons*, E.H.R., 1926 . CCXXIII
CLEDAT (LÉON), *Rôle historique de Bertrand de Born (1175–1200)*, Paris, 1879 (B. Ec. Ath. et Rome, fasc. vii) CCXXIV
COHN (E. S.), *The manuscript evidence for the letters of Peter of Blois*, E.H.R., 1926 . . . CCXXV
COLLIETTE (L. P.), *Mémoires pour servir à l'Histoire du Vermandois*, Cambrai, 1771–2, 3 vol. . . CCXXVI
COLLINET (PAUL), *La frontière d'Empire dans l'Argonne et l'Ardenne au Moyen âge* (extrait de *Revue d'Ardenne et d'Argonne*, xi, 1903.) . . CCXXVII
COMPAIN (L.), *Étude sur Geoffrey de Vendôme*, Paris, 1891 (B.E.H.E., fasc. 86) . . . CCXXVIII
COVILLE (ALF.), *Les états de Normandie, leurs origines et leur développement au XIVe siècle*, Paris, 1894 . CCXXIX
—— *Jean Petit, La question du tyrannicide au commencement du XVe siècle*, Paris, 1932 . . CCXXX
DAUMET (G.), *Mémoires sur les relations de la France et de la Castille de 1255 à 1320*, Paris, 1913 (B.E.H.E., fasc. 118) CCXXXI
DAVID (C. W.), *Robert Curthose, Duke of Normandy*, Cambridge (Mass.), 1920 (H.H.S., xxv) . . CCXXXII
DAVIDSOHN (ROBERT), *Philipp II. August von Frankreich und Ingeborg*, Stuttgart, 1888 . . CCXXXIII
DAVIS (H. W. C.), *The Anarchy of Stephen's reign*, E.H.R. 1903 CCXXXIV
—— *The Anglo-Saxon Laws*, E.H.R., 1913 . CCXXXV
—— *England under the Normans and Angevins*, London, 1905 (Oman, *History of England*, vol. ii) CCXXXVI

REFERENCES

Dechelette (J.), et Grenier (A.), *Manuel d'archéologie préhistorique, celtique et gallo-romaine*, Paris, 1908–1931, 5 vol. CCXXXVII
Degert (A.), *Un ouvrier de la réforme au XIe siècle, Amat d'Oloron*, R.Q.H., lxxxiv, 1908 . . . CCXXXVIII
—— *Le pouvoir royal en Guyenne sous les derniers Carolingiens et les premiers Capétiens*, R.Q.H. lxxii, 1902 CCXXXIX
Delaborde (H. F.), *Les classements du trésor des Chartes antérieurs à la mort de saint Louis*, B.E.C., 1901 . CCXL
—— *Jean de Joinville*, Paris, 1894 CCXLI
—— *Philippe le Borgne, roi de France*, Mél. Schl. . CCXLII
Delcambre (Étienne), *L'Ostrevent du IXe au XIIIe siècle*, M.A., 1927 CCXLIII
—— *Relations de la France avec le Hainaut, 1280–1297*, (Thèse), Paris, 1929 CCXLIV
Delisle (Léopold), *Chronologie des baillis et sénéchaux royaux*, H.F., xxiv, 1re partie, 1904 . . . CCXLV
—— *Chronologie historique des comtes d'Eu issus de la maison de Lusignan*, B.E.C., xvii, 1856 . . CCXLVI
—— *Le Clergé normand au XIIIe siècle*, B.E.C. viii, 1846 CCXLVII
—— *Étude sur la condition de la classes agricole en Normandie au Moyen âge*, Paris, 1851 . . CCXLVIII
—— *Liste des compagnons de Guillaume le Conquérant à la Conquête de l'Angleterre*, Caen, 1862 (Extr. du Bull. Monumental) CCXLIX
—— *Mémoire sur les opérations financières des Templiers*, Mém. A.I., xxxiii, 2e partie, 1889 . CCL
—— *Des revenus publics en Normandie au XIIe siècle*, B.E.C., x (2e série, v), 1848-9, xi (3e série, i), 1849, xiii (3e série, iii), 1852 CCLI
Depoin (J.), *Recherches sur quelques maréchaux de Philippe Auguste et de saint Louis*, B.H.P., 1912 . CCLII
Dept (G. G.), *Les influences anglaise et française dans le comté de Flandre au début du XIIIe siècle*. Travaux de l'Université de Gand, fasc. 59, 1928 . . CCLIII
—— *Les Marchands flamands et le roi d'Angleterre*, Revue du Nord, xii, 1926 CCLIV
Despois (L.), *Histoire de l'autorité royale dans le comté de Nivernais*, Paris, 1912 CCLV
Dickinson (John), *The Medieval conception of Kingship in the Policraticus of John of Salisbury*, S., July, 1926 CCLVI
Dieudonné (Ad.), *Les conditions du denier parisis et du denier tournois sous les premiers Capétiens*, B.E.C., 1920 CCLVII
—— *Histoire monétaire du denier parisis jusqu'à saint Louis* (Extrait de Mémoires de la S.A.F., lxxi, 1912) CCLVIII
Dieudonné (M. A.), *L'ordonnance de 1204 sur le change des monnaies en Normandie*, Mél. Schl., ii . CCLIX
Dmitrevski (Michel), *Notes sur le Catharisme et l'Inquisition dans le Midi de la France*, A.M., 1923–4 CCLX

DOBIACHE-ROJDESTVENSKI (OLGA), *La vie paroissiale en France au XIIIe siècle d'apres les actes épiscopaux*, (Thèse univ.) Paris, 1911 CCLXI
DOELLINGER (IGNACE DE) et FRIEDRICH (J.), *La Papauté*, trad. GIRAUD TEULON, Paris, 1904 . . . CCLXII
DOGNON (PAUL), *Les institutions politiques et administratives du pays de Languedoc, du XIIIe siècle, aux guerres de religion*, Toulouse, s.d. (Bibl. Mérid., 2e s., iv) CCLXIII
DOUAIS (C.), *L'Inquisition, ses origines, sa procédure*, Paris, 1906 CCLXIV
—— *Les sources de l'histoire de l'Inquisition dans le Midi de la France*, Paris, 1881 CCLXV
DOUËT D'ARCQ (LOUIS), *Recherches sur les anciens comtes de Beaumont-sur-Oise*, Mém. S.A.P., Doc. inéd., iv, Amiens, 1855 CCLXVI
DUBOIS (GASTON), *Recherches sur la vie de Guillaume des Roches*, B.E.C., xxx, xxxii, xxxiv (1869, 1871, 1873) CCLXVII
DUBOIS (PIERRE), *Les assurements au XIIIe siècle dans nos villes du Nord, Recherches sur le droit de vengeance* (Thèse droit), Paris, 1900 CCLXVIII
DUCOUDRAY (G.), *Les origines du Parlement de Paris*, Paris, 1902 CCLXIX
DUFAYARD (CH.), *La réaction féodale sous les fils de Philippe le Bel*, R.H., lix et lv, 1894 . . . CCLXX
DUFOUR (CH.), *Situation financière des villes de Picardie sous saint Louis* Mém. S.A.P., 2e série, v, 1858 . CCLXXI
DUMAS (AUG.), *Encore la question fidèles ou vassaux* N.R.H.D., xliv, 1920 CCLXXII
DUPLÈS-AGIER, *Notice sur une pièce concernant la ville de Sens au XIIIe siècle*, Bull. Soc. Archéol. de Sens., année, 1851 CCLXXIII
DUPONT (ÉTIENNE), *Recherches historiques et topographiques sur les compagnons de Guillaume le Conquérant*, Saint-Servan, 1907-8, 2 vol. . . CCLXXIV
DUPONT-FERRIER (G.), *Études sur les institutions financières de la France à la fin du Moyen âge*, Paris, 1930-2, 2 vol. CCLXXV
—— *Les officiers royaux des bailliages et sénéchaussées et les institutions monarchiques locales en France à la fin du Moyen âge*, Paris, 1902 (B.E.H.E., fasc. 145.) CCLXXVI
DUVIVIER (CH.), *La querelle des d'Avesnes et des Dampierre*, Brussels, 1894, 2 vol. . . . CCLXXVII
ELLIS (HENRY), *General Introduction to Domesday-Book*, London, 1833, 2 vol. CCLXXVIII
ESMEIN (A.), *Cours élémentaire d'histoire du droit français*, Quatorzième edit., mise à jour par R. GÉNESTAL, Paris, 1921 CCLXXIX
—— *L'unanimité et la majorité dans les élections canoniques*, Mél. F., t. i CCLXXX
ESPINAS (G.), *Les guerres familiales dans la commune de Douai aux XIIIe et XIVe siècles, les trêves et les paix*, N.R.H.D., 1899 CCLXXXI
ESPINAY (G. D'), *La sénéchaussée d'Anjou*, Extrait des Mém. Soc. nat. d'Argric., d'Angers, 1892 . . CCLXXXII

REFERENCES

EYTON (R. W.), *Court, Household and Itinerary of King Henry II*, London, 1878 CCLXXXIII
FAGNIEZ (G.), *Études sur l'industrie et la classe industrielle à Paris aux XIIIe et XIVe siècles*, Paris, 1877 (B.E.H.E., fasc. 33) CCLXXXIV
FARRER (W.), *Honors and Knight's fees*, vol. i, London, 1923 CCLXXXV
FAURE (J. A. FELIX), *Histoire de saint Louis*, Paris, 1866, 2 vol. CCLXXXVI
FAWTIER (R.), *L'histoire financière de l'Angleterre (à propos de quelques travaux récents)*, M.A. xxxviii, 1928 CCLXXXVII
FLACH (JACQUES), *Les Origines de l'ancienne France*, Paris, 1886–1917, 4 vol. CCLXXXVIII
FLAMMERMONT (JULES), *De concessu legis et auxilii tertio decimo saeculo* (Thèse), Paris, 1883 . . CCLXXXIX
—— *Histoire des Institutions municipales de Senlis*, Paris, 1881 (B.E.H.E., fasc. 45) . . . CCXC
FLICHE (AUGUSTIN), *La réforme Grégorienne*, Paris, 1924–5, t. i et ii CCXCI
—— *Le règne de Philippe Ier, roi de France* (Thèse), Paris, 1912 CCXCII
FLOQUET (A.), *Histoire du Parlement de Normandie*, Rouen, 1840, t. i CCXCIII
FOURGOUS (J.), *L'arbitrage dans le droit français aux XIIIe et XIVe siècles*, Paris, 1906 . . CCXCIV
FOURNIER (PAUL), *Les collections canoniques romaines de l'époque de Grégoire VII*, Mém. A.I., xli, 1920 . CCXCV
—— *Le royaume d'Arles et de Vienne*, Paris, 1891 . CCXCVI
—— *Les officialités au Moyen âge*, Paris, 1880 . CCXCVII
—— *Un tournant de l'histoire du droit*, N.R.H.D., xli, 1917 CCXCVIII
FREDERICHS (JULES), *Robert le Bougre*, Trav. Fac. Phil. de Gand, vi, 1892 CCXCIX
FREEMAN (EDWARD A.), *History of the Norman Conquest of England*, Oxford, 2e édit. 1870–1876, vol. i–iv . CCC
—— *The reign of William Rufus and the Accession of Henry I*, Oxford, 1882, 2 vol. CCCI
FRÉVILLE (R. DE), *Étude sur l'organisation judiciaire en Normandie aux XIIe et XIIIe siècles*, N.R.H.D., 1912 CCCII
FROIDEVAUX (H.), *De regiis conciliis Philippo II Augusto regnante habitis* (Thèse), Paris, 1891. . CCCIII
FUNCK-BRENTANO (F.), *Les pairs de France à la fin du XIIIe siècle*, Mél. G.M. CCCIV
GASQUET (F. A.), *Henry III and the Church*, London, 1905 CCCV
GAUTIER (LÉON), *L'idée politique dans les chansons de geste*, R.Q.H., vii, 1869 CCCVI
GAVRILOVITCH (MICHEL), *Étude sur le traité de Paris de 1259 entre Louis IX, roi de France, et Henri III, roi d'Angleterre*, Paris, 1899 (B.E.H.E., fasc. 125.) . CCCVII
GENESTAL (R.), *Le " privilegium " fori en France, du décret de Gratien à la fin du XIVe siècle*, Paris, 1921–4, 2 vol. (B.E.H.E., Sciences relig., fasc. 35 et 39) CCCVIII

GEORGE (R. H.), *The contribution of Flanders to the Conquest of England*, R.B.P., v, 1926 . . . CCCIX
GÉRAUD (HERCULE), *Ingeburge de Danemark, reine de France*, B.E.C. vi, 1844 CCCX
—— *Mercadier, les routiers au XIIIe siècle*, B.E.C., iii, 1841-2 CCCXI
—— *Les Routiers au XIIe siècle*, B.E.C., iii, 1841-2 CCCXII
GERMINY (MAXIME DE), *La réunion des provinces septentrionales à la Couronne par Philippe Auguste*, R.Q.H., lxvii, 1900 CCCXIII
GIRY (ARTHUR), *Les établissements de Rouen*, Paris, 1883-5, 2 vol. (B.E.H.E., fasc. 55 et 59) . . CCCXIV
—— *Histoire de la ville de Saint-Omer et de ses institutions jusqu'au XIVe siècle*, Paris, 1877 (B.E.H.E., fasc. 31.) CCCXV
—— *Manuel de Diplomatique*, Paris, 1894 . . CCCXVI
GNEIST (RUDOLF), *Englische Verfassungsgeschichte*, Berlin, 1882 CCCXVII
GRAS (N. S. B.), *The early English Customs System*, Cambridge (Mass.), 1918 (Harvard economic Studies, xviii) CCCXVIII
GRAVIER (H.), *Essai sur les prévôts royaux du XIe au XIVe siècle*, Paris, 1904. (Extrait corrigé de la N.R.H.D.) CCCXIX
GREEN (J. R.) *The making of England*, London, 1900, vol. i, 5e edit. CCCXX
GREEN (Mrs. J. R.), *Henry the Second*, London, 1903 . CCCXXI
GRENIER (P. L.), *La cité de Limoges, son évêque, son chapitre, son consulat*, Paris, 1907 (Bull. soc. Archéol. du Limousin, t. lvii) . . . CCCXXII
GROSDIDIER DE MATON (MARCEL), *Le comté de Bar, des origines au traité de Bruges, 950-1301*, Paris, 1922 . CCCXXIII
GROSS (CH.), *The Gild Merchant*, Oxford, 1890, 2 vol. . CCCXXIV
GUILHIERMOZ (P.), *Les deux condamnations de Jean sans Terre*, B.E.C., 1899 CCCXXV
—— *Essai sur l'origine de la Noblesse en France au Moyen âge*, Paris, 1902 CCCXXVI
—— *Note sur les poids du Moyen âge*, B.E.C., 1906 . CCCXXVII
—— *De la persistance du caractère oral dans la procédure civile française*, N.R.H.D., série, xiii, 1889 . CCCXXVIII
—— *Remarques diverses sur les poids et mesures au Moyen âge*, B.E.C., 1919 CCCXXIX
—— *Saint Louis, les gages de bataille et la procédure civile*, B.E.C., 1887 CCCXXX
GUINARD (PAUL), *Les idées de Jean de Salisbury sur l'Église et la Papauté*, 1920 (memoire inédit). . CCCXXXI
GUIRAUD (JEAN), *Étude sur l'albigéisme languedocien aux XII et XIIIe siècles*, in *Cartulaire de Notre-Dame de Prouille*, Paris, 1907, to. i . . . CCCXXXII
—— *L'Inquisition mediévale*, Paris, s.d. . . . CCCXXXIII
GUIZOT, *Histoire de la civilisation on France*, Paris, 1840, 4 vol., 3e édit. CCCXXXIV
GUTSCHOW (ELSE), *Innocenz III und England* (Thèse Strasbourg), Munich, 1904. CCCXXXV
GUY (HENRY), *Adan de le Hale*, Paris, 1898. . . CCCXXXVI

REFERENCES

HALL (HUBERT), *Court life under the Plantagenets (Reign of Henry the Second)*, London, 1890 . . CCCXXXVII
—— *History of the Custom revenues in England*, London, 1885, 2 vol. CCCXXXVIII
HALPHEN (LOUIS), *Le comté d'Anjou au XIe siècle*, Paris, 1906 CCCXXXIX
—— *Les débuts de l'Université de Paris*, Studi medievali, nuova serie, ii, Turin, 1929 CCCXL
—— *L'essor de l'Europe (XIe-XIIIe siècle)*, Paris, 1932. (Peuples et civilisations, t. vi) . . . CCCXLI
—— *La lettre d'Eude II de Blois au roi Robert*, R.H., xcvii, 1908 CCCXLII
—— *Paris sous les premiers Capétiens (987–1223) Étude de topographie historique*, Paris, 1909 (B.H.P.) CCCXLIII
—— *La Royauté française au XIe siècle, à propos d'un livre récent*, R.H., lxxxv, 1904 . . . CCCXLIV
—— *Les Universités au XIIIe siècle*, R.H., clxvi, 1931 . CCCXLV
HARCOURT (L. W. VERNON), *His Grace the Steward and Trial of Peers*, London, 1907 CCCXLVI
HARDEGEN (F.), *Imperialpolitik König Heinrichs II von England* (Thèse) Heidelberg, 1905 . . CCCXLVII
HASKINS (CH. H.), *England and Sicily in the twelfth century*, E.H.R., 1911 CCCXLVIII
—— *The Normans in European History*, London, 1916 CCCXLIX
—— *Norman Institutions*, Cambridge, Mass., 1918, H.H.S., xxiv CCCL
—— *Robert le Bougre and the beginnings of the Inquisition in the Northern France*, A.H.R., vii, 1902 . . CCCLI
HAURÉAU (B.), *Les propos de maître Robert de Sorbon* (Extr. des Mém. A.I., xxxi, 2e partie, 1884 . . CCCLII
HAVERFIELD (F. J.), *Introductory Sketch of Roman Britain*, V.H., Hampshire, i, 1900 . . . CCCLIII
—— *The Romanisation of Roman Britain*, Oxford, 1923, 4e édit. CCCLIV
HAVET (JULIEN), *Les couronnements des rois Hugues et Robert*, R.H., xlv, 1891 CCCLV
—— *L'hérésie et le bras séculier au Moyen âge jusqu'au XIIIe siècle*, B.E.C., 1880 CCCLVI
D'HERBOMEZ (A.), *Le Voyage de Philippe Auguste à Tournay en 1187*, R.Q.H., nouv. série, vi, 1891 . CCCLVII
HIRSCH (RICHARD), *Studien zur Geschichte König Ludwigs VII von Frankreich* (Thèse), Leipzig, 1892 . CCCLVIII
HODGKIN (TH.), *History of England from the earliest times to the Norman Conquest*, London, 1906 (Political History of England, vol. i) CCCLIX
HODGSON (C. E.), *Jung Heinrich, König von England* (Thèse), Iéna, 1906 CCCLX
HOEFFT (C. TH.), *France, Franceis, Franc, im Rolandsliede* (Thèse), Strasbourg, 1891 . . . CCCLXI
HOLDSWORTH (W. S.), *History of English Law*, vol. ii, London, 1923, 3e édit. CCCLXII
HUCHON (R.), *Histoire de la langue anglaise*, ii, Paris, 1930 CCCLXIII
HUISMAN (G.), *La Juridiction de la Municipalité parisienne de saint Louis à Charles VII*, Paris, 1912 (B.H.P.) CCCLXIV

HUNT (W.), *The English Church from its foundation to the Norman Conquest*, London, 1899 (Stephens and Hunt, History of the English Church, vol. i) . . CCCLXV
HUTTON (W. H.), *Thomas Becket, Archbishop of Canterbury*, Cambridge, 1926, 2ᵉ édit. CCCLXVI
HYAMSON (A. M.), *A History of the Jews in England*, London, 1908 CCCLXVII
ILWAIN (CH. H. MC), *The High Court of Parliament and its supremacy*, New Haven, 1910 (Y.H.P.) . . CCCLXVIII
IMBART DE LA TOUR (PIERRE), *Les élections épiscopales dans l'Église de France du IXᵉ au XIIᵉ siècle*, Paris, 1890 CCCLXIX
JACOB (E. F.), *The reign of Henry III, some suggestions*, T.R.H.S., 4ᵉ série, x, 1927 CCCLXX
—— *Studies in the period of baronial reform and rebellion (1258-1267)*, Oxford, 1925 (O.S., viii) . . CCCLXXI
—— *What were the Provisions of Oxford*, H., ix, 1925 . CCCLXXII
JARMAN (TH. LECKIE), *William Marshal, first earl of Pembroke and regent of England*, Oxford, 1930 . CCCLXXIII
JENKINSON (H.), *Financial Records of the reign of King John*, M.C.C.E.. CCCLXXIV
JENKS (EDWARD), *The Myth of Magna Carta*, Independant Review, November, 1904 . . . CCCLXXV
JORDAN (E.), *Les Origines de la domination angevine en Italie*, Paris, 1909 CCCLXXVI
—— *Le Saint-Siège et les banquiers italiens*, Compte-rendu du 3ᵉ congres scient. des Catholiques, 5ᵉ sec., Sciences hist., 1895 CCCLXXVII
JOUON DES LONGRAIS (F.), *La conception anglaise de la saisine*, Paris, 1925 CCCLXXVIII
JOYCE (P. W.), *Social History of Ancient Ireland*, New York, 1903, 2 vol. CCCLXXIX
JULLIAN (CAMILLE), *Histoire de Bordeaux depuis les origines jusqu'en 1895*, Bordeaux, 1895 . . CCCLXXX
KECHNIE (W. S. MC), *Magna Carta*, Glasgow, 1914, 2ᵉ édit. CCCLXXXI
KERN (FRITZ), *Die Anfange der franzosischen Ausdehnungspolitik*, Tubingen, 1910 . . . CCCLXXXII
KERVYN DE LETTENHOVE, *Histoire de Flandre*, Bruges, 1853-4, 4 vol. CCCLXXXIII
KIENAST (W.), *Die Deutschen Fursten im Dienste der Westmachte* (Utrecht, 1924-1931, 2 vol.) . . CCCLXXXIV
KIMBALL (MISS E. G.), *The judicial aspects of Frank Almoign Tenure*, E.H.R., 1932 . . . CCCLXXXV
KÖNIG (LUDWIG), *Die Politik des Grafen Balduin, V. von Hennegau*, B.C.H.B., lxxiv, 1905 . . CCCLXXXVI
KREHBIEL (EDW. B.), *The interdict, its history and its operation*, Washington, 1909 . . . CCCLXXXVII
KURTH (G.), *La France et les Francs dans la langue politique du Moyen âge*, R.Q.H., lvii, 1895 . CCCLXXXVIII
LABANDE (L. H.), *Avignon au XIIIᵉ siècle*, Paris, 1908 CCCLXXXIX
—— *Histoire de Beauvais et de ses institutions communales*, Paris, 1892 CCCXC
LA BORDERIE (ARTHUR LE MOYNE DE), *Histoire de Bretagne*, Paris, 1896-1913, 5 vol. . . . CCCXCI

REFERENCES

Lair (Jules), *Étude sur la vie et la mort de Guillaume Longue Epée, duc de Normandie*, Paris, 1893	CCCXCII
Lane-Poole (Stanley), *A History of Egypt in the Middle Ages*, New York, 1901.	CCCXCIII
Langlois (Ch. V.) et Stein (Henri), *Archives de l'Histoire de France*, Paris, 1891-2, 2 vol.	CCCXCIV
Langlois (Ch. V.), *Doléances recueillies par les Enquêteurs de saint Louis*, R.H., xcii, 1906.	CCCXCV
—— *De monumentis ad priorem Curiae Regis judiciariae historiam pertinentibus*, Paris, 1887	CCCXCVI
—— *Les origines du Parlement de Paris*, R.H., xlii, 1890	CCCXCVII
—— *Le règne de Philippe III le Hardi*, Paris, 1887	CCCXCVIII
—— *Saint Louis, Philippe le Bel, les derniers Capétiens directs*, Paris, 1901 (E. Lavisse, Histoire de France, t. iii, 2ᵉ partie)	CCCXCIX
Lapsley (Gaillard), *Buzones*, E.H.R., 1932	CD
Lapsley (G. T.), *The County Palatine of Durham*, London and New York, 1900 (H.H.S., viii)	CDI
Laroière (C. de), *Recherches sur la limite de la Flandre et de l'Artois*, Ann. du Comité flamand de France, iv, 1859	CDII
Larson (L. M.), *Canute the Great*, New York and London, 1912	CDIII
—— *The King's Household in England before the Norman Conquest*, Bull. de l'Univ. de Wisconsin, No. 100, 1904	CDIV
Latouche (R.), *Histoire du comté du Maine pendant le Xᵉ et le XIᵉ siècle*, Paris, 1910 (B.E.H.E., fasc. 183)	CDV
Lazard (L.), *Les revenus tirés des Juifs de France dans le Domaine royal (XIIIᵉ s.)*, R.E.J., xv, 1887	CDVI
Lea (H. Ch.), *Histoire de l'Inquisition au Moyen âge*, Trans. S. Reinach, Paris, 1900-2, 3 vol.	CDVII
Leclère (Léon), *La Grande Charte de 1215 est-elle une illusion?* Mél. P., t. i	CDVIII
Lecoy de la Marche (A.), *La France sous saint Louis et sous Philippe le Hardi*, Paris, s.d.	CDIX
Lefèvre (A.), *Les baillis de la Brie au XIIIᵉ siècle*, B.E.C., 5ᵉ serie, i, 1860	CDX
Lefranc (Abel), *Histoire de la ville de Noyon et de ses institutions jusqu'à la fin du XIIIᵉ siècle*, Paris, 1888 (B.E.H.E., fasc. 75)	CDXI
Legrand (Léon), *Les Quinze-Vingt depuis leur fondation jusqu'à leur translation au faubourg Saint-Antoine*, Mém. S.H.P., xiii, 1886	CDXII
Legrand (Michel), *La chapitre cathédral de Langres*, 1931	CDXII bis
Le Nain de Tillemont, *Vie de saint Louis, roi de France*, publ. by J. de Gaulle, Paris, 1847-1851, 6 vol. (S.H.F.)	CDXIII
Lépinois (E. de), *Recherches sur l'ancien comté de Clermont*, Mém. Soc. Acad. de l'Oise, x	CDXIV
Lespinasse (René de), *Le Nivernais et les comtes de Nevers*, Paris, 1909-1914, 3 vol.	CDXV

LEVÉ (A.), *La tapisserie de la reine Mathilde, dite la tapisserie de Bayeux*, Paris, 1919 . . . **CDXVI**
LEVETT (MISS A. E.), *The summons to a great council, 1213*, E.H.R., 1916 . . . . **CDXVII**
LEX (LÉONCE), *Eudes II, comte de Blois*, Troyes, 1892 . **CDXVIII**
L'HUILLIER (DOM. A.), *Saint Thomas de Cantorbéry*, Paris, 1891–2, 2 vol. . . . . . **CDXIX**
LIEBERMANN (FÉLIX), *The National Assembly in the Anglo-Saxon period*, Halle, 1913 . . **CDXX**
—— *The text of Henry's Coronation Charter*, T.R.H.S., new series, viii, 1894 . . . . . **CDXXI**
—— *Ueber Pseudo-Cnuts Constitutiones de Foresta*, Halle, 1894 . . . . . . **CDXXII**
LLOYD (JOHN EDWARD), *A History of Wales from the earliest Times to the Edwardian Conquest*, London, 1911, 2 vol. . . . . . . **CDXXIII**
LODGE, (Mrs. E. C.), *Gascony under English Rule*, London, 1926 . . . . . . **CDXXIV**
LOEB (ISIDORE), *La controverse de 1240 sur le Talmud*, R.E.J., t. i à iii, 1880–1 . . . . **CDXXV**
LONGNON (AUG.), *Atlas historique de la France depuis César jusq'à nos jours*, Paris, 1882–9 . . **CDXXVI**
—— *Atlas historique, texte explicatif des planches* 1re partie, de 58 av. J.C. à 1380 ap. J.C., Paris, 1907 . . . . **CDXXVII**
—— and DELABORDE (H. F.), *La formation de l'unité française*, Paris, 1922 . . . . **CDXXVIII**
—— *L'Île-de-France*, Mém. S.H.P., i, 1875 . . **CDXXIX**
LOT (FERD.), *Bretons et Anglais aux Ve et VIe siècles*, P.B.A., xvi, 1930 . . . . . . **CDXXX**
—— *Les derniers Carolingiens*, Paris, 1891 (B.E.H.E., fasc. 87) . . . . **CDXXXI**
—— *Études sur le règne de Hugues Capet et la fin du Xe siècle*, Paris, 1903 (B.E.H.E., fasc. 147) . . **CDXXXII**
—— *Fidèles ou vassaux ?* Paris, 1904. . . **CDXXXIII**
—— *La frontière de la France et de l'Empire sur le cours inférieur de l'Escaut*, B.E.C., 1910 . . **CDXXXIV**
—— *Hengist, Hors, Vortigern : la conquête de la Grande-Bretagne par les Saxons*, Mél.B. . . . **CDXXXV**
—— et FAWTIER (R.), *Le premier budget de la monarchie française*, Paris, 1932 (B.E.H.E., fasc. 259) . . **CDXXXVI**
—— *Quelques mots sur l'origine des pairs de France*, R.H., liv, 1894 . . . . . **CDXXXVII**
LUCHAIRE (ACH.), *Les communes françaises*, Paris, 1890 **CDXXXVIII**
—— *Un diplomate*, Trav. et Mém., A.S.M., t. clxxi, 1909 . . . . **CDXXXIX**
—— *Histoire des institutions monarchiques de la France sous les premiers Capétiens*, Paris, 1891, 2e edit., 2 vol. . . . . **CDXL**
—— *Hugues de Clers et le " de Senescalcia Franciae "*, Mél. d'Hist. du moyen âge, t. i (Bibl. de la Fac. des Lettres de l'Univ. de Paris, t. iii, 1897). . **CDXLI**
—— *Innocent III*, Paris, 1907–8, 6 vol., 3e edit. . **CDXLII**
—— *Lettre sur la question de l'origine des pairs de France*, R.H., liv, 1894 . . . . . . **CDXLIII**

REFERENCES

LUCHAIRE (ACH.), *Louis VI le Gros, annales de sa vie et de son règne*, Paris, 1890 . . . . **CDXLIV**
—— *Les premiers Capétiens*, Paris, 1901 (Lavisse, Hist. de France, ii, 2ᵉ partie) **CDXLV**
—— *Louis VII, Philippe Auguste, Louis VIII*, Paris, 1901 (Lavisse, *Hist. de France*, iii, 1ʳᵉ partie) **CDXLVI**
—— *Manuel des Institutions françaises, période des Capétiens directs*, Paris, 1892 . . . **CDXLVII**
—— *Les milices communales et la Royauté capétienne*, Séances et Trav., A.S.M., cxxix, 1888 **CDXLVIII**
—— *Recherches historiques et diplomatiques sur les premières années de la vie de Louis le Gros (1081–1100)*, Paris, 1886 . . **CDXLIX**
—— *La Société française au temps de Philippe Auguste*, Paris, 1909 . . . . . **CDL**
LUNT (W. S.), Introduction to his edition of *The Valuation of Norwich*, Oxford, 1926 . . **CDLI**
MACKENZIE (HUGH), *The anti-foreign movement in England, 1231–2*, Mél. H. . **CDLII**
MAITLAND (F. W.), Introduction to his edition of *Bracton's Note Book*, London, 1887, vol. i . . **CDLIII**
—— *Domesday-Book and beyond*, Cambridge, 1897 . **CDLIV**
—— *Henry II and the criminous Clerks*, E.H.R., 1892 . **CDLV**
—— Introduction to his edition of *Select Pleas of the crown (1200–1225)*, London, 1888 (Selden Society) **CDLVI**
MALDEN (H. E.), Introduction to M.C.C.E. **CDLVII**
MALO (HENRI), *Un grand feudataire, Renaud de Dammartin*, Paris, 1898 . . . . . **CDLVIII**
DE MANTEYER (G.) *L'Origine des douze pairs de France*, Mél. G.M. **CDLIX**
MARGRY (A.), *Nouvelles recherches sur les origines des grandes baillies royales*, Comité archéol. de Senlis, comptes rendus et mém., 4ᵉ serie, ii, 1897–8. . **CDLX**
MARSH (F. B.), *English Rule in Gascony, 1199–1259*, Ann-Arbor, 1912. (Univ. of Michigan histor. Studies.) . . . . **CDLXI**
MARTIN (F. E.), *L'affaire de Pierre de Dalbs, abbé de Saint-Pierre-de-Lezat*, 1253–4, M.A. xiii, 1900 . **CDLXII**
MARTIN (FELIX OLIVIER), *Études sur les régences. I. Les régences et la majorité des rois sous les Capétiens directs et les premiers Valois, 1060–1375*, Paris, 1931 . . . . **CDLXIII**
MARTIN (OLIVIER), *Histoire de la coutume de la prévôte et vicomté de Paris*, Paris, 1922–6, 2 vol. **CDLXIV**
MATHOREZ (J.), *Guillaume aux blanches mains, évêque de Chartres*, Chartres, 1911 (Arch. hist. du diocèse de Chartres) . . . . . **CDLXV**
MATROD (HENRI), *Le voyage de frère Guillaume de Rubrouck*, Couvin, 1910 (Extr. des Études franciscaines) . . **CDLXVI**
MAUGIS, (ED.), *Recherches sur les transformations du régime politique et social de la ville d'Amiens*, Paris, 1906 . . . . **CDLXVII**
MEYER (PAUL), *Les premières compilations françaises d'histoire ancienne*, R., xiv, 1885 . . . **CDLXVIII**

MEYER VON KNONAU (G.), *Jahrbücher des Deutschen Reiches unter Heinrich IV und Heinrich V*, t. vii, Leipzig, 1909 . . . . **CDLXIX**

MEYNIAL (EDOUARD), *Roman Law*, in The Legacy of the Middle Ages, edited by C. G. Crump and E. F. Jacob, Oxford, 1926 . . . . . **CDLXX**

MICHEL (ROBERT), *L'administration royale dans la sénéchaussée de Beaucaire au temps de Saint Louis*, Paris, 1910 . . . . **CDLXXI**

MILLS (MISS MABEL H.), *Adventus vicecomitum*, E.R.H., 1921 . . . . **CDLXXII**

—— *The reforms at the Exchequer, 1232–1242*, T.R.H.S., 4th series, x, 1927 . . . . . . **CDLXXIII**

MITCHELL (S. K.), *Studies in taxation under John and Henry III*, New Haven, 1914 (Y.H.P.) . . **CDLXXIV**

MOLINIER (AUG.), *Étude sur l'administration de Louis IX et d'Alphonse de Poitiers*, in *Hist. du Languedoc*, nouv. éd., vii, note lix . . . . . **CDLXXV**

—— " *L'expédition de Trencavel,*" in *Hist du Languedoc*, nouv. éd., vii . . . . . . **CDLXXVI**

MOLINIER (CH.), *L'Église et la Société cathares*, R.H., xciv–xcv, 1907 . . . . **CDLXXVII**

—— *L'Inquisition dans le Midi de la France aux XIIIᵉ et XIVᵉ siècles*, Paris, 1880 . . . . **CDLXXVIII**

MONOD (BERNARD), *Essai sur les rapports de Pascal II et de Philippe 1ᵉʳ*, Paris, 1907 (B.E.H.E., No. 164) **CDLXXIX**

—— *Le moine Guibert et son temps*, Paris, 1905 . . **CDLXXX**

MONOD (GABRIEL), *Le rôle de Paris dans la France du moyen âge*, R.H., cxix, 1915 . . . . **CDLXXXI**

MORICE (DOM.), *Histoire de Bretagne*, Paris, 1750 . **CDLXXXII**

MORRIS (J. E.), *The Welsh wars of Edward I*, Oxford, 1901 . . . . **CDLXXXIII**

MORRIS (W. A.), *The Medieval English Sheriff*, Manchester, 1927 . . . . **CDLXXXIV**

MUGNIER (FR.), *Les Savoyards en Angleterre au XIIIᵉ siècle*, Paris et Chambéry, 1890 . . . **CDLXXXV**

NEWMAN (W. M.), *The kings, the Court and the Royal Power in France in the eleventh century*, Toulouse (Thèse lettres), 1929 . . . . . . **CDLXXXVI**

NORGATE (Miss KATE), *The alleged condamnation of King John by the Court of France in 1202*, T.R.H.S., N.S., xiv, 1900 . . . . . . **CDLXXXVII**

—— *England under the Angevin kings*, London, 1887, 2 vol. . . . . **CDLXXXVIII**

—— *John Lackland*, London, 1902 . . . . **CDLXXXIX**

—— *The minority of Henry the Third*, London, 1912 . **CDXC**

—— *Richard the Lion Heart*, London, 1924 . . **CDXCI**

NOWÉ (H.), *Les baillis comtaux de Flandre, des origines à la fin de XIVᵉ siècle*, Brussels, 1929 . . **CDXCII**

OHEIX (ANDRÉ), *Essai sur les sénéchaux de Bretagne, des origines au XIVᵉ siècle*, Paris, 1913 . . **CDXCIII**

ORPEN (G. H.), *Ireland under the Normans, 1169–1333*, Oxford, 1911–1920, 4 vol. . . . . **CDXCIV**

PABST (VON), *Die aussere Politik der Grafschaft Flandern unter Ferrand von Portugal, 1212–1233*, B.C.H.B., lxxx, 1911 . . . . **CDXCV**

REFERENCES

PACKARD (S. R.), *King John and the Norman Church*, Harvard Theological Review, xv, 1922 . . CDXCVI
—— *The Norman Communes under Richard and John, 1189-1204*, Mél.H. . . . . . CDXCVII
PAGART D'HERMANSART, *Histoire du bailliage de Saint-Omer (1193-1790)*, Saint Omer, 1898, 2 vol. . CDXCVIII
PAGE (WILIAM), *London, its origin and early development*, London, 1913 . . . . CDXCIX
PALGRAVE (Sir FR.), *History of Normandy and of England*, Cambridge, 1919-1921, vols. i à iii . D
PANGE (MAURICE DE), *Les Lorrains et la France au moyen âge*, Paris, 1919. . . . . DI
PARIS (GASTON), *L'esprit normand en Angleterre*, in *La poésie du moyen âge*, 2ᵉ série, 1895 . . . DII
—— *Histoire poétique de Charlemagne*, Paris, 1865, Notes additionnelles, 1905 . . . . DIII
—— *La littérature normande avant l'annexion*, Dics. lu à la séance publ. de la S.A.N., 1ᵉʳ déc., 1898, 1899 . . . . . . DIV
—— *Le roman de Richard Cœur de Lion*, R., xxvi, 1897 . DV
PARISOT (R.), *Les origines de la Haute-Lorraine et sa première maison ducale*, Paris, 1909 . . DVI
PAROW (DR.), *Compotus vicecomitis, Die Rechenschaftslegung des sheriffs unter Heinrich II. von England*, Berlin, 1906 . . . . . . DVII
PARSLOE (C. J.), *Roman Britain*, Hi., x, 1925-6 . . DVIII
PASQUET (D.), *Essai sur les origines de la Chambre des Communes*, Paris, 1914 . . . . DIX
—— *An essay on the origins of the House of Commons*, English translation. Notes by G. Lapsley, Cambridge, 1925 . . . . . DX
PERRICHET (LUCIEN), *La Grande Chancellerie de France des origines à 1328*, Paris, 1912 . . . DXI
PERROT (ERNEST), *Les cas royaux*, Paris, 1910 . . DXII
PETIT (ERNEST), *Hist. des ducs de Bourgogne de la race capétienne*, Paris, 1885-1894 . . . DXIII
—— *Saint Louis en Bourgogne*, Bull. Soc. Sciences de l'Yonne, 1893 . . . . . DXIV
PETIT-DUTAILLIS (CH.), *Le Déshéritement de Jean sans Terre et le meurtre d'Arthur de Bretagne*, Paris, 1925 (ou dans R.H., cxlvii-cxlviii, 1924-5) . . . DXV
—— *Documents nouveaux sur les moeurs populaires et la droit de vengeance*, Paris, 1908 . . . DXVI
—— *Étude sur la vie et le règne de Louis VIII*, Paris, 1894 (B.E.H.E. fasc. 101) . . . . DXVII
—— *Les origines france-normandes de la Forêt anglaise*, Mél.B. . . . . . . DXVIII
—— *Querimoniae Normannorum*, Mél.Tout . . DXIX
—— et LEFEBVRE (G.), *Studies and Notes, supplementary to Stubbs's Constitutional History*, Manchester, 1908-1929, 3 vol. . . . . . DXX
PFISTER (CHR.), *Études sur le règne de Robert le Pieux*, Paris, 1885. (B.E.H.E. fasc 64) . . . DXXI
PHILLIPS (G. J.), *Das Regalienrecht in Frankreich*, Halle, 1873 . . . . . . DXXII

PIRENNE (H.), *Histoire de Belgique*, t. i, Bruxelles, 1900, 5ᵉ éd., 1929 . . . . . . **DXXIII**
PISSARD (H.), *La guerre sainte en pays chretien*, Paris, 1912 (Bibl. d'Hist. religieuse) . . . **DXXIV**
PITON (C.), *Les Lombards en France et à Paris*, Paris, 1892—3, 2 vol. . . . . . . **DXXV**
PLANIOL (MARCEL), *L'assise au comte Geoffroi. Étude sur les successions féodales en Bretagne*, N.R.H.D., xi, 1887 . . . . **DXXVI**
PLUMMER (CH.), *The life and times of Alfred the Great*, Oxford, 1902 . . . . . **DXXVII**
POCQUET DU HAUT JUSSÉ (B. A.), *Les papes et les ducs de Bretagne*, Paris, 1928, 2 vol. . . . **DXXVIII**
POETE (MARCEL), *Une vie de cité, Paris, de sa naissance à nos jours*, Paris, 1924, t. i . . . **DXXIX**
POLLARD (A. F.), *The Evolution of Parliament*, London, 1920 . . . . **DXXX**
—— *Henry VIII*, London, new ed., 1905 . **DXXXI**
POLLOCK, F., et MAITLAND (F. W.), *The history of English Law before the time of Edward I*, Cambridge, 1898, 2 vol., 2ᵉ éd. . . . . **DXXXII**
POOLE (R. L.), *The Exchequer in the twelfth century*, Oxford, 1912 . . . . . **DXXXIII**
—— *Henry II, Duke of Normandy*, E.H.R., 1927 **DXXXIV**
—— *Illustrations of the History of medieval thought and learning*, 2nd ed., London, 1920 . . **DXXXV**
—— *The publication of Great Charters by the English kings*, E.H.R., 1913 . . . . **DXXXVI**
POUPARDIN (R.), *Le royaume de Bourgogne, 888–1038*, Paris, 1907 (B.E.H.É., fasc. 163) . . **DXXXVII**
POWICKE (F. M.), *Alexander of Saint-Albans, a literary muddle*, Mél. Poole . . . . **DXXXVIII**
—— *The Angevin administration of Normandy*, E.H.R., 1906 et 1907 . . . . . **DXXXIX**
—— *The Chancery during the Minority of Henry III*, E.H.R., 1908 . . . . . **DXL**
—— *The Honour of Mortain in the Norman Infeudationes Militum of 1172*, E.H.R., 1911 . . **DXLI**
—— *The loss of Normandy (1189–1204)*, Manchester, 1913 . . . . . . **DXLII**
—— *Per judicium parium, vel per legem terrae*, M.C.C.E. **DXLIII**
—— *Some observations on the baronial Council, 1258–1260, and the Provisions of Westminster*, Mél. Tout **DXLIV**
—— *Stephen Langton*, Oxford, 1928 . . **DXLV**
PRENTOUT (H.), *Essai sur les origines et la fondation du duché de Normandie*, Paris, 1911 . . **DXLVI**
—— *Étude-critique sur Dudon de Saint-Quentin et son Histoire des premiers ducs normands*, Paris, 1916 . **DXLVII**
—— *Études sur quelques points d'histoire de Normandie*, 1ʳᵉ série, Caen, 1926 ; 2ᵉ série, Caen, 1929 . **DXLVIII**
—— *Guillaume le Conquérant. Légende et Histoire*, Caen, 1927 . . . . . . **DXLIX**
PROU (MAURICE), *L'acquisition du Gâtinais par Philippe Iᵉʳ*, Ann. de la Soc. Histor. et Archéol. du Gâtinais, 1898 . . . . . . **DL**

REFERENCES

PROU (MAURICE), *Les coutumes de Lorris et leur propagation aux XII⁰ et XIII⁰ siècles*, Paris, 1884	DLI
—— *Esquisse de la politique monétaire des rois de France du X⁰ au XIII⁰ siècle*, dans Eetre Camarades, Paris, 1901 (Public. de l'Assoc. des anciens élèves de la Fac. des Lettres du Paris)	DLII
PUYMAIGRE (DE), *La legende de Blondel*, R.Q.H., t. xix, 1876	DLIII
RAMSAY (J. H.), *The Angevin Empire, 1154–1216*, London, 1903	DLIV
—— *The Foundations of England, 55–1154*, London, 1898, 2 vol.	DLV
—— *A History of the revenues of the Kings of England (1066–1399)*, Oxford, 1925, 2 vol.	DLVI
—— *The origin of the name Pipe Roll*, E.H.R., 1911	DLVII
RASHDALL (HASTING), *The Universities of the Middle Ages*, Oxford, 1895, 2 vol. en 3 parties	DLVIII
RÉGNÉ (JEAN), *Étude sur la condition des Juifs de Narbonne du V⁰ au XIV⁰ siècle*, Narbonne, 1912	DLIX
—— *Histoire du Vivarais*, t. ii (1039–1500), Largentière, 1921	DLX
REID (Miss R. R.), *Barony and Thanage*, E.H.R., 1920	DLXI
RHODES (W. E.), *Edmund, Earl of Lancaster*, E.H.R., 1895	DLXII
RHYS (JOHN), *Celtic Britain*, London, 1904, 3rd ed.	DLXIII
—— et JONES (D. B.), *The Welsh people*, London, 1900	DLXIV
RICHARD (ALFRED), *Histoire des comtes de Poitou*, Paris, 1903, 2 vol.	DLXV
RICHARDSON (H. G.), *The origins of Parliament*, T.R.H.S., series iv, vol. xi, 1928	DLXVI
—— *Richard Fitz-Neal and the Dialogus de Scaccario*, E.H.R., 1928	DLXVII
RICHEMOND (EM.), *Recherches généalogiques sur la famille des seigneurs de Nemours*, Fontainebleau, 1907–8, 2 vol.	DLXVIII
RIESS (LUDWIG), *The reissue of Henry I's Coronation Charter*, E.H.R., 1926	DLXIX
—— *Zur Vorgeschichte der Magna Carta*, Historische Vierteljahrschrift, xiii, 1910	DLXX
ROHRICHT (R.), *Études sur les derniers temps du royaume de Jérusalem. Les combats du sultan Bibars*. Archives de l'Orient latin, ii, 1884	DLXXI
—— *Die Pastorellen*, Z.K., vi, 1884	DLXXII
ROLAND (E.), *Les chanoines et les élections épiscopales du XI⁰ au XIV⁰ siècle*. (Thèse Inst. Cath. Paris), Aurillac, 1909	DLXXIII
ROMEFORT (J. DE), *Le Rhône de l'Ardèche à la mer, frontière des Capétiens au XIII⁰ siècle*, R.H., clxi, 1929	DLXXIV
RONY (ABBÉ), *La Politique française de Grégoire VII*, R.Q.H., 3ᵉ série, xiii, 1928	DLXXV
ROSSLER (O.), *Kaiserin Mathilde, Mutter Heinrichs von Anjou, und das Zeitalter der Anarchie in England*, H.S.E., Heft vii, 1897	DLXXVI

ROUND (J. H.), *La bataille de Hastings*, R.H., lxv, 1897 . . . . DLXXVII
—— *The Commune of London and other studies*, Westminster, 1899 . . . . DLXXVIII
—— *The date of the Grand Assize*, E.H.R., 1916 . . DLXXIX
—— *The Domesday Survey*, V.H., Essex, i, 1903 . . DLXXX
—— *The Domesday Survey*, V.H., Hampshire, i, 1900 . DLXXXI
—— *The Domesday Survey*, V.H., Hertford, i, 1902 . DLXXXII
—— *The Domesday Survey*, V.H., Worcester, i, 1901 . DLXXXIII
—— *The early sheriffs of Norfolk*, E.H.R., 1920 . . DLXXXIV
—— *Feudal England*, London, 1895 . . . . DLXXXV
—— *Geoffrey de Mandeville*, London, 1892 . . DLXXXVI
—— *King John and Robert Fitz Walter*, E.H.R., 1904 . DLXXXVII
—— *The officers of Edward the Confessor*, E.H.R., 1904 DLXXXVIII
—— *The Saladin Tithe*, E.H.R., 1916 . . . DLXXXIX
RUSSEL (JOSIAH C.), *The canonization of Opposition to the King in Angevin England*, Mél.H. . . . DXC
SACKUR (ERNST), *Die Cluniacenser*. Halle, 1892–4, 2 vol. DXCI
SALZMAN (L. F.), *Henry II*, London, 1917 . . . DXCII
SAYLES (G. O.), *Representation of cities and boroughs in 1268*, E.H.R., 1925 . . . . . . DXCIII
SAYOUS (ANDRÉ-E.), *Les mandats de saint Louis sur son trésor et le mouvement international des capitaux pendant la septième Croisade*, R.H., clxvii, 1931 . DXCIV
SCHEFER-BOICHORST (PAUL), *Deutschland und Philipp II. August in den Jahren 1180 bis 1214*, Forschungen zur Deutschen Geschichte, 1868 . . . . DXCV
—— *Die Streit über die pragmatische Sanction Ludwigs des Heiligen*, Mittheilungen des Instituts für oesterreichische Geschichtsforschung, viii, 1887 . DXCVI
SCHMIDT (CH.), *Histoire et doctrine de la secte des Cathares ou Albigeois*, Paris, 1849, 2 vol. . . . DXCVII
SCHREIBER (A.), *Drei Beiträge zur Geschichte der deutschen Gefängenschaft des Königs Richard Löwenherz*, Historische Vierteljahrschrift, xxvi, 1931 . . DXCVIII
SCHREUER (HANS), *Die rechtlichen Grundgedanken der französischen Königskronung*, Weimar, 1911 . DXCIX
—— *Ueber altfranzösische Kronungsordnungen*, Weimar, 1909 (Zeitschrift der Savigny Stiftung für Rechtsgeschichte Germ. abt. xxx) . . . . DC
—— *Noch einmal über altfranzösische Kronungsordnungen* (Zeitschrift der Savigny Stiftung für Rechtsgeschichte Germ. abt. xxxii) . . . DCI
SCHWARTZ (W.), *Der Investiturstreit in Frankreich*, Z.K. xlii–xliii, 1923–4 . . . . . DCII
SÉE (H.), *Étude sur les classes serviles en Champagne* (Extrait de la R.H., lvi–lvii, 1894–5) . . . DCIII
SEEBOHM (F.), *English Village Community*, London, 3rd ed., 1884 . . . . DCIV
—— *Tribal Custom in Anglo-Saxon Law*, London, 1902 . . . . DCV
SEIGNOBOS (CH.), *Le régime féodal en Bourgogne jusqu'en 1360*, Paris, 1882 . . . . . . DCVI
SMETS (G.), *Henri I, duc de Brabant* (Thèse), Brussels, 1908 DCVII
SMITH (R. A.), *Anglo-Saxon remains*, V.H., Hampshire, t. i, 1900 . . . . DCVIII

REFERENCES

SOEHNEE (F.), *Étude sur la vie et le règne de Henri Ier, roi de France*, Positions de thèse des élèves de l'École des Chartes, 1891 . . . . DCIX

STAPLETON (TH.), *Observations on the great Rolls of Exchequer of Normandy* (Introduction à "Mag. rotuli Scaccarii Normanniae," t. i, London, 1840, Soc. of Antiq. of London) . . . . DCX

STEIN (H.), *La Palais de justice et la Sainte-Chapelle de Paris*, Paris, 1912 . . . . . DCXI

—— *Recherches sur quelques fonctionnaires royaux des XIIIe et XIVe siècles originaires du Gâtinais*, Paris, 1919 (Extr. des Ann. de la Soc. hist. et arch. du Gâtinais) . . . . . DCXII

STENTON (Miss DORIS M.), Introduction to her edition of *Chancellor's Roll for the eighth year of the reign of King Richard I, 1196* (Pipe Roll, 42), London, 1930 . . . . . DCXIII

—— Introduction to *The Earliest Lincolnshire Assize Rolls, 1202–9*, Lincoln Record Society, 1926 . . DCXIV

STENTON (F. M.), *The Danes in England*, Hi. t. v, 1920–1 . . . . . . DCXV

—— *Domesday Survey*, V.H., Derbyshire, t. i, Westminster, 1905 . . . . . DCXVI

—— *William the Conqueror*, London, 1908 . DCXVII

STEPHENS (W. R. W.), *The English Church from the Norman Conquest to the accession of Edward I*, London, 1901 (History of the English Church, ed. by Stephens and. Hunt, t. ii) . . . DCXVIII

STEPHENSON (CARL), *Les aides des villes françaises aux XIIe et XIIIe siècles*, M.A., t. xxxiii, 1922 . DCXIX

—— *The aids of the English Boroughs*, E.H.R., 1919 . DCXX

—— *Taxation and representation in the Middle Ages*, Mél.H. . . . . . DCXXI

STERNFELD (RICHARD), *Karl von Anjou als Graf der Provence (1245–1265) Historische Untersuchungen* hgg. von J. Jastrow, Heft X. Berlin, 1888 . . DCXXII

—— *Ludwigs des heiligen Kreuzzug nach Tunis, 1270, und die Politik Karls I von Sizilien*, H.S.E., Heft IV, 1896 . . . . . . DCXXIII

STEVENSON (F. S.), *Robert Grosseteste*, London, 1899 . DCXXIV

STEVENSON (W. B.), *The Crusaders in the East*, Cambridge, 1907 . . . . . DCXXV

STRAYER (J. R.), *Knight Service in Normandy in the thirteenth century*, Mél.H. . . . . DCXXVI

STUBBS (WILLIAM), *Histoire constitutionnelle de l'Angleterre*, French edition by Ch. PETIT-DUTAILLIS et G. LEFEBVRE, Paris, 1907–1927, 3 vol. . . DCXXVII

TAIT, J., *The firma burgi and the Commune in England, 1066–1191*, E.H.R., 1927 . . . . DCXXVIII

—— *Medieval Manchester and the beginnings of Lancashire*, Manchester, 1904 . . . DCXXIX

—— *Studies in Magna Carta, Waynagium and Contenementum*, E.H.R., 1912 . . . DCXXX

TANON (L.), *Histoire des tribunaux de l'Inquisition en France*, Paris, 1893 . . . . DCXXXI

TARDIF (AD.), *Date et caractère de l'ordonnance de Saint Louis sur le duel judiciaire*, N.R.H.D., xi, 1887 . DCXXXII
—— *La procédure civile et criminelle aux XIIIe et XIVe siècles*, Paris, 1885 . . . . . DCXXXIII
TARDIF (J.), *Le procès d'Enguerran de Coucy*, B.E.C., 1918 . . . . DCXXXIV
THAYER (J. B.), *A preliminary Treatise on evidence at the Common Law*. Part I, *Development of trial by jury*, Boston, 1896 . . . . . DCXXXV
THOMPSON (FAITH), *The first century of Magna Carta*, Minneapolis, 1925 . . . . . DCXXXVI
THOMPSON (J. W.), *The development of the French Monarchy under Louis VI*, Chicago, 1895 . . DCXXXVII
TIXIER (O.), *Essai sur les baillis et sénéchaux royaux*, Orléans, 1898 . . . . . DCXXXVIII
TOECHE (THÉODOR), *Kaiser Heinrich VI.*, Leipzig, 1867 (J.D.G.) . . . . . . DCXXXIX
TOUT (T. F.), *Chapters in the administrative History of Medieval England*, vol. i, Manchester, 1920 . . DCXL
—— *The Communitas bacheleriae Angliae*, in E.H.R., 1902 . . . . DCXLI
—— *History of England from the accession of Henry III to the death of Edward III*, London, 1905 (Political History of England, t. iii) . . . . DCXLII
—— *Wales and the March during the Baron's Wars*, London, 1902, (Hist. Essays, Owens College, Manchester) . . . . DCXLIII
TURNER (G. J.) *The Minority of Henri III*, T.R.H.S., new series, xviii, 1904 ; 3rd series, i, 1907, . DCXLIV
—— *The Sheriff's Farm*, T.R.H.S., N.S., xii, 1898 . DCXLV
VACANDARD (ABBÉ E.), *Le Divorce de Louis le Jeune*, R.Q.H., xlvii, 1890 . . . . . DCXLVI
VACANDARD (E.), *Vie de saint Bernard*, Paris, 1927, 2 vol. new ed. . . . . . . DCXLVII
VAISSETE (DOM.) et DOM DEVIC, *Histoire générale de Languedoc*, New ed. Toulouse, 1874–1889, 12 vol. DCXLVIII
VALAT (GEORGES) *Poursuite privée et composition pécuniaire dans l'ancienne Bourgogne* (Thèse Droit), Dijon, 1907 . . . . . . DCXLIX
VALIN (LUCIEN), *Le duc de Normandie et sa Cour*, Paris, 1910 . . . . DCL
VALOIS (NOËL), *Guillaume d'Auvergne*, Paris, 1880 . DCLI
VIARD (JULES), *La Cour au commencement du XIVe siècle*, B.E.C., 1916 . . . . . DCLII
—— *La Cour et ses " Parlements " au XIVe siècle*, B.E.C., 1918 . . . . . . DCLIII
—— *L'Ostrevant, enquête au sujet de la frontière française sous Philippe VI*, B.E.C., 1921 . DCLIV
VIDAL (J. M.), *Les derniers ministres de l'albigéisme en Languedoc*, R Q.H., lxxix, 1906 . . . DCLV
—— *Doctrine et morale des derniers ministres albigeois*, R.Q.H., lxxxv, lxxxvi, 1909 . . . . DCLVI
VILLEPELET (R.), *Périgueux et ses institutions municipales jusqu'au traité de Brétigny* (Thèse lettres, Bordeaux), Périgueux, 1908 . . . . . DCLVII

REFERENCES

VINOGRADOFF (PAUL), *English Society in the Eleventh Century*, Oxford, 1908 . . . . DCLVIII
—— *The Growth of the Manor*, London, 1905 . . DCLIX
—— *Magna Carta*, cap. 39, M.C.C.E. . . . DCLX
—— *Quelques problèmes d'histoire du Droit anglo-normand*, N.R.H.D., 4ᵉ série, 5ᵉ année, 1926 . DCLXI
—— *Villainage in England*, Oxford, 1892 . . . DCLXII
VIOLLET (PAUL), " *Guillaume de Mandagoust, canoniste*," Hist. littér. de la France, xxxiv, 1915 . . DCLXIII
—— *Histoire des institutions politiques et administratives de la France*, Paris, 1890–1903, 3 vol. . . DCLXIV
—— *La Pragmatique Sanction de saint Louis*, B.E.C., année 1870, Paris, 1871 . . . . . DCLXV
VUITRY (AD.), *Études sur le régime financier de la France*, Paris, 1878, v. i . . . . . . DCLXVI
DE WAILLY, *Dissertation sur les dépenses et les recettes ordinaires de saint Louis*, H.F., xxi . . . DCLXVII
—— *Note sur la monnaie Tournois et la monnaie Parisis de St. Louis*, H.F, xxi . . . . . DCLXVIII
WALKER (C. H.), *The date of the Conqueror's ordinance separating the ecclesiastical and lay courts*, E.H.R., 1924 . . . . DCLXIX
WALKER (WILLISTON), *On the increase of royal power in France under Philip Augustus* (Thèse), Leipzig, 1888 DCLXX
WALLENSKÖLD (A.), Introduction to the critical edition of *Les chansons de Thibaut de Champagne, roi de Navarre*, Paris, 1925 (Soc. des Anc. Textes) . . DCLXXI
WALLON (H.), *Saint Louis et son temps*, Paris, 1875, 2 vol. . . . . DCLXXII
WAQUET (HENRI), *Le bailliage de Vermandois aux XIIIᵉ et XIVᵉ siècles*, Paris, 1919 (B.E.H.E., fasc. 213) . . . . DCLXXIII
WARNKÖNIG and STEIN, *Französische Staats und Rechtsgeschichte*, Bâle, 2ᵉ éd., 1875, 3 vol. . . . DCLXXIV
WEINBAUM (MARTIN), *Verfassungsgeschichte Londons, 1066–1268*, Stuttgart, 1929 (Beihefte zur Vierteljahrschrift für Sozial und Wirtschaftsgeschichte hgg. von H. Aubin, XV Heft.) . . . DCLXXV
WHITE (A. B.), *The name Magna Carta*, E.H.R., 1915 DCLXXVI
—— *Some early instances of concentration of representatives in England*, A.H.R., xix, 1914 . . . DCLXXVII
—— *Was there a ' Common Council ' before Parliament ?* A.H.R., xxv, 1919–1920 . . . DCLXXVIII
WHITWELL (R. J.), *Italians Bankers and the English Crown*, T.R.H.S., new series, xvii, 1903 . . DCLXXIX
—— *The revenue and expenditure of England under Henry III*, E.H.R., 1903 . . . . . DCLXXX
WINKELMANN (EDUARD), *Kaiser Friedrich II*, Leipzig, 1889–1897, 2 vol. . . . . . . DCLXXXI
YVER (JEAN), *L'interdiction de la guerre privée dans le très ancien droit normand.* (Semaine de Droit normand, 1927, N.R.H.D., 4ᵉ série, vi) . . DCLXXXII
ZELLER (GASTON), *La Réunion de Metz à la France*, Paris, 1926 (Public. de la Fac. des Lettres de Strasbourg, fasc. 35). . . . . . DCLXXXIII

INDEX

Abbon de Fleury, 28 (note), 32, 121
Abelard, 96
Adalberon, Archbishop of Rheims, 27–8, 204
Adam, Clerk of Ph. Augustus, 182
Adam de Marsh, 367
Adams, G.-B., 74 (note)
Adelaide, sister of Ph. Aug., 110
—— de Maurienne, 77
Adèle de Champagne, wife of Louis VII, 180–2, 204, 229
Adela, wife of Stephen Count of Blois, 102
Ademar de Chabannes, 16
Administration of church lands by king, 18
Agen, 174
Agnes de Meran, wife of Ph. Aug., 209, 228–9
Aide, 142–3, 188, 251, 334, 337, 354, 359
Aigues Mortes, 285, 315
Aimar, Viscount de Limoges, 217
Aimard, Templar, 236
Aimery de Thours, 222, 248
Aire, 203, 224
Alais, Dame of, 298
Albigensian, 256, 269, 275, 284
Alençon, Town, 176
—— County, 245, 305 (note 3)
Alexander III, Pope, 149, 194, 206–8
—— IV, Pope, 275
—— de Macon (The Mason), 356
Alfred the Great, King of England, 37, 42, 46
Alphonse of Poitiers, brother of St. Louis, 247, 256, 258, 283, 293, 294, 295, 296, 299, 300, 314, 318, 504
—— the Noble, King of Castile, 260
—— X of Castile, 323
—— 4th son of Louis VIII, 222
Amaury de Chartres, 277 (note)
—— de Craon, 304
—— de Montfort, 280
Amiens, Town, 197
—— County, 17, 184, 201
—— Mise of, 326, 347
Anduze, Lords, 296
Anet, 234
Angers, Town, 132
—— Bishopric, 267
Anglican Church, 329 (note)

Anglo-Saxons, 39 (note), 60, 74, 75
Angoulême, Town, 170
—— Counts, County, 170, 173, 217
Anjou, Counts, County, 16, 99, 100, 157, 158, 167, 213, 222, 227, 242, 245, 246, 248
Anseau de Garlande, 312
Anselm, Archbishop of Canterbury, 72–3
Apanages, 246–7, 376
Appeal, 310
Aquitaine, Dukes and Duchy, 15, 29, 85, 99, 105, 107, 157, 158, 167–172, 176, 201, 210, 230, 240
Aragon Kings, 108, 246, 293, 323–4
Arbitration, 239, 325–6
Archambaud de Bourbon, 236
—— Sub Dean of Sainte Croix d'Orleans, 95
Architecture, Military, 17, 254
—— Religious, 323
Archives, 132, 234. See Trésor des Chartes
Arles, Kingdom, 177, 269, 325
Armies, 43, 54, 59, 61, 68, 69, 144, 145, 184, 193, 255, 291, 306
Armorica, 13
Arnaud Amalric, Legate, 278
Arnoul, Archbishop of Rheims, 22
Arpajon, 18
Arques, 163
Arras, Town, 197
—— Bishop, 267
Arthur, grandson of Henry II, 117, 119, 167, 171, 173, 213, 220
Artois, 184, 196, 202, 264, 295, 311
Arundel, County of, 332
Assemblies, see Courts, Parlement, Witena Gemot, 237, 241, 360, 362
Assizes, 137, 141, 145, 158, 165 (note), 167, 186, 193, 336
Association in the Throne, 28, 43, 116, 180, 311, 375
Assurance, 290, 313
Athelstan, King of England, 42
Aubains (foreigners), 250
Audebert de Perigord, 16
Audemar, Count of Angoulême, 217
Augustine, Missionary, 41, 44
Auvergne, 170, 194, 205, 212, 222, 245, 246, 291
Auxerre, Bishop of, 267

410

INDEX 411

Avesnes, Feudal House, 238
Avignon, 281
Avignonet, 282
Avranches, 150, 151, 163

Bachelors of England, 346, 368, 370
—— of Poitou, 170
Baillifs, 162, 185-6, 243, 247-8, 254, 288, 294, 299, 301, 321, 377
—— Comtal of Flanders, 186
Baldwin IV and V, Counts of Flanders, 15
—— VIII, 203
—— IX, 220
—— (False), 306
Bapaume, 197
Bar, County, 13, 325
Barcelona, County, 10, 15, 177
Barons, 69, 302, 331-2, 347 *passim*
Barthelemy de Roye, Chamberlain, 235, 321
Basque language, 13
Bayeux, Town, 176
—— Tapestry, 59
Bayonne, 176
Beadles, 295
Beatrix of Provence, wife of Charles of Anjou, 271
Beaucaire, Town, 279, 281, 316
—— Seneschalship, 246, 282, 296-7
Beaugency, Council, 107
Beaujeu, Lords of, 12, 240-1
Beaulieu, Abbey of, 12
Beaumanoir, 2, 308, 313, 315
Beaumont, Countess of, 182, 221, 236, 245, 305 (note)
Beauvais, Town, 37, 196, 252, 316
—— Bishop, Count, 240, 265
Bellème, 246
Bemont, Ch., 333 (note)
Benon, 170
Berengaria of Navarre, wife of Richard I, 177
Bernard, Prior of Grandmont, 182
—— Saint, 79, 93, 96
Berry, 170, 194, 205, 212-13
Bertrade, Queen of France, 77, 86, 99
Bertrand de Born, 173
Bethisy, family of officials, 186
Beziers, 279, 282
Bigod, English family, 343. *See* Hugh
Bigorre, Counts, 173, 343
Blanche, of Castile, Queen, 213, 227, 246-7, 256, 259, 262, 282, 291, 301, 306-7, 312, 315, 317, 319, 377
—— of Navarre, wife of Thibaud III of Champagne, 204, 221, 307
Blasphemers, 275, 308 (note)
Blois, County, 15, 16, 204, 221, 251, 303

Blosseville, 163
Bohun, English family, 343
Boniface of Savoy, Archbishop of Canterbury, 344, 365
Bordeaux, Archbishop and Town, 174
Boson de Bordeille, 314 (note)
Boulogne, County, 221, 223, 245, 304
Bourgeoisie, 179, 181, 195, 199, 238, 291, 316, 346, 353, 369, 377
—— Foreign, Royal, 309
Bourges, Town, 83, 205
—— Eccles. Prov., 20-1
—— Council, 281
Bouvines, Battle of, 225, 331
Burgundy, Duke, Duchy, 10, 15, 18, 183, 194, 199, 221, 224, 240, 283, 307
—— Franche Comté, 10, 325
—— Kingdom, 33, 117
Butler, 80, 94, 161, 235,
Brabant, Duke, Duchy, 202, 226
Bracton, 351, 352, 397-8
Brémule, Battle of, 84
Breteuil, 175, 322
Bretons, 37, 38, 39, 42
Brittany, County and Duchy, 67, 81, 158-9, 173, 213, 220, 222, 264, 292, 303, 305, 325
Brunner, H., 139 (note)
Brussel, 244 (note)
Bulgares, 283
Bury St. Edmunds, Abbey of, 366, 410
Byzantium, 33, 177
Booty of war, 254

Cadoc, Mercenary and Bailiff, 255, 296
Caen, 132, 164
Cahors, Bishop, 263
Cahour, Chancellor, 95
Cambrai, 10
Canterbury, Archbishop, 41, 45, 328. *See* Anselm, Boniface, Edmund Rich, Hubert Walter, Lanfranc, Robert Champart, Stephen Langton, Stigand, Theodore, Thomas Becket
Canute, King of Denmark and England, 43, 56, 212
Capet, Capetian, 21 (note)
Capitularies, 145
Carcassonne, Town, 281
—— Seneschalship, 246, 282, 296
—— Viscounty, 279
Carolingians, 2, 7, 18, 21, 33, 43, 80, 214
Carolinus, 191, 214
Cartellieri, Al., 180 (note), 191 (note), 220 (note)

Carucage, Tax, 143, 191
Castile, 108, 323. See Blanche of Castile
Catalonia, 325. See Barcelona
Cathares, see Albigensian
Celestin III, Pope, 207
Celts, 11, 13, 37, 38
Centaine, see Hundred
Chalon, Counts of, 12, 325
Chalons sur Marne, Bishop, Count of, 240
Chalus, 173
Chamberlains, 80, 235
—— Chambrièr, 80, 234–5
Chamber, 63, 80, 133 (note). 140 (note), 234
—— of Pleas, 243
Chambre des Comptes, Origins of the, 244
Champagne, Counts, County, 10, 12, 95, 204, 239, 240, 283, 292, 306, 307. See Blanche of Navarre, Thibaud (Fair), 198, 315
Chancellor, Chancery, 81, 94, 112, 114, 132, 163, 235, 351
Charlemagne, 23, 26, 128, 178, 265
Charles of Anjou, brother of St. Louis, 246 (note), 269, 270–1, 286, 311, 317, 324, 325
—— the Bald, 23
—— the Fat, 27
—— the Simple, 51
—— VII, 13, 275
Charter of Henry I, 74
—— of Stephen, 101
—— of Henry II, 107
—— Great, 136, 150, 331–9, 358, 362, 366, 369, 370, 374
—— Unknown of English liberties, 331, 331 (note)
Charters of Franchises, see Towns, Communes
Chartres, County of, 15, 34, 234, 303
Chase, see Forest
Chateaudun, Viscounty, 303
Chatelains, 162, 295, 302, 335
Chatellerault, Viscounty, 251
Chaumout, 196
Chester, County of, 151
Chichester, Bishop, 348
Chinon, 237
Christchurch, Canterbury, 328
Christianity, 41, 290
Church, 3, 19, 30, 41–2, 44, 72, 75, 86, 95, 106, 114, 122, 146, 152, 174–5, 190, 194–5, 259, 286, 290, 328, 333, 364, 367, 393, et passim
Cinque Ports, 145, 348, 349
Cité (île de la—at Paris), 198–9
Citeaux, Order of, 87

Clarendon, Constitutions of, 137, 146–9, 264
Clément, Family of Marshals, 182, 236
—— IV, Pope, 10, 270, 274–5, 350
Clermont en Beauvaisis, Counts, 182, 245, 305 (note)
Clermont Ferrand, Bishop, 263
Clovis, 23
Cluny, Order of, 20, 87, 94
Commendation, 49, 50, 65
Committee of twenty-five Barons, 337
Common Council of the Realm, 336 (art. 12), 360
—— Law, see Law
Communes, 86, 196–7, 302, 314
Compiègne, 234, 252
Conan of Brittany, 167
Concilium, Magnum, 352, 362
Conrad, Emperor, 33
Conradin, grandson of Frederick II, 270–2
Consecration, 3, 4, 23, 27–30, 43–4, 117, 180, 182, 200, 249
Consent to the aid, 129, 143, 188, 251–2, 316, 336, 342, 359, 362
—— to the Danegeld, 46
Constables, 80, 161, 164, 235, 375
Constance, 29
Corbeil, County, 17
—— Treaty, 324
Corbie, 83
Coronation, 24, 27, 30, 166, 174
Coucy, Lords of (Sires), 221, 236
Council, 66, 131, 242, 342, 352, 356, 362, 371
—— of Twelve, 341, 346, 363
—— of Nine, 348
—— of Fifteen, 344–5, 346, 363
—— of Twenty-four, 344
Counts, Counties in England, 63, 69, 70. See Shire
—— Palatine, 71
County Courts, 64, 134 passim
—— in France, 162 (note), 302
Courts of Early Capetians, 31–80
—— of Phillip I and Louis VI, 80, 82, 83
—— of Louis VII, 182
—— of Phillip Augustus, Louis VIII, and St. Louis, 182, 219, 235, 245, 321, 377 passim
—— ducal of Normand, 53, 65, 127, 159
—— of King of England, 65, 66, 72, 113, 127, 135, 351, 355
—— of Common Pleas, 135, 336, 351
Crusades, 181, 188, 207, 212, 220, 238, 252, 256, 276, 286, 319
Curia Regis, see Court
Custodes pacis, 349
Cyprus, 177

INDEX

413

Damietta, 318
Dampièrre, Feudal House, 238, 325
Danegeld, 42, 46, 63, 129, 130 (note), 143 *passim*
Danelaga, 139 (note)
Danish, 37, 42, 51
Dapiferat, Office of, *see* Seneschal
Dauphin of Auvergne, 304
Davis, H. W. C., 177 (note)
Decretals, False, 19
Delisle, Leopold, 320
Demesne, Royal, in France, 17, 82, 245, 307
—— in England, 62
Deposition of Kings, 43, 121
Dialogus de Scaccario, 114, 122, 133
Dieppe, 163
Dijon, 196
Diplomacy, 200, 255
Doellinger, Ignace de, 88 (note)
Domesday Book, 40, 48, 62, 63, 70, 133, 165
Domestici, 120
Dominicans, 283, 364
Doullens Chatellany, 245
Dreu de Mello, 182, 235
Dreux, Counts of, 236, 251
Dublin, Archbishops of, 3, 332
Duel, Judicial in France, 309
—— in England, 138, 336
Dukes, 302
Durham, Bishop of, 151
Dynasties, Seignorial, 14

Ealdorman, 42, 45, 58
Ebrouin the Changer, 200
Ecclesiastical Courts, 71, 147-9, 263-4
Edgar, King of England, 42
Edinburgh, 156
Edmund, son of Henry III, 323, 341
—— Rich, Archbishop of Canterbury, 364, 365
Edward the Elder, King of England, 47
—— the Confessor, id., 1, 48, 57
—— I, id., 36, 347, 349, 350
Egbert, id., 42
Egypt, 285
Eleanor of Aquitaine, 85, 95, 105-6, 129, 131, 151, 157, 167-171, 173, 174, 179, 201, 211, 213, 222, 260, 312, 328
—— of Provence, wife of Henry III, 340
Election of Bishops and Abbots, 20, 71, 86, 92, 122, 147, 174, 194, 267, 333
—— of the Jury, 153. *See* Monarchy
Ellis, 49 (note)

Empire, 8, 33, 86, 202, 206, 208
English idiom, 357
Enguerran de Coucy, 239 (note), 312
Enjeuger, Chatelain, 99
Escheats, 142
Escurolles, 196 (note)
Etablissements de Rouen, 176
Etablissements pour le commun profit, 378
Etampes, 18, 196
Ethelred, King of England, 43, 57 (note), 155
Etienne Boileau, 315
—— de Garlande, 94-5
—— de Montfort, Master in Parlement, 243
—— de Senlis, 94
Eu, County of, 251, 305
Eudo, King of France, 27
—— I, Count of Blois and Chartres, 16
—— II, 16, 33-4
—— de Lorris, Master in Parlement, 243
—— Rigaud, Archbishop in Rouen, 236, 290
Eugenius III, Pope, 106
Evesham, Battle of, 350
Evreux, Town, 176
—— County, 213
—— Bishopric, 268
Exchequer in England, 63, 113-14, 133-4, 351, 356
—— in Normandy, 159, 163-4, 247, 320-1

Falais, 176
Farmers (Bailes), 294, 296-7, 300
Fécamp, 163, 176
Feudalism, Feudal Spirit, 17, 36, 51-3, 62, 82, 123, 151, 201, 206, 211, 220-1, 226, 233, 262-3, 288, 292, 301, 310, 326, 330, 359, 368, 372
Feudal Guarantees, 303-4
—— Succession, 305
—— Ward, 331, 333
Feuds, 290, 313
Ferrand, Count of Flanders, 224-6, 306
Ferry Paté, 273
Finances, 63, 162, 164, 187, 192 (note), 244, 249, 257-8
Fix, 18 (note)
Flanders, Counts and County, 12, 15, 16, 84, 181, 202, 212, 223-4, 225, 240, 283, 303, 304, 306
Fontenoy le Comte, 170
Forest, 74, 101, 140-1, 150, 331, 335
Forester, 295, 335

Forez, 10
Fougères, Sire of, 304
Fournier, Paul, 88 (note)
France, French, 8, 30, 167, 322, 379
Franciscans, 298, 364, 367
Frank almoin, see Free alms
Frederick I, Barbarossa Emperor, 12, 194, 204, 206, 211
—— II, Emperor, 210, 224, 226, 265, 269, 323, 366
Free alms, Tenure in, 71, 148, 150
Freeholder, Free tenant, 69, 334
Freeman, E. A., 56 (note)
French, see France
—— Literature, 323, 370
Fréteval, Battle of, 192
Friars, 364
Frontiers, 10, 13, 33
Fulbert of Chartres, 29, 31
Fulk the Black, Count of Anjou, 16, 99
—— the Red, id., 99
—— the Surly, id., 215
—— the Young, id., 100
Fyrd, 61, 69, 144

Gael, 38
Gallican, Church, 329 (note)
Galon, Legate, 338
Gascons, 13
Gascony, Duchy of, 15, 341, 344, 386
Gatinais, 83
Gautier de Coutances, Archbishop of Royen, 112
—— de Ligne, 312
—— de Nemours, Chamberlain and Archivist, 234
—— Map, see Map Walter
Geoffrey, bastard son of Henry II, 172
—— brother of Henry II, 172
—— of Brittany, son of Henry II, 117, 211, 213
—— de la Celle, Seneschal of Gascony, 172
—— de la Chapelle, Master of Parlement, 243
—— de la Mandeville, 105
—— du Lauroux, Archbishop of Bordeaux, 174
—— Martel, Count of Anjou, 99
—— Plantegenet, 100, 159, 174
Germains, 37-8, 40-1
Germany, 11, 22, 207, 323. See Empire
Gervais of Canterbury, 113, 216
Gevaudan, 296
Gilles de Paris, 191, 214
Giraud de Cambrie, 215
Gisors, 234, 321

Gloucester, see Richard and Gilbert de Clare
Gneist, R., 65 (note)
Godwin, 45, 50, 58
Goulet, Peace of, 213
Granville, 112, 135, 138, 159
Gratian, Decree of, 208
Great Britain, 13, 37, 145
Gregory VII, Pope, 54, 71, 88, 92
—— IX, Pope, 265, 283
Guelfs and Ghibellines, 210
Guerin, Bishop of Senlis, 225, 234-5, 321
Guibert de Tournay, 319
Guigues, Dauphin, 325
Guilhiermoz, P., 193 (note), 220 (note), 239 (note)
Guillaume aux Blanches Maines, Archbishop of Rheims, 182, 204
Guy de Dampierre, 221, 307
—— de Fulquoi, see Clement IV
Guyenne, Duchy of, 227, 290

Hadrian, Pope, 156
Hainault, County of, 10, 11, 202, 317, 325
Hanse of Paris, 200 (note)
Hardegen, F., 177 (note)
Harfleur, 176
Harold, King of England, 50, 58-9
—— Hardrada, King of Norway, 59
Harthacnut, King of England, 57
Haskins, Ch.-H., 139 (note)
Hastings, Battle of, 60
Haverfield, F. J., 38 (note)
Hélie de Malmort, Archbishop of Bordeaux, 174
Henry I, Beauclerc, King of England, 61-3, 66, 73, 74, 84, 100, 115, 153, 159, 165, 175, 374
—— II, Plantegenet, id., 105, 178, 186, 190, 193, 201, 211, 260, 374, 375
—— III, id., 111, 214, 227, 293, 309, 325, 338, 351, 353, 356, 362, 371, 374-5
—— the Young, son of Henry II, 117, 131, 201, 211, 376
—— I, King of France, 7, 16, 18, 29, 33, 35, 76, 81, 86, 92
—— II, Emperor, 33
—— IV, Emperor, 88
—— V, Emperor, 85, 93, 110, 377
—— VI, Emperor, 177, 181, 207
—— Duke of Burgundy, 18
—— I, Duke of Brabant, 23
—— de Sully, Butler, 235
—— the Liberal, County Champagne, 204
—— the Lion, Duke of Saxony, 207-211

INDEX

Heretics, 277 (note), 281–5, 308 (note)
Hervé de Donzy, 205, 307
Hesdin, 197, 201
Hidage, hide, 143
Hildebert de Lavardin, Archbishop of Tours, 94
Hincmar, 31
Holland, 223
Holy Land, see Crusade
Honorius III, Pope, 227, 269, 280, 338
Honour, 34
Host, see Army
House of Commons, 353, 368
Household, 63, 234, 254, 340, 351
Hubert de Burgh, Grand Justiciar, 365
Hubert Walter, Archbishop of Canterbury, 117–18, 130, 328
Hue de la Ferté, 241
Hugh Bigod, Grand Justiciar, 345
—— Capet, 1, 7, 16, 18, 20, 22, 27, 28, 80
—— III, Duke of Burgundy, 205
—— IV, id., 304
—— de Die, Legate, 91
—— de Langres, 92
—— de Lusignan, 217, 222, 293, 340
Hundred, 40–1, 64, 134, 139, 373, 376

Indivisibility of the Kingdom, 376
Ingeburg, see Isambour
Innocent III, Pope, 208–210, 218, 221, 224–5, 268, 277–9, 338, 374
—— IV, id., 265–6, 269–273, 283–4, 341, 367, 374
Inquest, Inquisitors, 161, 165–6, 247, 298, 300, 301, 310
Inquisition, 282–4
Investitures, 22, 88, 92
Ireland, 108, 155–6
Isabella d'Angoulême, wife of John Lackland and then of Hugh de Lusignan, 217, 293, 340
—— of Aragon, wife of Philip III, 325
—— of Hainault, wife of Philip Augustus, 202–3, 206, 214
Isambour of Denmark, id., 181, 209, 212
Issoudun, Seigniory, 245
Italy, 55, 181

Jaime, King of Aragon, 324
Jeanne, Countess of Flanders, 223, 306
Jerusalem, 284–5
—— Kingdom of, 177, 212, 285
Jews, 142, 187, 191, 194, 238, 250, 256, 275, 299, 307, 333

Joan of Arc, 12
John d'Avesnes, 325
—— Lackland, 110, 111, 117–18, 123, 128–9, 131, 156, 172, 174–5, 201, 211, 214, 226, 327–332, 356, 362, 369, 374–5, et passim
—— of Salisbury, 106 (note), 115, 119–120, 156
Joinville, Jean, Sire de, 236, 243, 255, 260, 286 (note), 295, 325
Jury, 139, 140, 143, 145, 148, 165–6
Justice, 40, 71, 113, 127, 128, 134, 138, 162, 164, 239, 242, 300, 309, 314, 335, 336
—— Chief, 300
Justices, Itinerant, 66 (note), 101, 127, 135–6, 142, 143, 145, 165, 328 (note), 336, 351
Justiciar, Grand, 131

Kenilworth, Dictum de, 350
King's Bench, 136
Knights, 69, 173, 186, 200, 236, 302, 303, 334, 353, 365, 368, 388
—— Bannerets, 302

La Borderie, A. Le Moyne de, 158 (note)
La Chapelle, family of Chamberlains, 186, 236
Lady of England, 104
Lambeth, Treaty of, 227, 338
Lanfranc, Archbishop of Canterbury, 71
Langres, 194
—— Bishop of, 183, 194, 240, 269
Languages, 13
Laon, Bishop of, 240
La Roche au Moine, Battle of, 225, 331
La Rochelle, 170, 176, 222
Law, Canon, 113, 148
—— Common in England, 69, 72, 137, 351, 357
—— Criminal in France, 284
—— Roman, 113, 378
—— Customary, 318
—— of Vengeance, 53, 290, 313
Lefebvre, G., 64 (note)
Legates, Papal, 90, 91, 104, 208, 209, 261–2, 266, 278, 280, 338, 350, et passim
Leicester, Count of, 151. See Simon de Montfort
Le Mans, Bishopric, 267
Lendit, Fair, 85, 198
Leo IX, Pope, 88
Leopold of Austria, 212
Lewes, Battle of, 348
Liebermann, F., 44 (note), 65 (note), 74 (note)

INDEX

Lillebonne, 54, 59, 163
Limoges, Town, 176, 219 (note)
—— Viscounts and Viscounty, 170-4, 217
—— Bishop, 263, 302
Lincoln, 349
Lions, 163
Llewelyn ap Griffith, Prince of the Welsh, 347, 350
—— Joverth, id., 223
Lombards, 250
London, 38, 129, 134, 146, 152, 226, 332-4, 337, 342, 348, 369
—— Bishop of, 365
—— Parliament of, 348
Lord, 50
Lorraine, 10, 15, 33, 325
Lorris, Customs of, 195
Lot, F., 22 (note), 140 (note)
Lothaire, King of France, 28
Louis V, King of France, 28
—— VI, the Fat, id., 77-8, 83-4, 93-5, 376
—— VII, 24, 77-9, 85, 95, 100, 105-7, 131, 169, 179-180, 183, 192, 207, 377, *et passim*
—— VIII, 213-19, 222, 225, 227, 234, 238, 247, 252, 262, 269, 279, 282, 301, 302, 306, 311
—— IX (Saint Louis), 12, 91, 214, 227, 230, 234, 326, 347, 377-9
—— X, 314 (note)
Louvre, 198 (note), 234, 244
Luchaire (Ach.), 8 (note), 77 (note), 92 (note), 204 (note)
Lusignan, 217, 222, 293, 340, 343
Luxembourg, Count of, 325
Lyons, 10, 21, 269, 272-4, 366

MacKechnie, W. S. 333 (note)
Macon, County, 12, 246
—— Bishopric, 267
Maine, 99, 167-8, 213, 220, 222, 227, 242, 246
Mainerius, Jurist, 183
Maitland, F. W., 39 (note)
Majority, the King's, 293 (note)
Manfred, bastard son of Frederick II, 270
Manorial System, 68
Mantes, 197, 234
Map, Walter, 84, 109, 113, 135
Marc sterling, 188 (note)
Marc of Troyes, 187 (note)
Marchands de l'eau, 198, 314
Marche, Counts and County, 170, 173, 217
Margaret, Countess of Flanders, 325
—— of Provence, wife of St. Louis, 260, 312, 377

Marmande, 280
Marie of France, daughter of Ph. Augustus, 219
Marlborough, Statute of, 371
Marquard de Annweiler, 207
Marriage, Right of, 331, 333
Marseilles, 271
Marshal, 235
Mathew de Montmorency, Constable, 235
—— Paris, Chronicler, 118, 241, 323, 366
Mathieu de Beaune Bailiff, 295
—— de Vendome, Abbe of St. Denis, 236
Matilda, Empress, 100-5, 116, 153, 159, 166
—— daughter of Henry II, 211
Maubeuge, 10
Maurice de Craon, 168
Mediterranean, 10, 177
Melun, Town, 234, 238, 262
—— County, 17
Mercadier, Mercenary leader, 171
Merovingians, 20
Meuse, 8, 11
Military Service, *see* Army
Monarchy, Anglo-Saxon, 42
—— Carolingian, 23
—— Capetian, 23
—— Anglo-Norman, 60
—— Angevin, 99
—— Primitive doctrines of, 3
—— Doctrine of Church and of the Policraticus, 2, 19, 23-5, 88-9, 115-16, 120-2
—— Doctrine of Bracton and the English Ministers, 114-16, 354-5
—— Doctrine of St. Louis, 261, 301, 310, 378
—— Ideas of the Barons on, 24, 123
—— Popular ideas on, 25, 379
—— Theory of the elective, 27-8, 43, 115-18, 375
Monasteries, 20, 21
Mongols, 284, 285
Monies, 187, 238, 252-3, 308
—— Power to strike, 187
Monod, G., 199 (note)
Montargis, 205
Montdidier, 184, 197
Montivilliers, 163, 176
Montpellier, Seigniory, 246, 293, 324
Montreuil sur Mer, 18, 184, 196
Mortimer, Feudal family, 343
Muret, Battle, 279
Myth, Carolingian, 25-6, 212-14
—— of the Great Charter, 358-9, 370
—— of Parliament, 36, 362, 374
—— of the Monarchy, 24-6

INDEX

Nantes, County, 169
Narbonne, Duchy, 279
Nationality, National sentiment, 12, 22, 25, 36, 41–3, 45, 47, 51, 75, 85, 379
Navarre, Kingdom of, 325
Navy, 145
Nevelon, the Marshal bailiff, 295
Nevers, Counts of, 183, 205, 221
—— Bishopric, 267
Nimes, 279, 316
Niort, 170, 176, 222
Nogent, Seigniory, 245
—— l'Erembert, 305 (note)
Norfolk, Count of, 151
Norgate, Miss K., 117 (note)
Normandy, 15, 17, 35, 51–5, 64, 68, 142, 159, 167, 219, 221, 227, 233–4, 241, 244, 320, 322, 328
Noyon, Town, 196, 316
—— Bishop of, 183, 240, 268

Officers, Great, of the Crown, 31, 80, 235
Oléron, Isle of, 176
Orderic Vitalis, 76
Ordinances, General, 306–8, 377
Orleans, 18, 31
Ostrevent, 11
Otto of Brunswick, Emperor, 210, 215, 223, 226
Ottoboni, Legate, 350
Oxford, Parliament of, *see* Provisions of, 342

Pacy, 234, 321
Paix à parties, 313, 314 (note)
—— de Dieu, 82, 183
—— Normande, 53
Palace, 79, 80, 127, 183, 198, 243
Pandolph, Envoy then Papal Legate, 225, 332, 333
Papacy, 206–210, 268, 283, 323, 328–330, 338, 340–1, 356, 371, 374
Paris, 18, 31, 83, 183, 197, 200, 233, 255
—— Assembly at, 281
—— Bishopric, 267
—— Provostship, 258
—— Treaties concluded at, 230, 282, 344
Parliament, Parlement, 242, 309, 342, 352, 371, 375, 377
Parow, 140 (note)
Pastoureaux, 319
Pêche, 335
Peers, Judgment by, 239, 309, 336
—— of France, 203, 219–220, 240–1, 292
Peitz, W. M., 88
Pelet, Seignorial Dynasty, 297

Perche, County, 245
Perigueux, Bishop of, 174
Perigord, Counts, County, 170, 173, 302
Peronne, 184
—— Dit de, 325
Petition, Barons', 332, 356, 360
Peter the Marshal, Pierre le Maréchal, 182, 192
Pfister, Chr., 80 (note)
Philip I, King of France, 8, 23, 76, 82, 86, 92
—— II, Augustus, 2, 28, 36, 123, 161, 177, 180, 321, 377–8
—— III, the Bold, 286 (note), 324
—— IV, Le Bel, 11, 36, 242, 251
—— of Alsace, Count of Flanders, 181, 203, 204
—— Hurepel, son of Philip Augustus, 292, 305
—— of Swabia, Emperor, 210
Pierre II, King of Aragon, 277, 279
—— Bertin, Seneschal of Poitou, 171
—— Charlot, bastard son of Philip Augustus, 268
—— Damien, 87–8
—— D'Athies, Seneschal, 297
—— de Blois, 108, 113–5, 127, 190
—— de Castelnau, Legate, 278
—— de Corbeil, Archbishop of Sens, 236
—— de Courtenay, Count of Nevers, 205
—— de Dreux, Mauclerc, Bailiff of Brittany, 222, 239, 292, 303, 305
—— de Fontaines, Jurist, 236
—— de Rivaux, 340
—— des Roches, Bishop of Winchester, 328, 340
—— des Vaux de Cernay, Chronicler, 276
—— de Chambellan, 325
Pipe Rolls, 63, 133, 140 (note)
Plantegenets, 100 (note)
Poissy, 18, 196
Poitiers, 15, 171, 174, 176
—— Bishopric, 267
Poitou, 170–4, 210, 218, 222, 227, 245–6, 248, 341
Poix, 314 (note)
Policraticus, 119–122
Pont Audemer, Bailiwick, 295
Pont de l'Arche, 234, 321
Pont Saint Maxence, 305 (note)
Ponthieu, County, 251
Pontoise, 196, 274
Potestas, 18 (note), 159, 307
Pound, Parisian, 253
—— Sterling, 140 (note)
—— Tournois, 140 (note), 253
Powicke, F. M., 220 (note)

418 INDEX

Pragmatic Sanction, 275
Primat, Chronicler, 323
Primogeniture, 29, 376
Principalities, 14, 35, 36
Prisée des sergents, 193
Private War, 53, 313
Prou, Maurice, 23 (note)
Provençal, Idiom, 14
Provence, County, 12, 279
Provincial Estates, 241, 300
Provision, Right of, 30, 187, 194, 201, 250, 302
Provisions, of Oxford, 325-6, 344-6, 357, 371
―― of Westminster, 346, 370, 371
Provosts, 162, 184-5, 249, 254, 294, 299
Puiset, le, 83
Pyrennees, 10

Quarantaine le Roi, 313
Queen, Political role of, 31, 77, 131
Quinze Vingts, 255

Ramsay, J. H., 140 (note)
Ransoms, 254
Raoul de Faie, Seneschal of Aquitaine, 171
―― de Nesle, Constable, 235
―― de Wanneville, Chancellor of Henry II, 112
Raymond V, Count of Toulouse, 205-6
―― VI, id., 206, 277, 280
―― VII, id., 279, 283, 293
―― Trencavel, Count of Carcassonne, 282
Regale, 187, 207, 251, 267
Regency, 78 (note), 292, 375
Relief, Right of, 142, 187, 213, 251, 331, 333
Renaud de Dammartin, Count of Boulogne, 220, 223, 225, 307
Representation at Assemblies, 361
Rheims, Town, 15, 20-1, 25, 29, 85, 249
―― Archbishop, 23, 27, 87, 240-1, 249, 265, 267
―― Ecclesiastical Prov., 20, 21, 317
Rhone, 10
Richard Cœur de Lion, 108, 110, 117, 123, 130-1, 132, 143-5, 152-3, 157, 168, 171-7, 181, 190, 191, 201, 207, 210-13, 374
―― de Clare, 343
―― of Cornwall, brother of Henry III, 323, 341, 348
―― de Lucy, Grand Justiciar, Regent, 107, 112, 135

Richard d'Ilchester, Grand Seneschal of Normandy, 112, 161, 164
―― Fitz-Neel, Treasurer, 112, 133
Richer, Chronicler, 27, 32
Rigord, id., 180 (note), 192, 195, 199
Robert Champart, Archbishop of Canterbury, 57
―― Courthose, 73, 81
―― of Artois, brother of St. Louis, 246, 269
―― de Béthune 359
―― de Courtenay, Butler, 235
―― Fitz Walter, 329
―― Grosstête, Bishop of Lincoln, 338, 364, 366-7
―― Guiscard, Duke of Calabria, 55
―― Passelew, Judge, 365
―― the Pious, King of France, 7, 16, 18, 20, 22-4, 28, 34, 80, 82
Roger de Hovenden, Itinerant Judge and Chronicler, 130, 135
―― Bishop of Salisbury, 104
―― of Wendover, Chronicler, 216, 356
Roland, Chanson de, 25-6, 376
Rollon, 51
Romain, Cardinal of St. Ange, Legate, 281
Romans, 11, 37-9
Roman de la Rose, 323
Rome, Council of, 269
―― Visits of Louis VII and Ph. Augustus, 106, 181. See Papacy
Roussler, O., 104 (note)
Rouen, Town, 132, 163, 175, 198, 220. See Establissements de Rouen
―― Archbishop and Church, 129, 320
Rouergue, County, 15
Round, J. H., 50 (note), 69, 70 (note)
Roussillon, 325
Royal Causes, 309
Roye, 184, 197
Runnymede, 332
Rural Communities, 196, 318
Russia, 33

St. Basle, Council of, 22
St. Corneille de Compiègne, Abbey, 21, 94 (note)
St. Denis, id., 21, 78, 85, 198, 238, 265
St. Geneviève de Paris, 198
St. Germain des Prés, id., 21, 198
―― en Laye, 234
St. Hilaire de Poitiers, Abbey, 173
St. James de Beuvron, 246
St. Jean d'Angely, 170, 176, 222
St. Martin de Tours, Abbey, 21, 168
St. Omer, 203
St. Paul's, London, 331

INDEX

St. Pol, Counts of, 236, 307
St. Quentin, 197
—— Countess of, 221
St. Riquier, 197, 245
St. Victor de Paris, Abbey, 94, 198
Sainte Chapelle, 234, 255
Saintes, Town, 176
—— Battle, 222, 282, 293
—— Bishop, 174
Saintonge, 173, 245
Saladin, Sultan, 212
—— Tithe, 189, 191, 252
Salisbury, Bishop of, 364
—— Oath of, 62
—— Count of, brother of John Lackland, 332
Sancerre, County and Counts of, 221, 236, 303
Saone, 10
Savoy, 177, 325
Scandinavians, 37, 52-3 (note), 139 (note)
Scheldt, 10
Schreuer, H., 23 (note), 27 (note)
Scotland, 108, 156, 335, 344
Scripta de feodis, 302
Scrofula, Royal cure of, 3, 115
Scutage, 143, 191, 250, 360-1
Seebohm, F., 39 (note)
Seneschal of England, 349
—— of Anjou, 167-8
—— of Aquitaine, 171
—— of France, 80, 94-5 (note), 168-9, 235
—— of Normandy, 161, 164, 248, 321
Seneschals of the Capetian demesne, 248, 288, 294, 301
Senlis, 18, 252
—— Lords of, 182
Sens, Town, 18, 196, 206
—— Counts and County, 17-18
—— Ecclesiastical Province and Archbishop, 20, 21, 23, 92, 252
Serfs, 49 (note), 67, 80 (note), 195, 318
Sergents, 295
Sheriff, 42, 64, 70, 101, 125, 127, 153, 162, 186, 346, 353, 369, 373
Shire, 41-2, 63-4, 126, 162 (note), 373, 376
Sicily, 55, 108, 177, 210, 252, 256, 270-1, 274, 324, 341
Sigebert de Gembloux, 207
Simon de Montfort, Leader of the Albigensian Crusade, 277, 279
—— Count of Leicester, 343, 349, 354, 363, 367-8, 370
Simon de Nesle, King's lieutenant, 236
Socmen, 49, 67
Soissons, Town, 196, 252

Soissons, Count of, 17, 221
—— Bishop of, 251
—— Council of, 209
—— Assembly of, 238
Sordel troubadour, 325
State, 2, 10, 12, 36, 40, 146, 374
States General, Origin of, 241
Statutarii, 266
Stenton, D. M., 131 (note), 135 (note)
Stephen of Blois, King of England, 99, 100-5, 125, 159
—— Langton, Archbishop of Canterbury, 328, 332, 337, 364
—— of Marsai, 168
Stewards, and Bailiffs, 294, 296
Stigand, Archbishop of Canterbury, 58
Stubbs, W., 40 (note), 61 (note), 65 (note), 140 (note), 357
Subjects, 302, 311
Suger, 77-9, 94, 106, 121, 169 (note), 181, 183, 188, 377
Sweyn, King of England and Denmark, 56
Syria, 285

Taillebourg, Battle, 222, 293
Talmud, 276
Taxation, 43, 63, 90, 129, 142, 188, 200, 249, *et passim*
Temple, Templars, 192, 244
Tenurial régime, 51, 66
Thames, 45, 47, 139 (note)
Thayer, J. B., 139 (note)
Theocracy, 90
Theodore, Archbishop of Canterbury, 41, 44
Theobald, Thibaud, Count of Blois and Champagne, 79, 204
—— Count of Blois, Seneschal of France, 182, 204
—— III, Count of Champagne, 204
—— IV, "The Minstrel," Count of Champagne and King of Navarre, 292, 304, 309
—— V, Count of Champagne and King of Navarre, 325
—— the Rich, 200
Therouanne, Bishop, 201
Thierry of Alsace, Count of Flanders, 84, 202
—— Galeran, Councillor of Louis VII, 181
Thomas a Beckett, Archbishop of Canterbury, 112, 115, 119, 130, 135, 139, 146, 150, 194
—— of Savoy, 304
—— Wykes, chronicler, 350
Thuringia, 223
Tostig, Harold's brother, 59

420 INDEX

Toulouse, Town, 211, 280, 318
—— County and Counts, 12, 15, 108, 157, 170, 177, 205, 212, 241, 246, 276, 283, 296, 306
Touraine, 99, 167–8, 213, 220, 222, 227
Tournai, 10, 194, 197, 203
Tournaments, Ban on, 123, 312
Tours, 20, 157, 168
—— Eccl. Province and Archbishop, 20, 265
Towns, 152, 154, 175–6, 196, 200, 250, 251, 290, 293, 314, 317, 334, 368
Townships, 40, 186
Treasure, 63, 140, 192, 234, 244
Tresor des Chartes, 234, 265–6, 301, 326
Tristan, Family of Chamberlains, 236
Truce, in customary law, 315, 316 (note)
—— of God, 53, 82
Tunis, 256, 286
Turenne, Viscount of, 302
Turks, 284
Tyrannicide, 121

University of Paris, 199, 262
Urban II, Pope, 72, 91
—— IV, Pope, 270–1

Valenciennes, 10, 225
Valentinois, County, 12, 303
Valois, County of, 245
Varaville, Battle of, 17
Varenne, Count of, 332
Vaucouleurs, Interview at, 224
Vavasseurs, mercenaries, 346
Velay, 296
Verdun, Bishop of, 12
—— Treaty of, 10–11
Vermandois, County, 17, 197, 245, 295
Verneuil, 175
Vernon, 321
Vexin, French, 83, 241
—— Norman, 210, 212–13
Vezelay, Abbe of, 183
—— Assembly at, 188
Victor IV, Pope, 206
Viennese, 10
Villebeon, family of Chamberlains, 236
Villeins, 49, 67
Villeneuves, 195, 318
Villeneuve le Roi, 238
Vincennes, 234, 239
Vinogradoff, P., 137 (note)
Viscounts, Norman, 53, 162
Vitry, 95

Vivarais, 10, 297
Viviers, Bishops of, 297
Voirie, 18

Wace Chronicler, 167
Waes, 10
Wages, 193, 255
Wailly, N. de, 244 (note), 258 (note), 260 (note)
Wallingford, Treaty, 125
Wapentake, 373
Weights and Measures, Uniformity of, 334
Welsh, 156, 223, 335, 344
Wessex, Kingdom of, 40–2, 44, 57
Westminster, 132, 134, 343, 351. *See* Provisions
Will, of Philip Augustus, in 1190, 181–2, 185, 191–2, 194, 200
—— —— in 1222, 257
—— of Louis VIII, 257
—— of Louis IX, 258
William, the Bastard, or Conqueror, King of England, 17, 40, 48, 52, 71, 139, 373
—— II, Rufus, id., 61, 71–2, 121, 374
—— V, Duke of Aquitaine, 15
—— VIII, id., 169, 171
—— of Auvergne, Bishop of Paris, 236
—— Clito, 84
—— de Briouse, 220
—— Dampierre, 325
—— Garlande, 182
—— Mauzé, 169 (note)
—— Saint Calais, Bishop of Durham, 73
—— des Orines, Seneschal, 297
—— Roches, Seneschal of Anjou, 168, 222, 248
—— du Hommet, Constable of Normandy, 161
—— Fils Raoul, Grand Seneschal, 161
—— le Breton, Chronicler, 190, 199 (note), 216, 218 (note), 321
—— the Lion, King of Scotland, 156
—— the Marshal, 113, 114, 123, 172, 332, 338, 358
—— Longchamp, Chancellor, 112, 128
Winchester, 63, 100, 134
Wisemen, 42. *See* Witan
Witan, Witenagemot, 44–7, 60, 65, 127
Women, 77, 142
Worcester, Bishop of, 344, 365

York, 349
—— Archbishop of, 45
Yves de Chartres, 86, 92, 92, 121

THE HISTORY OF CIVILIZATION

Titles in the series

Pre History	Language - A Linguistic Introduction to History	J Vendryes
	A Geographical Introduction to History	Lucien Febvre
	The Dawn of European Civilization	V Gordon Childe
	The Aryans	V Gordon Childe
	From Tribe to Empire	Moret & Davy
	Death Customs	Effie Bendann
	The Migration of Symbols	D Mackenzie
	The History of Witchcraft and Demonology	Montague Summers
	The History of Medicine	C G Cumston
	Money and Monetary Policy in Early Times	A R Burns
	Life and Work in Prehistoric Times	G Renard
	Social Organization	Rivers & Perry
Greek Civilization	The Ægean Civilization	G Glotz
	Ancient Greece at Work	G Glotz
	The Formation of the Greek People	A Jardé
	Art in Greece	de Ridder & Deonna
	Macedonian Imperialism	Pierre Jouguet
	Greek Thought and the Origins of the Scientific Spirit	Léon Robin
	The Greek City and its Institutions	G Glotz
Roman Civilization	Primitive Italy	Leon Homo
	Rome the Law-Giver	J Declareuil
	The Roman Spirit	Albert Grenier
	The Roman World	V Chapot
	Roman Political Institutions	Leon Homo
	The Economic Life of the Ancient World	J Toutain
Eastern Civilization	The Nile and Egyptian Civilization	A Moret
	The Peoples of Asia	L H Dudley Buxton
	Mesopotamia	L Delaporte
	A Thousand Years of the Tartars	E H Parker
	Ancient Persia and Iranian Civilization	Clement Huart
	Chinese Civilization	Marcel Granet
	The Life of Buddha	Edward J Thomas
	The History of Buddhist Thought	Edward J Thomas
	Ancient India and Indian Civilization	Masson-Oursel et al
	The Heroic Age of India	N K Sidhanta
Judaeo Christian Civilization		
	Israel	Adolphe Lods
	The Prophets and the Rise of Judaism	Adolphe Lods
	The Jewish World in the Time of Jesus	Charles Guignebert
	The History and Literature of Christianity	Pierre de Labriolle
European Civilization	The End of the Ancient World	Ferdinand Lot
	The Rise of the Celts	Henri Hubert
	The Greatness and Decline of the Celts	Henri Hubert
	Life and Work in Medieval Europe	P Boissonnade
	The Feudal Monarchy in France and England	C Petit-Dutaillis
	Travel and Travellers of the Middle Ages	Arthur Newton
	Chivalry	Edgar Prestage
	The Court of Burgundy	Otto Cartellieri
	Life and Work in Modern Europe	Renard & Weulersse
	China and Europe	Adolf Reichwein
	The American Indian Frontier	W Christie Macleod

For Product Safety Concerns and Information please contact our EU representative GPSR@taylorandfrancis.com
Taylor & Francis Verlag GmbH, Kaufingerstraße 24, 80331 München, Germany